P9-CLR-705

Cisco®:
A Beginner's Guide,
Third Edition

Cisco®:
A Beginner's Guide,
Third Edition

ANTHONY T. **VELTE**, CISSP
TOBY J. **VELTE**, PH.D.

McGraw-Hill/Osborne
New York   Chicago   San Francisco
Lisbon   London   Madrid   Mexico City   Milan
New Delhi   San Juan   Seoul   Singapore   Sydney   Toronto

The McGraw·Hill Companies

McGraw-Hill/Osborne
2100 Powell Street, 10th Floor
Emeryville, California 94608
U.S.A.

To arrange bulk purchase discounts for sales promotions, premiums, or fund-raisers, please contact **McGraw-Hill/Osborne** at the above address. For information on translations or book distributors outside the U.S.A., please see the International Contact Information page immediately following the index of this book.

Cisco®: A Beginner's Guide, Third Edition

Copyright © 2004 by The McGraw-Hill Companies. All rights reserved. Printed in the United States of America. Except as permitted under the Copyright Act of 1976, no part of this publication may be reproduced or distributed in any form or by any means, or stored in a database or retrieval system, without the prior written permission of the publisher, with the exception that the program listings may be entered, stored, and executed in a computer system, but they may not be reproduced for publication.

34567890 CUS CUS 0198765

ISBN 0-07-225635-4

Publisher
  Brandon A. Nordin
Vice President & Associate Publisher
  Scott Rogers
Editorial Director
  Tracy Dunkelberger
Project Manager
  Janet Walden
Project Editors
  Claire Splan
  Emily Rader
Acquisitions Coordinator
  Jessica Wilson
Technical Editor
  Tony Martin

Copy Editor
  Mike McGee
Proofreaders
  Judy Wilson
  Paul Medoff
Indexer
  Claire Splan
Composition
  International Typesetting
  and Composition
Illustrator
  International Typesetting
  and Composition
Series Design
  Peter F. Hancik

This book was composed with Corel VENTURA™ Publisher.

This material is not sponsored by, endorsed by, or affiliated with Cisco Systems, Inc. Cisco®, Cisco Systems®, CCDA™, CCNA™, CCDP™, CCNP™, CCIE™, CCSI™, the Cisco Systems logo, and the CCIE logo are trademarks or registered trademarks of Cisco Systems, Inc., in the United States and in certain other countries. All other trademarks are trademarks of their respective owners.

Information has been obtained by **McGraw-Hill**/Osborne from sources believed to be reliable. However, because of the possibility of human or mechanical error by our sources, **McGraw-Hill**/Osborne, or others, **McGraw-Hill**/Osborne does not guarantee the accuracy, adequacy, or completeness of any information and is not responsible for any errors or omissions or the results obtained from the use of such information.

This book is dedicated to
Luke, Jack, Joey, Olivia, and their mothers,
Anne Marie and Sandra.
We'd also like to dedicate this book to
Robert Elsenpeter, his wife Janet, and their son Henry.
To the wives, we say thank you for
holding down the fort… again. We love you.

ABOUT THE AUTHORS

Anthony Velte, CISSP, MCSE+I, CCDA, is cofounder of Velte Publishing, Inc. In addition to writing and publishing a variety of technology books, Mr. Velte finds joy in spending time with his sons Luke, Jack, and Joey. He has founded several companies and has more recently led several large-scale network, security, and disaster recovery projects. He can be reached at atv@velte.com.

Toby Velte, Ph.D., MCSE+I, CCNA, CCDA, is cofounder of Velte Publishing, Inc. Dr. Velte is an international, best-selling author of technology articles and books. He is a self-proclaimed techno-geek and has started several high-tech companies in the Minneapolis area. He can be reached at tjv@velte.com.

ABOUT THE TECHNICAL EDITOR

Tony Martin is a Sales Systems Engineer for Level 3 Communications, Inc. His network certifications and licenses include the CCNA and Civil Engineering License. Tony has delivered simultaneous large-scale, mission-critical merger and acquisition integrations. His experience includes designing, implementing and optimizing SONET, MPLS, IP, VPN, and VOIP solutions for Fortune 500 clients. He formerly worked as a Naval Engineering Systems School Instructor and served over nine years in the United States Navy. He completed a Bachelor of Science degree in Corporate Education, Training, and Development. He has published white papers and was a speaker at SuperComm 2003 on CALEA in Next-Generation Carrier Networks. Mr. Martin also was an editor for the title *Juniper and Cisco Routing: Policy and Protocols for Multivendor IP Networks* by Walter J. Goralski (Wiley & Sons, 2002).

AT A GLANCE

CONTENTS

Part II

Cisco Internetworking Tools

Part III

Cisco Business Solutions

Part IV

Designing Cisco Networks

FOREWORD

When it comes to networking, Cisco® rules the roost. Internet infrastructure, corporate networks—they all involve those green boxes. Knowing how they work, what they can do, and how to implement things is key to working on today's computing infrastructure.

Choosing a network career path means learning about certifications, security, and network design issues. Fortunately, you can gain the critical knowledge you'll need without spending countless hours trying to figure things out all by yourself—an impractical move at best.

I still remember setting up my first screening routers in front of my first firewall. Even now, many, many networks and routers later, there's something about building a new network that fills me with a sense of purpose. Putting access lists on a live, running router to help secure a network is still a skill that comes in handy, many years after I first learned how. Confidently assuring an executive that his network won't go down because of the change is about the only real difference time has added.

When I connected usatoday.com to the Internet, I'd already learned enough about Cisco routers to proclaim confidently that the site would be ready for demonstrating during the Windows 95 launch day, even though we had less than 48 hours to perform the entire operation, from ordering a circuit to having visitors access the site. Knowing how to set up the routers gave me that confidence.

Building and understanding networks is the key to keeping a modern company running. Like laying the train tracks of yesteryear, these are the connections that keep the economy flowing. Network design and operations are a rewarding career. Learning the ins and outs and the fundamentals can be a challenge. Fortunately, you've picked the best way to start—a comprehensive book that's easy to understand and easy to reference.

Computer networks are amazing things. The ability to communicate with people you've never met, order products from companies around the globe instantly, keep in instant touch with friends on another continent—all of these things are taken for granted by people all over the world. A relative few understand the technology that allows them to sit at their desks and do these things. Web sites, e-mail, instant messaging, and voice and video communications all require a network.

It used to be said "You can't go wrong buying IBM." In today's corporate world, the same is said of Cisco. Knowing how Cisco gear works is the only real way to get a good networking job. Knowing how networks work is fundamental to today's corporate and Internet infrastructure. Here, you'll learn both at once.

This book is your first step in learning how to work with the equipment that powers most of those networks, and in understanding how it all works. Like any good journey, this one promises to be a grand adventure.

Paul D. Robertson
Director of Risk Assessment, TruSecure® Corporation
Moderator, Firewall-Wizards® Security Mailing List

Paul Robertson has been in information technology and security for over 20 years; highlights include being stationed at the White House while in the United States Army and putting *USA Today*'s Web site on the Internet. Paul currently helps manage risk for hundreds of corporate clients at TruSecure®, and he participates in computer forensics, advocating www.personalfirewallday.org and moderating the Firewall-Wizards mailing list.

ACKNOWLEDGMENTS

The first edition of this book would never have taken off without the enormous contributions of author Tom Shaughnessy. To him we owe a wonderful basis from which to build. For both the second and third editions, we called upon the talents of author Robert Elesenpeter. He corrected typos, edited and reworked text and art so that it was clear and current, and contributed some original work to flesh out both editions. We also extend our appreciation to technical editor Tony Martin. His careful review has helped ensure a high level of technical accuracy in this edition.

It was yet again a pleasure working with the team at Osborne/McGraw Hill. To this edition's acquisitions editor, Tracy Dunkleberger, and acquisitions coordinators, Jessica Wilson and Athena Honore, we say thank you very much. To the Osborne illustration team, we say thank you for your patience. And to this edition's project editors, Claire Splan and Emily Rader, and copy editor Mike McGee, we say thank you so very much for your light but incisive touch with the wordsmith's ever necessary scalpel.

INTRODUCTION

The volume in your hands is the third edition of the worldwide, best-selling introduction to Cisco networking. Since its introduction, this book has sold over 60 thousand copies, has been translated into numerous languages, and is distributed all over the world. This level of interest confirms what you already know—Cisco is, and continues to be, a huge player in the communications industry, and people want to better understand how this behemoth works.

Although three years have passed since writing the second edition, the book has remained quite popular, and we felt that another refresh was in order. As with the second edition, we took the book apart and reexamined each chapter. If you place this book next to the first edition and second editions, the first thing you'll probably notice is that it is getting progressively thicker. Although we were hard-pressed to find material we thought was no longer pertinent, we certainly found new subjects that just had to be discussed. For instance, we have again followed Cisco's changes to its certification program and updated our coverage of which Cisco certifications are current and how to get them. In the second edition, we added a new chapter that focused on Cisco business solutions, including Voice over IP (VoIP), storage area networks (SANs), and content distribution networks (CDNs). In this edition, we expanded the content in all three areas, making each into its own chapter. Because security has become ever more important, we also beefed up the security content, which is now covered in two chapters. Of course, all chapters were updated to cover the latest hardware and software offerings from Cisco.

So what's the reason for all of this work and revision? We continue to think that there is an enormous need by networking professionals for a clear, concise introduction to Cisco and its technology. In offices and conference rooms throughout the world, scenarios like the one described next are enacted—with abysmal outcomes. What is truly needed is a simple understanding of networking and Cisco's role in networking to make sense of many IT issues. So the story begins…

Almost two million dollars spent so far, thought the VP, yet the board was forced to seriously contemplate pulling the plug on the project. He'd been sent to identify the problem and to identify how to fix it. "OK," he said, as he took a seat at the head of the table, "I'm throwing open the agenda. I want to know what the project's major problems are, what is causing them, and how long and how much it'll take to fix them." Turning toward the CIO and his network manager, the VP went on, "We all know that this project is central to our corporate strategy; nothing else has had a higher priority or consumed more resources during the last year. Yet our two primary competitors have already successfully expanded their Web site capacity, implemented load balancing, and upgraded their business-to-business environments. But we can't see the light at the end of the tunnel. Let me remind you that this isn't just another little departmental application; the board wants the Internet to become our primary place of business. Our competition has already cut their cost of sales by 15 percent or more, and we've lost 5 percent market share in the last quarter alone. We aren't thrilled with having a half-finished network that runs like a dog, not to mention being over budget, but this weekend's security breach may have been the last straw. What's wrong with this project?"

The CIO spoke up, saying the contractors weren't adhering to the three-level hierarchical design he'd requested, complaining that back doors and chains were choking performance. The consultant shot back that if the company had retained the contractors for project management, things would be under better control using their rigorous management methodology. A person from the Web programming team snidely noted that the context-based access control algorithm was "puking back hosed code every time the implicit deny rule hit bottom." Another complained that the so-called strong cryptography chosen for the VPN was using an overwrought DES key. The consultants disputed that statement, noting that RMONs were probably chewing up too many CPU clicks with MIB collection and that the NMS was overpolling SNMP anyway.

The Network Manager then took exception, pointing out that the original EtherChannel wire-speed benchmark could be attained only if "major upgrades" were made to the blades jacked into the backplanes of the various LAN switches, especially the ones feeding the ATM LANE adapters, because they were blocking broadcasts within VLANs. Sure, *now* they all agreed that the route switch processor modules on the "big honker" Cisco 7500 were grossly underconfigured, but that wasn't the story during the big "to route or to switch" debate during the design phase. Fact is, if the backbone routers had PIM sparse mode implemented, everything would be cool, but now multicasts were bringing the network to its knees because there were too many unknown groups, especially going through the IGX switch fabric. Without that humming, QoS—especially for traffic shaping and CAR—didn't have a snowball's chance in summer, at least not without a serious commitment being made to multilayer switching, as had been recommended. This was the case given all the subnet masks, DHCP, and DNS to handle at the access layer.

The consultants begged to disagree, pointing out that propagation delays were spawning loops, especially in the RIP domains, something they had specifically recommended against. IGRP was the superior choice or, better yet, EIGRP. However, once the routing metrics were properly tuned, the RIP versus IGRP thing would fall to the wayside. Then traps could at long last be set to alarm for out-of-band operations, freeing the team to tweak the CBAC and ASA algorithms to assure that last weekend's security debacle didn't repeat itself.

The VP felt trapped and alarmed. Sensing the VP's growing discomfort, the head consultant blurted out an offer to reduce the billing rate for the nine people engaged full-time on the project from $160 to $150 an hour. At the end of his rope, the VP said, "I must tell you that I've never heard so much bull in my entire life. I've been in data processing for over twenty years, and I haven't understood a thing said in this meeting. It really bothers me that you network people can't speak plain English. This project is caught in a loop, and I've gotta get a grip on things here. Let's adjourn for now and get together after lunch."

At the back of the room sat two young staffers who were in the meeting just in case the network performance statistics they'd gathered needed explanation. They hadn't understood much of what was said, either. But without saying a word, they looked at one another and raised their eyebrows at the same thought: $160 per hour?

WHO SHOULD READ THIS BOOK

This book is designed for anybody new to internetworking. It covers what one might refer to as the Internet's technical infrastructure. The software on your desktop—the Web browser, FTP software, or ICQ messenger—is only the tip of the iceberg. Over the past 30 years, an ever-growing group of dedicated computer scientists, telecommunications engineers, and programmers have been busy designing and building a global infrastructure that is revolutionizing commerce and culture alike. As you saw in the earlier meeting scenario, internetworking has taken on a language all its own—separate even from that used by the computer industry at large.

This book is for aspiring professionals interested in learning about the networking giant, managers in the computing industry whose knowledge of internetworking is weak, computer platform and software pros, and even individuals in the general public with a taste for technology.

This book is for those interested in the Internet and internetworking, not just in Cisco. Technology basics are covered generically before delving into Cisco particulars. Cisco is used for all examples in this book because it has the biggest and most comprehensive product line in the industry and is still the most important player in the field.

For those of you interested in pursuing Cisco certification, read this book to be introduced to industry background, concepts, terms, and technology. Then go on to a test preparation book to nail down your CCNA test. Indeed, the publisher of this book also publishes the best CCNA test prep book, *CCNA Cisco Certified Network Associate Study Guide, Second Edition,* by Syngress Media, Inc. (**McGraw-Hill**/Osborne, 2000).

WHAT THIS BOOK COVERS

The following is a chapter-by-chapter breakdown of the subject matter covered in this book.

Part I, "Cisco Overview"

Chapter 1, "Cisco and the Internet"—The Internet represents the biggest and fastest economic change in history, and sooner or later all our lives will be profoundly affected by it (if they haven't been already). This chapter surveys the Internet as a phenomenon, with a particular eye toward Cisco Systems and how its IOS operating software has vaulted the company to a position among the computer industry elite, alongside Microsoft, Intel, and IBM. The internetworking industry is outlined, and how Cisco's product line matches up to industry niches is explained.

Chapter 2, "Networking Primer"—Modern internetworking is the culmination of dozens of sophisticated technologies. This chapter explains things from the wire up, starting first with electrons passing over cables, up through binary bits and bytes. The major LAN technologies such as Ethernet and Token Ring are explained, right down to how they differ and which are rising or fading from use, including high-speed backbone technologies such as ATM and Gigabit Ethernet. The seven-layer Open Systems Interconnection (OSI) reference model is explained, including the inner workings of the TCP/IP protocol suite—the software used to run the Internet. You'll learn the difference between connection-oriented and connectionless networking, and how domain names are translated to numerical IP addresses. The important networking fundamentals of IP addressing and subnet masks are explained in detail. Dial-in technologies such as DSL and ISDN are covered, as are WAN trunk technologies like T1 and T3, Frame Relay, and ATM.

Chapter 3, "Cisco Certifications"—Like Microsoft and Novell, Cisco has a full-fledged certification program for technicians working on their products. This chapter details the three paths—Cisco Certified Network Associate (CCNA), Cisco Certified Network Professional (CCNP), and Cisco Certified Internetworking Engineer (CCIE)—along with the sundry other areas in which Cisco certifies network professionals. Complete explanations are given of exam objectives for each certification. We also highlight a number of ways you can find help preparing for the Cisco exams. A must-read for anyone interested in pursuing a career in internetworking or anyone faced with recruiting and managing Cisco-certified personnel.

Part II, "Cisco Internetworking Tools"

Chapter 4, "Router Overview"—This chapter focuses on Cisco router basics. We cover router hardware components from the printed circuit board up through the CPU, and explain how network administrators can log into Cisco routers to work on them, even rebooting to perform such basic tasks as password recovery. The major software components in Cisco routers are also surveyed, including the Cisco IOS command interface and feature sets. Cisco's router product line is reviewed here, including some tips on how to select the best router to solve a particular internetworking problem.

Chapter 5, "Configuring Routers"—Now it's time to delve into the heavier stuff, especially the configuration file. This chapter goes into the Cisco IOS operating mode, command hierarchy, utilities, and how to use the IOS help subsystem. But most of the focus is on the all-important configuration file, and how it's used to set up Cisco routers and configure networks. Reading this chapter introduces you to essential Cisco router commands, command syntax, how to read device status, and how to configure key router parameters. Cisco's ConfigMaker and FastStep configuration software tools are reviewed.

Chapter 6, "Switches"—The so-called *access layer* is where host devices such as PCs and servers plug into internetworks. This chapter explains internetwork topology basics, cabling specifications, what bandwidth is, what distinguishes collision and broadcast domains, and how hubs and access switches differ. High-end LAN backbone switches are also covered, from the perspective of one of the most important subjects in the industry today—whether to design routed or switched networks. The more technical dimensions of switched networking are introduced, including switching protocols, virtual LANs (VLANs), and multilayered switching. Cisco's switch product lines are reviewed.

Chapter 7, "Quality of Service"—As more and more applications become bandwidth hogs, mission critical data can find itself mired down in the ether. Providing fast, reliable service is essential for any internetwork. Throwing more bandwidth at the problem isn't the solution. Rather, organizations need good Quality of Service (QoS) technologies and policies in place. This chapter discusses the issue of QoS and tells you how you can implement a good QoS solution using Cisco tools. We cover the philosophy behind different QoS techniques and introduce you to Cisco's QoS hardware and software offerings.

Chapter 8, "Security Overview"—Network security that exists beyond firewalls is user-based security, used to set and enforce passwords to access networks and authorizations to use network resources. This chapter first covers the underlying industry standards for security, especially the AAA (Authentication, Authorization, and Accounting) standard. AAA is covered at the command level, and then the CiscoSecure ACS product suite is reviewed. Cisco offers two user-based security products: RADIUS, an industry standard, and its proprietary TACACS+. Both are reviewed in detail.

Chapter 9, "Security Building Blocks"—There are three types of technologies through which internetworks can be accessed: firewalls, access servers, and virtual private networks (VPNs). This chapter explains each of the three, with a particular focus on firewalls. The access list is explained, as are adaptive firewall security algorithms, the technology at the heart of internetwork security at the packet level. Cisco sells two firewall products: the Cisco PIX Firewall hardware/software combination and the IOS

Firewall software feature set, and both are explained in detail. The VPN—the wide area network (WAN) of the future—is covered. How access servers work, and the role they play is also surveyed. Further, Cisco's access server product line is reviewed.

    Chapter 10, "Cisco Wireless"—Until recently, the only way to connect to an internetwork was via a thin piece of cable snaking into the back of your PC. As efficient as this has been, it was only a matter of time until someone figured out how to cut the cord and let devices communicate with each other in a wireless medium. In this chapter, we cover the fundamentals of wireless networking, and then delve into Cisco's solution. Wireless networking is not just a "gee-whiz" technology. Wireless networking brings the power of computing and network connectivity to a range of useful applications and is beneficial to such fields as health care and education. Cisco offers solutions for both wireless LANs and wireless WANs with its Aironet series that we discuss and then show you how to configure.

Part III, "Cisco Business Solutions"

Chapter 11, "Cisco IP Contact Center"—Networks and internetworks are great ways to move data from place to place. However, it isn't just text files and the fourth-quarter earnings statement that can traverse a Cisco-based network infrastructure. Thanks to Voice over IP (VoIP), your organization can use its internetwork as the backbone of your telecommunications system. Additionally, customers who need to get in contact with your organization will benefit from Cisco Intelligent Contact Management, a system allowing customers to contact an organization through its Web site and request telephone or text chats.

    Chapter 12, "Storage Tools"—With benefits of the Information Age comes a hefty issue—where do we *keep* all that information? In this chapter, we examine storage area networks (SANs), which are akin to LANs but are built with the goal of storing information. We'll talk about SAN designs and construction and then look at the products Cisco offers for its SAN solutions, including its Multilayer Datacenter Switches (MDS) line.

    Chapter 13, "Cisco Content Networking"—Organizations are offering more and more information on their Web sites. However, as more people request that data from various locations, the need arises to direct the client to the closest, fastest repository of that information. Content delivery networks (CDNs) help resolve congested networks because clients are given the data they need from the ideal location. This chapter covers CDN basics, along with Cisco's product line for this technology. Additionally, we cover the topic of caching, a way in which service providers and large organizations can maintain frequently accessed Web information so that it can be delivered without having to repeatedly go to the Internet to access it.

Part IV, "Designing Cisco Networks"

Chapter 14, "Routing Protocols"—Large internetworks, or for that matter the Internet, wouldn't be possible without routing protocols. This chapter covers fundamental problems confronting any internetwork, as well as how routing protocols are used to adapt to shifting traffic patterns, emerging problems, and topology changes. Basic routing protocol technology is covered here, as are the various major routing protocols in use today—both open standard protocols (RIP, OSPF, BGP) and Cisco-proprietary protocols (IGRP and EIGRP). Cisco's routing protocols are overviewed, down to the command level where routing metrics are set to modify network behavior to meet enterprise requirements.

Chapter 15, "Network Management"—Network management has become a major issue as internetworks have grown in size and complexity. This chapter covers the standards and technologies that underlie network management systems: the Simple Network Management Protocol (SNMP), remote monitor instrumentation (RMON), and the management information base (MIB). Issues surrounding network management standards are covered, as is Cisco's approach to implementing them. SNMP configuration is introduced at the command level. Cisco's suite of network management software products—Resource Management Essentials and CWSI Campus—are also reviewed.

Chapter 16, "Network Design Process"—There are basics that must be covered when considering any network design decision, whether for a whole new internetwork or a modest expansion of an existing one. The classic three-layer hierarchical design model is reviewed in terms of what to look for in the access, distribution, and backbone layers. Key design subjects such as topology meshing and load balancing are reviewed. How to perform a comprehensive network needs analysis and how to translate it into design solutions using Cisco products is explained, covering such design factors as routing protocols, address design, routing versus switching, WAN services, and traffic load balancing.

Chapter 17, "Troubleshooting Cisco Networks"—You've arrived as a network pro when you can troubleshoot an internetwork. This chapter surveys typical internetwork problems and the proper methodology for diagnosing and fixing them. Key Cisco IOS troubleshooting commands are reviewed in terms of how to handle connectivity problems, performance bottlenecks, and other problems. Particular attention is paid to how to track down and isolate configuration problems, how to tune routing protocol metrics, and how to troubleshoot WAN services such as serial line links. Additionally, we cover common wireless network problems, along with how to troubleshoot network performance issues.

HOW TO READ THIS BOOK

This book can be picked up and read from the beginning of any chapter. Chapters covering technology start out with the basics and give explanations from the standpoint of the technology's historical background, how it developed, and what the issues and trends surrounding it are. Only then is Cisco specifically covered in terms of IOS commands, Cisco software tools, and Cisco hardware and software products.

This book doesn't try to reinvent the wheel by publishing yet another glossary on internetworking terms and acronyms. Every term introduced in this book is defined and explained in context. But the book should be read with the reader's browser pointed to Cisco's Web site at www.cisco.com. While this book stands on its own, it never hurts to browse around to help reinforce newly learned subject matter. Cisco's Web site contains a wealth of product illustrations, white papers, and other materials. In particular, readers of this book should use the Universal Resource Locator (URL) for two excellent online glossaries that complement this book:

▼ **Cisco Systems Terms and Acronyms**
www.cisco.com/univercd/cc/td/doc/cisintwk/ita/cisco12.htm

▲ **Internetworking Terms and Acronyms**
www.cisco.com/univercd/cc/td/doc/cisintwk/ita/index.htm

PART I

Cisco Overview

CHAPTER 1

Cisco and the Internet

The Internet is amazing. There's just no other word to describe a technology that few had even heard of 15 years ago, yet now dominates so much of our collective consciousness. The gold fever surrounding the Internet makes the 1849 California gold rush seem insignificant in comparison. You've no doubt heard the analogies and the clichés—the Internet is the fastest-growing market in history; the fastest-growing technology in history; the first truly global, real-time marketplace of goods, services, and ideas. The Internet will bring profound change to all sectors, from business to education to entertainment. The Internet is the information superhighway that's our road to the future.

INTERNETWORKING

The most surprising thing about all the breathless Web hype is that most of it's true. In the next few years, it's estimated that the number of people on the Internet will exceed *one billion*—putting onto one system a population about *three* times the size of the U.S. population. The number of registered Internet domain names more than doubles annually. There are now about 313 *billion* Web pages, up from a million a decade ago. In 1998, U.S. businesses alone spent over $10 billion upgrading their internetworks. A thousand American households sign up for Internet access every *hour*. No matter how tired we are of hearing this litany, the numbers are awesome.

Although most press coverage dotes on visible technologies such as browsers and cellular Internet phones, the real action is in Internet infrastructure. Billions are being invested by serious players who foresee a day when virtually all mass media—radio, telephone, and television—converge onto the Internet. This convergence will use the Internet as a single "pipe" through which virtually all communication travels. There's disagreement about whether the Internet pipe will run over wireless, telephone lines, cable TV wires, or even satellites. In fact, it seems that for the time being, it's all of the above. However, battle lines are being drawn every day by a multitude of businesses, and a lot of money is being invested. The bets are large because winning the Internet infrastructure game promises untold riches.

But there's trouble in paradise. As more people have hopped onto the bandwagon, the diameter of the pipe—called *bandwidth*, a measure of how much data can be moved over a link—has come under increasing scrutiny. New users and bigger applications are chewing up bandwidth as fast as additional network equipment can be added to the Internet's infrastructure, the global maze of telecommunications links and internetworking devices that makes it all go. Let's face it, with all of the advances, the Internet can still be slow, can't it? The Internet has undergone perennial bandwidth scares, with pundits worrying that additional loads finally may bring the whole thing to a grinding halt. That hasn't happened yet, but a huge amount of money and attention is focused on Internet infrastructure.

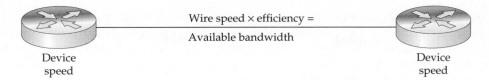

Wire speed × efficiency =
_____
Available bandwidth

Device   Device
speed   speed

Users connect to servers over this Internet infrastructure, yet few are aware of how it works. Bandwidth isn't just a matter of telecommunications media running over high-speed fiber-optic cable. The networking devices sitting at each end of the cables are every bit as important. In many situations, the speed of these devices is as big a factor in the Internet's bandwidth as telecom media.

This book surveys internetworking's infrastructure from the ground up, starting with underlying technology up through the product level. If you're a beginner, read this book and you'll know the basics of internetworking. It's written from the perspective of the premier manufacturer of internetworking technology, Cisco Systems. Because the technologies are covered generically, you'll understand the technologies and components needed to make any internetwork run, not just one built from Cisco products. But make no mistake; this book is about *infrastructure*—that is, about the devices over which internetworks operate.

▼ **Routers**   These devices route data between local area networks (LANs). Routers put the *inter* in internetworking; without them, the Internet would not be possible. Routers use Internet Protocol (IP) addresses to figure out how to best route packets through internetworks.

■ **Switches**   These devices also forward data between LANs and have replaced the hub as the de facto standard for connecting workstations and servers to the network. Switches are faster than routers, but most don't use IP addresses and, therefore, don't have the capability routers do for finding paths through large internetworks. There are, however, switches that incorporate routing—we'll discuss that in more detail later.

■ **Firewalls**   Although these can be understood simply as special routers that filter packets to secure data connections between internal and external networks, they are highly evolved security devices.

▲ **Access Servers**   These dedicated devices answer phone calls from remote users and connect them to the internetwork. Most access servers are used by Internet service providers (ISPs) to connect home users and small businesses to the Internet.

Collectively, these devices make up the Internet's infrastructure. The only other major ingredient is telecommunications links to make wide area network (WAN) connections. In this book we'll cover each device type as it exists within Cisco's product line and review WAN technologies also. Doing so (from the perspective of Cisco's product line) will give you a more detailed look at the inner workings of internetwork devices.

Cisco's Position in the Computer Industry

We all know that Microsoft Windows is the world's most important computer operating system. But here's a pop quiz: Can you name the second most important OS? Choose one:

▼ **MVS**   IBM's proprietary OS used to run mainframe computers. MVS still has a stranglehold on the central corporate and government data centers that handle financial accounting and other sensitive transactions.

■ **UNIX/LINUX**   There are actually about a dozen proprietary versions of UNIX from such computer manufacturers as Sun, HP, Compaq, Novell, and IBM. LINUX, the "new" kid on the block, has seen a boom in popularity. Nevertheless, "good old" UNIX is still the predominant server OS in enterprise class client-server applications.

▲ **IOS**   Short for Internetwork Operating System; this is Cisco Systems' proprietary OS for its line of internetworking hardware.

Since this is a Cisco book, this is a pretty easy question. IOS is the second most important operating system, and by a wide margin. We assert this partly because UNIX and MVS have both lost some of their edge—UNIX having lost market share to Microsoft Windows, and MVS still a mission-critical technology but one that has stopped growing altogether. However, the main reason IOS is so important is that Cisco has over an 80 percent share of the Internet router market, and the Internet is the fastest-growing market in history.

To put that in perspective, Cisco has about the same market share in router technology as Intel enjoys in Windows, or *Wintel*, hardware platforms. The Wintel regime has been attacked as a monopoly by competitors and the U.S. Department of Justice. Not so with Cisco. IOS is their proprietary OS architecture, and it runs on their hardware only. This means that Cisco's market leadership garners both hardware and software revenues and gives the company total architectural control over its products.

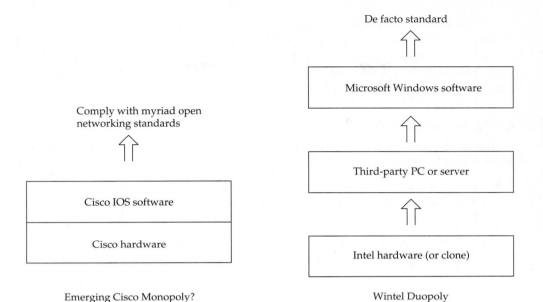

Emerging Cisco Monopoly?　　　　　　Wintel Duopoly

Cisco's present position has its strengths and weaknesses compared to the Wintel duopoly. On the negative side of the ledger, Cisco products are largely used to run truly open-standard protocols, which reduce the extent to which they can leverage product architecture to assert market control. Cisco can't freeze any competitor out of design cycles to prepare products that implement emerging technologies because the technologies implement open standards. On the positive side, Cisco is a single company that makes its own products. This contrasts favorably to Wintel, a pair of companies that rely on hundreds of PC manufacturers to deliver their respective products to a highly fragmented market.

Financially speaking, by the turn of the millennium, Cisco was riding a gravy train with biscuit wheels. Even though you could mention the company name to someone and they couldn't tell Cisco from Crisco, chances are some part of their life was touched by a Cisco product. Maybe their computer network at work utilized Cisco gear; maybe the ISP they used for Internet connectivity relied on Cisco gear. But the fact of the matter is that at one point in history, Cisco was the most valuable company on the face of the planet. In March 2000—less than two decades after the company was founded—the company reached a value of half a trillion dollars.

More than a year later, however, all that changed. When the dot-com bubble burst, Cisco fell hard. Many companies no longer needed Cisco's gadgets and by spring of 2001, Cisco faced a $2 billion write-off. From its leadership position with stocks trading at a high of $146 per share in March 2000, the stocks dipped to a low of a little more than $8 per share in October 2002. Though Cisco fell, it didn't fall as hard as those companies that had to close up shop. Cisco has hung in there and has made a steady climb back to profitability. At the end of 2003, Cisco stock was trading at $24 per share and by the end of fiscal year 2003 revenues rose 5 percent to $5 billion and net income rose 76 percent to $1.09 billion. The upshot of this lesson in finances? Cisco was down, but they weren't out.

This book is not an endorsement of Cisco, however. Like any industry powerhouse, the company has its faults and is duly criticized in these pages when appropriate. But whether you're an individual mulling a career move or a manager weighing your company's Internet strategy, learning how Cisco technology works is your best possible introduction to the world of internetworking.

The Internet Landscape

The Internet isn't a single technology, it's a collection of related technologies that make internetworking possible:

▼ **Physical media**   From connectors to high-speed fiber-optic cables, the physical links that connect everything together are the foundation of networking.

■ **Network technologies**   LAN protocols run what happens over the wire. The best known is Ethernet, but there are other important ones.

■ **TCP/IP**   The Transmission Control Protocol/Internet Protocol is what binds the Internet together. IP handles addressing and TCP handles messaging.

■ **Operational technologies**   Internetworks rely on a number of underlying standards and protocols to operate themselves, without which internetworking wouldn't be practical.

▲ **Application protocols**   Network applications define the kinds of useful work internetworks can do, from file transfers to Web page downloads.

To engineer its products, the networking industry uses a seven-layer architectural guideline called the Open Systems Interconnection (OSI) reference model. It's no coincidence that the preceding list of enabling technologies more or less adheres to the OSI model, from the physical level up.

Before we proceed, a quick word to make sure our terminology is clear: the *Internet* is a global interconnection of individual internetworks. An *internetwork* is any collection of local area networks (LANs) under a single administrative regime—usually an enterprise or an ISP. A private internetwork is mechanically the same as the open Internet. A *host* is a user device such as a PC, server, mainframe, or printer. A *device* is a piece of networking equipment such as a router. The generic terms *node* and *station* refer to both hosts and devices. A *LAN segment* is a network medium that hosts share. An *application protocol* is a software standard to operate such things as Web browsers, file transfers, e-mails, and other useful functions. An *intranet* is an internal internetwork operating as a private Web, with enterprise applications software used through Web browsers instead of a more traditional graphical user interface (GUI) such as Microsoft Windows.

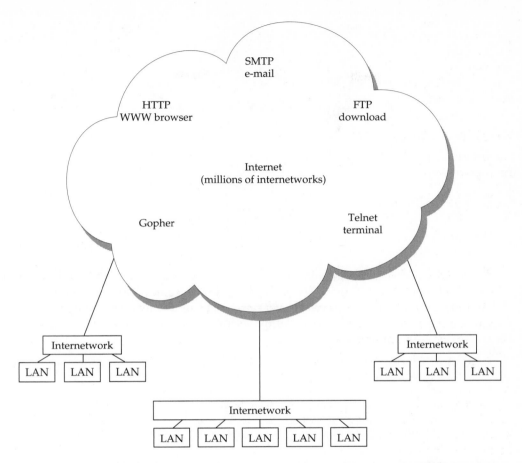

From a technical standpoint, private internetworks are composed of the same pieces as the Internet itself. The only thing that distinguishes the Internet from a large internetwork is its openness.

Internetworking's Four Major Device Types

A *switch* connects hosts to the internetwork, much like a hub. However, switches are fundamentally different in that they form a virtual circuit between the sending and receiving hosts. In other words, the switch's bandwidth is reserved for a single switched connection between two hosts as if it were 100 percent dedicated to that virtual circuit. Switches are able to do this by using better electronics than those used by hubs to "slice" bandwidth time into slivers—called *channels*—large enough to service each switch port. Switches have almost all but replaced hubs.

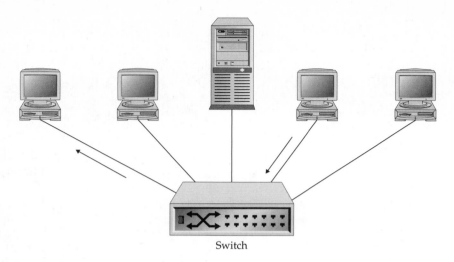

Switch

An *access server* is a specialized device that, stated roughly, acts like a modem on one side and a hub on the other. Access servers connect remote users to internetworks. The majority of the millions of access server ports in the world are operated by ISPs to take phone calls from Internet subscribers. Some perform more specialized functions, but the access server's main purpose is to connect remote dial-in users to an internetwork.

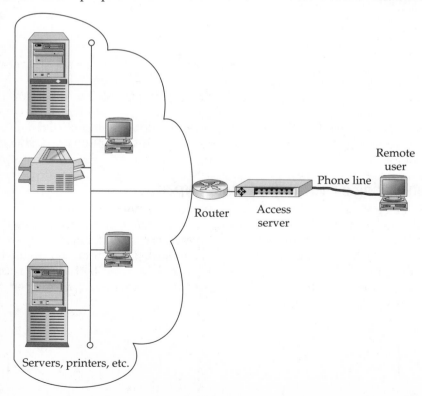

A *router* is an intelligent device that forwards traffic based on the IP address of a message. Whereas switches have ports into which individual hosts plug, routers have interfaces to which LAN segments attach. In simple terms, a router's job is to move *packets* of data between attached LAN segments.

The router is the single most important type of device in internetworking. It provides the flexibility and decision-making power that make it possible to run complicated internetworks. Without the logical capability routers provide, the Internet would be hundreds of times slower and much more expensive. As detailed in the next chapter, internetwork architectures have seven layers: switches predominantly operate at layer 2, and routers at layer 3. Routers also have the capability to filter traffic based upon source and destination addresses, network application, and other parameters.

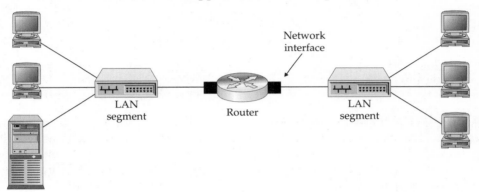

Firewalls are specialized routers that act as checkpoints between an internetwork and the outside. They work by checking each packet for compliance with security policies they have been programmed to enforce. A firewall forms an intentional traffic choke point and persistently monitors internal/external connections for security compliance. Any enterprise connected to the Internet should have a firewall configured.

The most powerful firewalls have specialized hardware, but they don't have to. A normal router can be programmed to perform many duties of a firewall, although a dedicated firewall device is preferred in most instances. Firewalls are increasingly being used internally to safeguard assets from potential internal threats.

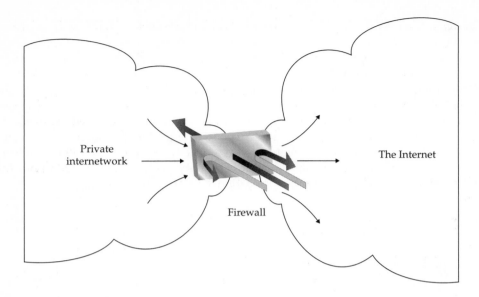

Private internetwork

The Internet

Firewall

Basic Internetwork Topologies

A *topology* is the physical arrangement of nodes within an internetwork. Usually, a topology is expressed as a logical map that graphically represents each node and the media links connecting the nodes. In fact, topology maps are used as the GUI through which most network management software tools operate. Figure 1-1 depicts the basic network elements that are combined in one way or another to make up internetworks.

The LAN segment is the basic building block of internetworks. Put another way, LAN segments are the network units that internetworks link together. The Internet itself is a collection of millions of LAN segments. The reason we use the formal term LAN *segment* is that a local collection of individual segments are commonly referred to as "LANs" even though, strictly speaking, they are actually local internetworks. This may seem like nit-picking, but you'll be happy for the distinction in later chapters.

Remote connections use phone circuits to tie physically removed hosts into the LAN segment. The telecom link can be anything from a regular analog voice line to a Digital Subscriber Line (DSL), the hot new telecom technology for small office/home office (SOHO) users.

The *campus LAN* is a double misnomer, but get used to it. Cisco uses it as a generic term to describe local enterprise internetworks. Most exist within a single building, not over an office campus, and all are composed of multiple LAN segments, not a single LAN. But campus LANs are distinguishable by the use of a high-speed backbone segment to interconnect the other local LAN segments. Most LAN backbones run over fiber-optic cabling.

WAN links are long-distance telecom links between cities, although some are strung across ocean floors to connect continents. Virtually all new WAN links being installed run over ultra-high-speed fiber-optic links. The current state of the art is OC-768, with a data rate of 40 Gbps. (OC stands for *optical carrier*; Gbps stands for *gigabits per second*.)

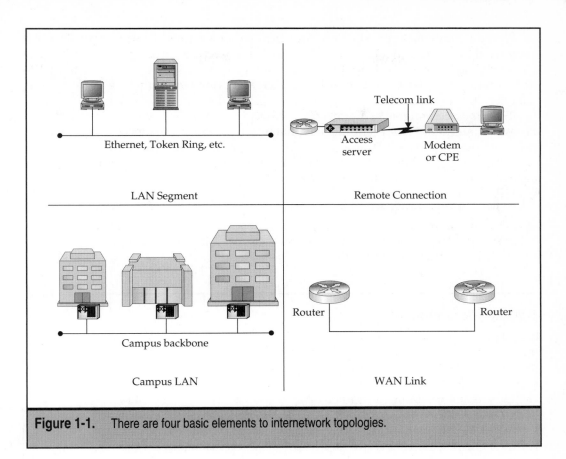

Figure 1-1.   There are four basic elements to internetwork topologies.

Slower WAN links run over technologies you've probably heard of—T1 and T3 (also called DS3), which run at 1.5 Mbps and 45 Mbps, respectively.

Internetwork Players

There is no "Internet network" as such. In other words, there is no separately owned dedicated trunk network operated under the auspices of some central management authority. The Internet is actually a free-for-all collection of individual networks bound together by two things:

▼　**Shared Enabling Technologies**　A complex of de facto standards and technologies that not only make the individual internetwork possible, but also enable internetworks to automatically interact with other internetworks.

▲　**Internet Protocol (IP)**　A globally accepted communication system that makes it possible to connect and exchange data with otherwise incompatible hosts anywhere on earth. IP unifies virtually all computer systems into a unitary data format and addressing system.

Figure 1-2 lays out approximately how the Internet is formed. The prerequisite is that users need to be on a network of some kind, and nowadays, in an office or plant, this usually means some type of Ethernet LAN. Desktop protocols such as Novell NetWare IPX and AppleTalk implement Ethernet, but an increasing number of enterprises are running vanilla IP LANs.

ISPs play a central role in Internet connectivity for enterprises, not just for home users. From the Internet's standpoint, the key juncture is where you connect to the so-called peer network—a group of thousands of high-speed routers that pass IP routes and traffic among one another. Although some very large enterprises (big corporations, government agencies, and universities) have their own connections to the peer network, most tap in via ISPs.

Entry to the peer network almost always takes place via a very high-speed fiber trunk line, usually controlled by so-called Internet backbone providers (IBPs), such as UUNET/MCI/WorldCom, PSINet, Sprint, and others. Only Tier 1 ISPs such as AOL and EarthLink can afford to contract directly with the IBPs.

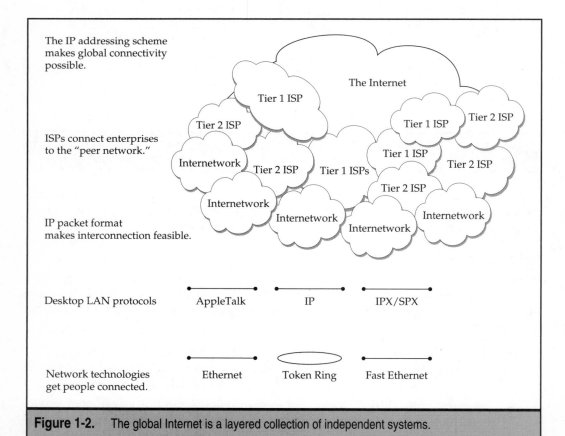

Figure 1-2.   The global Internet is a layered collection of independent systems.

Internetworking Protocols

Protocols are the key to internetworking. A networking *protocol* is an agreed-upon data format and set of rules for message exchange to govern a specific process. The Internet's two most fundamental protocols exist at the lower layers of the OSI model, layers 2 and 3. These are the various network (or LAN) protocols and the IP protocol. (In case you're wondering, layer 1 covers cabling and other physical transport media.)

Layer 3	IP	Internetworking
Layer 2	Ethernet, Token Ring, etc.	LAN segment media access

Layers 2 and 3 are the primary focus of this book, because that's where Cisco and its competitors bring physical network infrastructures to life as internetworks. Layer 2 connects the host to its home LAN segment, and layer 3 interconnects LAN segments.

However, that's just the beginning of the protocol story. There are literally dozens of supplementary protocols large and small to do everything from checking whether a neighboring device is still running to calculating the best path to send packets to the other side of the world.

For example, consider the Session Initiation Protocol (SIP). SIP is an Internet Engineering Task Force (IETF) standard managing how voice, video, and data can exist on the same network. Most often, you'll see SIP at work as the protocol involved in Voice over IP (VoIP) technologies and devices. Because of this protocol, VoIP can be used on desktop computers, personal digital assistants, IP phones, and other devices.

These supplementary protocols can be roughly divided into three groups: maintenance, management, and routing.

Routing protocols	Best paths	Exchange updates, calculate the best current routes
Management protocols	Health and security	Monitor performance, trip alarms, reconfigure
Maintenance protocols	Housekeeping	Discover devices, trace routes, notify neighbors

The maintenance protocols tend to be more proprietary (vendor-specific) the closer they are to the network device hardware. For example, the Cisco Discovery Protocol keeps track of devices—but only Cisco devices. The management protocols are more generic. However, Cisco is so big that they support the industry-standard security protocol in addition to pushing their own proprietary security protocol. A third kind of maintenance protocols called routing protocols are what make large, complicated networks possible.

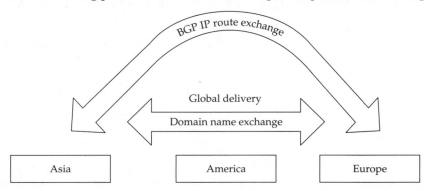

Routing protocols wring much of the labor and complexity out of very large networks by automatically tracking which routes to use between IP addresses. The Border Gateway Protocol (BGP) is the top-level routing protocol that connects everything within cities, between cities, and between continents. There are several other routing protocols used to track routes within private internetworks. Cisco supports industry-standard routing protocols in addition to pushing a couple of internal routing protocols of their own.

Routing vs. Switching

Over the last few years, a technology war was waged between routing and switching. As devices became less expensive and more powerful, switching emerged as a viable alternative to hubs on the low end and routers on the high end. Because switching is inherently faster, there was a push on to replace routed networks with switched networks. The battle took place at both ends of the internetworking landscape. At the low end—called the *access layer* because this is where hosts gain access to the internetwork—switches have replaced hubs as the device of choice to connect hosts because of switches' higher bandwidth. Switches have also displaced routers as backbones that connect LANs within a building or a campus. Figure 1-3 shows the three different types of switching.

Switching has always been the norm over WAN trunks such as the fiber-optic links Internet backbone providers operate between cities. In fact, voice telephone systems are switched networks built over permanent physical circuits in the form of the telephone cables running to businesses and homes.

Data switches, of course, don't have dedicated cabling—the switched circuits they create are virtual. That is, they create temporary logical (not hard-wired) end-to-end circuits that are set up and torn down on an as-needed basis. But nonetheless, data switches are inherently faster than shared networks. The phrase "switch where you can, route where you must" has emerged as the industry motto—the translation being that wherever possible, you should use access switches in place of hubs for host access and LAN switches instead of routers for internetwork connections.

Looking at Figure 1-3 tells you that the two technologies have their respective trade-offs. In a nutshell, routers are slower and more expensive, but are much more intelligent. Indeed, large internetworks will never be able to entirely do away with routing functionality of some sort. Thus, the industry is seeing the melding of switching's physical layer speed with routing's network layer intelligence. Hybrid devices have been rolled out that incorporate some IP routing intelligence into hardware. These hybrids are variously called layer-3 switches, multilayer switches, and so on.

Other Internetworking Trends

Beyond the routing versus switching technology war, a number of other trends are afoot in the internetworking industry:

▼ **Network management**   A big push is under way to make large, complicated internetworks more reliable and manageable. Enterprises are adopting so-called management console or network management station (NMS) software products from which their network teams can centrally monitor and troubleshoot internetworks. These NMS consoles are being fed by a couple of established but still-developing network management protocols.

■ **Network security**   To date, most industry effort has been on securing access to network packets. The trend now is turning toward encrypting their contents to virtually guarantee data security and integrity. Tight security requires a harsh trade-off in expense, performance, or both.

■ **Virtual private networks (VPNs)**   Traditional leased-line WAN links are quickly being replaced by VPN links. VPNs use encryption to enable enterprises to operate private WANs over the Internet—at a fraction of the cost. Again, encryption exacts a trade-off in lowered performance.

■ **Faster dial-in links**   Remote dial-in access technology to the home or small office is being upgraded by replacing plain old telephone line circuits with digital circuits. At one time, Integrated Services Digital Network (ISDN) looked like the answer, but now DSL and cable are viewed as the most likely way to travel the "last mile" from the local phone company switching office to the small office or home.

■ **Faster WAN trunks**   Trunk lines running the Synchronous Optical Network (SONET) standard are advancing at a breakneck pace. The original 52-Mbps OC-1 has been improved over several increments to the present state-of-the-art 40-Gbps OC-768 standard.

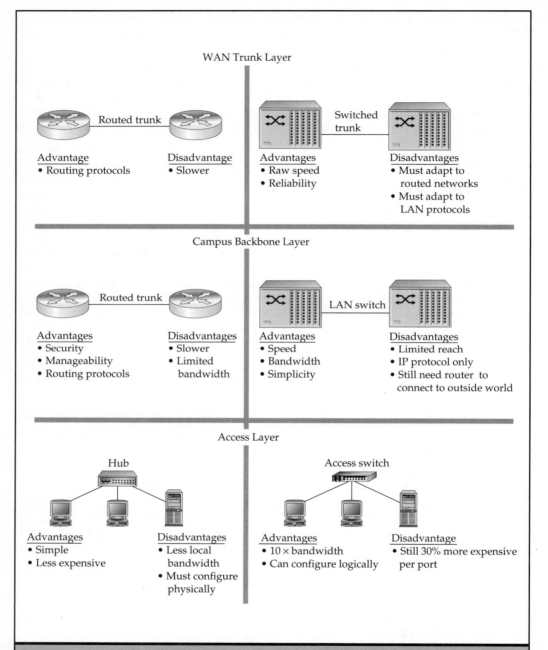

WAN Trunk Layer

Routed trunk

Advantage
• Routing protocols

Disadvantage
• Slower

Switched trunk

Advantages
• Raw speed
• Reliability

Disadvantages
• Must adapt to
  routed networks
• Must adapt to
  LAN protocols

Campus Backbone Layer

Routed trunk

Advantages
• Security
• Manageability
• Routing protocols

Disadvantages
• Slower
• Limited
  bandwidth

LAN switch

Advantages
• Speed
• Bandwidth
• Simplicity

Disadvantages
• Limited reach
• IP protocol only
• Still need router to
  connect to outside world

Access Layer

Hub

Advantages
• Simple
• Less expensive

Disadvantages
• Less local
  bandwidth
• Must configure
  physically

Access switch

Advantages
• 10 × bandwidth
• Can configure logically

Disadvantage
• Still 30% more expensive
  per port

Figure 1-3. Switching is encroaching on hubs at the low end and routers at the high end.

- ■ **Backbone technologies**   A showdown is under way between two high-bandwidth network protocols to take ownership of the campus backbone market: Asynchronous Transfer Mode (ATM) versus Gigabit Ethernet. ATM is a 622-Mbps non-IP standard that is ideal for multimedia traffic and has the ability to guarantee quality of service. However, it must be adapted for use with Ethernet networks. As the name implies, Gigabit Ethernet is the 1,000-Mbps successor to the 100-Mbps Fast Ethernet specification.

- ■ **IP Telephony**   For years, conventional telephone lines have been used to facilitate WAN connections, or even the SOHO user, calling an ISP to log into the network. The street runs both ways, however. Thanks to IP telephony, computer networks can be used to transport voice calls. In essence, the calls are converted into the popular Internet Protocol (IP) and the packets sent across the network to their destination where they are converted back into sound. A primary benefit of IP telephony is a cost savings—with a data network already in place, it's a simple matter to add an IP telephone system. IP telephony is nothing new—it's how telephone companies send calls between regional offices.

- ▲ **Wireless**   Conventional computer networks have had a major obstacle—computers having to be tethered to switches and hubs with Category 5 cabling. Obviously, this is not ideal in environments where mobility and computation must meet. The solution is wireless technology. This allows computers to be connected to the network, without having to be tied down with cabling. In recent months, wireless technology has taken impressive strides forward, allowing cable-free connectivity with increasing data rates.

These emerging technologies and standards have all the internetworking industry vendors jumping. Smaller competitors have tended to focus on a particular niche and choose sides, betting that one technology will prevail over the others. The big players have the resources and clout to take a more agnostic view of things; this is true of Cisco in particular.

CISCO'S OFFERINGS

Cisco Systems has the broadest and deepest product line in the internetworking business. You'll be surprised the first time you hold their product catalog—so thick and heavy that it's reminiscent of a catalog from a big computer company like IBM or Hewlett-Packard.

The product line has been in a constant state of flux over the last several years. This is partly due to the industry's relentless introduction of new standards and technologies, causing perpetual product-line turnover. But the flux has as much to do with Cisco's fervid pursuit of technology by acquisition.

The Cisco product line can be broken down into two categories:

▼ **Devices** Specific hardware products outlined at the beginning of this chapter

▲ **Solutions** The combination of hardware, software, and services to fit certain customer requirements

The industry solutions piece is part hype, but it's a good indication of where and how Cisco sees its individual products put to use. For example, a strategic focus now is on Voice over IP (VoIP). Should the much-touted data/voice convergence take hold, the potential exists for Cisco as the predominant IP device maker to become a key manufacturer of equipment used in telephone company back offices, and even of desktop data phones.

Competition

As mentioned earlier, the salient feature of Cisco's product line is that every class of device runs the Internetwork Operating System. Cisco will tell you that this enables customers to do a better job of configuring and managing internetworks. Cisco's competitors will tell you that IOS makes devices more expensive and takes away customer options in making future technology decisions. Both sides are right, of course—everything's a trade-off.

Although Cisco is well entrenched in the internetworking products battle, there are other companies out there firing their own salvos, hoping to gain enough ground on the field to make a name for their own companies.

Nipping at Their Tail

Cisco isn't bulletproof. The company has seen an increase in ambitious organizations trying to eat off of its plate. There are a number of examples showing where competitors are gaining ground in the service provider networking race. Challenging the leader are Juniper Networks in high-speed core Internet routers, Nortel Networks in optical networking gear, and Redback Networks in edge switching.

One of the major reasons Cisco is losing ground in selling to service providers, say analysts, is that service providers are looking for the very best product available. Conversely, in the enterprise market—where Cisco maintains its dominance—a strong brand and a solid distribution channel are normally the deciding factors. Furthermore, service providers also are willing to cobble their networks together using equipment from a range of suppliers. This is not the preferred *modus operandi* of many corporate network managers—they'd rather use the same supplier across the board.

Customer service is also a factor in Cisco's slippage. Smaller networking companies can more easily give the one-on-one service to individual service providers than Cisco: It's impossible for Cisco to personally manage 50,000 enterprise accounts. This can be made up for, on the other hand, by giving a half-dozen carrier customers their undivided attention.

Case Study

One such upstart that is making a name for itself is Juniper Networks, of Mountain View, California, which makes its own line of high-speed routers. Since its June 1999 IPO through 2001, its shares rose 494 percent, dwarfing Cisco's 118 percent rise during the same period. For the pessimists who think this is baseless dot-com speculation, think again. Juniper has real sales. In 1998, Cisco controlled 86.6 percent of the $175-million-a-year market for high-speed routers. At the same time, Juniper had a 6 percent share. Just one year later, Juniper had risen to a 17.5 percent slice of the $578 million pie. According to Dataquest, Cisco dipped to 80.7 percent. Juniper followed a value roller coaster ride, similar to Cisco's, through the early part of this decade. However, like Cisco, Juniper managed to weather the storm.

Juniper's gain on Cisco, say analysts, is because of its reliable hardware and corporate administration. Also, Juniper's JUNOS traffic management software is sometimes credited as being more reliable than Cisco's IOS system. Naturally, Cisco disagrees with this assessment, but the numbers are still cause for concern in San Jose.

What matters most, though, is that Cisco's IOS is far and away the most widely installed internetwork device operating system there is. This is leading many decision makers to view Cisco as the safe decision, given that the members of the internetworking labor market are more likely to be trained in IOS than another environment.

Who Wants to Be a Millionaire?

For many tech companies, the Holy Grail of success isn't discovered just in the development and sale of a great product that people will use every day. Rather, it's having Cisco wave its hand across the company's brow in blessing, then acquiring it. In turn, this transforms the company's executives and employees into instant millionaires—without even having to be the last one voted off the island.

Cisco continues to expand and develop its technology and product offerings by acquiring promising companies with impressive technology or services. Oftentimes, Cisco's acquisitions can make or break a technology. For example, when the speculation started as to whether ATM could or should take over as the backbone technology of choice, many observers assumed that Cisco—a company with deep roots in Ethernet—would side with Gigabit Ethernet. Cisco instead went out and acquired StrataCom, the premier ATM technology company, in one of the largest technology mergers ever at that point. Cisco has also acquired software providers focused on providing solutions in such areas as network design and management. Cisco has spent years hyping itself as the industry's premier enterprise internetworking solutions vendor, and the company's willingness to adapt to technology trends instead of fighting them has impressed observers.

Table 1-1 shows Cisco's acquisitions for 1999 through 2003, along with a brief description of each company and the market it serves.

Date of Acquisition	Company Name	What They Do	Market Served
Nov. 12, 2003	Latitude Communications, Inc.	Provider of conferencing products. Their MeetingPlace software integrates with existing desktop scheduling applications as well as data collaboration and instant messaging applications.	Enterprise conferencing
March 20, 2003	Linksys Group, Inc.	Provider of consumer/SOHO networking equipment, including wireless devices.	Consumer/ SOHO
March 19, 2003	SignalWorks, Inc.	Developer of high-performance audio software for IP telephony systems.	IP telephony
Jan. 24, 2003	Okena, Inc.	Developer of threat protection software for desktop and servers.	Host-based intrusion detection systems (HIDS)
Oct. 22, 2002	Psionic Software, Inc.	Developer of network security software. Products enhance intrusion detection efficiency by reducing false alarms.	Intrusion detection systems
Aug. 20, 2002	Andiamo Systems, Inc.	Developer of multilayer, intelligent storage switches. Provided Cisco with an entry into the Fibre Channel storage area networking (SAN) market.	Storage
July 25, 2002	AYR Networks, Inc.	Provider of network technologies that are expected to enhance and accelerate time-to-market delivery of Cisco's network operating system and routing software (IOS).	IOS

Table 1-1.   Cisco's Acquisitions from 1999 Through 2003

Date of Acquisition	Company Name	What They Do	Market Served
May 1, 2002	Hammerhead Networks, Inc.	Developer of software integrating with and accelerating time-to-market delivery of hardware solutions for IP aggregation. Specifically, broadband, leased-line, and cable markets.	IP aggregation
May 1, 2002	Navarro Networks, Inc.	Developer of ASIC components for Ethernet.	Ethernet switching
July 27, 2001	Allegro Systems	Developer of virtual private network (VPN) acceleration technologies used in high-bandwidth networks where simultaneous VPN connections are necessary.	VPNs for high-bandwidth networks
Jul. 11, 2001	AuroraNetics, Inc.	Developer of 10-Gbps silicon technology for metropolitan fiber networks. The technology is used by service providers to create high-speed metropolitan networks using fiber rings known as resilient packet rings (RPRs).	Metropolitan networks
Dec. 14, 2000	ExiO	Developer of in-building wireless technologies, based on Code Division Multiple Access (CDMA) technologies. The acquisition is to augment Cisco's existing wireless offerings.	Wireless LAN
Nov. 13, 2000	Radiata	Supplier of chipsets for high-speed wireless networks. The acquisition will help Cisco develop next-generation wireless networks.	Wireless LAN

Table 1-1.   Cisco's Acquisitions from 1999 Through 2003 *(continued)*

Date of Acquisition	Company Name	What They Do	Market Served
Nov. 10, 2000	Active Voice Corporation	Unified messaging consolidates voicemail, e-mail, and fax messages on a single IP network, making them accessible on any device at any time.	Unified messaging
Oct. 20, 2000	CAIS Software Solutions	Develops software for the management of high-speed, broadband Internet services. Their application, IPORT Broadband Provisioning System, provides features including security, authorization, accounting, and billing.	Broadband service management solutions
Sept. 28, 2000	Vovida Networks, Inc.	Communications software provider that offers a family of open source packet telephony networking software.	Voice over IP
Sept. 28, 2000	IPCell Technologies, Inc.	Developed software for VoIP packet applications.	Voice and data integrated access services
Oct. 31, 2000	PixStream, Inc.	Developed hardware and software solutions for distributing and managing streaming video across broadband networks.	Digital video
Oct. 1, 2000	IPMobile, Inc.	Developing wireless technology for next-generation networking.	Mobile wireless Internet
July 27, 2000	NuSpeed Internet Systems, Inc.	Connects storage area networks and IP networks.	IP-enabled storage area networking technology

Table 1-1.   Cisco's Acquisitions from 1999 Through 2003 *(continued)*

Date of Acquisition	Company Name	What They Do	Market Served
July 25, 2000	Komodo Technology, Inc.	Developer of VoIP devices that allow analog telephones to place calls over IP-based networks. Cisco expects this to ease the transition from circuit-switched networks to packet-based networks.	VoIP devices for analog phones
July 7, 2000	Netiverse, Ltd.	Providers of content acceleration technology for enhancing the performance of networking devices.	Content-aware switches
June 5, 2000	HyNEX, Ltd.	Developer of intelligent access devices for ATM network providers.	ATM and IP solutions
May 12, 2000	Qeyton Systems, Inc.	Developer of Metropolitan Dense Wave Division Multiplexing (MDWDM) technology, which allows for comprehensive end-to-end optical networking.	Metropolitan DWDM technology
May 5, 2000	ArrowPoint Communications, Inc.	Provides content switches that optimize the delivery of content across a network.	Content networking technology
April 12, 2000	Seagull Semiconductor, Ltd.	Developer of silicon technology, which will be used to develop terabit routers.	High-speed silicon for terabit routers
April 11, 2000	PentaCom Ltd.	Provides products that allow IP-based metropolitan networks to provide the same benefits as SONET-based networks while doubling bandwidth efficiency.	Metro IP networks
March 29, 2000	SightPath, Inc.	Provides appliances for developing intelligent content delivery networks.	Content delivery optimizers

Table 1-1.   Cisco's Acquisitions from 1999 Through 2003 *(continued)*

Date of Acquisition	Company Name	What They Do	Market Served
March 16, 2000	infoGear Technology Corp.	Provides hardware and software for managing information appliances for Internet access.	Software to manage information appliances
March 16, 2000	JetCell, Inc.	Develops in-building wireless networking for corporate networks.	In-building wireless telephony
March 1, 2000	Atlantech Technologies, Ltd.	Provides software to help configure and monitor network hardware.	Network element management software
Feb. 16, 2000	Growth Networks, Inc.	Developer of high-performance networking silicon that has the potential to scale capacities from 10s of Gbps to 10s of Tbps.	Internet switching fabrics
Jan. 19, 2000	Altiga Networks	VPN solution developer for remote access applications.	Enterprise VPN solutions
Jan. 19, 2000	Compatible Systems, Corp.	Develops standards-based VPN solutions for service providers.	Service provider VPN solutions
Dec. 20, 1999	Pirelli Optical Systems	Develops DWDM equipment.	Optical internetworking
Dec. 17, 1999	Internet Engineering Group, LLC	Develops high-performance software for next-generation networks.	Optical internetworking
Dec. 16, 1999	Worldwide Data Systems, Inc.	Data/voice networking consulting and engineering service.	Consumer advocacy
Nov. 11, 1999	V-Bits, Inc.	Digital video processor for video processing and cable television service providers.	Cable television
Nov. 9, 1999	Aironet Wireless Communications, Inc.	Develops high-speed wireless LAN hardware.	Wireless LANs

Table 1-1.   Cisco's Acquisitions from 1999 Through 2003 *(continued)*

Date of Acquisition	Company Name	What They Do	Market Served
Oct. 26, 1999	Tasmania Network Systems, Inc.	Develops network caching software, which accelerates content delivery and network performance.	Web scaling
Sept. 22, 1999	WebLine Communications Corp.	Provides customer service and e-business software.	Intelligent contact management
Sept. 15, 1999	Cocom A/S	Develops access solutions for cable TV networking.	Cable
Aug. 26, 1999	Cerent Corporation	Provides next-generation SONET equipment, which is used for voice and data networking.	Optical internetworking
Aug. 26, 1999	Monterey Networks, Inc.	Provides next-generation optical transport networking technology.	Optical internetworking
Aug. 18, 1999	MaxComm Technologies, Inc.	Develops DSL technology.	DSL
Aug. 16, 1999	Calista, Inc.	Develops technology that allows legacy digital telephones to interoperate with Cisco's New World voice-enabled switches and routers.	IP telephony
June 29, 1999	StratumOne Communications, Inc.	Develops semiconductor products for high-speed, wide-area networking.	Optical internetworking
June 17, 1999	TransMedia Communications, Inc.	Provider of media gateway technology that brings together different types of networks (ATM, IP).	Media gateway technology
April 28, 1999	Amteva Technologies, Inc.	Middleware developer that consolidates voicemail, e-mail, and fax on a single IP network.	IP-based unified communications software

Table 1-1.   Cisco's Acquisitions from 1999 Through 2003 *(continued)*

Date of Acquisition	Company Name	What They Do	Market Served
April 13, 1999	GeoTel Communications Corp.	Application developer that integrates enterprise data applications with voice devices (like PBXs) to deliver integrated data and voice to call centers.	Network-based call routing solutions for distributed call centers
April 8, 1999	Sentient Networks, Inc.	Developed a high-density ATM circuit emulation services gateway to deliver circuit-based private line services across packet-based ATM networks.	ATM circuit emulation services gateway
April 8, 1999	Fibex Systems	Developed products that combine voice services with data services using ATM.	Integrated access digital loop carrier

Table 1-1.   Cisco's Acquisitions from 1999 Through 2003 *(continued)*

Cisco Hardware Devices

Cisco's product line is aligned according to customer scale. In other words, they package and price product models according to the size and sophistication of the customer market. For example, Tier 2 ISPs may not be that big in revenue, but the amount of traffic coursing through their internetworks rivals that of a Fortune 1000 company, and so does the sophistication of the members of their network teams. On the other hand, a small-office customer wants things kept simple and doesn't want to pay a premium for a product that's expandable when more capacity is unlikely to be needed.

SOHO Routers

SOHO is an industry term for very small network users—small office/home office. Typical SOHO customers have only one or two LAN segments in their facility and an ISP connection to the Internet.

The linchpin of Cisco's SOHO strategy is low-end routers. Allowing small companies to tap into ISPs router-to-router instead of as dial-in users saves money on telephone connections, upgrades performance, and improves reliability. Table 1-2 outlines Cisco's SOHO product series. The term *series* here means a chassis that is variously configured at the manufacturing plant into several product models—usually depending on the printed circuit cards installed in them.

Product Series	Description
Cisco 70 Series	DSL or cable access router to connect multiple users. Includes user-configurable IOS.
Cisco 90 Series	Broadband routers featuring such security measures as VPN and firewall protection. Includes user-configurable IOS. Capable of supporting up to five users.
Cisco 600 Series	DSL access routers for a single user. Doesn't have user-configurable IOS.
Cisco 800 Series	ISDN, DSL, and serial access routers to connect up to 20 users. Includes IOS and has VPN encryption capability.
Cisco uBR900 Series	Cable access router. Integrated VoIP, VPN, and router functionality for telecommuters and small offices. Includes user-configurable IOS.

Table 1-2.   Cisco's Five Series of SOHO Routers

SOHO products emphasize dial-in technologies (DSL, cable, and ISDN) because small offices and home offices don't have dedicated WAN links connecting them to their ISP or enterprise internetwork.

Midrange Cisco Routers

The small- to medium-sized network requires a wide variety of solutions. Cisco has several tiers of access router products designed to fit the customer's capacity needs and type of telecom link.

The series in Table 1-3 represent dozens of individual product numbers. Depending on the product series, various combinations of LAN technologies and WAN media can be configured. *Modular* means that the chassis can be upgraded in the field by inserting one or more modules. Non-modular devices are fixed in configuration.

Backbone Routers

When Cisco claims that over 70 percent of the Internet is run using its routers, these are the models they're talking about. The Cisco 4000 series is perhaps the most widely distributed router chassis there is. The 7000 and 12000 series are bigger, resembling dorm refrigerators in shape and size, and have data buses into which *blades* (whole devices on a board) can be installed.

Product Series	Description
Cisco 1700 Series	Ethernet access router to connect to a broadband, ISDN, or DSL WAN link. VPN encryption, VoIP (Voice over IP), and VoFR (Voice over Frame Relay) capability.
Cisco 2500 Series	Ethernet or Token Ring router/hub or dial-access server models to connect one or two LAN segments to an ISDN or a serial link.
Cisco 2600 Series	Modular and cost-effective solution for duty as access router, voice/data gateway, or dial-access server. Connects one or two Ethernet or Token Ring LANs to ISDN, channelized T1, Ethernet, analog modems, or ATM links. Also supports voice/fax and Frame Relay.
Cisco 3600 Series	Modular high-density router for dial-access or router-to-router traffic. Supports ISDN, serial, channelized T1, digital modems, and ATM links. Also supports voice/fax and Frame Relay.
Cisco 3700 Series	Modular routers, targeted at branch offices. Supports Frame Relay, ISDN, LL, X.25, ATM, fractional T1/E1, xDSL, T3/E3, HSSI WAN protocols.

Table 1-3.   Cisco's Midrange Routing Solutions

Because they're not access routers, Cisco's backbone routers can take as many users as they can handle packets. All of the products (described in Table 1-4) are modular, letting customers install modules according to the LAN technology being run and the capacity needed. In fact, these routers can operate more than one protocol simultaneously, such as Ethernet and Token Ring. A *slot* is an electronic bay into which a printed circuit board module is inserted.

HSSI stands for high-speed serial interface, a specialized I/O standard mainly used in conjunction with supercomputers. The behemoth Cisco 12000 router and uBR10012 router are carrier-class devices, in that local equipment carriers' telecommunications network operators use them in their back-office data-switching operations.

All the backbone Cisco routers have extensive capabilities for VPN, security, Quality of Service (QoS), and network management.

Cisco Access Switches

Access switches have ports on their front into which individual host devices plug, and an "uplink" port on the back leading up the hierarchy to a router or a LAN switch. Cisco's access switch is described in Table 1-5.

Product Series	Description
Cisco 6400 Series	DSL router for ISPs and corporations. Supporting Ethernet, Fast Ethernet, Gigabit Ethernet, ATM, DSL, and broadband.
Cisco 7200 Series	Four to six slot routers. Features include support for up to 8,000 concurrent sessions, multiprotocol support, and voice/video/data integration.
Cisco 7300 Series	Four slots. Targeted at service providers and enterprise users. Includes support for copper or optical Gigabit Ethernet.
Cisco 7400 Series	Ideal for application-specific routing deployments. Supports a range of WAN protocols, from DS0 to OC3. MPLS VPN, MPLS provider edge, and full L2TP to MPLS supported.
Cisco 7500 Series	Five to thirteen slots. High port density, supports for a number of interface processors and port adapters. Designed for service providers and enterprises.
Cisco 7600 Series	Routing solutions for optical metropolitan area networks and WANs. Up to 720 Gbps switching fabric. 32,000 PPPoE connections, 16,000 L2TP connections, and 16,000 SSG connections per MWAM module.
Cisco 10000 Series	Ten-slot Gigabit Ethernet switch router. Can accommodate OC-48 card. Offers IPSec and MPLS VPN and Quality of Service (QoS) capabilities.
Cisco 12000 Series	Eight- or twelve-slot Gigabit Ethernet switch router optimized for IP. Has special cards for OC-12 and OC-48 WAN links.
Cisco uBR7200 Series	Two- to four-slot broadband, carrier-class routers. Designed for cable operators and service providers, this series connects residential subscribers for high-speed data, broadband, and IP telephony.
Cisco uBR10012 Series	Broadband, carrier-class router. Designed for cable operators and service providers, this series connects residential subscribers for high-speed data, broadband, and IP telephony.

Table 1-4.   Cisco's Series of Backbone Routers

Product Series	Description
Catalyst 2820	Designed for aggregating hubs or servers. Has 24 Fast Ethernet ports plus two slots for a choice of high-speed modules—Fast Ethernet, FDDI, or ATM. Not stackable.

Table 1-5.   Cisco's Access Switch

MicroSwitches are fixed-configuration devices with no access to the IOS command-line interface (they self-configure). As the popularity of access switches grows, some expect the low-cost MicroSwitch line to be expanded. Low-end Catalyst switches have more robust configurability.

Cisco Catalyst LAN Switches

A *LAN switch* is a high-speed layer-2 device that forwards traffic between LAN segments. They are not to be confused with access switches such as the MicroSwitch or a low-end Catalyst switch, which are devices that connect hosts to internetworks much like hubs. Put another way, access switches *form* LAN segments; LAN switches switch *between* them.

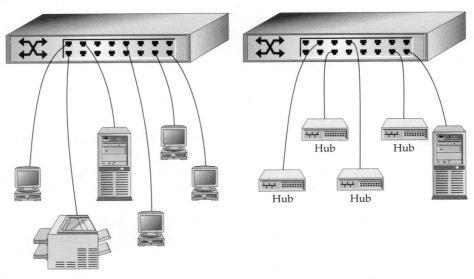

Access Switch   LAN Switch

Because hubs form LAN segments with multiple hosts attached to each segment, a switch powerful enough to connect hubs is regarded as a LAN switch. Keep in mind, though, that LAN switches can and do also connect such bandwidth-intensive hosts as servers and high-speed network printers.

The Cisco Catalyst Series family of LAN switches is the broadest in the industry. Catalyst models range from a four-port model all the way up to the carrier-class Catalyst 8500. The first tier of the Catalyst LAN switch line contains the 2900s, outlined in Table 1-6.

Multilayer switching (also called layer-3 switching) first appears in the middle range of the Catalyst switch line, as you see in Table 1-7. To reiterate, multilayer switches are devices with IP routing capability built into the switch hardware, thereby combining some of the logical capabilities of IP routing with the raw speed of switching.

Cisco offers two high-end backbone switches, one for Gigabit Ethernet and the other for ATM. Table 1-8 outlines them.

The Catalyst 6500 and 8500 are carrier-class switch devices. They have very high port density to interconnect hundreds of LAN segments. The 6500 has a special blade that

Product Series	Description
Catalyst 2900 Series	Three models with 12–48 ports for Ethernet/Fast Ethernet 10/100 auto sensing. Not stackable.
Catalyst 2900XL Series	24 ports and two module slots for 10Base-T/100Base-TX, 1000Base-X, 1000Base-T, Gigabit Ethernet, and Asynchronous Transfer Mode (ATM) modules. Not stackable.
Catalyst 2900XL LRE Series	Two switch models with either 12 or 24 ports delivering Long Range Ethernet (LRE) across existing telephone lines, up to 5,000 feet.
Catalyst 2940 Series	Two models with eight 10/100 Ethernet ports. The 2940-8TF model offers Gigabit Ethernet.
Catalyst 2950 Series	Fourteen models with between 12 and 48 ports of 10/100 Ethernet and (on most models) 2 ports of Gigabit Ethernet uplinks. Offers intelligent functionality, including security services and quality of service.
Catalyst 2970 Series	Two models of 24-port Gigabit Ethernet switches. The 2970G-24TS model also offers four small form-pluggable (SFP) ports.

Table 1-6.   Midrange 2900 Catalyst Switches Have Higher Port Densities

Product Series	Description
Catalyst 3500XL Series	One model with 24 10/100BaseT Ethernet ports and 2 Gigabit Ethernet uplink ports, and one model with eight Gigabit Ethernet ports. 3500XLs are stackable up to nine units running a switch fabric up to 10 Gbps. The 3500 Series is positioned as Cisco's premier solution for low-end Gigabit Ethernet connectivity.
Catalyst 3550 Series	Nine models of stackable, multilayer Ethernet switches. Models offer 24 or 49 10/100 Ethernet ports and two Gigabit Ethernet uplinks.
Catalyst 3750 Series	Four models of stackable switches offering 24 or 48 10/100 Ethernet ports. One model offers 12 Gigabit Ethernet ports. The switches utilize StackWise technology, which allows stacking with nine other 3750 units.
Catalyst 4000 Series	Three models with three-slot modular chassis supporting 10/100/1000 Ethernet. One module has 48 10/100 ports and another, 32 10/100 ports with a variety of Gigabit Ethernet uplink options.
	The third model offers 40 ports of 10/100 Ethernet and two ports of 1000BaseX Gigabit Ethernet. Not stackable.
Catalyst 4500 Series	Three models of switches with 3, 6, or 7 slots. Each slot is capable of accepting various switching modules offering 10/100 or Gigabit Ethernet with up to 240 ports.

Table 1-7.   Some Midrange Catalyst LAN Switches Incorporating Multilayer Switching

Product Series	Description
Catalyst 6500 Series	Five models with three to thirteen slots. The switches can be customized by adding various modules, including Ethernet, Gigabit Ethernet, 10 Gigabit, voice, ATM and other modules.
Catalyst 8500 Series	Four models with five to thirteen slots supporting multiservice ATM switching optimized for aggregating multiprotocol traffic. Not stackable. Cisco's choice for ATM backbone switches.

Table 1-8.   Cisco's Two High-End Catalyst Switches Covering Gigabit, 10 Gigabit, and ATM Backbones

handles multilayer switching functionality. The 8500 line is tuned for multimedia traffic types, such as VoIP, videocasting, and other specialized types.

Cisco Solutions

Cisco touts itself as the premier "end-to-end enterprise solutions provider" in internet-working. What this means in English is that Cisco has the breadth of product line functionality to fulfill virtually any customer requirement, whether integrated voice/data, ATM backbones, or integration to IBM SNA environments, and so on. In practical terms, Cisco has been able to do this because of its foresight and raw cash. Having over $180 billion in market capitalization at the end of 2003 has given the company the financial muscle to fill product-line gaps and enter emerging areas by either intensive internal R&D or going out and acquiring the best-of-breed provider. As mentioned, Cisco has acquired well over 70 companies over the past several years. Each acquisition seems to have been made to assimilate an emerging technology, not to buy the smaller company's installed customer base.

Not all of Cisco's solutions technologies were buyouts; some were developed in-house. However, many of the major technology additions were via acquisition. The key factor in each is whether Cisco can successfully integrate the new technology into the company's unifying IOS architecture. Despite the wishes of certain competitors, so far Cisco has done fairly well at that, with some exceptions. Here's an overview of the major solutions areas:

▼ **IOS feature sets** IOS can be purchased *a la carte* for many devices, to obtain the functionality needed to deal with the customer's installed environment, whether IBM SNA, Novell NetWare, AppleTalk, or vanilla IP.

■ **ATM** Cisco has invested heavily in ATM technology, with the StrataCom buyout bringing a full line of ATM WAN switches, multiservice ATM switches, and edge concentrators. Cisco also purchased a company called LightStream to obtain the LightStream 1010 ATM module for connecting to ATM campus LANs.

■ **Voice/data integration** To consolidate its position in the emerging VoIP market, Cisco offers the VCO/4K open programmable voice/data switch, Cisco-to-circuit switched gateways, and other voice integration products.

■ **Network management** Several disparate management software applications, both homegrown and acquired, are slowly being melded together under the CiscoWorks2000 banner. Right now things are still a bit of a mess, with three more-or-less stand-alone products: Resource Manager Essentials for managing routed networks, CWSI Campus for managing switched networks, and NetSys Baseliner for designing network topologies. CWSI and NetSys were acquisitions.

■ **ISP connectivity** Cisco offers "director" products for use by ISPs in managing their high-volume traffic loads. Cisco LocalDirector is a sophisticated server connection management system that manages traffic based on service requested, distribution method, and server availability. Cisco DistributedDirector is similar, but provides dynamic, transparent Internet traffic load distribution management between geographically dispersed servers.

- **Security** CiscoSecure is the company's integrated client-server security management system. IOS itself incorporates many security commands at the client device level, and CiscoSecure keeps a central database of users, user authorizations, and security event history. Cisco offers the PIX Firewall for traffic-level security. For those accessing a network across the Internet, Cisco offers VPN solutions that are matched with Cisco's products, which are including more and more VPN functionality. Cisco also offers an IOS feature set called IOS Firewall, which is an expanded set of IOS commands that allows configuration of most midrange and high-end Cisco routers with firewall functionality.

- **Storage area networking (SAN)** The extent to which a computer network is functional goes beyond whether everyone in an organization has a computer on his or her desktop or whether the network is faster than greased lightning. The material that courses through the network—namely, the data—must be stored somewhere. For organizations that have a need to store and maintain a great deal of data, storage area networks (SANs) are an increasingly popular option. SANs are communications platforms that interconnect servers and storage devices at gigabit speeds. Products like the Cisco MDS 9000 Series of multilayer switches help provide an environment in which data can be maintained.

- **Content networking** In order to provide access to specific network content, many organizations are implementing content networking solutions. Content networking provides an intelligent way to route content where it is needed. For example, content networking can help feed e-learning, streaming media, and file distribution. Cisco has developed a number of tools and technologies to help facilitate content networking, including the 7300 Content Engine, which accelerates content delivery, improving scalability and content availability.

- **Wireless** A few years ago, wireless networking technology might have seemed too expensive to be a feasible option for networking. Now, however, wireless is within everyone's grasp, and many computers come with wireless cards already installed. Cisco is no stranger to the world of wireless, having developed its own enterprise products. However, the company has also extended its reach into the realm of home and small business wireless networking through the acquisition of Linksys in 2003.

- **Voice over IP (VoIP)** Computer networks aren't just useful for transporting data between servers and clients. By utilizing the popular Internet Protocol (IP), telephone conversations can take place across computer networks by utilizing IP telephony. Cisco offers a number of devices to help facilitate Voice over IP (VoIP), from handsets plugged into switches to wireless IP phones to VoIP-capable routers and switches. VoIP is a popular technology because it allows low-cost telephony within an organization—whether the organization is situated within one building or at branch locations spread across the world.

These and other Cisco solutions are covered throughout this book. We won't go into them in any detail here; you need to get technical first. That process starts in the next chapter—a primer on internetworking technology basics.

CHAPTER 2

Networking Primer

Ever wonder how the Internet really works? Most of us at one time or another have wondered what happens behind the scenes when surfing Web pages, sending e-mail, or downloading files. You know instinctively that there must be many devices linking you to the other computer, but how exactly is the connection made? What makes up a message, and how does it find its way through the seemingly chaotic Internet back to your desktop? After all, it wasn't that long ago that incompatibility between various makes and models of computers made exchanging data a headache. Now everybody can connect to the Internet to share data and services without a second thought. How did the computer industry pull it off?

Most laypersons think the answer is technology, and to a point they're right. But the whole answer is that the Internet was brought together by a combination of technology and standards—specifically, *de jure* and *de facto* technical standards. De jure standards are set by trade associations; de facto standards are set by brute economic force. All the routers and switches in the world couldn't form the Internet without standards to make hardware, software, and telecommunications equipment compatible.

The products fueling the Internet were introduced in Chapter 1. Now we'll cover the underlying architectures that made all that technology possible, from telecommunications infrastructure all the way up to inside your PC. An understanding of the technologies and standards underpinning an internetwork will give you a clear picture of what happens in the background when you click in your browser.

BITS AND BYTES

Before going into details on internetworking, it's necessary to cover the basic concepts that explain how computer technology works. We'll do this "from the wire up" to help you understand why systems work the way they do.

The Internet's infrastructure is composed of millions of networking devices—routers, switches, firewalls, access servers, and hubs—loosely hooked together through a sophisticated global address system. They're linked mostly by twisted-pair copper cable to the desktop and big trunk lines running over very high-speed fiber-optic cable. But mostly the Internet is a matter of millions of individual hardware devices loosely tied together by a global addressing scheme.

How Computers Understand Data

Networking devices are more or less the same as normal computer platforms such as your PC. The biggest differences are in configuration: most types of network equipment have no CRT or disks because they're designed to move data—not store it or present it. However, all network devices are computers in the basic sense that they have CPUs, memory, and operating systems.

Bits Compose Binary Messages

Computing is largely a matter of sending electrical signals between various hardware components. In a normal computer platform, the signals shoot around tiny transistors inside the CPU or memory and travel over ultra-thin wires embedded in printed circuit boards. Once on the outside, electrical signals travel over cables in order to move between devices.

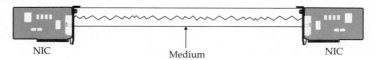

NIC   Medium   NIC

As signals are passed over the cable, network interface cards (NICs) at each end keep track of the electrical pulse waveforms and interpret them as data. The NIC senses each electrical pulse as either an On or Off signal. This is called *binary* transmission—a system in which each On pulse is recorded as the number 1 and each Off signal as the number 0. In machine language, these zeros and ones are *bits*, and a file of bits is a *binary* file.

Whether a signal represents a zero or a one is sensed by fluctuations in the voltage of electrical pulses (or light pulses, over fiber-optic media) during miniscule time intervals. These tiny time intervals are called *cycles per second,* or Hertz (Hz) in electrical engineering circles. For example, the CPU in a 100-Mbps NIC can generate 100 million cycles per second. In practical terms, the payoff is that the computer can process 100 million pulses per second and interpret them as either zeros or ones.

How Order Is Maintained Among Bits

All computers use binary transmission at the machine level. Bits are the basic raw material with which they work, usually as a collection of bits in a binary file. Binary files are the stuff that gets put into memory, processed through CPUs, stored on disks, and sent over cables. Both data and software programs are stored as binary files. If you were to look at a data file in any type of machine in binary format, you'd be staring at a page full of 0's and 1's. Doing so might make your eyes glaze over, but machines can handle binary format because of *ordinality*—a fancy term for knowing what piece of information is supposed to appear in a certain field position.

The computer doesn't keep track of ordinal positions one by one. It instead keeps track of the bit position at which a field begins and ends. A *field* is a logical piece of information. For example, the computer might know that bit positions 121 through 128 are used to store a person's middle initial.

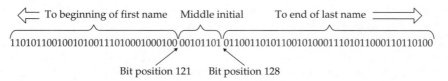

To beginning of first name   Middle initial   To end of last name

110101100100101001110100010001000 00101101 011001101011001010001110101100011011 0100

Bit position 121   Bit position 128

Computers are able to track bit orders with great precision by using clocks that time exactly where a CPU is in a stream of bits. By knowing where fields are, computers can build data from the wire up.

Computer Software Operates on Bytes

For simplicity, however, computers don't operate one bit at a time. There's an interim level one step up from bits called bytes—thus the expression "bits and bytes." A *byte* is a series of eight consecutive bits that are operated upon as a unit.

10110111	00110100	11001100	101110110	11000100
Byte	Byte	Byte	Byte	Byte

3-byte field   2-byte field

From a logical standpoint, the basic unit making up a data field is bytes. This not only makes systems run faster, but also makes them easier to program and debug. You'll never see a programmer declare how many bits long a field should be, but declaring byte lengths is routine. Keeping track of individual bit positions is often left to the computer.

Computer Words

Unlike software, CPUs must deal in bits. At the lowest level, computer hardware deals with On/Off electrical signals pulsing through its circuitry in bits. It would take too long to perform bit-to-byte translations inside a CPU, so computers have what's called a *word size*. The step up from a byte is a *word*, which is the number of bytes a CPU architecture is designed to handle each cycle.

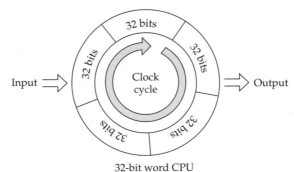

32-bit word CPU

For example, an Intel Xeon-based PC or server is a 32-bit word machine, meaning that it processes 32 bits per clock cycle. But as hardware miniaturization techniques have advanced—and the need to process data faster has grown—the industry has settled on 64-bit word architectures as the way to go. A variety of 64-bit machines are available from IBM, Sun, and manufacturers using Intel's Itanium 2 architecture. Cisco devices use both 32- and 64-bit CPUs.

Compiled Software

The last step up is from bytes to something we humans can understand. As you probably know, software takes the form of source code files written by computer programmers. The commands that programmers type into source code files are symbols instructing the computer what to do. When a program is written, it's changed into machine language—bits and bytes—by a *compiler*, which is a specialized application that translates software code into machine language files referred to as *executables* or *binaries*. For example, if code is written using the C++ programming language, it is translated through a C++ compiler.

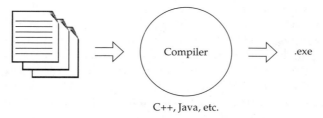

C++, Java, etc.

You may have noticed the .exe and .bin file extensions in your PC's directory. They stand for *executable* and *binary*, respectively. The Cisco IOS is executable software. Actually, it's a package containing hundreds of executables that operate device hardware, forward packets, talk-to-neighbor network devices, and so on.

Computing Architectures

A *computing architecture* is a technical specification of all components that make up a system. Published computing architectures are quite detailed and specific, and most are thousands of pages long. But in certain parts they are abstract by design, leaving the exact implementation of that portion of the architecture up to the designer.

Function
Functionality
Arrangement
Look and feel
Abstract Interface
Dependencies
Extensions
Products
Implementation

What separates an architecture from a regular product specification is the use of abstract layering. An *abstraction layer* is a fixed interface connecting two system components, and it governs the relationship between each side's function and implementation. If something changes on one side of the interface, by design it should not require changes on the other side. These layers are put in to help guarantee compatibility in two directions:

▼ Between various components within the system

▲ Between various products implementing the architecture

Abstraction between components stabilizes system designs, because it allows different development groups to engineer against a stable target. For example, the published interface between the layers in networking software allows hundreds of network interface manufacturers to engineer products compatible with the Fast Ethernet specification.

There are several important computing architectures—some more open than others. The Microsoft Windows/Intel 80x86 Wintel architecture is the stuff of legend. Other important computing architectures include RAID (redundant array of inexpensive disks), Java, CORBA (Common Object Request Broker Architecture, a vendor-independent architecture and infrastructure that applications use to work together over networks), and dozens more. Yet perhaps the most important computing architecture ever devised is the one that created the Internet: the OSI reference model.

OSI REFERENCE MODEL

The International Organization for Standardization (ISO), an international engineering organization based in Paris, published the Open Systems Interconnection (OSI) reference model in 1978. This seven-layer model has become the standard for designing communication methods among network devices and was the template used to design the Internet Protocol (IP).

The goal of the OSI reference model was to promote interoperability. *Interoperability* means the ability for otherwise incompatible systems to operate together in such a way that they can successfully perform common tasks. A good example of interoperability would be an Ethernet LAN transparently exchanging messages with an IBM Token Ring LAN.

The Seven-Layer Stack

The OSI model divides networks into seven functional layers and thus is often called the *seven-layer stack*. Each layer defines a function or set of functions performed when data is transferred between applications across the network. Whether the network protocol is IP, Novell NetWare, or AppleTalk, if it adheres to the OSI model, more or less the same rules are applied at each of the seven layers. The seven layers are outlined in Figure 2-1.

As depicted in Figure 2-1, each layer is a protocol for communications between linked devices. Concerning network operations, the key thing to understand is that each layer on each device talks to its counterpart to manage a particular aspect of the network connection. Concerning interoperability, the key is the fixed interface sitting between each layer. Abstract layering reduces what would otherwise be daunting complexity.

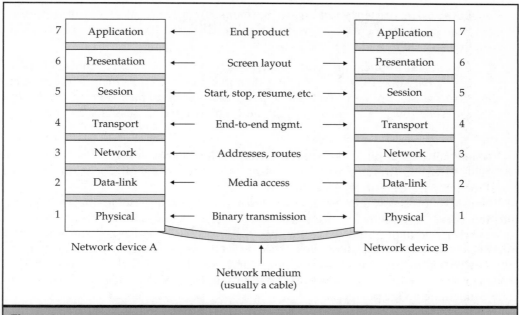

Figure 2-1.   Each OSI layer runs a protocol to manage connections between devices.

▼ **Layer 1, the physical layer**   Controls the transport medium by defining the
electrical and mechanical characteristics carrying the data signal. Examples include
twisted-pair cabling, fiber-optic cabling, coaxial cable, and serial lines.

■ **Layer 2, the data-link layer**   Controls access to the network and ensures the
reliable transfer of frames across the network. The best known data-link
specification is Ethernet's Carrier Sense Multiple Access with Collision Detection.
Token Ring and FDDI adhere to the token-passing data-link architecture.

■ **Layer 3, the network layer**   Manages the movement of data between different
networks. Protocols at this layer are responsible for finding the device for which
the data is destined. Examples include IP, IPX, and AppleTalk.

■ **Layer 4, the transport layer**   Makes sure that data reaches its destination intact
and in the proper order. The Transmission Control Protocol (TCP) and User
Datagram Protocol (UDP) operate at this layer.

■ **Layer 5, the session layer**   Establishes and terminates connections and arranges
sessions between two computers. Example session layer protocols include Remote
Procedure Call (RPC) and the Lightweight Directory Access Protocol (LDAP).

- ■ **Layer 6, the presentation layer**   Formats data for screen display or printing. Examples of presentation layer protocols include the Lightweight Presentation Protocol (LPP) and NetBIOS.

- ▲ **Layer 7, the application layer**   Contains protocols used to perform useful tasks over a network. Examples of network application protocols include the Simple Mail Transfer Protocol (SMTP) for e-mail, the Hypertext Transfer Protocol (HTTP) for Web browsers and servers, Telnet for remote terminal sessions, and hundreds of others.

Layer 7 network applications are the reason the lower six layers exist. Many of these protocols saw their first use in UNIX systems, given that the UNIX operating system developed in parallel with the Internet.

Intensive effort is now under way to develop new network applications that more tightly integrate normal applications with the network. The goal is for all kinds of applications—PC, client-server, and mainframe—to communicate transparently with other computers over internetworks. For example, it would be nice if a UNIX server-based financial accounting software package could automatically query foreign exchange rate databases—sitting on IBM mainframe computers in New York, London, and Hong Kong— in order to automatically recalculate hedge positions.

NOTE: Don't be misled by the name "application layer." This layer runs network applications, not applications software such as spreadsheets or inventory. Network applications include e-mail, Web browsing (HTTP), FTP, and other useful network tasks.

Peer Layers Form Protocol-Independent Virtual Links

Each layer in the stack relies on the layers above and below it to operate, yet each operates independently of the others, as if it were having an exclusive conversation with its counterpart layer on the other computer. Each layer on the device is said to have established a *virtual link* with the same layer on the other device. With all seven virtual links running, a *network connection* (or *session*) is established, and the two devices are talking as if they were wired directly together.

For example, in Figure 2-2 the sending computer, the Wintel PC on the left, processes downward through the stack to send a message, and the IBM mainframe receives the message by processing the message upward through its stack to understand the data—an FTP download request, in this example. The computers then reverse the process by working through their stacks the other way, this time for the IBM mainframe to download a file to the Wintel PC via the FTP application.

In Figure 2-2, you begin to see how the Internet was able to interconnect the world's computers. Because the layers are abstracted and operate independent of one another, the FTP application can successfully run over different implementations of the OSI model—in this example, Ethernet and Token Ring. You can see that the FTP application

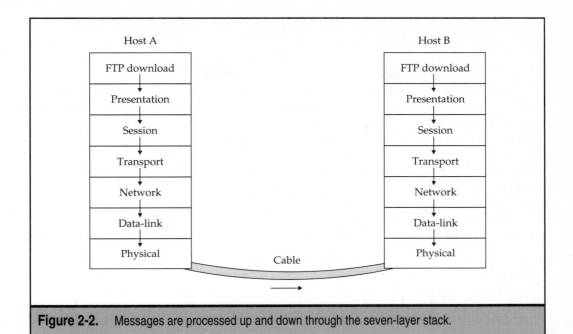

Figure 2-2.   Messages are processed up and down through the seven-layer stack.

doesn't care about the incompatibilities inherent between Windows XP and IBM mainframes, or even those between the Ethernet and Token Ring network technologies. Its only concern is whether the connected devices are talking FTP in compliance with OSI rules.

OSI Implementation by Layer

Although the seven-layer stack is expressed in vertical terms, looking at things horizontally might help you understand how it works. This is because as a message is processed through the stack, its horizontal length changes.

The first three layers handle the network application being run (application layer), data representation formats (presentation layer), and connection logistics (session layer). These first three layers represent very little of the message. For example, which application to run is defined by a port number—the HTTP HTML Web page application is identified by port number 80.

NOTE: The name "port number" was an unfortunate choice by the IETF engineers. It takes a while to get used to the fact that an IP port number refers to a software type, not a hardware port. On a related note, the term "socket" is an IP address paired with a port number.

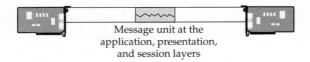

Message unit at the
application, presentation,
and session layers

At the transport layer, the message gets wider. Tasks performed here include making sure the receiver knows the message is coming, ensuring that the receiver won't be overwhelmed with too many packets at a time, making sure that packets sent were indeed received, and retransmitting packets that were dropped. Transport protocols include the Transmission Control Protocol (TCP) and User Datagram Protocol in the TCP/IP suite and the Sequenced Packet Exchange (SPX) layer of the NetWare IPX/SPX suite.

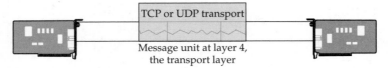

Message unit at layer 4,
the transport layer

At the network layer, the message gets a bit wider and becomes a *packet* (also called a *datagram*). Each packet's header has a logical (not physical) network address that can be used to route the message through the internetwork. Network layer protocols include the IP portion of the TCP/IP protocol suite and the IPX layer of the Novell NetWare IPX/SPX protocol suite, among others.

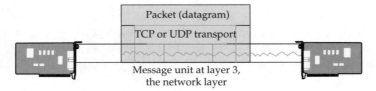

Message unit at layer 3,
the network layer

At the data-link layer, the binary information is read and encased into a format called a *frame*. The precise format for a frame is specified by the network protocol on which the NIC is operating—Ethernet or Token Ring, for example. Each frame's header contains so-called media access control (MAC) addresses, which are unique identifiers that act as a kind of serial number for hardware devices.

At the physical level, a message is a series of pulses. The device works to encode or decode the pulses into binary 0's or 1's to begin sorting out discrete message units. This signal processing is done in hardware on the network interface card, not in software.

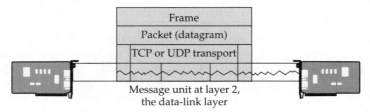

Message unit at layer 2,
the data-link layer

Once all the message-handling protocol information has been stripped away, you're left with payload data. There are many individual message units within a transmission. A network connection is made using a stream of packets, and each individual packet's data cargo contributes to the complete data file the connection needs—a Web page download, for example.

Payload data differs by application. For example, a Telnet session will send tiny data files to indicate a keystroke or a carriage return, which may be all contained in a packet or two. At the opposite extreme, an FTP file transfer may send millions of bytes of data spread across thousands of packets.

NETWORK TECHNOLOGIES

Network technologies (also called LAN technologies or network specifications) are used to run the basic unit of all internetworks—the LAN segment. The most widely known network technology is Ethernet, but there are several others, including Token Ring, Asynchronous Transfer Mode (ATM), and Fiber Distributed Data Interface (FDDI).

Network technologies are implemented at the data-link layer (layer 2) of the seven-layer OSI reference model. Put another way, network technologies are largely characterized by the physical media they share and how they control access to the shared medium. This makes sense, if you think about it. Networking is connectivity; but to be connected, order must somehow be maintained among those users doing the sharing. For that reason, layer 2 (the data-link layer) is also called the *media access control* layer, or MAC layer for short. The message unit format at this level is the *data frame*, or frame.

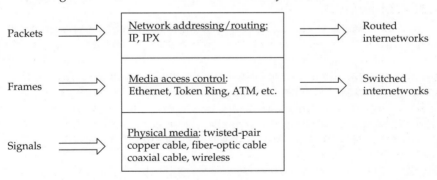

As such, network technologies in and of themselves can only deal with MAC addresses—those serial number-like device identifiers mentioned earlier. A network layer protocol such as IP is needed to route messages through the internetwork. Network technologies alone can only support switched internetwork operation—good only for local areas or simple paths over longer distances, where not much guidance is needed. Network technologies are used at opposite ends of the spectrum:

▼ **Access LANs**   Accept cabling from devices, tie workgroups together, and share resources such as departmental printers and servers

▲ **Backbone LANs**   Link access LANs, and share resources such as database servers, mail servers, and so on

Access LANs, formed by hubs or access switches, give users and devices connectivity to the network at the local level, usually within a floor in an office building. Backbone LANs, formed by routers or LAN switches, tie together access LANs, usually within a building or office campus. Routed internetworks are typically used to distribute traffic between the two.

Ethernet

Version 1 of Ethernet was developed by Xerox Corporation in 1970. Over the subsequent decade, Xerox teamed with Intel and Digital Equipment Corporation (now Compaq) to release Version 2 in 1982. Since that time, Ethernet has become the dominant network technology standard. Thanks mostly to economies of scale, the average cost per Ethernet port is now far lower than that of a Token Ring port. Indeed, it has become so much a de facto standard that many manufacturers are integrating Ethernet NICs into computer motherboards in an attempt to do away with the need for separate NIC modules.

Ethernet Architecture

Ethernet operates by contention. Devices sharing an Ethernet LAN segment listen for traffic being carried over the wire and defer transmitting a message until the medium is clear. If two stations send at about the same time and their packets collide, both transmissions are aborted, and the stations back off and wait a random period of time before retransmitting. Ethernet uses the Carrier Sense Multiple Access with Collision Detection (CSMA/CD) algorithm to listen to traffic, sense collisions, and abort transmissions. CSMA/CD is the traffic cop that controls what would otherwise be random traffic. It restricts access to the wire in order to ensure the integrity of transmissions. Figure 2-3 illustrates the CSMA/CD process.

Because the medium is shared, every device on an Ethernet LAN segment receives the message and checks it to see whether the destination address matches its own address. If it does, the message is accepted and processed through the seven-layer stack, and a network connection is made. If the address doesn't match, the packets are dropped.

Ethernet is implemented as the IEEE 802.3 specification. The IEEE, the Institute of Electrical and Electronics Engineers, has been around since the 19th century and contributes to the computer industry by setting standards for layers 1 and 2 (the physical and

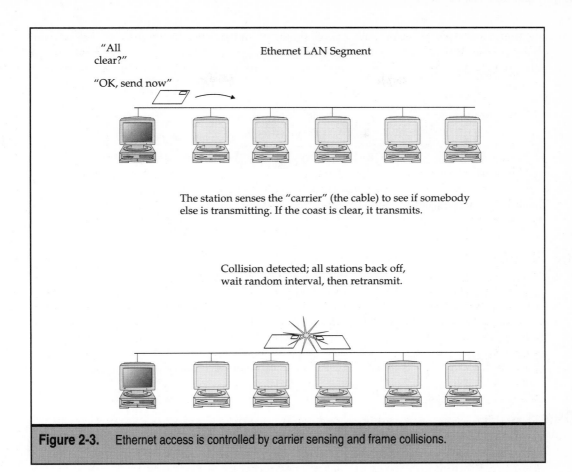

Figure 2-3. Ethernet access is controlled by carrier sensing and frame collisions.

data-link layers, respectively) of the OSI reference model. The IETF's work picks up at layer 3 and above.

NOTE: An algorithm is a structured sequence of rules designed to handle variable processes in an orderly manner automatically. Algorithms are commonplace in computing and networking because things move so fast that there isn't time for a human to intervene.

Ethernet Implementations

Even apart from economies of scale, Ethernet is inherently less expensive, thanks to the random nature of its architecture. In other words, the electronics needed to run Ethernet are easier to manufacture because Ethernet doesn't try to control everything. In rough terms, it only worries about collisions.

The obvious disadvantage of Ethernet is that a lot of raw bandwidth is sacrificed to aborted transmissions. Theoretical maximum effective bandwidth from Ethernet is estimated at only 37 percent of raw wire speed. However, the equipment is so inexpensive that Ethernet has always been on balance the cheapest form of effective bandwidth. In other words, its simplicity more than compensates for its inherent bandwidth inefficiency.

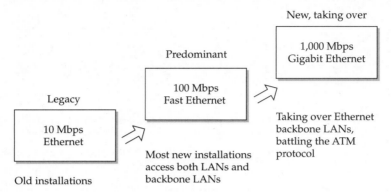

Ethernet has several implementation options. The original Ethernet specification ran at 1 Mbps over coaxial cable or 10BaseT twisted-pair cable (*T* stands for twisted-pair—we'll cover cabling specifications in Chapter 6). Fast Ethernet runs at 100 Mbps and runs over 100BaseTX or 100BaseFX fiber-optic cable (*F* stands for fiber). Gigabit Ethernet runs at 1,000 Mbps (or 1 Gbps) over 1000BaseTX or 1000BaseFX cable. A popular configuration choice right now is Fast Ethernet access LANs interconnected through a Gigabit Ethernet backbone LAN.

Token Ring

Token Ring is Ethernet's main competition as a LAN (networking) standard—or it was. Token Ring differs sharply from Ethernet in its architectural approach. The IEEE has defined Token Ring as a published standard in the IEEE 802.5 specification (much as Ethernet is the 802.3 specification).

As its own LAN standard, Token Ring is incompatible with Ethernet in terms of the type of NICs, cable connectors, and software that must be used. Although Token Ring was widely installed in enterprises dominated by IBM, it never caught on as an open standard.

Token Ring takes its name from the fact that it defines attached hosts into a logical ring. We use *logical* to describe Token Ring here because the LAN segment behaves like a ring by passing signals in a round-robin fashion as if the devices were actually attached to a looped cable. Physically, though, Token Ring LANs may be configured in a hub-and-spoke topology called a *star topology*. Figure 2-4 shows this. Note that in Token Ring parlance, the access concentrator is called a *media access unit (MAU)* instead of a hub.

Token Ring avoids contention over a LAN segment by a *token-passing* protocol, which regulates traffic flow by passing a frame called a *token* around the ring. Only the host in possession of the token is allowed to transmit, thereby eliminating packet collisions. Token Ring's architecture in effect trades wait-time for collisions, because each station must wait its turn before capturing the token in order to transmit. Nonetheless, eliminating packet collisions greatly increases Token Ring's effective utilization of raw bandwidth.

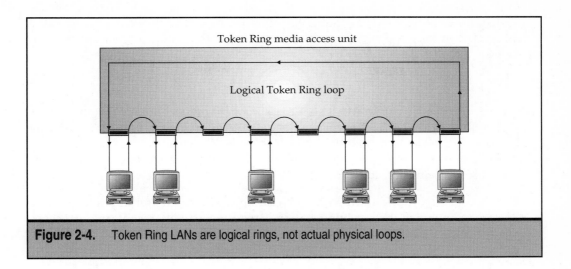

Figure 2-4. Token Ring LANs are logical rings, not actual physical loops.

Tests show that Token Ring can use up to 75 percent of raw bandwidth, compared to Ethernet's theoretical maximum of about 37 percent. The trouble is that Token Ring only begins to pay off above certain traffic volumes.

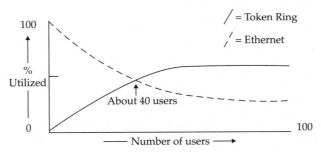

Persuading the market to accept a new technology as a de facto standard requires volume. Token Ring is a great technology, but it lost out to Ethernet's immense edge in total number of LANs installed. From a market standpoint, Token Ring's need for large LAN sizes to pay off was probably fatal. Most LANs are small because most enterprises are small. Moreover, even big companies have mostly small LANs, whether in branch offices or even departments in large buildings. Remember, we're talking LAN *segments* in this context—the actual shared medium, not the "local network" that is a collection of all LAN segments attached to the LAN backbone.

Another problem is that Token Ring requires expensive electronics to operate its deterministic processes. If you think about it, it's only natural that manufacturing a NIC that transmits packets "at will" would be cheaper than making one to participate in an orderly regimen in which a token is required.

When Token Ring was introduced, it ran at 4 Mbps, but most LANs were upgraded to 16-Mbps media. If this seems slow compared to Fast Ethernet's 100-Mbps speeds, keep in mind that Token Ring yields far more effective bandwidth from rated wire speed. A 100-Mbps Token Ring specification was also offered to the public but was not broadly deployed.

ATM

ATM (Asynchronous Transfer Mode) is a data-link network technology that, like Ethernet, Token Ring, and FDDI, is specified at layer 2 of the OSI model. But that's where the similarities end. ATM transmissions send 53-byte cells instead of packets. A *cell* is a fixed-length message unit. Like packets, cells are pieces of a message, but the fixed-length format causes certain characteristics:

▼ **Virtual circuit orientation** Cell-based networks run better in point-to-point mode, in which the receiving station is ready to actively receive and process the cells.

■ **Speed** The hardware knows exactly where the header ends and data starts in every cell, thereby speeding processing operations. Currently, ATM networks run at speeds of up to 40 Gbps.

▲ **Quality of Service (QoS)** Predictable throughput rates and virtual circuits enable cell-based networks to better guarantee service levels to types of traffic that are priority.

ATM doesn't have a media access control technology, per se. ATM is a switching technology, in which a so-called virtual circuit is set up before a transmission starts. This differs sharply from LAN technologies such as Ethernet and Token Ring, which simply transmit a message without prior notification to the receiving host, leaving it up to routers to figure out the best path to take to get there.

Compared to the tiny size of ATM cells, Ethernet packet size can range from 64 bytes to over 1,500 bytes—up to about 25 times larger per message unit. By being so much more granular, ATM becomes that much more controllable.

ATM is designed to run over fiber-optic cable operating the SONET (Synchronous Optical Network) specification. SONET is an ANSI standard specifying the physical interfaces that connect to fiber-optic cable at various speeds. SONET specifications are set up for various cable speeds called *optical carrier levels*, or OC for short:

▼ **OC-1** 52-Mbps fiber-optic cable

■ **OC-3** 155-Mbps fiber-optic cable

■ **OC-12** 622-Mbps fiber-optic cable

■ **OC-24** 1.2-Gbps fiber-optic cable

■ **OC-48** 2.5-Gbps fiber-optic cable

■ **OC-192** 10-Gbps fiber-optic cable

■ **OC-256** 13.27-Gbps fiber-optic cable

▲ **OC-768** 40-Gbps fiber-optic cable

Like token-passing architectures, ATM's deterministic design yields high effective bandwidth from its raw wire speed. In fact, ATM's effective yield is said to be well above even Token Ring's 75 percent. Most ATM backbone LANs run OC-3 or OC-12. Most intercity links run OC-12, although major Internet backbone providers are now wiring OC-48 and higher to meet ever-increasing bandwidth demands.

Most intercity Internet trunks are OC-12 running ATM, with OC-48 and higher taking over the heavier trunks. For example, UUNET—one of the largest Internet backbone providers—uses 622-Mbps fiber-optic cabling to connect Chicago with Atlanta, and 2.5-Gbps OC-48 to link New York with Washington, D.C.

Latency and Sequence Sensitivity

Certain types of traffic need predictability more than others. For example, a phone conversation can't tolerate delays because each party would start talking before the other is finished. This is called *latency sensitivity*—the reason why wireless telephone systems are cellular. Another type of traffic sensitivity is *priority sensitivity*, where the order in which data is received is critical. For example, a video transmission's message units must be received in the proper order so that complete video frames can be displayed in sequence. Figure 2-5 depicts how latency and sequence problems harm service quality in priority-sensitive applications such as videocasting.

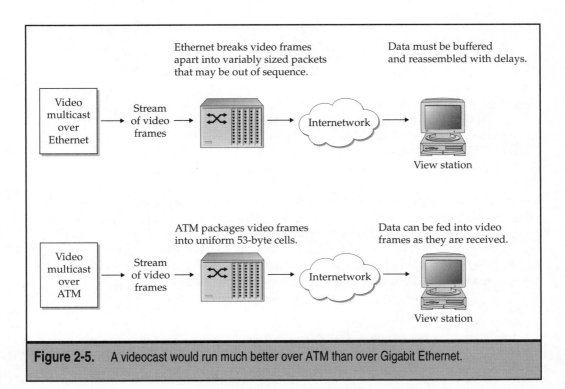

Figure 2-5.   A videocast would run much better over ATM than over Gigabit Ethernet.

Videocasts are becoming a popular solution for such applications as distance learning and internal corporate communications. Many envision the day when Internet-based (broadband) television will completely displace broadcast television. This brings up the important distinction between broadcast and multicast messaging.

Multicasting vs. Broadcasting

A *broadcast* message goes to every station within the broadcast domain. By default, a broadcast domain includes all stations attached to the shared medium of a LAN segment, although it can be purposely extended using routers.

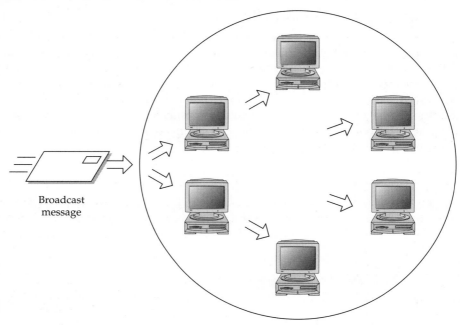

Broadcast message

Broadcast domain

Each station must receive and examine the broadcast message, but can drop it at the interface if programmed to do so. For example, broadcasts can be beneficial to a network by keeping stations updated on such changes as new addresses or downed links. Too many broadcasts, however, can mire bandwidth in useless traffic.

A *multicast* message goes to a subset of stations within a broadcast domain. In basic terms, each station "signs up" for the types of multicasts it wishes to receive.

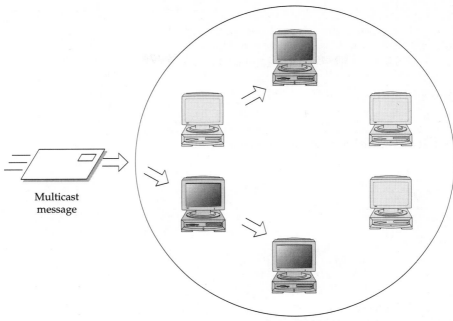

Multicast
message

Multicast domain

The new classic example of multicasting is videocasting, in which a lot of bandwidth is used to move video images, so only those stations that want to participate receive it. It makes sense for bandwidth-intensive applications to use multicasting to avoid needless congestion. ATM is heavily identified with multicasting because its fixed-cell format is ideal for multimedia applications.

If ATM is so much better than other network protocols, why aren't all networks running it? The answer lies in the fact that most traffic is not sensitive to transmission latency. The added expense and complexity of ATM can be hard to justify in the absence of a lot of multimedia traffic, because there is sufficient time to repackage messages at the receiving end. Figure 2-6 shows examples of both types of traffic.

Normal messages aren't particularly sensitive to intermittent delays or the sequence of delivery. For example, an e-mail with a document attached might be 20,000 bytes long (20KB). The user doesn't care about the order in which various chunks of the message are received and wouldn't even be aware of any delays. Therefore, the network can deliver the e-mail as it sees fit.

Virtual Circuits

Because they're so small, ATM cells don't contain the amount of address information found in the header of an Ethernet packet. In fact, ATM uses an addressing scheme entirely different from other network technologies. This is why ATM needs to set up a virtual circuit to the remote end before communicating. A *circuit* is a connection between

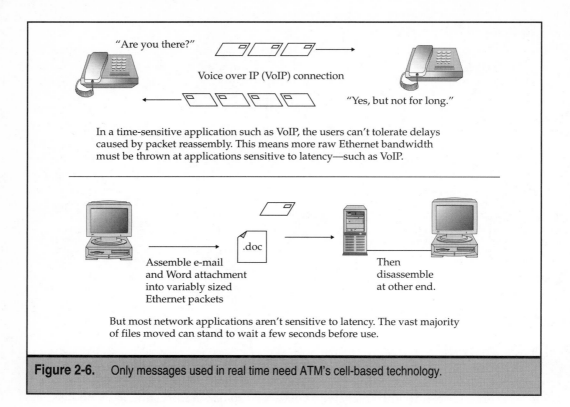

Figure 2-6. Only messages used in real time need ATM's cell-based technology.

two points. For example, your home phone circuit is wired directly to the central switching office in your neighborhood. A *virtual circuit* behaves like a real one, but isn't hard-wired, passing instead through various network devices such as hubs, switches, and routers along its way, as shown here:

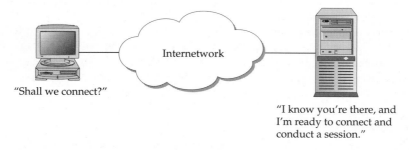

Before transmission can begin over a virtual circuit, each end must agree to execute the transmission and the path over which it will travel. This is markedly different from internetwork messages that simply send off to a destination address, leaving the details about how to get it there up to one or more routers sitting between sender and receiver.

LAN Emulation (LANE)

Although it can be configured all the way out to the desktop, ATM is primarily used for backbones, either as backbone LANs within an office campus or long-haul Internet links between cities. ATM is a natural for backbone duty because its underlying cell switching technology is ideal for high-speed point-to-point links.

But at some point, a backbone should speak the same language as the access LANs it serves—usually Ethernet or Token Ring. Because ATM deals in cells instead of packets, it uses an encapsulation technique called LANE (for LAN emulation). In networking, *encapsulation* is the technique of placing a message unit of one format inside that of another format in order to let it traverse an otherwise incompatible network. LANE encapsulates frames at the data-link layer (layer 2) to set up so-called emulated LAN circuits, called ELANs for short. In other words, LANE breaks down Ethernet or Token Ring packets into ATM cells on one side and reassembles them on the other.

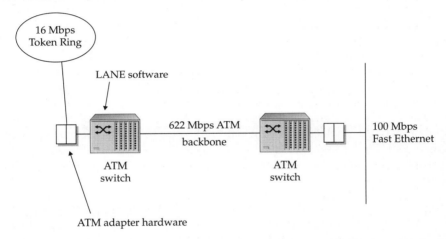

ATM is regarded by many as the answer to the Internet's bandwidth shortage. It's been installed by many enterprises to replace overtaxed FDDI backbones. Not only is ATM fast, but also its inherent predictability lends itself to guaranteeing Quality of Service (QoS)—especially for multimedia applications, which by nature cannot tolerate latency. However, because of the need for LANE adaptation, ATM has a relatively high cost per port. It also introduces a new protocol into the mix, thereby increasing complexity.

The ATM standard is coordinated by an international nonprofit industry group called the ATM Forum. The ATM Forum, based in Silicon Valley, publishes technical specifications and promotes the use of ATM products.

Gigabit and 10 Gigabit Ethernet

Gigabit Ethernet is a 1,000-Mbps extension of the Ethernet standard. The IEEE 802.3 committee adopted the Gigabit Ethernet 802.z specification in 1998. Gigabit Ethernet is sometimes also referred to as 1000BaseX in reference to the specification for the required copper or fiber-optic cabling. Gigabit Ethernet is being promoted by the Gigabit Ethernet Alliance, a nonprofit industry group much like the ATM Forum. The push for Gigabit Ethernet is largely motivated by its inherent compatibility with other Ethernet specifications (the original 10-Mbps Ethernet and 100-Mbps Fast Ethernet).

Gigabit Ethernet is ATM's main competition to replace FDDI as the backbone of choice. Its greatest advantage is familiarity, given that Ethernet is the pervasive technology. Originally designed as a LAN technology, at 1,000 Mbps, Gigabit Ethernet can scale to WAN configurations. Because Ethernet uses variable frame sizing—ranging between 64 bytes and over 1,400 bytes per frame—it does not enjoy the inherent QoS characteristics of ATM. However, many network managers are biased in favor of Gigabit Ethernet because their staffs are familiar with the technology, and it presumably doesn't introduce the added layer of complexity that LANE adaptation requires. Like ATM, Gigabit Ethernet backbones operate over a variety of fiber-optic cable types.

As speedy as a Gigabit Ethernet connection is, there is an even faster connection available on some Cisco gear, namely 10 Gigabit Ethernet. As the name suggests, 10 Gigabit Ethernet runs ten times faster than Gigabit Ethernet, at 10,000 Mbps. Where Gigabit Ethernet was a natural extension of Fast Ethernet, 10 Gigabit Ethernet differs in an important way, namely the physical medium required to transport its packets. The difference comes in that 10 Gigabit Ethernet does not run across twisted-pair cable, as does its Ethernet brethren. Rather, because of the sheer speed of 10 Gigabit Ethernet, single-mode or multimode fiber optics are required.

10 Gigabit Ethernet is used for WAN and MAN connections where high amounts of data need to be moved (although it can still be used in LANs). Further, 10 Gigabit Ethernet devices don't come cheap. The list price for a Catalyst 10GBase-EX4 Metro 10 Gigabit Ethernet module is $79,995.

The benefit of these zippier implementations of Ethernet is that network administrators can leverage their investments in Ethernet networks by easily upgrading from 10/100 Mbps up to Gigabit and 10 Gigabit Ethernet without having to reinvest in infrastructure.

FDDI

FDDI stands for Fiber Distributed Data Interface, a 100-Mbps protocol that runs over fiber-optic cable media. Like IBM's Token Ring, FDDI uses a token-passing architecture to control media access, yielding high effective bandwidth from its 100-Mbps wire speed. If you've never heard of FDDI, you're not alone. FDDI has experienced a relatively low public profile because it has traditionally been used for backbones, not access LANs.

FDDI Was the Standard Backbone Network Technology

For years, FDDI was the network technology of choice for backbone LANs. This could be partially attributed to its speed. During the era of its introduction, FDDI was the first major fiber-based network technology, and its 100-Mbps speed set the standard.

However, backbone LANs are mission critical. If the backbone goes down, the access LANs can't internetwork. For this reason, the FDDI specification was designed from the ground up for guaranteed availability, with a physical architecture configuring dual-redundant fiber-optic rings. Each station is connected to both rings, having two effects:

▼ The station can fail over to the backup ring if the primary ring fails.

▲ The station nearest the point of failure on the primary ring serves as a loop-back connector, effectively becoming a ring-connecting device that keeps the ring unbroken.

The FDDI Architecture Provides Dual-Ring Redundancy

FDDI's architecture made it attractive for use as backbone LANs, especially for office campuses and other large area applications. The dual rings provide redundant paths. Under normal operation, the secondary ring sits idle, passing only enough frames to keep itself running. The secondary ring goes into action when the primary ring fails. (Failures are usually caused by a break in the fiber or a faulty NIC somewhere in the network.) As Figure 2-7 shows, FDDI isolates the damaged station by wrapping around to the secondary ring and looping back in the other direction—thus keeping the ring intact.

The first official FDDI standard was published by the American National Standards Institute (ANSI) in 1987. The current FDDI specification is ANSI X3T9.5. Because of its design, an FDDI can have as much as 100 kilometers (60 miles) in fiber-optic cabling configured—a scale sometimes referred to as a metropolitan area network (MAN). The distance reach comes from the combined use of fiber-optic cabling and token-passing media access—both of which inherently support longer distances. In reality, though, most FDDI networks are located within a building or office campus. The few MANs that do exist generally belong to electrical utilities, which use them to centrally manage their power grids. FDDI is chosen for its fail-safe characteristics.

FDDI Can Now Be Run over Copper as CDDI

In an attempt to expand market acceptance, FDDI was adapted to run over unshielded twisted-pair media using a technology called CDDI (Copper Distributed Data Interface). CDDI is actually a trade name, not a standard, and Cisco acquired CDDI from Crescendo Communications in 1993. Even with Cisco's imprimatur, CDDI never really caught on as an alternative to Ethernet LANs. After a fairly long run of popularity as the backbone of choice with reliability-conscious large enterprises, FDDI itself has started to fade from the scene, with ATM and Gigabit Ethernet usurping it as the backbone technologies of choice.

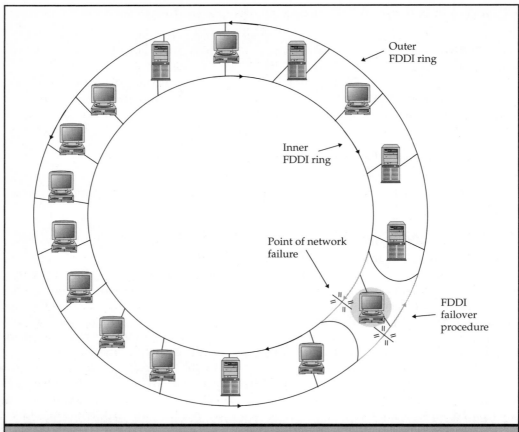

Figure 2-7. FDDI was the backbone of choice for years because of its speed and redundancy.

WAN TECHNOLOGIES

Most internetworks involve at least some remote users. Enterprises need to connect telecommuters and remote offices, ISPs need to take dial-ins from subscribers, and so on. There are two basic kinds of wide area networks (WANs):

▼ **Dial-ins** A dial-in line establishes a point-to-point connection between a central location and one user, or a few at most. When the dial-in connection is no longer needed, the phone circuit is terminated.

▲ **Trunks** A *trunk* is a high-capacity point-to-point link between offices. Usually, a trunk will connect a number of remote users to a central site. Most trunks run over T1 (1.5 Mbps) or T3 (45 Mbps) telephone lines, although new technologies have come on the scene.

Looked at another way, telephone networks exist on two planes: between telephone switching stations, and between the switching station and the home or office. The zone between the neighborhood switching station and the home or business is often called the *last mile* for its relatively slow telecommunications infrastructure. The term isn't meant literally, of course—the zone between endpoints and the switching station sometimes can be several miles.

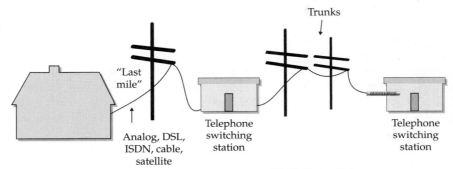

In case you didn't know, telephone switching stations are those small windowless buildings that sit inconspicuously in every neighborhood. Downtown switching stations are much bigger, usually taking up a few floors of the local telephone company building.

The so-called last mile has become a key battleground among internetwork vendors. This is because, with the boom in the Internet, more and more dial-ins are now individuals connecting to their ISPs from home. This includes telecommuters going to work in the corporate intranetwork, not just Web surfers. A huge technology battle has been joined to take over as the preferred medium for the last mile. The fray has largely been between DSL and ISDN—two digital telephony technologies. However, cable TV operators and even satellite companies have joined the fray, bypassing the telephone grid altogether.

Dial-in Technologies

Two technologies have been introduced to bring digital bandwidth into the home and small office: ISDN and DSL. ISDN was introduced in the 1980s, but local telephone carriers have been slow in making it available. DSL is the hot new technology, promising even better speeds and wider availability.

Dial-in technologies differ from other WAN media in that connections made using them are temporary. In other words, once the computer user has finished with the session, the circuit is terminated by hanging up the telephone. To this day, most homes are connected via analog phone circuits. Because normal lines are analog, they require modems at each end to operate, and for that reason are referred to by some as *analog/modem* circuits.

The major problem with analog/modem circuits is that they're slow. What slows them down is that the acoustical signals use only a tiny fraction of the raw bandwidth available in copper telephone system cables, because they were designed for voice, not data. This is why the state-of-the-art analog home connection is now 56 Kbps—glacially slow compared to 100-Mbps Fast Ethernet now standard inside office buildings.

ISDN

ISDN, which stands for Integrated Services Digital Network, was proposed as the first digital service to the home. ISDN requires a special phone circuit from a local telephone carrier and is unavailable in many areas. The key improvement over analog/modem lines is that ISDN circuits are digital, and for that reason they use so-called CPEs (customer premise equipment) instead of modems—CPE is an old-time telephony term.

ISDN creates multiple channels over a single line. A *channel* is a data path multiplexed over a single communications medium. (To *multiplex* means to combine multiple signals over a single line.) The basic kind of ISDN circuit is a BRI circuit (for Basic Rate Interface) with two so-called *B*, or bearer, channels for payload data. Figure 2-8 contrasts an analog/modem circuit with an ISDN BRI circuit.

Each B-channel runs at 64 Kbps for a total of 128-Kbps payload bandwidth. Having separate B-channels enhances throughput for symmetrical connections—in other words,

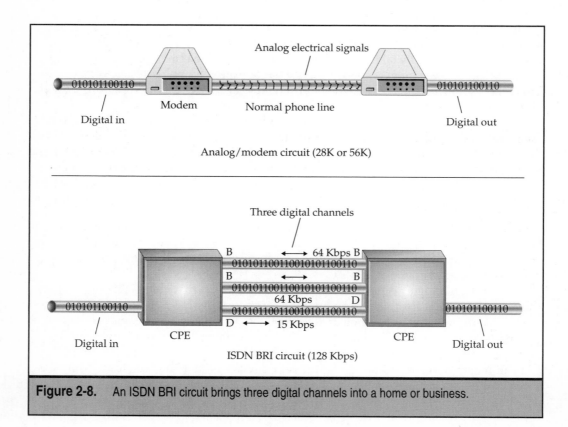

Figure 2-8. An ISDN BRI circuit brings three digital channels into a home or business.

sessions characterized by the bidirectional simultaneous flow of traffic. A third channel, called the *D* (or delta) channel, carries 16 Kbps. The D-channel is dedicated to network control instead of payload data. Separating control of overhead signals enhances ISDN's performance and reliability.

A second kind of ISDN circuit is a PRI circuit (for Primary Rate Interface). PRI is basically the same as BRI, except that it packages up to 23 B-channels plus one 64-Kbps D-channel for up to 1.544 Mbps total payload bandwidth. Small businesses use PRI circuits to connect multiple users, competing at the low end of T1's traditional market niche.

DSL

DSL stands for Digital Subscriber Line. As the name implies, DSL also runs digital signals over copper wire. DSL uses sophisticated algorithms to modulate signals in such a way that much more bandwidth can be squeezed from existing last-mile telephone infrastructure.

DSL is an inherently asymmetric telecommunications technology. What this means is that data can be moved much faster downstream (from the local phone carrier to your home) than upstream. There are several types of DSL; two are important to this discussion:

▼   **aDSL**   Asymmetric DSL, a two-way circuit that can handle about 640 Kbps upstream and up to 6 Mbps downstream.

▲   **DSL Lite**   Also called G.Lite, a slower, less expensive technology that can carry data at rates between about 1.5 Mbps and 6 Mbps downstream and from 128 Kbps to 384 Kbps upstream. The exact speeds depend on the equipment you install.

DSL's inherent asymmetry fits perfectly with the Internet, where most small office/ home office users download far more data than they upload.

The key fact to know is that DSL requires a special piece of equipment called a DSL modem to operate. It's the DSL modem that splits signals into upstream and downstream channels. The major difference with DSL Lite is that the splitting is done at the telephone switching station, not in the home or small office. Figure 2-9 depicts this.

Not requiring DSL signal splitting in the home makes DSL much more affordable than ISDN. To use most DSL circuits, you must be located no farther than about four or five miles from the telephone switching station.

Compaq, Microsoft, and Intel are cooperating on a new DSL standard in hopes that it will replace ISDN as the last-mile technology of choice. DSL's fat bandwidth is necessary to realize the goal of continuous-transmission video, audio, 3-D animation, and other multimedia applications many envision for the Web.

Cable Modems and Satellite Connections

Two more ways to gain dial-in access are more popularly found running into the back of your television set on a length of coaxial cable. Cable modems and satellite connections are gaining popularity as ways to access the Internet at high speeds.

Cable Modem   A cable modem connects to an existing cable television feed and to an Ethernet network card in the computer. Though cable modems and dial-up modems share a

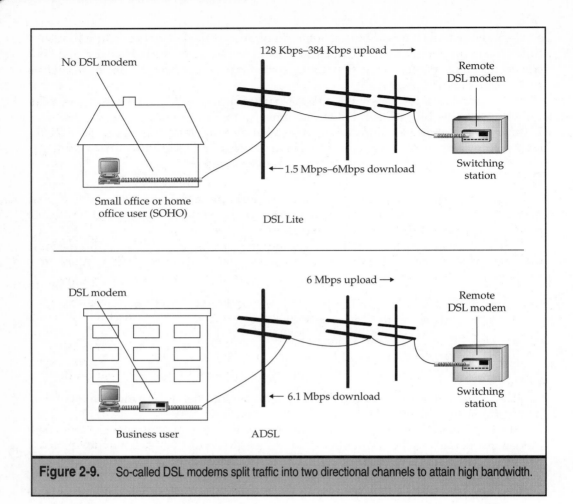

Figure 2-9. So-called DSL modems split traffic into two directional channels to attain high bandwidth.

common functionality, the two are very different devices, primarily in the realm of speed. Top-of-the-line dial-in modems over a POTS will give up to 56 Kbps. Cable modem downloads range from 384 Kbps to several million bps, depending on the service provider and the package purchased.

When cable modems made their debut, there were no standards and different brands of cable modems could not talk to each other. However, recently the industry has united on the Data Over Cable Service Interface Specification (DOCSIS) standard. This allows third-party vendors to make compliant cable modems, and should result in lower equipment costs.

Satellite Connection   If cable or DSL aren't options and you still feel the need for speed, you need look no further than the heavens.

Companies like Hughes Network Systems offer satellite delivery of Internet content. Much like the 18-inch dishes bolted to the sides and roofs of millions of houses for digital television and movies, these services utilize the high-bandwidth broadcasts to deliver high-speed Internet access.

The downside of satellite connections is that the speed works in one direction—from the satellite to your computer. When it comes to sending information—like e-mails, URLs, and any other data sent from your computer—that must be sent across a POTS.

Of course, like all technology, this is a field that is rapidly expanding. Look for faster speeds and two-way satellite transmissions in the coming months.

WAN Trunk Technologies

As stated earlier, a *trunk* is any high-capacity point-to-point data link. Trunks can exist within buildings and office campuses, but they're best known as wide area network links between buildings, cities, regions, and even continents.

WAN technology has evolved markedly over the past decade, and not just with the Internet boom. For example, Frame Relay packet-switching technology proved dramatically less expensive than dedicated leased WAN lines. We'll briefly review the WAN technologies in use today. They all share common characteristics in that they're dedicated circuits (not dial-in and hang-up) with high bandwidth used to connect locations with many users, as opposed to small office/home office sites with one or two users.

Most enterprises are replacing leased-line WAN services that shared infrastructure services. Their primary motive is to save money, but flexibility is also a big benefit.

T1 and T3 Leased Lines

T1 and T3 are the predominant leased-line technologies in use in North America and Japan today. (There are rough equivalents in Europe called E1 and E3.) A leased-line circuit (or part of a circuit) is reserved for use by the enterprise that rents it—and is paid for on a flat monthly rate regardless of how much it is used.

T1 is the most commonly used digital line technology. It uses a telecommunications technology called *time-division multiplexing (TDM)* to yield a data rate of about 1.5 Mbps. TDM combines streams of data by assigning each stream a different time slot in a set and repeatedly transmitting a fixed sequence of time slots over a single transmission channel. T1 lines use copper wire, both within and among metropolitan areas. You can purchase a T1 circuit from your local phone carrier or rent a portion of its bandwidth in an arrangement called *fractionalized T1*. Some ISPs are connected to the Internet via T1 circuits.

T3 is the successor to T1. T3 circuits are dedicated phone connections that carry data at 45 Mbps. T3 lines are used mostly by *Tier 1 ISPs* (ISPs who connect smaller ISPs to the Internet) and by large enterprises. Because of their sheer bandwidth and expense, most T3 lines are leased as fractional T3 lines. T3 lines are also called *DS3* lines.

Frame Relay

Frame Relay switches packets over a shared packet-switching network owned by a carrier such as a regional telephone company, MCI, or AT&T. As depicted in Figure 2-10,

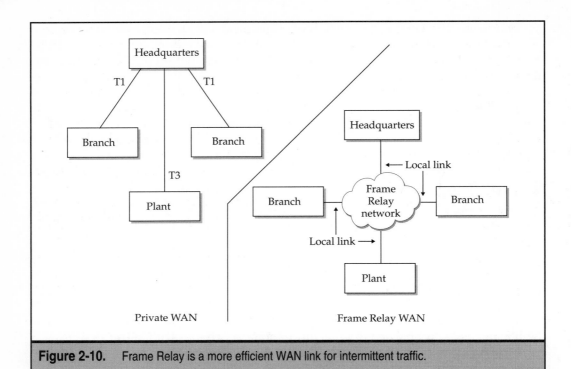

Figure 2-10. Frame Relay is a more efficient WAN link for intermittent traffic.

Frame Relay uses local phone circuits to link remote locations. The long-distance hauls are over a telecommunications infrastructure owned by the Frame Relay provider, shared among a number of other customers.

The primary benefit of Frame Relay is cost efficiency. Frame Relay takes its name from the fact that it puts data into variable-sized message units called frames. It leaves session management and error correction to nodes it operates at various connection points, thereby speeding network performance. Most Frame Relay customers rent *permanent virtual circuits*, or *PVCs*. A PVC gives the customer a continuous, dedicated connection without having to pay for a leased line, which uses dedicated permanent circuits. Frame Relay customers are charged according to level of usage. They also have the option of selecting between service levels, where QoS is programmed based on what priority the customer's frames are given inside the Frame Relay cloud.

Frame Relay networks themselves sit atop T1 or T3 trunks operated by the Frame Relay network operator. Use of Frame Relay makes economic sense when traffic isn't heavy enough to require a dedicated ATM connection.

VPN

VPNs, which stand for virtual private networks, are enterprise internetworks operated over the Internet. VPNs work by using encryption to "tunnel" through switched virtual circuits (SVCs) that navigate over a number of intermediary LANs in order to reach remote enterprise locations. *Encryption* is the technique of scrambling data so that only a receiving station with the key to decode it can read it. Other techniques are applied to make sure data integrity is intact (all the contents are still there and unaltered) after a message has traversed a VPN tunnel. Figure 2-11 depicts how an enterprise might use a VPN to interconnect its sites.

A typical VPN scenario is for an enterprise to go to a Tier 1 ISP and purchase SVCs to each remote site. The SVCs assure that messages will be routed in such a way that performance and security are optimized, and that backup paths are available in case a primary SVC experiences a link failure. Routers must be configured at each enterprise site to perform the encryption and decryption operations.

VPNs are exploding in popularity because of their cost efficiency, geographical reach, and flexibility. The extra expense required to beef up router configuration to handle encryption is more than made up by money not spent for leased lines or even Frame Relay service.

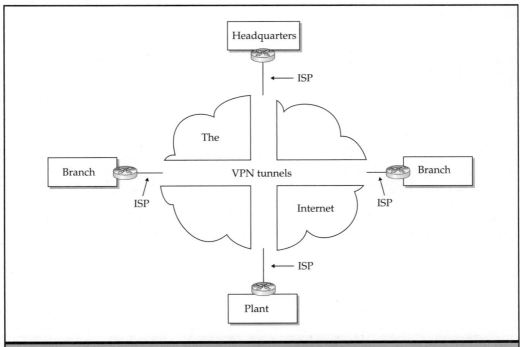

Figure 2-11.   VPNs rely on tunneling and encryption to operate over the Internet.

TCP/IP

The Internet runs over TCP/IP, the Transmission Control Protocol/Internet Protocol. TCP/IP is actually a suite of protocols, each performing a particular role to let computers talk the same language. TCP/IP is universally available and is almost certainly running on the computers you use at work and at home. This is true regardless of LAN protocols, because LAN vendors have implemented TCP/IP compatibility in their products. For example, the latest Novell NetWare product can talk TCP/IP.

TCP/IP was designed by the Defense Advanced Research Projects Agency (DARPA) in the 1970s—the design goal being to let dissimilar computers freely communicate regardless of location. Most early TCP/IP work was done on UNIX computers, which contributed to the protocol's popularity as vendors got into the practice of shipping TCP/IP software inside every UNIX computer. As a technology, TCP/IP maps to the OSI reference model, as shown in Figure 2-12.

Looking at Figure 2-12, you can see that TCP/IP focuses on layers 3 and 4 of the OSI reference model. The theory is to leave network technologies to the LAN vendors. TCP/IP's goal is to move messages through virtually any LAN product to set up a connection running virtually any network application.

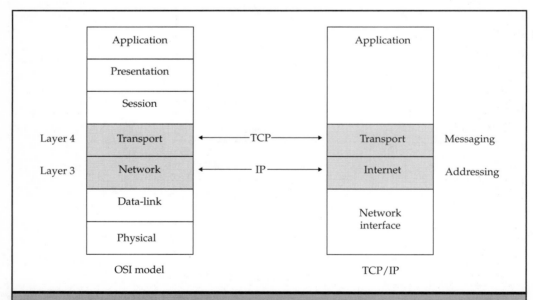

Figure 2-12. The TCP/IP stack is compliant with the OSI seven-layer reference model.

TCP/IP works because it closely maps to the OSI model at the lowest two levels—the data-link and physical layers. This lets TCP/IP talk to virtually any networking technology and, indirectly, any type of computer platform. Here are TCP/IP's four abstract layers:

▼ **Network interface**   Allows TCP/IP to interact with all modern network technologies by complying with the OSI model

■ **Internet**   Defines how IP directs messages through routers over internetworks such as the Internet

■ **Transport**   Defines the mechanics of how messages are exchanged between computers

▲ **Application**   Defines network applications to perform tasks such as file transfer, e-mail, and other useful functions

TCP/IP is the de facto standard that unifies the Internet. A computer that implements an OSI-compliant layer network technology such as Ethernet or Token Ring has overcome incompatibilities that would otherwise exist between platforms such as Windows, UNIX, MAC, IBM mainframes, and others. We've already covered layers 1 and 2 in our discussion of LAN technologies that connect groups of computers together in a location. Now we'll cover how computers internetwork over the Internet or private internetworks.

TCP/IP Messaging

All data that goes over a network must have a format so that devices know how to handle it. TCP/IP's Internet layer—which maps to the OSI model's network layer—is based on a fixed message format called the *IP datagram*—the bucket that holds the information making up the message. For example, when you download a Web page, the stuff you see on the screen was delivered inside datagrams.

Closely related to the datagram is the packet. Whereas a *datagram* is a unit of data, a *packet* is a physical message unit entity that passes through the internetwork. People often use the terms interchangeably; the distinction is only important in certain narrow contexts. The key point is that most messages are sent in pieces and reassembled at the receiving end.

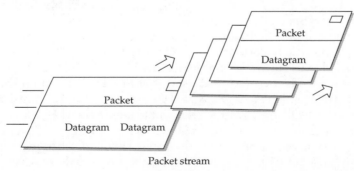

Packet stream

For example, when you send an e-mail to someone, it goes over the wire as a stream of packets. A small e-mail might be only ten packets; a big one may be split into thousands. At the opposite extreme, a request-for-service message might take only a single packet.

One advantage of this approach is that if a packet is corrupted during transmission, only that packet need be resent, not the entire message. Another advantage is that no single host is forced to wait an inordinate length of time for another's transmission to complete before being able to transmit its own message.

TCP vs. UDP as Transport Protocols

An IP message travels using either of two transport protocols: TCP or UDP. TCP stands for Transmission Control Protocol, the first half of the TCP/IP acronym. UDP stands for User Datagram Protocol, used in place of TCP for less critical messages. Either protocol provides the transport services necessary to shepherd messages through TCP/IP internetworks. TCP is called a *reliable* protocol because it checks with the receiver to make sure the packet was received. UDP is called *unreliable* because no effort is made to confirm delivery.

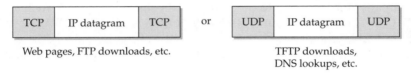

Web pages, FTP downloads, etc.　　　　　TFTP downloads,
　　　　　　　　　　　　　　　　　　　DNS lookups, etc.

Don't let the name TCP/IP throw you. TCP has no involvement in a UDP message. And while we're at it, don't let the name User Datagram Protocol throw you either. An IP message sent via TCP contains an IP datagram just like a UDP message does.

A key point to know is that only one transport protocol can be used to manage a message. For example, when you download a Web page, the packets are handled by TCP with no involvement from UDP. Conversely, a Trivial File Transfer Protocol (TFTP) upload or download is handled entirely by the UDP protocol.

Which transport protocol is used depends on the network application—e-mail, HTTP Web page downloads, network management, and so on. As we'll discuss, network software designers will use UDP where possible because it generates less overhead traffic. TCP goes to greater lengths to assure delivery and sends many more packets than UDP to manage connections. Figure 2-13 shows a sampling of network applications to illustrate the division between the TCP and UDP transports.

Figure 2-13's examples highlight a few good points. First, FTP and TFTP do essentially the same thing. The major difference is that TFTP is mainly used to download and back up network device software, and it uses UDP because failure of such a message is tolerable (TFTP payloads aren't for end users, but for network administrators, who are lower priority). The Domain Name System (DNS), the service that translates from URLs to IP addresses, uses UDP for client-to-server name lookups and TCP for server-to-server lookups. However, it may use only one of the two for a particular DNS lookup connection. Notice that FTP uses two port numbers—one to manage the request and the other to manage the download. This is because it can take hours to download a big file, so measures are taken to assure that FTP downloads are completed successfully.

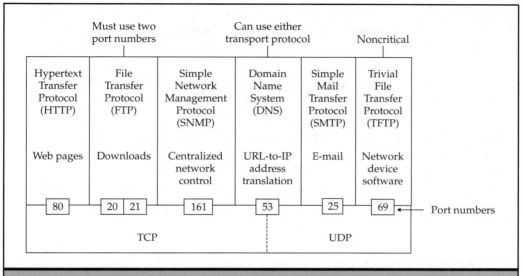

Figure 2-13. TCP and UDP handle different network applications (port numbers).

The IP Datagram Format

The datagram is the basic unit of data inside IP packets. The datagram's format provides fields both for message handling and for the payload data. The datagram layout is depicted in Figure 2-14. Don't be misled by the proportions of the fields in the figure; the data field is by far the largest field in most packets.

When you connect to another computer, the packets making the connection contain your IP address in addition to the destination addresses and, obviously, a field containing any data being sent (such as an instruction to download a Web page). The other 12 packet fields are for handling purposes.

A key fact about IP packets is that they are variable in length. For example, in Ethernet LANs, one packet might be 200 bytes long, another 1,400 bytes. IP packets can grow as large as 4,000 bytes in Token Ring packets.

NOTE: We're talking bytes instead of bits in this context because datagrams contain data, and computers prefer dealing with bytes. On the other hand, when discussing traffic streaming, say, over a cable, the unit of measure is bits—the preferred measure of networking.

Keep in mind that the CPU handling the packet needs to know where each field starts down to the exact bit position; otherwise, the entire thing is just a bunch of meaningless 0's and 1's. Notice that the three fields that can vary in length are placed toward the right side

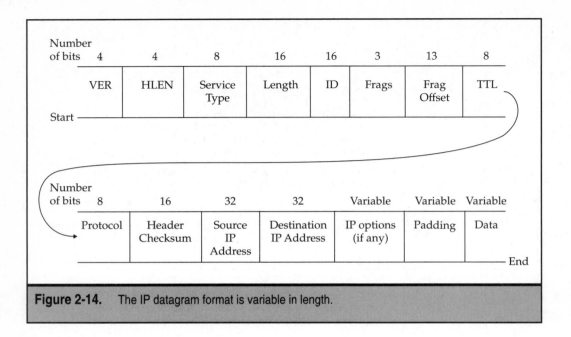

Figure 2-14. The IP datagram format is variable in length.

of the format. If variable-length fields were to the left in the format, it would be impossible for machines to know where the subsequent fields begin. Here are the IP datagram fields:

▼ **VER** The version of IP being used by the station that originated the message. The current version is IP version 4. This field lets different versions coexist in an internetwork.

■ **HLEN** For *header length*, this tells the receiver how long the header will be so the CPU knows where the data field begins.

■ **Service Type** A code to tell the router how the packet should be handled in terms of level of service (reliability, precedence, delay, and so on).

■ **Length** The total number of bytes in the entire packet, including all header fields and the data field.

■ **ID, Frags, and Frags Offset** These fields identify to the router how to packet fragmentation and reassembly, and how to offset for different frame sizes that might be encountered as the packet travels through different LAN segments using different networking technologies (Ethernet, FDDI, and so on).

■ **TTL** Stands for Time to Live, a number that is decremented by one each time the packet is forwarded. When the counter reaches zero, the packet is dropped. TTL prevents router loops and lost packets from endlessly wandering internetworks.

- **Protocol**   The transport protocol that should be used to handle the packet. This field almost always identifies TCP as the transport protocol to use, but certain other transports can be used to handle IP packets.

- **Header Checksum**   A *checksum* is a numerical value used to help assure message integrity. If the checksums in all the message's packets don't add up to the right value, the station knows that the message was garbled.

- **Source IP Address**   The 32-bit address of the host that originated the message (usually a PC or a server).

- **Destination IP Address**   The 32-bit address of the host to which the message is being sent (usually a PC or a server).

- **IP Options**   Used for network testing and other specialized purposes.

- **Padding**   Fills in any unused bit positions so that the CPU can correctly identify the first bit position of the data field.

▲ **Data**   The payload being sent. For example, a packet's data field might contain some of the text making up an e-mail.

A packet has two basic parts: header information and data. The data portion of the packet holds the cargo—the payload that's being sent across the network. The header contains housekeeping information needed by routers and computers to handle the packet and keep it in order with other packets making up the whole message.

The Transport Layer

The way packets are handled differs according to the type of traffic. There are two techniques for sending packets over a TCP/IP internetwork: connection-oriented and connectionless. In the strict sense, of course, a connection is made whenever a packet reaches its destination. *Connection-oriented* and *connectionless* refer to the level of effort and control that is applied to handling a message.

Every packet that goes over an internetwork consumes bandwidth, including overhead traffic. Connection assurance mechanisms are not used for certain types of TCP/IP traffic in order to minimize overhead packets where tolerable. Discrimination in packet handling is achieved by the choice of transport protocol:

▼ **TCP**   The connection-oriented mechanism to transport IP packets through an internetwork

▲ **UDP**   The connectionless mechanism for transporting packets

The primary difference between the two is that TCP requires an ACK message from the receiver that acknowledges the successful completion of each step of a transmission, while UDP does not. That's why UDP is often called the connectionless transport. Because UDP is connectionless, it's faster and more efficient than TCP. UDP is used for network applications where it is considered tolerable to retransmit should the message fail.

Both TCP and UDP operate at layer 4 of the OSI stack, just above the IP network layer. Internetworks run TCP and UDP traffic simultaneously, but an individual message may be sent using only one of the two. The difference between the two is manifested in the format of the IP datagram's transport wrapper, called a *segment*. When a stream of packets is sent over an IP network, the packets are wrapped in either a TCP segment or a UDP segment and handled according to the rules of that particular transport protocol. These segments hold the data used to transport the packet through the internetwork. Keep in mind that this is not payload data, but information used to manage transportation of the packets.

A packet sent via a TCP connection has a much longer header than one traveling via UDP. The extra fields in the TCP header contain information used for establishing connections and handling errors. TCP is the subsystem responsible for establishing and managing IP connections, and it uses a sophisticated handshake procedure to make sure the two end-stations are properly set up for the transmission. For example, when you click a hyperlink to jump to a new Web page, TCP springs into action to "shake hands" with that Web server so the page is downloaded properly. TCP also has procedures for monitoring transmissions and error recovery.

The TCP Segment Format

IP datagrams are placed inside TCP segments when transport is managed by the TCP protocol. The TCP segment format, depicted in Figure 2-15, holds certain pieces of data for establishing TCP connections and managing packet transport.

The data fields in the TCP segment reflect the protocol's focus on establishing and managing network connections. Each is used to perform a specific function that contributes to assuring that a connection runs smoothly:

▼ **Source port**   The application port used by the sending host.

■ **Destination port**   The application port used by the receiving host.

■ **Sequence number**   Positions the packet's data to fit in the overall packet stream.

■ **Acknowledgment number**   Contains the sequence number of the next expected TCP packet, thereby implicitly acknowledging receipt of the prior message.

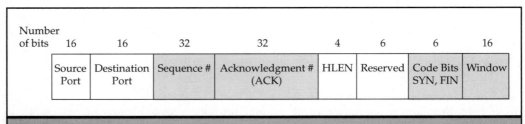

Figure 2-15.   The TCP packet segment holds data used to closely manage packet transport.

- **HLEN**   For *header length*, tells the receiver how long the header will be so the CPU knows where the data field begins.

- **Reserved**   Bits reserved for future use by the IETF.

- **Code bits**   Contains SYN (synchronize) bits to set up a connection or FIN (finish) bits to terminate one.

▲ **Window**   Contains the number of bytes the receiving station can buffer or the number of bytes to be sent. This field sets a "capacity window" to ensure that the sender does not overwhelm the receiver with too many packets all at once.

Establishing a TCP Connection

The TCP connection process is often referred to as the "three-way handshake" because the second step involves the receiving station sending two TCP segments at once. The steps in Figure 2-16 show a couple of the TCP segment fields in action. The first TCP segment's sequence number serves as the initial sequence number—the base number used to keep subsequent packets in proper sequence. The Sequence field is used for reassembling out-of-sequence packets into a cogent message at the receiving end.

Figure 2-16's example shows a PC connecting to a Web server. But any type of end-stations could be talking—a server connecting to another server to perform an e-commerce transaction, two PCs connecting for an IRC (Inter-Regional Connectivity) chat session, or any connection between two end-stations over an IP network.

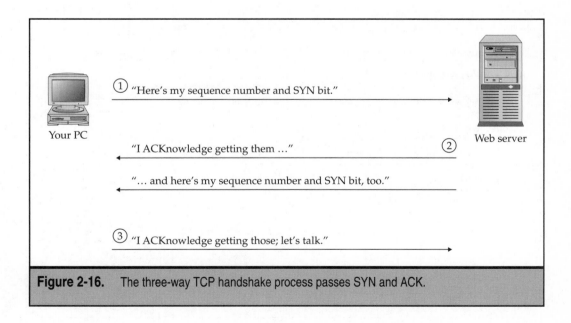

Figure 2-16.   The three-way TCP handshake process passes SYN and ACK.

TCP Windowing

It's not enough just to establish the connection; the session must be dynamically managed to make sure things run smoothly. The major task here is to ensure that one station doesn't overwhelm the other by transmitting too much data at once.

This is done using a technique called *windowing*, in which the receiving station updates the other as to how many bytes it's willing to accept. Put another way, the station is saying how much memory buffer it has available to handle received packets. The TCP windowing process is depicted in Figure 2-17, with a too-small window size shown on the left, and a proper window size on the right.

Window size is communicated via the ACK messages. Looking at Figure 2-17, obviously, a 1,000-byte window size is no good because it causes a one-to-one ratio between incoming packets and outgoing ACKs—way too much overhead in relation to payload traffic. The right half of Figure 2-17 shows a better window size of 10,000 bytes. As the illustration shows, this lets the sending station fire off as many packets as it wants, as long

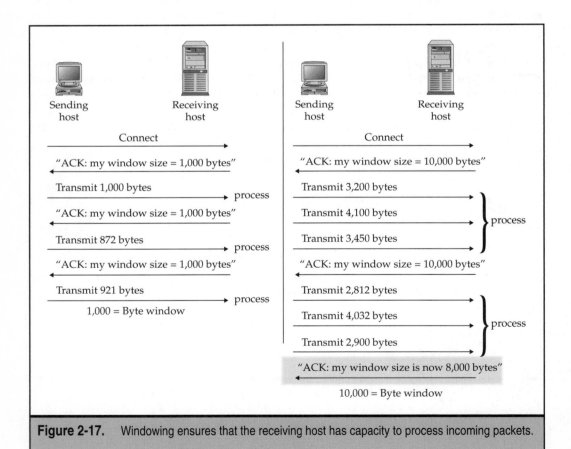

Figure 2-17.   Windowing ensures that the receiving host has capacity to process incoming packets.

as the cumulative total stays beneath the 10,000-byte window size limit. This permits a more favorable payload-to-overhead message ratio.

The message at the lower right is shaded to highlight the fact that window sizes are adjusted dynamically during a session. This is done because of changing conditions within the receiving station. For example, if a Web server suddenly picks up connections from other sending hosts, it has less memory buffer available to process your packets, and it adjusts your window size downward.

Connectionless IP Packet Handling via UDP

The User Datagram Protocol is connectionless in that it doesn't use acknowledgments or windowing. Compared to TCP, UDP is a "best effort" transport protocol—it simply transmits the message and hopes for the best. The UDP segment format is shown in Figure 2-18. Besides the port numbers to tell which network applications to run, UDP segments basically just declare packet size. The only reliability mechanism in UDP is the checksum, used to verify the integrity of the data in the transmission. The odds that the checksum of a received packet containing altered data will match the checksum of the sent packet are miniscule.

Port Numbers

A port number identifies the network application to the upper layers of the application. For example, each packet in an e-mail transmission contains the port number 25 in its header to indicate the Simple Mail Transfer Protocol. There are hundreds of assigned port numbers. The Internet Assigned Numbers Authority (IANA) coordinates port number assignments according to the following system:

▼ **Numbers 255 and below**   Assigned to public applications (such as SMTP)

■ **Numbers 256 to 1023**   Assigned to companies to identify network application products

▲ **Numbers 1024 and above**   Assigned dynamically by the end-user application using the network application

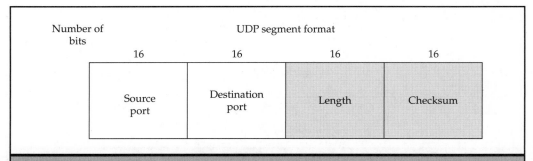

Figure 2-18.   The UDP segment format doesn't have Sequence or Acknowledgment fields.

Port numbers help the stations keep track of various connections being processed simultaneously. For example, for security reasons, most firewalls are configured to read port numbers in every packet header.

Many beginners are confused as to exactly how port numbers are used. For example, if you're trying to connect to a Web server from your PC, you might think that both end-stations would use port 80 (HTTP) to conduct a Web page download. In fact, the requesting client uses a random port number in the request packet's source port field and uses assigned HTTP port number 80 only in the destination port field. Figure 2-19 demonstrates how port numbers are used during a transmission.

The client uses a random port number to help keep track of conversations during a connection. A *conversation* is a discrete port-to-port transaction between end-stations. There can be any number of conversations within a single connection.

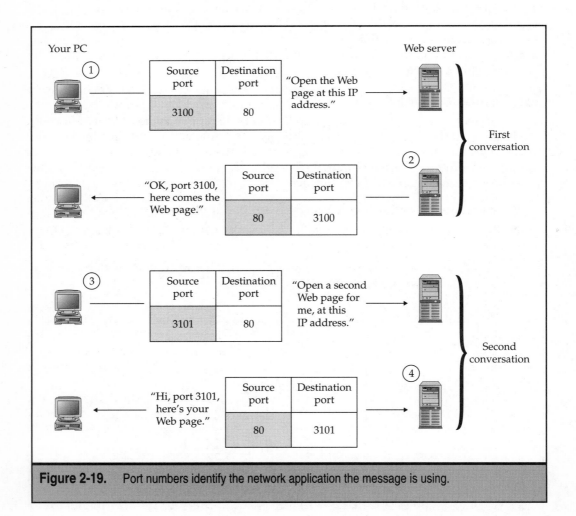

Figure 2-19.   Port numbers identify the network application the message is using.

Looking at Figure 2-19, the page downloaded in step 2 may have included one of those annoying embedded HTML commands that automatically creates a new browser window without your asking for it (a *pop-up*). The pop-up window requests that a new page be downloaded, thereby creating a whole new stream of HTML code, text, GIFs, and JPEGs to handle—a second conversation, in other words.

At the server end, however, a widely recognized port number such as 80 for HTTP must be used—otherwise, the thousands of hosts hitting the Web server would have no idea what application to ask for.

IP ADDRESSING

To go somewhere on the Internet, you must type a Uniform Resource Locator (URL) into the Address field on your browser. A unique domain name combines with its organization category to form a URL such as velte.com. Actually, you seldom even have to type in a URL; you just click a hyperlink that has the URL stored in the HTML that makes up the Web page you're leaving.

URLs only exist to make surfing the Internet easier; they aren't true IP addresses. In other words, if you type the URL **velte.com** into your browser, a query is sent to the nearest DNS server to translate the URL to an IP address, as shown in Figure 2-20.

Translation to IP addresses is necessary because the routers and switches that run the Internet don't recognize domain names. Indeed, an IP address must be used just for your query to get as far as the DNS server.

All Internet addresses are IP addresses. The IANA issues IP addresses. Domain names were issued by an organization called InterNIC (Internet Information Center). The primary responsibility of these organizations is to assure that all IP addresses and domain names are unique. For example, velte.com was issued by InterNIC; and its IP address at the time, 209.98.208.34, was issued by the ISP, which for its part was issued the IP address from the IANA. Internet Corporation for Assigned Names and Numbers (ICANN) was started in early 1999 to take over assignment duties. Now, domain names are issued by a large number of organizations that roll up under ICANN.

The IP Address Format

Every node on the Internet must have an IP address. This includes hosts as well as networks. There's no getting around this rule because IP addressing is what ties the Internet together. Even stations connected to a LAN with its own addressing system (AppleTalk, for example) must translate to IP in order to enter the Internet.

It's somewhat ironic that, despite the requirement that every IP address be unique to the world, at the same time all IP addresses must be in the same format. IP addresses are 32 bits long and divided into four sections, each 8 bits long, called *octets*.

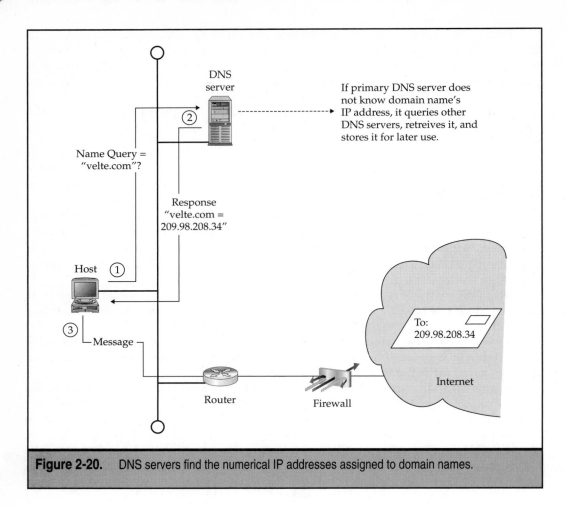

Figure 2-20. DNS servers find the numerical IP addresses assigned to domain names.

Routers use IP addresses to forward messages through internetworks. Put simply, as the packet hops from router to router, it works its way from left to right across the IP address until it finally reaches the router to which the destination address is attached.

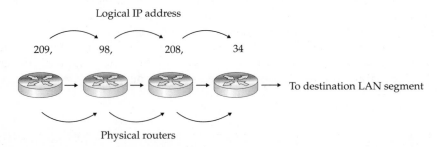

Of course, sometimes a message will go through several router hops before moving closer to its destination. More frequently, messages skip over entire octets and move to the destination LAN segment in just one or two hops. Sometimes hops are needed to find the next destination.

From Bits to Dotted-Decimal Format

As discussed earlier, machines only understand instructions and data in binary format. This goes for IP addresses, too, but the dotted-decimal format was invented so people could read binary IP addresses. *Dotted-decimal* takes its name from the fact that it converts bits to decimal numbers for each octet, punctuated with periods. Figure 2-21 shows the conversion of an IP address to dotted-decimal format.

Figure 2-21 also shows the two reserved addresses. All 1's in an octet are for broadcast, where the router automatically forwards a message to all hosts attached to networks

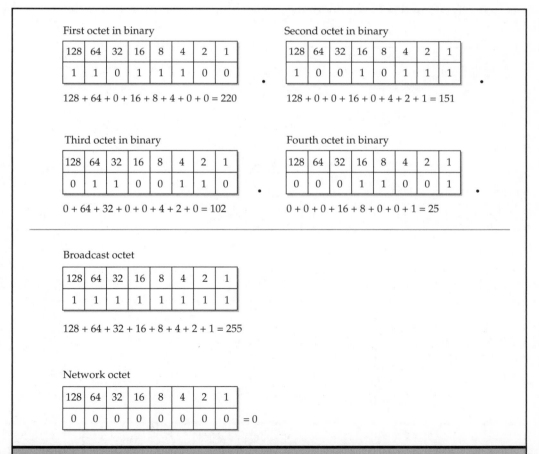

Figure 2-21. Thirty-two bits define the IP addresses you see in dotted-decimal format.

addressed thus far in the address. For example, messages addressed to 220.151.102.255 will be forwarded to all interfaces whose first three octets are 220.151.102. The other reserved address—called the "this network" address—is used for technical purposes not discussed here. Just understand that an address like 220.151.102.0 means "this interface" on network 220.151.102.

IP Address Classes

The IETF divides IP addresses into three general classes (plus two specialized ones). As mentioned earlier, IP addresses are divided into four dotted-decimal octets. Each class differs in the way the octets are designated for addressing networks, as opposed to hosts. Figure 2-22 shows the first octet number ranges. The shaded octets show how much of the IP address space is reserved for addressing networks. As the shaded portion moves to the right, there are more possible networks, but fewer possible hosts.

This designation of ranges is called the *first octet rule*. Any router in the world can read the first octet of an IP address and know which bits to interpret as part of the network

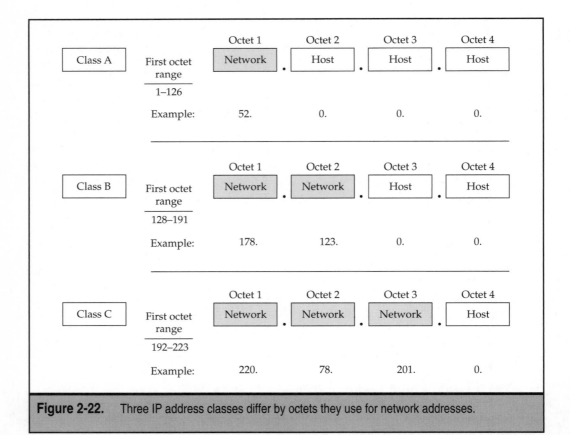

Figure 2-22. Three IP address classes differ by octets they use for network addresses.

address versus the host address. If routers weren't able to make this distinction, the Internet couldn't work at all.

The majority of networks are numbered using either Class B or Class C IP addresses. The first octet ranges for each class are as follows:

▼ **0 to 127**   Class A, range of network numbers is 0.0.0.0 to 127.0.0.0 for 128 networks. However, the network must not consist of only 0's, and 127.0.0.0 is reserved for loopback. Left are 126 networks—1 to 126. There are 16,777,214 possible host addresses (16,777,216 minus 2).

■ **128 to 191**   Class B, range of network numbers is 128.0.0.0 to 191.255.0.0 for 16,384 networks. There are 65,534 possible host addresses (65,536 minus 2).

▲ **192 to 223**   Class C, range of network numbers is 192.0.0.0 to 223.255.255.0 for 2,097,152 networks. There are 254 possible host addresses (256 minus 2).

All host calculations must use the "minus 2" calculation to deduct two reserved addresses: 0 for "this network" and 255 for broadcast. Addresses 1 through 254 may be assigned to hosts. In case you're wondering, first octet numbers 224 through 254 are reserved for two special classes not discussed here (multicasting and research).

As you look at the above list, you can imagine that only a few very large organizations have Class A addresses—only 126 of them, in fact. Most of us connect to the Internet via either Class B or Class C IP addresses.

NOTE: Don't forget that a network by strict definition is a LAN segment—an individual, shared-access medium. That's what is meant by the word "network" in the context of IP addressing. A network (or LAN segment) is also identified as a network interface (or interface, for short), because only one network may connect to a router's interface. For example, Ford Motor Company's intranet is probably referred to as a network by its employees, but Ford's network manager must assign unique IP addresses to the tens of thousands of individual networks (LAN segments) connected to the company's router interfaces.

Private Addressing

The IANA reserved three blocks of IP addresses for private addresses. A private IP address is one that is not registered with the IANA and will not be used beyond the bounds of the enterprise's internetwork—in other words, not on the Internet. Privately numbered internetworks are also sometimes called *private internets*, but we term them "internetworks" in this book to avoid confusion. The three blocks of reserved private address space are as follows:

▼ **10.0.0.0 through 10.255.255.255**   The *10 block* is a single Class A network number.

■ **172.16.0.0 through 172.31.255.255**   The *172 block* is 16 contiguous Class B network numbers.

▲ **192.168.0.0 through 192.168.255.255**   The *192 block* is 256 contiguous Class C network numbers.

Edge devices, such as firewalls and boundary routers, must be assigned public IP addresses to conduct business with the outside. Private addresses are assigned only to hosts that make most or all of their connections within the private internetwork.

That's not to say, however, that a privately addressed host cannot connect to the outside world. Two IP address translation services are used to assign valid public Internet IP numbers temporarily to hosts with permanent private IP addresses. One technique is Network Address Translation (NAT), and the other is Port Address Translation (PAT). How the two work is depicted in Figure 2-23.

Address translation is usually done by a firewall. Keep in mind that these private-to-public translations are temporary. In NAT, when the internal host terminates its connection to the outside, the public IP address is returned to the pool for reuse.

The obvious advantage of private addressing is to have virtually unlimited address space for numbering internal networks and hosts. With a properly configured firewall or edge router to perform NAT or PAT address translation, these privately addressed hosts are still afforded connectivity to the Internet. Moreover, because their actual addresses are "spoofed" by a temporarily assigned pool number, hackers see no indication of the private internetwork's topology.

Subnetting

Subnetting is the practice of squeezing more network addresses out of a given IP address than are available by default. As discussed, IP address classes define which bits, by default, will address networks versus hosts. What *by default* means here is that upon reading the first octet in an address, a router knows which bits to treat as network address bits. Taking a Class C address as an example, the router will, by default, see the first three octets as network bits, and the final octet as host bits.

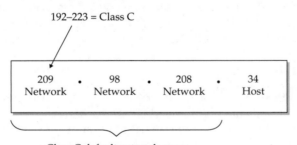

Class C default network space

However, in the real world, most enterprises need more network address space than they are assigned by their ISPs. This creates the need to "cheat" by claiming some of the default host bits for use in addressing networks. This is done by inserting a third zone between the default network and host address spaces. Figure 2-24 shows two IP addresses,

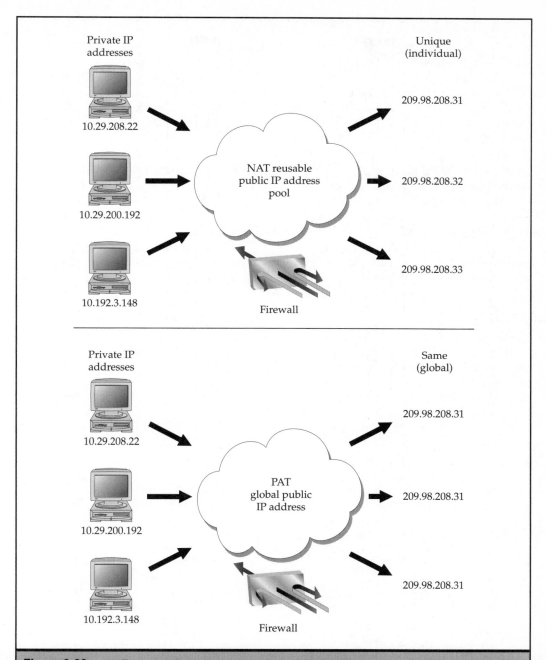

Figure 2-23.   NAT temporarily assigns unique reusable public IP addresses; PAT assigns a global IP address.

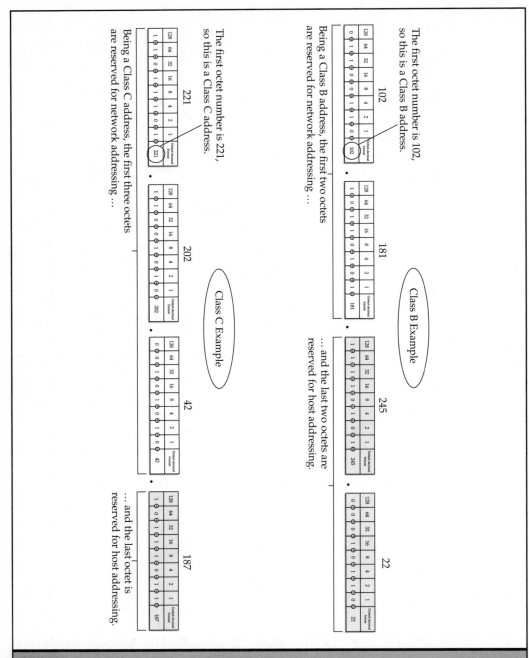

Figure 2-24.   Subnetting extends network address space rightward.

one a subnetted Class B and the other a Class C address. They're shown in both dotted-decimal and binary format.

Which class an IP address belongs to is important, because subnets extend to the right, starting from the leftmost bit in the default network address space. In other words, only bit positions in the shaded portions of Figure 2-24 may be encroached for subnet addressing.

Be aware that the majority of enterprises are assigned Class C addresses, meaning that they have at most only eight bits with which to work. Indeed, most networks are assigned only a range of host numbers, for example, 221.198.20.32-47.

Whole Octet Subnet Example

Subnetting makes more efficient use of public IP addresses without changing them. Take the network in Figure 2-25 as an example. The enterprise was issued the Class B public IP address 151.22.0.0 and subnetted the entire third octet.

Looking at Figure 2-25's configuration, you can see that there is address space for 254 subnetworks, with space for 254 hosts per subnetwork. The shaded host at the bottom right shows a complete subnet address—in this example host number 1 attached to subnet number 2 within IP address 151.22.0.1. The key feature of this example is that an entire octet—the third octet—is subnetted.

As remote routers work their way rightward through Figure 2-25's subnetted addresses, the packets will automatically fall through the correct interface in the edge router at the bottom center of the cloud.

What Subnet Masks Look Like and Where They Exist

All subnet masks are 32 bits in length. Take note that masks are not addresses; they are overlays that define how an IP address is to be used. They differ from normal IP addresses in two key ways:

▼   **Form**   A subnet mask is represented as a string of 1's in binary, or 255 in dotted-decimal format.

▲   **Location**   A subnet is applied to a specific network interface within the configuration file of the router to which the subnetwork is attached.

The configuration file sits inside the IOS software of the Cisco router. An attached LAN segment is subnetted by entering a statement like this:

```
MyRouter(config-if)#ip address 151.22.1.1 255.255.255.0
```

The MyRouter(config-if)# prompt means "configure this network interface on this router," where the command is being entered into a Cisco router named MyRouter. The **ip address** command is used to set the IP address for the network interface in question.

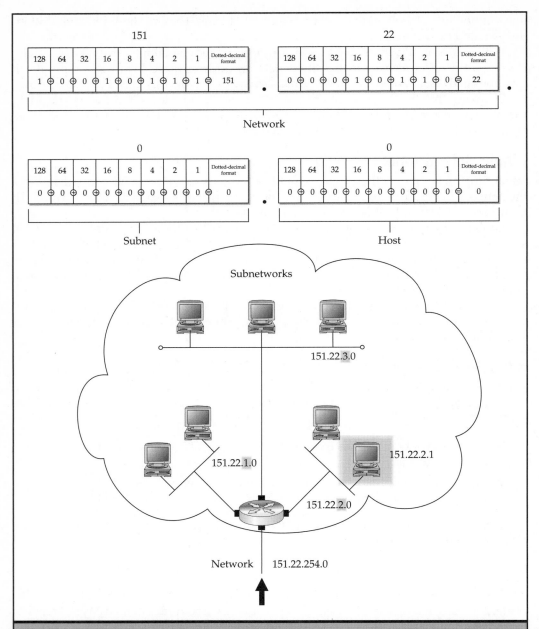

Figure 2-25. Subnetting makes efficient use of address space; this Class B example has room for 254 subnets.

The interface's proper IP address is 151.22.1.1 (a Class B address), and the subsequent 255.255.255.0 tells the router to subnet the entire third octet, represented in bits as:

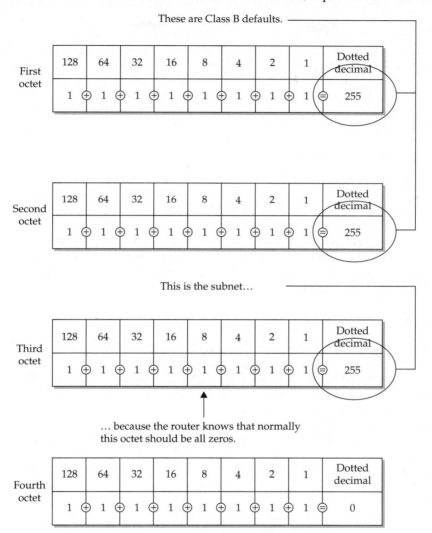

That's not too complicated. A subnet mask is the contiguous string of 1-bits extending from the end of the network address space into the host portion. Where that point is depends on the address class (the preceding example is a Class B). The subnet mask is entered into the router's config file using the **ip address** command to append the subnet mask to the normal IP address and apply it to a specific network interface—and in so doing, a specific LAN segment.

Partial Octet Subnetting

In most cases, however, subnets aren't quite so simple. This is because most enterprises are issued Class C IP addresses, where only the fourth octet is reserved by default as host address space. In these cases, the subnet mask extends only partway into the host address space, and is thus represented by some dotted-decimal number less than 255.

The shaded portion in Figure 2-26 represents the bits claimed for subnetting from the fourth octet. Notice that only half the bits were claimed, not all eight. This is the so-called .240 mask, which permits up to 14 subnets, each subnet with enough address space for 14 hosts—for a total of 196 possible hosts. This example would be input into the router's config file as follows:

```
MyRouter(config-if)#ip address 209.98.208.34 255.255.255.240
```

This command instructs the router that the interface is a subnet with 28 network ID bits and 4 host ID bits. From there, packet delivery into the subnet is automatic.

There are several subnet masks from which to choose, as illustrated in Table 2-1. The farther right a mask extends into the host address space, the lower the number of possible hosts per subnet. Which mask to use depends entirely on the application. For example, if a network interface on a router is attached to a point-to-point connection with a remote office, only two host addresses are required—one for each end. In this scenario, it would make sense to use the .252 mask, which has only two host addresses.

IP Version 6

While Internet addressing seems to run smoothly and without incident, the shocking truth is that we are running out of IP addresses. It might seem that IPv4, the current 32-bit addressing system, provides more than enough addresses. In fact, using IPv4, there are about four billion addresses available. However, it turns out we need more.

When the IP addressing scheme was developed in the 1980s, no one had a clue that the Internet would become the behemoth that it has grown into. The sheer pervasiveness of the Internet is gobbling up IP addresses—not only are computers, servers, and other network equipment using IP addresses, but as other devices, such as Internet-enabled cellular telephones and PDAs, gain in popularity, more and more IP addresses will be sucked up.

Enter IPv6, also known as IPng ("ng" standing for "next generation").

IPv4 utilizes a 32-bit binary number to identify unique networks and end stations. This allows for around four billion unique addresses. IPv6 is different in that it uses a 128-bit hexadecimal format (numbers range from 0000 to FFFF). This addressing scheme allows for 10^{15} unique hosts, or 340,282,366,920,938,463,463,374,607,431,768,211,456 total addresses. Basically, that's one address for every grain of sand on the planet.

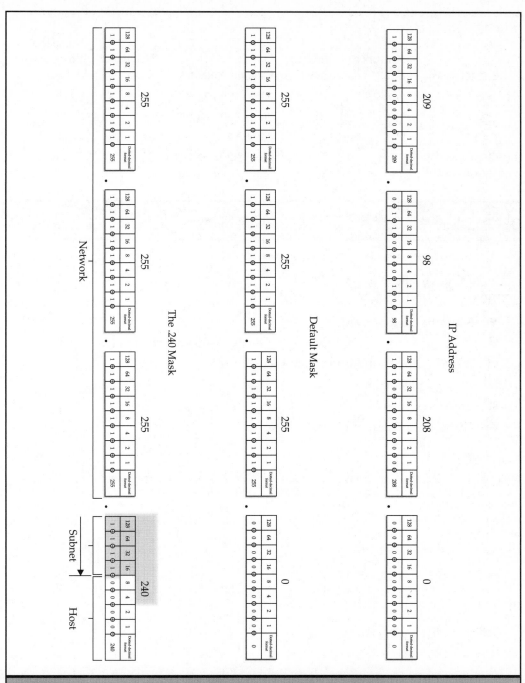

Figure 2-26.   Usually, only part of an octet is subnetted, as in this Class C example.

Subnet Mask	Network ID Bits	Host ID Bits	Example Notation	Number of Subnets	Number of Hosts per Subnet
.192	26	6	209.98.208.34/26	2	62
.224	27	5	209.98.208.34/27	6	30
.240	28	4	209.98.208.34/28	14	14
.248	29	3	209.98.208.34/29	30	6
.252	30	2	209.98.208.34/30	62	2

Table 2-1.   Subnet Masks Listed by Number of Network ID Bits

In addition to the exponential growth of IP addresses, IPv6 makes some functional improvements over IPv4, including:

▼ Simplified header format

■ Routing efficiency improved with hierarchical network architecture

■ IPv6's support for popular routing protocols

■ Auto configuration

■ Embedded IPSec

▲ Greater number of multicast addresses

Format

As noted earlier, IPv6 addresses are 128 bits in size. They are expressed as eight fields of 16-bit, hex notation numbers (0000-FFFF), in this format:

x:x:x:x:x:x:x:x

Examples of this format are

FEDC:BA98:7654:3210:FEDC:BA98:7654:3210

or

1080:0:0:0:8:800:200C:417A

IPv6 addresses can be presented in three ways:

▼ The most straightforward method is to simply enter the values in each of the eight fields, like:

    1070:200:0:0:900:300C:618A

You'll note that it is not necessary to use the leading 0's in an individual field. That is, "200" is the same as "0200."

■ In some cases, IPv6 addresses will contain long strings of zero bits. As such, crafters of the IPv6 addressing scheme have figured out a way to save the "0" button on your keyboard. Rather than enter "0000:0000:0000:0000:0000:0000:0000:1" or even "0:0:0:0:0:0:0:1," it is acceptable to indicate two or more groups of 0's using "::". As such, the aforementioned example can be abbreviated as "::: 1."

The only hitch to this shorthand is that the "::" notation can only be used once in the address. By using the "::" notation, IPv6 is able to determine that the "missing" number of values must all be 0's. However, if the "::" notation is used more than once, it would be impossible to tell how many sets of 0's are missing from each section.

    Table 2-2 shows how different IPv6 addresses can be abbreviated.

■ Finally, given that there will be a fair amount of transition time before IPv6 is completely adopted, there is a format that is used in mixed IPv6/IPv4 environments. That format combines both formats and is represented as:

    x:x:x:x:x:x:d.d.d.d

Address Type	IPv6 Address	Representation Using ::
Unicast	1070:200:0:0:900:300C:618A	1070:200::900:300C:618A
Multicast	FF01:0:0:0:0:0:0:100	FF01::100
Loopback	0:0:0:0:0:0:0:1	::1
Unspecified Address	0:0:0:0:0:0:0:0	::

Table 2-2. Abbreviating IPv6 Addresses

In this case, the "x" values are the hexadecimal values of the six high-order 16-bit pieces of the address and the "d" values are the decimal values of the four low-order 8-bit pieces of the address. For example:

0:0:0:0:0:FFFF:129.144.40.20

To throw a bit of a curveball at you, you are still allowed to utilize the compressed form of the address, even in the mixed format. For instance:

::FFF:129:144:40:20

IP Prefix

The IPv6 prefix is the portion of the address representing the left-most, high-order bits. These bits represent the network identifier. The IPv6 prefix is represented using the prefix/prefix length notation. For example, 2001/16 identifies the Internet, while 2001:AB18/32 might identify an ISP. 2001:4637:0:2930/64 identifies a specific network.

Header Formats

One of IPv6's most impressive improvements is its streamlining of the IPv4 header size, making it a simpler format. While an IPv4 header is only 20 octets, the variable length of the Options field increases the overall size of the IPv4 packet.

IPv6, on the other hand, has a fixed size of 40 octets. IPv6 maintains some of IPv4's header fields, but many of these fields have different names and the new protocol introduces new fields. Removed from IPv4 are

▼ Header Length

■ Identification Flags

■ Fragment Offset

■ Header Checksum

▲ Padding

With these fields removed, processing of the header is much faster. The removal of these fields means less work for the routers and less duplication of work. For example, with no fragmentation or checksum responsibilities, routers can focus on transmitting packets, not fixing faulty packets. And, since most checksum is performed at the link layer, it is not necessary for the router to duplicate this work.

Further, all fields in an IPv6 header are 64 bits, which makes them more agreeable with 64-bit processors.

The format for an IPv6 header is shown in Figure 2-27. The following explains the fields and their duties:

▼ **Version Number**   As in IPv4, this field contains a number identifying the IP version. In IPv6, this field will contain the number 6, rather than the 4 used in IPv4.

■ **Traffic Class**   Identical to the ToS field in IPv4.

■ **Flow Label**   New to IPv6, this 20-bit field is used to tag packets of a specific flow to distinguish them at the network layer. This aids identification of individual flows and per-flow processing by routers along the path. Because of this field, a router can easily identify a flow, rather than having to dig into the packet for identification information. This allows easier Quality of Service for packets that have been encrypted.

■ **Payload Length**   Same as the Total Length field in IPv4.

■ **Next Header**   Comparable to the Protocol field in IPv4. In IPv6, however, optional information in the header is managed differently. Extension headers are defined and are daisy-chained together by the Next Header field, then are stored in each extension header. (We'll explain extension headers in more depth in a moment.) By doing so, extension headers are processed more efficiently, allowing a faster forwarding rate and giving the router less processing work to do.

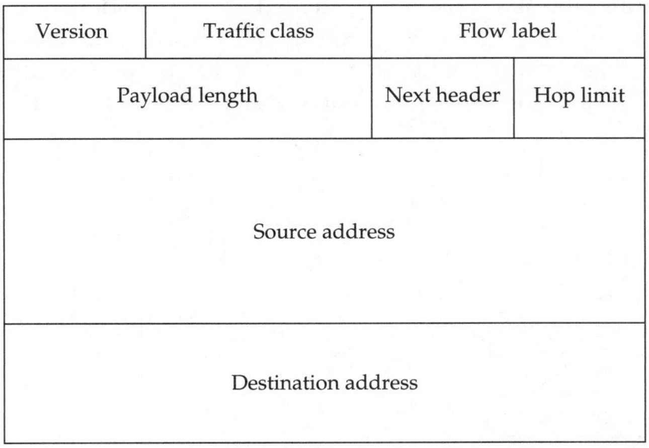

Version	Traffic class	Flow label	
Payload length		Next header	Hop limit
Source address			
Destination address			

Figure 2-27.   An IPv6 header is simplified over IPv4 headers.

■ **Hop Limit**   Like the Time to Live field in IPv4, the Hop Limit field is used to identify the maximum number of router hops that a packet can pass through before the packet is deemed invalid. Each router hop decrements the Hop Limit field value by 1.

■ **Source Address**   Similar to the Source Address field in an IPv4 packet, except this field will contain the 128-bit source IPv6 address, rather than a 32-bit IPv4 address.

▲ **Destination Address**   Similar to the Destination Address field in an IPv4 packet, except this field will contain the 128-bit source IPv6 address, rather than a 32-bit IPv4 address.

In IPv6, options are handled by the extension header. Extension headers are a good thing, because they can be added if needed, but left off if they're not needed. Under IPv4, a router would always have to check the IPv4 header and check to see if there were options. That's not the case in IPv6 because the router can see if there are extension headers that merit further examination.

Figure 2-28 shows the IPv6 extension header format. The following are different types of extension headers and, if multiple extension headers are used, they should be used in this order.

▼ **Hop-by-Hop Header**   Used for the Router Alert and the Jumbogram and is processed by all hops in the path. This header always follows after the IPv6 packet header. (Value = 0)

■ **Destination Options Header**   Processed at the final destination and at each address specified by a routing header. This header can also follow any Encapsulating Security Payload (ESP) header. In this case, the Destination Options header is processed only at the final destination. (Value = 60)

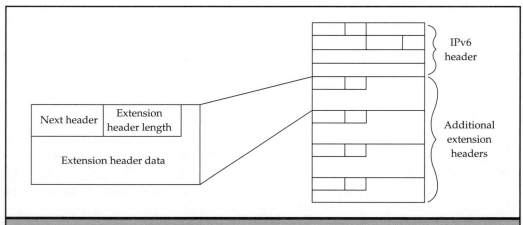

Figure 2-28.   The IPv6 extension header allows options to be added to a packet.

- **Routing Header**   Used for source routing and mobile IPv6. (Value = 43)
- **Fragment Header**   Used when a source must divide a packet that is larger than the maximum transmission unit (MTU). This header is used in each fragmented packet.
- **Authentication Header and Encapsulating Security Payload Header**   Used within IPSec for authentication, reliability, and security of a packet. (Value = 50)
- ▲ **Upper-Layer Header**   Used inside a packet for data transport. The protocols used are TCP (value = 6) and UDP (value = 17).

Types of Addressing

There are three types of addressing available in IPv6:

- ▼ **Unicast**   One host transmits to another on a network. Cisco supports five types of unicast addresses:

   - **Global unicast addresses,** which are comparable to IPv4 global unicast addresses. That is, it is an IPv6 address from the global unicast prefix. Global unicast addresses move upward through organizations, then to ISPs. Global unicast addresses contain a global routing prefix, a subnet ID, and an interface ID. With the exception of addresses beginning with 000, all global unicast addresses have a 64-bit interface ID. Currently, the global unicast allocation uses a range of addresses starting with the value 001 (2000::/3). Global unicast addresses use one-eighth of the total IPv6 address space and make up the largest block of assigned addresses.

     Figure 2-29 shows the global unicast address format.

   - **Site-local unicast addresses,** which are similar to private addresses (like 10.0.0.0, 172.16.0.0, and 192.168.0.0) in IPv4.

   - **Link-local unicast addresses,** which are used for neighbor discovery and autoconfiguration.

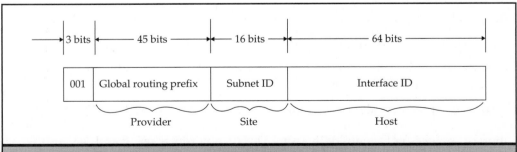

Figure 2-29.   The format of a global unicast IPv6 address

- **IPv4-mapped IPv6 addresses,** which are used to represent the address of an IPv4 node as an IPv6 address.

- **IPv4 compatible IPv6 addresses,** which are used transitionally as IPv6 is used over existing IPv4 networks.

- **Anycast**   One host transmits to the closest destination host. Anycasting is designed to let one host initiate router table updating for a group of hosts. IPv6 can determine which gateway host is closest and sends packets to that host, singly. In turn, that host can anycast to another host in the group and so on until all routing tables are updated. An anycast address is a global unicast address assigned to a set of interfaces belonging to different nodes.

- **Multicast**   One host transmits to multiple hosts on a network. The multicast address scheme uses addresses with a prefix of FF00::/8. In total, the multicast address range uses 1/256 of the total IPv6 address space. The second octet following the prefix establishes the lifetime and scope of the multicast address. Permanent multicast addresses have a lifetime parameter set to 0; temporary addresses are set to 1. The next four bits are used to establish the scope of the address.

Figure 2-30 not only shows the multicast address, but also includes the values of these bits. In order to identify specific functions, each block of multicast addresses within the range of FF00:: to FF0F:: is used accordingly:

- **FF01::1**   All nodes within the node-local scope.

- **FF02::1**   All nodes on the local link.

- **FF01::2**   All routers within the node-local scope.

- **FF02::2**   All routers on the link-local scope.

- **FF05::2**   All routers in the site.

- **FF02::1:FFXX:XXXX**   Solicited-node multicast address (XX:XXXX represents the last 24 bits of the IPv6 address of node).

Configuration

Using IPv4, addresses are assigned one of two ways:

- ▼ **Statically**   The address must be entered manually.

- ▲ **Dynamically**   DHCP/BOOTP automatically assigns IP addresses to a host when they boot onto the network.

IPv6 uses a feature called *stateless autoconfiguration*. This is similar to DHCP in that IP addresses are automatically assigned; however, it differs because a special DHCP application or server is not required. By using DCHP, any router using an IPv6 address becomes a "provider" of IP addresses to the network to which it is attached. To prevent duplicate addresses from being doled out, IPv6 uses a feature called *duplicate address detection (DAD)*.

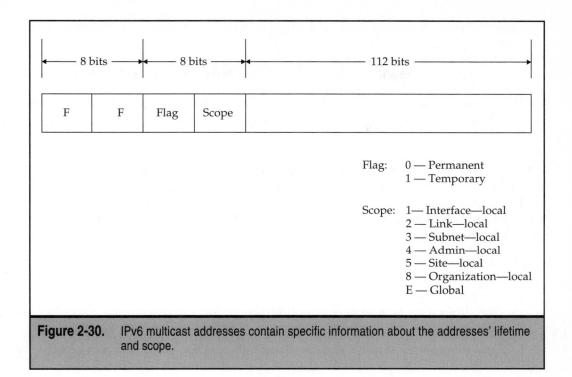

Figure 2-30.   IPv6 multicast addresses contain specific information about the addresses' lifetime and scope.

NAT and PAT

One of the downfalls of the lack of addresses available under IPv4 is that mechanisms such as NAT and PAT had to be used to stretch out IP addresses. Though this is an acceptable bandage, it is not perfect.

There are two schools of thought as to whether to upgrade to IPv6 or continue using NAT or PAT.

On the pro upgrade side of the ledger, one of the problems in using NAT and PAT is that there isn't the true interconnectivity available that the Internet promises. NAT and PAT allow a company or user to share a single IP address among multiple private addresses (which are not controlled by any addressing authority). This is fine as a means of stretching out IP addresses (and, as a bonus, preserving a user's anonymity), but independence suffers.

For example, a desktop workstation in Ely, Minnesota, may not truly be able to connect with another workstation in Nice, France. If both computers are using NAT or PAT because their organization needs to stretch out IP addresses, then they are not able to connect seamlessly. If each had its own, unique IP address, they would be able to connect with few obstructions.

On the other hand, using NAT and PAT provides a certain level of security. Since packets travel to a lone address for multiple-end stations, your individual IP address isn't being broadcast across the Internet.

However, if the thought of a unique IP address on the entire Internet for a single computer is frightening, don't worry too much. IPv6 provides enough address space for every device on the planet, and it also comes with built-in security features (namely IPSec) to keep the bad guys out.

Address Allocation

Like IPv4, you can't just decide on an IP address and call it your own—even if there is a seemingly limitless amount. IANA is managing IPv6 addresses much in the way it has managed IPv4 addresses. It has allocated addresses from 2001::/16 to registries from the full address space. Each registry gets a /23 prefix within the 2001::/16 address space. The addresses are allocated as follows:

▼ **2001:0200::/23 and 2001:0C00::/23**   For use in Asia. These addresses were allocated to Asia Pacific Network Information Centre (APNIC).

■ **2001:0400::/23**   For use in the Americas. The addresses were allocated to American Registry for Internet Numbers (ARIN).

▲ **2001:0600::/23 and 2001:0800::/23**   For use in Europe and the Middle East. These addresses were allocated to Reseaux IP Europeens – Network Coordination Center (RIPE NCC).

Next, the registries allocate a /32 prefix to the IPv6 ISPs, then the ISPs allocate a /48 prefix to each customer. The /48 prefix of each site could be further allocated to each LAN, using a /64 prefix. Each site could have a maximum of 65,535 LANs.

IPv6 Addresses in a URL

Since the colon (:) is already used to identify a specific port number in a URL (for instance, www.thisisjustatest.com:8080), it cannot be used within the address. As such, it is necessary to find a workaround to use this in Web browsers. The chosen way to make IPv6 addresses work as URLs is to enclose them in brackets, like this:

http://[2001:0401:3:4F23::AE35]

If we wanted to go to a specific port using an IPv6 address, the colon and port number would simply follow the address, like this:

http://[2001:0401:3:4F23::AE35]:8080

That having been said, using IPv6 as a URL is a giant pain. Best just to use the fully qualified domain name than mess around with the IPv6 address. After all, isn't it easier to remember www.thisisjustatest.com than 2001:0401:3:4F23::AE35?

IPv6 isn't going to phase out IPv4 anytime soon (even the most optimistic speculation sees IPv6 phasing in between 2004 and 2010). There are plenty of pundits out there who think IPv4 won't run out of address space for more than a decade and that IPv6 doesn't really bring anything new and revolutionary to the IP party. Agree or disagree, this is relevant information to know because many Cisco devices are ready to go using IPv6 for addressing. At this point in time, however, the vast majority of Internetworking is achieved using the 32-bit, four-octet, IPv4.

PUTTING IT ALL TOGETHER

So, what happens behind the scenes when you make a connection across the Internet? Let's take the most common scenario of all, a Web page download.

Your PC sends UDP packets to your local DNS server to translate the domain name into an IP address and returns the results. If there's a problem, the DNS lookup will time out, and the browser will complain that the server was not found.

The destination IP address is inserted into the header of your packets, along with your IP address and the port number for HTTP (80). Your request is sent over the TCP transport to the destination host to set up a connection. The route taken to the destination is left up to the routers, who read the IP address and hop from router to router to get there. If the packets can't find the destination host, you will likely see a "destination unreachable" error, or if there is a routing loop in the network, the Time-to-Live (TTL) counter will reach zero and the connection attempt will be timed out.

If the routers find the router on which the destination host resides, the packets go through the network interface to enter the host's LAN segment using the destination IP address' subnet mask, if there is one.

The receiving host reads your message and decides whether to respond. To answer your service request, it answers using the TCP three-way handshake and windowing techniques, the connection is established, and the requested Web page download is executed under the management of TCP windowing.

In simplified terms, that's what happens when you click a hyperlink in your browser.

CHAPTER 3

Cisco Certifications

The boom in internetworking has created an urgent need for more technical talent to install and manage network infrastructure. Industry growth is the biggest factor. The number of installed routers, switches, and other internetworking devices has grown explosively over the last decade, and more qualified technicians are needed to take care of them. But industry growth isn't the only factor driving the talent shortage; another driver of the shortfall is that internetworking technology itself has become a lot more complicated. What used to be a fairly straightforward proposition of hubs and routers has given way to switched networks, virtual LANs, ATM emulated LANs, virtual private networks (VPNs), optical telecommunications media, firewalls, management tools, and more. The onslaught of new and better internetworking technology is coming so fast that it's even hard for established pros to stay current.

If you're considering a career move into a technical area, the advice here is to take a serious look at network engineering. Internetworking professionals—often referred to as *wireheads* or *networkers*—are the people who work with the infrastructure that's largely invisible to network users. This is an entirely different group from the people who code HTML pages or write Java applets. Wireheads are the people who work with routers, switches, firewalls, access servers, and other internetworking devices. Some of them help run office or campus networks, and others work with wide area networks (WANs). A growing number of wireheads work for ISPs and other provider organizations instead of end-user enterprises. In addition, an increasing number of them are with internetwork consulting firms, not as full-time, permanent employees.

Talent shortages are nothing new to the computer business, and they're recognized as a threat. If demand for a vendor's products is hot but customers can't find anybody to install and maintain the products, the vendor's growth is curtailed. Another pitfall is having unqualified personnel working on the vendor's equipment. This inevitably leads to technical disasters large and small, and the vendor often ends up taking the brunt of customer dissatisfaction.

The industry response has been vendor certifications. A *certification* is a stamp of approval that a person has a certain level of technical competency with the vendor's products. It is obtained by passing a battery of tests specifically geared to the vendor's product line. These tests sometimes include hands-on lab exercises in addition to written exams. Vendors typically farm out their certification programs to approved training organizations that must adhere to the vendor-designed curriculum. Most vendor certification programs are arranged into a career track with certifications by level (beginner, intermediate, and expert) and sometimes also by area of specialization.

Interestingly, the first well-known certification program came from a network company, not a computer company—the major LAN software vendor, Novell. Novell's theory was that not only are networks quite complicated, but one that malfunctions is highly visible within the customer organization. So, in the 1980s, Novell instituted its Certified Network Administrator (CNA) and Certified Network Engineer (CNE) programs. The idea was a huge success, and soon the want ads were filled with the CNA and CNE acronyms. The certifications became such a standard job requirement that even veteran Novell technicians were forced to qualify.

Other vendors followed Novell's lead with programs of their own to the point that now the computer section of the Sunday want ads is an alphabet soup of certification acronyms. Perhaps the best-known certification program is Microsoft's, ranging from the Microsoft Certified Professional (MCP) to the high-end Microsoft Certified Systems Engineer (MCSE).

Certification programs work both ways for the vendor. On one hand, they help keep customers happy; on the other, the vendor's market position is enhanced by having a qualified workforce ready to install and maintain its products. A certification program is a way for vendors to reduce risk and secure market position, and some even make money off their programs. For these reasons, all the major computer companies now have certification programs of one type or another.

However, certifications make just as much sense for the individual. Even the lowest-ranking certification is a virtual pass to a good job with lots of opportunity. For example, a person holding a Cisco Certified Network Associate (CCNA) with little or no real-world experience can get an entry-level job paying $35,000 or more. A CCNA with hands-on Cisco experience can expect to make $50,000 or more depending on the local job market. These figures vary according to region and the type of employer, of course, but that kind of money at the bottom rung speaks to how important certifications have become. Some observe that nowadays the right certification carries more weight than a college degree.

CERTIFICATIONS OVERVIEW

Cisco has one of the most extensive certification programs in the computer industry. This may surprise you, but as you read this book, you'll come to understand just how big and complicated the field of internetworking is. Cisco's program certifies three tiers of expertise: Associate, Professional, and Expert. Within these tiers, you can be certified in any of several specialties. The overall program is called Cisco Career Certifications, although sometimes the company uses the term "CCIE pathway" as a generic reference to all three program tiers.

Cisco Career Paths Overview

Cisco offers and recommends training courses for its Career Certifications program. Recommended courses are taught by Cisco Training Partners, who must use a standardized college-level instruction curriculum designed by Cisco. The training companies may not deviate from the approved curriculum. Cisco Training Partners are authorized on a country-by-country basis, but they may not administer certification exams or issue Cisco certifications. Two companies, Prometric and Pearson VUE, are retained by Cisco as the exclusive test administrator in the United States. Most tests cost $100 or $300 to take. Because many people don't have access to Cisco equipment to use for practice, the company sponsors a number of practice labs. However, there are a limited number of them, and they cost $500 to $1,000 per day to use.

The certification program is designed to encourage participants by offering a progressive learning path:

▼ **CCNA   Cisco Certified Network Associate**   The entry-level certificate requires proficiency in basic internetworking concepts, terminology, technologies, products, and rudimentary configuration skills.

■ **CCNP   Cisco Certified Network Professional**   The intermediate certificate requires working proficiency in the Cisco product line, advanced technologies, device configuration, troubleshooting, and management.

▲ **CCIE   Cisco Certified Internetwork Engineer**   The top-level certificate requires best-of-breed proficiency that only years of experience and sustained training can bring.

Cisco touts the CCIE as better than other computer industry certification programs. Some wags call it the black belt of network certifications. Cisco claims that "experience is the number one factor" in earning a CCIE certification. And they have a point, in that the CCIE exam has a grueling two-day hands-on lab exam that is very difficult. The train-cram-test routine so many use to qualify for top-rung technical certifications isn't an option with the CCIE. Much of the exam can only be learned from extensive job experience. Cisco emphasizes that the CCIE certification is "experience-based, not training-based" as are most other certifications. This shouldn't dissuade the beginner, however, because the CCNA requires only one written exam, and that's a start.

Certain other top-level vendor certifications have been criticized for failing to assure quality. The loudest complaining has been about Microsoft's top-of-the-line MCSE certification. Many employers complain that because the MCSE is only a battery of multiple-choice written exams with no hands-on proof, tens of thousands of inexperienced people are cramming their way through to certification with little or no applied knowledge and poor knowledge retention after the tests.

THE CCIE PATHWAY

A CCIE is the most respected certification in the networking industry, affording its holder status among the elite in practitioners of advanced internetworking technology. There are about 10,000 CCIEs worldwide, but more are now working their way through the CCIE program, hoping to cash in on the benefits the certification brings. In fact, the number of CCIEs has doubled in just the last few years.

CCIE Overview

The CCIE program was instituted in 1993. The intermediate CCNA and CCNP certifications were created in 1998 in response to customer demand for more Cisco talent. Each certification requires passing a supervised test. The candidate is not required to have a CCNA or CCNP before attempting to become a CCIE, but the intermediate certificates are intended as stepping stones to that status. Given the intensive long-term training and experience required to pass the CCIE, most candidates earn their CCNA and CCNP certifications anyway as they work through the CCIE learning track. Doing so boosts the person's employability and market value, so why not take the tests?

Employers can verify a person's certification by e-mailing the CCIE program at www.cisco.com. Once certified, individuals must requalify every two years for CCIE and specializations, and every three years for CCNA, CCDA, CCNP, and CCDP to help assure that they have stayed current with technology and product developments.

Cisco's term for the certification program, CCIE pathway, is partly marketing hype to encourage those earning a CCNA or CCNP to think of themselves as partway through the process of earning a CCIE. That's not necessarily the case, of course. Many generalists will take one or both of the intermediate certifications to round out their credentials with no intention of going for the CCIE.

CCIE Tracks

Internetworking technology is an expansive subject area, which is why several areas of specialization have emerged. The field has grown so big and complicated that it's no longer feasible for even a motivated industry veteran to maintain expertise in all areas. This is especially the case for technicians working with Cisco's product line, by far the biggest in the business. For that reason, Cisco has instituted so-called technology tracks that represent fields of study much like a college major:

▼ **Routing and Switching** This is the most popular CCIE track. By achieving this certification, network professionals are proving an expert level of knowledge of networking and internetworking. The routing and switching track covers both LAN and WAN technologies and uses a variety of routers and switches. Experts with this certification are able to solve complex connectivity problems and improve overall network performance.

■ **Service Provider** This certification shows that a network professional has expert skills and understanding to technologies relevant to a service provider. Such skills include unicast IP routing, QoS, multicast, MPLS, MPLS VPNs, and multiprotocol BGP. CCIE certification at this level also requires knowledge of a technology area specific to service providers, like dial, DSL, cable, optical, or IP telephony.

■ **Security** This certification shows that a network professional has expert skills and understanding of network and internetwork security. The CCIE in security will be an expert in the basics of IP and IP routing, in addition to having a specialized understanding of security.

▲ **Voice** This certification shows that the network professional is an expert in the field of configuring and maintaining VoIP deployments. The CCIE in voice must be knowledgeable about the different Cisco VoIP products and technologies. Though service provider CCIEs must also have a solid understanding of VoIP, this track is different because it is highly focused on VoIP.

ASSOCIATE

The first stop in acquiring Cisco certification is to complete the exams necessary for either CCNA or CCDA certification. This shows an understanding of Cisco internetworking and can be thought of as an apprentice level of knowledge and skills.

CCDA

The CCDA certification (Cisco Certified Design Associate) shows that the networking professional has a foundation in the Cisco internetwork infrastructure. CCDA certified professionals are able to design routed and switched networks using LANs, WANs, and dial access services.

To achieve a CCDA certification, it is necessary to pass the exam listed in Table 3-1.

NOTE: Out of necessity, the exam outlines in this chapter introduce many acronyms, technologies, and products without defining or explaining them. Don't worry about the technical details here; most will be covered in later chapters. The exam outlines are intended to give you a flavor of the nature and scope of each certification.

CCNA

The Cisco Certified Network Associate (CCNA) shows a network professional's knowledge of networking. Professionals with a CCNA certification are capable of installation, configuration, and operation of LANs, WANs, and dial access services for networks with 100 or fewer nodes. They must have a solid understanding of IP, IGRP, serial, frame relay, VLANs, RIP, and Ethernet, among others.

To achieve this certification, it is necessary to pass the exams listed in Table 3-2 *or* Table 3-3.

Exam Name and Number	Description
Designing for Cisco Internetwork Solutions Exam (DESGN 640-861)	This test is used to assess a candidate's skills and understanding as they pertain to the design of Cisco internetworks. Topics on the exam include network analysis, modeling, and planning.

Table 3-1.   CCDA Exam

Exam Name and Number	Description
CCNA Exam (CCNA 640-801)	This test is used to assess and evaluate a candidate's knowledge and skills to select, connect, configure, and troubleshoot various Cisco devices. Topics on this exam include extended switched networks with VLANs, determining IP routes, managing IP traffic with access lists, and establishing both point-to-point and Frame Relay connections.

Table 3-2.   CCNA Exam

Exam Name and Number	Description
INTRO Beta Exam (INTRO 641-821)	This test is used to assess a candidate's ability to describe and identify network and WAN components, including their function and purpose. Topics on this exam include network types, network media, switching fundamentals, TCP/IP, IP addressing and routing, WAN technologies, operating and configuring IOS devices, and managing network environments.
Interconnecting Cisco Networking Devices Exam (ICND 640-811)	This test is used to assess a candidate's ability to choose, connect, configure, and troubleshoot various Cisco networking devices. Topics on this exam include extending switched networks with VLANS, determining IP routes, managing IP traffic with access lists, and establishing both point-to-point and Frame Relay connections.

Table 3-3.   Alternate CCNA Exams

PROFESSIONAL

The mid-level in Cisco Career Certifications is the professional level of certification. The CCNP, CCSP, CCDP, and CCIP certifications can be equated to a journeyman level of skill and knowledge. This is the level achieved once the associate level has been accomplished and the stopping point until CCIE certification has been earned.

CCDP

The Cisco Certified Design Professional (CCDP) certification is used to designate an advanced knowledge of network design. With a CCDP certification, a network professional is able to design routed and switched LANs, WANs, and dial access services. The CCDP certified technician is able to apply design theory in a modular manner, and then ensure that the entire configuration works properly and is highly available.

A prerequisite to CCDP certification is achievement of CCNA and CCDA certification. Once CCNA and CCDA certificates have been earned, the CCDP candidate must complete the tests in Table 3-4 *or* Table 3-5.

Exam Name and Number	Description
Building Scalable Cisco Internetworks Exam (BSCI 642-801)	This test is used to demonstrate that the candidate has the ability to use advanced IP addressing and routing to develop scalable solutions for Cisco routers connected to a WAN or LAN. The test covers such topics as advanced IP addressing, configuring the EIGRP, configuring the Open Shortest Path First protocol, and configuring basic BGP.
Building Cisco Multilayer Switched Exam (BCMSN 642-811)	This test is used to demonstrate that the candidate has the ability to build scalable, multilayer switched networks. Further, it will ensure the candidate can design and deploy a global intranet and utilize troubleshooting techniques for networks using Cisco multilayer switches for client hosts and services. Topics on this exam include switching technology, planning, design, implementation, operation, and troubleshooting.
Designing Cisco Network Service Architectures Exam (ARCH 642-871)	This test is used to demonstrate that a candidate has an understanding of recent trends in network design and technologies. Topics on this exam include network infrastructure, intelligent network services, and converged network solutions.

Table 3-4. CCDP Exam

Exam Name and Number	Description
Composite Exam (642-891)	This exam is a composite of both the BSCI and BCMSN tests, explained in Table 3-4. Most often, this test is used for recertification, but it can also be used for first-time certification, assuming the candidate passes both sections on routing and switching.
Designing Cisco Network Service Architectures Exam (ARCH 642-871)	(See Table 3-4)

Table 3-5.   Alternate CCDP Exams

CCIP

The Cisco Certified Internetwork Professional (CCIP) is a certification for individuals working in service provider organizations. CCIP certified individuals must have a thorough understanding of networking technologies, especially as they relate to service providers, including:

▼   IP routing
■   IP
■   QoS
■   BGP
▲   MPLS

A prerequisite to taking the CCIP exam is to have earned CCNA certification, and then complete the exams listed in Table 3-6.

CCNP

The Cisco Certified Network Professional (CCNP) certification is for individuals with advanced knowledge of networks. CCNP certified individuals can install, configure, and troubleshoot LANs and WANs for organizations with between 100 and 500 nodes.

Topics that must be mastered to achieve this certification include

▼   Security
■   Converged networks

Exam Name and Number	Description
Building Scalable Cisco Internetworks Exam (BSCI 642-801)	(See Table 3-4)
Configuring BGP on Cisco Routers Exam (BGP 642-661)	This test is used to assess a candidate's understanding of BGP, his or her ability to configure BGP on Cisco routers, and his or her troubleshooting skills.
Quality of Service Exam (QoS 642-641)	This test is used to assess a candidate's knowledge and skills as they pertain to QoS, specifically configuring and troubleshooting Cisco IOS routers utilizing QoS protocols. Topics covered in this test include IP QoS, classification, queuing, traffic shaping, congestion avoidance, link efficiency, signaling, and QoS and IP over ATM.
Implementing Cisco MPLS (MPLS 640-910)	This test is used to assess a candidate's knowledge and skills as they pertain to MPLS, using Cisco equipment. Topics covered in this test include core MPLS technology, frame-mode MPLS implementation on Cisco IOS platforms, MPLS VPN technology, and running OSPF inside a VPN.

Table 3-6.   CCIP Exams

- ■ QoS
- ■ VPNs
- ▲ Broadband technologies

The prerequisite for CCNP certification is to have earned a CCNA certification. Next, candidates must pass the exams listed in Table 3-7 *or* Table 3-8.

CCSP

A Cisco Certified Security Professional (CCSP) certification is used to indicate network professionals with skills necessary to design and build secure Cisco networks. Prerequisites for this certification are having earned either a CCNA or a CCIP certification, and completion of the tests in Table 3-9.

Exam Name and Number	Description
Building Scalable Cisco Internetworks Exam (BSCI 642-801)	(See Table 3-4)
Building Cisco Multilayer Switched Exam (BCMSN 642-811)	(See Table 3-4)
BCRAN Exam (BCRAN 642-821)	This test is used to assess a candidate's ability to describe, configure, operate, and troubleshoot WAN and remote access connections. Topics on this exam include general WAN knowledge, planning, design, implementation, operation, and troubleshooting WANs.
Internet Troubleshooting Support Exam (CIT 642-831)	This test is used to assess a candidate's ability to troubleshoot converged networks that are not operating optimally. Topics in this exam include baselining; developing a troubleshooting strategy; ameliorating problems at the physical, data link, network, transport, and application layers.

Table 3-7.   CCNP Exams

Exam Name and Number	Description
Composite Exam (642-891)	(See Table 3-5)
BCRAN Exam (BCRAN 642-821)	(See Table 3-7)
Internet Troubleshooting Support Exam (CIT 642-831)	(See Table 3-7)

Table 3-8.   Alternate CCNP Exams

Exam Name and Number	Description
Securing Cisco IOS Networks (SECUR 642-501)	This test is used to assess a candidate's ability to secure Cisco IOS router networks. Topics include basic Cisco router security, advanced AAA security for Cisco router networks, Cisco router threat migration, firewall authentication proxy configuration, and building basic IPSec.
Cisco Secure PIX Firewall Exam (CSPFA 642-521)	This test is used to assess a candidate's ability to describe, configure, verify, and manage Cisco's PIX firewall product family. Topics include overall PIX firewall products and features, access control lists, advanced protocol handling, failover, VPNs, and Cisco PIX Device Manager.
Cisco Security Intrusion Detection Systems Beta Exam (CSIDS 643-531)	This test is used to assess a candidate's ability to design, install, and configure a Cisco Intrusion Protection system for enterprises of all sizes. Topics include identifying Cisco IDS systems and their features, performing maintenance, and monitoring an IDS.
Cisco Secure Virtual Private Networks (CSVPN 642-511)	This test is used to assess a candidate's ability to describe, configure, verify, and manage the Cisco VPN 3000 Concentrator, Cisco VPN Software Client, and Cisco VPN 3002 Hardware Client feature set.
Cisco SAFE Implementation Exam (CSI 642-541 CSI)	This test is used to assess a candidate's ability to understand and implement the tenets of Cisco's SAFE Small, Midsize, and Remote (SMR) User White Paper. The test will assess the candidate's knowledge of using IOS routers, PIX Firewalls, VPN Concentrators, Cisco IDS Sensors, Cisco Host IDS, and the Cisco VPN Client in an end-to-end solution.

Table 3-9.   CCSP Exams

CISCO QUALIFIED SPECIALIST

Once a person earns a CCNP within a chosen technology track, the option exists to take a certification in one of ten specialties. This is the Cisco Qualified Specialist program—a grouping of several specialty certifications in such niche areas as Cisco VPN and Network Security and Cisco Network Management. Specialization certificates aren't stand-alone; you must possess a CCNA, CCNP, or CCIE to qualify for one.

These specializations are meant to assure solid knowledge within a narrow skill area, as opposed to having only a passing familiarity, perhaps obtained by working occasionally with a particular subset of the technology. Acute talent shortages exist in each of the areas. For example, CCNPs with some real-world experience and a Cisco VPN and Security certification are among the hottest recruits in any sector of the computer business.

There are dozens of standard tests in the Cisco Qualified Specialist program. The tests you must take depend on the career path and specialization (if any). The course work is matched to the certification's required exams. Cisco also offers so-called beta exams, which are tests under development by the company. Cisco encourages candidates to take the beta exams at no charge. They want to use you as a guinea pig, in effect, to "test the test" before releasing it for use by Prometric and VUE. Many candidates like taking the tests for practice.

NOTE: With many of these certifications, Cisco also offers a unique certification for sales staff. The discussion of those specific certifications are out of the scope of this book. However, if you would like to get more information, visit Cisco's Web site at www.cisco.com.

Access Routing and LAN Switching Certification

The Cisco Access Routing and LAN Switching certification is meant to identify network professionals who can develop and maintain LAN and WAN networks. These professionals must be able to scale IP addresses with NAT, manage network performance, configure PPP, PAP, CHAP, and interVLAN routing in a network that utilizes both switches and routers.

Candidates must pass either exam 642-801 BSCI (see Table 3-4 for a description of this test) or 642-891 Composite (see Table 3-5).

They must also pass exam 9E0-541, which is explained in Table 3-10.

Cable Communications Certification

The Cisco Cable Communications specialist certification shows that the network professional is able to implement and support Cisco cable two-way data services. The prerequisite for this certification is a CCDA, CCDP, CCNA, CCNP, CCIE, or CCIP. The exam required for this certification is listed in Table 3-11.

Exam Name and Number	Description
Routing and Switching Exam (RSS 9E0-541)	This test is used to assess a candidate's skills in the realm of routing and switching, using Cisco equipment. Topics on this test include trunking, VLANs, PPP, PAP, CHAP, LAN technologies and products, and WAN technologies and products.

Table 3-10.   Access Routing and Switching Exam

Content Networking Certification

The Cisco Content Networking Specialist certification shows that a networking professional has knowledge of content networking technology, including content edge delivery, content distribution, content management, content switching, and content routing. The prerequisite for this certification is a CCDA, CCDP, CCNA, CCNP, CCIE, or CCIP. The exam required for this certification is listed in Table 3-12.

Exam Name and Number	Description
Cable Communications Specialist 1 (9E0-701)	This test is used to assess a candidate's skills necessary to verify a cable head end and hybrid fiber coaxial (HFC) infrastructure. The test also verifies the candidate's knowledge of Cisco cable IP network solutions.

Table 3-11.   Cable Communications Exam

Exam Name and Number	Description
Content Networking Specialist v1.1 Exam (9E0-600)	This test is used to assess a candidate's skill in content networking using Cisco technology. Topics on the test include caching, ECDN, and CSS.

Table 3-12.   Content Networking Specialist Exam

IP Telephony Certification

Cisco offers several specific certifications within the realm of IP telephony. Rather than a blanket certification, Cisco offers certifications in IP telephony design, operations, and support. These certifications show the networking professional's skills in IP telephony design, installation, and support on a multiservice network.

IP Telephony Design

The IP Telephony Design certification is used to demonstrate a candidate's skill and knowledge in the design of networks, utilizing IP telephony. The prerequisite for this certification is a CCDA. The exams required to earn this certification are listed in Table 3-13.

IP Telephony Express Specialist

The Cisco IP Telephony Express Specialist certification is used to show that a networking professional has the knowledge and skills to install and support a multiservice network with an emphasis on IP telephony and CallManager Express. Prerequisites for this certification are either a CCNA or CCDA rating. The exams required for this certification are listed in Table 3-14.

IP Telephony Operations Specialist

The Cisco IP Telephony Operations Specialist certification is used to prove the network professional's skill in multiservice network operation and troubleshooting. The prerequisite for this certification is a CCNA certification. The exams required for this certification are listed in Table 3-15.

Exam Name and Number	Description
Enterprise Voice Over Data Design (EVODD 9E0-412)	This test is used to evaluate a candidate's skills on the subject of voice over data networks. The candidate must be able to explain methodology for addressing problems that a systems engineer would face. This test covers both IOS-based and CallManager-based voice systems.
Deploying Quality of Service in Enterprise Networks Exam (DQOS 9E0-601) or (QOS Beta 643-642)	This test is used to evaluate a candidate's skills and abilities to deploy QoS in an enterprise network. Topics in this test include a QoS overview, classification, congestion management, congestion avoidance, policing and shaping, and QoS design and management.

Table 3-13.   IP Telephony Design Exams

Exam Name and Number	Description
Cisco Voice Over IP Exam (CVOICE 9E0-431)	This exam is used to test a candidate's knowledge of voice over IP technology and equipment. Topics on the test include analog and digital voice connections, configuring voice interfaces, voice dial peers, introduction to VoIP, VoIP signaling, and improving and maintaining voice quality.
IQoS Exam (644-201) *or* Deploying Quality of Service in Enterprise Networks Exam (DQOS 9E0-601) or (QOS Beta 643-642)	The IQoS exam (644-201) is used to demonstrate that a candidate can deploy IP telephony using various QoS principles. Topics in this exam include IP QoS, classification and marking, queuing, traffic shaping and policing, congestion avoidance, and campus LAN QoS. The description of DQOS 9E0-601 can be found in Table 3-13.
CallManager Express Exam (CME 644-141)	This test is used to assess a candidate's skills in the operation of CallManager Express (CME). Topics on this exam include an overview of CME, its architecture, provisioning and planning, technical features, and troubleshooting.

Table 3-14. IP Telephony Express Exams

Exam Name and Number	Description
IP Telephony Troubleshooting Exam (9E0-422 IPTT)	This test is used to assess a candidate's ability to troubleshoot Enterprise CallManager, Unity, and IP network deployments. Topics include design, deployment, and configuration of AVVID solutions.
Deploying Quality of Service in Enterprise Networks Exam (DQOS 9E0-601) or (QOS Beta 643-642)	(See Table 3-13)

Table 3-15. IP Telephony Operations Specialist Exams

IP Telephony Support Specialist

The Cisco IP Telephony Support Specialist certification is used to certify that a network professional is competent in the support of multiservice networks. A prerequisite for this exam is CCNP certification. The exams required for this certification are listed in Table 3-16.

Multiservice Switching Certification

The Cisco Multiservice Switching Specialist certification is used to show a network professional's skills and knowledge in the installation, configuration, support and troubleshooting of ATM-based, service provider networks. The prerequisite for this certification is a CCNA certification. The exams required for this certification are listed in Table 3-17.

Network Management Certification

The Cisco Network Management certification is used to show a network professional's skill in the implementation and support of LAN and WAN networks, utilizing CiscoWorks to manage Cisco LANs and WANs, and utilizing LAN Management Solution (LMS) and Routed WAN (RWAN) to manage network performance. The prerequisite to this certification is a CCNP certification. The exam required for this certification is listed in Table 3-18.

Exam Name and Number	Description
IP Telephony Exam (CIPT 9E0-441)	This test is used to assess a candidate's knowledge of Cisco IP telephony technologies. Topics on the exam include an overview of AVVID and CIPT components, CallManager, and the installation and support of IP telephones. Additionally, the test includes coverage of Cisco switches and routers, route planning, and telephony class of service.
Cisco Voice Over IP Exam (CVOICE 9E0-431)	(See Table 3-14)
Deploying Quality of Service in Enterprise Networks Exam (DQOS 9E0-601) or (QOS Beta 643-642)	(See Table 3-13)

Table 3-16. IP Telephony Support Specialist Exams

Exam Name and Number	Description
ATM Multiservice Switching Exam (ATMMS 9E0-911)	This test is used to assess the candidate's understanding of ATM Multiservice networks. Topics include WANs, WAN switch installation, BPX switches, MGX ATM concentrator configuration, and Cisco WAN Manager installation and operation.
PNNI and MPLS Networking Exam (PNNIMPLS 9E0-921)	This test is used to assess a candidate's understanding of PNNI and MPLS in Cisco networks. Topics include MGX ATM edge switch configuration, SES controller configuration, MGX and SES PNNI network planning, implementing MPLS, and designing ATM MPLS networks.

Table 3-17. Multiservice Switching Exams

Optical Certification

The Cisco Optical Certification is used to show a network professional's skill in optical network design, installation, operation, and maintenance. Networking professionals who earn this certification must understand basic optical network technologies such as SONET/SDH, DWDM, DPT.RPR, POS, optical cross connects, and Ethernet over optical. Unlike the other Cisco Qualified Specialist tracks, there are no prerequisites required for this certification. The exams required for this certification are listed in Table 3-19.

Exam Name and Number	Description
Network Management Exam (NM 9E0-300)	This test is used to assess the candidate's ability to manage Cisco networks. Topics on this exam include CiscoWorks2000 Server, CiscoView, Resource Management Essentials, the Integration Utility, Campus Manager, Internet Performance Manager, and Access Control List Manager.

Table 3-18. Network Management Exam

Exam Name and Number	Description
Optical SONET (641-311) For candidates in the U.S., Canada, and Korea. *or* Optical SDH (641-321) For candidates in the Americas, APAC (except Korea), EMEA, and Japan.	The Optical SONET and SDH exams are specific to the region of the world in which optical technology will be deployed (SONET for the U.S. and Canada and SDH for Japan, for example). Topics on the exams include Cisco ONS 15454 Turn Up, Text, Provisioning, and Operation Training (OCTPO); Cisco ONS 15216 Provisioning and Operation Training (OPODA); and optical fundamentals. The exam also covers optical technologies like SONET, SDH, DWDM, and optical cross connects. A Cisco Optical Specialist will be able to design, build, configure, and manage Cisco optical networking products.

Table 3-19. Optical Certification Exams

Public Access Certification

There are two specific certifications within Cisco's Public Access certification: Public Access Design Specialist and Public Access Support Specialist. The following explain each of these certifications and the requirements to earn them.

Public Access Design Specialist

The Cisco Public Access Design Specialist is used to demonstrate that a network professional is able to design networks using Cisco Broadband Service Manager (BBSM) and Cisco Long Reach Ethernet (LRE) with a Cisco wireless LAN. These solutions are used in high-performance multiunit buildings, enterprise campuses, and similar facilities. The prerequisite for this certification is a CCDA certification. The exams required for this certification are listed in Table 3-20.

Public Access Support Specialist

The Cisco Public Access Support Specialist is used to demonstrate a network professional's skills and knowledge necessary to support BBSM, LRE, and wireless LANs. The prerequisite for this certification is a CCNA certification. The exams required for this certification are listed in Table 3-21.

Exam Name and Number	Description
Wireless LAN for System Engineers (WLANSE 9E0-576)	This test is used to assess a candidate's ability and knowledge in the design, construction, and maintenance of wireless LANs. Topics in this exam include radio frequency fundamentals, antennas, RF technologies, WLAN fundamentals, WLAN topologies and deployment, configuration, and security.
Long Reach Ethernet Exam (LRE 9E0-821)	This test is used to assess the candidate's understanding of long reach Ethernet. Topics include LRE fundamentals, components, configuration, and performance and operational challenges.
Building Broadband Service Manager Exam (BBSM 9E0-811)	This test is used to assess the candidate's understanding of Cisco Building Broadband Service Manager. Topics on this exam include an overview of BBSM, installation, operation, configuration, and troubleshooting.

Table 3-20.   Public Access Design Specialist Exams

Exam Name and Number	Description
Wireless LAN for Field Engineers (WLANFE 9E0-581)	This test is used to assess a candidate's ability and knowledge in the design, construction, and maintenance of wireless LANs. Topics in this exam include radio frequency fundamentals, antennas, RF technologies, WLAN fundamentals, WLAN topologies and deployment, configuration, and security.
Long Reach Ethernet Exam (LRE 9E0-821)	(See Table 3-20)
Building Broadband Service Manager Exam (BBSM 9E0-811)	(See Table 3-20)

Table 3-21.   Public Access Support Specialist Exams

VPN and Security Certification

Security is a hot topic, and for good reason. Organizations want to know that their networks are secure enough to hold their sensitive data. There has been no dearth of security technologies to keep that data safe. Within the realm of security certifications, Cisco offers specific tracks specializing in intrusion detection systems (IDSs), virtual private networks (VPNs), and firewalls.

Firewall Specialist

The Cisco Firewall Specialist certification is used to demonstrate the network professional's skill and understanding of complete security solutions, with an emphasis on securing networks using Cisco IOS software and PIX Firewall technologies. The prerequisite for this certification is a CCNA certification. The exams required for this certification are listed in Table 3-22.

IDS Specialist

The Cisco IDS Specialist certification is used to demonstrate the network professional's skill and understanding of security solutions, with an emphasis on Cisco IDS. The certification requires knowledge of Cisco IOS software and IDS technologies. The prerequisite for this certification is a CCNA certification. The exams required for this certification are listed in Table 3-23.

VPN Specialist

The Cisco VPN Specialist certification is used to show the network professional's skill and understanding of security solutions, with an emphasis on VPNs. VPN specialists are able to configure VPNs across shared public networks and use Cisco IOS software and VPN 3000 Concentrator technologies. The prerequisite for this certification is CCNA certification. The exams required for this certification are listed in Table 3-24.

Exam Name and Number	Description
Securing Cisco IOS Networks (SECUR 642-501)	(See Table 3-9)
Cisco Secure PIX Firewall Exam (CSPFA 642-521)	(See Table 3-9)

Table 3-22.   Firewall Specialist Exams

Exam Name and Number	Description
Securing Cisco IOS Networks (SECUR 642-501)	(See Table 3-9)
Cisco Security Intrusion Detection Systems Beta Exam (CSIDS 643-531)	(See Table 3-9)

Table 3-23.   IDS Specialist Exams

Wireless LAN Certification

Cisco offers two certification tracks in wireless LANs. The certifications are used to exhibit the network professional's skill in either the design or support of wireless LANs. Wireless LAN specialists must understand radio technologies as they pertain to 802.11 standards, WLAN and bridge topologies, and applications. They must also be able to configure WLAN products, including access points, bridges, and clients, specifically Cisco's Aironet hardware and software.

Wireless LAN Design Specialist

The Cisco Wireless LAN Design Specialist certification is useful for network professionals who want to show their understanding and skills in the design of wireless LANs. The prerequisite for this certification is a CCDA certification. The exam required for this certification is listed in Table 3-25.

Wireless LAN Support Specialist

The Cisco Wireless LAN Support Specialist certification is useful for network professionals who want to demonstrate their understanding and skills in the support and troubleshooting

Exam Name and Number	Description
Securing Cisco IOS Networks (SECUR 642-501)	(See Table 3-9)
Cisco Secure Virtual Private Networks (CSVPN 642-511)	(See Table 3-9)

Table 3-24.   VPN Specialist Exams

Exam Name and Number	Description
Wireless LAN for System Engineers (WLANSE 9E0-576)	(See Table 3-20)

Table 3-25.   Wireless LAN Design Specialist Exam

of WLANs. The prerequisite for this certification is CCNA certification. The exam required for this certification is listed in Table 3-26.

WHERE TO GET HELP

With the certification tracks ranging from Cisco to Microsoft to Novell, forward-minded, entrepreneurial individuals and organizations have found a niche to help the hopeful wireheads. If digging through stacks of white papers and dry texts is just too much to stomach, there are a number of interactive alternatives that can help you achieve that much-sought-after Cisco certification.

Web Sites

If you haven't already taken a peek into cyberspace, there are a number of Web sites out there willing to help you earn that Cisco Certification. Like any topic represented on the World Wide Web, sites range in their slickness, complexity, and usefulness. Some seem to have been slapped together as an afterthought; others are chock full of information and have a slick, professional layout and design.

Some sites simply require you to register; others charge a fee; and some others are completely free. Be wary of the Web sites where a group of people who recently took the test are sharing answers. It's akin to buying used college textbooks just so you can cut to the highlighted bits—how do you know the person who had the book before you knew what he was doing? It's the same deal for testing. Sometimes, posters will claim to have the exact test questions along with the correct answers. As attractive as this is, don't bet your testing fee on what an anonymous person out in the ether tries to tell you.

Exam Name and Number	Description
Wireless LAN for Field Engineers (WLANFE 9E0-581)	(See Table 3-21)

Table 3-26.   Wireless LAN Support Specialist Exam

If you can't afford to set up a brand new Cisco router in your living room, some sites offer access to test routers so you can experiment with commands and see their results. One such site is Clickx3, which isn't especially fancy, but is full of information for the CCNA exam (along with several other companies' certifications). Some sites, like Clickx3, offer this service for free; others charge for online lab time.

Table 3-27 lists a number of Web sites that can help you prepare for the certification.

Classes

A number of independent learning centers offer classes to bone up for the Cisco Certification exams. The classes' format will guide what kind of educational experience you can expect.

Some classes are formulated around quarter and semester formats and require an hour or so a couple times a week, with the final exam in the form of the actual Cisco Certification exam. But for those who don't want to wait three or four months, there are accelerated courses—or "boot camps"—that can pound the information into your head in less than a week.

Don't worry too much—I'm quite certain there are no push-ups required, and not many dogfaces have had to push a rack of routers and switches up a muddy hill at 4:00 A.M. while calling cadence. Different boot camps are suited for different people. Some are very intense and are best for those with little or no experience. These usually require you to live, eat, and breathe Cisco. Still others are designed for people who have some previous experience and aren't nearly as severe.

Boot camps aren't cheap. In the real Army, you have to pay with blood, sweat, and tears. But for certification, the only price you'll pay is in cold, hard cash—many cost around $7,000 plus hotel and other transportation expenses (at least in the Army you get three hots and a cot).

Name	URL
CCPrep	www.ccprep.com
Certification Zone	www.certificationzone.com/cisco
Learn Key	www.learnkey.com
Clickx3	www.clickx3.com
Boson	www.boson.com
Group Study	www.groupstudy.com
Cisco	www.cisco.com/en/US/learning/index.html

Table 3-27.   Web Sites That Can Help With Certification Preparation

It's in your best interest to compare boot camps and other training courses—first, to find the course that matches with your skill level and needs, and second to make sure you're actually learning, not just studying to pass the test. Without getting an understanding of the technologies and tools, you could still pass the tests. However, you would have the certification in name only, and would be in trouble the first time you had to do something that wasn't asked on the test.

Table 3-28 lists some companies offering Cisco classes and boot camps.

Don't forget your local community and technical colleges. Years ago, Cisco started a program through community and technical colleges to train certified techs. The courses emphasize learning, they are endorsed by Cisco (many other training programs are not), and you're likely to come away with more than you would at a boot camp. Not only will you get the training and the certification you're after, but you also get a bullet point for your résumé, acknowledging your training. You may also score some college credit.

No matter what your Cisco certification goal or the means by which you choose to achieve that goal, the end result will be most beneficial. Certification puts you in a select class that understands and can be counted on to design, build, and maintain the plumbing of the Internet.

Name	URL
Global Knowledge	www.globalknowledge.com
CCPrep	www.ccprep.com
Intense School	www.intenseschool.com

Table 3-28. Cisco Boot Camps

PART II

Cisco Internetworking Tools

CHAPTER 4

Router Overview

A dizzying array of hardware, software, telecommunications media, and technical expertise goes into internetworking. Switches, hubs, firewalls, packets, gateways, ports, access servers, interfaces, layers, protocols, serial lines, ISDN, frames, topologies—the list can seem endless. But there is a way to simplify things. A single, tangible entity makes sense of it all: the router.

In the most basic terms, internetworking is about nothing more than linking machines and people through a maze of intermediary telecommunications lines and computing devices. This takes routing, which in essence involves just two fundamental missions: determine a path along which a link can be made and transmit packets across that path. It is within these two functions—which take place inside the router—that internetworking becomes easier to understand. This is because the router itself must cut all the complexity down to a level it can deal with. The router does this by working with everything, one IP packet at a time.

Looked at in this way, the router is the basic fabric of internetworks. Indeed, without the router, the Internet as we know it couldn't even exist. This is because of the router's unique and powerful capabilities:

▼ Routers can simultaneously support different protocols (such as Ethernet, Token Ring, ISDN, and others), effectively making virtually all computers compatible at the internetwork level.

■ They seamlessly connect local area networks (LANs) to wide area networks (WANs), which makes it feasible to build large-scale internetworks with minimum centralized planning—sort of like Lego™ sets.

■ Routers filter out unwanted traffic by isolating areas in which messages can be "broadcast" to all users in a network.

■ They act as security gates by checking traffic against access permission lists.

■ Routers assure reliability by providing multiple paths through internetworks.

▲ They automatically learn about new paths and select the best ones, eliminating artificial constraints on expanding and improving internetworks.

In other words, routers make internetworks possible. They do so by providing a unified and secure environment in which large groups of people can connect. However, there are obstacles to bringing users together on internetworks, whether on a corporate intranet, a virtual private network, or the Internet itself. Figure 4-1 depicts how routing technology is the key to overcoming these obstacles.

Routers are like mini Towers of Babel. The router's ability to support different protocols simultaneously is probably its most important feature because this capability lets otherwise incompatible computers talk with one another regardless of operating system, data format, or communications medium. The computer industry spent decades and billions of dollars struggling to attain compatibility between proprietary systems and met with limited success. Yet, in less than a decade, TCP/IP internetworking has built a common

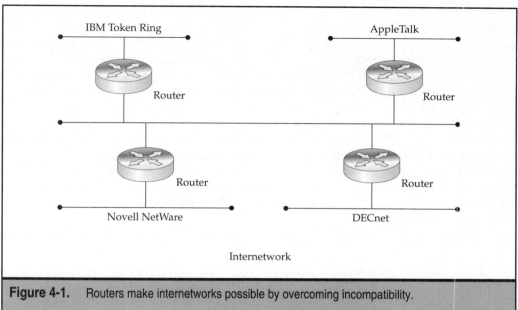

Figure 4-1.   Routers make internetworks possible by overcoming incompatibility.

platform across which virtually all computer and network architectures can freely exchange information.

The router's ability to filter out unwanted traffic is also important to internetworking. If users are bombarded with volumes of unwanted messages or if they feel their systems can be easily broken into, they will resist linking up to internetworks. Traffic filtering and access control provided by routers give users sufficient privacy and confidence to participate in internetworks.

There are other important types of network devices besides the router, but understanding how a router works will go a long way toward your understanding the whole of internetworking. Before you can learn how to configure and manage routers, however, you need to know the basics of what makes one up. This chapter gives a general review of Cisco router hardware and software.

HOW ROUTERS WORK

In a nutshell, routers do exactly what their name says: They route data from a LAN to another router, then another router, and so on until data is received at its destination. Routers also act as traffic cops, allowing only authorized machines to transmit data into the local network so that private information can remain secure. In addition to supporting these dial-in and leased connections, routers also handle errors, keep network usage statistics, and handle security issues.

Routing for Efficiency

When you send an e-mail to your Aunt Sadie on the other side of the country, it's routing technology that ensures she and she alone gets the message, and not every computer hooked up to the Internet. Routers direct the flow of traffic among, rather than within, networks. For instance, let's consider how routers can be used within a LAN to keep information flowing.

Design-O-Rama, as shown in Figure 4-2, is a computer graphics company. The company's LAN is divvied into two smaller LANs—one for the animators and one for the administration and support staff. The two subdivisions are connected with a router. Design-O-Rama employs eight people—four animators and four other staffers. When one animator sends a file to another, the large file will use a great deal of the network's capacity. This results in performance problems for the others on the network.

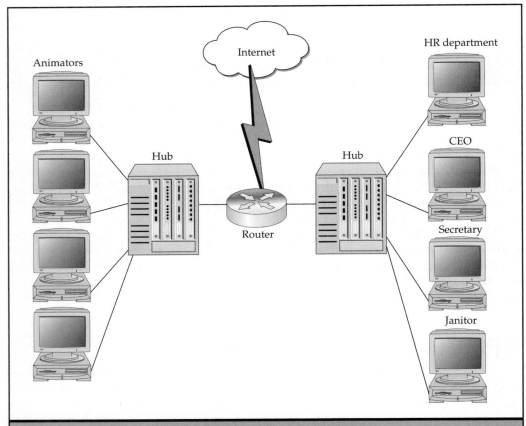

Figure 4-2.   Routers can be used to improve efficiency within a LAN.

NOTE: Remember how Ethernet works. A single user can have such a dramatic impact on the network because each information packet sent by one computer is broadcast to all the other computers on the LAN. Then each computer examines the packet and decides if it was meant for them.

To keep the animators from constantly slowing down the network, the network was divided into two—one for the animators and one for everybody else. A router links the two networks and connects them both to the Internet. The router is the only device on the network that sees every message sent by any computer on either network. When an animator sends a file to a colleague, the router looks at the recipient's address and keeps that piece of traffic isolated on that LAN. On the other hand, if the animator wants to query the human relations department about vacation time, the router knows to let that piece of traffic through to the HR department.

Routers and the Internet

In our previous example, we examined how a router could be used locally. Now, let's broaden the scope of what routers do to include their functionality across the entire Internet.

For the sake of comparison, let's first talk about how a telephone call is routed across the country. Say it's Aunt Sadie's birthday and rather than send an e-mail, you want to call her. When you make a long-distance call, the telephone system establishes a stable circuit between your telephone and Aunt Sadie's. The circuit may involve hopping through a number of steps, including fiber-optics, copper wires, and satellites. This end-to-end chain ensures that the quality of the line between you and Aunt Sadie will be constant. However, if the satellite goes offline or work crews cut the fiber-optic cable, your conversation with Aunt Sadie will be cut short. The Internet avoids this problem by making its "calls" in an entirely different way.

Packets and Paths

Whatever information is sent across the Internet (e-mail, Web page, and so on) is first broken into 1,500-byte packets. The packets are transmitted across a number of routers, each one sending the packet to the destination device. The packets will be transmitted via the best available route. This type of network is called a *packet-switched* network. Each packet could take the same route, or none of the packets could take the same route. Once the packets show up at the destination computer, they are reassembled. This process goes so quickly that you wouldn't even know that the file was chopped into 1,500-byte packets and then reassembled.

Figure 4-3 illustrates how a packet-switched network operates. The routers in the Internet are linked together in a web. The packets follow the path of least resistance to ensure they arrive at their destination in a reasonable amount of time. It seems logical that the packets would go through the least number of routers to get to its destination. However, sometimes that isn't feasible, because there may be congestion clogging the ideal path. Routers send the traffic around the congested portions of the Internet for increased speed and efficiency.

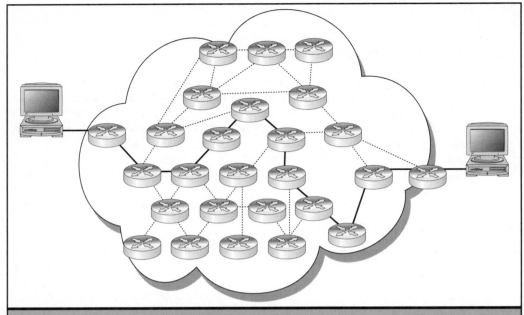

Figure 4-3. Routers send packets across the path of least resistance.

This may seem like a very complicated system—as compared to the process followed when placing a telephone call—but the system works for two important reasons:

▼ The network can balance the load across different pieces of equipment on a millisecond-by-millisecond basis.

▲ If there is a problem with one piece of equipment in the network while a message is being transmitted, packets can be routed around the problem to ensure that the entire message is received.

The routers that make up the main backbone of the Internet can reconfigure the paths that packets take because they look at all the information surrounding the data packet, and they tell each other about line conditions, like problems sending and receiving data on various parts of the Internet.

All Shapes and Sizes

Not every router is responsible for the fate of packets whizzing across the Internet. Routers come in different sizes and do more or less, depending on how big and sophisticated they are. For instance:

▼   If you have enabled Internet Connection Sharing between two Windows XP-based computers, the computer that is connected to the Internet is acting as a simple router. This router does very little—it just looks at data to see which computer it's meant for.

■   Routers that are used to connect small offices to the Internet do more. They enforce rules about security for the office LAN, and they generally handle enough traffic that they tend to be stand-alone devices.

▲   The biggest routers (the ones used to handle data at the major traffic points on the Internet) handle a lot of information—millions of packets each second. These are stand-alone devices that look more like Maytag made them than a computer company.

Let's consider the medium-sized router—it's probably something humming away in a small room at your business. This router only has two networks to deal with—your LAN and the Internet. The office LAN connects to the router via an Ethernet connection. The router might also have two connections to your company's ISP—a T3 and an ISDN connection. For the most part, your traffic comes and goes via the T3 line. However, the ISDN line is used in the event something goes awry with the T3 line. In fact, the router is configured to send data across the ISDN line, because the configuration table has been programmed to switch over in case of an emergency.

This router is also tasked with another function—it's a layer of security against outside attacks. Although firewalls are routinely used to prevent attacks, the router is also configured to keep the bad people out.

However, the backbone of the Internet uses the third kind of router we listed. Cisco's Gigabit Switch Router 12000 Series of routers is the kind of equipment used to run the Internet. These routers are designed and built like supercomputers. For instance, the 12000 Series uses 200 MHz MIPS R5000 processors, which are the same kind of processors used in the computers that make special effects for the movies. Cisco's largest router—the 12816—can handle up to 1.28 trillion bits of information per second.

Optical Routers

In a conventional internetwork, information would be transmitted across great distances using twisted-pair copper wire, across a WAN or even a LAN. As useful and utilitarian as twisted-pair cabling and an electrical network have been, fiber-optics allow information to be transferred at immensely higher rates. In the past, when computers shared only brief conversations across the miles, electrical networks could handle the load. But now, as information is shared as it has never been shared before, there is a clear need for an upgrade in network capacities.

Comparing the bit rates in electrical networks to optical networks is like putting Woody Allen in a prison yard fist fight with Mike Tyson—there's just no comparison. The greatest thing that optical networking has going for it is raw speed.

Designation	Speed
OC-12	622 Mbps
OC-24	1.244 Gbps
OC-48	2.488 Gbps
OC-192	9.952 Gbps
OC-768	40 Gbps

Table 4-1.   Optical Networking Speeds

Common WAN links that move across electrical networks are T-1 (1.544 Mbps) and T-3 (45 Mbps). On the LAN front, things get a little better. Most organizations use 10 or 100 Mbps Ethernet. The top-of-the-line Ethernet clocks in at 10 Gbps. However, once fiber-optics get into the race, look out.

At their slowest, fiber-optic networks speed along much faster than a T-1 or a T-3. Once fiber shifts out of first gear, there ceases to be a comparison. When discussing optical networking speeds, you'll hear the terminology change from T-1 or T-3 to OC. OC stands for *optical carrier*. OC takes over where T leaves off. Once the optical carrier gets involved, speeds not only reach 1 Gbps but even leave 1 Gbps in the rearview mirror.

Table 4-1 shows how optical networking line speeds increase.

As you can see, the speed rates in optical networks (not to mention their development) are increasing at an amazing velocity. Thanks to *dense wavelength division multiplexing (DWDM)* optical bandwidth will only increase, because more than one stream of data can be introduced on a single run of fiber. More on that in a moment.

Optical Technologies

There are two prevalent technologies in the world of optical routing: SONET and DWDM. SONET is the oldest and most popular technology, while DWDM is somewhat of a new kid on the block, but supports capacities much greater than SONET. Let's examine these technologies in a little more depth.

SONET   The most basic and popular architecture for an optical network is the Synchronous Optical Network (SONET).

SONET is a standard for optical telecommunications transport developed by the Exchange Carriers Standards Association (ECSA) for the American National Standards Institute (ANSI), the body that sets industry standards in the U.S. for telecommunications and other industries. The comprehensive SONET standard is expected to provide the transport infrastructure for worldwide telecommunications for at least the next two or three decades.

NOTE: In Europe, SONET is known by another acronym, SDH, which is short for Synchronous Digital Hierarchy.

SONET is so speedy that you could transmit an entire 650MB CD-ROM from New York to Seattle in less than one second. Not only is SONET fast, but it's also rather versatile. Voice calls from one office to another can be multiplexed along with data and fired out across the same fiber. Further, because of the generous bandwidth SONET affords, compression and encapsulation into Internet Protocol (IP) packets is unnecessary. For comparison's sake, a single OC-3 connection can carry more than 2,000 simultaneous voice calls. Further, all types of data can be multiplexed alongside the calls.

SONET offers a top-end bandwidth of OC-192 (9.952 Gbps) and can carry a diverse range of information. In addition to high speeds, SONET features bit-error rates of one error in 10 billion bits. Compare this with copper transmission methods that have bit-error rates of one error in 1 million bits.

DWDM   In its beginning, SONET delivered bandwidth that was previously unimaginable. At the time, delivering OC-3 levels (155.52 Mbps) provided more bandwidth than anyone knew what to do with. Of course, those were in the mid-1980s, a decade before the Internet and high-bandwidth applications. Technology kept delivering faster and faster optical carriers. After OC-3, there were OC-12, OC-48, and beyond.

OC-48 (2.5 Gbps) is a popular speed for SONET; however, the next level, OC-192 (10 Gbps) is about the best SONET will be able to deliver. Sure, ten years ago no one knew what a gigabit was, but now we do and we can't get enough of them. The problem is that 10 Gbps is about SONET's limit. The solution is to jump to DWDM.

DWDM is a technique in which multiple signals can traverse a single strand of optical fiber. The lasers used in optical networking can be tuned to different wavelengths (think of them as different colors). As such, it is possible to put multiple colors on a single fiber. When the receiving router sees the various colors, it knows which colors to separate out for which data streams, as shown in Figure 4-4.

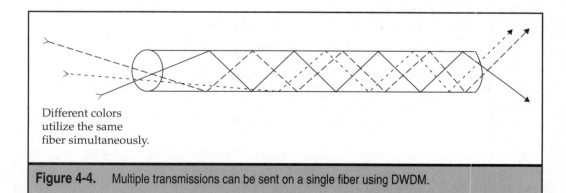

Different colors
utilize the same
fiber simultaneously.

Figure 4-4.   Multiple transmissions can be sent on a single fiber using DWDM.

Cisco's Optical Offerings

Cisco utilizes both SONET and DWDM with its optical routers. For example, the Cisco ONS 15808 optical router supports DWDM technology. This carrier class router supports speeds between 2.5 and 10 Gbps and is capable of transmitting up to 2,000 kilometers. The router is able to be upgraded so that 160 channels are transmitted across the fiber with speeds up to 40 Gbps.

Cisco also provides a certain level of modularity with its devices. Rather than make a few models with a predetermined number of ports set up for Gigabit Ethernet and another amount dedicated to SONET or DWDM, the company has developed cards and modules that can be plugged into a router, making it customizable. That is, you can decide to load the router with SONET modules, DWDM modules, or any combination of optical and electrical you please.

COMMUNICATING WITH A ROUTER

Most users of internetworks don't communicate with routers, they communicate *through* them. Network administrators, however, must deal directly with individual routers in order to install and manage them.

Routers are purpose-built computers dedicated to internetwork processing. They are important devices that individually serve hundreds or thousands of users—some serve even more. When a router goes down, or even just slows down, users howl and network managers jump. As you might imagine then, network administrators demand foolproof ways to gain access to the routers they manage in order to work on them.

Routers don't come with a monitor, keyboard, or mouse, so you must communicate with them in one of three other ways:

▼ From a terminal that's in the same location as the router and is connected to it via a cable (the terminal is usually a PC or workstation running in terminal mode).

■ From a terminal that's in a different location as the router and is connected to it via a modem that calls a modem connected to the router with a cable.

▲ Via the network on which the router sits.

In large networks, network administrators are often physically removed from routers and must access them via a network. However, if the router is unreachable due to a network problem, or if there's no modem attached to the router itself, someone must go to its location and log directly into the router. The three ways to gain administrative access to routers are depicted in Figure 4-5.

Even when network administrators manage routers in the same building, they still prefer to access them by network. It doesn't make sense to have a terminal hooked up to each router, especially when there are dozens of them stacked in a data closet or computer room. Also, it's much more convenient to manage them all from a single PC or workstation.

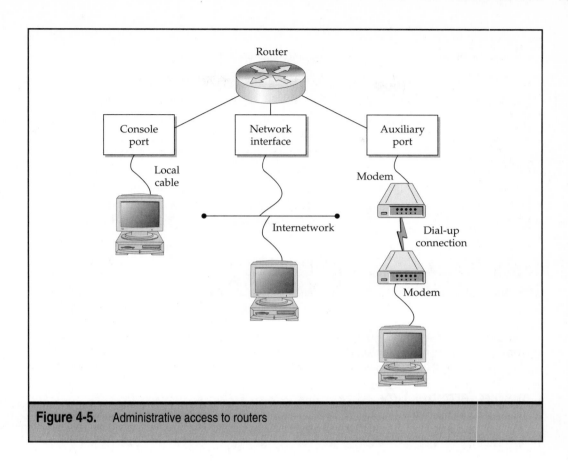

Figure 4-5. Administrative access to routers

There are several ways to communicate with a router, each made possible by a particular communications protocol. Table 4-2 lists each method, the protocol, and how each is used.

The Console Port

Every Cisco router has a console port on its back. It is there to provide a way to hook up a terminal to the router in order to work on it. The console port (sometimes called the management port) is used by administrators to log into a router directly—that is, without a network connection. The console must be used to install routers onto networks because, of course, at that point there is no network connection to work through.

Long term, the console's role is to be there as a contingency in case of emergency. When a router is completely down—in other words, when it is no longer able to process network packets—it cannot be accessed via the network. If the router is up and processing packets, but the network segment through which the technician must access it is

Access Method	Protocol	Communication Method
Console port	EIA/TIA-232	Serial line connection from local terminal.
Auxiliary port	EIA/TIA-232	Serial line terminal connection via modem.
Telnet	Telnet	Virtual terminal connection via TCP/IP network.
HTTP Server	HTTP	Web browser connection via TCP/IP network.
SNMP	SNMP	Simple Network Management Protocol; virtual terminal connection made via a TCP/IP network. (SNMP is covered in Chapter 15.)

Table 4-2. How Network Administrators Access Routers

down, going over a network to fix the router is not an option. This is when the console port provides a sure way to log into the router to fix things. The drawback, of course, is that someone must be in the same physical location as the router in order to connect to it.

Console Terminal Types

A stand-alone CRT, PC, or workstation can be used as a console. Console terminals must run a character-based user interface. They cannot run a graphical user interface (GUI) such as Microsoft Windows, Mac OS, or X-Windows. In order to use a PC or workstation as a console, you must use terminal emulator software. For example, one of the best-known terminal emulators is HyperTerminal from Hilgraeve, Inc., which ships with all versions of Windows. Start up HyperTerminal (or one of the many other terminal emulator products) and log into the router from there.

Console Connector Types

Console ports in Cisco routers use a variety of connector types (25-pin, RJ-45, 9-pin, and so on), but all provide a single terminal connection. A word of warning: make sure you have the proper cable before trying to hook up a console terminal to work on a router. Many a network administrator has spent a half hour fiddling with cables to finally find one that could connect to a router just to do 15 minutes of productive work.

NOTE: Console ports on Cisco devices are usually labeled "Console"—but not always. On some products, console ports are labeled "Admin," and on others they are labeled "Management." Don't be confused by this; they are all console ports.

The Auxiliary Port

Most Cisco routers have a second port on the back called the auxiliary port (usually called the AUX port, for short). Like the console port, the AUX port makes possible a direct, nonnetwork connection to the router.

How does the AUX port differ from the console port? The AUX port uses a connector type that modems can plug into (console ports have connectors designed for terminal cables). If a router in a faraway data closet goes down, the network administrator asks somebody in the area to go to the router and plug in a modem so it can be serviced remotely. In more critical configurations, a modem is often left permanently connected to a router's AUX port. Either way, the AUX port affords console-like access when it isn't practical to send a technician to the site to work on a router through a local console.

Figure 4-6 shows the console and AUX ports on the back of a Cisco 4500 router.

NOTE: Cisco's smaller routers do not have AUX ports, only console ports. These devices support remote management logins by connecting a modem to the router using an auxiliary/console cable kit.

Telnet

Once a router is installed on a network, access to it is almost always made via Telnet sessions, not via the console or AUX ports. Telnet is a way to log into a router as a virtual terminal. "Virtual" here means that a real terminal connection is not made to the device via a direct cable or a modem, as with the console or AUX ports. Telnet connections are instead made through the network. In the most basic terms, a real terminal session is composed of bits streaming one by one over a serial line. A virtual terminal session is composed of IP packets being routed over a network, pretending to be bits streaming over a serial line.

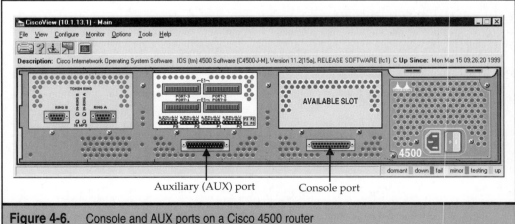

Auxiliary (AUX) port   Console port

Figure 4-6.   Console and AUX ports on a Cisco 4500 router

Telnet is a network application, not a terminal emulator. It was developed in the early days of the UNIX operating system as a way to log into remote computers to manage them. Later, internetwork pioneers incorporated Telnet directly into the TCP/IP networking protocol as a way to get to and manage internetwork devices. Telnet ships with every copy of Cisco's IOS software and most computer operating systems.

When using Telnet to access a router, you do so over a virtual line provided by the Cisco IOS software. These are called *VTY lines*. Don't let the word "line" confuse you. It does not refer to an actual communications circuit; it means a virtual terminal session inside the IOS software. IOS supports up to five virtual terminal lines (numbered VTY 0–4, inclusive), making it possible to have up to five virtual terminal sessions running on a router at the same time. This is probably design overkill, however. It's rare to have more than one virtual terminal session running on a router at the same time. Some routers have even more than five VTY lines, and with the Enterprise version of the IOS, you can even assign more than that.

Cisco's IOS software is used mostly in character-based interface mode, which is to say that it's not a point-and-click GUI environment such as we've grown accustomed to using on our Microsoft Windows PCs, Apple Macs, or X-Windows UNIX workstations. Whether logging into a router via the console port, AUX port, or Telnet, you are delivered to the character-based IOS software interface. The following shows character-based IOS output:

```
!
line con 0
 exec-timeout 0 0
line aux 0
 transport input all
line vty 0 2
 exec-timeout 0 0
 password 7 1313041B
 login
line vty 3
 exec-timeout 5 0
 password 7 1313041B
 login
line vty 4
 exec-timeout 0 0
 password 7 1313041B
 login
!
```

The preceding example is a listing of the seven IOS lines—*con* for console, *aux* for auxiliary, and *vty* for the virtual terminal. The seven lines are

▼   The console port, accessed through a local cable connection

■   The AUX port, accessed through a modem connection

▲   Five VTY lines, accessed through TCP/IP network connections

The HTTP Server User Interface

A more recent router access method is HTTP Server. Don't be misled by the name; no computer server is involved in using HTTP Server. The "server" in HTTP Server refers to a small software application running inside the Cisco IOS software. HTTP Server first became available with IOS Release 10.3. HTTP Server makes it possible to interact with the router through a Web browser. Figure 4-7 shows an HTTP Server screen.

Using HTTP to handle IOS command-line input and output isn't particularly ergonomic. The majority of network administrators still prefer using the IOS software in character-based

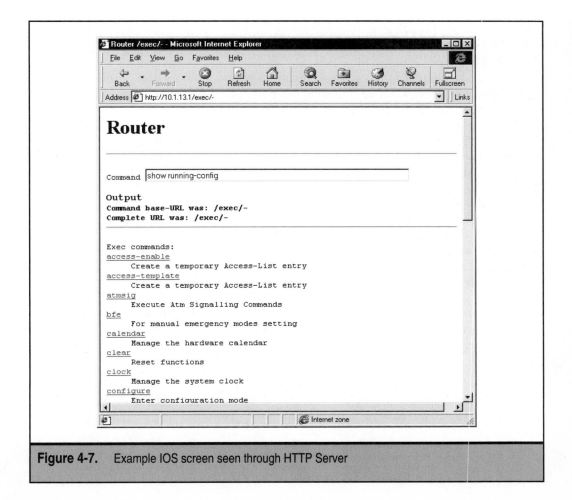

Figure 4-7.   Example IOS screen seen through HTTP Server

mode because it's faster and more direct than pointing and clicking. This is not unlike those old hands who jump into Microsoft Windows' MS-DOS prompt window to type in system-level commands, but Cisco may gradually move IOS toward a graphical user interface for a couple of reasons. The most obvious reason to at least offer a GUI-based alternative to working with IOS is that Cisco devices are increasingly being tended to by nonexperts. The other is that as complexity increases, the need for system visualization even inside a single router grows. Using visualization tools (to show load conditions, isolate errors, and so on) will, of course, require a browser instead of the old-fashioned "green screen" character-based command-line interface.

NOTE: To use the command-line interface, you must know what commands to type. You may want to use HTTP Server to get started and phase over to character-based mode as you become comfortable with the IOS command structure.

ROUTER SECURITY

Routers aren't very visible on internetworks, mainly because they usually don't have addresses such as www.yahoo.com or www.amazon.com. Routers don't need to have human-friendly addresses, because normal internetwork users never need to know that a router is there; they just need the connectivity it provides them.

The only people who ever need to log directly into a router are members of the network team responsible for managing it. In TCP/IP networks—the protocol on which most internetworks run—routers identify themselves to internetworks only with their IP addresses. For this reason, to log into a router you must first know that it exists and then what its IP address is. The network administrators responsible for the router will, of course, know this information.

The potential for abuse by hackers still exists. As you will learn in Chapter 14, routers constantly send messages to one another in order to update and manage the internetworks on which they operate. With the proper skills and enough determination, a hacker could discover a router's IP address and then attempt to establish a Telnet connection to it. Given that routers are the links that stitch internetworks together, it's easy to understand why Cisco and other internetwork equipment manufacturers design many security measures into their products. As shown in Figure 4-8, security must restrict access to areas within an internetwork and to individual devices.

NOTE: Router passwords only control entry to the router devices themselves. Don't confuse router passwords with passwords normal internetwork users must type in to enter certain Web sites or to gain admittance to intranets (private internetworks). Restrictions put on normal users are administered through firewalls and access lists, which are covered in Chapter 8.

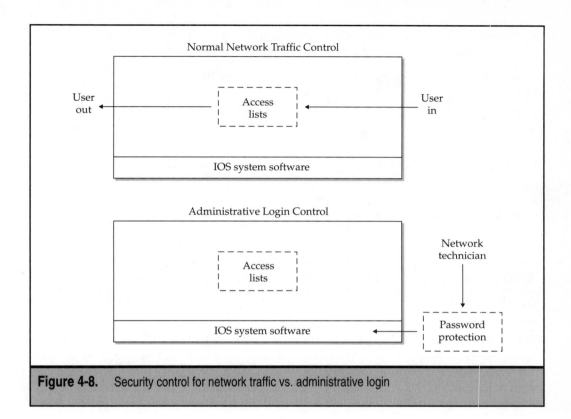

Figure 4-8.   Security control for network traffic vs. administrative login

Router Passwords

Router passwords aren't intended only to keep out hackers. Password protection is administered on a router-by-router basis. Passwords to get into a router are stored inside the router itself in most cases. Large internetworks have dozens or even hundreds of routers—some more critical to network operations than others—so it's a common practice for network managers to allow only select network team members access to certain routers, or even to command levels within routers. Table 4-3 lists router passwords and what they do.

In Cisco routers, passwords are used to control access to

▼   The router device itself

■   The Privileged EXEC (enable mode) portion of the IOS software environment

▲   The use of specific IOS commands

Line Passwords

Line passwords are used to control who can log into a router. They are used to set password protection on the console terminal line, the AUX (auxiliary) line, and any or all of the five virtual terminal (VTY) lines.

Control Point	Password Type	What's Restricted
Console port	Line	Logging into the router via a local line connected via the console port
AUX port	Line	Logging into the router via a modem (or local) line connected via the auxiliary port
Network login	Line	Logging into the router via a network connection using Telnet on a VTY line
Privileged EXEC	Enable or Enable Secret	Entry into the more powerful Privileged EXEC level of IOS environment

Table 4-3. Overview of Router Passwords and Their Uses

You must set at least one password for the router's VTY lines. If no Line password is set, when you attempt to log into the router via Telnet, you will be stopped by the error message "password required but none set." Remember, anyone on the Internet can conceivably Telnet into any router, so setting Line passwords will stop all but the best hackers from getting a foothold. Here, IOS is prompting for a password:

```
User Access Verification

Password:
Router>>
```

When you enter passwords into IOS, no asterisks appear to mask the letters typed—something to which most of us are accustomed. In the preceding example, at the prompt Router>> (the router's host name in this example), the correct password was entered, the host router was successfully logged into, but no asterisks appear to the right of the password prompt. This might throw you off at first, but you'll grow accustomed to it.

NOTE: You may have noticed that the password examples in this chapter are not made person-specific with usernames. While it is possible to have usernames with Enable and Enable Secret passwords, it is rarely done. This is because Enable and Enable Secret passwords are stored in router configuration files. Network managers find it more practical to simply issue generic passwords to avoid the administrative nightmare of maintaining username/passwords across dozens or even hundreds of routers. Refer to Chapter 8 to find out how user accounts and passwords can be centrally maintained using TACACS+ and CiscoSecure.

Enable and Enable Secret Passwords

Once you get past the Line password, you are logged into the router's IOS software environment. IOS is divided into two privilege levels, EXEC and Privileged EXEC (which is usually called enable mode).

The EXEC level contains only basic, nondestructive commands. Being in enable mode provides access to more commands. EXEC-level commands basically allow you to view a router. Enable mode commands are more powerful in that they let you reconfigure the router's settings. These commands are potentially destructive commands, the **erase** command being a good example.

Two types of passwords can be used to restrict access to Privileged EXEC (enable mode): the Enable password and the Enable Secret password. The idea of a "secret password" seems silly at first. *Of course* all passwords are secret, or at least they should be. What the Cisco engineers are alluding to here is the level of encryption used to mask the password from unauthorized users.

The Privileged EXEC Level of IOS   Enable and Enable Secret passwords both do the same thing: they restrict access to Privileged EXEC (enable mode). The difference between the two is in the level of encryption supported. *Encryption* is a technique used to scramble data, making it incomprehensible to those who don't have a key to read it. Enable Secret passwords are scrambled using an advanced encryption algorithm based on 128 bits for which there is no known decoding technique. Encryption for the Enable password relies on a less powerful algorithm. Cisco strongly recommends using Enable Secret instead of the Enable password.

Enable Secret was introduced in 1997, so a fair amount of hardware and software that can support only Enable passwords is still in use, and servers storing backup IOS images frequently service both old and new routers. When both are set, the Enable Secret password always takes precedence over the Enable password. IOS will only put the Enable password to use when running an old version of IOS software.

IOS passwords are stored in the configuration file for a router. Configuration files routinely cross networks as routers are updated and backed up. Having an Enable Secret password means that a hacker using a protocol analyzer (a test device that can read packets) will have a tougher time decoding your password. The following sample configuration file illustrates this:

```
version 11.2
service password-encryption
service udp-small-servers
service tcp-small-servers
!
hostname Router
!
enable secret 5 $1$C/q2$ZhtujqzQIuJrRGqFwdwn71
enable password 7 0012000F
```

Note that the encryption mask of the Enable password on the last line is much shorter than the encryption mask of the Enable Secret password (on the second-to-last line).

The Service Password-Encryption Command Certain types of passwords, such as Line passwords, by default appear in clear text in the configuration file. You can use the **service password-encryption** command to make them more secure. Once this command is entered, each password configured is automatically encrypted and thus rendered illegible inside the configuration file (much as the Enable/Enable Secret passwords are). Securing Line passwords is doubly important in networks on which TFTP servers are used, because TFTP backup entails routinely moving config files across networks—and config files, of course, contain Line passwords.

ROUTER HARDWARE

At first glance, routers seem a lot like a PC. They have a CPU; memory; and, on the back, ports and interfaces to hook up peripherals and various communications media. They sometimes even have a monitor to serve as a system console.

But there's one defining difference from a PC: routers are diskless. They don't even have floppy disks. If you think about it, this makes sense. A router exists to do just that: route. They don't exist to create or display information or to store it, even temporarily. Routers have as their sole mission the task of filtering incoming packets and routing them outbound to their proper destinations.

Another difference is in the kind of add-on modules that can be plugged into routers. Whereas the typical PC contains cards for video, sound, graphics, or other purposes, the modules put into routers are strictly for networking (for obvious reasons). These are called *interface modules*, or just plain *interfaces*. When people or documents refer to a router interface, they mean an actual, physical printed circuit board that handles a particular networking protocol. EO and E1, for example, probably mean Ethernet interface numbers 1 and 2 inside a router. Interface modules are always layer-2 protocol specific. There is one protocol per interface.

Interfaces are added according to the network environment in which they will work. For example, a router might be configured with interface modules only for Ethernet. A router serving in a mixed-LAN environment, by contrast, would have interfaces for both the Ethernet and Token Ring protocols, and if that router were acting as a LAN-to-WAN juncture, it might also have an ISDN module.

There is one last difference between routers and general-purpose computers—a more subtle one. Computer product lines are almost always based on a common central processor (CPU) architecture, for example, Wintel PCs on the venerable Intel *x*86 architecture, Apple's Motorola 68000 variants, Sun's SPARC, and so on.

In contrast, Cisco routers use a variety of CPUs, each chosen to fit a particular mission. Cisco SOHO 70 Series routers, for example, employ 50 MHz CPUs. Cisco probably made this selection because the 70 Series is designed for small office or home office use, where activity loads are light. The Motorola MPC 855T RISC chip is reliable; capable of handling the job; and, perhaps most important, inexpensive. Moving up the router product line, Cisco uses progressively more powerful general-purpose processors from Motorola, Silicon Graphics, and other chip makers.

Router Memory

Routers use various kinds of memory to operate and manage themselves. Figure 4-9 depicts the layout of a motherboard in a Cisco 4500 router (a good example because it's one of the most widely used routers in the world today). All Cisco router motherboards use four types of memory, each dedicated to performing specific roles.

Each Cisco router ships with at least a factory default minimum amount of DRAM and flash memory. Memory can be added at the factory or upgraded in the field. As a general rule, the amount of DRAM can be doubled or quadrupled (depending on the specific model), and the amount of flash can be doubled. If traffic loads increase over time, DRAM can be upgraded to increase a router's throughput capacity.

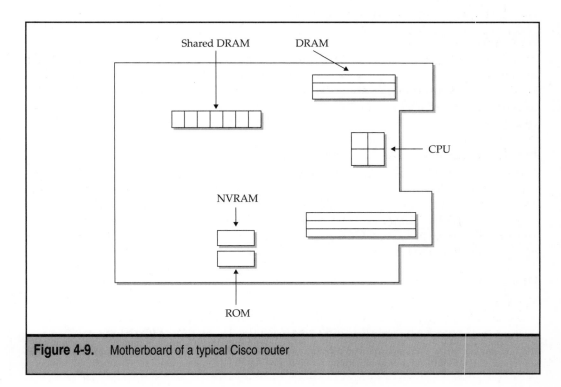

Figure 4-9. Motherboard of a typical Cisco router

RAM/DRAM

RAM/DRAM stands for random access memory/dynamic random access memory. Also called *working storage*, RAM/DRAM is used by the router's central processor to do its work, much like the memory in your PC. When a router is in operation, its RAM/DRAM contains an image of the Cisco IOS software, the running configuration file, the routing table, other tables (built by the router after it starts up), and the packet buffer.

Don't be thrown by the two parts in RAM/DRAM. The acronym is a catch-all. Virtually all RAM/DRAM in Cisco routers is DRAM—dynamic random access memory. Nondynamic memory, also called *static memory*, became obsolete years ago. But the term RAM is still so widely used that it's included in the literature to avoid confusion on the subject.

Cisco's smallest router, the 70 Series, ships with a minimum of 16MB of DRAM. At the other end of the spectrum, the 12816-gigabit switch router, one of Cisco's largest, supports up to 4GB.

NOTE: Shared memory (also called packet memory) is a specialized type of DRAM. Shared memory DRAM is dedicated to handling the router's packet buffer. Cisco's designers separate out shared memory to help assure I/O throughput. Shared memory is even physically nearer to the interface modules to further boost performance.

NVRAM

NVRAM stands for nonvolatile RAM. Nonvolatile means memory that will retain information after losing power. Cisco routers store a copy of the router's configuration file in NVRAM (configuration files are covered later in this chapter). When the router is intentionally turned off, or if power is lost, NVRAM enables the router to restart in its proper configuration.

Flash Memory

Flash memory is also nonvolatile. It differs from NVRAM in that it can be erased and re-programmed as needed. Originally developed by Intel, flash memory is in wide use in computers and other devices. In Cisco routers, flash memory is used to store one or more copies of the IOS software. This is an important feature because it enables network managers to stage new versions of IOS on routers throughout an internetwork and then upgrade them all at once to a new version from flash memory.

ROM

ROM stands for read-only memory. It, too, is nonvolatile. Cisco routers use ROM to hold a so-called *bootstrap program*, which is a file that can be used to boot to a minimum configuration state after a catastrophe. ROM is also referred to as ROMMON. In fact, when you boot from ROM, the first thing you'll see is the rommon>> prompt. ROMMON (for ROM monitor) harks back to the early days of the UNIX operating system, which relied on ROMMON to reboot a computer to the point at which commands could at least be typed into the system console monitor. In smaller Cisco routers, ROM holds a bare-bones subset of the Cisco IOS software. ROM in some high-end Cisco routers holds a full copy of IOS.

Router Ports and Modules

A router's window to the internetwork is through its ports and modules. Without them, a router is a useless box. The ports and modules that are put into a router define what it can do.

Internetworking can be intimidating, with the seemingly endless combinations of products, protocols, media, feature sets, standards—you name it. The acronyms come so fast and so hard that it might seem hopeless to learn how to properly configure a router. But choosing the right router product can be boiled down to manageable proportions. Table 4-4 lays out five major requirement areas that, if met, will lead you to the best router solution.

Cisco obviously can't manufacture a model of router to match every customer's specific requirements. To make them more flexible to configure, routers come in two major parts:

▼ **Chassis** The actual box and basic components inside it, such as power supply, fans, rear and front faceplates, indicator lights, and slots

▲ **Ports and modules** The printed circuit boards that slide into the router box

Area	Description	Configuration Requirement
1	Physical	It must be hardware compatible with the physical network segment on which the router will sit.
2	Communication	The router must be compatible with the transport medium that will be used (Frame Relay, ATM, and so on).
3	Protocol	It must be compatible with the protocols used in the internetwork (IP, IPX, SNA, and so on).
4	Mission	The router must provide the speed, reliability, security, and functional features the job requires.
5	Business	It must fit within the purchase budget and network growth plans.

Table 4-4. Five Major Factors in Selecting a Router

Cisco's router product-line structure tries to steer you to a product—or at least to a reasonably focused selection of products—meeting all five requirement areas in Table 4-4.

Finding the right router for your needs is basically a three-step process. The following illustrates the process of selecting a router for a large branch office operation:

Router Series

Cisco	SOHO	Series
Cisco	800	Series
Cisco	1000	Series
Cisco	2000	Series
Cisco	3000	Series
Cisco	6000	Series
Cisco	7000	Series
Cisco	10000	Series
Cisco	12000	Series

First, Cisco's routers are grouped into product families called *series*. Choosing a router product series is usually a matter of budget, because each series reflects a price/ performance tier. Models within series are generally based on the same chassis, which is the metal frame and basic components (power supply, fans, and so on) around which the router is built. We'll select the Cisco 2000 Series because it fits both the purchase budget and performance requirements for our large branch office.

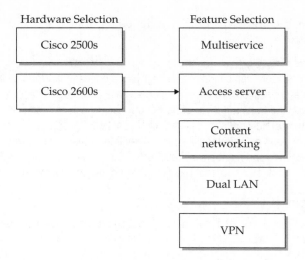

From the 2000 Series, we'll take the Cisco 2600 Series. The 2600 chassis is versatile enough to fit a lot of situations, making it a popular brand of branch office router.

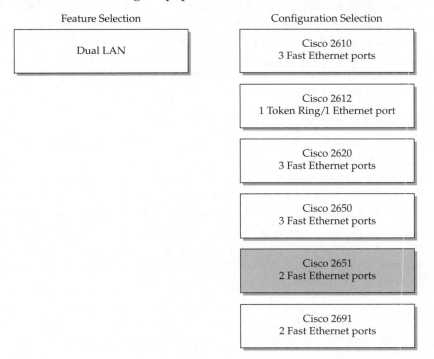

Third, we'll select the Cisco 2650 because it has two Ethernet ports; and our imaginary branch office will operate two subnets, one for the customer service office and another for the front office. The two Ethernet ports will let us separate the two departments, thereby isolating traffic.

NOTE: The term "port" can cause confusion if you're not careful. When speaking of hardware, port means a physical connection through which I/O can pass (a serial port, for example), but there are also so-called ports at the transport layer of network protocols. These "ports" are actually port numbers used to identify what network application packets contain. These ports (port numbers) are also referred to as TCP ports or "listeners," because they inform the receiver what's inside the message. Example TCP-defined port numbers include Port 25 for Simple Mail Transfer Protocol and Port 80 for HTTP. Refer to Chapter 2's section, "The Transport Layer," for more on TCP ports.

Router Packaging

Three major categories of modules can be configured into Cisco routers to support either LAN or WAN connectivity:

▼ **Ethernet modules**   To support any of the many Ethernet LAN variants on the market, including Novell NetWare, Banyan VINES, and AppleTalk.

■ **Token Ring modules**   IBM's LAN technology, which is well established in banks, insurance companies, and other Fortune 1000 corporate environments.

▲ **WAN connectivity modules**   To support a wide variety of WAN protocols, some old and some new. Example WAN technologies include newer protocols such as ISDN, Frame Relay, Asynchronous Transfer Mode (ATM), and legacy protocols such as SDLC and X.25.

Configuration options depend mainly on the specific Cisco router:

▼ Lower-end routers tend to be "fixed configuration" in that the modules are factory integrated only (preconfigured).

■ Midrange routers, such as the Cisco 3600 Series, are "modular" in that they can accept a variety of modules, often packaging different protocols in the same box. Interface modules are plugged into this class of routers' motherboards.

▲ High-end routers, the Cisco 7300 Series and Cisco 12000 Series, have buses (also called *backplanes*). Bus-based routers accept larger modules—usually referred to as *blades* or *cards*—that are effectively self-contained routers (they have their own CPUs, memory units, and so on).

Figure 4-10 is a view of the back of a Cisco 4500 configured with two Token Ring modules (Ring A and Ring B) and four serial ports. Notice that an empty slot is available on the right. It's a common practice to purchase a router model with room for adding an interface as network traffic grows.

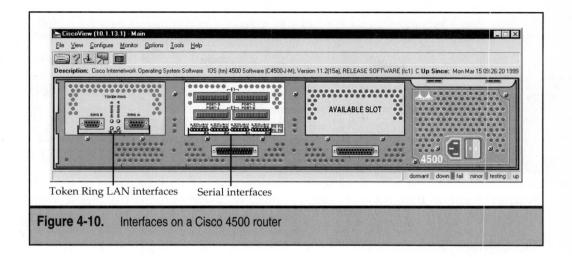

Figure 4-10.   Interfaces on a Cisco 4500 router

ESSENTIAL FILES

In contrast to normal computers, Cisco routers have just two main files:

▼   The configuration file

▲   The Cisco IOS software

Cisco IOS software contains instructions to the router. IOS acts as the traffic cop, directing activity inside the router. IOS manages internal router operations by telling the various hardware components what to do, much like Windows XP or LINUX with a general-purpose computer. Customers cannot alter the contents of the IOS file.

The configuration file contains instructions to the router input by the customer, not Cisco. It contains information describing the network environment in which the router will run and how the network manager wants it to behave. In a phrase, the configuration file tells it *what* to do; IOS tells the router *how* to do it.

As will be covered in the next chapter, routers also use dynamic files, which are not stored in the router's flash memory, NVRAM, or ROM. Dynamic files instead are built from scratch when a router is booted and are strictly reactive in the sense that they only hold live information, not operational instructions.

IOS: The Internetwork Operating System

We usually don't think of an operating system as a file. After all, your PC's operating system is made up of many thousands of files (they sit in your directory with file extensions such as SYS, EXE, DRV, and DLL).

However, IOS is indeed contained in a single file. When you ship an IOS file somewhere, it holds everything necessary to run a router. Depending on the version, an IOS software image will have a footprint from 3MB to over 10MB in size.

NOTE: Less sophisticated Cisco internetworking devices get their intelligence in the form of factory-installed software called *firmware*. Firmware is a subset of IOS itself. It can be field-upgraded to keep the device's software current with the rest of the network.

IOS needs to be tightly constructed because copies of it, referred to as *system images*, are routinely shipped across internetworks. System images are uploaded and downloaded over routers in order to back up routers, upgrade their capabilities, and restart them after a failure. It wouldn't be practical to send thousands of 50MB files. Being able to send a single, small, self-contained IOS file makes effective network management possible.

IOS Feature Sets

Feature sets are packages that try to simplify configuring and ordering IOS software. There is no single IOS software product, per se. IOS is actually a common software platform on which a suite of IOS implementations is based, each packaged to fulfill a specific mission. Cisco calls these IOS packages *feature sets* (also called *software images* or *feature packs*). When you order a Cisco router, you choose an IOS feature set that contains all the capabilities your particular situation requires. Most of these requirements have to do with maintaining compatibility with the various hardware devices and network protocols in the environment in which the router will operate.

As depicted in Figure 4-11, variants of the Cisco IOS software are defined two ways: by feature set and by release. Feature sets define the job a version of IOS can do; releases are used to manage the IOS software through time.

Cisco IOS feature sets are designed to

▼ Be compatible with certain router platforms

■ Enable interoperability between disparate networking protocols (Novell NetWare, IBM SNA, AppleTalk, and so on)

▲ Provide functional features in the form of network services and applications for such things as network management, security, and multimedia

Packaging and selling IOS software in this way simplifies things for Cisco and customers alike. For the customer, having a single part number to order simplifies figuring out what software to buy. For Cisco, it helps the company's product engineers to figure out what goes where so that their support personnel figure out who has what. Remember, internetworking can get hopelessly complicated because the nature of the business is to enable disparate computer platforms and networking protocols to interoperate and coexist.

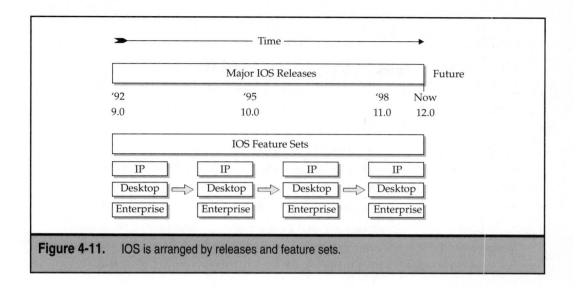

Figure 4-11.   IOS is arranged by releases and feature sets.

How Feature Sets Are Constructed   Because IOS feature sets have dependencies on the router hardware on which they run, two rules of thumb apply:

▼   You can't run all feature sets on all router platforms.

▲   Sometimes, specific features within a feature set will or will not run, depending on the router platform.

If you look at a Cisco product catalog, understanding Cisco's feature sets can seem tough at first glance. Feature sets do nothing more than put functionality groupings into logical packages that customers can use. All feature sets, in one way or another, derive their functionality from about a dozen categories, listed in Table 4-5.

Don't worry about the examples on the right side of this table or all the acronyms you don't know. The important thing here is to understand that IOS software's myriad features and functions can be grouped into about a dozen categories.

Cisco IOS feature sets try to combine features into groups most likely to match real-world customer requirements. Cisco offers dozens of point-product feature sets in the form of IOS software product numbers you can put on a purchase order. They are grouped by general characteristics into the four general feature set families shown in Table 4-6. Notice in Tables 4-5 and 4-6 that proprietary computer platforms, such as IBM, DEC, and Apple, and proprietary networking platforms, such as Novell and SNA, drive much of the need for feature sets. Each Cisco router must deal with the customer's real-world compatibility requirements, which means being able to run with legacy hardware and software. Nearly all legacy architectures exist at the "network's edge." Which is to say most of the proprietary equipment with which IP must maintain compatibility sits either on LANs or on computers sitting on the LANs. This is where compatibility issues with proprietary legacy computer architectures or specialized platforms are manifested.

Category	Examples of Features
LAN support	IP, Novell IPX, AppleTalk, Banyan VINES, DECnet
WAN services	PPP, ATM LAN emulation, Frame Relay, ISDN, X.25
WAN optimization	Dial-on-demand, snapshot routing, traffic shaping
IP routing	BGP, RIP, IGRP, Enhanced IGRP, OSPF, IS-IS, NAT
Other routing	IPX RIP, AURP, NLSP
Multimedia and QoS	Generic traffic shaping, random early detection, RSVP
Management	SNMP, RMON, Cisco Call History MIB, Virtual Profiles
Security	Access lists, extended access lists, lock and key, TACACS+
Switching	Fast-switched policy routing, AppleTalk Routing over ISL
IBM support	APPN, Bisync, Frame Relay for SNA, SDLC integration
Protocol translation	LAT, PPP, X.25
Remote node	PPP, SLIP, MacIP, IP pooling, CSLIP, NetBEUI over PPP
Terminal services	LAT, Xremote, Telnet, X.25 PAD

Table 4-5.   IOS Software Feature Categories

Tables 4-5 and 4-6 also show which software functionality groupings go into what IOS feature set products. For example, multinational enterprises are likely to be interested in IBM functionality, such as NetBEUI over PPP and Frame Relay for SNA, and would probably be interested in one of the Enterprise/APPN feature sets. By contrast, an advertising agency heavy into Apple and Windows would focus on the Desktop feature sets.

Feature Set Family	Target Customer Environments
IP	Basic IP routing
Desktop	IP, Novell NetWare IPX, AppleTalk, DECnet
Enterprise	High-end functionality for LANs, WANs, and management
Enterprise/APPN	Same as Enterprise, but with many IBM-specific features added

Table 4-6.   IOS Feature Set Families

Grouping feature sets into families is Cisco's way of bringing a semblance of order to pricing policies and upgrade paths. Ordering a single IOS part number instead of dozens helps everybody avoid mistakes. Figure 4-12 depicts the process of feature set selection.

Last, feature sets are further grouped into software product variants:

▼ **Basic**   The basic feature set for the hardware platform

■ **Plus**   The basic feature set and additional features, which are dependent on the hardware platform selected

▲ **Encryption**   The addition of either a 40-bit (Plus 40) or a 56-bit (Plus 56) data encryption feature atop either the Basic or Plus feature set

The ultimate goal of feature sets is to guide you through the process of ordering, say, IOS Feature Set Enterprise 56 for a Cisco 7500/RSP running Release 11—without making a mistake that costs your network upgrade project a two-week delay.

The Anatomy of Cisco Release Numbers   Cisco IOS software release numbers have four basic parts, as shown in Figure 4-13.

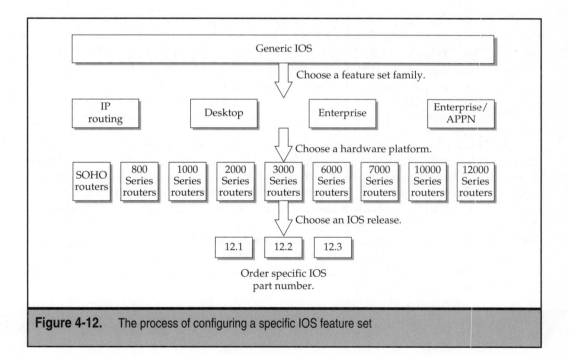

Figure 4-12.   The process of configuring a specific IOS feature set

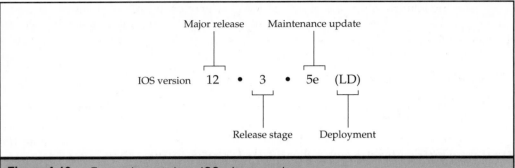

Figure 4-13.   Four major parts in an IOS release number

The first part is a major release—the "12" in Figure 4-13—which marks First Customer Shipments (FCS) of an IOS version of stable, high-quality software for customers to use in their production networks. Major releases are further defined by the following:

▼ **Stage**   The "3" in Figure 4-13, which marks FCS of various major release stages (first release, general deployment release, short-lived release, and so on). Stage releases are often referred to in the future tense, when they are still planned but have not yet taken place.

▲ **Maintenance Update**   The "5e" in Figure 4-13, which denotes support for additional platforms of features beyond what was available in the major release's FCS.

The fourth part of the release number is the deployment. A general deployment (GD) release is for unconstrained use by all customers. Early deployment (ED) releases are to deliver new functionality or technologies to customers to deploy in a limited manner in their networks. Limited deployment (LD) denotes a limited lifecycle between FCS and GD.

At any given time there can be several major releases in use in the field. For example, three versions of IOS 12 are available, but 11.2 and 11.3 are still widely used. Most network managers are content to stick with a release they know works for them. Early adopters use advanced IOS releases because they need platform or feature support not available before. Most users are happy to let the early adopters help Cisco shake things out before general release.

NOTE: The terms "version" and "release" are sometimes used interchangeably in connection with editions of IOS software. In this book, version is used to specify a particular release of a particular IOS feature set.

Using TFTP for IOS Backups and Updates

In the event of a network catastrophe, it is possible for a router's IOS system image to be corrupted or erased from flash memory altogether. Standard procedure is to maintain a backup image of every IOS version in use in the network being managed. These backup IOS images are maintained on TFTP servers or within network management applications such as CiscoWorks (covered in Chapter 15).

TFTP stands for Trivial File Transfer Protocol. TFTP is a TCP/IP application derived from the early days of the UNIX operating system. As you may have guessed, TFTP is a stripped-down version of FTP, the command many of you have used to download files over the Internet. IOS uses TFTP instead of FTP because it's speedier and uses fewer system resources.

So-called TFTP servers are computer platforms on an internetwork that store and download IOS system images and configuration files. It is recommended that more than one TFTP server be used to back up a network. This is in case the TFTP server itself goes down or the network segment connecting it to the devices it backs up becomes unavailable.

To load a new IOS image to a router's flash memory, use the **copy tftp flash** command following the procedure, shown here:

```
Router#copy tftp flash

System flash directory:
File   Length   Name/status
  1    4171336  c4500-j-mz_112-15a.bin
[4171400 bytes used, 22904 available, 4194304 total]
Address or name of remote host [10.1.10.40]? 10.1.10.40
Source file name? c4500-j-mz_112-15a.bin
Destination file name [c4500-j-mz_112-15a.bin]? <cr>
Accessing file 'c4500-j-mz_112-15a.bin' on 10.1.10.40...
Loading c4500-j-mz_112-15a.bin from 10.1.1.12 (via TokenRing1): [OK]

Erase flash device before writing? [confirm]yes
Flash contains files. Are you sure you want to erase? [confirm]yes

Copy 'c4500-j-mz_112-15a.bin' from server
  as 'c4500-j-mz_112-15a.bin' into Flash WITH erase? [yes/no]yes
Erasing device... eeeeeeeeeeeeeeee ...erased
Loading c4500-j-mz_112-15a.bin from 10.1.1.12 (via TokenRing1): !
  !!!!!!!!!!!!!!!!!!!!!!!!!!!!!!!!!!!!!!!!!!!!!!!!!!!!!!!!!!!!!!!!!!!!!
  !!!!!!!!!!!!!!!!!!!!!!!!!!!!!!!!!!!!!!!!!!!!!!!!!!!!!!!!!!!!!!!!!!!!!
  !!!!!!!!!!!!!!!!!!!!!!!!!!!!!!!!!!!!!!!!!!!!!!!!!!!!!!!!!!!!!!!!!!!!!
```

```
!!!!!!!!!!!!!!!!!!!!!!!!!!!!!!!!!!!!!!!!!!!!!!!!!!!!!!!!!!!!!!!!!!!!
!!!!!!!!!!!!!!!!!!!!!!!!!!!!!!!!!!!!!!!!!!!!!!!!!!!!!!!!!!!!!!!!!!!!
!!!!!!!!!!!!!!!!!!!!!!!!!!!!!!!!!!!!!!!!!!!!!!!!!!!!!!!!!!!!!!!!!!!!
!!!!!!!!!!!!!!!!!!!!!!!!!!!!!!!!!!!!!!!!!!!!!!!!!!!!!!!!!!!!!!!!!!!!
!!!!!!!!!!!!!!!!!!!!!!!!!!!!!!!!!!!!!!!!!!!!!!!!!!!!!!!!!!!!!!!!!!!!
!!!!!!!!!!!!!!!!!!!!!!!!!!!!!!!!!!!!!!!!!!!!!!!!!!!!!!!!!!!!!!!!!!!!
!!!!!!!!!!!!!!!!!!!!!!!!!!!!!!!!!!!!!!!!!!!!!!!!!!!!!!!!!!!!!!!!!!!!
[OK - 4171336/4194304 bytes]

Verifying checksum...  OK (0x29D5)
Flash copy took 00:00:30 [hh:mm:ss]
Router#
```

You can see that the TFTP server confirmed that it had the IOS system image before overwriting the one in the router's flash memory. Each exclamation point in the display indicates that a block of the file was successfully copied over the network from the server to the router.

NOTE: If you are copying a file to a TFTP server, be sure the name of the file that you are attempting to transfer already exists in the TFTP directory. Create the file on UNIX systems using the **touch** command. On Microsoft platforms, open Notepad to create the file and save it under the filename.

The Configuration File

Managing a router involves installation, upgrades, backups, recovery, and other event-driven tasks, but the biggest part of router management is the care and feeding of a router's configuration file. The configuration file is the cockpit from which the network administrator runs the router and all the traffic going through it. As will be detailed in the next chapter, configuration files contain access lists, passwords, and other important router management tools.

Viewing the Configuration File

The most common way to examine the status of a router is to view its configuration file. To view most anything in IOS is to ask for a view of the configuration. The main IOS command for viewing such information is the **show** command.

The following example uses the **show running-config** command to view a router's running configuration. There are two types of configuration files. The *running* configuration file is an image running in DRAM (main memory) at a given time. The *backup* configuration file is stored in NVRAM and is used to boot the router.

```
Router#show running-config
Building configuration...
```

```
Current configuration:
!
version 11.2
service password-encryption
service udp-small-servers
service tcp-small-servers
!
hostname Router
!
enable secret 5 $1$C/q2$ZhtujqzQIuJrRGqFwdwn71
enable password 7 0012000F
!
vty-async
!
interface Serial0
 no ip address
 no ip route-cache
 no ip mroute-cache
 shutdown
! interface Serial1
 no ip address
 .
 .
 .
```

In the next chapter we will go into greater depth on what the configuration file does and how to edit it.

Using TFTP for Configuration File Backups and Updates

As with IOS system image backups and updates, TFTP servers are used to back up and update configuration files. For example, the **copy running-config tftp** command is used to back up the router's running configuration file (named tomtest in this example) to a TFTP server, using the following procedure:

```
Router#copy running-config tftp
Remote host []? 10.1.10.40
Name of configuration file to write [router-confg]? test
Write file tomtest on host 10.1.10.40? [confirm]<cr>
Building configuration...

Writing test !! [OK]
Router#
```

The other TFTP commands to back up or update configuration files are

▼ **copy tftp running-config** Configures the router directly by copying from the TFTP directly into the router's DRAM

■ **copy startup-config tftp** Backs up the startup configuration from the router's NVRAM to the TFTP server

▲ **copy tftp startup-config** Updates the router's startup configuration file by downloading from the TFTP server and overwriting the one stored in the router's NVRAM

Note that **tftp** goes *in front of* the file type—**running-config** or **startup-config**—to download (update from the server) and *behind* the file type to upload (back up to the server). Think of the **copy** command as copying *from* somewhere *to* somewhere.

CHAPTER 5

Configuring Routers

The router is the centerpiece of internetworking. It's the device that stitches networks together into internetworks and makes them useful. So, if you can learn how to manage routers properly, you can pretty much manage an internetwork. The network administrator's single point of control over router behavior is the configuration file, called the *config file* for short. The config file is one of only two permanent files on a router. The other is the IOS software, which is general in nature and cannot be altered by customers. The config file, then, is the network administrator's single point of control over the network. It's at the center of the router operations, with IOS referring to it hundreds of times per second in order to tell the router how to do its job.

Although the config file is the key tool, at first it can seem hard to understand. This is because the config file is unlike the kinds of files most of us are used to. You can't put a cursor inside one and edit it in real time like you would, say, a word processor document. You can't compile it and debug it the way computer programmers turn source code into executable code. Config files are modified by entering IOS commands and then viewing the new configuration to see if you achieved the desired results.

THE CONFIGURATION FILE'S CENTRAL ROLE

Most network problems are caused by configuration problems, not by glitches in hardware or errors in telecommunications circuits. This is not surprising if you think about it. The config file is where all the network administrator's input goes and, by implication, where human error is most likely to be manifested. As we saw in the previous chapter, a router in and of itself is a sophisticated device. Put one on an internetwork—where a router interacts with other routers—and you understand how the average router's config file is rife with interdependencies. Every router added to an internetwork increases complexity exponentially. It follows, then, that each time you make a change to a config file, the complexity becomes that much harder to track.

Configuration mistakes don't necessarily make themselves immediately apparent in the form of operational problems. Many problems are harder to see (and thus harder to avoid) because they remain latent—lying in config files across a network, waiting to rear their ugly heads at the worst possible moment.

So when internetworking people talk about "configuring" a router, the subject isn't what parts to put into the box. They're talking about making a change to a router's behavior and considering everything that might flow from that change. Internetworks, by their very nature, tend to magnify things by passing them down the line. This is why network administrators put a lot of thought and planning into what might seem inconsequential to the uninitiated. Network administrators spend most of their time either changing or reviewing config files because that's where the action is.

Further magnifying the importance of config file design is the fact that the average config file controls more than one router. By and large, network management isn't performed one router at a time. Config files are generally maintained for groups of routers *en masse*. Mass distribution of config files is done as much for design control as for convenience. It's a way of assuring consistency that internetworks need to run smoothly.

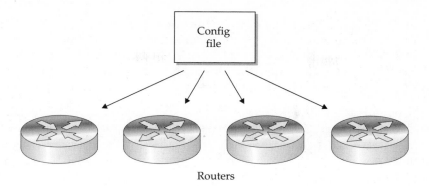

Routers

Network designers typically divide router populations into subgroups—or classes—with common characteristics having to do with network areas, equipment software version levels, or security requirements. Therefore, it makes sense to implement network policy changes, upgrades, tests, and so on en masse in config file downloads and uploads. A router's config file is usually dealt with individually only when there is a problem with that particular machine.

Three Types of Cisco Router Files

Three types of files are used to run a Cisco router: the two permanent files—the IOS image and config file—and files created and maintained by the router itself. It's important to have an idea about how they fit together.

Like any operating system, IOS is dedicated to running the machine on which it sits. It differs from other operating systems in that its predominant focus is moving transient packets in and out of the box. Where other kinds of operating systems are concerned with interacting with users, crunching numbers, printing output, and the like, IOS is almost solely concerned with forwarding packets unchanged to their next destination. It cares about supporting a user interface only insofar as one is necessary to let network administrators perform housekeeping chores.

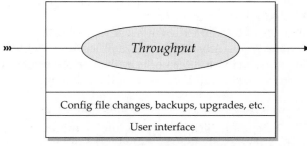

Priorities of IOS Operations

The config file is where management instructions are put to tell IOS how to function properly in the internetwork. The config file defines the network interface hardware in the router box, the protocols to support, what packets get through, and so on. In short, the config file is where network administrators store all their work. Once you learn to work well with config files, you've mastered the basics of internetwork management.

Config file	External (network behavior)
IOS	Internal

But the router creates a number of files on its own. These files—as a class sometimes called *dynamic files*—come into existence only after the router is turned on. Turn the router off and the dynamic files disappear (only the IOS image and config file are permanently stored).

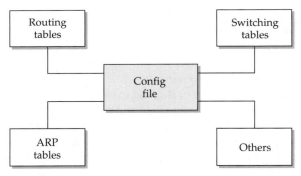

Dynamic files are created and maintained by the router in order to adapt on a moment-by-moment basis, which is why it wouldn't be practical for a person to keep them updated. But while network administrators cannot put instructions into dynamic files, they can control behavior of dynamic files indirectly by setting parameters in the config file. Also, administrators frequently examine dynamic file contents in order to troubleshoot network problems. The ins and outs of how the various dynamic files work will be covered in later chapters. For now, just remember the following:

▼ You cannot put things directly into dynamic files.

■ The contents of dynamic files change minute by minute in response to trends in network traffic—that's why they're called "dynamic."

▲ Control over dynamic files is indirect, through parameters set in the config file.

IOS	Config file	Dynamic files
Releases, feature sets	Operational instructions	Temporary info

Taken together, IOS, the config file, and dynamic files make up the router's operational environment. The config file is the focal point of control over routers and, by implication, control over whole networks. IOS is left to the Cisco software engineers; you control it only by loading new versions every year or so. You control dynamic files only indirectly. Thus, all network management changes go into the config file.

Given that you cannot edit config files directly, the process of administering Cisco routers tends to be more indirect than what most of us are accustomed to. Figure 5-1 depicts the typical process of modifying a config file.

To some, the combination of a character-based user interface and the indirect management process that routers involve seems complicated. But internetworking is simpler than it seems. Understanding these basic facts will help the beginner get started in analyzing and troubleshooting network problems:

▼ IOS is your interface; you use IOS commands to interact with the router.

■ The config file and the various dynamic files hold the information you need to analyze network problems.

■ The config file tells you how a router is set up; dynamic files show how the setup is working in the network environment.

■ The config file is your single point of control.

▲ You can't directly edit the config file; you change it through IOS commands and then review the results.

Now that you know your way around a router, it's time for some hands-on work. If you have access to a Cisco router, log in and follow along.

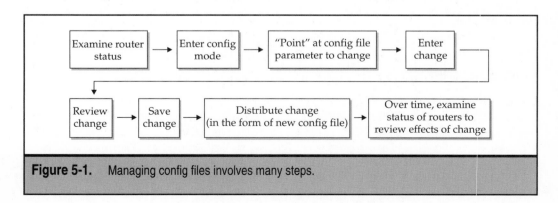

Figure 5-1. Managing config files involves many steps.

GETTING STARTED WITH CISCO ROUTERS

To configure and manage Cisco routers, you need to be able to interact with them through some kind of connection. First, you must somehow communicate with a router, either by logging into it or by downloading and uploading files to and from it. Once you're successfully hooked up to a router, you must then be able to speak its language, which in Cisco routers are IOS commands.

Communicating with IOS

You can gain access to a router either directly through the console or AUX ports or via a network using either the Telnet or HTTP protocol. Network pros generally use Telnet for convenience. Whatever method is used, you need to get into the IOS environment in order to review files and enter commands. Telnet is distributed with all Microsoft Windows operating systems. You can run it by clicking the Start button (in the Microsoft Windows desktop), and then Run. Afterward, enter **telnet** at the command prompt, and a blank Telnet screen will appear. Click Connect at the far left of the menu bar, and then enter the IP address of the router you want to log into under the Remote System option. This brings you to the Line password prompt of the target router.

Notice in Figure 5-2 that either remote or local hosts can be accessed. The IP address highlighted in Figure 5-2 is for a router on the local area network (LAN) in the same office as our imaginary network administrator. One of the remote IP addresses would be used if the router were located at a remote site (that is, beyond the LAN). Even if you are on the same network with the router, a valid password must be entered in order to gain entry into the router.

Just in case you ever encounter it, Figure 5-3 shows an error condition that commonly befuddles beginners typing in their first IOS commands.

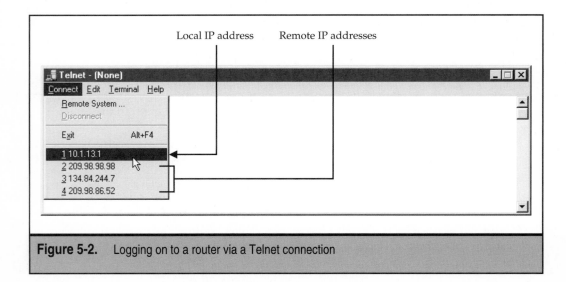

Figure 5-2.   Logging on to a router via a Telnet connection

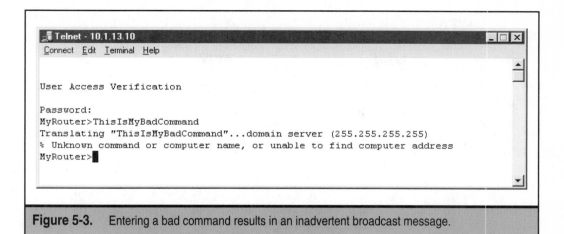

Figure 5-3.   Entering a bad command results in an inadvertent broadcast message.

What's happening in Figure 5-3 is this: When you enter text that IOS cannot interpret as a command, it assumes that it's a symbolic name for an IP address. IOS has no choice in the matter. After all, one purpose of a router is to communicate with other routers, and no single router has all existing addresses on file. Here, the router attempts to send the symbolic address name to all addresses within its broadcast domain. Broadcasts are always addressed 255.255.255.255 (as you no doubt remember from Chapter 2). After ten seconds or so, the router gives up, displays an error message, and returns to the prompt.

NOTE: If you enter a bad command into most computer operating systems, you get an error message. Give IOS a bad command and it assumes the input is a network address and tries to Telnet to it. Normal operating systems know all possible input values that can go into them, but IOS doesn't have that luxury. It deals in network addresses, and routers never assume they know all possible addresses because networks change constantly.

Meet IOS 12.3

Cisco's most recent version of IOS is Major Release 12.3. This version offers a number of enhancements and improvements over previous IOS releases, mainly in the realm of security and provisioning.

However, one of the biggest changes with IOS 12.3 isn't so much in the technology involved with the release, as in how it sells the software. With IOS 12.3, Cisco has also revamped the way it packages devices. Rather than offering 44 packages, 12.3 has just eight. This makes the whole process of selecting a package less of a headache for customers.

IOS 12.3 is aimed at enterprise and access users, and is included on the following router families:

▼ 800

■ 1700

■ 2600

■ 3600

■ 3700

▲ 7000

As with any new operating system, it isn't wise (or even necessary) to immediately make the switch to a new release without first understanding the impact it might have on your network. Cisco recommends upgrading to 12.3 for customers who are using Release 12.2T, since 12.3 provides maintenance for the 12.2T release, once it reaches its end of engineering stage. Beyond that, however, it's a good idea to consider what you're using and determine whether the new features in 12.3 are worth your while.

Cisco has arranged its packages for IOS 12.3 in a hierarchical organization (as shown in Figure 5-4). That is, more comprehensive feature sets include the features of those beneath them. The eight Cisco IOS packages include the following:

▼ **IP Base**   The baseline of IOS software required to operate a Cisco IOS router. This includes DSL connectivity, Ethernet switching, 802.1q routing, and trunking. It's the default IOS image on most routers.

■ **IP Voice**   This package adds voice features, including support for VoIP and VoFR. It also includes functionality for Cisco IOS Telephony Services and Survivable Remote Site Telephony (SRST).

■ **Enterprise Base**   Adds support for improved data connectivity, QoS and other routed and IBM services, like AppleTalk and Novell.

■ **Advanced Security**   Adds security and VPN features, including IOS Firewall, Intrusion Detection System (IDS), Secure Shell, and support for Easy VPN Client and Server.

■ **SP Services**   Adds data connectivity with voice encapsulation and transport services. Provides support for voice and data over IP and ATM. This package also includes NetFlow and IPv6.

■ **Advanced IP Services**   Combines data and voice support with security and VPN features. It combines the features from the SP Services package and adds security support found in the Advanced Security package.

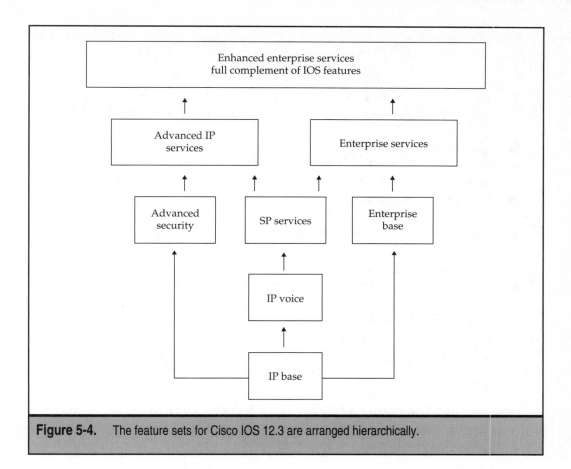

Figure 5-4.   The feature sets for Cisco IOS 12.3 are arranged hierarchically.

- ■ **Enterprise Services** Combines support for services, like AppleTalk and IPX, with voice and ATM services. It includes features found in the SP Services package, as well as support for L3 routed protocols included in the Enterprise Basic feature set.

- ▲ **Advanced Enterprise Services** This is the highest level of IOS packaging and includes the features from all the aforementioned feature sets.

Overall, it's best to check the Cisco Web site to determine which feature set is best for you. However, as you move through the feature sets, you add security, multiple protocol support, ATM, and combinations of these features. Naturally, as you progress through the feature sets, the more comprehensive sets demand more of your wallet.

Cisco has introduced a number of new technologies and features with IOS 12.3. These provide improved security, ease of use, and overall functionality. Let's take a look at some of these features:

▼ **AutoSecure** The idea behind AutoSecure is that it provides "one touch device lockdown." This allows a macro to be deployed, causing the router to reconfigure itself with a variety of security features.

■ **Easy VPN Remote** Provides server support for the Cisco VPN client. The idea here is that it will be easier to use Cisco IPSec with the VPN gateways. IPSec for the client is managed by the server.

■ **Stateful NAT Failover** Allows NAT routers to track state and retain services if one of the routers should fail.

■ **Nonstop Forwarding (NSF)** NSF is a support mechanism for dual route processor failover. When a routing neighbor sees a dual route processor fail, it will continue forwarding packets using existing routing information.

■ **Survivable Remote Site Telephony (SRST)** Provides remote site redundancy for IP telephony, even allowing a voice call to continue at a branch office when the WAN link fails.

▲ **AutoQoS** Provides VoIP QoS configuration of routers and switches using just one or two commands. Later, you can go back in and fine-tune your QoS configuration. AutoQoS is a good mechanism to get one's feet wet in the world of QoS.

These are just a handful of the new features in IOS 12.3. Whether or not these new features are desirable for your organization is something you'll have to decide before making any changes to your network's operating system.

Using IOS Commands

Any computer software environment has its quirks, and IOS is no exception. On one hand, IOS is a purpose-built operating system that has been stripped of all but the bare essentials in order to keep things simple and fast. That's a good thing, but you won't see the plush conveniences that a Mac, X-Windows (UNIX), or Microsoft Windows graphical user interface (GUI) offers. On the other hand, IOS is one of the world's most widely distributed and important operating systems. So, everything you need to operate is inside if you look.

The IOS Command Hierarchy

IOS has hundreds of commands. Some can be used anywhere in IOS, others only within a specific area. Even Cisco gurus haven't memorized all the IOS commands. So, like any good operating system, IOS arranges its commands into a hierarchy. Figure 5-5 is an overview of how IOS commands are structured.

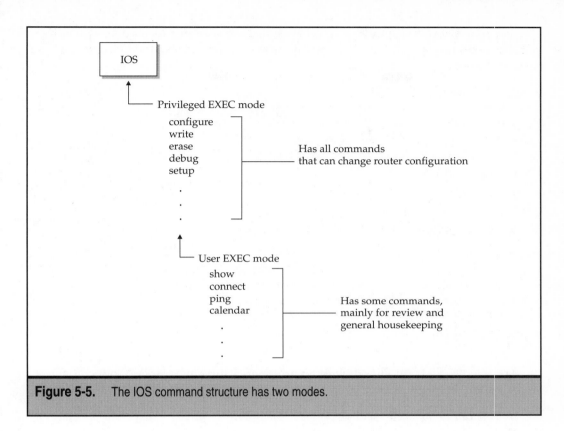

Figure 5-5.   The IOS command structure has two modes.

The first division within IOS is between the User EXEC and Privileged EXEC levels of IOS. User EXEC, of course, contains only a subset of Privileged EXEC's commands. The less powerful User EXEC mode is where **connect**, **login**, **ping**, **show**, and other innocuous commands reside. These are in Privileged EXEC too, but privileged mode is where the more powerful, and potentially destructive, commands—such as **configure**, **debug**, **erase**, **setup**, and others—are exclusively available.

Depending on the IOS feature set installed, there are about twice as many commands in Privileged EXEC as in User EXEC. The commands in User EXEC mode tend to be "flat." In other words, they don't have branches leading to subset commands underneath, as the following example shows:

```
Router>>connect ?
  WORD  IP address or hostname of a remote system
  <cr>
```

As a rule, User EXEC mode commands go, at most, just two levels deep. Being more powerful, Privileged EXEC mode commands can go deeper, as the following example sequence shows:

```
MyRouter#show ip ?
  access-lists          List IP access lists
  accounting            The active IP accounting database
  aliases               IP alias table
  arp                   IP ARP table
  .
  .
  .
```

The **ip** root command has many available arguments (subcommands):

```
MyRouter#show ip arp ?
H.H.H                 48-bit hardware address of ARP entry
Hostname or A.B.C.D   IP address or hostname of ARP entry
  Null                Null interface
  Serial              Serial
  Token Ring           IEEE 802.5
  <cr>
```

Arguments can be modified by other arguments still deeper in the root command's "subcommand" tree:

```
My Router#show ip arp serial ?
  <0-3>   Serial interface number
  <cr>
```

The end of the branch is announced with the <cr> symbol, which is IOS telling the user to enter the completed command with a carriage return. For example, after you've pieced together a full command from the preceding options—**ip access-lists serial2**, for example—you would enter a carriage return after the "2" for serial line number 2.

Piecing together straightforward command lines is one thing. The real trick is knowing where to find arguments to root commands so you can put together complete and correct command lines. This is where the IOS help system comes into play.

Traversing IOS with the Help System

IOS has a built-in, context-sensitive help system. *Context-sensitive* means the help system responds with information based on where you are in the system at the time. You can get the broadest kind of context-sensitive help by simply entering a question mark at the prompt. Here, for example, is a listing of all the root commands available in the User EXEC level of IOS:

```
Router>>?
Exec commands:
  <1-99>           Session number to resume
  access-enable    Create a temporary Access-List entry
  atmsig           Execute Atm Signaling Commands
  clear            Reset functions
  connect          Open a terminal connection
  disable          Turn off privileged commands
  disconnect       Disconnect an existing network connection
  enable           Turn on privileged commands
  exit             Exit from the EXEC
  help             Description of the interactive help system
  lat              Open a lat connection
  lock             Lock the terminal
  login            Log in as a particular user
  logout           Exit from the EXEC
  .
  .
  .
```

You can also get what some call "word help" by entering part of a command you don't know followed immediately by a question mark:

```
Router>>sh?
show
```

Word help is a great way to get definitions and is especially handy for figuring out what truncated commands are, as with **show** in the preceding example. Another way to get help on a partial command is to simply enter it, whereupon the system will come back with an instruction on how to obtain complete help on the command:

```
Router>>sh
% Type "show ?" for a list of subcommands
```

Notice that in help's suggested command **show ?** there is a space between the command and the question mark. As you've by now noticed, there is always a space between a command and its modifier (called an *argument*). Doing this in a help request is the way to ask for a list of arguments available for the command. In the following example, the question mark asks for all arguments available for the **show** command:

```
Router>>show ?
  bootflash       Boot Flash information
  calendar        Display the hardware calendar
  clock           Display the system clock
  context         Show context information
  dialer          Dialer parameters and statistics
  history         Display the session command history
  hosts           IP domain-name, lookup style, nameservers,
                  and host table
  kerberos        Show Kerberos Values
  location        Display the system location
  .
  .
  .
```

Sometimes using help in this way is called *command-syntax* help, because it helps you properly complete a multipart command. Command-syntax help is a powerful learning tool because it lists keywords or arguments available to you at nearly any point in IOS command operations. Remember, the space must be inserted between the command and the question mark in order to use command-syntax help.

In IOS, help plays a more integral role than help systems in normal PC or business application software packages. Those help systems, also context-sensitive, are essentially online manuals that try to help you learn a whole subsection of the application. IOS help is terse: It just wants to get you through the next command line. That's refreshing. Most help systems nowadays seem to assume that you're anxious to spend hours reading all about an entire subsystem when, in fact, you just want to know what to do next.

NOTE: Don't be confused by the **show** command's name. **show** displays running system information. It is not an all-purpose command to "show" help information; the **?** command does that. The **show** command is used to examine router status.

Command Syntax

There's more to operating IOS commands than simply "walking rightward" through the root command's subcommand tree. To run IOS, you must learn how to combine different commands, not just modify a single command, in order to form the command lines it takes to do the heavy lifting that network administration requires. But IOS isn't rocket science, as the following example sequence demonstrates:

```
MyRouter#config
Configuring from terminal, memory, or network [terminal]?
```

In the preceding prompt, we're entering config mode, and IOS wants to know if the configuration will be delivered via network download, copied from an image stored in the router's NVRAM memory, or typed in from the terminal. We just as easily could have bypassed the prompt by concatenating the two commands into one command line:

```
MyRouter#config terminal
```

Don't let this throw you: we're not configuring a terminal as IOS's phrasing seems to imply. In IOS command shorthand, **config terminal** means we're "configuring from a terminal." The next step is to "point" at the thing to be configured. We'll configure an interface:

```
MyRouter(config)#interface
% Incomplete command.
```

Instead of asking, "What interface would you like to configure?" IOS cruelly barks back that our command is no good. This is where some user know-how is required:

```
MyRouter(config)#interface tokenring1
MyRouter(config-if)#
```

IOS wanted to know what physical interface module was to be configured. Told that port number 1 of the Token Ring interface module was the one to be configured, the IOS prompt changes to MyRouter(config-if)#, where the "if" is shorthand for "interface." (Configuration modes will be covered later in this chapter.)

NOTE: Always keep track of the device you're pointing at when configuring. The IOS config prompt is generic and doesn't tell you at which network interface the (config-if)# prompt is pointed. IOS does not insert the interface's name into the prompt.

Once pointed at the network interface to be configured, from there router configuration is simply a matter of supplying IOS the configuration parameters for that interface, which we'll cover in a few pages.

An understanding of how IOS syntax works, combined with the help system, is enough for anyone to begin entering correct command lines—with some time and hard work, of course.

Command Completion

Sooner or later you'll encounter IOS command lines filled with seemingly cryptic symbols. Don't be intimidated by them; they are only commands that expert users have truncated (cut off at the end) to speed the process of typing commands—and maybe to impress people a bit. IOS is like DOS and most other editors in that it will accept truncated commands. But if the truncated command is not a string of letters unique to the command set, it will generate an error message. For example, if you type the first two letters of a command that another command starts with, you'll get an error message, such as the following:

```
Router#te
% Ambiguous command:   "te"
```

This error is displayed because IOS has three commands beginning with the letter string *te*: **telnet**, **terminal**, and **test**. If the intent was to Telnet somewhere, one more character will do the job:

```
Router>>tel
Host:
```

NOTE: If you run across a truncated command you don't understand, simply look it up by using word help in the online help system. Type in the truncated command followed immediately by a question mark. Unlike command-syntax help, when using word help no space should precede the **?** command.

Recalling Command History

IOS keeps a running record of recently entered commands. Being able to recall commands is useful for:

- ▼ Avoiding having to type commands that are entered repeatedly
- ▲ Avoiding having to remember long, complicated command lines

The history utility will record anything you enter, even bad commands. The only limit is the amount of buffer memory you dedicate to keeping the history. Here's an example:

```
Router#show history
  test
  tel
  exit
  enable
```

More recently entered commands are toward the top of **show history** lists. They are not listed in alphabetical order.

Arrow keys can also be used to display prior commands. Using arrow keys saves having to enter the **show history** command, but only shows prior commands one at a time. Press the UP ARROW (or CTRL-P) to recall the most recent commands first. If you're already somewhere in the sequence of prior commands, press the DOWN ARROW (or CTRL-N) to recall the least recent commands first.

Overview of Router Modes

Cisco routers can be in any one of seven possible operating modes, as illustrated in Figure 5-6. Three of them are startup modes. In the other four, network administrators are in either User EXEC mode or Privileged EXEC (enable) mode. You must go through the password prompt in User EXEC to enter Privileged EXEC. Once inside Privileged EXEC, configuration changes can be made either to the entire device or to a specific network interface.

You must keep track of what router mode you are in at all times. Many IOS commands will execute only from a specific mode. As can be seen in Figure 5-6, router modes get more specific—and powerful—as the user traverses toward the center of IOS. It pays to keep an eye on IOS prompts because they'll always tell you which mode you're in.

Three Types of Operating Modes

Cisco router operating modes exist to perform three general tasks:

▼ Boot a system

■ Define what commands can be used

▲ Specify which part(s) of the router will be affected by changes made to the config file

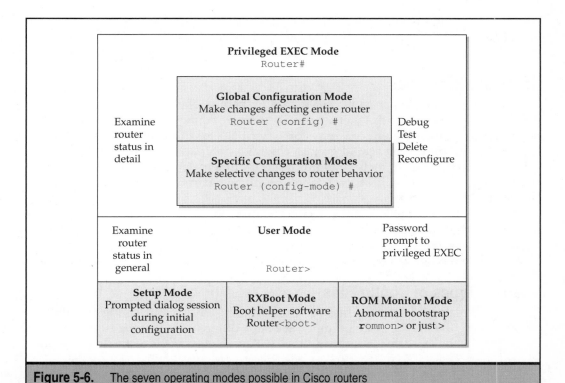

Figure 5-6. The seven operating modes possible in Cisco routers

Mode Type	Purpose
Boot	*Setup mode* is used to make a basic working configuration file.
	RXBoot mode assists router boot to rudimentary state when a working IOS image can't be found in Flash memory.
	ROM monitor mode is used by the router if the IOS image can't be found or the normal boot sequence was interrupted.
User	*User EXEC mode* is the first "room" one enters after login; it restricts users to examining router status.
	Privileged EXEC mode is entered using an Enable password; it allows users to change the config file, erase memory, and so on.
Configuration	*Global config mode* changes parameters for all interfaces.
	Config-command mode "targets" changes at specific interfaces.

Table 5-1. Three General Kinds of IOS Software Modes

Table 5-1 outlines the various IOS modes and what they are used for. As you become more familiar with Cisco internetworking in general, and the IOS software in particular, you will see that most of the action takes place inside the various configuration modes.

Configuration Modes

Configuration modes differ from user modes by nature. The two EXEC modes define what level of IOS commands you may use. By contrast, configuration modes are used to target specific network interfaces—physical or virtual—to which a configuration change applies. For example, you would go into configure interface mode—identified by the (config-if)# prompt—in order to configure a specific Ethernet interface module. There are eight configuration modes in all, each targeting different parts of the configuration file, as enumerated in Table 5-2.

A look at Table 5-2 tells you that configuration mode is all about instructing IOS on what to do with packets flowing through the device. Some modes apply to packets flowing through specific connection points such as interfaces, lines, and ports. The other IOS configuration modes deal with routing protocols and tables needed to handle that flow.

The Two Types of Config Files

There are two types of config files for every router: the running-config file and the startup-config file. As their names imply, the basic difference is that the running-config file is "live" in the sense that its image is in RAM. Any changes made to the running-config

Configuration Mode	Router Port Targeted	Applies to
Global	Router(config)#	Entire config file
Interface	Router(config-if)#	Interface module (physical)
Subinterface	Router(config-subif)#	Subinterface (virtual)
Controller	Router(config-controller)#	Controller (physical)
Line	Router(config-line)#	Terminal lines (console, aux, or virtual)
Router	Router(config-router)#	IP routing (protocol)
IPX-Router	Router(config-ipx-router)#	IPX routing (protocol)
Route-Map	Router(config-route-map)#	Routing tables

Table 5-2. Config Modes and the Parts of the Router Targeted

file go into effect immediately. The startup-config file is stored in the router's NVRAM, where the IOS bootstrap program goes to fetch the router's running configuration parameters when starting up.

The **copy** command is used to save and distribute config file changes. As can be seen at the bottom of Figure 5-7, a master config file can be distributed to other routers via a TFTP server.

ESSENTIAL ROUTER COMMANDS

A few major root commands handle most tasks associated with configuring routers. They include the following:

▼ **show** Examine router status.

■ **configure** Make changes to config file parameters.

■ **no** Negate a parameter setting.

▲ **copy** Put config file changes into effect.

The **show** command is the bread-and-butter command of IOS. It's used to examine nearly everything about a router. The following example shows who's logged into the router, which is moment-to-moment information:

```
Router>>show users
   Line      User      Host(s)          Idle Location
*  2 vty 0             idle                00:00:00
```

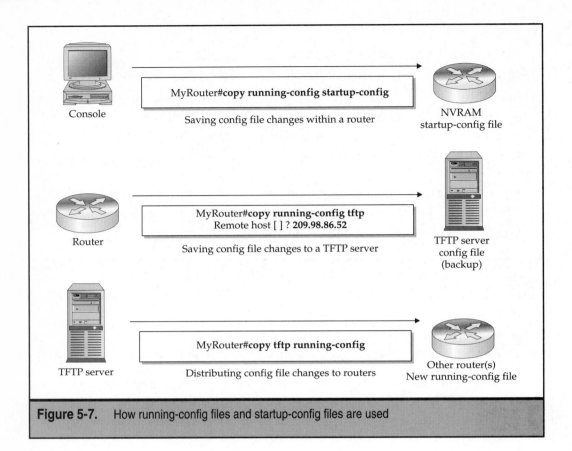

Figure 5-7. How running-config files and startup-config files are used

The **show** command can also be used to show information that might change once every year or so, such as the version of IOS software installed:

```
MyRouter>>show version
Cisco Internetwork Operating System Software
IOS (tm) 4500 Software (C4500-J-M), Version 11.2(15a), RELEASE
 SOFTWARE (fc1)
Copyright (c) 1986-1998 by Cisco Systems, Inc.
Compiled Mon 24-Aug-98 01:47 by amarie
Image text-base: 0x600088A0, data-base: 0x607C4000

ROM: System Bootstrap, Version 5.2(7b) [mkamson 7b], RELEASE SOFTWARE
 (fc1)
BOOTFLASH: 4500 Bootstrap Software (C4500-BOOT-M), Version 10.3(7)
 .
 .
 .
```

The **no** command is used to reverse an existing parameter setting. For example, if we turned on IP accounting for Token Ring port number 1 and now want to turn it off, we point to that interface in configure interface mode—indicated by the MyRouter(config-if)# prompt—and then simply precede the command used to turn it on (**ip accounting**) with the **no** command, as shown here:

```
MyRouter(config-if)#no ip accounting
```

Any IOS command can be turned off using the **no** command syntax.

Knowing how to navigate within an operating system environment is always half the battle. This is especially so in command-line interfaces because there are no graphical icons to show the way. Table 5-3 lists commands used to move around within the IOS environment.

"Hot key" commands are useful because some config-file command lines can get long and complicated.

STEP-BY-STEP ROUTER CONFIGURATION

A router can be configured by one of the following:

▼ Entering changes directly to a router's running-config file

■ Downloading a new config file from a TFTP server

▲ Setting up the config file from scratch

Command	Purpose
Enable	Move from User EXEC to Privileged EXEC mode.
Disable	Return to User EXEC mode from Privileged EXEC mode.
Exit	Exit configuration mode or terminate a login session.
CTRL-A	Move to the start of a command line.
CTRL-B	Move backward one character position.
CTRL-F	Move forward one character position.
CTRL-Z	Exit or quit a process (such as a login or a multipage display).
ESC-B	Move to the beginning of the prior word (good for making corrections).
ESC-F	Move to the beginning of the next word.

Table 5-3. IOS Navigation Commands

The best way to learn how to configure a router is to set one up from scratch. We'll step through setup mode here, not because the procedure is performed that often, but because it's an excellent way to review the fundamentals of router configuration.

Setup Mode

Setup is run to get the router up to a basic level of operation. If the device is new (and therefore has never been configured) or the config file in NVRAM has been corrupted, the IOS software defaults into setup mode to rebuild the config file from scratch. Once that's accomplished, setup mode can be exited and the router rebooted in normal IOS mode, whereupon a complete config file can be built. Setup mode doesn't run by itself; a network administrator must be present to respond to setup's long sequence of questions about how to configure the router. Also, given that the router isn't configured, you cannot run setup via a network connection. Setup must be run through either the console or AUX port.

A router doesn't have to be new or corrupted to run setup. Setup can also be useful in non-emergency situations. Network administrators sometimes use setup when a config file has become so jumbled that it makes more sense to start anew—sort of like a blank sheet of paper. Used in this way, the parameter settings given as answers during a setup session overwrite the existing config file.

Setup mode is entered using the **setup** command. But before starting, hook your PC's COM port to the router's console port. Then start whatever terminal emulator software you prefer to use (remember, you'll be logged into the router's operating system, not your PC). The following instructions assume you're running on a Microsoft Windows PC. If you're not, you'll need to know how to start your terminal emulator. This shouldn't be a problem, because if you're running Apple, you're a survivor; if you're running X-Windows from a UNIX computer, you don't need our advice on such a trifling technical issue in the first place:

1. Click the Start button.
2. Select Programs | Accessories | Communications | HyperTerminal.
3. A HyperTerminal window will open, with a blinking cursor in the upper-left corner.
4. Press ENTER, and you should be looking at the router's prompt.
5. Go into Privileged EXEC mode by entering **enable** and then the Enable Secret password (**setup** is essentially a configuration command, and config files cannot be modified from the user EXEC level of IOS).
6. Type **setup**, and setup mode is started.

Once setup is started, a banner appears with command instructions, an option to quit, and an option to review a summary of the interface modules on the router. Figure 5-8 shows the System Configuration Dialog banner.

If you decide to proceed, setup starts by configuring global parameters. This is basic information, such as giving the router a name and passwords. If it's a new router or the

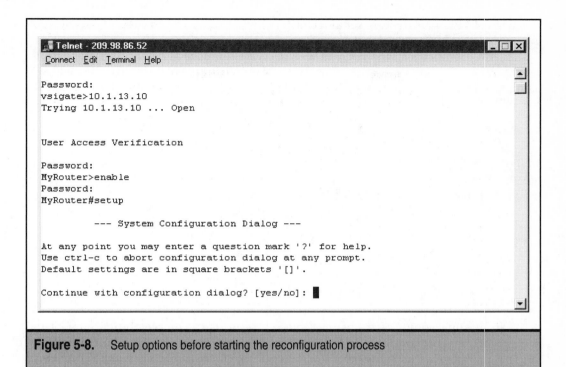

Figure 5-8. Setup options before starting the reconfiguration process

config file in NVRAM has been corrupted, you must enter new parameters for these things, as shown in the following:

```
Configuring global parameters:

  Enter host name [MyRouter]: MyRouter

The enable secret is a one-way cryptographic secret used
instead of the enable password when it exists.

  Enter enable secret [<use current secret>]: test

The enable password is used when there is no enable secret
and when using older software and some boot images.

  Enter enable password [02101752]: test1
  Enter virtual terminal password [02101752]: test1
```

Once the fundamentals are covered, setup takes you through a list of protocols that you might want to globally configure. This gives a picture of the protocols supported in the IOS feature set on our example router. If, for example, this router had an image of the

Enterprise/APPN IOS feature set in its flash memory, setup would present a list including many IBM SNA protocols at this point.

Several prompts ask whether you want to configure legacy protocols. For example, LAT (local area terminal) is an old-time protocol for wiring terminals into a DECnet LAN using terminal servers. In today's world, the protocols you're most likely to use are IP, Novell IPX, AppleTalk, and VINES, in about that order.

```
Configure LAT? [no]:
  Configure AppleTalk? [no]:
  Configure DECnet? [no]:
  Configure IP? [yes]:
    Configure IGRP routing? [yes]:
      Your IGRP autonomous system number [1]:
  Configure CLNS? [no]:
  Configure IPX? [no]:
  Configure Vines? [no]:
  Configure XNS? [no]:
  Configure Apollo? [no]:
  Configure bridging? [no]:
```

If an existing config file is being replaced, setup isn't completely ignorant of the router's current configuration. In the preceding example, you can see from the **[yes]** default prompts that setup senses that the pre-existing global config file is configured with IP using the IGRP routing protocol configured to use the IGRP autonomous system number 1. If, however, the router were new or the existing config file had been corrupted, no pre-existing parameter settings would be sensed, and all prompts would have **[no]** as the default. (Don't sweat the IGRP terminology here; we'll cover it in Chapter 14.)

After these global configuration parameters are done, setup turns to interface-specific configuration and begins prompting for settings for specific interface modules.

Looking at the following example, setup automatically detects interface modules physically present in the router's slots. One by one, it asks whether each "interface is in use," as shown in the following example. Don't be confused by the phrase "in use" here. It doesn't mean whether a cable is attached to the port; it means whether the port's administrative status setting is turned on inside the config file.

```
Configuring interface Serial1:
  Is this interface in use? [no]:

Configuring interface Serial2:
  Is this interface in use? [no]:

Configuring interface Serial3:
  Is this interface in use? [no]:

Configuring interface TokenRing0:
  Is this interface in use? [no]:
```

```
Configuring interface TokenRing1:
  Is this interface in use? [yes]:
  Tokenring ring speed (4 or 16) ? [16]:
```

By answering yes to any of these prompts currently showing a **[no]** default answer, you are opting to change that parameter setting from being "administratively down" to online. The last prompt in the preceding example is for the router's second Token Ring port, which is administratively up. This demonstrates that setup can sense not only presence and up/down status but also interface settings (for Token Ring speed, in this case), which it senses as being set to 16 Mbps.

NOTE: The reason interfaces are set to administratively down is that if you leave one administratively up but physically unused, IOS will sense that it's not signaling and assume there's a problem with it. This will cause the router to repeatedly generate alerts of the apparent error until the interface port is either reset to administratively down or properly cabled so it can begin signaling.

When an interface is detected, setup wants its parameters to be set:

```
Is this interface in use? [yes]:
  Tokenring ring speed (4 or 16) ? [16]:
  Configure IP on this interface? [yes]:
    IP address for this interface [10.1.13.1]: 10.1.13.254
    Number of bits in subnet field [0]:
```

Parameters are changed by simply typing in a new value instead of taking the default with a carriage return. In the preceding example, the IP address of Token Ring interface number one was changed from 10.1.13.1 to 10.1.13.254.

When all the interfaces have been dealt with, setup will present the user with a "script" recapping the router's new config file, including any changes, and then ask you whether to go ahead and put the just-completed config file into force.

```
Use this configuration? [yes/no]: yes
Building configuration...
```

If you go ahead, setup then takes a few seconds to "build" the config file (as we said earlier, config files are not edited interactively, like a word processor file). Once the build is done, you're delivered to IOS in "normal mode," and advised that if you want to continue configuring, you must do so using the **config** command:

```
[OK]
```

Once the setup session is done, a basic configuration file has been created. From there you would follow normal procedure and use the **configure** command to input a complete configuration file.

Giving a Router an Identity

Taking the time to name and document each router properly helps make networks easier to manage. Identifying information can be assigned by:

▼ Giving the router a meaningful name

■ Individually documenting router interfaces

▲ Putting a message of the day (MOTD) on the router

You will frequently see the example name "Router" used in configuration examples. Don't let that confuse you; "Router" is not a mandatory part of the Cisco IOS prompt. A router could just as easily be named "MainOffice" or "R23183" or anything else. Routers should be given meaningful names that inform network administrators where the router is and what it does. You must be in global configuration mode and use the **hostname** command to change the device name, as shown here:

```
Router(config)#hostname MyRouter
MyRouter(config)#
```

Because the new name was input into the running-config file, the new router name MyRouter is used immediately in the next command prompt. However, unless you use the **write** or **copy** command to store the new name (or any other change) in NVRAM, if the router were rebooted, IOS would come back up using the old name.

NOTE: The term "host" can confuse computer industry veterans new to internetworking. In the computer applications world, a host is a full-fledged computer system acting as a server, and network devices are nodes. In the internetworking context, host can mean any networked device, including routers, switches, and access servers, in addition to servers. We try to keep all this clear by referring only to computers as "hosts" and calling network equipment "devices"—but beware, the term "host" can take on different meanings in internetworking documents.

A router interface can be specifically documented using the **description** command. Using descriptions is a great way to keep track of the network (and users) serviced by an interface. This may not sound like much, but big networks have thousands of interfaces, and they are reconfigured frequently. To enter an interface-specific description, you must first go to that interface—in this example, TokenRing0:

```
MyRouter(config)#interface TokenRing0
MyRouter(config-if)#
```

Then enter the **description** command followed by the description:

```
MyRouter(config-if)#description Token Ring for finance department
MyRouter(config-if)#
```

Descriptions can be up to 80 characters in length. To close the loop, the description can be seen in part of the config file for the interface:

```
MyRouter(config-if)#
MyRouter#show running-config
.
.
.
interface TokenRing0
 description TokenRing for finance department
```

Router names and interface descriptions are only seen by network administrators. A third router identification tool—the message-of-the-day banner—is a way to announce information to all terminals connected to a router. MOTD banners are a good way to make sure housekeeping announcements are seen by all users on the network. Banners are commonly used to warn against unauthorized use, announce scheduled system downtime, and make other types of announcements. Use the **banner motd** command to put a banner on a router:

```
MyRouter(config)#banner motd $MyRouter will be down tonight$
```

The dollar sign was arbitrarily chosen for use here as the delimiter marking the start and end of the banner message. Any character can be used; just make sure to use a character that will not appear in the banner text itself.

The banner will display whenever someone either logs directly into the router or hits the router from a Web browser:

```
MyRouter will be down tonight
User Access Verification
Password:
```

Fancy multiline banners can be built using extended mode commands for VT terminals. VT is a de facto standard for terminal programming from Digital Equipment Corporation (now part of Compaq Computer).

CAUTION: Do not put any sensitive information in MOTD banners, because anybody can see them. In addition, there could be legal implications if a "Welcome to..." message greets a hacker who is breaking into your network.

Examining Device Status

Examining network interfaces is a basic technique for getting critical status information. The **show interface** command does this. Figure 5-9 shows example output.

Keepalive messages are sent by interfaces to one another at the data link layer to confirm that the virtual circuit between them is still active.

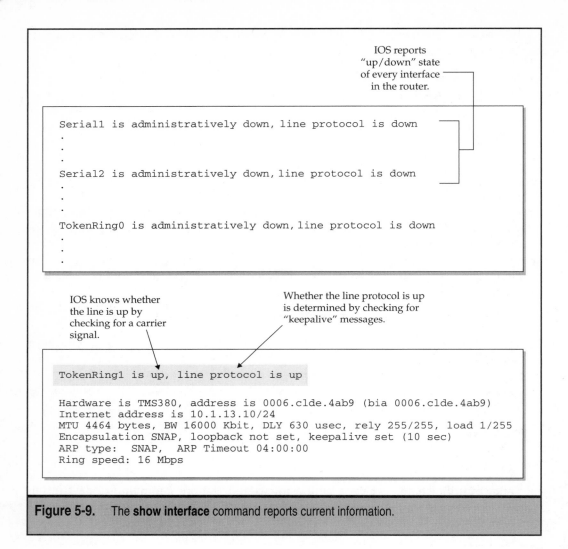

Figure 5-9. The **show interface** command reports current information.

Table 5-4 summarizes what the various status reports mean (using an interface named TokenRing1 as an example).

Cisco Discovery Protocol

Cisco has a proprietary troubleshooting tool called the Cisco Discovery Protocol (CDP). It ships with all Cisco equipment, including routers. CDP is used by devices to discover and learn about one another. It is media and protocol independent. Cisco devices use CDP as a way to advertise their existence to neighbors on a LAN or on the far side of a WAN connection. Think of CDP as a sort of "show configuration" command for a neighborhood of Cisco routers and other devices.

Message	Meaning
TokenRing1 is up, line protocol is up	Running OK
TokenRing1 is up, line protocol is down	Interface OK, but no active connection
TokenRing1 is down, line protocol is down	Interface problem
TokenRing1 is administratively down, line protocol is down	Disabled

Table 5-4.   Interface Status Report Definitions

CDP runs at the data link layer in order to be compatible with devices running different network layer protocols (IPX, IP, AppleTalk, and so on). CDP can communicate with any physical media supporting the Subnetwork Access Protocol (SNAP), including LANs, Frame Relay, and ATM media. SNAP is a protocol designed to let devices pass messages within a subnetwork, allowing them to keep track of what's operating in the neighborhood.

CDP is automatic. You can connect any combination of Cisco devices, power them up, stand back, and let them automatically identify one another—even prior to being assigned network addresses. CDP is able to do this using a proprietary standard called the Cisco Proprietary Data-Link Protocol. Figure 5-10 shows how CDP spans otherwise incompatible protocols.

CDP is enabled by default in all Cisco devices. It works by having all Cisco devices in a directly connected network pass CDP frames to one another. The key to understanding CDP's outer limit lies in the words "directly connected." CDP can discover devices beyond a LAN, but only as long as the WAN connection does not go through any non-Cisco (and therefore non-CDP) devices to make the connection. CDP frames must be able to pass through internetwork connections in order to keep extending its map of what's connected to its home LAN.

Use the **show CDP** command to see what its current operating settings are.

```
MyRouter>>show CDP
Global CDP information:
        Sending CDP packets every 60 seconds
        Sending a holdtime value of 180 seconds
```

High-level protocols	TCP/IP Novell AppleTalk DECnet Others IPX
Cisco Proprietary Data-Link Protocol	Discover other Cisco devices, show information about them
SNAP	Ethernet Token Ring ATM Frame Others Relay

Figure 5-10.   CDP bypasses incompatible protocols to keep track of networks.

Asking for command-syntax help for the **show CDP** command displays the kind of information CDP can provide:

```
MyRouter>>show CDP ?
  entry      Information for specific neighbor entry
  interface  CDP interface status and configuration
  neighbors  CDP neighbor entries
  traffic    CDP statistics
  <cr>
```

The most common usage of CDP is probably to show other devices directly connected to the device requesting the CDP information:

```
vsigate>>show cdp neighbors
Capability Codes: R - Router, T - Trans Bridge, B - Source Route
Bridge, S - Switch, H - Host, I - IGMP, r - Repeater

Device ID          Local Intrfce     Holdtme        Capability
Platform           Port ID
tacacsrouter       Tok 0             168            R
4500               Tok 0
Switch.velte.com   Eth 1             129            S
WS-C2924M          Fas 0/1
vsitest7           Tok 1             169            R
RSP2               Tok 6/0
```

To look in greater detail at a specific neighbor, use the **show cdp entry** command:

```
vsigate>>show cdp entry vsitest7
------------------------
Device ID: vsitest7
Entry address(es):
  IP address: 10.1.12.2
Platform: cisco RSP2,  Capabilities: Router
Interface: TokenRing1,  Port ID (outgoing port): TokenRing6/0
Holdtime : 138 sec

Version :
Cisco Internetwork Operating System Software
IOS (tm) RSP Software (RSP-JSV-M), Version 11.2(12a)P, RELEASE
SOFTWARE (fc1)
Copyright (c) 1986-1998 by cisco Systems, Inc.
Compiled Sun 15-Mar-98 22:14 by etleva
```

As you can see, CDP is able to gather fairly detailed configuration information on devices remotely. CDP was designed to be an efficient, low-overhead protocol so as not to gobble precious bandwidth and thereby render Cisco's entire product line slow. Because CDP is proprietary, it is able to gather a lot of information using a tiny amount of overhead. Other tools exist for discovering "locally connected" devices. The SNMP network management tools are great for centralized management, but gather less granular configuration information than CDP can on Cisco devices (SNMP is covered in Chapter 7).

PASSWORD RECOVERY

Sometimes situations occur that make it necessary to recover a router's password. Two of the most common such situations are

▼ A password is forgotten, and a record of it cannot be found.

▲ A router is bought used, and it came with passwords on it.

Password recovery naturally involves somehow getting into the router's configuration file to find the lost password, change it, or erase the entire configuration file and reconfigure the router from scratch.

The trouble is that the configuration file sits inside the Privileged EXEC (enable mode) level of IOS, which itself is password-protected. For that reason, recovering a password means getting to the base level of the IOS software. This is why password recovery procedures are so involved.

There are several procedures for recovering passwords from Cisco routers, depending on whether a Line or Enable password was lost, the model of router hardware, and the version of IOS software. All the procedures involve resetting settings that tell the router how to boot. Older Cisco routers use physical hardware jumpers, so you need to go inside the router box to reset them. Newer Cisco routers have "soft jumpers," called *configuration registers,* where settings can be changed. An example configuration register setting is 0x2102. The first four bits (0–3) are the ones that select the boot mode.

▼　When the four bits are 0000 (0), it indicates the router will enter rommon>> mode upon reboot.

■　When the four bits are 0001 (1), it means the router will boot from the IOS system stored in ROM.

▲　When the four bits are 0010 (2), it indicates the router will look to the configuration file in NVRAM to find which IOS system image to boot from.

Recovering Enable Passwords

Two procedures are used to recover Enable passwords (Enable and Enable Secret). The one to use depends on the router model, and sometimes the CPU or IOS software version the router runs on.

To recover a password, you must get to a base level of IOS: the rommon>> prompt to recover Enable or Enable Secret passwords, and the test-system>> prompt to recover a Line password. This is done by sending a Break signal from the console terminal to the router to interrupt the normal boot process.

NOTE:　The router may not respond to the Break signal sent from PC terminal emulators. You must understand how the terminal emulator you're using generates Break signals. In some emulators, Break is generated with the ALT-B key combination; in others, CTRL-B. Check the help documentation for your emulator if you have problems interrupting the router's boot process with Break.

Getting to the rommon>> Prompt

For either of the two procedures to recover Enable/Enable Secret passwords, the first part—getting to the rommon>> prompt level of IOS—is the same:

1.　Attach a terminal, or a PC running terminal emulation software, to the router's console port using these settings:

■　9600 baud rate

■　No parity

■　1 stop bit

■　No flow control

2. Go to the >> prompt and type the **show version** command. (Remember, you lost either the Enable or Enable Secret password, which only locks you out of enable mode, not out of the IOS entirely.)

```
TN3270 Emulation software.
2 Token Ring/IEEE 802.5 interface(s)
4 Serial network interface(s)
128K bytes of non-volatile configuration memory.
4096K bytes of processor board System flash (Read/Write)
4096K bytes of processor board Boot flash (Read/Write)

Configuration register is 0x2102
```

The last line of the **show version** display is the configuration register. The factory default setting is usually 0x2102; sometimes it is 0x102. Write down the settings in your router for later use.

3. Reboot the router by turning off the power and then turning it back on.

4. Press the BREAK key on the terminal (or combination of keys required to send Break from your terminal emulator) within 60 seconds of having turned the router back on.

5. The rommon>> prompt—without the router's name showing—should appear.

Now that you've gotten to the rommon>> prompt, the battle of password recovery is half won. From this point on, the router model will determine what you need to do to recover the password (in some cases, the IOS version and CPU also come into play). Look at Tables 5-5 and 5-6 to determine which procedure to follow, and pick up step 6 from there.

Recovery Procedure	Platforms Using Procedure 1
Enable Password Recovery Procedure 1	Cisco 2000
	Cisco 2500
	Cisco 3000
	Cisco 4000
	Cisco AccessPro
	Cisco 7000 (RP)
	Cisco AGS
	Cisco IGS
	Cisco STS-10x

Table 5-5. Platforms Using Enable Password Recovery Procedure 1

Recovery Procedure	Platforms Using Procedure 2
Enable Password Recovery Technique 2	Cisco 806
	Cisco 827
	Cisco uBR900
	Cisco 1003
	Cisco 1004
	Cisco 1005
	Cisco 1400
	Cisco 1600
	Cisco 1700
	Cisco 2600
	Cisco 3600
	Cisco 4500
	Cisco 4700
	Cisco AS5x00
	Cisco 6x00
	Cisco 7000 (RSP7000)
	Cisco 7100
	Cisco 7200
	Cisco 7500
	Cisco uBR7100
	Cisco uBR7200
	Cisco uBR10000
	Cisco 12000
	Cisco LS1010
	Catalyst 2948G-L3
	Catalyst 4840G
	Catalyst 4908G-L3
	Catalyst 5500 (RSM)
	Catalyst 8510-CSR
	Catalyst 8510-MSR
	Catalyst 8540-CSR
	Catalyst 8540-MSR

Table 5-6. Platforms Using Enable Password Recovery Procedure 2

Recovery Procedure	Platforms Using Procedure 2
	Cisco MC3810
	Cisco NI-2
	Cisco VG200 Analog Gateway
	Route Processor Module

Table 5-6.   Platforms Using Enable Password Recovery Procedure 2 *(continued)*

Enable Password Recovery Procedure 1   Use this procedure for routers that belong to the Cisco router series listed in Table 5-5 (and its CPU and/or IOS release, if applicable).

1. Type **o/r 0x2142**, then press ENTER at the > prompt. This loads from Flash memory without loading the router's configuration file.

2. Type **i** at the prompt, and then press ENTER.

3. You will be asked a series of setup questions. Answer **no** to each question, or press CTRL-C to skip this sequence altogether.

4. At the Router> prompt, type **enable.**

5. Type **configure memory** or **copy startup-config running-config.** This copies the NVRAM into memory.

6. Enter **write terminal** or **show running-config.** These commands show the router's configuration. This will show that all the interfaces are currently shut down. Additionally, you will see the passwords, either encrypted or unencrypted. Unencrypted passwords can be reused, while encrypted passwords must be changed with a new password.

7. Enter **configure terminal** and make desired changes. Now, the prompt will be **hostname(config)#.**

8. To change a given password, enter **enable secret <password>** to change the enable secret password, for instance.

9. On each interface, enter the **no shutdown** command.

10. Type **config-register 0x2102** (or whatever value you wrote down in step 2).

11. Press CTRL-Z or END to exit configuration mode. The prompt should now be **hostname#.**

12. Enter **write memory** or copy **running-config startup-config** to save your changes.

13. Enter **Reload** to restart the router with the Cisco IOS software booting from Flash memory.

Enable Password Recovery Procedure 2   Use this procedure for routers that belong to the Cisco router series listed in Table 5-6 (and its CPU, if applicable).

1. Enter the **confreg 0x2141** command at the rommon>> prompt. (Note that **confreg** is not a mistyping of **config.** It stands for *configuration register*). When the "do you wish to change configuration?" prompt appears, answer **yes.**

2. Type **reset** at the rommon 2> prompt. The router will reboot, but ignore the saved configuration.

3. A number of setup questions will appear. Enter **no** for each one. Alternatively, you can press CTRL-C to skip the initial setup sequence.

4. Type **enable** at the Router> prompt. This will put you into the enable mode and you'll see the Router# prompt.

5. Enter **configure memory** or **copy startup-config running config.** This copies the nonvolatile RAM into memory.

6. Enter **write terminal** or **show running-config.** These commands show the router's configuration, and will show that all the interfaces are currently shut down. Additionally, you will see the passwords, either encrypted or unencrypted. Unencrypted passwords can be reused; encrypted passwords must be changed with a new password.

7. Enter **configure terminal** and make any desired changes. Now, the prompt will be **hostname(config)#.**

8. To change a given password, enter **enable secret <password>** to change the enable secret password, for instance.

9. On each interface, enter the **no shutdown** command.

10. Type **config-register 0x2102.**

11. Press CTRL-Z or END to exit configuration mode. The prompt should now be **hostname#.**

12. Enter **write memory** or copy **running-config startup-config** to save your changes.

13. Enter **Reload** to restart the router with the Cisco IOS software booting from Flash memory.

Recovering a Line Password

The router must be forced into factory diagnostic mode in order to recover a lost Line password. Refer to the hardware installation/maintenance publication for the router product for specific information on configuring the processor configuration register for factory diagnostic mode. Table 5-7 summarizes the hardware or software settings required by the various products to boot into factory diagnostic mode.

Once the router has been forced into factory diagnostic mode, follow these steps:

1. Answer **yes** when asked if you want to set the manufacturer's addresses. The test-system>> prompt appears.

Recovery Procedure	Platforms Using Procedure
Change the setting to 0x8000 to boot in factory diagnostic mode. Use the **reload** command to restart; then change configuration settings back to 0x2102 when finished.	Cisco AS5100, AS5200, AS5300 Cisco 1600 Series, 2500 Series, 3000 Series, 3600 Series
Set jumper in bit 15 of the configuration register, restart, and reset the jumper when finished.	Modular products

Table 5-7. Configuration Register Settings to Enter Factory Diagnostic Mode

2. Enter the **enable** command to get the test-system>> enable prompt.
3. Type **config term,** and then **show startup-config.** You should now be looking at the system configuration file. Find the password and write it down. Do not attempt to change the password.
4. Restart the router.
5. Use the recovered Line password (the one you wrote down) to log into the router.

Recovering Passwords from Older Cisco Routers

To recover passwords from legacy Cisco routers—and there are millions of them still out there, installed and running—it is necessary to change the configuration register setting using a hardware jumper switch. Those procedures are not covered here. Refer to www.cisco.com to find password recovery procedures for legacy products listed in Table 5-8.

Recovery Procedure	Legacy Cisco Platforms Using Procedures
Technique 3	IG routers running software earlier than Cisco IOS 9.1
Technique 4	CGS, MGS, AGS, AGS+, and any Cisco 70x0 Series running ROMs earlier than Cisco IOS 10.0
Technique 5	500-CS Communication Servers
Technique 6	Cisco 1020

Table 5-8. Cisco's Password Recovery Procedures for Legacy Router Protocols

USING APPLICATIONS TO HELP CONFIGURE ROUTERS

Thus far in this chapter, we've dealt with configuring routers by hand. Cisco makes two software applications to serve as tools:

▼ **ConfigMaker**   A midrange tool that runs on Windows. It's used for configuring Ethernet LANs as well as WAN connectivity, targeted for use by reasonably proficient network managers or consultants.

▲ **Fast Step**   A low-end tool that runs on Windows. It is used to configure and install small Cisco routers and access servers, targeted for use by less sophisticated users.

We'll quickly run through configuring a router using each tool. In doing this, we'll cover some router configuration concepts not discussed during the setup procedure.

Both tools use a graphical user interface to assist with the task of getting routers up and running. Neither tool addresses large or complex internetworking problems. A separate product called NetSys Baseliner is used for enterprise internetwork modeling and management. ConfigMaker and Fast Step are meant for use by intermediates and beginners only.

ConfigMaker

ConfigMaker is a Microsoft Windows–based tool used to design and configure small networks. It works both for LAN configurations and WAN connectivity, with support for a wide range of Cisco devices and protocols. ConfigMaker provides a clean and intuitive desktop work environment that strikes a good balance between ease of use and functionality. But it isn't intended for power users since it has no support for high-end devices such as Cisco 7000 Series routers or high-end switches. Nor does ConfigMaker support the Token Ring LAN protocol or any router utilizing a version of IOS prior to 11.2.

ConfigMaker runs on Windows 98, Windows Me, Windows 2000, Windows XP, or Windows NT 4.0 with at least Service Pack 3. Cisco makes it available at no charge. To try it out, download a copy from Cisco's Web site at www.cisco.com/en/US/products/sw/netmgtsw/ps754/index.html.

For the growing number of technical staff in small- and medium-sized enterprises who want to handle their own network configurations, ConfigMaker is probably the solution—as long as their networks are made up of all or nearly all Cisco devices.

The ConfigMaker Desktop Environment

At the center of ConfigMaker's desktop is a network diagram area into which network "objects" are placed, configured, and linked together. At the outset, the network diagram area is empty, like a sheet of drafting paper before the first line is drawn. The network diagram area is surrounded by three windows, each put there to help you build a network through to completion:

▼ **Device Window**   Source for devices to drag and drop into Network Diagram; located in the upper-left pane.

■ **Connections Window**   Source for wide area network connections to drag and drop into Network Diagram; located in the lower-left pane.

▲ **Cisco ConfigMaker**   Checklist of the chronological steps that must be completed in network configuration, located in the rightmost pane.

The first step is to drag and drop devices from the Device window onto the Network Diagram area. It's a simple proposition; just choose whatever devices are to be part of the network: routers, hubs, LAN cables, and so on. As each device is put into the diagram, ConfigMaker prompts for settings needed to make it functional. The prompt routines are similar to the Add New Hardware routine in the Microsoft Windows Control Panel.

Once the devices have been put into the diagram, it's time to connect them into a network. This is done by dragging one or more connections into the diagram from the Connections window. To connect a device to the network, first click the connection, and then the device to be connected. Figure 5-11 shows the ConfigMaker desktop with the

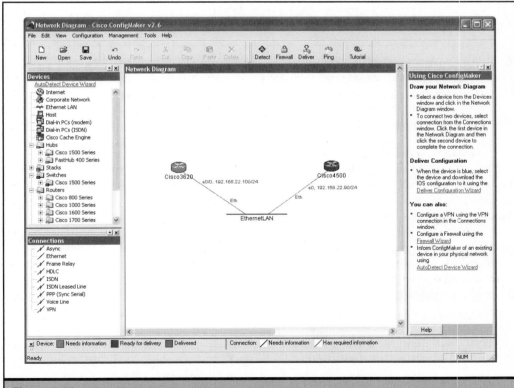

Figure 5-11.   The ConfigMaker desktop

beginnings of an Ethernet network displayed in the network diagram area, with two Cisco routers connected to an Ethernet LAN. The user keeps adding devices and connections until the entire network is depicted in the diagram.

ConfigMaker's Methodology

Building a network through this graphical interface is great for conceptualizing network topology, but ConfigMaker is more than merely a network-diagramming program. Every item put into the diagram drawn in the Device window has intelligence behind it. As each network object (device or network connection) is put in, ConfigMaker asks for line item details such as settings, names, and so on. This information is stored in a database hidden behind the diagram, and is used by ConfigMaker to check for completeness and internal consistency. ConfigMaker enforces a quality assurance methodology over the network design process, as described in the following:

▼ As a device is added to the network, information is collected about it.

■ The information is checked for consistency with the rest of the database.

■ If an error is made, ConfigMaker prompts the user to correct it right away.

▲ ConfigMaker's rules-based logic keeps checking the entire network for correctness as each new object (device or connection) is added.

NOTE: As the perceptive beginner you are, you're probably wondering why Ethernet is in both the Device and Connections windows. If you drag the Ethernet icon from the Device window, it's defined to your diagram as a local area network segment; drag Ethernet from the Connections window, and it becomes a wide area network link. In other words, the Ethernet LAN segment—a cable or a hub box—is treated as a physical device, while the Ethernet connection logically represents an internetwork link.

To see the database kept by ConfigMaker, right-click any device and select Properties. A dialog box with multiple tabs will appear, presenting all the information known about a device. Figure 5-12, for example, shows the hardware configuration tab. The tab's left window contains all the possible modules that can be plugged into the device. The right window shows the current configuration. In this example, the Cisco 4500 is configured with one six-slot Ethernet module and a one-port T1/ISDN module. ConfigMaker has the logic to catch most configuration errors before they happen: the user is prevented from inserting a network module into an incompatible device, and a proper interface must be in a device before it can be connected to the network. Glancing at our example in Figures 5-11 and 5-12, the Cisco 4500 router was allowed to connect to the Ethernet network because it was first configured with its six-port Ethernet interface, and it could also be hooked up to a T1/ISDN connection.

The boxes along the bottom of the ConfigMaker screen (Figure 5-11) make up a legend of color-keyed status conditions (only three colors are shown in Figure 5-11, but there

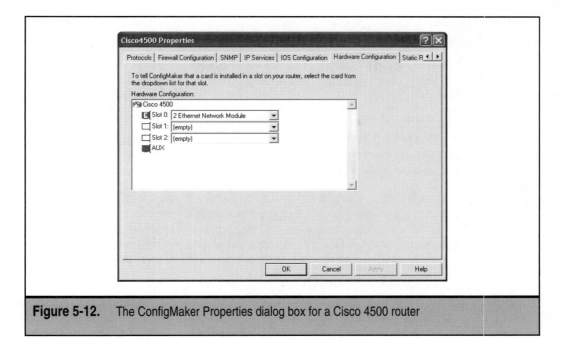

Figure 5-12.   The ConfigMaker Properties dialog box for a Cisco 4500 router

are six colors used). Table 5-9 gives a legend for the color keys. A device icon or connection line will change colors on the screen as the configuration status of the object changes.

Building a Network with ConfigMaker

The Using Cisco ConfigMaker pane is a help system and checklist all in one. Located to the right of the Network Diagram, it uses wizards to guide the user through the major

Color	Configuration Status
Gray	Additional information is needed on the device or connection.
Black	Addresses (IP addresses, submasks, and so on) are needed for the device.
Blue	The device config file is ready for delivery (or the connection has the required information).
Red	The device config file was delivered and encountered an error.
Green	The device config file was delivered successfully.

Table 5-9.   Color Keys that Track Configuration Status

steps of network configuration. The Using Cisco ConfigMaker pane is divided into three parts, two of which contain wizards dedicated to a particular job:

▼ **AutoDetect Device Wizard**   A series of "Add New Hardware" dialog box prompts that gather necessary description and settings information for network devices

■ **Deliver Configurations Wizard**   Automatically downloads config files to devices

▲ **Firewall Wizard**   Allows you to establish firewall policies and determine which LANs can access the Internet or corporate network, as well as which internal LANs can access each other

The AutoDetect Device Wizard   Using the AutoDetect Device Wizard is optional. If you use it, it will automatically sense and identify the type of hardware to be configured. AutoDetect Device is handy if you're configuring devices remotely and aren't there to physically inspect hardware components for model numbers, installed interface modules, and so on. The AutoDetect Device Wizard supports both network and virtual terminal (VTY) connections to the devices being configured.

The Firewall Wizard   The Firewall Wizard is used to configure and define firewall policies. That is, it is a mechanism you can use to decide which LANs can access the Internet and, within a network, which LANs can access each other. This is a useful tool because it allows you to establish policies for each LAN in your network. Figure 5-13 shows the Firewall Wizard screen, where you can set and manage firewall policies.

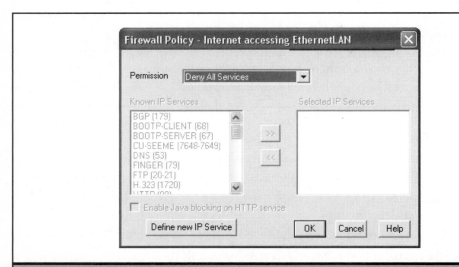

Figure 5-13.   The Firewall Wizard is used to configure firewalls in ConfigMaker.

The Deliver Configuration Wizard   The Deliver Configuration Wizard does just that: It automatically downloads config files created by ConfigMaker into the target devices. To use this, the devices must be connected (via the console port or network) to the PC on which ConfigMaker is running.

ConfigMaker Product Review

An important benefit of ConfigMaker is that users will find it hard to make mistakes. Many configuration mistakes involve wrong choices for particular devices. In ConfigMaker—which is Cisco specific—if you try to put an incompatible device in a particular router, an error message will stop you. If you leave out something necessary, ConfigMaker will prompt you. This capacity for quality assurance not only helps avoid mistakes, but also helps keep the user up-to-date on product options (which change constantly).

Perhaps the most important benefit of ConfigMaker is that you don't need to know the Cisco IOS software command-line interface to be able to configure network devices and connections. When you need to input something, the correct choices are right there in front of you. The Windows-based GUI makes that possible. The use of Windows conventions (the "Add New Hardware" prompts, the menu bar, and so on) and color keys makes it easy to learn and use.

ConfigMaker strikes a good enough balance between capability and ease of use that both nonexperts and those with internetworking expertise can use it. It's a godsend for the uninitiated, not only for getting a network up and running, but also for learning internetworking basics.

ConfigMaker has limits, however. It's not meant for designing and managing large or complicated networks. For example, only routers up through the Cisco 4000 Series are supported, not the high-end router series, and its functionality won't let you simulate network behavior.

Fast Step

Cisco Fast Step is a configuration utility that ships with low-end routers and access servers. It is targeted for use by the novice network user to configure end-to-end connections between a PC and an Internet service provider (ISP) or corporate intranets. Fast Step runs on Microsoft Windows 95, 98, NT 4.0, 2000, or XP. It ships on a CD-ROM for installation on a Windows PC, and can be used two ways:

▼ To configure the router interactively while connected to the router either over a serial cable from its PC COM port to the router console port, or via an Ethernet link

▲ To build a configuration file for later download to the router or as a base to configure other routers (the file can be read by Fast Step's Setup Wizard)

After installing Fast Step, clicking the icon starts a sequence of dialog boxes prompting the user to input the information needed to configure and install the router. The sequence can go over a dozen dialog boxes, depending on the options taken. To help sort things out, every Fast Step screen has a Tasks window on the left side. You can see where you are in the process by finding which task is highlighted in the Task window on the left side of any Fast Step screen. As outlined in Table 5-10, Fast Step groups configuration tasks into four major steps.

Find and Connect

Fast Step starts by asking for general information about the configuration session, such as the model of the router to be configured and whether a new config file is to be created or a preconfigured file will be used.

Then more specific information is requested. Fast Step asks you to enter the PPP (Point-to-Point Protocol) username issued to you by the ISP or your corporate intranet administrator. The PPP username is case sensitive, so be sure to type it in exactly as it appears on the information given by your ISP or network administrator.

Next, enter your PPP password. This isn't your network login password. The PPP password is only for dial-in remote access over a router-to-router connection. Be sure that the password complies with the requirements set by your ISP or corporate network (minimum number of characters, and so on). This password is sometimes called a "PAP" or "CHAP" password and is also case sensitive. Last, enter the central router or PPP name of the router to which you'll be connecting (not the name of the router you're configuring). PPP, CHAP, and PAP are covered in Chapter 8.

Step	Description of Tasks
Find and Connect	Provide router number; select setup mode (interactive or download); define connection type (ISP or corporate); give settings; access provider IP address and phone numbers, username, password, and so on
Security	Specify router name, router read-only password, and router Enable Secret password; specify the types of services (Web server, mail server, FTP server)
Local Addressing	Specify IP address for LAN connection provided by ISP or corporate intranet
Setup and Test	Save config file to router and run, save config file for use with other routers

Table 5-10.   Fast Step Divides Configuration Tasks into Four Parts

The second half of the Find and Connect step is to provide the information and settings needed to hook the router up to the Internet. To do this, Fast Step prompts for more involved parameters such as switch type, ISDN SPIDs, and access phone numbers. (SPID stands for service provider ID, usually an ISP.)

Then things get really involved—at least by a beginner's standards. Figure 5-14 shows Fast Step prompting for IP address information.

Only one of the three options can be taken:

▼   Don't provide any address because you don't have them yet.

■   Give a range of addresses provided to you by your ISP or corporate network administrator.

▲   Give an IP network address and subnet mask.

This information is meant to identify the LAN segment the user will be connected to with an address unique to the Internet. Fast Step needs this information to make the connection to the Internet. These settings are, in essence, the user's address as it is presented to the rest of the Internet (or corporate intranet community). Fast Step can automatically discover the address but lets the user input it directly if desired.

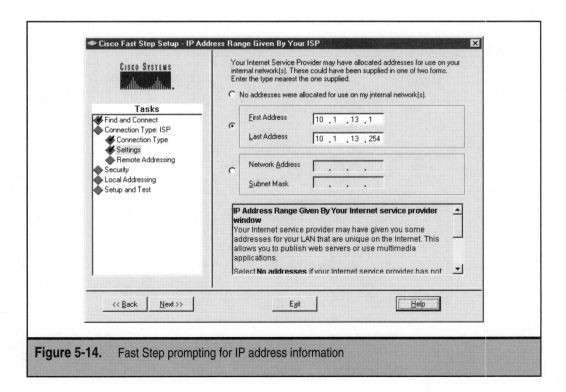

Figure 5-14.   Fast Step prompting for IP address information

Security

Fast Step next asks for parameters having to do with router security and router server publishing. Figure 5-15 shows the user being prompted to give the router a name, a read-only password, and an enable password.

A number of rules apply to the names and passwords here—violate one and an error message stops you. The online help system tells the user what the rules are. These passwords apply to gaining access to the router itself for administrative purposes. Fast Step then lets the user configure one or all of four Internet services options:

▼ Single Server (both a Web server and mail server—the most common option)

■ Web server (a Web page but with no e-mail service)

■ Mail server (only Internet e-mail services)

▲ FTP server (the ability for Internet users to download information from your site)

Internetworking pros often call these options "servers." For example, if the parameter to offer FTP downloads from the user's LAN was set to yes, that LAN is running an FTP server. Don't be put off by this; it's just a fancy term for a service.

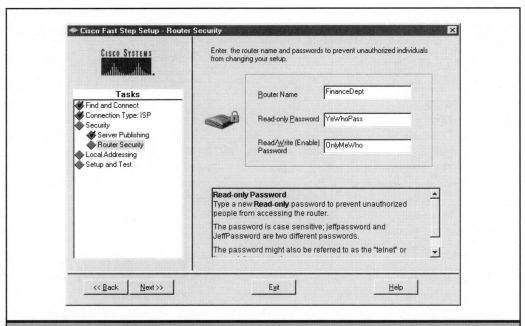

Figure 5-15. Fast Step prompts for a router name and administrative passwords.

Local Addressing

Finally, Fast Step prompts for the IP addresses of the wide area network to which the user's LAN is connected. These addresses, shown in Figure 5-16, identify the ISP or corporate network on the Internet.

Looking at Figures 5-14 and 5-16, we see that Fast Step wants two sets of addresses, which are used to identify two separate network segments to be involved in connecting the user's remote LAN to the Internet. This can confuse the beginner. Keep in mind here that the router will connect to the ISP/intranet by way of a point-to-point, router-to-router connection—not over some nebulous Internet IP address. The address information provided in Figure 5-14 is used to identify the router being configured using Fast Step. This router is what connects the user's LAN to the Internet. Because that LAN will presumably have more than one user operating on the Internet at any given time, Fast Step asked for a range of IP addresses—one per user (Figure 5-14). On the other hand, the *remote* address prompted for in Figure 5-16 will be used to identify the network segment identifying the ISP/intranet through which the user will connect.

Figure 5-17 helps sort out these addresses. The LAN local to the user (and the router being configured using Fast Step here) is usually issued a block of IP addresses. The example in Figure 5-14 has a block of 254 addresses issued for the user's internal network (10.1.13.1–10.1.13.254, inclusive).

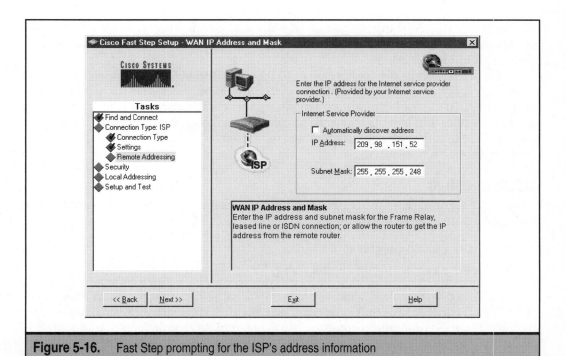

Figure 5-16. Fast Step prompting for the ISP's address information

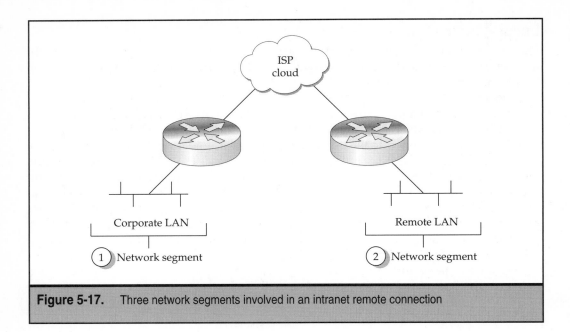

Figure 5-17.   Three network segments involved in an intranet remote connection

The ISP or corporate intranet has an IP address to identify its network segment, and a subnet mask for that IP address—255.255.255.248—allows for up to six possible host addresses within that subnetwork.

If the scenario calls for hooking up to a corporate intranet, a third network segment comes into play: the corporation's main network segment, which is on the left side of Figure 5-17. To the user configuring the router, the internetwork cloud in the middle is the same service whether the connection is made through a private corporate network or an ISP, and the corporate network segment on the left side likely can be reached only by passing through a firewall.

Setup and Test

In the last part of the configuration, Fast Step lets you complete the router configuration process by doing one of the following:

▼   Loading the config file into the router

▲   Making a separate copy of the config file

If the user opts to make a separate copy, the file must, of course, be given a name. The choice exists either to save the file as is in Fast Step's CFG format for use on other routers, or save it in IOS command format for use as a template from which to build slightly different config files for other routers. Here's the top portion of a Cisco 801 router config file created using Fast Step:

```
! Cisco IOS router configuration file
! Automatically made by Cisco Fast Step v2.0
! Designed for Cisco C801
! March 31, 1999
! Cisco Fast Step Template

no service udp-small-servers
no service tcp-small-servers
service password-encryption
hostname veltepub003
username tonyv password Password
enable secret SuperSecret
no ip source-route
isdn switch-type basic-5ess
.
.
.
```

Fast Step Product Review

Fast Step's series of dialog boxes prompt the user to give all the information required to configure an end-to-end connection between a home or small office PC and an ISP (or corporate intranet). That's good because, like it or not, network configurations can get complicated.

Compared to ConfigMaker, the prompts leave more room for omission and error. This is largely because Fast Step's job is different from ConfigMaker's. For example, to decide which interface to configure into a slot in a Cisco router, ConfigMaker gives you a window containing only interfaces compatible with the router being configured. By contrast, Fast Step asks mostly for open-ended answers that come from outside sources—rather than providing an input selection window inside the Fast Step screen. The user must refer to outside documents for such things as phone numbers, control numbers, usernames, IP addresses, and so on. Cisco knows this, which is why they provide worksheets in the Quick Start Guide to help users gather required configuration parameters before starting.

Extensive input edits are in force throughout Fast Step. This helps the user catch mistakes as they happen. If the user tries to input something illegal, an exclamation point will appear to the right of the field, and an error message will appear in the prompt box. The edits can be both a blessing and a curse. For example, if you try to input a bad PPP password, the prompt box informs you that it "does not meet the accepted rules." Fair enough, but what *are* the rules? Push the Help button, and your answer is "Password is a login password given to you by your Internet service provider or network administrator," when what you really need to know is what the syntax rules are. The Fast Step help subsystem is generally good, but at times uneven.

However, with Fast Step's prompts and abundant choices, as well as a little effort, a novice can configure and install a low-end router to the Internet. Without Fast Step, a layperson would have little chance of configuring and rolling out a router. Fast Step may not be perfect, but it gives you more than a fighting chance.

CHAPTER 6

Switches

The two previous chapters discussed routers, which operate between networks. An internetwork is, by definition, a collection of local area networks connected by routers. In other words, a packet that has to traverse one or more routers has traveled across an internetwork. Eventually that packet will arrive at the destination network—home of the destination IP address.

But what then? At that juncture, the message has gotten past the last router and must worm its way through the destination network's wiring. In other words, it must drop out of the internetwork cloud and look not for yet another router interface, but for the specific connection port into which the destination host is plugged. Since most PCs and servers do not have network connections directly to a router, there is one last leg of the journey.

So, they don't have their own router ports. Well, hosts—PCs and servers, for example—need to hook up to networks somehow. The router is designed to connect networks to other networks, so it is of little use when it comes to physically connecting hosts. That's where switches come in. Switches provide local connectivity to hosts, and are the building blocks with which LANs are pieced together.

The last leg of a message's journey takes place inside a building or within an office campus. Here, the transition must be made from the internetworking cloud's telecom lines, down into the cabling strung through the walls and ceilings of the building, all the way out to a wall plate, and finally to the host device itself. This final stage requires making the transition to the destination host's physical address. This address is called the media access control address, or MAC for short. The IP address gets you to the neighborhood, while the MAC address gets you to the front door of the house. MAC addresses, which are always unique, identify the actual NIC (network interface card) connecting the destination device to its LAN. They serve as a kind of serial number for a physical device, so any device on any network in the world can be uniquely identified.

But a one-step shift from a worldwide IP address down to an individual host's MAC address would be too abrupt. There needs to be an intermediary step separating the high-speed router level from slow-speed NICs. Having no buffer zone would, in effect, put side-street traffic onto the interstate highway. Even if NICs and hosts were lightning fast, a middle level would still be necessary just to make things manageable. A switch provides that intermediary step. Figure 6-1 shows where they fit in.

In this chapter, we delve into that local zone sitting between the desktop and the router that links it to the LAN. This is the realm of cables and connectors. We realize eyes tend to glaze over when talk turns to cable plants and patch panels, as if these things are for some reason best left to the building janitor, but the subject of local connectivity is not as mundane as you might think. As high-tech networking equipment inches outward from the backbone toward the desktop, deciding how to connect individual hosts and workgroups has become strategic to the big picture of enterprise internetworking. Technology advances are happening quickly in the field of local connectivity. Thus, it's important that you understand the basics of this subject area, including some specifics on how Cisco switches work.

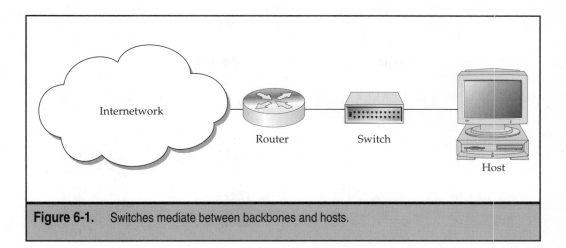

Figure 6-1. Switches mediate between backbones and hosts.

NETWORK TOPOLOGIES

The physical layout of a network is referred to as its *topology*. Twenty or so years ago, there was little if any choice in designing a network's topology.

To build a LAN, you ran a fat coaxial cable called a *Thicknet* through your building and tapped hosts directly into it. The Thicknet cable was the network backbone. Connecting hosts directly to the network backbone resulted in a so-called bus topology. A *bus* is a cable (or a printed circuit board acting like a cable), and a bus topology is where most or all of a network's devices are connected to a single cable—which is like having everybody's driveway empty into one major thoroughfare instead of side streets. Two typical early network topologies are depicted in Figure 6-2.

As network technology developed, topologies evolved a bit with the introduction of terminal servers, which made it possible to indirectly connect dumb terminals to the LAN. This was a good thing because it gave individual users easy access to more than one minicomputer or mainframe. Another advance was the introduction of a thinner kind of coaxial cable called *Thinnet*, which was cheaper and far easier to work with than Thicknet cabling. But these improvements were only incremental; network layouts were still basically a bus topology.

The trouble with bus topologies was that if something failed along the trunk, the whole network went down (or at least a big part of it). Another drawback was that connecting hosts meant crawling into the ceiling plenum, finding the trunk cable, making the tap, dropping a second cable from the tap down to the device, and then testing the connection to see if it worked. Not only were early networks prone to failure and hard to install, but the equipment was also bulky and expensive.

Things have changed a lot since then. Nowadays, most hosts are connected to networks through switches. Switches give network administrators more choices in both the physical and logical layout of networks. They are modular in the sense that devices and

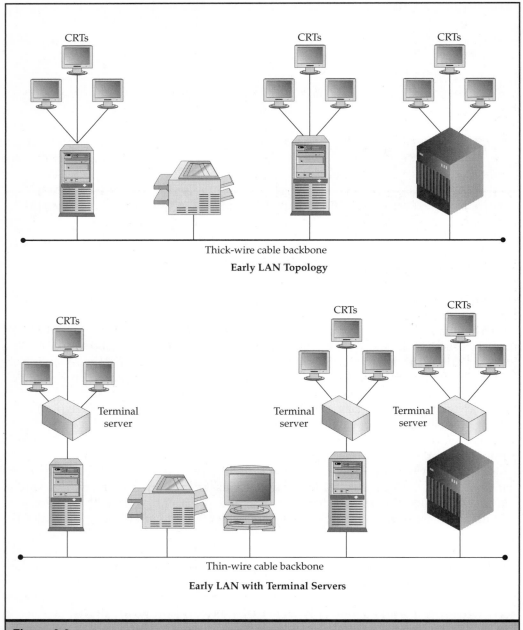

Figure 6-2.   A look at early network topologies

hosts can be added without having to change anything on the network backbone. But above all, switches do away with bus topologies by allowing the easy installation and management of multiple LANs. Today, network designers use star topologies in place of one overtaxed LAN.

> **NOTE:**   The term "LAN" can be confusing. In the old days, a LAN was a central trunk running through a building with everything on the network connected directly to it. Today, that same building might have dozens of switches serving as host connection points, with the switches in turn connected to a backbone. Any shared network medium is a LAN. A switch is a shared medium, and so is the backbone's central trunk cable. Even experts use the term "LAN," or "local area network," to loosely describe a local network comprised of multiple LANs. To avoid confusion, in this book we use the term "LAN segment" to describe a shared network medium, which is the basic building block of network topologies. A LAN segment is defined by a switch, or cable. Nowadays, the term "LAN" most often refers to a collection of LAN segments within a building or campus.

Breaking things up into smaller LANs makes it easier to meet current needs and still leave room for future change and growth. Network segmentation improves network performance by isolating traffic. Users within a workgroup or department are most likely to send messages to one another, so putting them on their own LAN segment means others won't get caught in their traffic. Reliability is better because what happens on one LAN segment doesn't affect the overall network; the fault is isolated within the segment where the trouble started. Network administrators can better identify where the trouble is because of the transition points between LAN segments—an important feature in complicated networks. Also, the modularity of hierarchical networks naturally enhances security and manageability because devices can be grouped in ways that best fit management needs.

For all these reasons, networks today use switches to concentrate multiple hosts into a single network connection point—an approach called the *star configuration.* Star configurations are the building blocks with which hierarchical networks are constructed. Figure 6-3 shows common variations on the basic star topology.

In stark contrast to the bad old days of trunk pulling and cable dropping, connecting a host to a network now is as simple as plugging in a phone-style jack. Each star-topology building block meets certain needs:

▼   A small business or department might use just one switch to form a LAN—in effect putting the entire network inside a box—which is called a *single-star topology.* With switches, backbone cabling is no longer necessary to form small networks.

▲   A *star-hierarchy topology* is used to make more connection ports available within an office. Plugging outlying switches into a master switch gives more hosts a place to plug in without having to pull additional cable into the area.

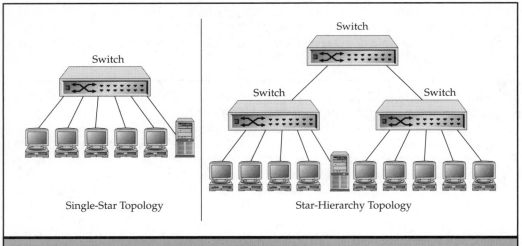

Figure 6-3.   The star topology is the network's basic building block.

NOTE: The terms "backbone" and "central trunk" evoke the image of a single, unbroken span of cable. In reality, most backbones are made up of many cable spans spliced together. At the other extreme, some backbones aren't made up of cable at all, but instead are contained inside a box entirely on circuit boards, which is called a collapsed backbone. By definition, though, a backbone is the part of a network that acts as the primary path routing traffic between LAN segments. In general, only switches and routers are connected directly to backbones. In large networks, a backbone usually runs at a higher speed than the LAN segments it connects.

The topology of a network is, of course, most closely tied to the enterprise's geography—who's on what floor, which server sits where, and so on, but other considerations also come into play. Table 6-1 lists network design factors and how they affect decisions about what to do when designing a network.

Network design decisions are most often constrained by the amount of money to be spent and such logistical issues as how long the enterprise plans to stay in a building. Platforms, on the other hand, are always strategic and are usually a condition that network designers have little or no control over. If the enterprise is heavily invested in Novell NetWare or IBM SNA or Apple, the network equipment must adapt to the hardware and software platforms already installed.

Nowadays, however, no matter what your budget is or which platforms you're using, segmenting networks is not only an option but is the preferred design approach.

The Importance of Network Domains

The *domain* is one of the most fundamental concepts in internetworking. Although the term has many uses, for our purposes what's important are the two most basic kinds of

Factor	Network Design Consideration
Pre-existing cable plant	To save time and money, network designers frequently try to run networks over wiring already installed in the walls and ceiling spaces of a building. Sometimes they have no choice and the type of network devices that can be used is dictated by pre-existing cabling.
Performance goals	Projected network traffic loads and end-user "need for speed" can influence the class of network devices and cabling plant used.
Platforms	The installed base of network operating systems and computer platforms frequently dictates network design decisions.
Security	Topology layout is often used as a way to help enforce security.

Table 6-1.   Topology Design Factors (Besides Geography)

domains: the collision domain (or the token domain in Token Ring LAN segments) and the broadcast domain.

LAN segments run over shared media. In physical terms, member hosts in a LAN segment share a switch. To stave off the electronic chaos that would otherwise ensue from sharing a medium and "talking" all at once, some form of control must be enforced over access to it. This is called *media access control* (from whence the MAC address takes its name, as mentioned earlier).

NOTE: For the literal-minded out there thinking that the name should be "medium access control" because LANs by definition share only a single switched segment, you're right—to a point. Keep in mind, though, that MAC addresses are routinely exchanged between segments. Besides, somehow "medium access control" sounds half-hearted in the world of strict networking rules.

Ethernet and Token Ring are both shared media LAN technologies, but they use two sharply contrasting access control methods: Ethernet's CSMA/CD method (Carrier Sense Multiple Access/Collision Detection) and Token Ring's token-passing method.

Ethernet Collision Domains

Ethernet lets network hosts randomly contend for bandwidth. A host may send a message at will, but if it collides with a message sent by another host, both must back off and retry after a random wait period. An Ethernet collision domain is any segment in which collisions can take place—the LAN's shared medium in the form of a switch. The more traffic there is on a collision domain, the more likely it is that collisions will occur. Increased collisions, in turn, result in hosts spending more and more time futilely attempting to retransmit.

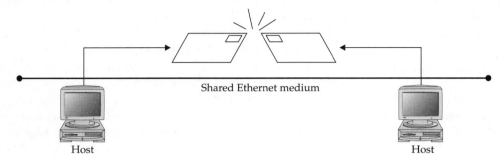

Shared Ethernet medium

Host   Host

Token Domains

A token domain is a Token Ring LAN's shared medium. Token Ring uses a deterministic method for controlling media access called *token passing*. In token passing, each host must wait for the token to be passed around the LAN's ring before it can grab it and transmit. Although they have no packet collisions, Token Ring LANs are not immune to traffic congestion. The more hosts connected to a ring, the longer each must wait for the token to come back around to be able to transmit. A good analogy to help understand Token Ring technology is a traffic light at the top of a highway on-ramp. You're forced to wait for a green light before entering the highway; thus, the heavier the traffic, the longer the wait. You're not going to be stuck in a jam down on the highway, but if traffic's heavy, you still must do your waiting up on the ramp.

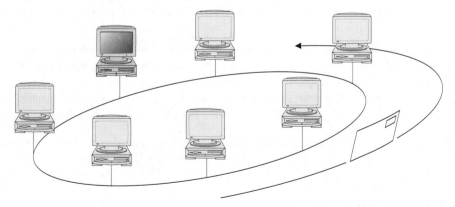

The majority of new LAN installations are Ethernet, so throughout the remainder of this chapter we'll focus on Ethernet switches and refer to Token Ring only where appropriate.

NOTE: There are three kinds of messages in IP-based networks, all ending in "cast": (1) a unicast message is a message sent to a single network address, (2) a multicast is a single message copied and sent to a specific group of network addresses, and (3) a broadcast message is sent to all nodes on a network. IPv6 networks, you might recall, introduces a fourth kind of message, called anycast. Anycast messages are transmitted by a host to the closest destination host.

Broadcast Domains

A broadcast domain is a set of all stations (network devices and hosts) that will receive any broadcast message originating from any device or host within the set. The key differentiation between broadcast and collision domains is that they are defined by the type of message they encompass. Collision domains encompass messages of any kind, while broadcast domains encompass only broadcast messages. As the lower-left part of Figure 6-4 illustrates, for two switches to join in the same broadcast domain, they must somehow be internetworked (routers usually block broadcasts).

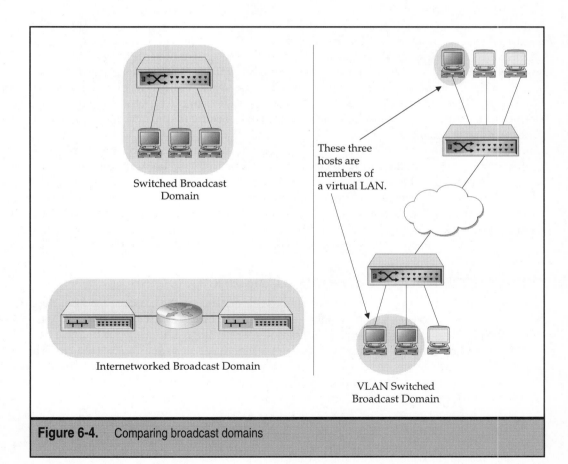

Figure 6-4. Comparing broadcast domains

The right side of Figure 6-4 shows how broadcast domains can be very different switched networks. Using switch technology, a broadcast domain can be specifically configured through logical connections instead of physical ones. This is called a *virtual LAN*, or VLAN for short. The "virtual" in VLAN means that the LAN's domain is not defined by a physical connection. In fact, VLANs usually aren't even local at all (more on that in the section "VLANs" later in the chapter).

Collisions waste bandwidth because they abort transmissions. In contrast, broadcast messages indeed reach their destinations, but are still wasted bandwidth if the receiving hosts discard them as irrelevant. Obviously, then, broadcasts also play a central role in traffic congestion. Think of broadcast domains as internetworking's version of the ZIP code: the more addresses within a ZIP code, the longer it takes to deliver all the mail. Internetworking is no different. The larger the broadcast domain is, the slower the network tends to be.

The Need to Segment Networks

LAN segments should be kept small in order to help guarantee throughput speed by limiting the frequency of collisions. Small is also good when it comes to network flexibility, security, and maintainability. The trend is to divide networks into more and more LAN segments as network bandwidth comes under increasing strain. More users are becoming members of networks, and, on average, individual users are generating more network traffic. In addition, the mix is changing to more bandwidth-intensive applications such as graphics, voice, and video. All this has combined to push network managers to deliver more bandwidth by both installing faster networking media and breaking up networks into ever smaller segments.

Network managers are doing both, but demand for bandwidth is outstripping the ability of network manufacturers to create faster technology, so network infrastructures are being reconfigured to incorporate more hierarchy and segmentation. This trend is reinforced as the cost of the hardware needed to segment networks plummets. The trend's greatest reinforcement is that the tools needed to integrate and manage heavily segmented networks have improved significantly. These tools are so good, in fact, that switches are being used to "microsegment" networks into tiny LAN segments.

Cabling Defines Network Speed and Distance

You can't appreciate traffic management without understanding the basics of road building. So, before we go into how Cisco switches address these problems, it's necessary to learn about the physical media over which networks operate: the cabling.

The most fundamental fact about networks is that they run over either of two kinds of physical transport media: copper wire or fiber-optic cable. The vast majority of all LANs installed in the world today are on some form of copper wire. Fiber-optic cabling—often called *fiber* or *glass* for short—is mostly used for high-speed backbones.

NOTE: Though copper and fiber are the most prevalent types of connecting media, wireless is picking up steam as a way to connect network hosts and devices without being tethered to a desk. We talk about wireless connectivity and networking in Chapter 10.

The proliferation of network users and bandwidth-hungry applications has driven the industry to introduce a steady stream of newer and faster transport technologies. A review of network cabling and terminology will help you keep things straight.

A Brief History of LAN Cabling

As mentioned, the earliest LANs ran over Thicknet coaxial cables. Thicknet was costly and hard to work with, so in the mid-1980s it was replaced by Thinnet coaxial cable (also called *Cheapernet*). When used to run 10-Mbps Ethernet, Thinnet has a maximum length of 185 meters. Thinnet LANs can be extended beyond that distance using repeaters to link segments. (*Repeaters* are devices placed along a LAN cable to amplify electrical signals and extend maximum operating length. Simple repeaters are rarely used now.) Also, coaxial cable requires that there be a certain minimum amount of spacing between connections, which cramps topology design choices.

Hubs were introduced in the late 1980s. Also called *concentrators*, hubs make hierarchical network topologies possible and simplify the installation and management of a cable plant. Hubs also hastened the introduction of a new type of cabling called *twisted-pair*, which is inexpensive and very easy to work with. One of the reasons using twisted-pair became possible is that its relatively short operating limit of 100 meters is extensible using hubs. For example, an office space 300 meters in length could be wired with twisted-pair by placing two hubs into the topology.

LAN Cabling Today

Most larger networks today use a combination of fiber and twisted-pair. Twisted-pair is used to connect hosts to switches, while fiber is used for network backbones. Thanks to technological advances, even though twisted-pair uses less copper and shielding than Thinnet coaxial cable, it supports faster data rates. About the same time twisted-pair was taking over desktop connectivity, fiber-optic cabling established itself as the preferred medium for high-speed network backbones. Fiber is used to connect floors or major areas within an office building, and twisted-pair is used to connect LAN segments spanning from the backbone. As Figure 6-5 depicts, switches funnel the LAN segments into the backbone via various star-hierarchy configurations. "Backbone" is a relative term, however. For example, the fiber trunk interconnecting the buildings of a campus LAN is referred to as its *backbone,* while the fiber-optic cable connecting the floors of one of the buildings is referred to as a *riser*.

Twisted-pair cable comes in two basic types:

▼ **STP (Shielded Twisted-Pair)**   A two-pair cabling medium encased in shielded insulation to limit electromagnetic interference of signals.

▲ **UTP (Unshielded Twisted-Pair)**   A four-pair cabling medium not encased in shielding. UTP is used in most networks.

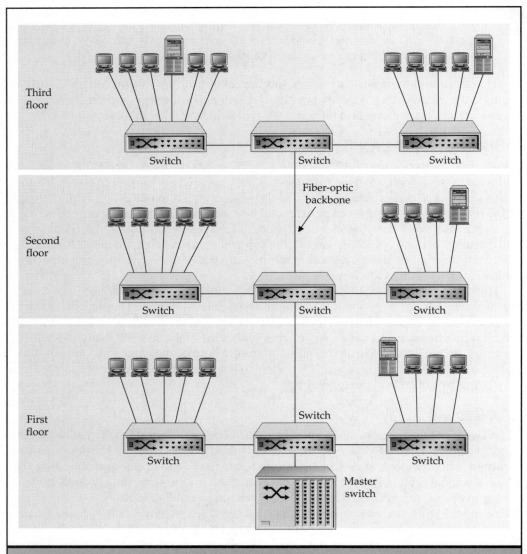

Figure 6-5. Enterprise networks today combine fiber and twisted-pair cable media.

Generally, the more tightly twisted the copper wire strands are, the less likely it is there will be interference or signal loss. STP has only two twisted-pairs, but compensates with its shielding. UTP, on the other hand, has no shielding, but compensates with an extra pair of wires. Because UTP is fast, reliable, and inexpensive, it has become the predominant type of cabling used in networking today. Use of the more expensive STP is limited to environments made hostile by high levels of electromagnetic interference.

Cabling Specifications   Table 6-2 explains the categories of twisted-pair specified by an international standards organization called TIA/EIA (Telecommunications Industry Association/Electronics Industry Association). These cabling specifications are important in that the rate at which data can be reliably transmitted is determined by a combination of factors, such as:

▼ How tightly twisted the copper wire is

■ The quality of the cable's copper

■ The type of insulation used to encase the cable

▲ The design and quality of the cable connectors

In Table 6-2, Categories 3 and 5 represent the lion's share of twisted-pair networks today—especially Cat 5.

Note that higher category numbers indicate higher speeds. Most new LAN installations use Cat 5 in order to accommodate 100-Mbps Fast Ethernet, but many still run on older Cat 3 because it's so widely installed in network infrastructures.

The alternative to copper cabling is fiber-optic cabling. Although it's employed mostly as a backbone medium, it's sometimes used all the way out to the desktop for demanding applications such as high-end graphics. The advantage of fiber is that it can sustain very high speeds over long distances, but its use is constrained by relatively high costs.

Network Technologies   Cabling specifications such as Cat 5 describe the physical medium. *Network specifications* describe what is to happen over a medium and are built around the capabilities and limitations of one or more cabling specifications.

There are several Ethernet specifications, each designed to guarantee efficacy on the physical medium over which it's designed to operate. Any networking technology's ability to function properly depends on how well matched it is to the physical medium. The faster a network must run—or the greater the distance over which it will operate—the better the underlying cable plant must be.

Network specification names seem mysterious until you've been introduced to the logic behind them. The following illustration breaks down the name of the Ethernet 10BaseT specification.

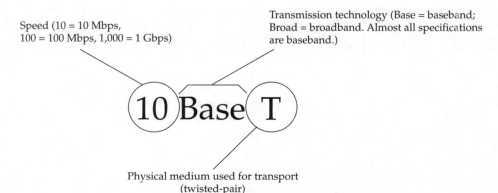

Speed (10 = 10 Mbps, 100 = 100 Mbps, 1,000 = 1 Gbps)

Transmission technology (Base = baseband; Broad = broadband. Almost all specifications are baseband.)

Physical medium used for transport (twisted-pair)

Category	Cable Description	Cable Application
Cat 1	Traditional telephone cable	Not usable for networking; no longer installed for telephones
Cat 2	Four twisted-pairs	4 Mbps; not recommended for networking
Cat 3	Four twisted-pairs with three twists per foot, rated up to 16 MHz	10 Mbps Ethernet and 4 Mbps for Token Ring; also used for new telephone cabling
Cat 4	Four twisted-pairs, rated up to 20 MHz	16 Mbps; used for Token Ring
Cat 5	Four twisted-pairs with eight twists per foot, rated up to 100 MHz	100 Mbps; used for Fast Ethernet; fast becoming ubiquitous in networked buildings
Enhanced Cat 5	Four twisted-pairs with eight twists per foot, but made of higher-quality materials and rated up to 200 MHz	Rated to have up to twice the transmission capability of regular Cat 5
Cat 6	Four twisted-pairs with each pair wrapped in foil insulation; the whole bundle wrapped in polymer	Rated to have up to six times the transmission capability of regular Cat 5
Cat 7	Four twisted-pairs, made of high-quality materials; rated up to 600 MHz	Super-fast broadband applications, like Gigabit Ethernet; allows multiple applications operating at different frequencies

Table 6-2. TIE/EIA Twisted-Pair Specifications

Sorting out the various network specifications shows that some media are used only for certain speeds, some are legacy specs no longer used in new installations, and others are specs that never quite caught on. Table 6-3 lists network specifications (mostly Ethernet) in their approximate order of importance, based on:

▼   Percentage of new LANs being installed

■   Percentage of all installations

▲   Probable future importance as a technology

The specifications reflect the worldwide trend toward Ethernet technologies. The two major exceptions are FDDI and ATM.

Table 6-3 shows that many network specifications are either old or are contending standards that meet with limited market acceptance. The trend in networking technology is, of course, toward ever faster speeds running over cheaper cabling plant. Not including high-speed backbones, most new LANs today use 100BaseTX Fast Ethernet running over Cat 5 cabling.

LAN Spec	Description
10BaseT	10-Mbps Ethernet using UTP Cats 3, 4, or 5 cabling; most new installations during the 1990s; in the process of being eclipsed by 100BaseT; 100-meter limit
100BaseTX	100-Mbps Fast Ethernet using UTP Cat 5 cabling; most new installations going in now are 100BaseT; 100-meter limit
100BaseFX	100-Mbps Fast Ethernet using two strands of multimode fiber-optic cable per link; most new high-speed backbones are 100BaseFX; 400-meter limit
FDDI	100-Mbps Fiber Distributed Data Interface token-passing LAN using either single-mode or multimode fiber-optic cabling (or sometimes either STP or UTP copper, called CDDI, for Copper Distributed Data Interface); 100-kilometer limit over fiber, 100-meter limit over copper
ATM	622-Mbps Asynchronous Transfer Mode over fiber-optic cabling; popular as a backbone for its sustained throughput and its proven ability to move multimedia applications at speed
1000BaseFX	1-Gbps Gigabit Ethernet over fiber-optic cabling; although 1000BaseX is now being reengineered to run over Cat 5 copper (to be called 1000BaseTX)
100VG-AnyLAN	100-Mbps Fast Ethernet and Token Ring using UTP Cats 3, 4, or 5 cabling; developed by Hewlett-Packard; can be run over any existing 10BaseT networks

Table 6-3.   LAN Specifications with Cable Types and Distance Limits

LAN Spec	Description
10Base2	10-Mbps Ethernet using Thinnet coaxial cabling; widely installed in the 1980s; eclipsed by 10BaseT; 185-meter limit
10Base5	10-Mbps Ethernet using Thicknet coaxial cabling; widely installed in 1970s and 1980s; 500-meter limit
100BaseT4	100-Mbps Fast Ethernet using four pairs of UTP Cats 3, 4, or 5 cabling; 100-meter limit
10BaseFB	10-Mbps Ethernet using fiber-optic cabling; used as a LAN backbone (not to connect hosts directly); 2-kilometer limit
10BaseFL	10-Mbps Ethernet using fiber-optic cabling; two-kilometer limit, one-kilometer with FOIRL (Fiber-Optic Inter-Repeater Link, a precursor signaling methodology that FL replaces)
10BaseFP	10-Mbps Ethernet using fiber-optic cabling; used to link computers into a star topology without using repeaters; 500-meter limit
10Broad36	10-Mbps Ethernet using broadband coaxial cable cabling; 3.6-kilometer limit

Table 6-3.   LAN Specifications with Cable Types and Distance Limits *(continued)*

Things are less clear about which technology is winning out as the backbone medium of choice. ATM supplanted FDDI, probably due in part to the recent sharp increase in the demand for multimedia applications. ATM's competition as the backbone of the future is 1000BaseX, commonly called Gigabit Ethernet. Planners not only like Gigabit Ethernet's rated speed of 1000 Mbps, but they also like its compatibility with most installed Ethernet networks. Chapter 2 discusses competing network technologies in detail.

NOTE: Ever wonder how data travels over a cable? In simple terms, electrical pulses going over a wire are measured for plus or minus voltages to track signals. Special encoding schemes—for example, the Institute of Electrical and Electronics Engineers (IEEE) schemes for Fast Ethernet and Gigabit Ethernet— are used to translate data from identifiable bit patterns represented by the voltage fluctuations. Fast Ethernet uses a three-level encoding scheme to track data; Gigabit Ethernet uses a five-level encoding scheme. The two major problems facing network communications are return-loss and far-end crosstalk. Without getting bogged down in engineering details, return-loss is when a signal echoes back to the transmitter, confusing it; crosstalk, on the other hand, is when signals leak between wire pairs, creating electrical noise. Network engineers are always looking for improved encoding schemes to squeeze more bandwidth into smaller wires. It ain't like connecting two tin cans with baling wire, is it?

Straight-Through vs. Crossover Cables and Devices

Network hardware documentation frequently refers to *straight-through* cables and *crossover* cables. Network devices have transmitter (TX) pins and receiver (RX) pins. In a straight-through cable, the wire pair does not cross from TX to RX between interfaces. In a crossover cable, however, wire pairs are crossed over from TX to RX between connections. You must use crossover cables to connect hosts with identical interfaces. If a straight-through cable is used, one of the two devices must perform the crossover function. If neither device has a crossover connector, then a crossover cable must be used. In other words, signals must be crossed over either in one of the devices or in the cable. Figure 6-6 illustrates the two ways.

Think of a signal traveling RX-to-RX or TX-to-TX as being like a conversation in which two persons mouth words, but no sound reaches their ears. Crossing over signals between devices makes networking possible by moving the signal from "mouth to ear."

CISCO SWITCHES

It's no exaggeration to say that switched network technology is revolutionizing how internetworks are designed and what they can do for users. Over the past decade, switches have begun pushing internetworks to size scales and service levels many considered infeasible not long ago.

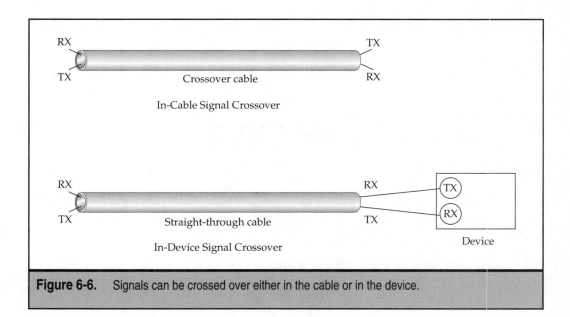

Figure 6-6.   Signals can be crossed over either in the cable or in the device.

But what exactly are switched networks? How do they work? As Cisco likes to put it, "switches deliver shared bandwidth." How can the switch do this? The answer is in the electronics:

▼ They run at very high speeds because they operate at the data-link layer (layer 2) instead of at the network layer (layer 3), where routers operate. This enables switches to process traffic without creating bottlenecks.

▲ They have many of the capabilities of a router, but sit between the host and the backbone, instead of between backbones as routers do. Switches can take control over traffic at or near its source, whereas the router usually doesn't take over until the message is ready to begin its trek to a remote LAN. Taking control at the source takes much of the randomness out of network operations.

How an Individual Switch Works

Almost all computer advances in one way or another come down to miniaturization and speed, and the network switch is no different. They are smart and fast enough to read both the source port and the destination port of each frame and "switch" messages between the two (thus the name). This is shown in Figure 6-7.

Much like routers, switches examine destination and source addresses as messages pass through. Switches differ from routers in that they're looking at layer-2 MAC addresses instead of layer-3 IP addresses.

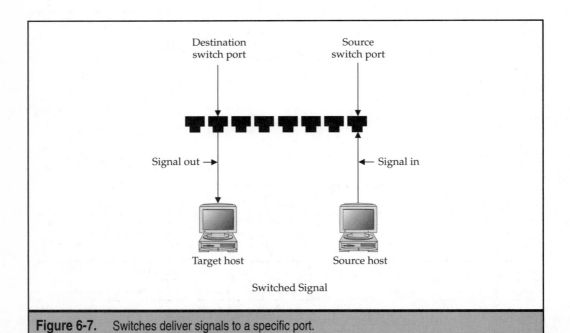

Figure 6-7.   Switches deliver signals to a specific port.

The switch provides a shared media LAN into which hosts can connect. But the switch is at the same time able to assume router-like duties, for two reasons:

▼ Switches have more powerful electronics than their predecessors, the hubs (they have more transistors crammed onto their printed circuit boards).

▲ They operate at the data-link layer (layer 2), which means they don't have to dig as deep into messages as layer-3 routers.

Beefed-up electronics give the switch the ability of a speed reader, but while switches are smart, they're not nearly as smart as routers. The switch is, in effect, assigned a lighter reading assignment than routers because it handles traffic at layer 2.

To illustrate this, Figure 6-8 traces a message through a hypothetical switched network. The first step takes place between the host sending the message and its switch port. To do this, the switch reads the incoming message's destination MAC address and instantly moves it to the outbound port it associates with that destination MAC.

Because the message is switched to a targeted outbound port instead of being replicated to all ports, it encounters no collisions. This makes more bandwidth available and moves messages at faster throughput speeds.

The same process holds for the message's second step. As the message pours out of the outbound port on Switch 1, it has dedicated bandwidth (no collisions) over the cable connecting it to the port in Switch 2. The switching process again repeats itself through the third step all the way out to the destination host.

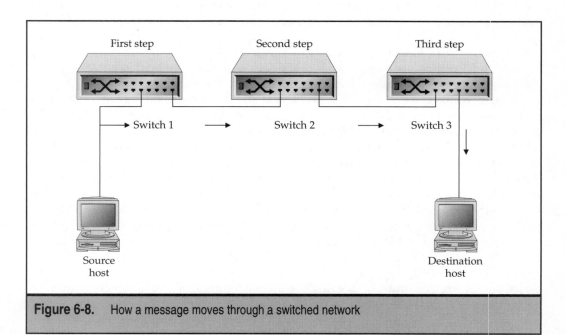

Figure 6-8. How a message moves through a switched network

When a switch receives a message seeking an address it doesn't know, instead of dropping the message, the switch broadcasts the message to all its ports. This process is called *flooding,* which is necessary for discovery-type messages. For example, Dynamic Host Configuration Protocol (DHCP) is used by a host when it boots up to locate nearby services such as network printers. Without flooding, switches could not support broadcast messages sent by DHCP and other utilities.

Switched Networking Basics

How is it possible to have dedicated bandwidth all the way through a multiple-device network connecting hundreds of hosts? The answer is that switched networks balance intelligence with raw power.

In simplified terms, routers move messages through an internetwork to their destinations by working from left to right across the destination's IP address, as depicted next:

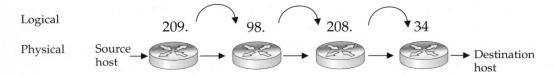

As the message hops between routers, it checks the routing table maintained in each new router, trying to match the next part of the destination IP address. When it finds a more complete match, the message physically moves through the internetwork to the router whose location is represented by that matched IP address information. Sooner or later, all the IP address parts are matched and the message arrives at the router serving as the gateway to the destination host.

In sharp contrast, a message must find its way through a switched network without the luxury of hierarchical IP addresses. Switched networks operate using MAC addresses, which are considered to be flat in topology. A MAC address—also called a physical address—is a sort of network serial number assigned to a host's NIC. The first half of every MAC address is a vendor code signifying the manufacturer of the NIC; the second half is the serial number of the actual device. If you move a device to the other side of the world, its MAC address remains unchanged. Switched networks are completely flat in that, because they rely solely on MAC addresses, they essentially think all devices and hosts are attached to the same cable. Beyond the friendly confines of the home LAN, a MAC address is a small clue. How, then, do switched networks manage to deliver messages?

When a switch is turned on, it begins building a dynamic address table. It does so by examining the source MAC address of each incoming frame and associating it with the port through which it came. In this way, the switch figures out what hosts are attached to each of its ports. Figure 6-9 shows a dynamic address table.

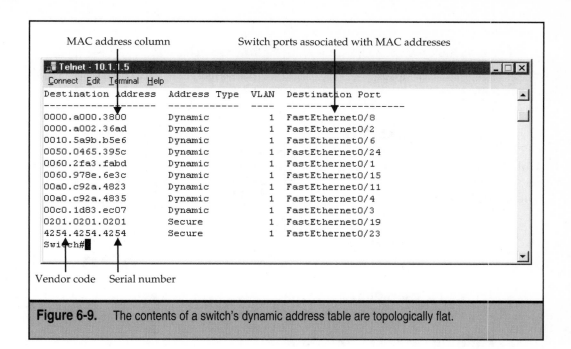

MAC address column   Switch ports associated with MAC addresses

Figure 6-9.   The contents of a switch's dynamic address table are topologically flat.

The switch also discovers and maps the surrounding neighborhood using Cisco Discovery Protocol (CDP), which was covered in Chapter 5. The switch uses CDP to discover nearby switches and begins sharing dynamic address table information with them. CDP only talks to those switches it can ping directly, but as Figure 6-10 shows, that doesn't matter. MAC addresses are passed back through a chain of cooperating switches until they reach the switch building its dynamic address table.

Theoretically, a switch could eventually compile a list containing the MAC addresses of every switch in the world. To prevent that from happening, switches drop unused MACs after a default period of five minutes. The dynamic address table isn't as smart as routing tables, which use all types of costing algorithms to choose optimal paths. A switch simply places the most frequently used MACs toward the top of its dynamic address table. Together, these two procedures guarantee that the switch's network path-finding intelligence is at least fresh, and more likely to be reliable.

Designing Switched Internetworks

Even if a switch's dynamic address table could identify a path through a very large switched internetwork, if that path required hundreds or even just dozens of hops, it would be too slow. Two technologies have been developed to solve this problem: switched backbones and multilayer switching.

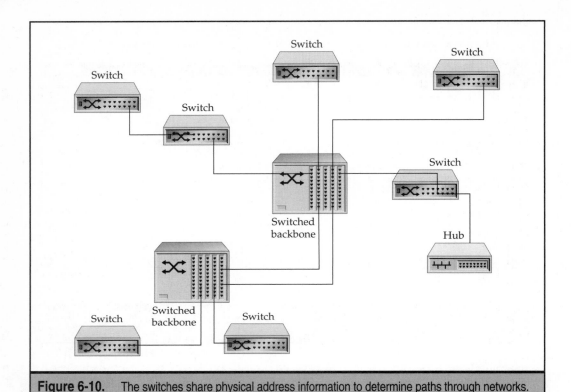

Figure 6-10.   The switches share physical address information to determine paths through networks.

Switched Backbones

Switched backbones are high-end switches used to aggregate bandwidth from other switches. The idea of a switched backbone is for it to have the biggest dynamic address table of all. Switched backbones are frequently configured with multiple high-end switches, both for purposes of redundancy and in order to attain blazingly fast throughput rates.

It'd be neat to tell you that switched backbones are fat, high-tech cables strung atop towering pylons in electrical utility power grids, or that they're meshed networks of very fast and expensive T3 high-speed phone circuits. But they're not. Even the biggest of the big switched backbones is an unglamorous collection of refrigerator-like boxes cabled together, quietly humming away in a computer room somewhere.

A switched backbone's job is to concentrate what would otherwise be many hops into a single hop through a single backbone LAN. This is what's meant by bandwidth aggregation. Switched backbones pack large amounts of memory and throughput into a single configuration. Not all switched backbones are behemoths. A switched backbone might be a device about the size of a pizza box sitting in a rack in a data closet. Remember, a backbone by definition is a relatively fast LAN interconnecting other LANs.

While switched backbones aren't absolutely necessary in smaller networks, they probably are in very large ones. You probably remember when AOL's network collapsed. After the headlines faded, gurus lambasted AOL for having stuck with its mostly router-based topology too long.

Switched backbones are implemented using any of four technologies:

▼   ATM (Asynchronous Transfer Mode)

■   Fast Ethernet or Gigabit Ethernet

■   FDDI

▲   Token Ring

Many large internetworks inevitably have subnets implementing a variety of technologies. For this reason, Cisco's Catalyst 6500 family of switches features any-to-any switching between ATM, Gigabit, Fast Ethernet, Token Ring, and FDDI.

Aggregating bandwidth, of course, means rolling up messages from a large number of subsidiary switches. Because switched networks deal only in MAC addresses, this cannot be done by hierarchical routing. The workaround is to create levels of switches through uplink ports. Figure 6-11 depicts how this configuration funnels the traffic from many hosts through the host switch out to the backbone switch.

This configuration technique enables designers to create a power hierarchy in lieu of a logical hierarchy. Switched networks aggregate traffic into the bandwidth of a single switch to help the message find its way. Described in basic terms, this is accomplished by a switched backbone machine having more switches connected directly to it and thus building a much larger dynamic address table.

Each Cisco switch's ability to aggregate bandwidth into a high-speed intelligent backbone relies on most or all of the advanced switching technologies introduced in Table 6-4.

The technology central to Cisco's switched backbone strategy is something called EtherChannel, which is a bus technology. Strictly speaking, a bus is a cable (or a printed circuit board functioning like a cable). What makes EtherChannel a full-blown technology is that it's an integrated package of high-speed cabling, connectors, controllers, software, and management tools designed to sustain high switching throughput rates. EtherChannel provides bandwidth scalability in increments from 200 Mbps to 800 Mbps.

EtherChannel works by setting up logical groups of ports to serve as high-speed connections between switches sitting in the same location—in effect letting multiple switch devices function as a single machine. An EtherChannel group can have up to 12 member ports. Ports are usually grouped to service a specific VLAN, which is why EtherChannel is central to Cisco's switched network strategy: aggregating bandwidth means interconnecting switches to switch servers that hold ever larger dynamic MAC address tables. Large-volume streams of switched messages flow within VLANs. EtherChannel is where the logical meets the physical. It funnels a VLAN's traffic through a dedicated high-speed bus into a collapsed switched backbone running at about the same speed. Balanced bus-to-switch throughput speed is increasingly referred to as a *switch fabric,* in which ports and even stack units share a common dynamic address table.

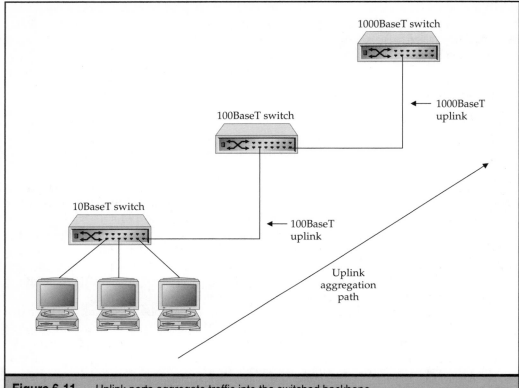

Figure 6-11. Uplink ports aggregate traffic into the switched backbone.

An added benefit is that EtherChannel groups provide load balancing and redundancy. If one port is overloaded or fails, traffic loads are transparently shifted to other ports in the group. EtherChannel is a design architecture Cisco is now using to deliver multigigabit capacity. The technology implements IEEE 802.3 100BaseX and 1000BaseX standards as Fast EtherChannel and Gigabit EtherChannel products, respectively.

Multilayer Switching

Multilayer switching is a hybrid of routing and switching technologies. Even the best-designed switched networks must still use routers at some level. The hierarchical topology of layer-3 IP addressing has a much better "aim" than switched network schemes, given that routers use hierarchical addresses instead of flat MAC addresses. This is why smart network designers are using multilayer switches to augment switched networks with the capabilities of a router to identify optimal paths to destinations. Depending on the manufacturer, multilayer switching is also called *IP switching, layer-3 switching, short-cut routing,* and *high-speed routing.*

Technology	Description
Address Cache	Also called MAC cache—the maximum number of MAC addresses a switch can maintain in its dynamic address table, which is a function of a combination of factors, including DRAM and CPU capacity
Wirespeed	Also called forwarding rate—the rate at which a switch can pick up a stream of packets from an incoming cable, usually expressed in packets per second (pps)
Backplane (Switch Fabric)	The data rate of the switch's bus, which services CPU, memory, and I/O controllers, expressed in megabits per second (Mbps) or gigabits per second (Gbps)
IP Multicast	Certain message types tend to be multicast, where, for example, one copy of a message is sent to 1000 hosts instead of 1000 copies being sent. Doing this through a switched network requires a switch with sufficient processing power, memory capacity, bus speed, and software to handle such large MAC addressing transactions. IP Multicast is becoming an important switch technology as the world moves to the type of traffic that lends itself to multicast messaging, such as video on demand.

Table 6-4.   Key Switching Technologies

Operators of very large internetworks—mainly corporations running big intranets—are offering services in which users can click a hyperlink in one place and suddenly create a message demanding information or services from a faraway server. As users increasingly move about an internetwork to use its remote services, strain is put on the capacity of its routers. Properly implemented, multilayer switching can deliver tenfold throughput improvements at heavily traveled connection points. It's a relatively new and immature technology.

Multilayer switching works by first determining the best route or routes through an internetwork using layer-3 protocols and storing what it finds for later reference. Users who come along later wanting to travel that route do so via switches, bypassing the router (and the bottleneck it would cause).

Even if multilayer switching technology is not integrated into a switched network, some routing should still be used to provide some form of hierarchical topology to the network. This is necessary not only to maintain network-wide performance, but also to enhance security. Switches will not displace routers from internetworks in the foreseeable future. However, multilayer switching could be the industry's first step toward melding what are now two technologies into one—much like how the bridge was subsumed by the router five to ten years ago.

VLANs

In a switched network, a host can participate in a VLAN (virtual local area network). Much as a group of hosts becomes a member of a physical LAN by plugging into a shared switch, they become part of a virtual LAN by being configured into it using switched network management software. In switched networks built using Cisco equipment, VLANs are created and maintained using the Visual Switch Manager software.

Within a VLAN, member hosts can communicate as if they were attached to the same wire, when in fact they can be located on any number of physical LANs. Because VLANs form broadcast domains, members enjoy the connectivity, shared services, and security associated with physical LANs.

Basing LANs on logical parameters instead of physical topology gives network administrators the option to align domains to parallel, geographically dispersed workgroups. Even temporary exigencies can be accommodated using VLANs. For example, if two computer programmers needed to run a week's worth of tests involving heavy upload and download activity, they could be temporarily configured into a VLAN so as not to drag down the network's performance for other members of the normal VLAN.

Domains are usually arranged by department or workgroup. However, the trend toward dynamic organizational structures in the business world has made planning and maintaining modern networks somewhat tougher than it would otherwise be. Contemporary business phenomena such as virtual offices, distributed teams, reorganizations, mergers, acquisitions, and downsizing cause near constant migration of personnel and services within networks. Figure 6-12 outlines what a VLAN topology might look like.

But VLANs are more than just an organizational convenience. They are a necessity in switched networks in order to contain broadcast domains. Don't forget that using only MAC addresses causes flat network topology. VLANs ameliorate most flat topology problems by creating virtual hierarchies.

Largely, VLANs are created using Cisco switches. However, if a device on one VLAN needs to communicate with a device on a second VLAN, it is necessary to get a router involved. This is because two or more VLANs can't communicate with each other (that sort of defeats the purpose of the VLAN) without a little help from a layer-3 device.

Consider the network shown in Figure 6-13. In this example, there are two switches connecting four VLANs. Switch 1 has been configured with VLAN A and VLAN B. Switch 2 has been configured with VLAN C and VLAN D.

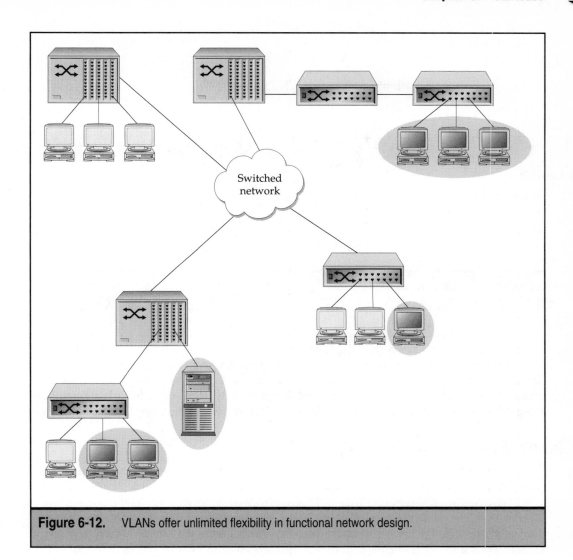

Figure 6-12.   VLANs offer unlimited flexibility in functional network design.

VLANs A and B are sent through a single port (this is called *trunking*) to the router and through another port to Switch 2. VLANs C and D are trunked from Switch 2 to Switch 1, then through Switch 1 to the router. This trunk is able to carry the traffic from all four VLANs. That single connection to the router allows the router to appear on all four VLANs.

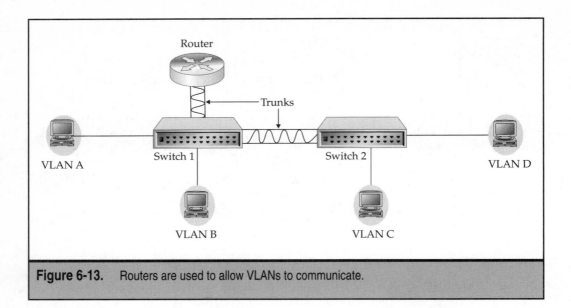

Figure 6-13.   Routers are used to allow VLANs to communicate.

Since the VLANs are connected to the router, they can communicate with each other via the trunking connection between the two switches, using the router. For instance, if a file is located on VLAN D and a computer on VLAN A needs access to it, the data must travel from Switch 1 to the router, then back to the Switch 1, then on to Switch 2. Because of the trunking, both computers and the router think they are on the same physical segment.

Cisco's Switched Network Products

Cisco's main line of switched network solutions are its Catalyst Switches, delivered in over a dozen different series of products. With the vast options available, you can "have it your way," at least when it comes to high-performance switching. The Catalyst line is similar to Cisco routers in that it includes fixed-configuration desktop models and configurable plug-and-play modular chassis models, all the way up to "dormitory refrigerator" packages with high-speed buses into which many cards can be inserted—each card packing as much as other fully configured Catalyst models.

In keeping with well-established trends in the networking marketplace, most Cisco LAN switches are Ethernet products. The lineup of Catalyst-switched backbone products incorporates the diversity of technologies competing at that level, with support for Fast Ethernet, Gigabit Ethernet, FDDI, and ATM.

Most Cisco switches run a full-blown image of the IOS software, different only in that it's tuned for switching rather than routing. Most Catalyst switches offer the regular command-line interface, but some have a menu-driven interface.

Cisco switched network products are packaged to:

▼ Deliver seamless migration from legacy technologies with tools such as 10/100 autosensing and high-speed uplink ports.

■ Enable interoperation between diverse technologies such as ATM, FDDI, Token Ring, and Ethernet.

■ Facilitate bandwidth aggregation through scalable configurations and powerful switch fabric technologies.

▲ Be manageable using remote monitoring, configuration, and security tools.

Table 6-5 outlines the Cisco switch product line at the time this was being written. Refer to **www.cisco.com** for current catalogs of information on Cisco switches and other products.

Configuring and Managing Cisco Switches

Cisco Catalyst switches can be configured using either the IOS command-line interface or the Visual Switch Manager, a tool operated through a Web browser interface. Which to use is a matter of user preference; neither configures anything the other doesn't. If you use the command-line interface, the normal rules apply as far as using Telnet to log in through the Console port. For simplicity's sake, we'll use Visual Switch Manager to explain Cisco switch configuration and management.

VISUAL SWITCH MANAGER

Visual Switch Manager (VSM) is a Web browser–based tool used to work with Cisco Catalyst switches. VSM presents real-time information measuring activity in a switch while it runs. This information is used to monitor and manage a switch. More important, the tool is also used to modify switch configuration.

Visual Switch Manager has six configuration management areas that lead to a combined total of 18 pages (browser screens). Figure 6-14 shows the Visual Switch Manager home page and a list of pages by area. The home page itself handles such housekeeping chores as naming the switch and setting its Line password.

An outstanding feature of Visual Switch Manager is that a device's status can be viewed by looking at a live image of it on the home page. Figure 6-15 shows the graphical image of a Cisco 2924XL switch. You can't see the color keys in this black-and-white book, but if the port is colored green, its status is Link Up; blue means No Link Status; and red indicates Link Faulty or Port Disabled.

Product Series	Description
Catalyst 2820	Designed for aggregating hubs or servers. Has 24 Fast Ethernet ports plus two slots for a choice of high-speed modules—Fast Ethernet, FDDI, or ATM. Not stackable.
Catalyst 2900 Series	Three models with 12–48 ports for Ethernet/Fast Ethernet 10/100 autosensing. Not stackable.
Catalyst 2900XL Series	Has 24 ports and two module slots for 10BASE-T/100BASE-TX, 1000BASE-X, 1000BASE-T, Gigabit Ethernet, and asynchronous transfer mode (ATM) modules. Not stackable.
Catalyst 2900XL LRE Series	Two switch models with either 12- or 24-ports delivering Long Range Ethernet (LRE) across existing telephone lines; up to 5000 feet.
Catalyst 2940 Series	Two models with eight 10/100 Ethernet ports. The 2940-8TF model offers Gigabit Ethernetworking.
Catalyst 2950 Series	Fourteen models with between 12- and 48-ports of 10/100 Ethernet and (on most models) two ports of Gigabit Ethernet uplinks. Offers intelligent functionality, including security services and Quality of Service.
Catalyst 2970 Series	Two models of 24-port Gigabit Ethernet switches. The 2970G-24TS model also offers four small form-pluggable (SFP) ports.
Catalyst 3500XL Series	One model with 24 10/100BaseT Ethernet ports and two Gigabit Ethernet uplink ports, and one model with eight Gigabit Ethernet ports. 3500XLs are stackable up to nine units, and run a switch fabric up to 10 Gbps. The 3500 Series is positioned as Cisco's premier solution for low-end Gigabit Ethernet connectivity.
Catalyst 3550 Series	Nine models of stackable, multilayer Ethernet switches. Models offer 24 or 49 10/100 Ethernet ports and two Gigabit Ethernet uplinks.

Table 6-5. Cisco's Switch Offerings

Product Series	Description
Catalyst 3750 Series	Four models of stackable switches offering 24 or 48 10/100 Ethernet ports. One model offers 12 Gigabit Ethernet ports. The switches utilize StackWise technology, which allows stacking with nine other 3750 units.
Catalyst 4000 Series	Three models with three-slot modular chassis supporting 10/100/1000 Ethernet. One module has 48 10/100 ports and another, 32 10/100 ports with a variety of Gigabit Ethernet uplink options. The third model offers 40 ports of 10/100 Ethernet and two ports of 1000BaseX Gigabit Ethernet. Not stackable.
Catalyst 4500 Series	Three models of switches with 3, 6, or 7 slots. Each slot is capable of accepting various switching modules offering 10/100 or Gigabit Ethernet with up to 240 ports.
Catalyst 5000 (5500) Series	High-performance switching coupled with NetFlow switching for layer-3 routing. The series supports Gigabit Ethernet and ATM with additional interface module options, including 10/100 Ethernet, Fast EtherChannel, fiber Fast Ethernet, and even Token Ring and CDDI/FDDI.
Catalyst 6500 Series	Five models with three to 13 slots. The switches can be customized by adding various modules, including Ethernet, Gigabit Ethernet, 10 Gigabit, voice, ATM and other modules.
Catalyst 8500 Series	Four models with five to 13 slots supporting multiservice ATM switching, optimized for aggregating multiprotocol traffic. Not stackable. Cisco's choice for ATM backbone switches.

Table 6-5.   Cisco's Switch Offerings *(continued)*

Notice in Figure 6-15 that Visual Switch Manager makes the distinction between a port and a link. A *port* is the physical connection where the cable is plugged in. A *link*, on the other hand, is the logical connection taking place over that port to a port on some other device—which could be another switch, router, server, or other device. A port could be operating properly, and at the same time the link running through it could be

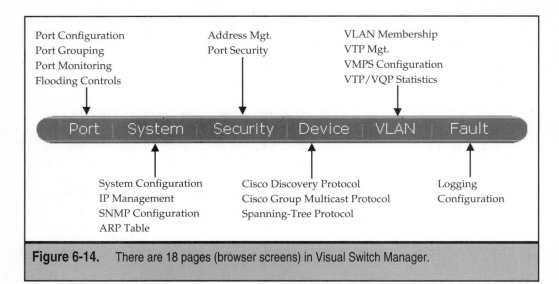

Port Configuration
Port Grouping
Port Monitoring
Flooding Controls

Address Mgt.
Port Security

VLAN Membership
VTP Mgt.
VMPS Configuration
VTP/VQP Statistics

Port | System | Security | Device | VLAN | Fault

System Configuration
IP Management
SNMP Configuration
ARP Table

Cisco Discovery Protocol
Cisco Group Multicast Protocol
Spanning-Tree Protocol

Logging
Configuration

Figure 6-14.　There are 18 pages (browser screens) in Visual Switch Manager.

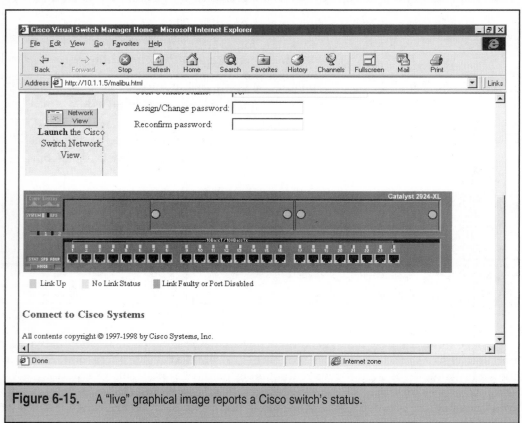

Figure 6-15.　A "live" graphical image reports a Cisco switch's status.

malfunctioning. You can see how Visual Switch Manager helps network administrators isolate and solve problems quickly.

The Port Configuration pages (or commands, if you're in the IOS command-line interface) allow you to enable or disable specific switch ports and to set duplex mode to full, half, or automatically selected, according to the capability of the host device making a link to the port. If the switch device being configured is 10/100, speed mode can be set in the same way. If a switch is participating in an EtherChannel, individual ports would be assigned to EtherChannel groups in the Port Grouping page.

The System area pages cover basic system-wide configuration parameters such as the version of IOS software installed, booting procedure, system console baud rate, and memory configuration options.

Perhaps the most important area of switch configuration and management has to do with VLANs. Visual Switch Manager includes pages for assigning ports VLAN memberships, as well as pages to set parameters for such specialized VLAN services as:

▼ **STP (Spanning Tree Protocol)**   A link management protocol that allows advertisement of redundant paths through switched networks, while at the same time preventing paths from looping back to their source. STP does for switched networks what routing protocols do for routed networks.

■ **VTP (VLAN Trunk Protocol)**   A way to create pathways serving a number of switches in a VLAN, accomplished by dynamically sharing MAC addresses and other information from a VTP server and VTP clients.

■ **VMPS (VLAN Membership Policy Server)**   A client-server based protocol that dynamically tracks the VLAN (or VLANs) to which a particular MAC address belongs.

▲ **VQP (VLAN Query Protocol)**   A protocol that continually runs statistics on VMPS queries sent by the VMPS server to its clients.

How switches can be configured and managed using SNMP and CiscoWorks is covered in Chapter 15.

Visual Switch Manager Software

VSM operates by talking to a switch through the HTTP protocol. HTTP is the IP protocol used to support Web browser–based applications. As a browser application, VSM overlays the switch's image of Cisco IOS software and runs IOS commands.

Initial switch installation is done while running a terminal session through the switch's Console port (not Visual Switch Manager). Notice that both Telnet and Visual Switch Manager are options in Figure 6-16. It is only after the switch is made a member of a LAN that management activity can begin through VSM.

The home page also provides access to other tools besides VSM. For example, clicking the Telnet hyperlink lets you log into the IOS command-line interface. Other hyperlinks connect to Cisco resources, such as Cisco's Web page and Technical Assistance Center.

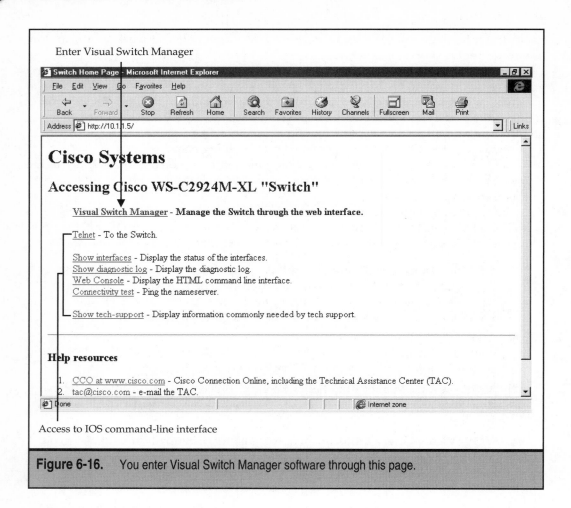

Figure 6-16.   You enter Visual Switch Manager software through this page.

The Visual Switch Manager Home Page

Basic housekeeping tasks are handled in the VSM home page. This is where the switch is given a name, where a network administrator responsible for the switch is assigned, where passwords are maintained, and so forth. Notice that the IP address and Cisco IOS Software version fields are display-only. They are defined elsewhere and cannot be input from this page.

Switches are almost always administered from inside the enterprise's private network. Figure 6-17 shows a private IP address (http://10.1.1.5), as opposed to a public address (such as http://209.98.86.52). For security reasons, administrative access to a switch from outside the private network is rare.

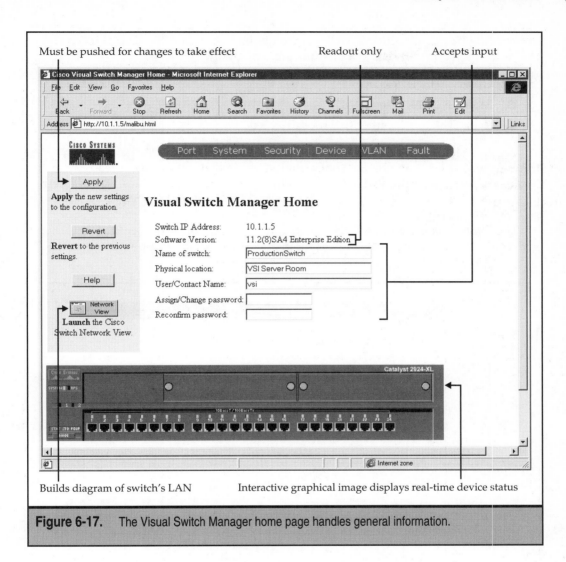

Figure 6-17.   The Visual Switch Manager home page handles general information.

For a parameter change to take effect in the switch's running-configuration file, the Apply button must be clicked. This causes the parameter change to be uploaded to the switch and be updated in the device's memory. The Revert button reverts switch parameter settings to what they were before the last change.

The Interactive Device Graphic in Visual Switch Manager

Visual Switch Manager takes its name from the interactive graphical image of a switch at the bottom of the home page. The image is of the actual switch device. The example in Figure 6-16 is logged into a Cisco Catalyst 2924-XL. The switch image is "live," in that status information displayed reflects what's currently happening on the device. Each switch port is lit up in one of three colors to indicate current device status:

▼ **Green** The link is up.

■ **Blue** No link is reported.

▲ **Red** The link is either faulty or disabled.

The switch image does more than just report status. It's an interactive interface through which you can change configuration parameters. If you've already read this book, you'll recognize the switch image as the same interactive graphical device interface used in CiscoView. CiscoView (covered in Chapter 17) is a superset of VSM, in that it handles all Cisco devices, not just switches.

The dialog box in Figure 6-18 comes up after the user clicks the FastEthernet0/8 port in the switch image in Figure 6-16. This input dialog is specific to the port that is clicked.

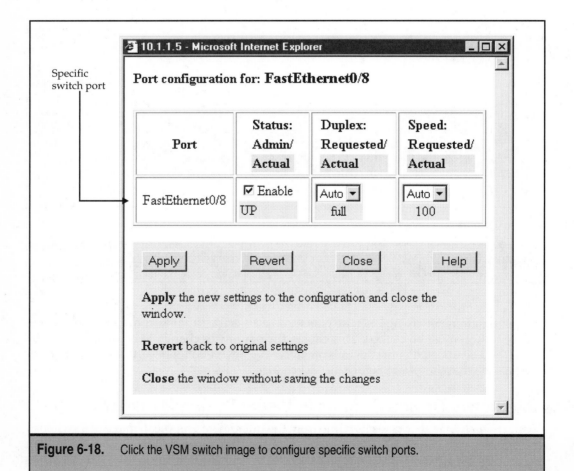

Figure 6-18.   Click the VSM switch image to configure specific switch ports.

The port's basic parameters are set here. The Enable checkbox turns the switch port on or off. The status below the Enable checkbox is a readout indicating whether connection to the LAN is working properly (up or down). Figure 6-18's example indicates UP.

Network View

The Network View feature is an application that discovers and diagrams surrounding network topology. Network View diagrams *only* Cisco devices. It provides reports on network devices and links and can be used as an interactive interface to change device configuration parameters. Network View diagrams include these features:

▼   **Visual Stack**   Use this to display a switch image of one or more members of a switch stack.

■   **Switch Manager**   Click the right mouse button on a switch in the image to show a pop-up menu with two options: to see a report on the switch or to launch a management software application that can be used to reconfigure the LAN.

■   **Link Report**   Click the right mouse button on a link (the line connecting devices in the diagram) to see that link's IP addresses, operating mode, VLANs, and other operating parameters.

▲   **Toggle Labels**   Use this to change device labels in the diagram from IP addresses to the Cisco device model numbers (for example, from IP address 10.1.1.5 to model number 2924M-XL) and to label network links (lines). Link labels contain the name of the device interface through which the link is running (for example, Ethernet1).

Be careful before launching Network View, though. It can be slow, because it uses CDP (Cisco Discovery Protocol) to find other devices. For example, it took something over 20 minutes to generate the diagram in Figure 6-19.

Switch Port Configuration

A port is where stations physically connect to the switch. Ports on switch devices are called *switch ports* or *switched ports*. They are the connections into which twisted-pair cables from hosts (such as PCs, servers, or printers) are plugged. Other network devices, such as routers and other switches, also connect to switch ports.

Switch ports have both administrative status and actual status, shown in Figure 6-20. Administrative status is set to enabled mode by default. The Enable setting means the port is ready for work. Actual status can be either Up or Down. It's possible for a port's administrative status to be enabled and its actual status to be Down. This would indicate that the port is operationally ready but is not at work (Down) because nothing is plugged into it.

Two parameters can be set to affect a switch port's effective operating speed: duplex mode and transmission speed.

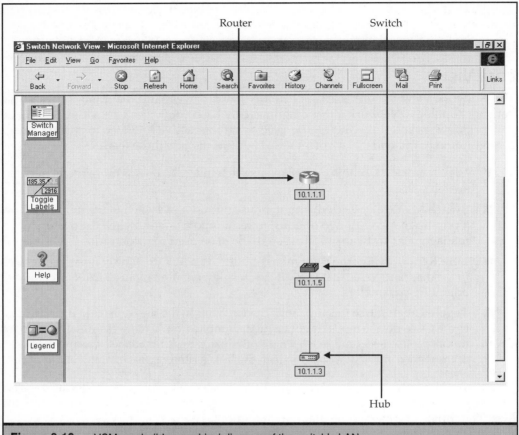

Figure 6-19. VSM can build a graphical diagram of the switch's LAN.

The Duplex parameter can be set so it automatically recognizes and sets either full-duplex or half-duplex. Duplex mode is whether transmission is one-way or two-way. If devices connected at both ends of a link have full-duplex capability, the Auto setting will automatically set to it, in effect doubling transmission speed. Unless configured otherwise, VSM always autonegotiates full-duplex mode when possible.

In switches with 10/100 autosensing, the Transmission Speed Requested parameter is usually set to Auto. The term 10/100 refers to the capability of a switch to sense automatically whether the device at the other end of a link is running 100 Mbps (Fast Ethernet) or 10 Mbps (plain Ethernet). Unless configured otherwise, VSM always autonegotiates a 100-Mbps connection when possible. Network administrators will override Auto and specify one speed over the other when the switch is having trouble correctly sensing a link's speed.

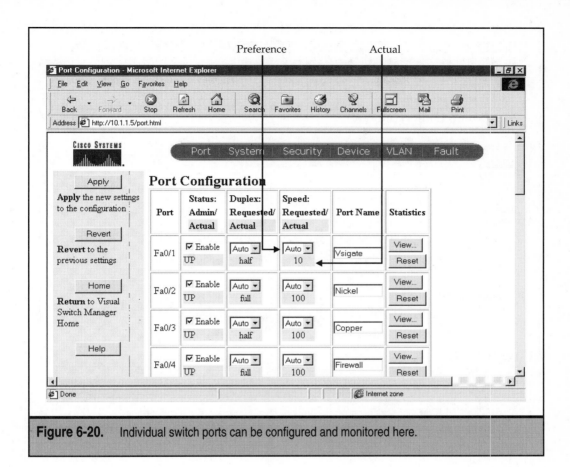

Figure 6-20. Individual switch ports can be configured and monitored here.

Port Grouping

Port groups are logical high-speed connections between switches. They are configured for either Fast EtherChannel or Gigabit EtherChannel connections. Port groups create redundant links between switches so that if there's a failure with one link in the group, its traffic will automatically move to the other links (an automatic process called *failover*).

A port group is treated as a single logical port. Forming port groups simplifies management and reporting. For example, configuration changes for a port group need to be made in just one place instead of for each individual port. Figure 6-21 shows the interface for forming port groups.

All ports in the group must belong to the same set of VLANs and must all be source-based or destination-based. *Source-based* switching is when the port group makes switching decisions based on the source MAC addresses. In *destination-based* switching, switching decisions are based on the destination MACs. It's OK to configure both source-based and destination-based port groups on the same switch, but not in the same group.

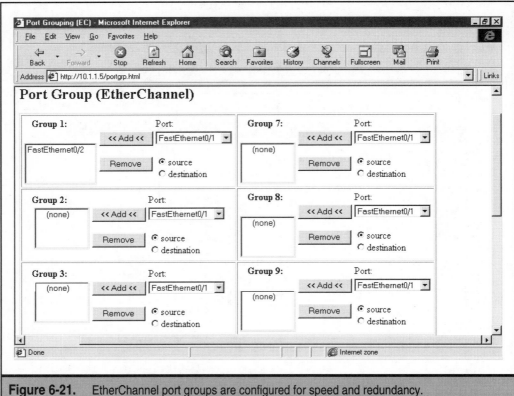

Figure 6-21.   EtherChannel port groups are configured for speed and redundancy.

Port Monitoring (SPAN)

SPAN (Switched Port ANalyzer) gathers real-time information for monitoring switch ports and diagnosing problems. Its purpose is to concentrate port activity information into a single port—the SPAN port—dedicated to troubleshooting. A SPAN port functions as a test instrument probe, but in the form of a dedicated switch port instead of separate hardware from an external test device.

SPAN operates by mirroring traffic from one or more switch ports to the SPAN port. If the ports being monitored are members of a VLAN, the SPAN port must be a member of the same VLAN. Figure 6-22 shows that three ports on the example switch are being monitored.

The SPAN port runs RMON probe software. *RMON* (for Remote Monitoring) is specialized probe software that tracks port performance statistics, traffic patterns, and alarms. Usually, a Network Management Module (NMM) card is inserted into the switch to provide electronics dedicated to monitoring and diagnosing problems. Sometimes a network management station reads data from the port instead of an NMM, which are

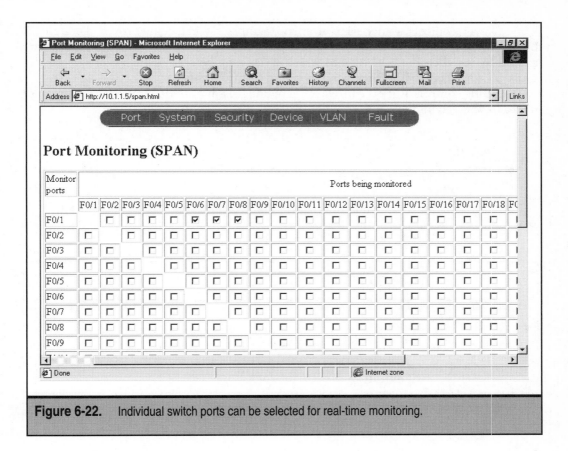

Figure 6-22.   Individual switch ports can be selected for real-time monitoring.

usually PCs or UNIX workstations. Having this type of information available across a switched network helps network administrators anticipate and solve network problems. Without SPAN, port network management in switched networks would require more time and effort.

Flooding Controls/Network Port

Flooding occurs when traffic received in one switch port is passed out all other ports. Switches flood when they receive messages with unknown destination addresses. Flooding is necessary in switched networks because they rely on MAC addresses of physical devices, not logical IP addresses, as do routers. Without flooding in switched networks, a message would be dropped by the first network, unaware of its destination MAC address, effectively terminating the transmission.

However, controls are necessary to ensure against a switch being drowned in a glut of flooded messages. The potential for flooding is made worse by the fact that messages are passed by a switch to all VLANs in which it has membership (switches are frequently multi-VLAN). Figure 6-23 shows the Flooding Controls page.

Flooding controls block the forwarding of unnecessary flooded traffic by using one of the following techniques:

▼ Sending all flooded messages to a single port (the *network port*) so only that port gets flooded

■ Enabling *broadcast storm thresholds* to limit how many flooded messages a port will accept

▲ Blocking the forwarding of unicast (one-to-one) and broadcast (one-to-all) messages, shown in the *Receive Unknown MACs* field

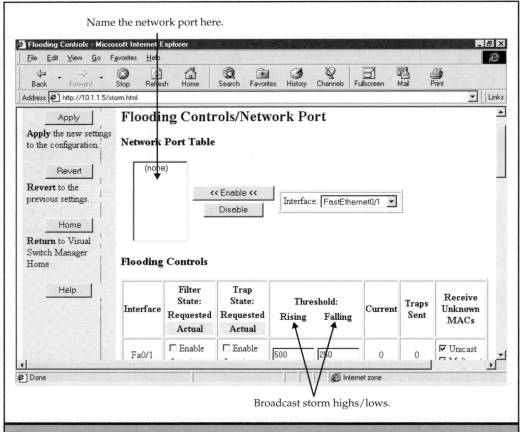

Figure 6-23.   Flooded and broadcast messages can be limited in switched networks.

System Configuration

Cisco switches run a full-blown image of the IOS software optimized for switching. An IOS config file must be created and maintained for the switch. The startup-config file tells it how to reconfigure itself when it reboots. Figure 6-24 shows the System Configuration page. It's used to maintain basic setup information on the IOS image running on the switch.

NVRAM stands for nonvolatile random access memory, and its buffer size tells the switch how many bytes to allocate for storing the startup-config file. The Boot Loader Flags field tells the switch to perform an extended self-test during reboot.

IP Management

For a switch to become operable on a network, it must have several IP addresses assigned. The IP Management page shown in Figure 6-25 is used to administer and update IP information. Three mandatory IP addresses include the following:

▼ **IP address** A 32-bit address assigned to hosts using TCP/IP, written as four octets separated by periods (for example, 209.98.86.52).

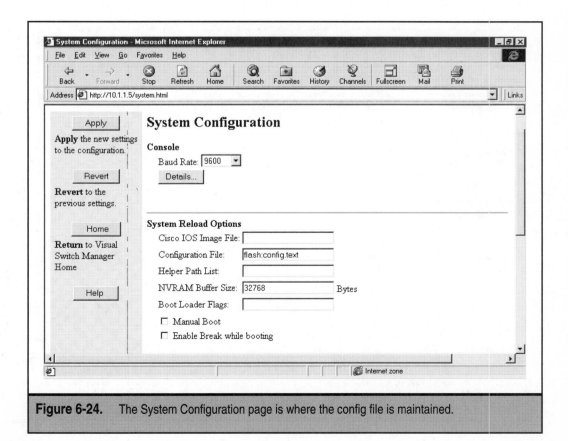

Figure 6-24. The System Configuration page is where the config file is maintained.

■ **IP subnet mask**   A mask overlaying a full IP address to indicate the bits of the full IP address used to address the local subnetwork, often simply called the *mask*. The mask is always some portion of the left side of the overall IP address (for example, 255.255.255.248). Refer to the blueprints section in the center of this book for an explanation of subnet masking.

▲ **Default gateway**   The switch sends traffic to an unknown IP address through the default gateway. When a message is sent outside the local network, it's routed through the default gateway, which has one or more external addresses. The default gateway address is frequently an Internet service provider (ISP).

Notice that the Management VLAN is read-only in this page. That's because the IP Management page controls only what goes into the config file of the individual switch device being managed. The Management VLAN that the device is a part of is specified in the config file of a higher-level device called the network management station (NMS). The NMS—usually a PC or UNIX workstation—is the master console used by the network management team.

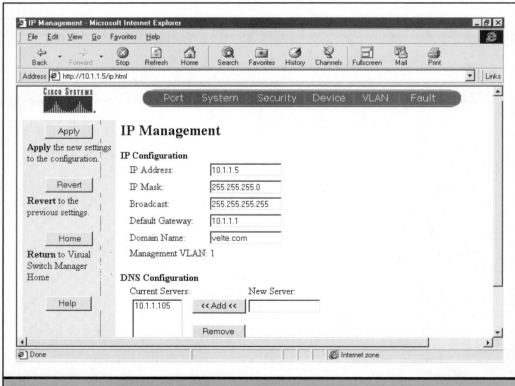

Figure 6-25.   The IP Management page is used to change IP address information.

SNMP Configuration

SNMP (Simple Network Management Protocol) is an IP application used to administer and troubleshoot network devices from a so-called network management station (NMS). SNMP is an industry standard, not a proprietary Cisco protocol. The interface shown in Figure 6-26 is, of course, Cisco's, but the parameters set via this page enable the creation of generalized SNMP information that can be used by any SNMP software product, not just Cisco's. You have the option of not enabling SNMP management for the switch. Disabling SNMP prevents SNMP-based network management applications from being able to monitor or reconfigure the switch.

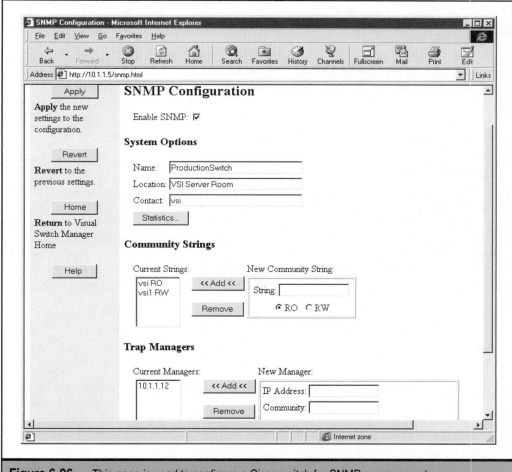

Figure 6-26.   This page is used to configure a Cisco switch for SNMP management.

SNMP works by setting up *agents* on a device. These agents are small software programs that observe activity on the switch and send alerts called *traps* to the NMS, informing it of significant events. A *community string* is a text string that acts as a sort of group password used to authenticate messages sent between the NMS and the devices it manages. The community string is sent in every packet between the manager and the SNMP agent. Refer to Chapter 15 to read about various Cisco products incorporating SNMP functionality.

ARP Table

ARP stands for the Address Resolution Protocol, which is an industry-standard protocol for mapping IP addresses to MAC addresses. Translating addresses is necessary because when a message reaches its destination LAN, it must resolve the logical IP address to a physical MAC address in order to know which physical host device to communicate with. In ARP tables inside Cisco switches, the IP address is on the left and the MAC address it is associated with is on the right.

Addresses are dynamically added to the ARP table as messages pass through the switch. To prevent infinite growth of the table, the ARP Cache Timeout Value field limits how long entries stay in the table prior to being dropped. The ARP table ages off of addresses that go unused for that specified period of time *except* those that were added to the table manually as permanent or static ARP entries. In the example in Figure 6-27, the aging period is set for 14,400 seconds (four hours).

Address Management

The address table (also called the address management table) is used by switches to decide where to forward incoming messages. The address table associates a list of MAC addresses with specific switch ports. Unlike IP addresses, MAC addresses are a sort of network serial number identifying physical network devices (usually the network interface card). Address tables are the centerpiece of switched network architecture because they guide messages to their destinations. MAC addresses function in switched networks the way IP addresses function in router-based networks. There are three kinds of address tables:

▼ **Dynamic address table**   Built by the switch by associating each message's incoming port number and source MAC address. (See Figure 6-28.)

■ **Secure address table**   A secure address has only one destination port; they're manually entered and don't age.

▲ **Static address table**   Like a secure address in that they're manually entered and don't age, but a static address applies to the entire switch instead of just a single port.

Most ports in switched networks use dynamic addressing, because that way the network can help operate itself without human intervention. Static addressing is used for port grouping, while secure addressing is used to protect valuable network resources and proprietary data.

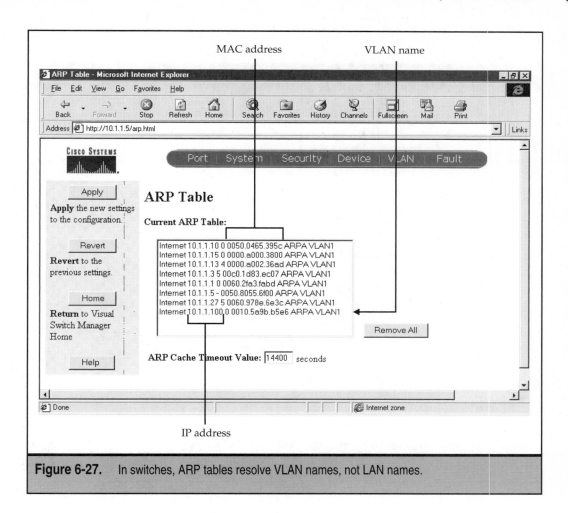

Figure 6-27. In switches, ARP tables resolve VLAN names, not LAN names.

Port Security

A *secure port* is established by creating a list of one or more source MAC addresses that may send traffic to it. In this sense, a secure port is a form of static-access port. Port security should not be mixed up with SNMP alerts and other security applications. Port security works by restricting access to a port to explicitly named links. This is often done as much for performance reasons as for data security. Figure 6-29 shows the Port Security page.

The advantages of securing a port are that unknown devices cannot connect to the port without your knowledge. It's also a good way to dedicate the port's bandwidth by setting the size of the port's address table to 1, thereby making available all the port's bandwidth to that device. A port is secured by checking the box in the Security column, and one or both of the Trap and Shutdown fields. Port security cannot be enabled on a multi-VLAN port.

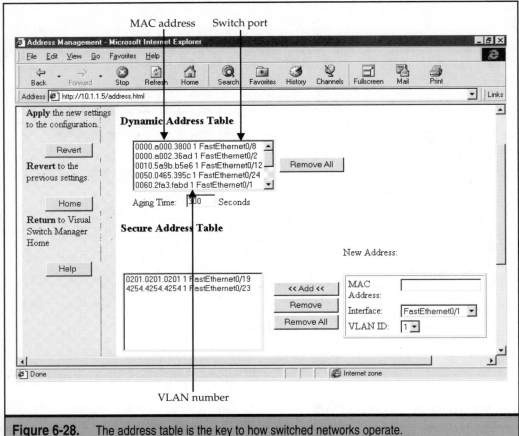

Figure 6-28.   The address table is the key to how switched networks operate.

Cisco Discovery Protocol

Cisco Discovery Protocol (CDP) is a proprietary Cisco protocol that automatically finds other Cisco devices on the same network. CDP is a low-level protocol that is independent of higher-level networking protocols such as IP or NetWare's IPX. In this way, it can draw an accurate picture of Cisco devices in a LAN—regardless of what protocols each is running. CDP enables various Web-based management software tools—including Visual Switch Manager's Network View application—to diagram networks graphically as they exist in real time.

Packet Hold Time is the number of seconds a neighboring device will retain the CDP neighbor information it receives (set to 180 seconds in the example in Figure 6-30). CDP can be enabled by individual port, which is a common practice done for security reasons or to conserve bandwidth.

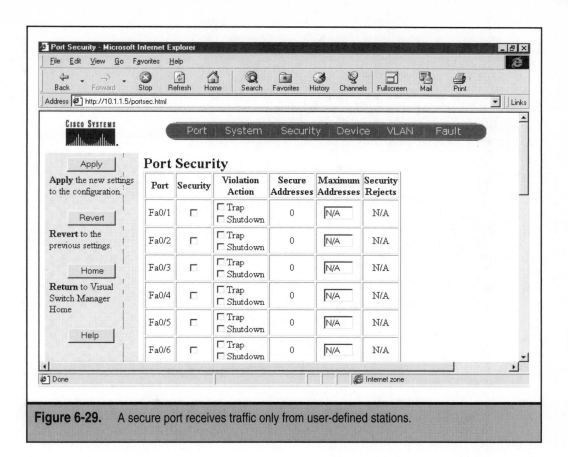

Figure 6-29. A secure port receives traffic only from user-defined stations.

Cisco Group Multicast Protocol

Cisco Group Multicast Protocol (CGMP) is a proprietary Cisco protocol used to limit the forwarding of IP multicast (one-to-many) packets in a network. For example, a switch might sign up to receive multicasts advertising new MAC addresses from networks outside the intranet. CGMP is sort of a subscription-processing service in which hosts enroll in a group that receives certain kinds of multicasts. Hosts issue *join* messages to join a multicast group and *leave* messages to quit. Like most table-building protocols, CGMP ages off of unused subscriptions to limit table size. The Router Hold Time parameter (set to 300 seconds in the example in Figure 6-31) removes an entry after a user-specified time period.

The CGMP table is maintained on a router. For CGMP to work, therefore, a switch must have a connection to a router that is running both CGMP and IGMP (Internet Group Management Protocol). IGMP is used by IP hosts to report their multicast group memberships to an adjacent multicast router. When the router receives an IGMP request (leave or join) from a client, it forwards this information to the switch in a CGMP packet. The switch uses this information to alter its forwarding behavior.

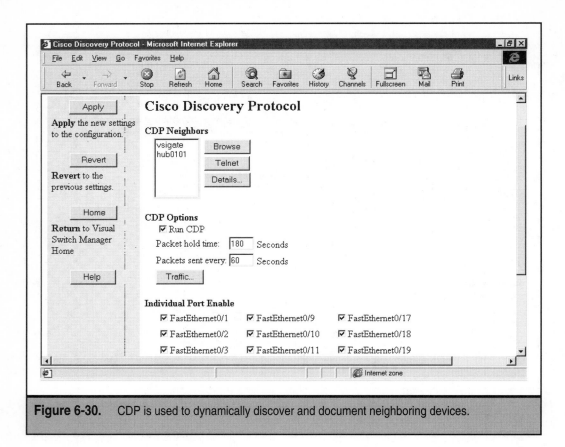

Figure 6-30.   CDP is used to dynamically discover and document neighboring devices.

Spanning-Tree Protocol

Spanning-Tree Protocol (STP) is an industry-standard technique for preventing loop-back paths in switched networks. Switched networks use MAC addresses in lieu of logical IP addresses. They work by forwarding a message to any switch containing the desired MAC address. Without STP, switched networks are susceptible to using paths that double back to the switch that sent the message—causing slow delivery and generating unnecessary traffic.

STP works by identifying redundant paths and blocking at least one of them. The Spanning-Tree Protocol page, shown in Figure 6-32, is used to enable a switch for STP and to define a root switch for each VLAN. Having a root switch for a VLAN helps the STP algorithm figure out which paths are best to block or not block. STP uses a *path costing* system not unlike the routing protocols discussed in Chapter 14. A lower path cost represents higher speed (for example, an STP cost value of 100 for 10 Mbps versus 4 for 1 Gbps). The Hello Time parameter sets the number of seconds between STP messages. The Max Age parameter sets how long the switch should wait between STP messages before reconfiguring STP on its own.

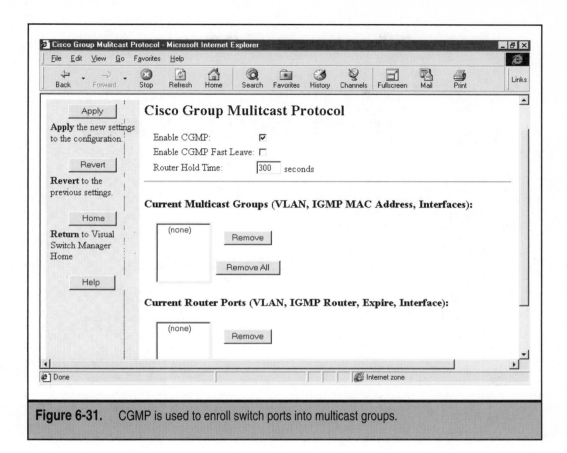

Figure 6-31. CGMP is used to enroll switch ports into multicast groups.

VLAN Membership

VLAN membership is a simple matter of assigning a switch port to one or more virtual LANs. The maximum number of VLANs a port may belong to is a function of the switch model. The example switch in Figure 6-33 is a Cisco Catalyst 2924-XL, which supports up to 64 VLANs per port. VLAN membership modes are as follows:

▼ Static-access VLAN membership mode

■ Multi-VLAN membership mode

■ Dynamic-access VLAN membership mode

▲ ISL trunk VLAN membership mode

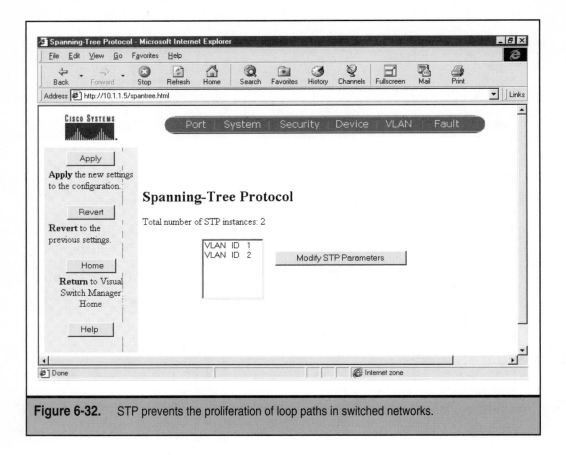

Figure 6-32. STP prevents the proliferation of loop paths in switched networks.

ISL, which stands for Inter-Switch Link, is a proprietary Cisco protocol for intercon-necting multiple switches and maintaining VLAN information as traffic goes between them. ISL provides VLAN capabilities while maintaining high performance on Fast Ethernet links in full- or half-duplex mode.

Special IOS software feature sets are required on a switch for it to operate advanced VLAN modes such as multi-VLAN and dynamic-access VLAN.

VTP Management

VLAN Trunk Protocol (VTP) enables network administrators to make configuration changes on a single switch and automatically communicate those changes to all the other switches in the network. Central configuration limits a number of problems, such as du-plicate VLAN names, incorrect VLAN-type specifications, and security violations. VTP works by sending advertisements over the switched network as a way to maintain VTP trunk memberships and transmit other VTP configuration changes. VTP configuration is maintained as a VLAN database stored in the NVRAM of member switches. A switch can be in any one of three VTP modes:

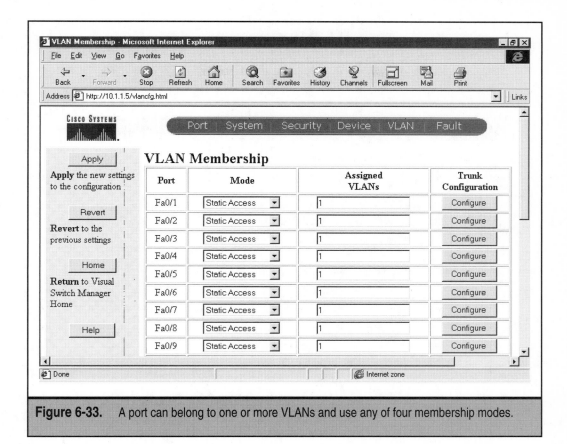

Figure 6-33. A port can belong to one or more VLANs and use any of four membership modes.

▼ **Client VTP mode** A switch that is enabled for VTP; can send advertisements but cannot configure VLANs

■ **Transparent VTP mode** A switch that is disabled from using VTP; cannot send its own advertisements but can receive and forward them to and from other switches

▲ **Server VTP mode** A switch that is enabled for VTP; can send advertisements and can configure VLANs

As shown in Figure 6-34, the VTP Management screen displays VTP status information at the top and inputs configuration parameter changes at the bottom.

ISL works by encapsulating frames going through a switch with an ISL header, letting other switches on the trunk filter through ISL encapsulated messages as "native" to the trunk. The IEEE 802.1Q tagging format, an open standard that is not proprietary to Cisco, supports simultaneous tagged and untagged traffic on a switch port.

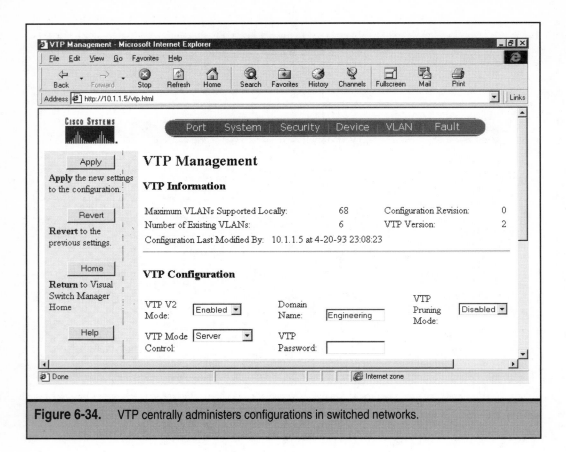

Figure 6-34. VTP centrally administers configurations in switched networks.

VMPS Configuration

VLAN Membership Policy Server (VMPS) dynamically assigns switch ports to VLANs based on the MAC address of the device connected to the port. When a host is moved from a port on one switch in the network to a port on another switch in the network, it's automatically assigned to the proper VLAN. A VMPS maintains a database that maps the MAC addresses of VMPS-enabled ports to VLANs. It's downloaded from the server via Trivial File Transfer Protocol (TFTP).

VMPS is useful in enterprises in which users move about between locations and use their laptop computers to jack into the intranet from wherever they are. The VMPS Configuration page (Figure 6-35) is used to set the VMPS server, add or remove VLANs, and set a primary VLAN.

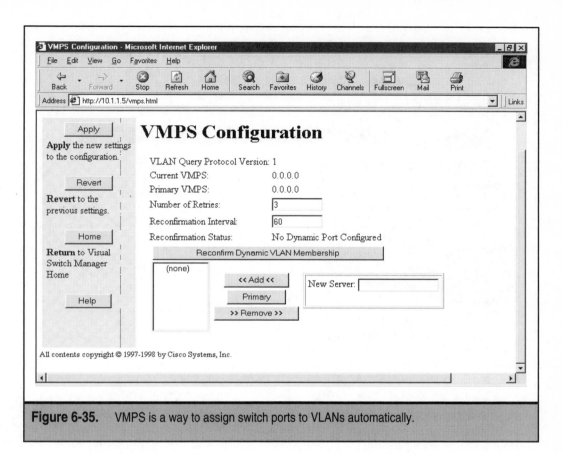

Figure 6-35.   VMPS is a way to assign switch ports to VLANs automatically.

VTP/VQP Statistics

VLAN Trunk Protocol and VLAN Query Protocol (VQP) gather VLAN policy statistics. A switch transmits advertisement messages on all its trunk ports after a VLAN configuration changes and transmits periodic summary advertisements on any trunk port for which it has not sent or received an advertisement for the last five minutes. By hearing these advertisements, other switches in the same management domain learn about new VLANs configured in the transmitting switch.

VTP statistics summarize advertisement messaging, while VQP statistics summarize message results such as the number of query messages, bad messages, changes, denied responses, and other totals, as shown in Figure 6-36.

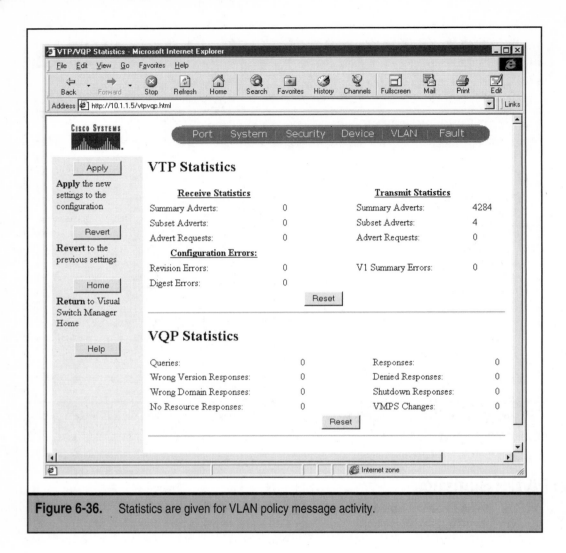

Figure 6-36. Statistics are given for VLAN policy message activity.

Logging Configuration

Switches log activity records as they operate, doing so by severity levels when network or switch events occur. You can display log information about switch activity on a console or write log messages to a buffer, file, or to the UNIX syslog facility.

The Logging Configuration page (Figure 6-37) configures how these things are done for a switch. The Logging Level field is where you select the minimum severity level you want reported. The options are as follows:

▼ Alerts

■ Critical

- Debugging
- Emergencies
- Errors
- Informational
- Notifications
- ▲ Warnings

The user cannot define which switch events belong to which severity levels. Cisco IOS software correlates events to a particular severity-level category.

Switches are an important means of providing connectivity in an organization's network. They not only unite devices on a network, but they also supply an important, intermediary step between the PC and the internetwork. In addition to a number of switch offerings for organizations large and small, Cisco also provides a powerful management tool in its VSM software.

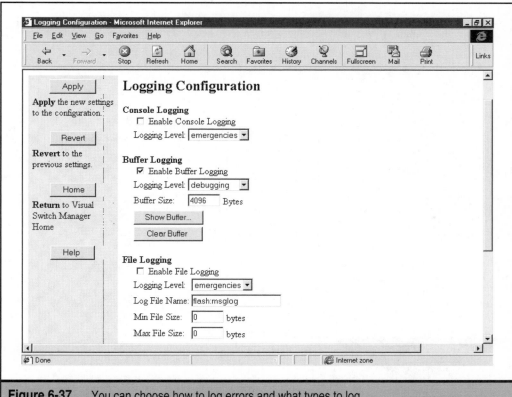

Figure 6-37.   You can choose how to log errors and what types to log.

CHAPTER 7

Quality of Service

Technology touches businesses and organizations of all sizes today as it never did before. And because of organizations' reliance on technology and networking, it's crucial for traffic to get where it's intended, and—sometimes more importantly—*when* it's intended.

WHAT IS QoS?

In a perfect world, we would have instantaneous access to all the information we wanted with the single click of a mouse. There would be no wait for files to come to us across the Internet, nor while waiting for a file to download would we be faced with enough time to prepare a Thanksgiving dinner.

Back here on earth, however, things aren't so utopian. Internetworking did not start with huge, inexpensive, wide-open pipes through which everyone could instantaneously transmit data. Because of the cost and speed issues inherent with modern networking—not to mention the greater and greater demand for bandwidth coming from new technology and applications—there must be a way to send the important data first.

Consider, for example, the blight at college campuses around the nation. With file-sharing services like Grokster and WinMX offering music, video, and software files, campus networks are choking because of all the students downloading gigabytes of data. With bandwidth being sucked up to download music files, network applications critical to the day-to-day academic and administrative functioning of the colleges are suffering. But how can you tell the network to let the administrative traffic go through the network before the Grokster traffic goes through? Easy. Just implement Quality of Service (QoS).

By utilizing QoS technology and policies, college network administrators can prioritize network traffic. This means that the academic and administrative functions can be given higher priority on the network than the music-hoarding kids, thereby ensuring the important traffic gets where it needs to go.

What exactly is QoS? Dozens of definitions are floating around, partly because the words "quality" and "service" have been subjected to significant abuse over the years. Join these two trendy words at the hip, and confusion can really kick in. A more serious problem is that QoS is somewhat of a nascent technology, with the Internet Engineering Task Force (IETF) still in the process of defining technical specifications for many important elements of QoS. Add to this the fact that there are competing commercial agendas for QoS, which are further complicated by the conflicting needs of ISPs and corporate intranets.

Nonetheless, QoS is a real technology, so it can be defined. An informative definition might be as follows: *QoS is a collection of run-time processes that actively manage bandwidth to provide committed levels of network service to applications and/or users. It implements a framework for service policy and action that extends end-to-end for serviced connections, even across autonomous systems.* From there, a seemingly endless parade of variations ensues, but suffice it to say that QoS is a collection of mechanisms designed to favor some types of traffic over others.

Why Your Organization Needs QoS

At first, QoS sounds like something networks sending streaming video or voice need, but that other networks can survive without. Such notions are misleading. You may not be planning on transmitting movies across your network, but you still must ensure that information is flowing swiftly through your pipes—and not getting stuck in any network clogs.

For instance, the market data applications that brokerage firms use are sensitive not only to average networking conditions, but also to peak rates. Brokers must be able to receive their information with minimal delay—they have to in order to be able to buy or sell, no matter if the market is booming or crashing.

It isn't just video or Voice over IP (VoIP) that relies on QoS. Especially if your organization is one that hosts customers, it's important that traffic comes and goes as expeditiously as possible.

Bandwidth Is Not Enough

Until recently, increasing bandwidth solved most network user satisfaction problems. When things slowed down, network managers simply put in a fatter pipe to speed things back up.

The amount of raw data that can be moved through a network is no longer the only issue, however. Now, timing and coordination can be just as important as raw throughput to satisfactory service quality. While it's true that most multimedia applications are bandwidth hogs, many also introduce operational requirements new to IP networks. To take an example, packet delay during a VoIP phone call can cause the speakers to talk out of sequence, robbing the conversation of its coherence.

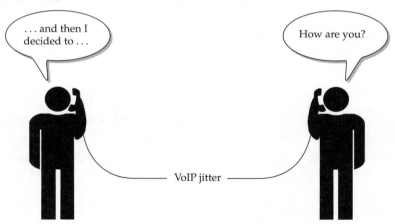

In the parlance, packet delivery delay that causes a signal to lose its timing references is called *jitter*. Because the effects of jitter on VoIP calls are so noticeable to users, they render the calls all but useless.

Traditional applications like e-mail, Web browsers, and FTP aren't much affected by jitter or the other by-products of best-effort IP packet delivery. They're "elastic" in that they're not sensitive to timing issues.

Throwing bandwidth at a media application such as VoIP won't necessarily help. Even with a high-bandwidth end-to-end pipe, sudden bursts of traffic would still be manifested as jitter.

Network applications vary in their signal delivery requirements. The more an application's signal pattern is sensitive to delivery delay, the greater difficulty it has with IP's best-effort service approach. (By the way, *delay* is when a message is delivered intact but slowly; in contrast, jitter is where delay harms message integrity.) Table 7-1 outlines various traffic types and their elasticity to packet delay or jitter.

Most traditional Internet applications are asynchronous and therefore very tolerant to jitter. For example, a user may not like waiting 30 seconds for a Web page to download (delay), but the HTTP application still works fine from a functional standpoint. Convergence applications aren't so forgiving, although some are more tolerant to the vagaries of IP than others.

Let's add some examples to the categories in Table 7-1:

▼ NetMeeting (nonvideo) is a good example of interactive traffic, in which delivery sequence is important but not critical.

■ VoIP is truly isochronous traffic because out-of-sequence speech causes information loss and may even annoy users enough to hang up.

■ Videocasting is another example of isochronous traffic, because each frame must be presented immediately after its predecessor in perfect sequence, and also in quick succession.

▲ The classic example of mission-critical traffic is a process control interrupt instruction to open a safety valve in a nuclear reactor's cooling system.

Tolerance to Delay	Traffic Type	Effect of Packet Delay on the Network Application
Very tolerant	Asynchronous	Fully elastic, delay causes no effect
	Synchronous	Delay can cause some effect, usually just slowness
Somewhat tolerant	Interactive	Delay annoys and distracts users, but application is still functional
	Isochronous	Application is only partially functional
Not tolerant	Mission-critical	Application is functionally disabled

Table 7-1.   Tolerance of Packet Delay (Jitter): A Function of the Type of Traffic

To take the Internet to the next level, IP must provide more reliable network service levels, and the industry is convinced QoS is the answer.

Changing Business Needs

As bigger, beefier, and time-sensitive applications become more intertwined with networking technology, it will be even more important to provide crucial services as fast as possible.

A decade ago, no one would have guessed we'd have Jetsons-like video chats across the country on our computer screens. Certainly no one thought we'd be able to view interactive online catalogs from our favorite retail stores or listen to CDs at our desks before we bought them. So, as the Internet and technology changes, so will business offerings and, as a result, network needs.

Whether your mission-critical applications are the bandwidth hogs or they are affected by the bandwidth hogs, a good QoS solution is important to keep your business traffic flowing both now and in the future.

Key QoS Concepts

Before charging ahead into the ups, downs, ins, and outs of the kinds of QoS out there, let's take in some fundamentals. We'll look at some of the concepts behind QoS, how it is applied to a network, and then how QoS is already being delivered.

Existing QoS

The industry has been using a QoS of sorts in WAN links for years. WAN links are costly and have historically been the biggest bottleneck in end-to-end connections. It simply costs more to pull a cable over long distances, across land belonging to others, under streets, and even under oceans. The only way to cut WAN costs is to install faster media, or to spread the cost among more users.

Both problems put intense pressure on the telecom industry to put various QoS mechanisms into their WAN transport technologies, which today are primarily ATM and Frame Relay. These mechanisms now serve as a model for the designers currently formulating QoS solutions for the Internet.

Frame Relay   Frame Relay is now the de facto standard technology for WANs. From the technical standpoint, Frame Relay is a data-link layer protocol that uses the High-Level Data-Link Control (HDLC) transport protocol for transport. By using HDLC encapsulation, Frame Relay is able to form multiple virtual circuits within a network cloud, making for a fast and reliable network that can be conveniently shared by otherwise unrelated enterprises.

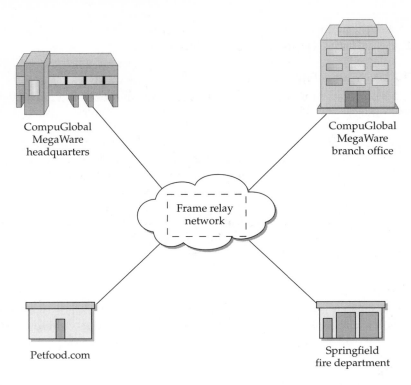

Within Frame Relay, Explicit Congestion Notification (ECN) is a form of flow control accepted by the Frame Relay standards committee as a way of preventing network congestion. ECN consists of two bits that are carried in the frame header. These bits are established by the network in the event of congestion. When congestion occurs, the user device must react by reducing the data rate sent onto the network. It reacts primarily to congestion at the source or destination of the Frame Relay connection.

When the source end of the circuit detects its input buffer filling up, it sets the Forward ECN (FECN) bit. This bit is carried "forward" through the network, toward the frame destination. At the same time, it also sets the Backward ECN (BECN) bit, which is sent back to the transmitting user device. FECN and BECN are worthless in reducing network congestion if the user device does not react (or is not capable of reacting) to the presence of the FECN and BECN bits.

ATM   Asynchronous Transfer Mode (ATM) has many QoS-enabling features built into it, especially in the form of the fixed-size, 53-byte cell it uses to transport information. This gives the hardware in ATM switches a big speed advantage over IP devices, which must process variable-size packets. Those variable-size packets force IP routers and switches to expend extra CPU cycles to figure out exactly where fields begin and end.

ATM switching works by combining multiple virtual circuits (VCs) into a virtual path (VP). Multiple VPs are, in turn, combined within a physical circuit, usually a fiber-optic cable operated by the Synchronous Optical Network (SONET) protocol at the physical level, as depicted in Figure 7-1.

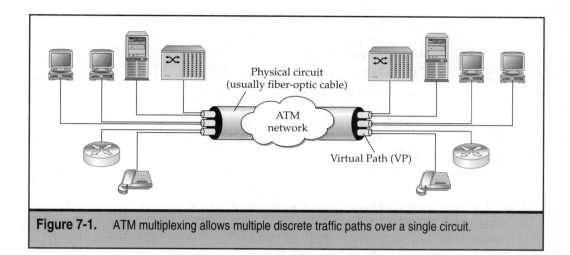

Figure 7-1. ATM multiplexing allows multiple discrete traffic paths over a single circuit.

Each ATM cell identifies itself with a VC identifier and a VP identifier (VCI and VPI) to tell ATM switches how it should be handled. As a cell hops between switches, its VCI and VPI values are rewritten to direct the cell to its next hop, thereby combining path integrity and adaptability.

ATM is, at its core, uniquely enabled to provide QoS. The primary responsibility of traffic-management mechanisms in ATM is to promote network efficiency and avoid congestion. It is also a critical design objective of ATM that the network utilization imposed by transporting one type of application data does not adversely affect the network's capability to deliver other data.

IP Convergence of the world onto IP for internetworking is a done deal, and the same goes for convergence onto Ethernet as the de facto LAN standard.

However, the convergence of virtually all communications media (telephone, television, radio) onto IP is still somewhat problematic because, as discussed, IP by its very nature is antagonistic to the determinism of QoS. The best-effort philosophy of IP is the fundamental result of the Internet Protocol's connectionless nature. When you send a packet, it's left up to IP as to what route will be taken to deliver it to its destination. In addition to its connectionless, best-effort architecture, IP QoS is a tough engineering proposition for other reasons as well:

▼ Network provisioning is a zero-sum game. Because bandwidth is a finite resource, every bit per second of capacity dedicated to one connection is consumed at the expense of all other simultaneous connections. QoS only finesses bandwidth; it doesn't create it.

■ Users will always take as much bandwidth as they can consume—so long as they don't have to pay extra for it. To be effective, QoS needs a way to authenticate users, and a way to record utilization for billing. These authentication and accounting mechanisms must be unobtrusive and resource efficient.

■ To remain universal, the Internet must be careful to not allocate so much bandwidth to inelastic applications such that time-independent applications like HTTP and FTP become bandwidth-starved.

▲ There is no infrastructure in place to support a run-time QoS environment. ATM and Frame Relay QoS work fairly well because they provide their own internal infrastructures. End-to-end QoS entails operation across a multiprotocol environment, implying an order-of-magnitude increase in complexity.

The QoS Framework

To operate properly, QoS needs a separate policy framework to layer atop IP networks. A service-level agreement (SLA) is a policy, not unlike a network security policy, but an SLA must be propagated to the devices that are to enforce it, and the policy must somehow be kept uniform across the topology.

Coordinating QoS across large internetworks can get complicated. A communications infrastructure is needed to serve as a framework coordinating QoS policy across the topology. Those familiar with routing protocols or SNMP will understand that a cohesive suite of technical elements—a freestanding subsystem, in other words—must be in place for QoS to work.

Without a framework, it would be necessary to separately maintain each QoS policy on a per-device basis. Forcing administrators to "touch" each device would make QoS within an internetwork both labor-intensive and mistake-prone.

In a typical internetwork, requests for service and changes in operating conditions take place several times a minute. With that kind of dynamism, it follows that network teams will need to tweak fixed QoS policies with some increasing frequency.

QoS needs a way to continually account for finite bandwidth resources. Also needed are automated mechanisms to make decisions between competing QoS requests and to set up and tear down QoS assignments as connections come and go. The mission of a QoS framework takes on high complexity as QoS services span autonomous systems.

ENSURING QoS

Now that you understand what QoS is and what its goals are, the natural question is, "so how do I implement it for my organization?" There are a number of techniques and tools to ensure QoS. In the case of bandwidth provisioning, using RSVP for instance, you chop a trail through the cyber-jungle by establishing a free path across all the routers between the two endpoints. Alternatively, you can ensure that the most important packets get priority and are sent across the network first. There are also a number of different ways to deal with packets both before and after they start piling up.

In this section, we'll look at the different ways QoS can be deployed across your internetwork. First, we'll look at a method that relies heavily on hardware, and then we'll take a look under the QoS hood to see what software can do to keep the packets flowing.

Bandwidth Provisioning

Our first method of ensuring QoS is to clear a path between the two communicating computers. With bandwidth provisioning, a connection is allocated a certain amount of bandwidth that is negotiated among routers and switches along its path.

As contrasted to bandwidth prioritization (which we'll talk about in the next section), reserved connections are far more complex. Reservation schemes must get all routers along a connection's path to agree on a QoS regimen before transmission can begin. Moreover, the path itself must be defined before the reservations must be made. Reserved path bandwidth may also need to make real-time adjustments to changing operating conditions, further adding to complexity. This process is shown in Figure 7-2.

RSVP

The Resource Reservation Protocol (RSVP) "reserves" an amount of bandwidth resources along a path connecting source and destination devices to assure a minimum level of QoS. Applications running on IP end systems will use RSVP to indicate the nature of the packet streams they want to receive, thereby "reserving" bandwidth that can support the required QoS. This is done by defining parameters for such characteristics as minimum bandwidth, maximum delay jitter, maximum burst, and the like.

RSVP is considered the enabling protocol for what is called *integrated services* QoS architecture, or *IntServ* for short. The "integrated" part comes from the notion that all devices—end hosts and interim devices alike—are integrated into a unitary QoS service regimen to be maintained in both directions for the life of the QoS-serviced flow.

RSVP is complicated. It defines *sender* and *receiver* hosts for each flow of data. The sender sends a so-called *PATH* message downstream to the receiver, with the PATH collecting a roster of devices along the route. Once the PATH message is received, the receiver sends a request called a *RESV* message back upstream along the same path to the RSVP sender. The RESV message specifies parameters for the desired bandwidth characteristics. Once all the interim devices are signed on to support the QoS levels, the session

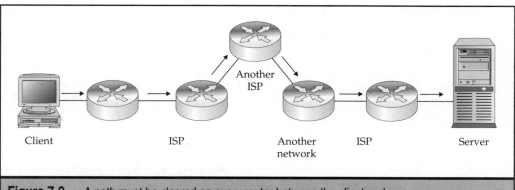

Figure 7-2.   A path must be cleared on every router between the client and server.

may begin. When the connection is terminated, an explicit tear-down mechanism is used to free up resources on the reserved devices. The RSVP process is depicted in Figure 7-3.

For the reservation to be fully guaranteed, each hop between network hardware must grant the reservation and physically allocate the requested bandwidth. By granting the reservation, the hop commits to providing the requested resources.

If the reservation is denied, the program receives a response that the network cannot support the amount and type of bandwidth or the requested service level. The program determines whether to send the data now using best-effort delivery or to wait and try the request again later.

RSVP is a *soft-state protocol,* which requires the reservation to be refreshed periodically. The reservation information, or *reservation state,* is cached at each hop. If the network routing protocol alters the data path, RSVP automatically installs the reservation state along the new route. If refresh messages are not received, reservations time out and are dropped, and the bandwidth is released.

NOTE: Many legacy routers and switches are not RSVP-compliant. In these cases, the reservation messages pass through each hop. End-to-end and low-delay guarantees for the requested service level are not available.

Route aggregation partially ameliorates RSVP complexity and overhead. For example, if thousands of RSVP receiver hosts were to receive a multicast (say, a Web TV videocast), the RESV messages would be rolled up and combined at aggregation points. Conversely, only

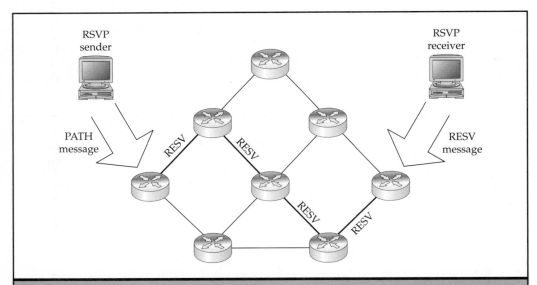

Figure 7-3.   RSVP uses a sophisticated, self-contained messaging system to reserve bandwidth.

one stream would be sent downstream from the videocaster, replicated at aggregation points to worm out to all endpoint destinations.

Shortcomings

Unfortunately, RSVP is not the best solution to deliver QoS in most environments. Since RSVP is based on establishing a path across the network, it is inherently weak.

Our biggest causes for concern with an RSVP-based solution are

▼ **Many weak links out there**   In a perfect world, everyone would have brand new network hardware, a homogenous Windows operating system, complete with Windows workstations. But in reality, networks tend to be cobbled together from Windows NT and 9x operating systems and use some hardware that's held together with duct tape and a couple stray Post-it™ notes that read "Never, EVER, press this button!" It is because of this inevitable combination of new equipment and legacy hardware that RSVP has problems. Though the bandwidth can be established with the QoS-compatible routers, there will probably be a couple in the network that aren't compatible and will provide that weak link in the chain. If that clear path cannot be guaranteed—even at one router—RSVP-based QoS won't work right. It isn't just the hardware that acts like sugar in the QoS gas tank. A good many applications are not QoS-aware yet. All in all, the environment is just not suited for an RSVP-based solution.

■ **Lack of scalability**   Because RSVP must reconfigure every router in its path, the onus is on the network to talk to the routers and tell them what to do. RSVP doesn't scale very well, and you're bound to have problems. Conversely, if you use packet prioritization, it really only takes a little extra effort on the part of a client computer to assign precedence to outgoing packets. As they pass through the network infrastructure, they are merely bumped ahead of the other packets that don't have the same level of prioritization. The amount of CPU overhead requirements on the routers is greater for RSVP versus Weighted Fair Queuing, for example.

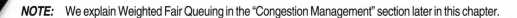

NOTE: We explain Weighted Fair Queuing in the "Congestion Management" section later in this chapter.

▲ **Waste of bandwidth**   Since RSVP plows a path across a network, if the reservation space is not used, some RSVP schemes won't allow other applications to use the allocated bandwidth—thus making the clogged pipe even worse.

Though RSVP is a popular QoS mechanism—Windows 2000 bases its solution on RSVP, for instance—there is a better way to assure services are delivered in a timely manner.

Bandwidth Prioritization

The better method—in our opinion—to ensure solid, reliable QoS comes from bandwidth prioritization. Rather than boring a big, wide tunnel through your pipe, bandwidth prioritization takes the packets that are rocketing through the pipe and sends the most important ones off to where they need to go first.

Simple prioritization QoS is packet-based. In other words, the treatment a packet deserves is in one way or another signified inside the packet itself. As shown in Figure 7-4, in a header on each packet is an IP Precedence bit. This is a number that assigns a certain level of priority to a packet. More important packets are placed ahead of those less important.

Though all QoS is priority-driven and operates packet-by-packet, prioritization QoS is distinguishable in that its implementation is constrained to a device that inspects packets. In other words, routers treat prioritization independently of other routers.

If operating conditions are changed when packets from another flow with the same or higher priority enter the same router, the original flow's packets are simply adjusted in its queue. As you'll see, some priority-based QoS mechanisms work by forming multiple output queues.

By contrast, reserving bandwidth requires all devices in the path to converse and collectively arrive at a QoS service-level commitment. Put another way, containing QoS in the packet itself does away with the need to set up and monitor connection flows across routers, across routing areas, and even across autonomous system boundaries. (An *autonomous system* is defined as a collection of routers under a single administrative authority using a common interior gateway routing protocol. For example, an ISP is an autonomous system.)

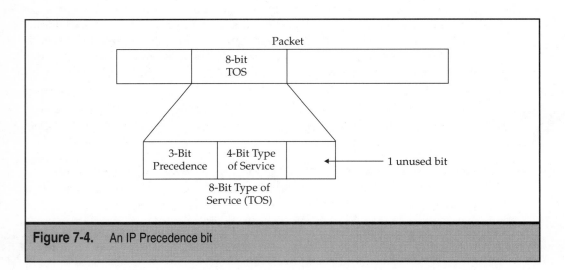

Figure 7-4. An IP Precedence bit

How It Works

Bandwidth prioritization works so well because it is very simple and can be used on almost any current Cisco-based network.

1. As information is sent onto the network, a software mechanism looks at the information's QoS policies and not only determines which packets are important, but just how important they are.

2. The computer then assigns each packet a number ranging from 1 to 7, depending on their order of importance, as shown in Figure 7-5.

3. At this point, the packets are lined up in the router in seven different queues as they wait to be sent.

4. By using a queuing mechanism, such as Weighted Fair Queuing, the most important packets (those at level 7) are transmitted first. After the level-7 packets are transmitted, for example, the packets in the sixth queue are sent, and so on.

5. This process repeats as long as data is being transmitted.

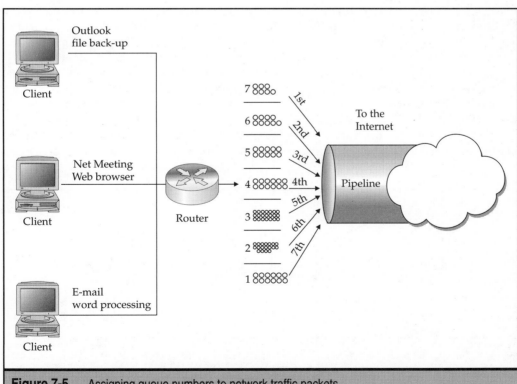

Figure 7-5. Assigning queue numbers to network traffic packets

Why It's Preferred

In addition to its ability to work with existing technology (a hurdle for any application that works on the Internet), another important reason bandwidth prioritization is the favored solution for QoS is that it is extremely efficient and wastes no bandwidth, unlike bandwidth provisioning.

Used with Existing Technology   As mentioned earlier, the biggest problem with bandwidth provisioning is that it must use modern, RSVP-capable routers to work. This is fine if you own and control all the routers from end to end. But realistically speaking, you will have control over only one router. After that, it's up to the whims of fate.

Routers that will make bandwidth provisioning work are recent models with QoS-specific features. Bandwidth prioritization, on the other hand, works because it operates with all kinds of routers, both new and legacy. Bandwidth prioritization relies on sending the packets in a specific, prioritized fashion; the packets don't care what kind of router they go through, because they are guaranteed to go through in a specific, mission-critical order. Remember, the most important packets arrive at their destination first because they were the first packets sent.

Efficiency   Delivering QoS through bandwidth prioritization is also the more efficient method, because it uses the bandwidth that's available, without hoarding it from other applications. For a contrast, consider Figure 7-6.

In this figure, you'll see that a decent-sized portion of the pipe has been set aside solely for videoconferencing. This is all well and good and does a fine job; however, when no one is videoconferencing, that section of the pipe is going to waste.

Bandwidth prioritization allows the entire pipe to be used; it merely puts the most important traffic first. Consider Figure 7-7.

You can see that all the traffic is getting into the pipe, and when the videoconferencing isn't taking place, the next bits of traffic on the prioritization tree are moved up and sent first.

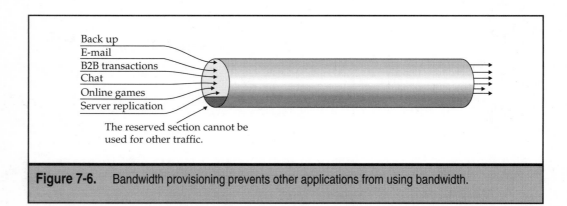

Figure 7-6.   Bandwidth provisioning prevents other applications from using bandwidth.

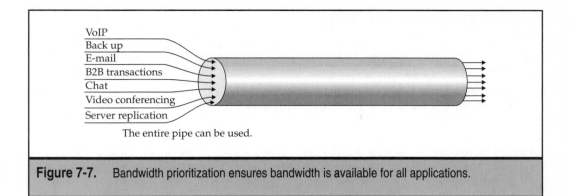

Figure 7-7.   Bandwidth prioritization ensures bandwidth is available for all applications.

DiffServ

A better-understood prioritization model is called Differentiated Services, or *DiffServ* for short. DiffServ is meant to provide a relatively coarse but simple way to prioritize traffic. DiffServ redefines the original IP ToS field bits into its own scheme, where two of the eight ToS bits are used for congestion notification, and the remaining six bits, for packet markings. This new scheme implements so-called *codepoints* within the six-bit marking space. Packets are marked for the DiffServ class as they enter the DiffServ QoS network.

DiffServ attempts only to control so-called "per-hop" behaviors. In other words, policy is defined locally, and DiffServ as a mechanism executes within a device to influence when and where the packet's next hop will be. Once policy is set across a topology, everything takes place in-device. DiffServ supports two service levels (traffic classes):

▼   **Expedited Forwarding (EF)**   Minimizes delay and jitter. Packets are dropped if traffic exceeds a maximum load threshold set by local policy.

▲   **Assured Forwarding (AF)**   Provides for four subclasses and three drop-precedences within each subclass for a total of 12 codepoints. If traffic load exceeds local policy, excess AF packets are not delivered at the specified priority but are instead demoted to a lower priority (but not dropped). This demotion procedure cascades through any configured drop-precedence codepoints.

Congestion Avoidance

If your intent is to avoid network congestion entirely, two prominent mechanisms are Random Early Detection (RED) and Weighted Random Early Detection (WRED). These two techniques are used when there is no existing throughput problem, but if one happens to be on the horizon. RED and WRED relieve overflowing traffic by using a queuing algorithm to sort the traffic, and then determining which packets will be sent and which packets will be dropped.

Random Early Detection (RED)

RED is a proactive measure to relieve congestion in TCP flows. Rather than wait for a full-blown congestion problem, the router drops packets as the congestion begins to form. RED monitors the queue depth, and as the queue begins to fill, it randomly selects TCP flows and starts dropping packets, as seen in Figure 7-8.

TCP contains a built-in feature that reacts to dropped packets by slowing the transmission rate at the source (the router sends a notification to the source telling it to slow down). If a workstation receives a dropped packet notification from the router, it will slow its transmission rate by half. Then, after a period where no packets have been dropped, it will double its rate of transmission (going back to the original rate). Because of this, RED can trigger the TCP mechanisms "early," or before the congestion is too high.

The threshold at which RED snaps into action and drops packets is configured by the network administrator, as well as the rate at which drops occur in relation to how quickly the queue fills. The more it fills, the greater the number of flows selected and the greater the number of packets dropped. As a result, a greater number of senders are signaled to slow down, which eases network congestion.

As the name implies, this is a random function with no regard for class, weight, or priority. As the congestion increases, more and more packets are dropped randomly until total throughput is reached, when all new packets are dropped. RED does not possess the same undesirable overhead characteristics as some of the non-FIFO queuing techniques. With RED, there is no packet reordering or queue management. Priority, class-based, and Weighted Fair Queuing require a significant amount of computational overhead, because of packet reordering and queue management. RED, on the other hand, requires much less overhead than more involved queuing mechanisms. Of course, the QoS it delivers is much different than other mechanisms.

Weighted RED

RED is a "nice" way to deliver QoS. No one's packets are selected preferentially over another and everyone is treated exactly the same. Some might call it outcome-based QoS, but do you want a happy, "everyone's the same" approach to your network's QoS? In the

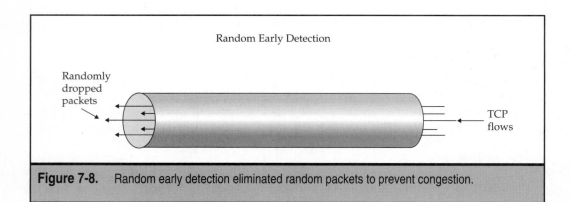

Figure 7-8.   Random early detection eliminated random packets to prevent congestion.

world of QoS, do you really want your critical VoIP traffic to vie for bandwidth alongside a dozen people using Napster or playing a LAN-based video game? Of course not, and that's why you need to introduce an element of unfairness into your QoS solution.

Weighted Random Early Detection (WRED) is basically the same as RED, but it takes into account the priorities (or weight) of packets when deciding which packets to drop. The combination of random packet drops and weighting provides for preferential traffic handling for higher-priority packets. It can selectively discard lower-priority traffic when the router gets congested, and provide differentiated performance characteristics for different classes of service. For instance, if the network administrator has decided that VoIP should have more precedence than e-mail, when congestion is approached, the router will drop more e-mail packets than VoIP packets.

WRED differs from other congestion management techniques, such as queuing strategies, because it attempts to anticipate and avoid congestion rather than controlling congestion once it occurs. Figure 7-9 shows how WRED works.

As with RED, by randomly dropping packets just before a network experiences congestion, WRED tells the source to decrease its transmission rate. However, WRED differs from RED because it drops packets selectively based on IP precedence. Packets that have been given a higher IP precedence are less likely to be dropped than packets with a lower precedence. Therefore, traffic with a higher level of priority is more likely to be delivered

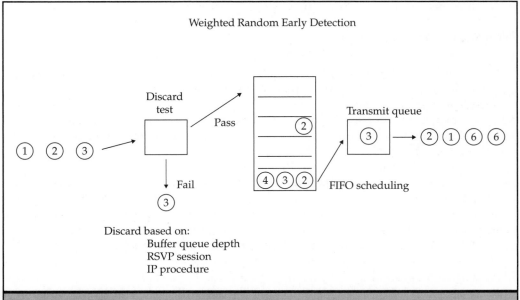

Figure 7-9.   WRED takes the importance of packets into consideration before dropping any.

than traffic with a lower level of priority. WRED is also an RSVP-aware mechanism, and can provide integrated services controlled-load QoS service.

WRED can be used on any router where you expect congestion to occur. WRED is primarily used in the core routers of a network, rather than at the network edge. Edge routers may assign IP precedence to packets as they enter the network, and then WRED uses these precedences to determine how it treats different types of traffic.

WRED is similar to RED because it drops some packets early rather than waiting until the buffer is full and the network is congested. By employing this technique, WRED allows full utilization of the transmission line at all times. Statistically speaking, WRED drops more packets that originate from large users than small. As a result, traffic sources generating the most traffic are more likely to be slowed down than traffic sources that generate little traffic. When comparing RED to WRED further, it's worth noting that Cisco internetworking favors WRED over RED (although RED is still supported).

Congestion Management

If you're in the midst of a bandwidth drought, you need something to take the pressure off your mission-critical applications and get the important traffic flowing. Weighted Fair Queuing and Class-Based Weighted Fair Queuing are mechanisms used when network congestion threatens your network. These two mechanisms look at your traffic and decide—based on criteria the network administrator establishes—which packets are sent out first, which ones have to wait, and which ones will get dropped.

Weighted Fair Queuing

Weighted Fair Queuing (WFQ) is a method of ensuring that packets are allowed throughput based on their precedence, or weight. In the event of congestion, the ToS bits are used to determine which packets are dropped and which are given priority. When the router becomes congested and more packets are trying to get through than can physically be allowed, the router will *tail drop,* or drop after congestion has been realized. Normally, the router will do this randomly, but WFQ ensures that the higher-priority packets are less likely to be dropped.

WFQ uses a statistical algorithm that has a linear effect. In other words, the eight packet priorities are issued numbers 0 through 7. This means that the packets with priority 5 are five times *less* likely to be dropped than priority 0 packets. As the packet's precedence increases, the algorithm sets aside more bandwidth for that conversation. This ensures that it will be served more quickly in the event of network congestion.

WFQ also assigns a weight to each flow. This factor determines the transmission order for the queued packets—thus, the system allows the lower weights to be served first. IP precedence acts as a divisor to this weighting factor. For instance, traffic with an IP precedence of 7 gets a lower weight than traffic with an IP precedence field value of 2, thereby having priority in the transmission order. WFQ is illustrated in Figure 7-10.

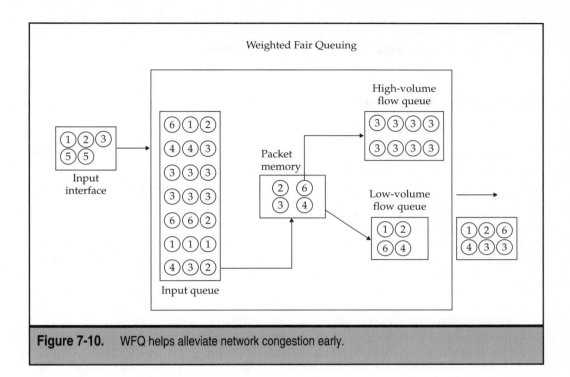

Figure 7-10. WFQ helps alleviate network congestion early.

WFQ is also RSVP-aware. RSVP uses WFQ to allocate buffer space and schedule packets, guaranteeing bandwidth for reserved flows.

WFQ ensures that queues aren't starved for bandwidth, and that traffic gets predictable service. Low-volume traffic streams—the most prevalent type of traffic on an internetwork—receive preferential service and are allowed to transmit their entire offered loads in a timely fashion. Conversely, high-volume traffic streams must share the remaining capacity proportionally between them.

Designed with the most common traffic flows in mind, WFQ minimizes configuration efforts, adapting automatically to the dynamism of an internetwork's traffic conditions. WFQ uses available bandwidth to "open the pipe" and forward traffic from lower-priority flows if there is no higher-priority traffic present. Compare this to Time Division Multiplexing (TDM), which simply divides the bandwidth and lets it sit idle if no traffic is present.

Class-Based Weighted Fair Queuing

Class-Based Weighted Fair Queuing (CBWFQ) is a more flexible version of WFQ. In this scenario, administrators are allowed more granular control of the *classes*, or priorities.

For example, a company can use CBWFQ for defining a more exponential algorithmic effect. In other words, instead of allocating weights using

```
1, 2, 3, 4, 5, 6, 7, 8
```

weighting could, instead, be allocated as:

```
1, 2, 4, 8, 16, 32, 64, 128.
```

As you can see in this example, the packets with priority 6 are now 32 times less likely to be dropped in times of congestion.

Overview   CBWFQ enhances WFQ functionality and allows network administrators to define specific weights for classes of traffic. For instance, you can define traffic classes based on such criteria as protocols, Access Control Lists, and input interfaces. A queue is then established for each class, and the packets are routed to the appropriate queue of its class.

As soon as a class has been defined (the criteria has been established), you assign it characteristics. To characterize a class, you assign bandwidth, weight, and maximum packet limits. Once network congestion begins, the bandwidth assigned to a class is the minimum amount of bandwidth delivered. Additionally, you must also specify the queue limit for each class. This number is the maximum number of packets that can accumulate in the class's queue. As soon as a queue reaches its specified queue limit, *enqueuing* of additional packets to the class causes tail drop.

Tail drop is the most typical means of eliminating overflow packets for CBWFQ, unless you decide to use WRED for specific classes.

NOTE: Be careful, however, if you use WRED instead of tail drop; you have to make sure that WRED is not configured for the interface to which you attach that service policy.

If you configure a default class, all unclassified traffic is automatically treated as if it is part of the default class (that's what default is all about). However, if no default class is specified, then unclassified traffic is given best-effort service.

Configuring a class policy and configuring CBWFQ involves three processes:

1. Establishing traffic classes, thereby specifying the classification policy. This process establishes how different packets are to be differentiated from one another.

2. Assigning policies to each class of traffic. This process configures policies to packets belonging to one of the predefined classes of traffic. For this process, you build a policy map, specifying the policies for each class of traffic.

3. Attaching policies to interfaces. This process requires you to associate an existing policy map with an interface to a new interface.

The additional control CBWFQ gives network administrators much more flexibility over QoS policies, which themselves can be difficult to implement and manage.

Benefits Employing CBWFQ allows you two important controls over your internetwork, namely bandwidth allocation and granularity of control. Let's take a closer look at how CBWFQ helps manage QoS policies:

▼ **Bandwidth allocation** CBWFQ lets you specify the precise amount of bandwidth you wish set aside for each class of traffic. By keeping track of available bandwidth on the interface, you can configure up to 64 classes and control distribution among them, which is not allowed with flow-based WFQ. Flow-based WFQ simply applies weights to traffic, thereby classifying it into conversations and determining how much bandwidth each conversation will be allowed, given the state of existing conversations on the internetwork.

▲ **Granularity** CBWFQ allows you the flexibility to decide what constitutes a class, based on criteria you establish. You use such tools as Access Control Lists and protocols to establish how traffic will be classified. Further, you are not required to maintain traffic classification on a flow basis. Finally, you can define up to 64 discrete classes in a service policy.

CBWFQ is more complex than the other techniques we've mentioned. However, it combines the best of both worlds when trying to relieve network congestion.

Packet Shapers

Rather than just regurgitate what the network sends its way, there are several mechanisms used to control the characteristics of traffic being allowed into a network. Called "traffic shaping," this method is primarily used at border routers. Network operators are starting to use traffic shaping to condition WAN links for better service quality.

By definition, *traffic shaping* is the practice of controlling the volume of packets entering a network and controlling the rate of transmission in order to make traffic conform to a desired pattern. The name comes from the fact that a traffic flow is said to have been *shaped* when its pattern is changed. There are two predominant mechanisms used to shape traffic:

▼ **The leaky bucket** A *leaky bucket* controls the rate at which packets enter a network. This mechanism works by manipulating inbound queues so as to smooth bursty traffic into less variable flows. ATM invented the leaky bucket as a way to control the rate at which ATM cell traffic is transmitted over an ATM link. It has more recently come into use to condition IP packet datagram flows.

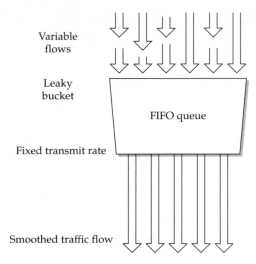

▼ **The token bucket mechanism**   Although the names are similar, the token bucket mechanism is quite different from the leaky bucket. A *token bucket* is the practice of controlling the rate of transmission based on the presence of so-called "tokens" in the bucket. In other words, a *token* is an abstract currency (measured in bytes) that must be available at any instant for the next First-In, First-Out (FIFO) packet to exit the network interface. There must be at least as many token bytes available as the number of bytes in the packet to be transmitted.

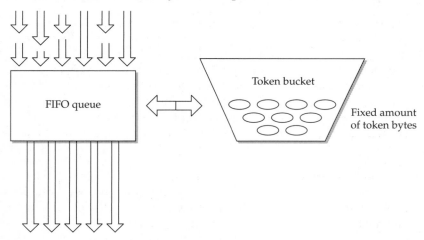

Packet shapers have limited use and application. They are best used by organizations with few WAN links since these hardware devices are required at both ends of every WAN link where you want QoS. Also, they are strategically set so changes to policy can only be accomplished infrequently.

Networking Scenarios

Obviously, your networking usage will greatly affect your need for QoS. For instance, if your network needs don't demand anything better than best-effort service, you can manage without QoS. On the other hand, if—like many networks—you are facing ever-increasing demand for bandwidth, or if packet latency will affect your organization's mission (for instance, you use VoIP), then it's important to have solid QoS practices in hand.

Research has shown that most QoS implementations done to date are within private (non-ISP) enterprise internetworks. This is somewhat ironic, given that ISPs adopted the SLA as a way to do business, not to mention the fact that ISPs operate most ATM networks, but it's understandable:

▼ When a packet passes through the ingress router to enter someone else's autonomous system, it becomes less of a priority. Why should they take on the added expense of the processing and administrative overhead needed to assure the packet a QoS service level?

■ Even if another autonomous system wanted to help—say, an ISP that wants to win your business—how can your policies be distributed to, and implemented in, its routers?

▲ If your policy was implemented in another autonomous system, what would assure that it was executed in accordance with a common understanding of which conditions are active and which actions should result?

A lot of Internet gurus are asking these very questions nowadays, and it's a tough nut to crack. As you travel between autonomous systems, you pass through differing policy domains with their own operating styles. Not only would a global policy framework holding uniform criteria be required, a global policy evaluation algorithm would also be needed. Rule sets, bit precedents, policies, and other elements of QoS execution in each autonomous system (AS) must be kept uniform.

Interoperable QoS regime: policy; interpretation; execution mechanics

Different hardware   Different directory systems   Different network management products

AS AS AS AS AS AS AS AS

Different operating systems   Different routing protocols

Compounding the problem of inter-autonomous system QoS is the lack of a uniform technical infrastructure. Any group of autonomous systems attempting to interoperate QoS are likely to be running a variety of routing protocols, network device hardware, computer platform operating systems, directory technologies, and network management systems. Their existence dictates that a truly interoperable QoS framework be in place in order for end-to-end QoS to work.

QoS works best and can be assured most effectively within the confines of a private or controlled network. Because this network is entirely under your control, you can have your say about how traffic is prioritized. The threat to QoS comes when traffic has to reach out across a public WAN or—worse yet—a public network, like the Internet.

Let's look at how both of these network scenarios play themselves out.

ISPs The most likely place for network traffic to get congested is when it leaves your router and heads to your ISP, as shown in Figure 7-11.

The biggest problem occurs when traffic leaves the guarantees established by your enterprise and hits the ISP or Internet proper. Just because the traffic is high priority to you doesn't mean that it's a high priority once it gets to your ISP or outside your ISP.

This is not to suggest that all ISP situations are going to provide choppy service. On the one hand, let's use the example of two companies set up in a B2B (business-to-business) arrangement. If the two companies have their own, independent ISPs, then there are many places between each end where network traffic can get bottlenecked.

Let's look at another scenario. Again, let's assume you and a business partner have a business-to-business solution in place. In this case, however, you're both contracting with the same ISP. You're more likely to be able to have an assured level of QoS, because the traffic will not leave the ISP and have to cross a multitude of routers. It remains within

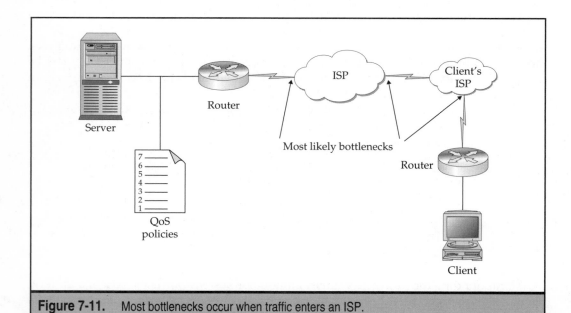

Figure 7-11. Most bottlenecks occur when traffic enters an ISP.

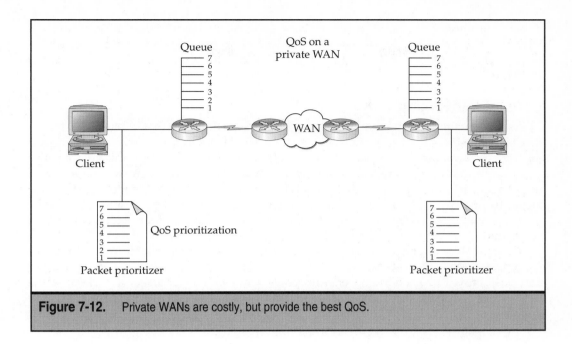

Figure 7-12.   Private WANs are costly, but provide the best QoS.

one autonomous system. Since most traffic snarls occur when they leave a single ISP, this problem will be mitigated.

Private WANs   The best-case scenario for supplying QoS across a wide area is across a private WAN. As compared to using a public network, this is a more costly option; however, (forgive the cliché) you get what you pay for. Take a look at Figure 7-12.

As you can see, there isn't anything in between the two ends to slow down traffic. There's nothing that can reprioritize your priority traffic, and there aren't the bottlenecks that come when you go through an ISP (or worse, two ISPs).

CISCO'S SOLUTION

QoS may be a concept that's been picking up steam just recently, but Cisco has been planning and developing solutions for years. In this section, we take a closer look at Cisco's hardware and software offerings, along with the technologies that help enable QoS within internetworks.

Services

Cisco's QoS solution is delivered through a marriage of hardware devices and software tools. But in a larger sense, Cisco delivers QoS in comprehensive internetworking technologies, like Content Networking and nBAR. Solutions such as Content Networking allow your network traffic to be streamlined and prioritized. nBAR—which we explain later in this section—is a mechanism that enables QoS within the larger content networking picture. The next two sections highlight how QoS is delivered using a larger, integrated technology.

Content Networking

Cisco Content Networking is an intelligent network architecture that dynamically recognizes Internet business applications and engages network services to achieve end-to-end security, performance, and availability. Your network must be able to dynamically recognize every application and provide the appropriate set of services. For example, if remote sites need to access Web pages hosted at corporate headquarters, the Web pages must be protected through security mechanisms and the bandwidth over the remote link must be properly managed. The network also needs to provide a variety of services, including security and QoS.

Content Networking technology optimizes internetworks to dynamically enable faster responses to Web requests and decrease bandwidth congestion. It allows for scalability and flash crowd protection and ensures content availability and security. Because the network is optimized to deliver specific content to specific users, QoS functions are enabled.

Cisco Content Networking has three components:

▼ Intelligent network devices that integrate Internet applications with network services

■ Intelligent network classification and network services delivered through Cisco IOS

▲ An intelligent policy management framework for configuration and monitoring

With these three components, QoS is enabled for growing networks that have specific content for specific users. For more information on Cisco Content Delivery Networks, flip ahead to Chapter 13.

Network-Based Application Recognition

Network-based application recognition (nBAR) solves the problems inherent in classifying applications by adding intelligent network classification to a network's infrastructure. nBAR can recognize a variety of applications, including Web-based and client/server applications that dynamically assign Transmission Control Protocol (TCP) or User Datagram Protocol (UDP) port numbers.

Once nBAR classifies an application, the network can apply preset policies based on the particular application. nBAR works with QoS features to ensure network bandwidth is used in the most efficient means possible. These features include the ability to:

▼ Guarantee bandwidth to critical applications

■ Limit bandwidth to other applications

■ Drop selective packets to avoid congestion

▲ Mark packets so that proper end-to-end delivery is ensured between your network and your service provider

In addition to classifying applications, nBAR can help in the development of your QoS policy. nBAR's protocol-discovery feature shows you which applications are currently running on the network so you will have a solid starting point and an understanding of your network's dynamics before implementing new policy.

Products

Augmenting Cisco's hardware are two pieces of software. Cisco's QoS Policy Manager (QPM) is used to control the bandwidth that people, organizations, and applications employ on your network. Cisco's QoS Device Manager (QDM) is used to control specific interfaces on your network. In this section, we take a closer look at these two pieces of software and discuss their functionality and how you can use them.

Naturally, Cisco offers a fleet of internetworking devices that are QoS-enabled. Table 7-2 lists some of Cisco's switches and routers that offer QoS functions.

Even though Cisco is a hardware-first company, they have developed two pieces of software to help manage both QoS policies and devices.

Router Models	Switch Models
SOHO 77 ADSL Router	MGX 8200 Series
800 Series	Lightstream 1010
1700 Series	IGX 8400
2600 Series	6000 Series IP DSL
3600 Series	BPX 8600 Series
6400 Series Broadband Aggregator	Catalyst 2900 Series
7200 Series	Catalyst 3500 Series XL
7500 Series	Catalyst 4500 Series
7600 Series	Catalyst 4840G Server Load Balancing Switch
10000 Edge Series Router	Catalyst 6500 Series
12000 Series Internet Router	Catalyst 8500 Series

Table 7-2.   Some QoS-Enabled Cisco Devices

QoS Policy Manager

QoS Policy Manager (QPM) offers features to expedite the flow of traffic across your network. From complete support of IOS devices to automatic management and deployment of QoS policies to integration with CiscoWorks 2000, QPM 3.1 is Cisco's top-line tool to keep QoS policies in line, without adding an abundance of work to the network administrator's load.

QPM also has enhanced reliability features, such as the ability to detect device configuration changes and to label and group devices, interfaces, and virtual LANs. Network administrators can roll back new policies to previous policies and redeploy them in a network if the new policies are inadequate. Another security feature lets users selectively block packets on a per-port basis. The software now supports more than 30 Cisco device series.

QPM consists of two products, Policy Manager and Distribution Manager, and provides distributed policy management and a centralized distribution. The software also includes enhanced support for IOS devices and eases the implementation of both low-latency queuing and congestion-management queuing.

The following list highlights some of the features of QPM:

▼ **Traffic monitoring for setting and validating QoS** Allows you to measure traffic throughput for applications and service classes and troubleshoot problems with real-time and historical data.

■ **User administration and security** Control user access, centrally, while using Cisco Secure Access Control Server (ACS) to manage privileges for policy view, modification, and deployment for different devices.

■ **Centralized Web-based control** Utilize a Web-based GUI to configure and manage QoS from anywhere.

■ **Application-level classification** Apply the necessary service levels to specific applications through the support of IP packet classification. Classification can be applied based on application signature, Web URLs, and ports.

■ **Differentiated service for mission-critical applications** Classes of service are applied to important applications.

■ **Service classification by user** Services can be specified for individual users and user groups.

■ **Voice QoS support** High-quality voice service is guaranteed under QPM.

▲ **Automated policy deployment** Policies are deployed to all QoS-enabled Cisco devices in your network.

A gratifying feature of QPM is the ease in which it is installed and enabled. With just a few mouse clicks, the software is installed and ready to dispense policy across your internetwork. However, you still need a thorough understanding of networking to use this tool.

Setting Up   Currently, the Policy Manager component runs on Microsoft Windows NT 4.0 and Windows 2000. During installation, network administrators are allowed to perform a complete install, loading both the Distribution Manager and the Policy Manager on the same machine or a remote install, which loads only the Policy Manager. The remote install demands minimal configuration, but the administrator must supply the IP address of the Distribution Manager to deploy QoS policies.

When you install the Distribution Manager, you'll need to set up two user groups:

▼   A group with permission to both read and write policies

▲   A group with permission to read policies only

Security is based on Windows credentials, and domain accounts can be used. The user interface is a tree-based view of all configured devices.

To retrieve device information, QPM uses SNMP queries, requiring only a device's IP address and proper authentication. If you are running CiscoWorks2000, you should take advantage of the import feature. Managers who must add devices manually will want to retrieve any existing QoS policies.

QPM in Action   QPM allows network administrators the ability to define Access Control Lists, with just a few mouse clicks. For instance, let's say you want to restrict access to a Web site that's heavy with multimedia content. By using QPM, you simply select the serial interface on the WAN router and add a "deny traffic to this IP address" policy.

Next, you save this new QoS policy in the database and launch the Distribution Manager via a menu option in the Policy Manager. From this point, the policy is distributed to all devices being managed. This policy is now in place, and no one using a managed device can visit the forbidden Web site.

In addition to new congestion management tools, QPM offers the ability to provision service levels via nBAR coloring (this allows nBAR to set priorities for classified applications) and rate limiting. The software adds another layer of usability by allowing management and deployment of QoS policies by virtual LAN (VLAN).

Cisco also streamlines the process of deploying QoS policies across an internetwork. Conventionally, this can be a brain-numbing task because commands have to be entered over and over for each interface on a group of devices. QPM employs a "device group" feature, which allows any policy set on the group to be automatically propagated over all the devices and interfaces in the group.

Priced at U.S. $12,000, QPM is a comprehensive tool that will allow you to set and manage rudimentary QoS policies easily and efficiently across a variety of internetworks.

Cisco AutoQoS

The notion of applying QoS to your network might be somewhat daunting. How do you know when to use RED versus WRED? Which packets should be given which precedence? When one considers all the QoS options and approaches for both LANs and WANs, it's easy to become lackadaisical about QoS and simply put the whole issue on the back burner. Because of this, Cisco has responded to customer perceptions that QoS is too difficult a technology to deploy by creating something called AutoQoS.

AutoQoS is a feature in recent versions of Cisco IOS and Cisco Catalyst Operating System software and is used to administer QoS on select routers and switches. AutoQoS is being released in phases. The first phase automates QoS for IP telephony. This is especially useful for those who want to deploy an IP telephony solution, but who lack the skills and expertise needed for IP QoS.

NOTE: Subsequent phases of AutoQoS will include support for video, voice, and data, dynamic policy recommendations, business policy specification, and active auto-monitoring.

AutoQoS simplifies network QoS provisioning and makes the process of QoS deployment much quicker. AutoQoS is used to:

▼ Quickly roll out a QoS deployment

■ Automate common QoS scenarios

■ Identify and classify applications

▲ Define alert conditions

In essence, AutoQoS is a feature built into various models of Cisco routers and switches that, using simple commands, fires up QoS functionality. Let's take a closer look at this feature and talk about how you can use it in your own networks.

Overview   It's easiest to think of AutoQoS as a macro. When you enter the AutoQoS command, the router or switch operating system starts a series of larger, more intricate configuration commands. This is a great tool and is useful, especially in initial IP telephony deployments.

The use of AutoQoS greatly simplifies the task of initial LAN and WAN QoS deployment. It is also a lot easier to specify settings and deploy QoS from QPM. When using QPM, it is only necessary to select the appropriate AutoQoS commands, rather than enter lots of details into the Policy Creation Wizard.

When used in conjunction with QPM, traffic throughput can be measured for top applications and service classes. Problems on the network (like dropped VoIP packets) can be troubleshot using real-time and historical QoS data. This data can be displayed as line or bar charts of bits and packets. Using QPM, charts can be displayed both before and after QoS deployment, and whenever QoS policies are altered, for easy comparison of the network's environment.

QoS is deployed differently in WANs and LANs. As such, AutoQoS offers different features for each environment.

In a WAN, AutoQoS offers

▼ Autodetermination of WAN settings, thus eliminating the need to understand QoS theory

■ Initial policy generation, which reduces the time needed to start their VoIP QoS deployment

■ Syslog and SNMP traps, which show the classes of service deployed and provides notification when abnormal events occur

▲ Cisco nBAR, which is used for stateful packet inspection; this simplifies QoS configurations by reducing the need for ACLs

In your LAN, AutoQoS offers

▼ Easy, one-command configuration that prioritizes VoIP traffic without interfering with other traffic

■ Automatic detection of Cisco IP phones (the network is automatically configured with QoS settings)

▲ End-to-end QoS when working with other Cisco AutoQoS-enabled devices

AutoQoS is available on the switches and routers utilizing the software listed in Table 7-3.

AutoQoS and Routers   AutoQoS employs nBAR on Cisco routers, allowing intelligent classification of packets as they enter and exit your network.

To set up AutoQoS on a router, simply enter the bandwidth, IP address, and then the AutoQoS command in the router's config file. This is shown next:

```
bandwidth 256
ip address 10.1.65.101 255.255.255.0
auto qos voip
```

If Frame Relay to ATM service is being used, add **fr-atm** to the end of the command.

	Device	Operating System
Switches	Catalyst 2950, 3550	12.1(12c)EA1
	Catalyst 4500	12.1(19)E
	Catalyst 6500	Catalyst OS 7.5.1
Routers	2600, 2600-XM, 3600, 3700, 7200 Series	12.2(15)T

Table 7-3.   Platforms supporting AutoQoS

By default, the AutoQoS command is untrusted. This means that all inbound traffic will be classified and marked. This setting can be changed if you want incoming traffic to be trusted. Simply add **trust** to the end of the command.

Untrusted links are automatically classified by AutoQoS and thus mark VoIP traffic, as well as MGCP and H.323 signaling traffic. This is possible because of new nBAR protocols, which have been extended to recognize various types of RTP traffic and signaling protocols. This accelerates the process, because the access lists no longer have to be analyzed, configured, and maintained.

AutoQoS on Switches   On supported Catalyst switches, AutoQoS is enabled with the command:

```
Set qos autoqos
```

Next, the ports must be configured with the commands:

```
set port macro <mod/port> [ciscosoftphone | ciscoipphone]
set port qos autoqos <mod/port> voip [ciscosoftphone | ciscoipphone]
```

To control the trust boundary (essentially the edge of your network where traffic enters), utilize the **port** command:

```
set port qos autoqos <mod/port> trust [cos|dscp]
```

As with Cisco routers, the switch can be instructed to trust inbound traffic by using the **trust** command:

```
auto qos voip trust
```

If a Cisco phone is detected on a switch port, the switch can be instructed to trust incoming traffic by entering:

```
auto qos voip cisco-phone
```

When the IP phone is disconnected from the network, AutoQoS automatically shuts down.

As bandwidth-hungry and latency-sensitive applications become more and more prevalent, the need for QoS will only increase. Cisco offers a number of useful QoS mechanisms to help ensure that packets arrive at their destination on time. This isn't the final word in the realm of QoS, however. QoS is an evolving technology, after all, so look for smarter and easier applications to help provision and manage QoS in the future.

CHAPTER 8

Security Overview

The concept of network security may seem somewhat of a moving target—or several moving targets. When we talk about "security" we know what we *want*, but describing it and making it happen can be different matters altogether. Network security has a natural conflict with network connectivity. The more an autonomous system opens itself up, the more risk it takes on. This, in turn, requires that more effort be applied to security enforcement tasks.

On top of that, add departmental budget constraints (and the personnel cuts that many companies have seen in recent years) and even reasonable security solutions might seem impossible to attain. Three trends have increased the bite that security takes out of the IT department's overall budget:

▼ Internetworks are getting bigger and more complicated.

■ New threats are always emerging.

▲ The typical network security system is usually not a system at all, but is a patchwork of vendor-specific tools (sound familiar?).

Network security is so pervasive a consideration that even network management consoles raise concerns. As we'll talk about in Chapter 15, some worry about whether the SNMP infrastructure itself is secure enough. After all, stealing the right SNMP community string would give a hacker a road map to an entire internetwork's configuration, and unless you've been living in a cave, you know about computer viruses spreading in various forms: e-mail bombs, Trojan horse Java applets, Denial-of-Service attacks, and other worrisome new threats to computer security. Suffice it to say that a lot of time, money, and effort go into network security.

NOTE: SNMP stands for Simple Network Management Protocol and, as you have probably deduced, it is used for network management. Don't worry about it too much at this point. We're mentioning it here as a bit of foreshadowing, before we talk about it in depth in Chapter 15. SNMP relates to some other protocols that are used for network security. Basically, all these protocols gather information from your network—whether for security or for network management.

In Chapter 9, we'll talk about Cisco's Internet access and security products. Just as a head's up, the focus will be mainly on how firewalls—and even routers—monitor internetwork traffic at the packet level to provide security. Traffic-based security runs on firewalls and routers and deals mainly in IP addresses.

But a second kind of security operates at the *people* level. This kind of security, called *user-based security*, employs passwords and other login controls to authenticate users' identities before they are permitted access. There are two basic types of user-based security:

▼ End-user remote access to servers, in which employees dial into their enterprise internetworks and subscribers dial into their Internet service providers (ISPs)

▲ Network administrator access to network devices, in which technicians log into IOS on various kinds of network devices in order to work on them

Security is the third major control system in internetworking, along with network management systems and routing protocols. Although the three control systems have distinct missions, you'll see a familiar pattern:

▼   **Embedded commands**   Application commands built directly into IOS that are used to configure individual devices to participate in a larger network control system

■   **Dedicated control protocol**   A communications protocol that coordinates the exchange of messages needed to perform the network control system's tasks

▲   **Server and console**   A server to store the messages and a workstation to provide the human interface through which the network control system is operated

Figure 8-1 illustrates the common architecture shared by network control systems. Looking at the figure, you see two new names listed next to SNMP—TACACS+ and RADIUS. These are the protocols used for security, not management, as is SNMP, but they're analogous in how they operate. Data is gathered from network devices and stored

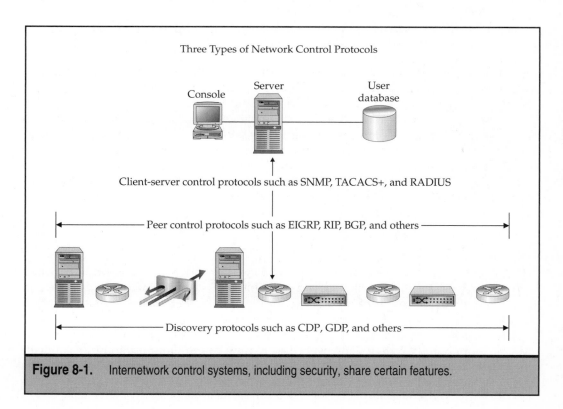

Three Types of Network Control Protocols

Console   Server   User database

Client-server control protocols such as SNMP, TACACS+, and RADIUS

Peer control protocols such as EIGRP, RIP, BGP, and others

Discovery protocols such as CDP, GDP, and others

Figure 8-1.   Internetwork control systems, including security, share certain features.

in a central database, and a console is used to configure devices from a central management workstation. Network management and security systems differ in what they do, but are basically the same in how they work.

The third internetwork control system, routing protocols, differs sharply. Routing protocols don't use servers because the information—route tables—is transient and doesn't need to be stored on disk. Additionally, they don't use consoles because they are largely self-operating.

The structural similarities between network management and security will make it easier to comprehend network security technology. Just swap in new names for protocols (TACACS+ and RADIUS) and consoles, and you understand the general setup.

OVERVIEW OF NETWORK SECURITY

There are two kinds of network security. One kind is enforced as a background process not visible to users; the other is in your face:

▼ **Traffic-based security**   Controls connections requested by a network application, such as a web browser or an FTP download

▲ **User-based security**   Controls admission of individuals to systems in order to start applications once inside, usually by user and password

One kind of traffic-based security is the use of firewalls to protect autonomous systems by screening traffic from untrusted hosts. The other kind of traffic-based security is router access lists, used to restrict traffic and resources within an autonomous system. User-based security is concerned with people, not hosts. This is the kind of security with which we're all familiar—login-based security that asks you for a username and password.

The two types complement one another yet operate at different levels. Traffic-based security goes into action when you click a button in a web browser, enter a command into an FTP screen, or use some other application command. User-based security, on the other hand, asserts itself when an individual tries to log into a network, device, or service offered on a device.

Traffic-Based Security

Traffic-based security is implemented in a Cisco internetwork by using firewalls or router access lists. This style of security—covered in Chapter 9—focuses mainly on source and destination IP addresses, application port numbers, and other packet-level information that can be used to restrict and control network connections.

Until recently, firewalls have focused strictly on guarding against intruders from outside the autonomous system. However, they're now coming into use in more sophisticated shops to restrict access to sensitive assets from the inside. Access lists have been the traditional tool used to enforce intramural security.

Access List Traffic-Based Security

Routers can be configured to enforce security in much the same way firewalls do. All routers have access lists, and they can be used to control what traffic may come and go through the router's network interfaces and what applications may be used if admitted. What exactly an access list does is left to how it's configured by the network administrator.

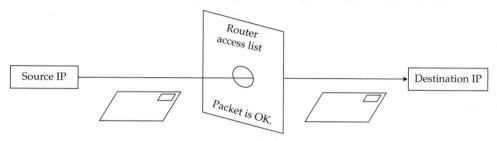

Mostly, access lists are used to improve network performance by isolating traffic in its home area, but a heavily configured access list can pretty much behave like an internal firewall, restricting traffic among departments.

Firewall Traffic-Based Security

Firewalls are basically beefed-up routers that screen processes according to strict traffic management rules. They use all sorts of tactics to enhance security: address translation to hide internal network topology from outsiders; application layer inspection to make sure only permitted services are being run; even high/low counters that watch for any precipitous spikes in certain types of packets to ward off Denial-of-Service attacks such as SYNflood and FINwait.

Firewalls intentionally create a bottleneck at the autonomous system's perimeter. As traffic passes through, the firewall inspects packets as they come and go through the networks attached to its interfaces.

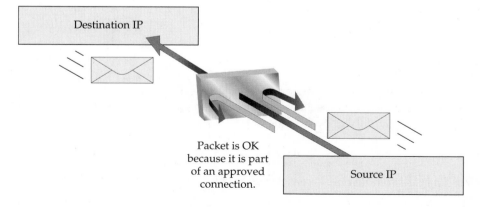

Firewalls read source and destination host addresses and port numbers (for example, port 80 for HTTP), and establish a context for each permitted connection. The context comes in the form of a session, where packets with a certain address pair and port number must belong to a valid session. For example, if a user tries to connect to a web server to download a file, the firewall will check the user's source IP address and the application service requested before permitting the packets to pass.

Think of traffic-based security as being like those "easy pass" automated tollbooths on major toll roads. Vehicles are funneled through a gateway where a laser reads each electronic ID, barely slowing the flow of traffic.

User-Based Security

User-based security evokes a different picture—this one of a gate with a humorless security guard standing at the post. The guard demands to know who you are and challenges you to prove your identity. If you qualify, you get to go in. More sophisticated user-based security systems also have the guard ask what you intend to do once inside and issue you a coded visitor's badge giving you access to some areas, but not others.

Thus, user-based security is employed where a person must log into a host, and the security comes in the form of a challenge for your username and password. In internetworking, this kind of security is used as much to keep bad guys from entering network devices such as routers or switches, as it is to restrict access to payload devices, such as servers.

Unlike firewalls, however, user-based security is nearly as concerned with insiders as outsiders. That security guard at the gate has colleagues on the inside, there to make sure nobody goes into the wrong area. You know the routine—there are employee badges and there are visitor badges, but the employee badges let you go more places.

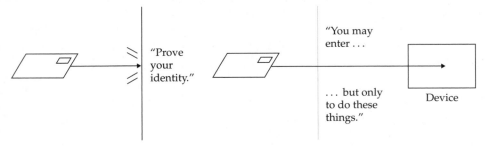

Login/password points are generally placed on every network device and all servers. Because user-based security mechanisms are software, not hardware, they can be deployed at will within an internetwork with little impact on performance or budget. The trade-off is how much inconvenience you're willing to put network users through, having to log in to gain access to various services. User-based security has four major applications:

▼ To grant remote employees access to the enterprise internetwork

■ To grant onsite employees access to protected hosts and services within the internetwork

■   To let network administrators log into network devices

▲   To let ISPs grant subscribers access to their portals

Because most user-based security involves remote dial-in connections, WAN technologies play an important role. The two most important pieces in WAN connections are access servers and dial-in protocols.

Access Servers

Entering an internetwork via a dial-in connection is almost always done through an access server. The access server is a dedicated device that fields phone calls from remote individuals trying to establish a connection to a network. *Access servers* are also called *network access servers* or *communication servers*. Their key attribute is to behave like a full-fledged IP host on one side, but like a modem on the other side. Figure 8-2 depicts the role access servers play in dial-in connections.

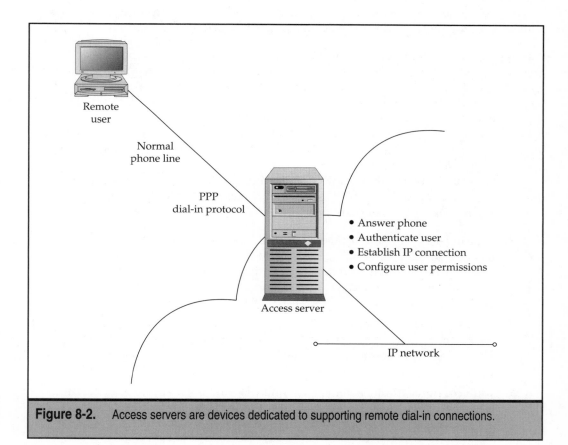

Remote
user

Normal
phone line

PPP
dial-in protocol

• Answer phone
• Authenticate user
• Establish IP connection
• Configure user permissions

Access server

IP network

Figure 8-2.   Access servers are devices dedicated to supporting remote dial-in connections.

When you connect to an internetwork's host from the enterprise campus, you usually do so over a dedicated twisted-pair cable that is connected to a hub or a switch. To make that same connection from afar, you usually do so over a normal telephone line through an access server—a device that answers the phone call and establishes a network connection. Besides making connections for remote dial-in users, access servers can also be used to connect remote routers.

User-Based Security for Local Connectivity   When you turn on your PC and log in at work, you're not dealing with TACACS+ or RADIUS. The username and password prompts are coming from your local server. Most LAN servers run Windows 2000/2003, Linux, UNIX, or Novell platforms. They have security subsystems and user databases of their own to authenticate and authorize users. RADIUS isn't used because it's a dial-in password protocol. TACACS+ isn't used because it controls entry into the Cisco network devices themselves—routers, switches, and access servers—in addition to providing dial-in security much like RADIUS.

In this chapter, discussions of local or "in-network" connections refer to network administrators logging into IOS to work on a Cisco network device.

User-Based Security for Remote Connectivity   Small office and home office users tap into their enterprise internetworks via an access server, making it perhaps the most basic device in any wide area network. Low-end access servers are inconspicuous desktop devices resembling a PC without a monitor. When you dial into your ISP to get into the Internet from home, the call is also answered by an access server. As you might imagine, an ISP's computer room is jammed with rack-mounted high-density access servers to handle connections made from thousands of subscribers. (As a reminder, *high density* means many ports per device.)

Access servers are intelligent devices that handle other tasks in addition to making a line connection. They provide special services to accommodate configurations frequently encountered in enterprise internetworks:

▼ **Routing service**   Run by access servers called *access routers*, this makes it seem as if the dial-in user is sitting directly on the campus network. The key feature of access routers is dial-on-demand routing (DDR), which makes it possible to route traffic from a remote LAN to the main network over low-cost, dial-up phone lines.

■ **Terminal service**   Many WAN connections still use terminal protocols. For that reason, most access servers support terminal protocols such as IBM's TN3270, UNIX rlogin, or Digital Equipment's Local-Area Transport (LAT). A PC could run terminal emulation software to make such a connection.

▲ **Protocol translation**   A remote user may be running a virtual terminal protocol and then connect to a system running another virtual terminal protocol. Most access servers still support protocol translation.

As computing infrastructure improves, terminal service and protocol translation are declining in use. In contrast, access routers are increasing in popularity as small offices build LANs of their own and turn to DDR for convenience and savings.

Dial-In Protocols

As you've learned by now, there's a protocol for just about every major internetworking task. Making dial-in network connections work properly presents special problems because most telephone company infrastructure was designed to handle voice, not high-speed data. Dial-in protocols exist to handle the point-to-point dial-in connections over normal telephone lines.

- ▼ **PPP** Point-to-Point Protocol is the de facto standard for remote dial-in connections to IP networks; virtually all dial-in connections to the Internet use PPP. Most PPP connections are over asynchronous lines, but a growing number are made over ISDN in areas where it's available.

- ■ **SLIP** Serial Line Internet Protocol is also used to make point-to-point dial-in connections to IP networks from remote sites. SLIP is the predecessor to PPP, but is still in use in some quarters. You may also encounter a SLIP variant called CSLIP, Compressed Serial Line Internet Protocol.

- ▲ **ARAP** AppleTalk Remote Access Protocol is Apple's tool for dial-in connectivity to remote AppleTalk networks.

In the old days, to make a remote connection, you dialed into a PBX or terminal server to connect to a mainframe or minicomputer as a dumb terminal. With the rise of internetworking, network-attached terminal servers took over the job of taking dial-in calls. As demand for remote computing grew even more, simple terminal connections were replaced by those made using the SLIP protocol. By that point, many desktops had PCs instead of terminals, but they emulated terminals in order to make dial-in connections. The boom in demand for Internet connectivity drove the market to replace SLIP with PPP, a protocol even more capable of computer-to-computer communications over phone lines. For our purposes, we'll assume PPP as the dial-in protocol unless otherwise noted.

AUTHENTICATION, AUTHORIZATION, AND ACCOUNTING

The framework for user-based security is called authentication, authorization, and accounting (AAA), pronounced *triple-a*. The AAA framework is designed to be consistent and modular in order to give network teams flexibility in implementing the enterprise's network security policy.

NOTE: Network security systems like CiscoSecure control access to LAN segments, lines, and network applications such as HTTP and FTP. Network access devices—usually access servers and access routers—control access to these network-based services, but an additional layer of security is sometimes configured into the server platform once it is reached. For example, an IBM mainframe will enforce security policies using its own mechanisms. Security for computer platforms and major application software packages is still performed using self-contained security systems resident in the application server, in addition to the network access device security measures covered in this chapter.

Overview of the AAA Model

AAA's purpose is to control who is allowed access to network devices and what services they are allowed to use once they have access. Here is a brief description of the AAA model's three functional areas:

▼ **Authentication**   Validates the user's identity as authentic before granting the login

■ **Authorization**   Grants the user the privilege to access networks and commands

▲ **Accounting**   Collects data to track usage patterns by individual user, service, host, time of day, day of week, and so on

Thankfully, the acronym makers put the three functions in sequential order, making the AAA concept easier to pick up: first, you're allowed to log in (your identity is authenticated); then you have certain privileges to use once you're in (you have predetermined authorizations); and finally, a running history is kept on what you do while logged in (the network team keeps an account of what you do).

The philosophy is to let network teams enforce security policy on a granular basis. Most AAA parameters can be put into effect per LAN segment, per line (user), and per protocol—usually IP.

AAA is a clearly defined security implementation framework that everybody can understand. The architecture is defined down to the command level. Indeed, the AAA concepts are actual IOS commands. Starting an AAA process on a Cisco device involves using the **aaa** prefix followed by one of the three root functions, such as **aaa authentication.** A whole AAA command line might read **aaa authentication ppp RemoteWorkers tacacs+ local**, for example. The purpose of AAA is to provide the client-side command structure on which CiscoSecure relies.

AAA Modularity

A security policy is a set of principles and rules adopted by an enterprise to protect system resources, confidential records, and intellectual property. It's the network manager's responsibility to implement and enforce the policy, but in the real world, security policy can get dragged down into the mire of office politics, budget constraints, and impatience. An end-user manager can have a lot of clout as to how the policy will be conducted on his or her turf. After all, the company, not the IT department, funds the network. Consequently, there can be a lot of variance among security policies—even within an enterprise's internetwork.

This means that security policies must be highly adaptable. CiscoSecure tries to satisfy this need with modularity—the ability to separately apply security functions by secured entity, independent of how they are applied to other resources. The AAA architecture gives you the option to implement any of the three functions independent of the other two. This includes whether they're activated on a device, which security protocol is used, and what security server or user database is accessed.

Authentication Controls   The **aaa authentication** command validates a user's identity at login. But once you're authenticated, exactly what can you access? That depends on the type of access being made:

▼   If you're a network administrator logging into a switch to tweak its config file, the authentication gets you into that switch's IOS command prompt.

■   If you're an employee sitting inside the enterprise and you were authenticated by a router, you get into a protected host to run Windows or browser-based internetwork client-server applications.

■   If you're a telecommuter and an access server authenticated you, you're admitted to your enterprise's internetwork to run the same client-server applications.

▲   If you dialed into the Internet from home, as a member of the general public, you were authenticated by one of your ISP's many access servers, and you enter the World Wide Web.

Security must protect three destination environments: the Internet, the internetwork, and, most of all, the internal operating system of the devices over which internetworks run. Figure 8-3 illustrates access types and destination environments.

The scenario of the network administrator logging into IOS devices is unique. In Cisco internetworks, that type of access is usually authenticated using TACACS+. Other types of access open into a Windows- or HTTP-based application service. Network administrators access a device's IOS environment in order to perform device maintenance tasks.

Users also require different dial-in services. Although almost everybody uses PPP nowadays, there still can be different requirements. Depending on the local network from which the call is made, different PPP services may be required, such as IP, IPX, NetBEUI, or just a plain terminal connection.

Whatever the issues may be, different requirements often call for a variety of authentication methods to be used in the same internetwork. CiscoSecure lets the network manager employ any of the major dial-in protocols and authentication techniques. In addition, it supports the ability to apply these different tools by network interface or line—even on the same device.

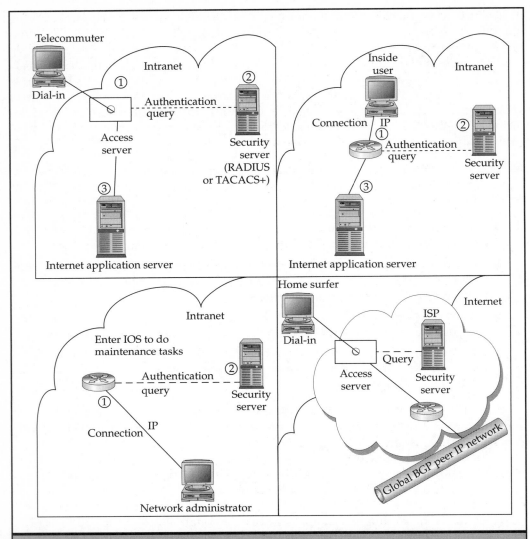

Figure 8-3. User authentication takes place in four scenarios that open into three worlds.

Authorization Controls AAA authorization limits services to the user. In other words, if authorization has been activated on a secured entity using the **aaa authorization** command, users must be explicitly granted access to it.

The person's user profile is usually stored in the security server and sometimes also in the device's local user database. When the administrator logs into the device and his or her user profile is checked, the device configures the authorizations to know what commands to allow the administrator to use during that session. Commands can be authorized by IOS command mode (the MyRouter> versus MyRouter# prompts) or by specific commands within a mode. Figure 8-4 lays out some of the various forms authorizations can take.

Authorization can be more complicated than authentication. After you've been authenticated, the security server must supply the access device configuration information specific to the user—for example, which networks the user may access, which applications may be run, which commands are okay to use, and so on. Without centralized maintenance of authorization information, it wouldn't be practical to assign authorizations by user. (It's hard enough just to keep usernames and passwords up-to-date.)

Accounting Controls   Accounting doesn't permit or deny anything, but instead keeps a running record of what users do. AAA accounting is a background process that tracks the person's logins and network use. Figure 8-5 shows how AAA security accounting tracks resource usage.

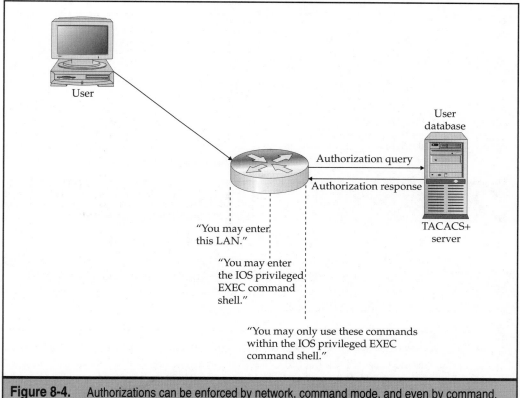

Figure 8-4.   Authorizations can be enforced by network, command mode, and even by command.

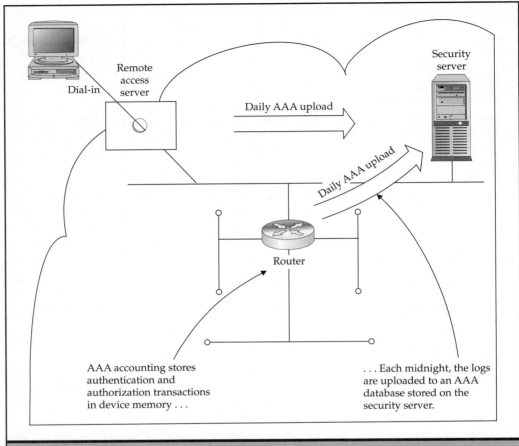

Figure 8-5. AAA accounting is a background process that tracks a user's network activity.

AAA accounting reflects events as they take place in entering systems and using services. Thus, the accounting commands more or less mirror the others. For example, accounting tasks can be enabled by system, command mode, network device interface, protocol, and connection—just like authorization commands.

NOTE: By default, AAA defines IOS as having two command modes: the user EXEC mode (sometimes also called Shell) and the privileged EXEC modes. The IOS **level** command can be used to further divide things up into 16 command levels (numbered 0–15), so access to commands can be authorized on a more fine-grained basis.

Trends Leading to Client-Server Security Systems

As with most network control systems, AAA uses the client-server model to manage security. In other words, there is a central security server holding the user profile information used by client access devices to enforce security. When a user makes a request to connect to a network, line, or service, the client device queries the server to check if it's okay. Centralization is necessary because it's no longer feasible to administer security one access device at a time; there are simply too many of them to keep track of.

In the 1970s, a natural by-product of remote users dialing into central mainframes was that user security profiles (accounts, passwords, and authorizations) were stored right there on the same computer where all the services sat. This made it easy for the security system to check on user permissions. Then, in the 1980s, departmental minicomputers became popular, spreading computers out into the organization. Terminal servers were invented to provide the additional entry points the distributed topologies required, but user databases were now spread across many access devices—making it much tougher to maintain the security system. By the time IP-based networking took off, it became apparent that security information had to be centralized. Figure 8-6 depicts this trend.

The rise of internetworking demands that an enterprise offer dial-in access throughout the organization. Doing so presents problems for enforcing consistent security controls across so many access servers. The AAA architecture is Cisco's game plan for meeting these challenges.

AAA's Two Security Protocols: TACACS+ and RADIUS

It's possible to use AAA security on a stand-alone basis, with no central security database. In the real world, few do this because it would require the extra effort of maintaining security parameters on a device-by-device basis—a labor-intensive and mistake-prone proposition. IOS supports stand-alone security because, in some cases, a security server is unavailable—for example, in a very small internetwork or during the period of time when a security server is being implemented but is still not operable.

AAA configures access devices as clients. Client devices include access servers, routers, switches, and firewalls. The clients query one or more security servers to check whether user connections are permitted. To do this, a protocol is needed to specify rules and conventions to govern the exchange of information. AAA security can use two protocols to handle client-server security configurations:

▼ **RADIUS**   A security protocol used mainly for authentication. RADIUS stands for Remote Authentication Dial-in User Service. RADIUS is an industry standard under the auspices of the IETF.

▲ **TACACS+**   A proprietary Cisco protocol that is largely the equivalent of RADIUS, but with stronger integration of authorization and accounting with authentication. TACACS stands for Terminal Access Controller Access Control System. Cisco has submitted TACACS+ to the IETF for consideration as a security protocol standard.

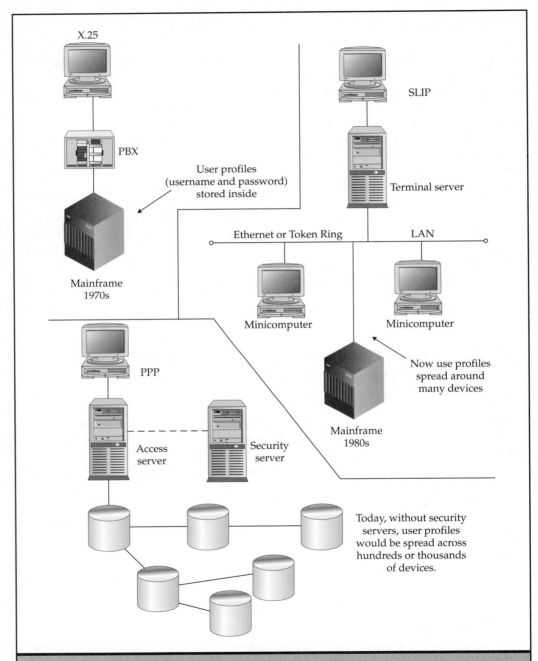

Figure 8-6.   Security systems have evolved along with the computing industry.

NOTE: There is a third security protocol called Kerberos. Developed at MIT, Kerberos is an emerging open standard for secret-key authentication that uses the Data Encryption Standard (DES) cryptographic algorithm. Microsoft, for example, integrated Kerberos into Windows 2000. Although more difficult to implement and administer, Kerberos is gaining in popularity in internetworks more sensitive to security. Its key benefits are that it can function in a multivendor network like RADIUS, but it doesn't transmit passwords over the network (it passes so-called tickets instead). IOS includes Kerberos commands in its AAA framework.

How AAA Works

AAA is the security infrastructure of IOS devices. AAA commands are located in the IOS privileged EXEC mode. Each client device is configured for security using the AAA commands from global configuration mode. Properly configured, the device can then make use of the CiscoSecure server via either the TACACS+ or RADIUS security protocols— or both.

In fact, AAA commands can be used stand-alone to secure a device. In other words, the device can use a local user database stored in NVRAM on the device itself, instead of one on a RADIUS or TACACS+ server. However, this is rarely done because it entails maintaining and monitoring user security data in hundreds, or even thousands, of device config files instead of in a single database.

TACACS+ and RADIUS are client-server network protocols used to implement client-server security over the network. In that sense, they are the equivalent of what SNMP is to network management.

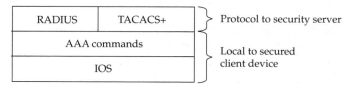

A user database changes every time users are added or deleted, passwords are changed, or authorizations are modified. Separating the user database from device config files reduces the number of places updates must be made. Most internetworks use a primary server and one or two alternate security servers, leaving only a few places in which user profile databases need to be updated.

Ensuring that the user databases contain identical data is called *database synchronization*. This can be done automatically by using Replication Partners in CiscoSecure. In the scenario with three security servers, the three user databases would be configured as replication partners, and the CiscoSecure ACS would automatically synchronize user profile records between the three on a daily basis.

The AAA Approval Process

AAA works by compiling attributes that specify a user's permissions. In the AAA context, an *attribute* is an entity (or object) to which the person may have access. For example, an authentication attribute might be a specific LAN segment to which the person is permitted access. An authorization attribute might be the limit on concurrent connections the person may have open at one time.

When a user attempts to connect to a secured service, the access device checks to see if the user has clearance per the security policy. It does so by sending a query to the server database to look for a match. The secured access device knows what to query for based on its config file parameter settings, and the query is to verify that the user has permission to do whatever is being attempted.

Attribute-Value Pairs   The query contains the attributes that are mandatory for the requested service, as defined in the access device's config file. The server processes the query by searching for the same attributes in the user's profile in the user database. The search is for so-called attribute-values. An attribute, called an *attribute-value pair* (or AV pair) in TACACS+ terminology, is a fancy term for a network entity that is secured.

For example, in someone's user profile, the password is an attribute, and the person's actual password, *imreallyme*, is the value paired with it. When the user enters the password, the access device handling the login first knows to check for a password because to do so is set as a parameter in the device's config file. By checking the person's user profile, it looks for a match between the value entered into the password prompt and what's on file in the user database for the username the person entered. Figure 8-7 shows the AAA procedure for handling a user's request for a connection.

How AAA Handles Authentication Transactions   When the connection is established, the access device contacts the security server to obtain a user prompt and displays it to the user. The user enters the information (usually just a username and password), and the protocol (RADIUS or TACACS+) encrypts the packet and sends it to the server. The server decrypts the information, checks the user's profile, forms and encrypts the response, and returns the response to the access device.

The rules of AAA approval are fairly simple: If an ACCEPT is returned, the requested connection is made. If a REJECT is returned, the user's request-for-connection session is terminated, but if an ERROR is returned and the access device is configured for multiple security servers, the query is then forwarded to an alternate server. If that server also fails to return a response, the process continues until the query runs out of servers. At that point, if the access device has been configured with a second method, it will iterate through the process again, first trying for approval with a query to the primary security server, and so on. If the access device exhausts authentication methods, it terminates the user's request-for-connection session.

The CONTINUE response is another optional configuration parameter that prompts the user for additional information. The prompts can be anything the network administrator arbitrarily defines. For example, prompting users for their mother's maiden name is a common challenge.

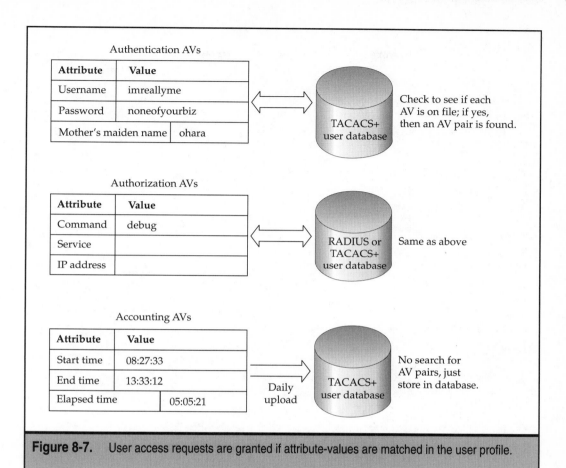

Figure 8-7. User access requests are granted if attribute-values are matched in the user profile.

NOTE: A daemon (pronounced either with long *e* or long *a*) is a process that runs on a server to perform a predefined task, usually in response to some event. The term comes from Greek mythology, in which daemons were guardian spirits. Daemons are called system agents in Windows parlance. A TACACS+ daemon sits on the security server and fields authentication or authorization queries from client access devices. It does so by searching the user database for required AV pairs and returning the results to the client in TACACS+ packets.

Authorization Transactions   If the user is authenticated, the daemon is contacted to check for authorization attributes on a case-by-case basis. Figure 8-8 depicts how authentication and authorization work together.

Authorization attributes can be issued for such services as connection type (login, PPP, and so on), IOS command modes (User EXEC or Privileged EXEC), and various connection parameters, including host IP addresses, user timeouts, access lists, and so on.

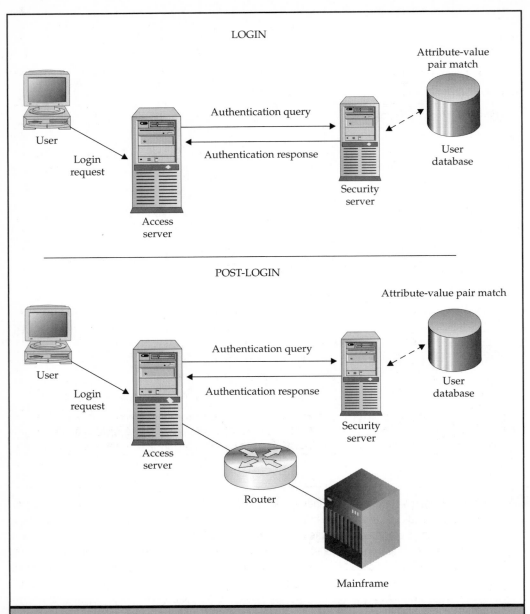

Figure 8-8.   Once authenticated, a user's authorizations are cleared as needed.

Authorization is, by nature, more sophisticated than authentication. More information than just username and password is involved, and the attributes have a state. For example, the Maximum-Time attribute requires the server to keep tabs on how long the user has been connected and to terminate the session when the value (number of seconds) for the user has been exceeded.

Authentication Protocols

CiscoSecure supports a number of authentication mechanisms. Also called *password configurations* or *password protocols*, authentication protocols make sure you are who you say you are when logging into a system. Here are four major authentication mechanisms supported by AAA:

▼ **ASCII**   American Standard Code for Information Interchange is the oldest authentication protocol. ASCII is a machine-independent technique for representing English characters and has many other uses besides authentication. ASCII authentication requires the user to type in a username and password to be sent in clear text (that is, unencrypted) and matched with those in the user database stored in ASCII format.

■ **PAP**   Password Authentication Protocol is used to authenticate PPP connections. PAP passes passwords and other user information in clear text. You know PAP as a protocol that lets you store your username and password in the dialog box so you don't have to type it during each login.

■ **CHAP**   Challenge Handshake Authentication Protocol provides the same functionality of PAP, but it is much more secure since it avoids sending the password and other user information over the network to the security server. Figure 8-9 depicts how challenge-response works.

▲ **Token-Card**   This authentication technique uses one-time passwords. A token-card is an electronic device that's a bit larger than a credit card. The card is used to generate an encrypted password that must match one filed for the user in the token-card database residing on the security server. The encrypted password is good for only one use; thus the name *token*. Token-card authentication systems provide the best access security.

AAA also supports NASI (NetWare Asynchronous Services Interface), an authentication protocol built into Novell LANs. Another vendor-specific password protocol is ARAP (AppleTalk Remote Access Protocol), with a double challenge-response authentication mechanism that goes CHAP one better by making the security server authenticate *itself* to the client as well. In addition, there are subtle variations in how the PAP protocol works with Windows NT/2000/2003.

Security comes at a cost—mostly in the form of increased inconvenience to users, but there's also additional expense to deploy and administer security measures. For example, CHAP requires some extra hardware and expertise, and token-cards are cumbersome to deploy. Can you imagine the giant Internet service provider AOL mailing token-cards to

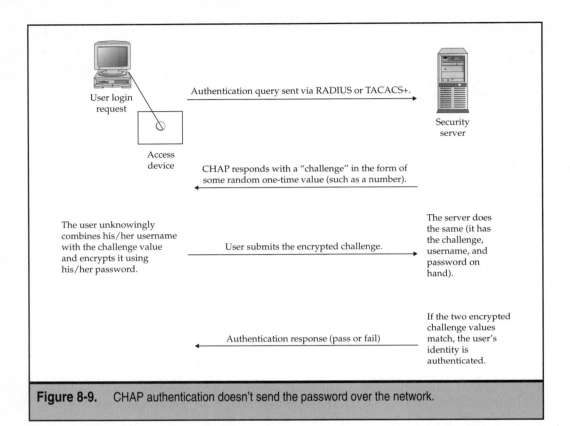

Figure 8-9.   CHAP authentication doesn't send the password over the network.

every new user and administering a token database of one-time passwords? The added expense and logistical complexity of advanced authentication protocols have discouraged their adoption.

PAP is by far the most widely used authentication protocol because it's simple for users and inexpensive for network operators. When you log into the Internet from home, you're almost certainly going through a PAP mechanism. Corporate internetworks are more likely to use CHAP, while token-cards are mainly used to protect high-security networks in the military, R&D, or banking. From an ISP's standpoint, preventing a hacker from gaining free Web access isn't worth the trouble and expense of replacing PAP with a better authentication technology.

Methods and Types

Certain pieces must be put in place before security can be enforced. As you just saw, the access device must be configured to query one or more security servers for authentication and authorization, and the user database must have profiles containing attributes that define what the user is permitted to do on the network. But what exactly happens when the query hits the TACACS+ or RADIUS database? What steps are taken to verify the user's identity and figure out what services that person is permitted?

AAA command statements in an access device's config file tell the device what to do when a user tries to log in. The root AAA commands **authenticate**, **authorization**, and **accounting** are used in conjunction with various keywords to code config file instructions on how connection attempts are to be handled. As mentioned earlier, these instruction parameters are modular in that they can be applied per user and per service. The instructions are implemented in the access device's config file using methods and types.

▼ A *method* is a prepackaged computer program that performs a specific function. For example, **radius** is a method to query a RADIUS server.

▲ A *type* is the entity to which the method applies. For example, a **radius** method is applied to a **ppp** type so that when a user attempts to make a connection using the PPP protocol, the access device queries its RADIUS server to authenticate the person's identity.

Because there are almost always multiple security parameters set for a device, AAA configurations are referred to as *named method lists.* They're called *named* methods because they are named by the administrator in the device config file and applied to one or more specific secured entity types. Figure 8-10 shows how named method lists and types work together to enforce security.

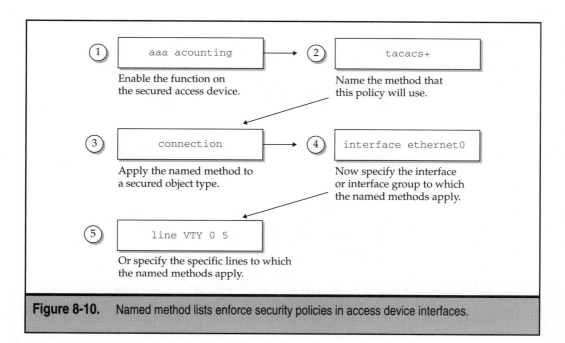

Figure 8-10.   Named method lists enforce security policies in access device interfaces.

NOTE: There are unnamed methods in the form of the default method list. If an interface or line has no named method list configured, a default method list is automatically put into force for it. To have no AAA security, it must be explicitly configured this way by using the **none** method. Cisco makes it hard to have no security in force.

Named method lists are entered into the config file of the access device being secured—usually an access server or a router. IOS applies methods in the sequence in which they appear in the configuration, initially trying the first method and then turning to the following ones until an ACCEPT or REJECT is returned. Figure 8-11 explains a typical named method list.

The last part of the AAA configuration in Figure 8-11 specifies lines because authentication deals with individual users. Traffic-based security can be applied on the interface level because the firewall or router monitors information in the header of each packet—a process that is done either to all or none of the packets passing through an interface. By contrast, user-based security controls individuals as they make a remote network connection via an access server, or log into IOS inside a router or switch within the network. Each of these two scenarios involves using a line.

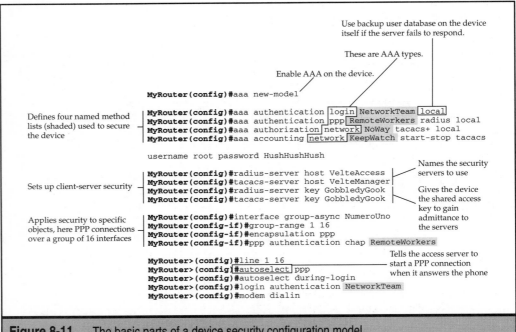

Figure 8-11. The basic parts of a device security configuration model

AAA Authentication Methods and Types   AAA has several methods to authenticate user identity. Only one method may be used per user line (except when the **Local** method is configured as backup to one of the three client-server methods). Table 8-1 lists Cisco's authentication methods.

The list of AAA methods in Table 8-1 varies slightly according to the password mechanism being used. Remember that AAA is an architectural model that must be adapted to differences in the way other vendors design their products. For example, AAA supports Guest and Auth-Guest methods for the password protocol in Apple's ARAP.

It's possible to configure different authentication methods on different lines within the same access device. For example, you might want to configure PPP connections to query the user database on a RADIUS server, but to check the local user database for login connections made from the console or AUX ports.

Connection Types   Because authentication is applied to user lines, named authentication methods are applied to connection types. A *connection type* is the communications protocol used to make a connection. To explain, remote connections to ISPs and internetworks nowadays are usually PPP connections. But when a network administrator logs into IOS in order to work on a device, that connection is via a Telnet session (if over the network) or a terminal emulator (if over the console or AUX port). Table 8-2 explains the authentication types.

IOS Command Keyword	AAA Authentication Method
RADIUS	Authenticates using the RADIUS protocol and user database.
TACACS+	Authenticates using the TACACS+ protocol and user database.
Krb5	Authenticates using the Kerberos 5 protocol and user database. (Note: Kerberos can only be used with the PAP password protocol.)
Local	Authenticates using a user database stored in memory in the access device, or for backup if the security server does not respond.
Enable	Authenticates using Enable Secret passwords in the access device's config file.
If-needed	Does not require authentication if the user has already been authenticated on a VTY or TTY line.
None	Uses no authentication.

Table 8-1.   Authentication Methods in IOS

IOS Command Keyword	AAA Authentication Type
Login	Line connections made to Ethernet or Token Ring network interfaces using Telnet, or to console or AUX ports using virtual terminal (VTY)
PPP	Dial-in line connections made to serial network interfaces using Point-to-Point Protocol
SLIP	Dial-in line connections made to serial network interfaces using Serial Line Internet Protocol
ARAP	Dial-in line connections made to serial network interfaces using AppleTalk Remote Access Protocol

Table 8-2. Entity Types Secured by AAA Authentication Methods

The following example statement illustrates a serial interface on an access server being configured to use TACACS+ to authenticate persons making PPP network connections:

```
MyAccessServer(config)#aaa new-model
MyAccessServer(config)#aaa authentication ppp MyList tacacs+ local
MyAccessServer(config)#interface serial0
MyAccessServer(config-if)#ppp authentication pap MyList
MyAccessServer(config-if)#tacacs-server host 10.1.13.10
MyAccessServer(config-if)#tacacs-server key DoNotTell
```

The **aaa new-model** command activates (enables) the AAA inside the device's IOS software. Then the statement specifies that a TACACS+ security protocol be used and that the local user database should be used if the TACACS+ server fails to respond. The **interface serial0** command points the configuration to all lines on the access server's serial network interface named serial0. The **ppp authentication pap MyList tacacs+ local** specifies that the PAP password protocol be used for PPP connections and applies the named method list **MyList** to be used as the test.

The next statement specifies that the TACACS+ server resides on the host computer at IP address 10.1.13.10. The next line specifies that the encryption key **DoNotTell** be used for all communications between the security server and the client access device being configured here. The shared encryption key also must be configured on the security server(s) with which the client access device will communicate.

NOTE: Three types of protocols play a major role in AAA: dial-in protocols such as PPP, security protocols such as RADIUS, and password protocols such as CHAP. Dial-in protocols are network protocols that handle signals over phone lines, keeping the IP packets together between the access server and the remote user. Security protocols provide the client-server messaging system to the centralized user database. Password protocols are relatively simple mechanisms to deal with the person logging in. Some dial-in protocols incorporate their own password protocol—ARAP, for example.

AAA Authorization Methods and Types   AAA has five methods for authorization. There are actually six, but the **none** method is a request not to do any authorization procedure. Table 8-3 explains the AAA authorization methods. Each method is a keyword for use as an argument with the root **aaa authorization** command. These, in turn, are applied to secured entity types.

As mentioned, RADIUS and TACACS+ can coexist on the same access device. Depending on the connection being attempted and how the device is configured, the client will query either the RADIUS or the TACACS+ servers, which are separate user databases.

The **if-authenticated** command waives authorization if the user has already been authenticated elsewhere. This is important, because during a single session a user may make dozens of connections to entities secured by AAA authorization (such as IOS command modes), and it would be unwieldy for the client device to query the TACACS+ or RADIUS server each time.

IOS Command Keyword	AAA Authorization Method
TACACS+	Sends a message requesting authorization information from the TACACS+ server.
RADIUS	Sends a message requesting authorization information from the RADIUS server.
If-authenticated	Allows access to the requested function if the user has already been authenticated. (*If* here is the word *if*, as in "depending on," not the mnemonic IOS uses for network interface in the config prompt.)
Local	Uses the local user database to execute the authorization program.
Krb5-instance	Uses an instance defined in the Kerberos instance map.
None	Does not execute any authorization methods on this access device.

Table 8-3.   AAA's Six Named Methods for User Authentication

Generally, a device's local user database contains only usernames and passwords. Remember that network devices don't have hard disks, and they must store permanent information in NVRAM memory, already burdened with storing a boot image of IOS and even daily AAA accounting logs. For this reason, local user databases generally do not hold authorizations for users. Therefore, if a security server were unavailable when a user logged in, that person would likely be unable to access any services configured to require authorization. Figure 8-12 shows how a local user database coexists with the server database(s).

If no authorization is to be executed on a secured entity, this should be explicitly configured by using the **none** command. Otherwise, the IOS software will automatically put the default authorization methods into force. The four types of secured objects to which AAA authorization methods can be applied are explained in Table 8-4.

The four authorization entity types can be broken down into two pairs:

▼ The EXEC and Command methods each deal with access to IOS commands.

▲ The Network and Reverse Access methods both deal with connections, but those which go in different directions.

On Cisco access devices, the **aaa authorization config-commands** command is enabled by default. That way the device has security right out of the box, in case the administrator installs it without configuring security. The following example statement illustrates a router being configured to require authorization for any type of network connection. This would apply, for example, whether the connection was being made via a console TTY login, a Telnet VTY login, or a PPP dial-in login:

```
MyRouter(config)#aaa new-model
MyRouter(config)#aaa authorization network NetTeam tacacs+ local
```

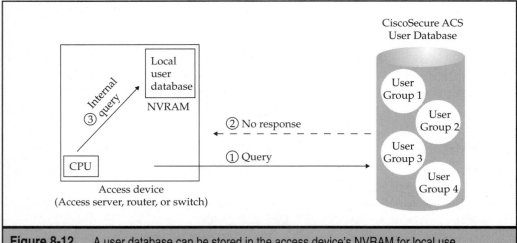

Figure 8-12.   A user database can be stored in the access device's NVRAM for local use.

Type	AAA Authorization Type
Network	Applies method to network-related service requests, including direct Login connections (via console or AUX), Telnet connections (via IP or IPX), or dial-in connections (via PPP, SLIP, or ARAP).
Reverse Access	Applies method to Telnet sessions in which the user attempts to connect from the secured access device to another host—a common maneuver by a hacker who has broken into a network device.
EXEC	Applies method to sessions in the User EXEC command mode and can be applied by user, date, and start and stop times.
Commands	Applies method to restrict access to specific commands. Command methods must be applied to an IOS command level group. There are two default groups, numbers 0 and 15 (user EXEC and privileged EXEC modes, respectively). The Command method can be applied by user, date, and start and stop times.

Table 8-4. IOS's Four Authorization Types

The preceding command specifies that the TACACS+ security protocol be used to check users against the NetTeam named method list, and to use the local user database for backup. By default, this authorization is applied to all network interfaces on the device (as opposed to authentication methods, which must be applied to specific lines).

But, as mentioned earlier, sometimes having authorizations stored on the device itself isn't practical. To accommodate this, the restriction could be loosened using the **none** command to allow a network connection if the TACACS+ server fails to respond:

```
MyRouter(config)#aaa authorization network NetTeam tacacs+ none
```

In the preceding command, the user's identity must have already been authenticated with a password to get this far into the AAA configuration. The **none** command goes into effect only when the TACACS+ server fails to respond. The following code statement configures a somewhat more sophisticated authorization:

```
MyRouter(config)#aaa authorization commands 15 SeniorTechs
MyRouter(config)#line vty 0 5
MyRouter(config-line)#authorization commands 15 SeniorTechs
```

The preceding statement shows an example of configuration by line, as opposed to network interface. Here, the six virtual terminal (VTY) lines are secured. In this example, the named method list SeniorTechs is declared as necessary for an administrator to use IOS command level 15 in this device. We mentioned earlier that the IOS **level** command can be employed to authorize the use of a group of commands. By default, all Privileged EXEC mode commands are grouped into level 15, and all User EXEC mode commands are grouped into level 0. Therefore, the preceding code snippet specifies that only administrators with user profiles configured with the SeniorTechs attributes will be permitted to use the Privileged EXEC commands.

Accounting Methods and Types   AAA accounting methods configure user activities to track within a secured access device. Accounting methods gather data from TACACS+ and RADIUS packets and log it into a file stored on the access device. The security server comes around each day and collects the data into a central AAA accounting database. Table 8-5 explains how the two work.

Notice that the only accounting methods are the security protocols themselves. This is because accounting data is, by default, collected for the entire device. The reason for the two methods is that the accounting data must travel either in TACACS+ or RADIUS packets to the server (AAA accounting isn't done without servers).

AAA has five accounting secured entity types, slightly different from those for authorization. Table 8-6 explains them.

The **system** accounting keyword only collects a default set of variables. It cannot be configured to collect only certain events. The reason for this is that a system event simply happens—a user does not request permission to cause it. An example system event would be a network interface going down at 11:32:28 Tuesday, January 9, 2005. AAA accounting does not automatically associate the system event with a security transaction, but comparing accounting and authorization logs for that date and time would make it easy for a system administrator to figure out who the culprit was.

Like authorization, AAA accounting named method lists must be applied to all network interfaces they are meant to secure, and then applied to an indicated accounting type. For example, the MyRouter(config)#**aaa accounting network tacacs+** command configures IOS to keep track of all SLIP, PPP connections made over a network interface that are authorized using TACACS+.

Command Keyword	AAA Accounting Method
TACACS+	Logs accounting information on TACACS+ in the CiscoSecure ACS database
RADIUS	Logs accounting information on RADIUS in the CiscoSecure ACS database

Table 8-5.   AAA Accounting Uses One Method per Security Protocol

Command Keyword	AAA Accounting Type
Network	Applies method to network connections, usually a PPP connection, but methods can also be named for logins, SLIP, or ARAP connections.
EXEC	Provides information on all User EXEC mode terminal sessions within the access device's IOS environment. EXEC accounting information can be collected by user, date, and start and stop times.
Commands	Provides information on any commands issued by users who are members of an IOS Privileged EXEC mode. Command accounting information can be collected by user, date, and start and stop times.
Connection	Provides information on all outbound connections attempted from the secured access device in sessions made using the Telnet, rlogin, TN270, PAD, and LAT terminal protocols.
System	Provides information about system-level events, such as reboots.

Table 8-6.   AAA Accounting Types that Track Asset Usage for Five Secured Entity Types

Accounting is a little more complicated in how it tracks requests, though. AAA accounting relies on so-called accounting notices to gather data. An *accounting notice* is a special packet notifying the accounting method of an event. This information is recorded in the accounting log file for upload to the appropriate security server. One of three AAA accounting keywords must be used to specify exactly when during the service request process the notices are to be sent. The terminology can get a bit confusing, but Figure 8-13 will help you visualize how the three work:

▼ **Stop-only**   For minimal accounting. Has RADIUS or TACACS+ send a stop recording accounting data notice at the *end* of the requested service. Stop-only accounting is good only for tracking who went where. This is important information for security purposes.

■ **Start-stop**   For more accounting. Has RADIUS or TACACS+ send a start accounting notice at the *beginning* of the requested service and a stop accounting notice at the end of the service. Start-stop accounting yields the elapsed time of a connection.

▲ **Wait-start**   For maximum accounting. Has RADIUS or TACACS+ wait until the start notice is received by AAA accounting *before* the user's request process begins. Most regard wait-start as overkill and an inconvenience to users, so its use is limited to very sensitive services.

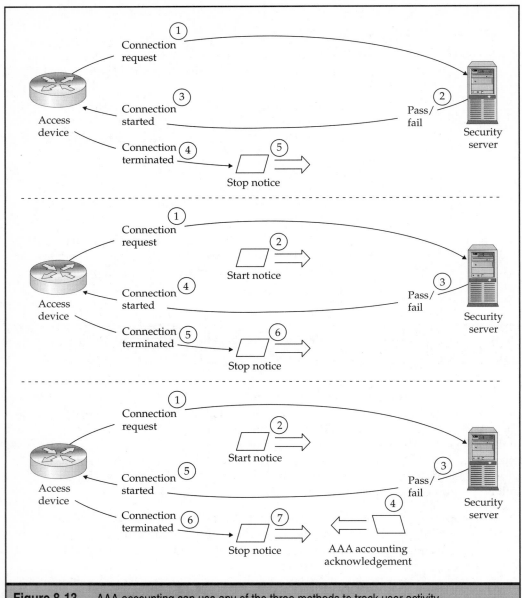

Figure 8-13. AAA accounting can use any of the three methods to track user activity.

To select a method, include any one of the three keywords as arguments to the root **aaa accounting** command in the configuration statement. The three options give differing levels of accounting control. For example, if an administrator requests entry into a secured device's User EXEC mode, the stop-only process records only the end of the administrator's session within User EXEC mode. The start-stop process records the beginning and the end of the session. The wait-start process ensures that no connection is made prior to the accounting notice having been received and acknowledged.

The following example shows an AAA accounting configuration. Lines 2, 3, and 4 show all three AAA functions being configured together, the normal practice in the real world.

```
MyAccessServer(config)#aaa new-model
MyAccessServer(config)#aaa authentication login NetTeam local
MyAccessServer(config)#aaa authentication ppp RemoteWorkers tacacs+ local
MyAccessServer(config)#aaa authorization network NetTeam tacacs+ local
MyAccessServer(config)#aaa accounting network WeWillBillYou
MyAccessServer(config)#
MyAccessServer(config)#tacacs-server host BigUnixBox
MyAccessServer(config)#tacacs-server key JustBetweenUs
MyAccessServer(config)#
MyAccessServer(config)#interface group-async 1
MyAccessServer(config-if)#group-range 1 16
MyAccessServer(config-if)#encapsulation ppp
MyAccessServer(config-if)#ppp authentication chap RemoteWorkers
MyAccessServer(config-if)#ppp authorization NetTeam
MyAccessServer(config-if)#ppp accounting WeWillBillYou
```

The accounting commands are woven in with the others, to give you an idea of how statements really look. As configured here, full start-stop accounting records will be logged for all network connections made by the network team through any of the 16 asynchronous ports on the device, MyRouter.

Exactly what gets logged depends on how the named method list WeWillBillYou is configured. Most network managers, at a minimum, would use the **network** command to account for connection times. Generally speaking, the command-oriented parameters **exec** and **commands** are useful only for security audits.

RADIUS and TACACS+ Attributes

A security protocol is largely defined by the attributes it supports. After all, they define the raw material used to operate the user-based security system. RADIUS and TACACS+ are separate protocols packaged into the AAA command structure within IOS. The major differences between the two come into play inside the user database, where each user has a security profile containing attributes that define what that person may do. As separate technologies, RADIUS and TACACS+ have their own attributes.

RADIUS is an open standard under the auspices of the IETF and defines nearly 60 attributes. We won't list them all here, but Table 8-7 shows several to help you see what's involved in user-based security.

Seventeen RADIUS attributes are so-called vendor-proprietary attributes. These are items that vendors can customize to extend functionality within their products. Table 8-8 shows a few Cisco extensions to give you an idea of what vendors like to customize.

RADIUS Attribute	Description
User-Name	The name of a person's user profile account. For example, Anne Marie's username might be "amarie."
User-Password	The secret pass code created by the person.
CHAP-Password	The encrypted value returned during the challenge-handshake exchange. This is the username mixed with a random number called a *challenge*.
NAS-IP Address	The IP address of the access server requesting authentication. (Recall that NAS stands for network access server, the same thing as an access server.)
NAS-Port	The physical port number on the access server. This includes the various types of interfaces possible, such as asynchronous terminal lines, synchronous network lines, ISDN channels, and other types of interfaces.
Service-Type	The service requested or granted—for example, an administrator might request the **enable** command in IOS in order to enter the Privileged EXEC command mode.
Login-Port	The TCP port with which the user is to be connected—for example, port 80 for HTTP Web browsing.
Acct-Session-Id	A unique accounting identifier used to match start and stop notices in an accounting log file.
Acct-Session-Time	The number of seconds the user remained connected.
Acct-Authentic	The way the user was authenticated, whether by RADIUS, the local user database, TACACS+, or Kerberos.

Table 8-7.   RADIUS Attributes Used to Enforce User-Based Security

Cisco-Specific RADIUS Attribute	Description
Password-Expiration	Specifies a time interval or event that forces the user to create a new password.
IP-Direct	The Cisco device will bypass all routing tables and send packets directly to a specified IP address. For example, IP-Direct might be used to make sure a user's WAN connection goes through a firewall.
Idle-Limit	Specifies the maximum number of seconds any session may be idle.

Table 8-8.   Cisco Extensions to the RADIUS Standard

TACACS+ has over 50 attributes (attribute-value pairs). While TACACS+ and RADIUS both support the three AAA functions, TACACS+ is more sophisticated. For example, it has attributes such as Tunnel-ID to help secure VPN connections. This is why internetworks that use RADIUS for authenticating dial-in users will frequently use TACACS+ for authorization and accounting. Table 8-9 shows example TACACS+ attributes to give you a feel for the protocol.

The sampling of AV pairs in Table 8-9 shows two areas in which TACACS+ is stronger than RADIUS. First, TACACS+ offers stricter internal security than RADIUS by locking down commands and access lists. The first thing a hacker would do upon breaking into an IOS device would be to make new entries into its access lists, which makes file transfers possible. These AV pairs not only help to stop hackers, they also let the network manager specify which devices, IOS commands, or access lists individual administrators may work with. Locking out certain team members helps avoid configuration errors.

The second area in which TACACS+ is stronger is protocol support. For example, TACACS+ has AV pairs to enhance security of VPNs, which are exploding in popularity. As would be expected, TACACS+ also has accounting attributes to go along with the areas where it expands beyond RADIUS. For example, the **cmd=**x AV pair lets you keep track of which IOS commands an administrator uses while working on a device. This can be useful information for diagnosing how a configuration error was made.

DYNAMIC ACCESS LISTS

Access lists are normally used to filter traffic at the packet level. In other words, when a connection is attempted through a router interface, packet headers are inspected for prohibited IP addresses or application port numbers, and traffic is passed or blocked. These

TACACS+ AV Pair	Description
service=x	Specifies the connection service to be authorized or accounted. For example, **aaa authorization service=ppp** would be used to authorize a person to make a remote PPP connection to a device. Another example would be **service=shell** to let an administrator get into a device's Privileged EXEC command mode.
protocol=x	A protocol is a subset of a service. For example, a PPP connection might use TN3270, VINES, Telnet, or other protocols. A key protocol nowadays is VPDN (Virtual Private Dialup Network). The AV pair **protocol=vpdn** would let a remote dial-in user establish an encrypted connection to the enterprise's VPN network.
routing=x	Specifies whether routing updates may be propagated through the interface used for the connection.
priv-lvl=x	Specifies the IOS command mode the person may use. For this to work, commands must first be grouped using the **level** command.
acl=x	Restricts connection access lists on a device. Connection access lists are also called *reflexive access lists,* and are used to track sessions.
inacl=x, inacl#=x, outacl=x, outacl#=x	Four AV pairs restricting access to per-user inbound and outbound access lists placed on an interface.
tunnel-id	Specifies a username for establishing remote VPN connections.
gw-password=x	Specifies the password placed on the home gateway into the VPN. Must be used where **service=ppp** and **protocol=vpdn.**

Table 8-9.   TACACS+ Authentication and Authorization AV Pairs

are called extended access lists, and they're discussed in Chapter 9. To review here, such access lists are *extended* in that they can filter based on network application port numbers instead of just addresses. They're also called *static* extended access lists, because the **permit** and **deny** commands are blindly enforced, regardless of the user. To make an exception for a particular person, an administrator would need to go into the router's config file and edit the list for that interface.

Dynamic access lists are configured using so-called lock-and-key commands. By employing these, a user who would otherwise be blocked can be granted temporary access to a network or subnet via a Telnet session over the Internet.

The Telnet session is opened to a router configured for lock-and-key. The dynamic access list prompts the user for authentication information. As with other user-based security protocols, lock-and-key can be configured to check against a user database on the router itself (local), or against a user database maintained on a TACACS+ or RADIUS server. If authenticated, the user is automatically logged out of the Telnet session and can start a normal application such as a browser.

Lock-and-Key Using a Local User Database

The following sequence of code snippets shows how lock-and-key could be configured on a router using a locally maintained user authentication file. To start, a particular network interface on the router is declared along with a subnetted IP address. The **ip access-group** command places the just-named interface and networks under the control of access list 103:

```
MyRouter(config)#interface ethernet1
MyRouter(config-if)#ip address 209.198.208.30 255.255.255.0
MyRouter(config-if)#ip access-group 103 in
```

The keyword **in** specifies that access control be applied only to inbound connections (lock-and-key can also be used to restrict outbound connections).

In the following statement, the first entry of access list 103 allows only Telnet connections into the router. The second entry of access list 103 is ignored until lock-and-key is triggered whenever a Telnet connection has been established in the router. The keyword **dynamic** defines access list 103 as a dynamic (lock-and-key) list.

```
MyRouter(config)#access-list 103 permit tcp any host 209.198.207.2 eq telnet
MyRouter(config)#access-list 103 dynamic InCrowd timeout 60 permit ip any any
```

This is the key juncture. If so configured, an attempted Telnet connection to the router causes it to check against its local user database to see if the user and password are valid for lock-and-key access to the router. If validated, the **timeout 60 permit ip any any** statement gives the user 60 minutes to use the router as a connection between any two IP addresses.

Finally, an **autocommand** statement creates a temporary inbound access list entry (named InCrowd in the previous statement) at the network interface Ethernet1 and line 0 on the router. The temporary access list entry will time out after five minutes.

```
MyRouter(config)#line vty 0
MyRouter(config-line)#login local
MyRouter(config-line)#autocommand access-enable timeout 5
```

The temporary access list entry isn't automatically deleted when the user terminates the session. It will remain configured until the timeout period expires.

Dynamic access lists can also be configured to authenticate users against a user database maintained on either a TACACS+ or RADIUS server. This, in effect, turns a router into an access server through which a user can gain entry into an internetwork, but only by logging in via a Telnet session.

It goes without saying, and is certainly a cliché, that network security is extremely important and necessary. However, understanding that it's important and understanding how to actually implement it are two different things. To be sure, an entire book can be (and many have been) written on the subject of network security in general, and Cisco security in particular. The object of this chapter was to show you various details behind some of the important components in securing your internetwork. In Chapter 9, we'll talk about some specific tools that Cisco offers in the realm of network access and security.

CHAPTER 9

Security Building Blocks

The last few chapters showed how data move over internetworks. It starts with the twisted-pair cable running from the desktop. Then we see messages traveling through hubs, switches, and routers. Quickly, the data makes it to destinations across buildings or on the other side of the world. All this technology has made it possible to do some amazing things. It's now routine for businesses to sell and support entire product lines from Web sites—unthinkable just a few short years ago. Just as impressive, whole companies are being managed within internetwork management platforms. It's even possible to operate private networks over the public Internet. But there's a catch to all this technology: networks are two-way streets. If good things can happen over internetworks, it follows that bad things can, too.

Hooking a computer up to any kind of network necessarily incurs risk. Hooking up an entire enterprise, as you might imagine, brings a boatload of security issues. Network security is a broad subject that encompasses policies, safeguards, techniques, standards, protocols, algorithms, and specialized hardware and software products. Security has been paramount in computing since the early years of central mainframes and green screen terminals. Experts now regard security as the single biggest hurdle to the Internet becoming the all-encompassing business environment that so many envision. Indeed, network security is such an important subject that it's an entire industry unto itself.

Good security is tougher to attain now because systems are so interconnected. In the old days, you either had a terminal hooked up to the mainframe or you were out. But in this era of connectivity, anybody with sufficient resources and time conceivably can break into any system. Vulnerability is a fact of life in internetworking, and the industry's response is a phalanx of security technologies.

All security starts with *access*. Even back in the misty days of cavemen, having good security meant not letting bad things in or valuable things out. Internetworking is no different. Running an internetwork is like running a storefront business: it's in your interest to let strangers freely enter and exit the store, but doing so inevitably means giving thieves and vandals a shot at your goods. You have to keep access open; all you can do is try to weed out the bad guys. Three network access technologies try to balance the conflicting needs for access and security:

▼ **Firewalls** Special routers that intercept and control traffic between a private network and public networks (especially the Internet).

■ **Virtual private networks (VPNs)** Private networks operating over a public network (usually the Internet).

▲ **Access devices** Dedicated devices used to connect remote users to internetworks over the Internet and normal telephone lines. These products include access servers and access routers.

Of the three technologies, only the firewall is solely concerned with security, and it doesn't provide access so much as permit it. The other two—VPNs and access devices—exist primarily to deliver cost-effective connectivity. Access servers provide remote persons a way to enter internetworks. The mission of a VPN is to run a wide area network (WAN) over the Internet, but both access servers and VPNs restrict unauthorized access and attempt to ensure data integrity.

> **NOTE:**   We won't talk about access servers, specifically, in this chapter. What's important to know is that these devices are used to accommodate dial-in access. Dial-in users call into the network and connect using the access server's modem bank. Once authenticated, they are able to access internetwork resources. This chapter covers Cisco access technology from both functional and security perspectives. Integrated security management tools were covered in Chapter 8.

FIREWALLS

A *firewall* is a traffic control point between a private network and one or more public networks. It's a gateway that selectively decides what may enter or leave a private network. To do this, a firewall must be the sole gateway between the network it protects and the outside. If traffic can go around a firewall, the security it provides is worthless. A basic tenet is that all external traffic must pass through the firewall. A normal router could serve as a firewall if it were configured as a choke point. Figure 9-1 shows how a firewall acts as a funnel through which all traffic must pass.

There is a necessary trade-off between security and network performance. If you substituted cars and trucks for IP packets in Figure 9-1, you'd see traffic from several highways squeezed through a single on-ramp. If security weren't a concern, to boost access, private internetworks would be surrounded on all sides by routers.

Firewall Basics

The firewall, in fact, is a kind of router. Traffic enters through one network interface and leaves through another, and messages are handled at the network layer (layer 3) of the seven-layer OSI model.

Firewalls operate by intercepting and inspecting each packet that enters any of their network interfaces. The inspections vary according to the firewall's sophistication and how tight the security policy is. But the goal is always to identify a match between each packet's contents and the security rules the firewall has been programmed to enforce. The basic steps of intercepting and inspecting packets are shown in Figure 9-2.

There's nothing fancy about how a firewall intercepts traffic. It does so by funneling all traffic entering its network interfaces over a single path (called a *data bus* in computer terminology). By having all traffic pass through the firewall's internal data bus and memory, software running on the central processing unit (CPU) is given the opportunity to check each packet against the security rules it's been programmed to enforce.

The actual inspection is done by reading the packet's header for conditions that match rules set up in security tables. Security tables usually include dozens of rules, each designed to explicitly accept or reject specific kinds of traffic by applying a pass/fail test to the packet. If the packet passes, it's forwarded to its destination. If it fails, the packet is dropped at the network interface and ceases to exist.

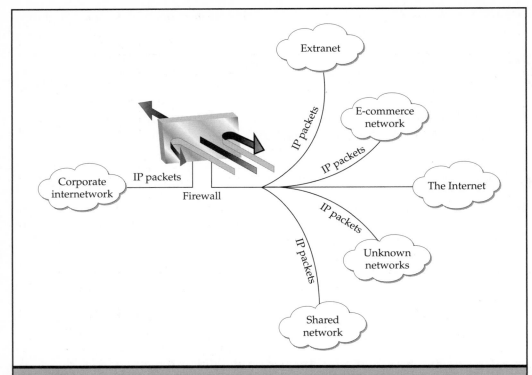

Figure 9-1. A firewall is partly defined by its position as a traffic bottleneck.

Firewalls Map Out a Defensive Landscape

Routers tend to take a friendly view of the world. They focus on addresses and the best routes to deliver messages to them. By contrast, firewalls take a militaristic view of things where addresses are still important, but for inspection and clearance instead of delivery. Firewalls define the world as either inside networks or outside networks, with the division made according to what lies beyond the security perimeter. The security perimeter itself is established by one or more firewalls placed between the secured network and the outside. The firewall places every network it encounters into one of three classifications:

▼ **Trusted network** Inside the security perimeter and under complete administrative control of the enterprise

■ **Untrusted network** Outside the security perimeter and known to the firewall, but beyond the enterprise's administrative control

▲ **Unknown network** A network that the firewall has received no information or instructions about—this includes almost the entire Internet

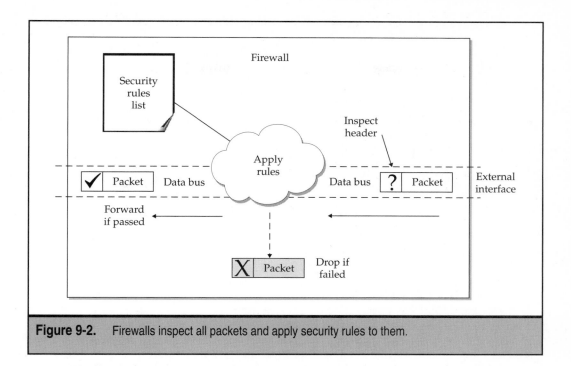

Figure 9-2.   Firewalls inspect all packets and apply security rules to them.

The security perimeter is drawn right down the middle of the firewall, with the physical configuration of the device itself defining what's internal and external. The network interfaces on the firewall are designated as either *inside* or *outside* interfaces. The network attached to each interface in turn takes on its interface's designation as either an *inside network* or *outside network.* In Figure 9-3, for example, network 10.1.13.0 is attached to an inside interface, and thus is defined as being inside the security perimeter, and therefore a trusted network.

In terms of network security, *administrative control* is the ability to do such things as assign IP addresses, issue user accounts and passwords, and maintain network device configuration files. Usually, the network media—LANs and WANs—over which a secured network operates are owned and controlled by the enterprise. The major exception to this is the VPN, which runs mostly over intermediate network segments that are operated by somebody else but that are still regarded as trusted networks.

Security Is a Matter of Policy, Not Technology

Internetwork security isn't just a matter of how much control you can exert, it's also how much you *choose* to exert. Much like the trade-off between security and performance, a trade-off also exists between security and connectivity. In theory, any LAN could have impenetrable security by simply unplugging all routers, switches, and modems leading to the outside.

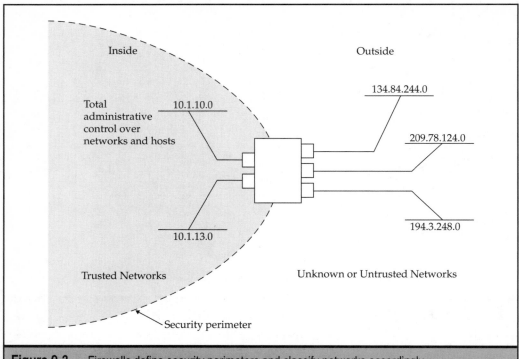

Inside

Outside

134.84.244.0

Total
administrative
control over
networks and hosts

10.1.10.0

209.78.124.0

194.3.248.0

10.1.13.0

Trusted Networks

Unknown or Untrusted Networks

Security perimeter

Figure 9-3. Firewalls define security perimeters and classify networks accordingly.

But enterprises are compelled to connect to the outside because the benefits of connectivity outweigh the risk it brings. In fact, almost all businesses are now connected to the most unknown and dangerous public network of all: the Internet. Every time you hit a company's Web site to look up information, download software, or place an order, that enterprise has taken a calculated risk by letting you access some part of its system. Most enterprises need to open their internal networks to the public to at least some degree. Businesses do it to sell and support, governments to serve, and educational organizations to teach. Firewalls try to help accommodate this intentional security compromise by defining a middle ground called a *demilitarized zone*, or DMZ for short. Figure 9-4 shows a typical DMZ configuration.

LAN segments on the firewall's outside are called the *external perimeter networks*, and ones on the inside are called *internal perimeter networks*. Usually, each perimeter network has a router attached, and access lists on these routers handle the bulk of traffic flow duties, allowing the firewall to focus on packet inspection and rules enforcement. The outside router is often referred to as the *shield router*, which usually has an Internet service

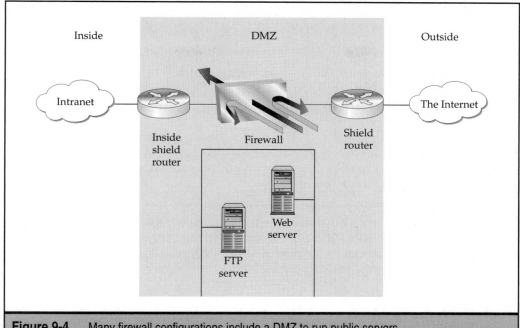

Figure 9-4.   Many firewall configurations include a DMZ to run public servers.

provider (ISP) attached to at least one of its interfaces. In addition to normal router duty, the shield router also protects the servers in the DMZ from attack by acting as an alarm system for the firewall. The router on the inside, called the *inside shield router*, is the last line of defense between the firewall and the inside networks. The key point to understand is that a firewall is defined as much by its physical configuration (what's connected to what) as the security rules it's programmed to enforce.

How Firewalls Work

Security rules are defined for each firewall network interface. This is true whether the firewall is a router trying to serve as a firewall or a high-tech dedicated device such as the Cisco PIX Firewall. Each packet is filtered based on rules applied to the specific network interface card through which it entered the firewall. The act of configuring a firewall, then, is largely a matter of assigning security rules to each firewall interface.

The Access List Is the Most Basic Internetwork Security Tool

The simplest form of network security technology is the access list. Also called an *access control list (ACL)*, or *filter*, the access list is a basic component of any router's configuration.

As the name implies, the access list restricts certain traffic from gaining access to a network. It provides a basic level of network security by filtering packets according to three criteria:

- ▼ **Source address**   The IP address from which the packet originated
- ■ **Destination address**   The IP address (or addresses) to which the packet is addressed
- ▲ **Port number**   The application-layer (layer 7) protocol the packet will use

Cisco calls these *extended access lists*—the extension being the port number. Early Cisco products used only source/destination addresses, which were referred to as *standard access lists*. But don't be misled by this terminology; extended access lists are the basic type of access lists being used now.

NOTE: Port numbers (also called network ports or just ports) aren't physical interface ports like S0 or E3. Messages sent using the TCP or UDP transport-layer protocols (layer 4) use port numbers to identify which application protocol the transmission will run. For example, the number for HTTP (WWW) is port 80, SMTP's port is 25, and FTP's port is 21.

Network administrators create access lists in the router's configuration file. One access list is created for each network interface. If an interface handles traffic in multiple network protocols—for example, IP, IPX, and AppleTalk—each network protocol has its own access list format. Therefore, a separate access list must be created for each protocol to run over that network interface. Regardless of the network protocol used, each criterion (access rule) occupies a line on the list. Figure 9-5 depicts how access lists work. This example uses a router restricting the flow of traffic between departments within an organization.

As each packet attempts to enter an interface, its header is examined to see if anything matches the access list. The router is looking for positive matches. Once it finds a match, no further evaluations are performed. If the rule matched is a *permit* rule, the packet is forwarded out a network interface on the other side of the router. If the matched rule is a *deny,* the packet is dropped right there at the interface.

If a packet's evaluation runs all the way to the bottom of the access list without a match, it is dropped by default. This mechanism is called the *implicit deny rule,* which provides an added measure of security by dealing with conditions not anticipated in the access list.

The router evaluates the packet one rule at a time, working its way from the top line to the bottom. The bottom part of Figure 9-6 is an example taken from a router's access list. Each line in the list is a rule that either permits or denies a specific type of traffic. The top of Figure 9-6 charts the parts of a rule's statement, starting with the **access-list** command followed by various modifiers. Keep in mind that this example is for IP, and syntax varies slightly for IPX, AppleTalk, and other non-IP network protocols.

A cohesive access list is created by using a common access list name at the beginning of each statement for an IP access list. Each statement must declare a transport protocol:

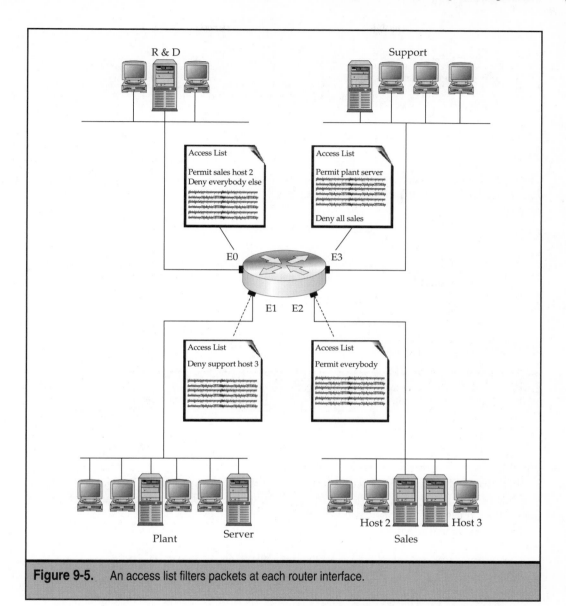

Figure 9-5.   An access list filters packets at each router interface.

the Transmission Control Protocol (TCP), the User Datagram Protocol (UDP), or the Internet Control Messaging Protocol (ICMP). If the rule involves a network application, the statement must first declare a transport protocol and end with the application protocol. In the example rule at the top of Figure 9-6, the transport protocol is TCP, and the application protocol is HTTP.

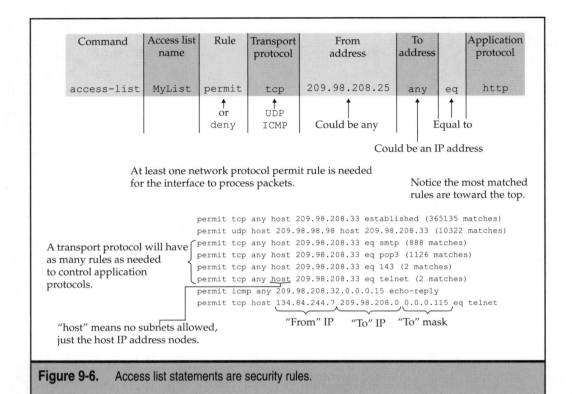

Figure 9-6. Access list statements are security rules.

To apply a rule to incoming traffic, you must put the outside host's IP address in the *from* position, which always precedes the *to* position. This order is reversed so as to restrict outbound traffic. The modifier **any** is used to indicate all networks. The statement at the top of Figure 9-6, then, is saying "permit host 209.98.208.25 to access any network in order to run the HTTP application over TCP."

The access list is activated on an interface by using the **access-group** command, as shown in the following code snippet. The first line "points" the IOS to serial0 interface, and the second line applies access list 100 to all incoming traffic trying to enter through serial0:

```
MyRouter(config)#interface serial0
MyRouter(config-if)#ip access-group 100 in
```

Routers look for matches between packet header content and the interface's access list. A catch would be a source address, destination address, or port number. If the matched rule is a permit rule, the packet is forwarded. If, however, a deny rule is matched, the packet is dropped without evaluating against any rules further down the list.

An access list can have as many filtering rules as desired, with the practical limit being the amount of router memory you wish to use for security filtering instead of productive routing. Because access list rules are evaluated from top to bottom, the most frequently encountered matches should be put toward the top of the list so as not to waste router CPU cycles.

Keep in mind that an access list alone doesn't turn a router into a firewall. The majority of standard access lists are used for basic traffic management within internetworks. However, you could physically configure a router as a choke point so that all traffic must pass an access list, thereby making it into a lightweight firewall. This is frequently done to restrict access among networks making up an internetwork. In fact, standard IOS has dozens of security-oriented commands beyond the **access-list** command that are also used in Cisco's firewall products. However, relying on the access list as the centerpiece of a firewall configuration results in questionable security.

Access lists make lousy security gateways because they're *stateless,* meaning that access rules are applied without the benefit of understanding the context of each connection made between hosts (called *sessions*). Simple packet filters have no idea which session's packets belong to, so decisions to forward or block them are based strictly on source address, destination address, or port number. Knowing which conversation a packet belongs to makes for better security.

Firewalls Track Internetwork Sessions

Firewall technology builds on access lists by keeping track of sessions. This technology is called *stateful* or *context-based* packet filtering, because an individual packet can be handled based on the larger context of its connection. This type of filtering uses what some call *reflexive access lists,* so named because their contents dynamically change in reflexive response to the state of individual sessions (whether the session was initiated from an inside host, how long it's been running, and so on). Figure 9-7 shows how context-based firewalls track sessions.

> **NOTE:**   TCP and UDP are protocols running at the transport layer (layer 4) of the seven-layer OSI reference model. TCP stands for Transmission Control Protocol, a connection-oriented protocol designed to deliver full-duplex communications with guaranteed delivery. The bulk of IP traffic goes via TCP connections. UDP stands for User Datagram Protocol—a no-frills, low-overhead, connectionless protocol that has no guaranteed delivery or error correction. UDP is used by relatively simple applications like TFTP (Trivial File Transfer Protocol). A third transport protocol is ICMP (Internet Control Message Protocol), a specialized protocol used by applications such as **ping** and **traceroute.** Transport protocols are covered in Chapter 2.

The astute reader might wonder how a firewall can track UDP sessions, given that UDP is a so-called connectionless transport protocol lacking the formal handshakes and acknowledgments of TCP. UDP filtering works by noting the source/destination address and port number of the session, and then guessing that all packets sharing those three characteristics belong to the same session. Because timeout periods are so brief for UDP sessions (usually a fraction of maximum times set for TCP sessions), the firewall almost always guesses right.

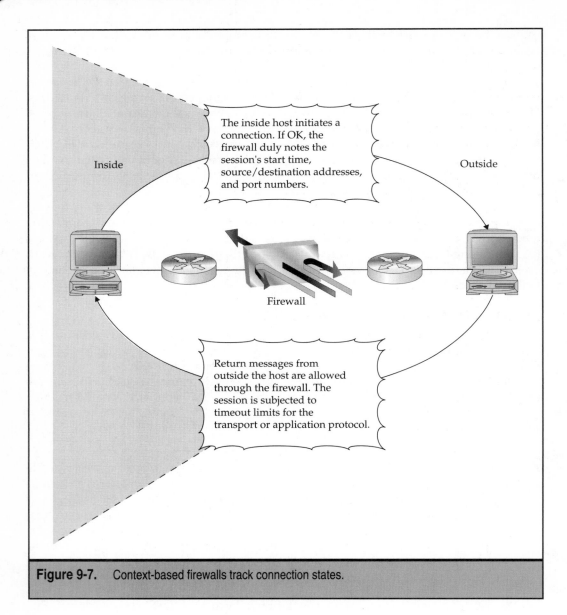

Figure 9-7.   Context-based firewalls track connection states.

Using Global Addresses to Hide Internal Network Topology

Cisco's IOS software has a capability called Network Address Translation (NAT) used by routers and firewalls to mask internal network addresses from the outside world. As discussed in Chapter 2, IP allows the use of private addresses instead of registered IP addresses—for example, 10.1.13.1 instead of 209.78.124.12. This is done for a variety of reasons, but mainly it's done to conserve addresses (sometimes called *address space*) because there simply aren't enough IP addresses to uniquely number all the hosts, devices, and LANs in most internetworks. It's possible to run an internetwork without private addresses, but it's rarely done.

As packets are forwarded to the outside, NAT overwrites the internal network address in the source address field with a full IP address. This is done from a pool of registered IP addresses made available to NAT, which then assigns them to outbound connections as they're established. NAT maps the inside local address to the pool address, deletes the mapping when the connection is terminated, and reuses the pool address for the next outbound connection that comes along. As you can see at the top of Figure 9-8, NAT translation takes place on a one-to-one basis. Therefore, although NAT hides internal addresses, it does not conserve address space.

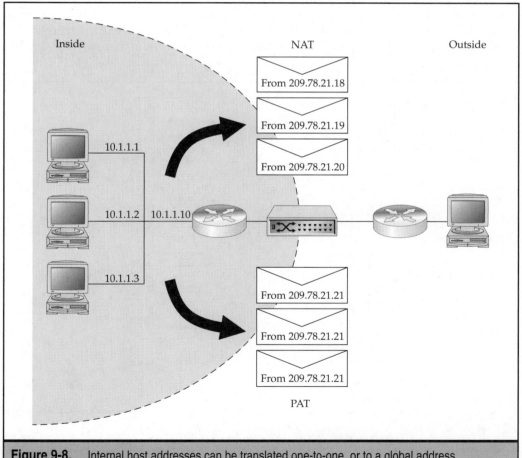

Figure 9-8.   Internal host addresses can be translated one-to-one, or to a global address.

The bottom of Figure 9-8 shows NAT can also be configured to use just one registered address for all internal hosts making outside connections. This function is called Port Address Translation (PAT), which differs from NAT by translating to one global outside address instead of to individual outside addresses. PAT provides additional security by making it impossible for hackers to identify individual hosts inside a private internetwork because everybody appears to be coming from the same host address. Beyond enhancing security, PAT also conserves address space.

Address translation is an example of the value of context-based session tracking. Without the ability to keep track of which session each packet belongs to, it wouldn't be possible to dynamically assign and map internal addresses to the public addresses.

Proxy Servers

A *proxy server* is an application that acts as an intermediary between two end systems. Proxy servers operate at the application layer (layer 7) of the firewall, where both ends of a connection are forced to conduct the session through the proxy. They do this by creating and running a process on the firewall that mirrors a service as if it were running on the end host. As Figure 9-9 illustrates, a proxy server essentially turns a two-party session into

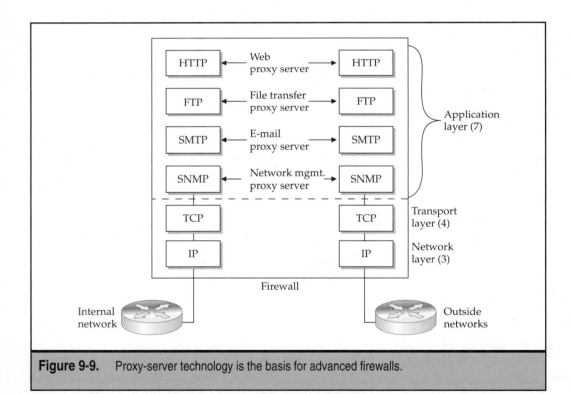

Figure 9-9. Proxy-server technology is the basis for advanced firewalls.

a four-party session, with the middle two processes emulating the two real hosts. Because they operate at layer 7, proxy servers are also referred to as *application-layer firewalls.*

A proxy service must be run for each type of Internet application the firewall will support—a Simple Mail Transport Protocol (SMTP) proxy for e-mail, an HTTP proxy for Web services, and so on. Proxy servers are almost always one-way arrangements running from the internal network to outside networks. In other words, if an internal user wants to access a Web site on the Internet, the packets making up that request are processed through the HTTP server before being forwarded to the Web site. Packets returned from the Web site in turn are processed through the HTTP server before being forwarded back to the internal user host. As with NAT, the packets go to the external Web server carrying the IP address of the HTTP server instead of the internal host address. Figure 9-9 depicts a firewall running several proxy servers at once.

Because proxy servers centralize all activity for an application into a single server, they present the ideal opportunity to perform a variety of useful functions. Having the application running right on the firewall presents the opportunity to inspect packets for much more than just source/destination addresses and port numbers. This is why nearly all modern firewalls incorporate some form of proxy-server architecture. For example, inbound packets headed to a server set up strictly to disburse information (say, an FTP server) can be inspected to see if they contain any write commands (such as the **PUT** command). In this way, the proxy server could allow only connections containing read commands.

Proxy server is another technology possible only in context-based firewalls. For example, if a firewall supports thousands of simultaneous Web connections, it must, of course, sort out to which session each of the millions of incoming packets with port number 80 (HTTP) belong.

Dual-Home Configurations

A *dual-homed* firewall configuration turns off routing between the network interface cards. Doing this forces all traffic to go through a proxy service before it can be routed out another interface, which is why proxy-server firewalls use dual-homed configurations, as depicted on the left side of Figure 9-10. Another use of dual homing is when you want users on two networks—say, the R&D and Sales departments—to access a single resource, but don't want any traffic routed between them. The configuration on the right in Figure 9-10 shows this.

Using a dual-homed configuration this way doesn't create a firewall gateway, per se, because inbound traffic isn't headed anywhere beyond the server. It's just an easy way to have one server take care of two departments that shouldn't exchange traffic. It's also a way of making sure traffic isn't exchanged, because routing services are turned off inside the router.

Event Logging and Notification

Record keeping is an important part of a firewall's overall role. When a packet is denied entry by a firewall, the event is duly recorded into a file called *syslog* (industry shorthand for

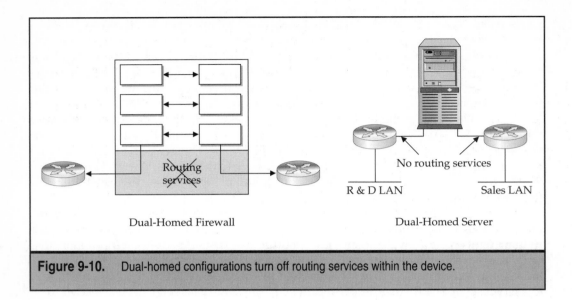

Figure 9-10.   Dual-homed configurations turn off routing services within the device.

system log). Most firewalls can be configured to upload log information to a security server elsewhere on the network, where it's analyzed against the enterprise's security policy.

Firewalls can also be configured to generate alert messages if specified thresholds are surpassed. In more sophisticated network operations, these alerts are immediately directed to a manned console so that the network team can respond to the event by any number of measures (usually shutting down the network interface where the apparent security breach is taking place).

The IOS Firewall Feature Set

The IOS Firewall is a value-added option to the Cisco IOS software. It is purchased as a so-called IOS *feature set* (feature sets are covered in Chapter 5). IOS Firewall is used to turn a standard Cisco router into a fairly robust firewall by adding several security functions over and above the basic traffic filtering of standard IOS software:

▼ **Context-Based Access Control (CBAC)**   An advanced form of traffic filtering that examines application-layer (layer 7) information such as HTTP to learn about the state of TCP or UDP connections.

■ **Address Translation (PAT and NAT)**   Disguises internal IP addresses by inserting disguised source addresses on packets sent outside the firewall. PAT and NAT hide internal network topology from hackers.

- **Security server support** The router can be configured as a client to TACACS+, RADIUS, or Kerberos security servers, where usernames and passwords can be stored in such a server's user authentication database.

- **Denial-of-Service attack detection** Detects the traffic patterns characteristic of so-called *Denial-of-Service* attacks and sends alert messages. (Denial-of-Service attacks attempt to deny service by overwhelming a network with service requests such as illegal e-mail commands or infinite e-mails.)

- **Network-Based Application Recognition (NBAR)** Recognizes many different applications and can use special services based on them.

- **Java blocking** The ability to selectively block Java messages from a network. (Java applets are downloadable self-operating programs, and applets can be programmed to harm any host system unfortunate enough to execute them.)

- **Encryption** The ability to make a packet's contents incomprehensible to all systems except those provided with a cipher (key) to decrypt it.

- **Neighbor router authentication** A command by which a router can force a neighboring router to authenticate its identity or block all packets routed from it.

- **Security alerts and event logging** Messages alerting network administration of a security problem, and the logging of all security events for later collation and analysis.

- **VPN and QoS support** Provides tunneling and QoS features to secure VPNs. This feature provides encrypted tunnels on the router while ensuring strong security, service-level validation, intrusion detection, and advanced bandwidth management.

- **Audit trail** Allows you a number of features for detailed tracking. It records the time stamp, source host, destination host, ports, duration, and total number of bytes transmitted for detailed reporting. It is configurable based on applications and features.

- **Dynamic port mapping** Permits CBAC-based applications to be run on nonstandard ports. This allows network administrators to customize access control for selected applications and services.

- **Firewall management** Firewalls are configured with a user-friendly interface that provides step-by-step help through network design, addressing, and IOS Firewall security policy configuration.

- **Integration with Cisco IOS software** This feature set seamlessly interacts with Cisco IOS features, integrating security policy features.

- **Policy-based multiinterface support** User access can be controlled based on IP address and interface. Access is determined by the security policy.

■ **Redundancy/failover** Automatically routes traffic to a secondary router in the event of failure.

▲ **Time-based access lists** Security policy can be established based on time of day and day of the week.

Most of these capabilities are enabled by Context-Based Access Control, which is the central technology in the IOS Firewall software.

How Context-Based Access Control Works

Context-Based Access Control is a set of IOS commands that can be used to inspect packets much more closely than normal access lists. CBAC works by tracking outside connections initiated from inside the firewall. CBAC identifies sessions by tracking source/destination IP addresses and source/destination port numbers gleaned from the packets. When a response returns from the session's remote host in the form of inbound traffic, CBAC determines the session to which the inbound packets belong. CBAC, in this way, maintains a dynamic list of ongoing sessions and is able to juggle security exceptions on a moment-by-moment basis. This dynamic list, called the *state table*, tracks the state of valid sessions through to termination. The CBAC state table maintains itself by deleting sessions when concluded by users or dropping them after a maximum allowable period of inactivity called a *timeout*. Timeout values are specified by the network administrator for each transport protocol. Figure 9-11 depicts the CBAC process.

CBAC uses the state table to make dynamic entries and deletions to the access list of the interface. Source/destination address or port numbers normally blocked by the access list are momentarily allowed, but only for a session CBAC knows to be a valid session initiated from inside the firewall security perimeter. CBAC creates openings in the firewall as necessary to permit returning traffic and thus is bidirectional. Once the session shuts down, the access list's prohibition is put back in effect until another session calls from the CBAC state table asking for a temporary exception of its own.

If it seems as if the router would be overwhelmed by the sheer complexity of it all, remember that state tables and access lists are maintained on a per-interface basis. Each interface on a Cisco router running IOS Firewall has its own access list, inspection rules, and valid sessions. Good firewall configuration design can cut down a big part of the complexity you must deal with, by grouping similar traffic types or sources onto specific network interfaces.

Major IOS Firewall Functions

IOS Firewall selectively enforces security rules based on the context of each session. To pull this off, IOS Firewall must inspect packets much more closely than simple access lists do.

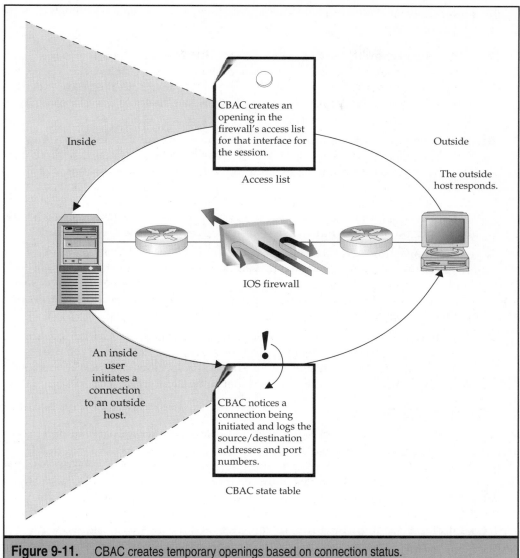

Figure 9-11.   CBAC creates temporary openings based on connection status.

For this reason, the IOS Firewall software is granular in its application of inspection rules. *Granular* here means inspection rules are applied much more selectively than the "all-or-nothing" permit/deny scheme used in access lists. This makes the firewall more flexible and a tougher security barrier to crack. We won't delve into IOS Firewall inspection features too deeply since this is a beginner's book, but a quick review will illustrate how firewall technology works at the packet inspection level:

▼ **SMTP inspection**   Many of the worst virus attacks inject themselves into secured internetworks via e-mail. Beyond just inspecting each packet for the SMTP port number, IOS Firewall inspects SMTP packets for illegal commands. Any SMTP packet containing a command other than the 15 legal SMTP commands will be discarded as subversive.

■ **Java inspection**   Some network security policies prohibit downloading Java applets from outside networks because of their potential destructive power. A security policy mandating that all internal users disable Java in their Web browsers is unenforceable. IOS Firewall allows you to block incoming Java applets at the firewall and also to designate a list of trusted (friendly) external sites from which downloaded Java applets will not be blocked (or you could permit applets from all sites except sites explicitly defined as hostile).

■ **H.323 inspection**   NetMeeting is a premier H.323 protocol application that requires use of a second channel (session) in addition to the H.323 channel maintained in the CBAC state table. IOS Firewall can be configured to inspect for a generic TCP channel in addition to the H.323 channel to allow NetMeeting connections to operate through the firewall.

▲ **RPC inspection**   The IOS Firewall RPC (Remote Procedure Call) inspection command accepts the entry of program numbers. For example, if the program number for NFS (Network File System Protocol) is specified in an RPC command, then NFS traffic may operate through that firewall interface.

Configuring IOS Firewall

Address translation is configured in IOS Firewall using the **nat** and **pat** commands. The first step of configuring IOS Firewall is to set up translations so as to mask internal IP addresses from the outside world. Example configurations for NAT and PAT (Port Address Translation) are given in the next part of this chapter, which covers the PIX Firewall.

Context-based security is configured in the IOS Firewall by creating inspection rules. Inspection rules (also called *rule sets*) are applied to access lists governing specific firewall network interfaces. Configuring IOS Firewall, then, is done mostly using two variations of two commands:

▼ **access-list**   A command used to define the basic access rules for the interface

▲ **ip inspect**   A command used to define what CBAC will look for at the interface

The access list specifies which normal rules apply to traffic entering the interface, and is used to tell the interface which network applications (port numbers) are prohibited, which destination addresses are blocked, and so on. CBAC inspection rules dynamically modify the access list as necessary to create temporary openings in the IOS firewall for valid sessions. CBAC defines a valid session as any TCP or UDP connection that matches its access-list criteria.

In addition to creating temporary openings in the firewall, CBAC applies inspection rules to detect various kinds of network attacks and generate alert messages, which are usually sent to the network management console.

NOTE: One of the best-known Denial-of-Service attacks is SYNflood, so named for the SYN bit used to consummate a three-way handshake used to set up TCP connections. SYNflood attacks try to drown the target network in a flood of connection attempts—thereby denying legitimate hosts network service. A command called **synwait-time** is used by the network administrator to tell IOS Firewall how long an unrequited SYN bit is retained before being discarded. By not letting SYN bits pile up, the **synwait-time** command can be used to thwart this type of Denial-of-Service attack.

IOS Firewall can be configured one of two ways, depending on whether the firewall configuration includes a DMZ. Figure 9-12 depicts this. The configuration on the right of Figure 9-12 shows the access list pulled back to the inside of the firewall.

Configuring CBAC on the internal interface relieves the firewall from having to create and delete context-based rule exceptions for traffic hitting the DMZ's Web (HTTP) server and DNS (Domain Name System) server. With this arrangement, CBAC can still selectively control access to HTTP and DNS services by internal users, but it doesn't have to worry about connections hitting the DMZ servers.

NOTE: IOS Firewall is a version of Cisco IOS software, so normal IOS conventions apply. To configure IOS Firewall, you must first gain access to the router via Telnet or the Web browser interface, enter Privileged Exec command mode, and then enter configuration mode with the firewall(config-if)# prompt pointing to the interface to which the CBAC configuration will apply.

The first step in configuring the IOS Firewall interface is to create an access list. To define an access list, use the following command syntax:

```
Firewall(config)#ip access-list standard access-list-name-or-number
Firewall(config-std-nacl)#permit ....
```

If a permit rule is matched, the packet is forwarded through the firewall. Deny rules are defined using the same syntax:

```
Firewall(config)#ip access-list standard access-list-name-or-number
Firewall(config-std-nacl)#deny ....
```

If a deny rule is matched, the packet is dropped. Figure 9-13 shows an example access list 100. This access list will be applied to the Ethernet0 firewall interface. Access list 100 permits all traffic that should be CBAC-inspected. The last line of the access list is set up to deny unknown IP protocols that a hacker might attempt to use.

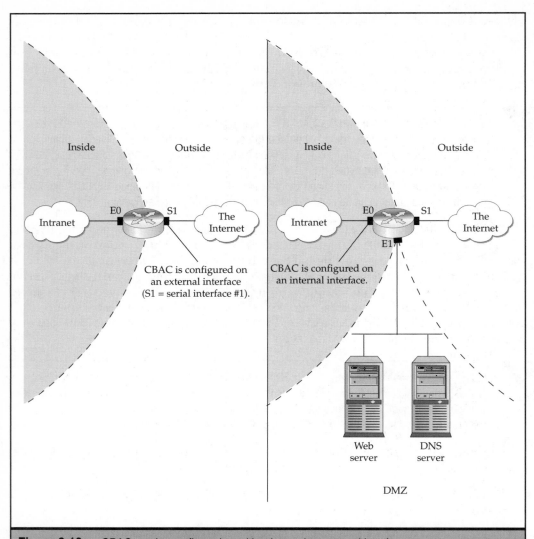

Figure 9-12.   CBAC can be configured on either internal or external interfaces.

The second step in configuring CBAC is to create inspection rules with the **ip inspect** command, using the following syntax:

```
Firewall(config)#ip inspect name inspection-name protocol [timeout
seconds]
```

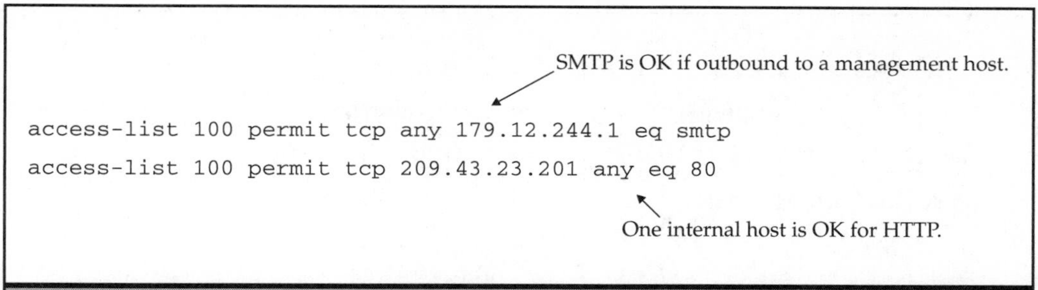

SMTP is OK if outbound to a management host.

```
access-list 100 permit tcp any 179.12.244.1 eq smtp
access-list 100 permit tcp 209.43.23.201 any eq 80
```

One internal host is OK for HTTP.

Figure 9-13.   This access list sets up traffic on Ethernet0 for CBAC inspection.

This command syntax tells IOS Firewall what to inspect packets for, and the maximum period of inactivity allowed before closing any session that was created using the inspection rule. Timeout periods are important in CBAC configurations. If timeout limits are set too high, the state table could become bloated, which could hurt router performance and even security. On the other hand, if timeouts are set too low, users could become frustrated at having to frequently reset connections made to Internet hosts.

A set of inspection rules is created by using the same *inspection-name* in all the commands to be included in the set. The following code snippet shows an inspection rule set being built under the name Rulz. By sharing the name Rulz, the six **ip inspect** commands included in this set can be invoked in a single statement. Table 9-1 gives the keywords used for protocol inspection commands.

```
Firewall(config)#ip inspect name Rulz ftp timeout 2000
Firewall(config)#ip inspect name Rulz smtp timeout 3000
Firewall(config)#ip inspect name Rulz tftp timeout 60
Firewall(config)#ip inspect name Rulz http java-list 99 timeout 3000
Firewall(config)#ip inspect name Rulz udp timeout 15
Firewall(config)#ip inspect name Rulz tcp timeout 2000
```

The timeout limits in the preceding example allow TCP applications about three to five minutes to respond, and UDP applications a minute or less. This reflects the fact that UDP applications are more concerned with causing minimal network overhead than with session integrity. The timeouts set for TCP and UDP are overridden in sessions running an application protocol. For example, any TFTP backup session running through this firewall would have the 60-second timeout limit set for TFTP in force (preempting the 15-second limit set for UDP-only sessions).

While it's true that timeouts help conserve system resources, the primary reason for configuring them in a firewall is security. The less time you give a hacker's attack program to try to worm through the firewall's interface, the better your internetwork security is. However, timeouts can't be set at too tight of a tolerance, or legitimate users will

Transport-Layer Protocols	Keyword
Terminal Control Protocol (TCP)	Tcp
User Datagram Protocol (UDP)	Udp
Application-Layer Protocols	
CU-SeeMe	Cuseeme
FTP	ftp
Java	http
H.323	h323
UNIX R commands (r-login, r-exec, r-sh)	Rcmd
RealAudio	Realaudio
RPC	Rpc
SMTP	Smtp
SQL*Net	Sqlnet
StreamWorks	Streamworks
TFTP	Tftp
VDOLive	Vdolive

Table 9-1. Keywords in IOS Firewall's **ip inspect** and **access-list** Commands

have to make several attempts to connect. Like everything else in internetworking, time-out strategy is a balancing act.

The last step in configuring an IOS Firewall interface is applying an inspection rule set to the access list. The following snippet taken from the config file for firewall interface Ethernet0 shows the inspection set Rulz has been invoked for access list 89. The rules have been applied to inspect and filter inbound traffic.

```
interface Ethernet0
  description Velte Extranet Gateway
  ip address 209.78.124.12 255.255.255.248
  ip broadcast address 209.78.124.1
  ip inspect Rulz in
  ip access-group 89 in
```

Without inspection rules to modify access lists, IOS Firewall behavior would revert to that of a normal router running normal access lists.

IOS Firewall Session Management Features

By now, you've seen how important time is to firewalls. This is not unlike the head of security in a bank maintaining strict control over how long the safe door may stay open as people enter and leave it. For obvious reasons, the security chief would frown on employees loitering about the safe door.

The max-incomplete Session Commands Like the bank's security chief, network administrators fret over connections pending at the firewall's interfaces—especially the outside interfaces. These incomplete connections are called *half-open sessions.* A rising number of half-open sessions at the firewall indicate that a Denial-of-Service attack is under way. IOS Firewall has several commands, called TCP intercept commands that intercept Denial-of-Service attacks before they can overwhelm a firewall's network interface.

IOS Firewall uses the **ip inspect max-incomplete** command to track and control half-open sessions. For TCP, *half-open* means that a session has not yet reached the established state. (In fact, it's entered into the CBAC state table as a pending request to start a session.) A UDP session is deemed half-open when traffic is detected from one direction only. (Remember, UDP is a connectionless protocol.)

CBAC monitors half-open sessions both in absolute numbers and in relative trends. Once every minute, CBAC totals all types of half-open sessions and weighs the total against an allowable threshold specified in the config file (500 half-open requests is the default limit). Once the threshold is exceeded, CBAC begins deleting half-open requests from its state table. It will continue deleting them until it reaches a minimum threshold, whereupon operations are returned to normal. The following code snippet shows a typical configuration of the **max-incomplete high** command. It's a good practice to keep the high-low spread narrow so CBAC can make frequent use of this control feature.

```
Firewall(config)#ip inspect max-incomplete high 1000
Firewall(config)#ip inspect max-incomplete low 900
```

The inspect one-minute Commands The other command to control half-open sessions is the **inspect one-minute** command. Instead of acting on the number of half-open connections, the rate of change in half-open sessions is what's measured. It works much like the **max-incomplete** command. Here's an example configuration (using the default values):

```
Firewall(config)#ip inspect one-minute high 900
Firewall(config)#ip inspect one-minute low 400
```

Other TCP Intercept Commands CBAC has other commands to thwart Denial-of-Service attacks. As mentioned earlier, the **inspect tcp synwait-time** command controls SYNflood attacks by deleting connection requests with SYN bits that have been pending longer than a specified time limit. (The default is 30 seconds.) The **inspect tcp finwait-time** command similarly controls FINflood attacks. (FIN bits are exchanged when a TCP connection is ready to close; its default is five seconds.) The **inspect tcp max-incomplete host** command is used to specify threshold and timeout values for TCP host-specific Denial-of-Service detection. It limits how many half-open sessions with the same host destination address are allowed and how long CBAC will continue deleting new connection requests from the host. (The defaults are 50 half-open sessions and 0 seconds.) Finally, generic protection is given by configuring the maximum idle times for connections with the **inspect tcp idle-time** and **inspect udp idle-time** commands (with default limits of 1 hour and 30 seconds, respectively).

Cisco Secure PIX Firewall

Cisco Secure PIX Firewall is Cisco's premier product for firewall duties. The IOS Firewall feature set is targeted at more price-sensitive customers or for duty in cordoning off access within enterprise networks. PIX is a total package positioned by Cisco to compete head-to-head with the major firewall products on the market today. PIX Firewall differs from IOS Firewall in these ways:

▼ **Integrated hardware/software** PIX Firewall is an integrated package on a hardware platform purposely built for heavy-duty firewall service. It doesn't come as a separate software package.

■ **Adaptive Security Algorithm (ASA)** Neither a packet filter nor an application proxy firewall, PIX implements a cut-through proxy architecture that delivers higher performance.

NOTE: Cut-through processing is a technique of forwarding the beginning of a message before its last packet has been received.

▲ **Integrated VPN option** A plug-in processor card configures virtual private networks supporting the advanced Internet Protocol Security (IPSec) encryption and Internet Key Exchange (IKE) standards.

Network administrators are increasingly turning to purpose-built devices such as Cisco Secure PIX Firewall to meet their network security needs. The electronics and software in the PIX firewall are tuned specifically to balance advanced security functionality with the need for high-throughput performance. PIX Firewall and dedicated products like it are called *network appliances*—the hip new term for devices built to serve a narrowly defined networking function. The most obvious advantage of using a firewall appliance is that the IOS software doesn't have to split its time between filtering and routing.

Beyond the appliance versus firewall-enabled router debate, Cisco is positioning PIX as a real-time embedded system against competitors' firewall appliances based on UNIX platforms. The argument is that UNIX-based firewall appliances must pay a price in performance and in security. The reasoning is that a general-purpose operating system kernel like UNIX not only has latencies and overheads inappropriate for firewall duty, but also has inherent security holes that hackers could use to break into the firewall itself.

PIX Firewall's Adaptive Security Algorithm

The Adaptive Security Algorithm is roughly equivalent to IOS Firewall's Context-Based Access Control. Both serve as the central engine for their respective firewall products. Both PIX and IOS Firewall run a version of IOS software, which is beneficial because network administrators are familiar with the environment and its basic commands (**configure**, **debug**, **write**, and so on). But ASA has a very different set of firewall-specific commands, and its architecture is radically different from that of IOS Firewall. ASA enables PIX Firewall to implement tighter security measures and to scale to higher-capacity gateway sizes.

NOTE: What's an algorithm? The term makes it sound as if writing one would involve quantum physics with a dash of quadratic equations thrown in. But algorithms aren't anything mysterious. An algorithm is nothing more than a carefully crafted set of rules rigorously applied to a repetitive process, and that is logically able to handle variable conditions. Yes, some algorithms contain mathematical equations, but most don't. Computers make heavy use of algorithms because nearly everything in computing is repetitive and driven by variables.

The nameif Command   The cliché is that the world is painted not in black and white, but in shades of gray. So, too, for the world of internetwork security, where the "good guys versus bad guys" model falls short because almost *everybody* is regarded as suspect. The trend in truly powerful network security, then, is the capability to designate networks and hosts as a spectrum of security levels instead of merely as "inside" or "outside."

PIX Firewall's **nameif** (name interface) command lets you specify relative security levels for interfaces both inside and outside of the firewall. Applying relative security levels on an interface-by-interface basis lets you draw a far more descriptive security map than you would be able to by defining all networks as either inside or outside.

To configure a firewall's interfaces with relative security levels, you enter a **nameif** command for each interface. You can choose any value for a security level between 0 and 99, and no two interfaces on a PIX firewall may have the same level. The common practice is to assign levels in tens, as shown in the following code snippet, which identifies eight interfaces in three security zones:

```
Firewall(config)#nameif ethernet0 outside security0
Firewall(config)#nameif ethernet1 outside security10
Firewall(config)#nameif serial0 outside security20
Firewall(config)#nameif ethernet2 dmz security50
Firewall(config)#nameif ethernet3 dmz security30
Firewall(config)#nameif ethernet4 inside security100
Firewall(config)#nameif ethernet5 inside security90
Firewall(config)#nameif serial1 inside security70
```

The way security levels work is that each host on a network takes on the security level assigned to it. A connection being made from a higher level to a lower network is treated by the software as outbound; one headed from a lower-level interface to a higher level would be treated as inbound. This scheme enables the network administrator to apply rules on a much more granular basis.

Because each zone has its own security scale, the option exists to implement intrazone security checks. For example, access lists could apply restrictions on traffic flowing between hosts attached to the two DMZ networks. Some possible uses of security levels are depicted in Figure 9-14.

As with the IOS firewall and other firewalls, packets may not traverse the PIX firewall without a connection and a state. The Adaptive Security Algorithm checks inbound packets using the following rules.

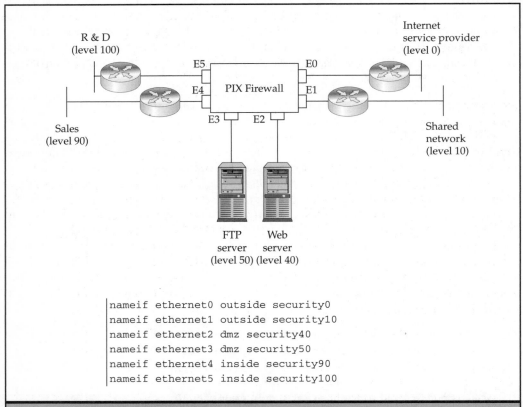

```
nameif ethernet0 outside security0
nameif ethernet1 outside security10
nameif ethernet2 dmz security40
nameif ethernet3 dmz security50
nameif ethernet4 inside security90
nameif ethernet5 inside security100
```

Figure 9-14.   The **nameif** command draws a more detailed and powerful security map.

▼ All inbound connections must be explicitly configured by a **conduit** command. *Conduits* specify which external IP addresses are allowed to connect to which internal addresses behind the PIX firewall.

■ All outbound connections are permitted except those configured as denied in outbound access lists.

▲ Static outbound connections can be configured using the **static** command, bypassing the dynamic translation pools created using the **global** and **nat** or **pat** commands.

PIX Firewall Translation Slots   As with the IOS Firewall, address translation and session tracking are at the center of the architecture. But the PIX Firewall uses a more formal system to implement IP address translation. Instead of simply creating a new translation and dynamically entering it into a reflexive access list like IOS Firewall, ASA assigns a *slot* to the new connection.

PIX firewalls are sold with connection licenses that limit the total number of connection slots that can be used simultaneously. Each session consumes a slot. Slots configured with both the **global** or **static** commands are sometimes referred to as *xlates* (as in *translates*), although they're usually just called slots. When a connection is initiated, ASA takes a slot from the license pool and enters the session into the state table. The slot is returned to the pool when the session terminates.

If an internetwork needs more simultaneous connections than it's licensed for, the operator must buy a bigger software license from Cisco. Table 9-2 shows the increments in which PIX firewall slots may be licensed.

To help manage slot consumption, you can specify a slot limit when configuring interfaces with the **nat** command. In this way, network administrators can prevent individual network users from consuming too many translation slots.

DRAM	Maximum Connections (Slots)
8MB	16,384
16MB	32,768
32MB	65,536
64MB	131,072

Table 9-2.   The Number of Maximum Simultaneous Connections Is a Function of Firewall Memory.

NOTE: Did you know that some applications use more than one connection at a time? For example, FTP takes two connections. A Web browser (which runs the HTTP application protocol) can take up to four or more connections, depending on whether it's in the process of loading a page or other objects such as Java applets. So don't think of Internet connections in terms of something the user consciously decides to start and stop. Sessions are launching and quitting without our even knowing it. Microsoft Internet Explorer is said to consume up to 20 TCP connections per user!

We'll run through a simple PIX firewall configuration to showcase some of the commands. Whole books have been written about firewalls, so we'll only cover those commands that will help you understand basic PIX firewall operations. The PIX firewall runs a special version of IOS, so the usual IOS command conventions apply. Figure 9-15 shows a three-interface PIX configuration with one shield router, one inside shield router, and one DMZ server attached. The configuration incorporates global address translation, restrictions on outbound traffic, and an outbound static route with an inbound conduit.

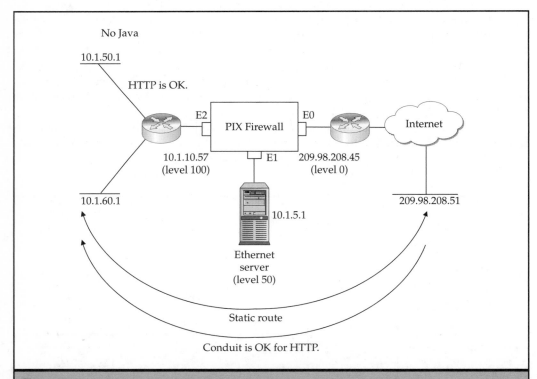

Figure 9-15.   This three-interface PIX firewall supports a static route with conduit.

The first step is to go into configure interface mode, pointing at each interface as it's being configured:

```
Firewall>enable
Password:******
Firewall#config t
Firewall(config)#
```

Then, **interface** commands are used to give the interfaces security zones and levels:

```
Firewall(config)#nameif ethernet0 outside security0
Firewall(config)#nameif ethernet1 Extranet security50
Firewall(config)#nameif ethernet2 inside security100
```

Next, **interface** commands determine the Ethernet specification that the interfaces will operate (autosensing 10/100 Mbps):

```
Firewall(config)#interface ethernet0 auto
Firewall(config)#interface ethernet1 auto
Firewall(config)#interface ethernet2 auto
```

The interfaces must be identified with IP addresses and masks, which is done using **ip address** commands. Notice that the names you just gave to the interface (outside, Extranet, and inside) are put to use, and the private internal IP addresses are used for the Extranet and inside interfaces (10.1.5.1 and 10.1.10.57):

```
Firewall(config)#ip address outside 209.98.208.45 255.255.255.240
Firewall(config)#ip address Extranet 10.1.5.1 255.255.255.0
Firewall(config)#ip address inside 10.1.10.57 255.255.255.0
```

The **nat** command is used to let all users in two inside user groups make outbound connections using translated IP addresses. The number following the **(inside)** arguments of the two statements is a NAT ID number or NAT reference number (1 and 2), used to link groups to global address pools:

```
Firewall(config)#nat (inside) 1 10.0.0.0 255.0.0.0
Firewall(config)#nat (inside) 2 10.0.0.0 255.0.0.0
```

Statements using the **global** command create two global address pools. They're assigned to users by way of the NAT ID numbers (1 and 2 here). The middle statement is the PAT address pool. What's happening here is that the system is being told to assign NAT addresses and, when they're all in use, to begin applying the PAT global address to sessions. All connections assigned a PAT address will show a source address of 209.98.208.50:

```
Firewall(Config)#global (outside) 1 209.98.208.46-209.98.208.49 netmask
255.255.255.240
Firewall(Config)#global (outside) 1 209.98.208.50 netmask
255.255.255.240
```

```
Firewall(Config)#global (outside) 2 209.98.210.1-209.98.210.254 netmask
255.255.255.240
```

A **static** statement is used to create an externally visible IP address. An accompanying **conduit** statement permits a specified host or network—a business partner, for example—through the PIX firewall. The following example statement permits users on an outside host access through the firewall to server 10.1.60.1 via TCP connections for Web access. The **eq 80** clause specifies that the TCP connection must be running (equal to) port 80—the port number for the HTTP application protocol. The **any** modifier lets any external host attach to 10.1.60.1:

```
Firewall(config)#static (inside, outside) 209.98.208.51 10.1.60.1
                  netmask 255.255.255.0
Firewall(config)#conduit permit tcp host 10.1.60.1 eq 80 any
```

This statement using the **outbound** command creates an access list that permits an inside host Web access (port 80), but forbids it from downloading Java applets. PIX uses the **outbound** command to create access lists and the **apply** command to apply them. Notice that the port number for Java is represented by the text string **java** instead of a port number. Using names instead of numbers is possible for some newer application-layer protocols like Java. It's obviously a lot easier to remember names instead of a cryptic number. The **outgoing_src** option denies or permits an internal address the ability to start outbound connections using the services specified in the **outbound** command:

```
Firewall(config)#outbound 10 permit 209.98.208.22 255.255.255.255 80
Firewall(config)#outbound 10 deny 209.98.208.22 255.255.255.255 java
Firewall(config)#apply (Extranet) 10 outgoing_src
```

There are many other commands to use when configuring a PIX firewall. Indeed, in most internetworking environments, there are several more that *must* be configured to get the firewall working properly. Properly configuring a PIX firewall with multiple servers, protocols, access lists, and shield routers would take days. The possible configurations are endless. But the simple statements we just went through demonstrate that configuring even a firewall—one of internetworking's most complex devices—isn't rocket science. It can get pretty deep, but doing it is just a matter of taking things one interface at a time, one command at time.

PIX OS 6.2   The latest version of the PIX Firewall OS software is version 6.2 and it offers a variety of improvements and upgrades over previous versions of the software. Some of its features include

▼   **LAN-based failover**   Allows failover information to be shared with its failover pair across a LAN connection, rather than a serial cable.

■   **Bidirectional Network Address Translation (NAT)**   Improves NAT functionality, supporting networks with overlapping private addresses.

- **Turbo ACLs**   Gives enhanced performance in deployments where large ACLs are used.

- **Enhanced small-packet performance**   Improves performance for 64- to 512-byte packets over earlier OS releases.

- **Object grouping**   Allows network objects to be grouped logically, simplifying the application and definition of rules.

- **Command-level authorization**   Allows organizations to create up to 16 administrative profiles for accessing the firewall. For example, specific administrative profiles could include monitoring-only, read-only access to configuration, VPN administrator, firewall administrator, and others.

- **Packet capture**   Allows administrators to troubleshoot by examining specific packets. Means of examining the packets include using the console, Web access, or exporting the file.

▲ **Easy VPN Remote**   For small office, telecommuter, and remote offices, the PIX 501 and 506E firewalls are able to act as hardware VPN clients. The VPN policy is dynamically downloaded from the Easy VPN Server once the connection is made, ensuring the latest security policies are put in place.

There are many other major elements of firewall configuration. One example is configuring two firewalls—one as the primary gateway server and the other as a hot backup box to which traffic will go if the primary server fails (configured using the **failover** command). Another is configuring the firewall to integrate with a security server such as TACACS+, which we covered in Chapter 8.

Makes and Models

Whatever the firewall need, Cisco offers its PIX line in five distinct flavors. At the low end of the scale is the Cisco Secure PIX Firewall 501. This model is aimed at the small office/home office market and is equipped with a 133-MHz processor, Ethernet connections, and a scant 16MB. On the other end of the spectrum is the big boy in firewalls. They should have named the Cisco Secure PIX Firewall 535 the Gigawall, because everything about this firewall screams "giga." Aimed at the enterprise and service-provider market, it boasts a 1GB processor, 1GB RAM, and Gigabit Ethernet connections.

As much as these firewalls seem to differ, they share the core functionality of the PIX firewall, namely, its hardware and software integration, VPN functionality, and extensibility. Table 9-3 compares Cisco's line of Cisco Secure Pix firewalls.

VIRTUAL PRIVATE NETWORKS

What is a virtual private network (VPN)? As so often happens in the computer business, marketing hype can muddle an otherwise clear term. In the case of VPNs, some confusion

	Cisco Secure PIX Firewall 501	Cisco Secure PIX Firewall 506E	Cisco Secure PIX Firewall 515E	Cisco Secure PIX Firewall 525	Cisco Secure PIX Firewall 535
Market	Small office/home office	Remote office/branch office	Small- to medium-sized businesses and enterprises	Enterprise and service providers	Enterprise and service providers
Processor	133-MHz Intel Pentium	300-MHz Intel Pentium	433-MHz Intel Pentium	600-MHz Intel Pentium III	1-GHz Intel Pentium III
RAM	16MB	32MB	32–64MB	Up to 256MB	1GB
Interfaces	Dual integrated 10BaseT Fast Ethernet	Dual integrated 10/100BaseT Fast Ethernet	Supports up to six 10/100 BaseT Fast Ethernet interfaces	Supports up to eight 10/100 BaseT Fast Ethernet or three Gigabit Ethernet interfaces	Supports up to ten 10/100 BaseT Fast Ethernet or nine Gigabit Ethernet interfaces
Connections	60-Mbps throughput; 7,500 concurrent connections	100-Mbps throughput; 25,000 concurrent connections	188-Mbps throughput; 130,000 concurrent connections	330-Mbps throughput; 280,000 concurrent connections	1.7-Gbps throughput; 500,000 concurrent connections; 2,000 simultaneous VPN tunnels
NIC Support	Fast Ethernet	Fast Ethernet	Fast Ethernet, Token Ring, FDDI	Fast Ethernet, Gigabit Ethernet, Token Ring, FDDI	Gigabit Ethernet, Fast Ethernet, Token Ring, FDDI

Table 9-3.   Cisco's Line of Cisco Secure PIX Firewalls

exists over what's *virtual* in a VPN—the privacy or the network? Here's the two-part definition of a virtual private network:

▼   VPN topology runs mostly over *shared* network infrastructure, usually the Internet, and has at least one private LAN segment at each end point.

▲   VPN sessions run through an encrypted connection.

To operate through encrypted connections across the Internet, the network segments at each end of a VPN must be under the administrative control of the enterprise (or enterprises) running the virtual network. In practical terms, this means that the endpoint routers must be under a common security and operational regimen. Above all, the endpoint routers in a VPN must operate a common encryption scheme.

Traditionally, long-distance connectivity to an internetwork relied on a WAN with a leased line. Further, a leased line is simply not an option for an individual who is traveling and cannot be in one place long enough for a leased line to be justified. The following are some reasons why VPNs are making an impact on the leased-line market:

▼   **Lower Costs**   Leased lines require expensive transport bandwidth and backbone equipment. Additionally, VPNs don't need in-house terminal equipment and access modems.

■   **Network Agility**   Relatively speaking, VPN links are easy and inexpensive to set up, change, and remove. Because of this, an organization's communications infrastructure won't be traumatized when a VPN is installed, reconfigured, or removed. Further, the availability of the Internet ensures that you can connect your VPN nearly anywhere.

▲   **Access**   Because of its availability, subscribers anywhere on the VPN have the same level of access and view of central services (like e-mail, internal and external Web sites, security, and so forth).

What Composes a VPN

Think of VPNs as wide area networks that operate at least partly over the Internet. Like most WANs, a VPN could provide a mixture of access types, as shown in Figure 9-16.

VPNs are steadily taking over the role of WANs in enterprise networking. All or part of a VPN can be an intranet, an extranet, or a remote access vehicle for telecommuters or mobile workers. A significant number of new VPNs are owned and operated by Internet service providers, who parcel out VPN bandwidth to enterprises. Outsourcing VPNs is becoming a standard practice for all but the largest enterprises because it's less expensive, and the enterprise can rely on the ISP to manage VPN infrastructure for them.

Encryption and other security measures largely define a VPN. This is for the simple reason that running enterprise WANs over the Internet is easy and inexpensive, but not feasible without appropriate security. Thus, security is part of what makes up a VPN. It is also defined by a suite of Internet-compatible access servers, network appliances (such as firewalls), and internetwork management techniques.

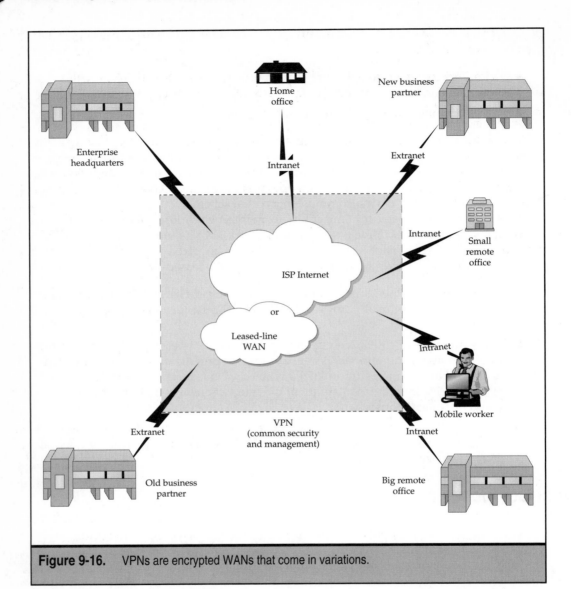

Figure 9-16. VPNs are encrypted WANs that come in variations.

NOTE: Encryption is a technique that scrambles the format of data in such a way that it can only be read by a system holding an authorized key with a mathematical formula needed to unscramble the payloads. (Packet headers are left unscrambled so that they can be routed.) Encryption and decryption take place between two peer encrypting routers, called *peer routers*. (Note that firewalls can also handle encryption.) Peer routers share a secret algorithm key used to unscramble the payload. Peer routers must authenticate each other before each encrypted session, using Digital Signature Standard (DSS) keys (unique character strings). When a signature is verified, the peer router is authenticated and the encrypted session begins. The actual scrambling is done using a temporary Data Encryption Standard (DES) key, which must be exchanged in the connection messages between the peer routers. When the encrypted session is over, the DES key is discarded.

The components making up a VPN are

▼ **Tunneling**   Point-to-point connections over a connectionless IP network—in essence, a set of predetermined router hops taken through the Internet to guarantee performance and delivery.

■ **Encryption**   The scrambling of an IP packet's contents (but not the header) to render it unreadable to all but those with a key to unscramble it. (Keys are held by authorized VPN senders and receivers only.)

■ **Encapsulation**   Placing a non-IP frame inside an IP packet to bridge dissimilar networks (the IP is unpacked on the other side), effectively allowing tunneling to take place across otherwise incompatible VPN network segments.

■ **Packet authentication**   The ability to ensure the integrity of a VPN packet by confirming that its contents (payload) weren't altered en route.

■ **User authentication**   User authentication, authorization, and accounting (AAA) capabilities enforced through security servers such as TACACS+, RADIUS, or Kerberos.

■ **Access control**   Firewalls, intrusion detection devices, and security auditing procedures used to monitor all traffic crossing VPN security perimeters.

▲ **Quality of Service (QoS)**   Cisco's QoS is a set of internetwork management standards and functions to assure interoperability of devices and software platforms, and to leverage the platform to guarantee end-to-end network performance and reliability.

This list shows how a VPN is as much about *seamlessness* as security. Forcing network administrators or users to go through multiple steps to accomplish simple tasks would make using a VPN as infeasible as poor security. In practical terms, therefore, a VPN must be configured using hardware and software devices with these required characteristics.

Cisco's Solution

To deliver VPN functionality, Cisco has used a broad sword to make a name for itself. Rather than focus on just the hardware side of the issue, Cisco developed an integrated solution relying on both hardware and software.

The Cisco solution doesn't put all of its VPN eggs in one basket. In addition to routers and PIX firewalls enabled with VPN functions, they have software designed to make use of that extra functionality. The following sections take a closer look at Cisco's hardware, software, and how the two can be used together to deliver VPNs for remote access, intranets, and extranets.

Hardware

To deliver VPN functionality, Cisco has built VPN features into a number of its router models. For instance, the Cisco 1721 VPN Access Router is used to connect small remote sites to a VPN. The 1721 is packaged to perform high-speed encryption and deliver tunnel-routing services in a single package. A conduit must be configured to operate a VPN through a PIX firewall.

VPNs have traditionally been software-based solutions. However, by building equipment with VPN functionality in mind, VPN services are improved over software solutions. For example, by adding VPN functionality to Cisco 2600 and 3600 series routers, VPN functionality is ten times greater than software solutions alone.

Some of Cisco's VPN-enabled hardware is listed in Table 9-4.

Cisco VPN Client

Though Cisco is building VPN functionality into its hardware, they haven't forsaken the software end of the solution. Cisco's VPN solution can start at a piece of equipment that has no earthly connection to a piece of Cisco hardware. When Cisco Secure VPN Client version 1.1 is installed on a Windows-based PC, a telecommuter, remote office, or traveler can connect across any internetwork with their own VPN tunnel.

The client—which can be placed on a PC anywhere in the world—worms its way through the Internet to find its way to its home router or PIX firewall.

Requirements   The VPN client is only available for Windows 9x, NT, 2000, Millennium Edition, and XP. Further, a Cisco VPN Client computer must contain the following attributes:

▼ PC-compatible computer with a Pentium processor

■ At least 16MB for Windows 9x, 32MB for Windows NT and Windows ME, 64MB for Windows 2000, and 128MB for Windows XP

■ 10MB available hard disk space

■ Internal/external modem or an Ethernet network connection with an NDIS-compliant driver

Product	Description
Cisco VPN 3000 Concentrator Series	Remote-access, scalable, aimed at the enterprise level. Features up to 100-Mbps 3Des-encrypted throughput.
Cisco Secure PIX Firewalls	Built-in software encryption, up to 440 Mbps of encrypted throughput.
Cisco 800 Series Routers	For the SOHO market, up to 128-Kbps ISDN, broadband.
Cisco uBr900 Series Router	For the SOHO market, T1 cable and broadband.
Cisco 1700 Series Routers	Small office market, up to T1/E1.
Cisco 2600 Series Router	For the branch office market, up to dual T1/E1.
Cisco 3600 Series Router	For the large branch office, scalable T1/E1 connectivity.
Cisco 7200 Series Routers	Central site, up to DS3 levels.
Cisco 7300 Series Routers	Central site, up to DS3 levels.

Table 9-4.   Some of Cisco's VPN-Enabled Hardware

- Microsoft TCP/IP communications stack and Microsoft dialer
- On the network, the following prerequisites exist:
    - Cisco IOS Release 12.2
    - Cisco Secure PIX Firewall version 6.2

Once these minimums have been met, installation is a simple process of double-clicking an icon on the installation CD-ROM. Once the client is installed, it sits quietly in an icon at the bottom of the screen until it is needed.

Features   Under the hood, Cisco's VPN client features a number of tools aimed at ensuring safe, stable IPSec tunneling. Some of the major features include

- ▼ The network administrator can export and lock the security policy.
- The client is IPSec-compliant. It also supports
    - Tunnel Mode or Transport Mode security
    - DES, 3DES, MD-5, and SHA-1 algorithms
    - IKE using ISAKMP/Oakley Handshake and Key Agreement

- It's compatible with most Windows communications devices, including LAN adapters, modems, PCMCIA cards, and so on.

- It's centrally configured for ease of use.

- It's compatible with X.509 Certificate Authorities, including

  - Windows 2000 Certificate Services

  - Verisign Onsite

  - Netscape Certificate Management System

  - GUI to make security policy and certificate management user-friendly

▲ It's transparent when in use.

Digging a Tunnel

When a combination of Cisco's VPN-enabled hardware and software come together, that's when the strength of the Cisco VPN solution is evident. For instance, by using a Cisco Secure PIX 515 Firewall along with the PIX v5.0 software, the PIX can create and/or terminate VPN tunnels between two PIXes, between a PIX and any Cisco VPN-enabled router, and between a PIX and the Cisco Secure VPN Client.

The following scenarios explain how different VPN needs can be met.

Remote Access   The most basic VPN comes when a user needs to access the network from a remote location. For instance, if a salesman is traveling and needs to access information on the company's network, he need only initiate a VPN back to the home office.

Let's look at how a remote access connection can be made. Figure 9-17 shows a pet food company's headquarters located in St. Paul, Minnesota, and a salesman, who is on a business trip in Boise, Idaho. To access his company's network, the remote user will be connected through a secure tunnel that is established through the Internet. This allows

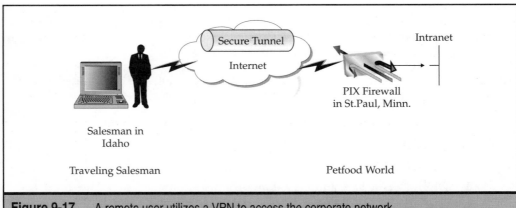

Figure 9-17.   A remote user utilizes a VPN to access the corporate network.

the salesman to access internal information as if his computer was physically connected to the corporate LAN.

In Figure 9-18 we add the hardware elements that will make the VPN possible.

In this scenario, we used a PIX firewall as the VPN device on the company's end. This same scenario can be configured with a router in place of the PIX firewall. Using the same construction, one of Cisco's VPN-enabled routers could be used in place of the PIX.

NOTE: Refer back to Table 9-4 for a list of Cisco's VPN-enabled hardware.

Of course, your internetworking needs and your means will feature prominently in your decision between a PIX firewall and a router. For maximum security, you should use the firewall. A VPN-enabled router provides much-increased performance over software-only VPN solutions.

This configuration works well for the "traveling salesman" scenario, but VPN functionality can also be established between two companies or a company and a branch office.

Site-to-Site Access   Even in an environment where a WAN is the preferred mode of connectivity, a substantial cost savings can still be realized by employing a VPN. Site-to-Site VPNs extend the classic WAN by replacing existing private networks utilizing leased lines, Frame Relay, or ATM to connect business partners and branch offices to the central site.

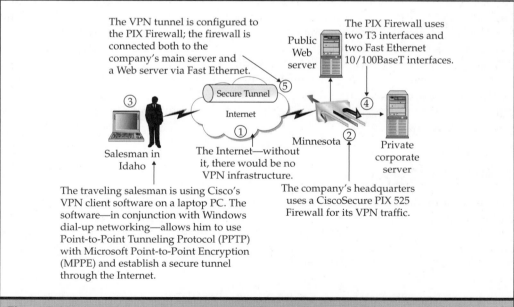

Figure 9-18.   Hardware components of a remote access VPN connection

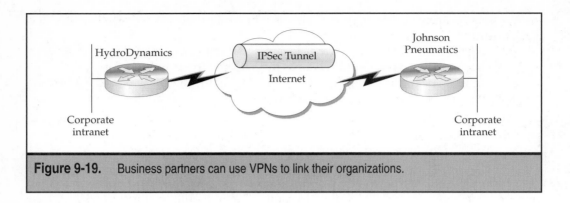

Figure 9-19.   Business partners can use VPNs to link their organizations.

In this capacity, VPNs don't change the requirements of private WANs, such as support for multiple protocols, reliability, and extensibility. Rather, they meet these requirements, but are more cost-effective and flexible. To deliver private WAN-style capabilities on a budget, site-to-site VPNs can use the Internet or Internet service providers by utilizing tunneling and encryption for privacy, and quality of service for reliability. The following scenario shows how a VPN can be established between a company's headquarters and a remote office (intranet) or between two business partners (extranet).

In this example, let's show how two business partners can link their respective networks together across the Internet. Figure 9-19 shows the headquarters of HydroDynamics, which needs to provide network access to extranet partner, Johnson Pneumatics. The two offices are connected through a secure IPSec tunnel, which connects through the Internet. Employees at Johnson Pneumatics are able to access the public Web server of their business partner across the country. Figure 9-20 shows the hardware and software details of the VPN link between HydroDynamics and Johnson Pneumatics.

As you can see, connecting two business partners or a branch office via VPN is much easier and less expensive than a WAN. By safely and securely tunneling though the Internet, connectivity can be delivered without taking too much of a bite out of an organization's bottom line.

ACCESS ROUTERS

Access to your network can come in many ways. As we explored in the last section, dial-up needs are served by access servers, for instance. However, branch offices, small offices, telecommuters, and road warriors may need higher performance and more robust access to the network. As such, access for these connections can be facilitated via access routers. Access routers are a subset of Cisco's router offerings.

Overview

Cisco's access router line provides the functionality for remote workers who need more powerful access to the network. To facilitate these connections, access routers include beefed-up security and performance features. Access routers offer secure Internet and

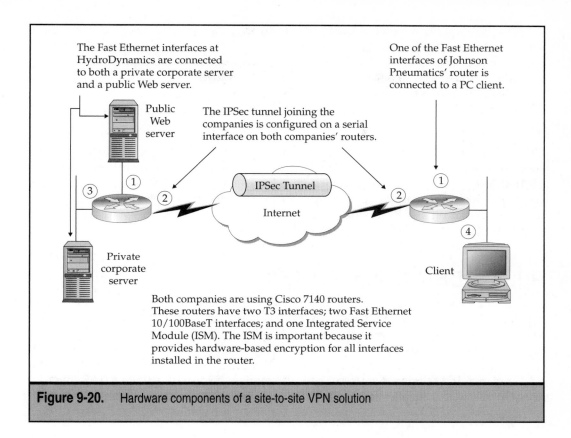

The Fast Ethernet interfaces at HydroDynamics are connected to both a private corporate server and a public Web server.

One of the Fast Ethernet interfaces of Johnson Pneumatics' router is connected to a PC client.

The IPSec tunnel joining the companies is configured on a serial interface on both companies' routers.

Public Web server

IPSec Tunnel

Internet

Client

Private corporate server

Both companies are using Cisco 7140 routers. These routers have two T3 interfaces; two Fast Ethernet 10/100BaseT interfaces; and one Integrated Service Module (ISM). The ISM is important because it provides hardware-based encryption for all interfaces installed in the router.

Figure 9-20.   Hardware components of a site-to-site VPN solution

network access through a variety of high-speed WAN access technologies. Benefits of the access routers include

▼   High-speed broadband and leased-line access.

■   Multiservice data/voice integration applications.

■   Integrated security capabilities, with IPSec VPN, a stateful inspection firewall, and intrusion detection.

▲   Higher-end models are modular, providing design and deployment flexibility.

Cisco's line of access routers covers the gamut of organizational needs, offering models from SOHO use to medium-sized businesses to huge enterprise deployments.

In addition to traditional router duties, access routers provide enhanced security, manageability, and Quality of Service (QoS) necessary for such applications as video-conferencing, e-learning, VPNs, and online collaboration.

An important feature on the access routers are their QoS capabilities. Since the routers will be asked to channel VoIP, multimedia content, and other applications that would suffer from packet latency, QoS is a necessary mechanism. These capabilities result in smoother, jitter-free conversations and transmissions than without QoS in place. For a more in-depth discussion of QoS, please flip back to Chapter 7.

Models

Cisco offers a number of access routers with varying levels of features. The lower-end access routers are fixed in their configuration—that is, they simply plug into a WAN connection, like a DSL line. However, when you start moving up the ladder of Cisco's access router products, there are more opportunities for modularity. That is, they can be configured to operate on an OC-3 connection, or T1 connection, for example, depending on which cards and modules you use to tweak it out.

INTRUSION DETECTION SYSTEM

Firewalls are great things to have in place. They are important safeguards against someone trying to attack your network. However, security doesn't stop there. Think of firewalls as security systems in banks. Sure, when the thugs come in, the security system offers a certain level of security, but that doesn't mean that no one can get in and that doesn't mean no one is going to try. That's why banks supplement the security system with a guard. If a criminal wants to go for the money, the guard is there to stop the robbery. In the world of internetworking, firewalls are good security systems, but there needs to be a guard. To serve this need, Cisco offers its Intrusion Detection System (IDS).

Components

Cisco IDS is used to monitor your Cisco network, looking for user-defined security breaches, and if found, informing security personnel, logging the incident, or both. IDS is comprised of three components:

▼ **Sensor** The Sensor is a network appliance that uses a rules-based engine to gather copious amounts of IP network traffic into security events, which it forwards to the Director. The Sensor can also be used to log security data, cut TCP sessions, and manage a router's access control lists to thwart intruders.

■ **Director** The Director is a central GUI for security management across a network. It is also used for other functions, including data management through third-party tools, access to the Network Security Database, Sensor management, and alerting security personnel when a security breach occurs.

▲ **Post Office** The Post Office is the communications backbone that allows IDS services and hosts to communicate with each other.

The Sensor captures network packets, and then compares them against its own rule set, indicating intrusion activity. When IDS analyzes traffic, it is looking for patterns of misuse. These patterns can be as simple as an attempt to access a specific port on a certain host, or as complex as operations distributed across a number of hosts over a lengthy period of time. If an attack is detected, a Sensor can generate an alarm—which can be sent to a Director, either for logging or notification.

The Director configures the Sensors, and then monitors them, garnering real-time security information. This information is displayed via icons shown on one or more network security maps. Further, the Director is used to remotely manage the Sensors' services, and then collect and analyze sensor data.

NOTE: For Sensor data analysis, third-party software is needed that provides relational database management, report writing, file management, and trouble-ticketing functionality.

The Post Office is the component that allows the Director and Sensor to communicate. The technology is based on a three-part address using "Organization," "Host," and "Application" as identifiers to locate each node. The Post Office can be layered on top of existing network protocols and addresses a larger domain than the conventional 32-bit IP protocol. Figure 9-21 shows how IDS components are deployed in a network.

Additionally, IDS can utilize software built into other Cisco devices to act as sensors. Cisco Secure Integrated Software includes the same sort of intrusion detection tools available in the Sensor devices. This software is included in Cisco's mid- and high-range router series, including the 2600, 2600, 7100, and 7200 series. As such, these devices can be set up as IDS Sensors, examining and analyzing traffic patterns for misuse and abuse.

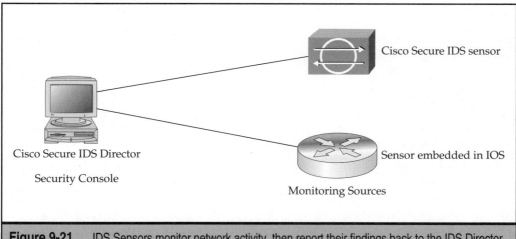

Figure 9-21. IDS Sensors monitor network activity, then report their findings back to the IDS Director.

Monitoring

An IDS is a good tool because it can be tweaked and modified, based on your organization's particular needs and goals.

Cisco's IDS is a network-based IDS. That is, it monitors an entire network segment, looking for violations of established rules. The sensors in the IDS monitor network traffic on the desired segment, and then perform a rules-based or expert system analysis of the traffic, using conditions established by the network administrator. These sensors examine packet headers to determine their source and destination addresses and the type of information being transmitted. Next, the sensors examine the packet payload to determine what type of information is being transmitted. If the sensor determines that there is a security breach, it can log the event, send an alarm to the management console, reset the connection, or order a router to block future traffic from the particular host or network.

NOTE: Other IDSes are so-called *host-based* solutions. That is, they monitor activity of individual hosts—PCs and servers—looking for suspect behavior. Cisco Secure IDS is a network-based solution that monitors entire network segments.

There are a number of ways to manage access to your network—either by setting up an access server for dial-in use or an access router for Internet-bound traffic. No matter which method you choose, it's vital to keep security in mind, and a network should have a properly configured firewall and IDS in place to thwart malicious individuals.

CHAPTER 10

Cisco Wireless

Conventionally speaking, internetworking has been accomplished by plugging cables into electronic boxes, then letting packets fly. But the latest, greatest addition to networking gives packets wings. They need no longer be constrained by the physical limit of the twisted-pair wiring. Thus, the era of wireless networking is indeed upon us.

INTRODUCTION TO WIRELESS NETWORKING

With all the advances in conventional, wired networking, it was only a matter of time before someone looked up into the sky and wondered, "What about wireless?" Truth be told, someone asked that question almost 20 years ago, but the practical, functional result of that question has only been realized in the last couple of years.

In this section, we take a look back at where wireless networking came from, how it works, and how you can benefit from it.

The Roots of Wireless Networking

To better understand the wireless networking of today, it's important to know its history and how we've gotten here from there.

The most popular LAN technology in the world is Ethernet. It is defined by the Institute of Electrical and Electronics Engineers (IEEE) with the 802.3 standard. Ethernet has provided an evolving, widely available, high-speed networking standard. Initially, Ethernet provided 1-Mbps, and then 10-Mbps transfer rates, which then grew to 100 Mbps. Speeds of 1 Gbps and even 10 Gbps are also available. Because IEEE 802.3 is an open standard, there is a broad range of suppliers and products for Ethernet users. The standard ensures a certain level of interoperability, no matter what the product or vendor.

The first wireless LAN (WLAN) technologies weren't as speedy as Ethernet at the time. They operated in the 900-MHz band and only clocked in at about 2 Mbps, max. Further, they were proprietary in nature, which eliminated any common communication between different vendors' products. In spite of these obstacles, wireless networking managed to carve out a respectable niche for itself in vertical markets like retail and warehousing. It was useful in these environments because the mobility and flexibility of the technology was necessary in environments where the workers used hand-held devices for such activities as inventory management and data collection.

Aironet, a wireless networking company, realized the need for standardization in wireless networking if the industry was to grow. They began pushing for standards in 1991.

NOTE: Cisco acquired Aironet in 2000 and uses its technology as the cornerstone of its WLAN products. We talk about Cisco's acquisition and their Aironet devices later in the chapter.

By establishing standards, they argued, wireless LANs would gain broad market acceptance. The next year, WLAN developers began developing products that operated in the unlicensed 2.4-GHz frequency band. This new technology was especially appealing to two particular markets:

▼ **Healthcare**   Wireless networking made it possible to transfer patient data to mobile computing devices. Rather than tote a computer from exam room to exam room, wireless networking puts patient information at a healthcare professional's fingertips.

▲ **Schools**   Not being constrained by wires made it possible for schools that were constructed without wiring conduits (remember the days) to construct computer networks without having to punch holes in walls and string cabling between floors.

In June 1997, the technology that serves as the core standard for the WLANs we know today was developed. The IEEE released the 802.11 standard for wireless local area networking. The standard supports data transmission in infrared light and two types of radio transmission within the unlicensed 2.4-GHz frequency band: Frequency Hopping Spread Spectrum (FHSS) and Direct Sequence Spread Spectrum (DSSS).

NOTE: We'll delve deeper into the specifics of 802.11 later in the chapter.

Benefits

If the simple ability to perform networking functions without being tethered to a switch or a hub isn't enough to stir your soul, let's take a closer look at the abilities of wireless data transmission, along with a few situations in which wireless networking is beneficial.

What It Can Do

Besides the "gee-whiz, this is kewl" aspect of a computer network that operates without wires, there are a number of important factors that make wireless networking a useful, productive technology:

▼ **Mobility**   With WLANs, users can get real-time access to their LAN from virtually anywhere. This ability comes without having to be hardwired into the network. Mobility of this kind gives users the freedom to access the network from anywhere at any time.

■ **Reduced cost-of-ownership**   Even though start-up costs for WLAN hardware are more than the cost of a traditional LAN, when the complete lifecycle expenses are considered, WLAN expenses can be considerably lower. The greatest long-term cost benefits are seen in dynamic environments where there are frequent moves and changes.

■ **Scalability**   WLANs can be easily configured in a number of networking topologies to meet the needs of specific applications and installations. Configurations are highly flexible, can easily be changed, and range from simple peer-to-peer networks that are ideal for a few users to full infrastructure networks of thousands of users that enable roaming across a broad area.

- **High-speed data rates**   WLAN transmission speeds are comparable to wired networks. Users can access information at 54 Mbps, which is on a par with conventional wire speeds. Though not yet touching the 100 Mbps and 1 Gbps that are possible in wired networks, wireless has a respectable, functional speed.

- **Interoperability**   Manufacturers (like Cisco) who build their products using the 802.11 standard ensure functionality with other compliant equipment or brands within the network.

- **Encryption for high-speed LAN security**   By incorporating wired equivalency privacy (WEP), network security can be ensured. WEP serves 54-Mbps access points, PC cards, ISA cards, and PCI adapters.

- **Installation speed and simplicity**   Before wireless technology, connecting computers to a LAN required stringing and plugging in a mess of wires. The task could be further complicated if the wiring needed to be strung through walls or between different floors. Wireless technology simplifies and speeds up the installation process.

- **Installation flexibility**   Because WLANs aren't restricted by the physical barriers that constrain wired LANs, wireless networks can provide network access to those users and workstations where connecting to a LAN is simply impossible.

Applications

Given the continually changing face of technology and its applications, it almost seems silly to pigeonhole a specific technology into specific fields. However, the following list will give you an idea of how wireless technology can be used in a number of different fields. Again, this list should not be considered as the extent of wireless' capabilities—your own circumstances and situations will be the best guide as to whether you benefit most from wireless or wired networking.

- **Corporate**   With a WLAN, corporate employees need no longer be tethered to their desks. By using laptops equipped with wireless NICs, they can take full advantage of e-mail, file sharing, and Web browsing regardless of where they are in the office or business campus.

- **Hospitality and retail**   Hospitality services—like restaurants—can use WLANs to enter and send food orders to the kitchen, directly from the table. Retail stores can use WLANs to set up temporary cash registers for special events, like the day after Christmas or the start of a sale.

- **Manufacturing**   WLANs link factory floor workstations and data collection devices to a company's network. They are mobile on the work floor and don't require more cabling on the factory floor.

- **Warehousing**   WLANs connect handheld and forklift-mounted computer terminals with barcode readers and wireless data links. This technology is used to enter and maintain the location of a warehouse's inventory.

■ **Education**   Schools, colleges, and universities benefit from mobile connectivity by enabling students, faculty, and staff with notebook computers to connect to the academic institution's network for collaborative lessons, and to the Internet for Web browsing and e-mail. Further, wireless technology can save desperately needed classroom space by making portable computer labs a reality.

■ **Financial**   Financial traders can use a handheld PC with a WLAN adapter, to receive pricing information from a database in real time, and speed up and improve the quality of trades.

▲ **Healthcare**   By using wireless handheld PCs, healthcare professionals have access to real-time information and can increase productivity and quality of patient care by reducing treatment delays, eliminating redundant paperwork, and decreasing transcription errors.

This is just the tip of the iceberg on how wireless networking can be used. To be sure, as technology changes the face of business, more and more uses for wireless networking will be apparent.

WLANS

A WLAN (wireless LAN) is just what the acronym suggests—a LAN that is accessed without having to be physically tethered to a server, switch, hub, or any other networking device. Using radio frequency (RF) technology, WLANs transmit and receive data out of midair, eliminating the need for conventional, wired connections. WLANs are becoming more and more popular in a number of specialized fields, including healthcare, retail, manufacturing, warehousing, and academia. These domains have benefited from the productivity gains of using handheld PCs and notebook computers to transmit and receive real-time information with the centralized network. WLANs are gaining recognition as a general-purpose network connectivity solution for a broad range of business users.

In this section, we'll take a closer look at how wireless networking is deployed in a practical manner. Then, we'll look at some of the core technologies fueling wireless networks. Finally, we'll gaze into our crystal ball and try to predict where wireless networking is going in the future.

How They Work

Like cordless telephones, WLANs use electromagnetic radio waves to communicate information from one location (your laptop, for instance) to another (an access point), without having to use any physical medium to transfer the message. Figure 10-1 illustrates this.

NOTE: Radio waves are often referred to as radio carriers because their function is delivering energy to a remote receiver. The transmitted data is superimposed on the radio carrier so that it can be extracted at the receiving end. This is known as modulation of the carrier by the transmitted information.

Figure 10-1. WLANs communicate information like wireless telephones.

Once data is added onto the radio carrier, the radio signal spills over, occupying more than a single frequency. This happens because the frequency—or bit rate—of the modulating data adds to the carrier.

This may seem to present a problem, especially in environments where several machines will be trying to access the wireless device. In reality, however, multiple carriers function just fine in the same area, as long as the radio waves are transmitted on different frequencies. In order to collect data, a radio receiver tunes in just one specific radio frequency, as in Figure 10-2, while ignoring all others.

In a WLAN, the device that physically connects to the wired LAN is a transceiver (a combination of a transmitter and receiver) and is commonly called an *access point.* The access point receives, buffers, and transmits data between the WLAN and the wired network. As shown in Figure 10-3, another way to think about an access point is to consider it as a wireless hub—a single access point can serve hundreds of clients. Depending on the range of the access point, clients can be located within a few feet, or up to 1,500 feet

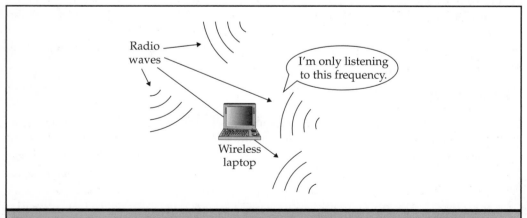

Figure 10-2. Wireless devices tune out unwanted frequencies and focus on the relevant one.

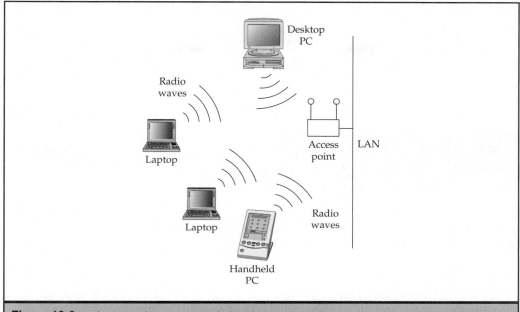

Figure 10-3.   Access points serve as wireless hubs, connecting one—or many—wireless devices to the WLAN.

away, from the access point. Optimally, the antenna for the access point would be situated high above the floor. However, the antenna could be located anywhere space permits.

To connect to the access point, client computers use WLAN adapters, which are small PC cards for notebook and palmtop computers, and cards in desktop computers. They can also be integrated within handheld computers. These cards have built-in antennas and transceiver components.

Architecture

Wireless LANs can be as simple as two computers talking or as complex as hundreds of computers in one location connecting to computers in another building miles away. Let's take a look at the three basic ways you can build your wireless networks.

Peer-to-Peer

The simplest, most basic wireless network consists of two PCs, equipped with wireless adapter cards. As shown in Figure 10-4, no access point is needed; and whenever these two computers get within range of each other, they form their own independent network. This is called a *peer-to-peer network*. On-demand networks like this are extremely simple to set up and operate. They require no administration or pre-configuration; and, in this case, each computer would only have access to the resources of the other computer, but not to a central server or the Internet.

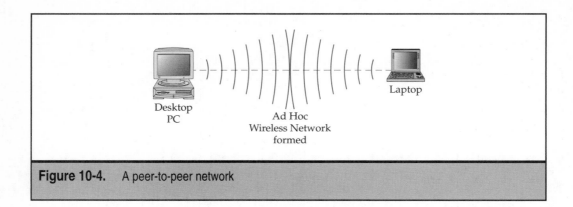

Figure 10-4.   A peer-to-peer network

This type of network is ideal for home networking or small businesses for spontaneous networking.

In-Building

Much like a conventionally wired network, in-building WLAN equipment consists of a PC card, Personal Computer Interface (PCI), and Industry-Standard Architecture (ISA) client adapters, as well as access points.

Like wired LANs for small or temporary networks, a WLAN can be constructed with just two computers in a peer-to-peer design or on-the-fly topology using only client adapters. To extend the range of your WLAN, as shown in Figure 10-5, or to increase functionality, access points can be used in the network's topology and will also function as a bridge to an Ethernet network.

By applying WLAN technology to desktop systems, an organization is afforded the flexibility that is simply impossible with a conventional LAN. Clients can be deployed in places where running cable is simply impossible. Further, clients can be redeployed anywhere at any time. This makes wireless ideal for temporary workgroups or fast-growing organizations.

Installing an access point can extend the range of a peer-to-peer or ad-hoc network. It would essentially double the range at which the devices can communicate. Because the access point is connected directly to the wired network, each client has access to the server's resources, as well as to other clients. Like hubs in a wired network, each access point can accommodate several clients—exactly how many depends on how many transmissions are involved, and the nature of those transmissions. It's not uncommon for access points to handle up to 50 clients.

NOTE: Be aware, however, that more clients connecting to an access point cuts into the amount of traffic an access point can handle. If an access point is handling 40 clients, don't expect it to be as speedy as an access point being used by only ten clients.

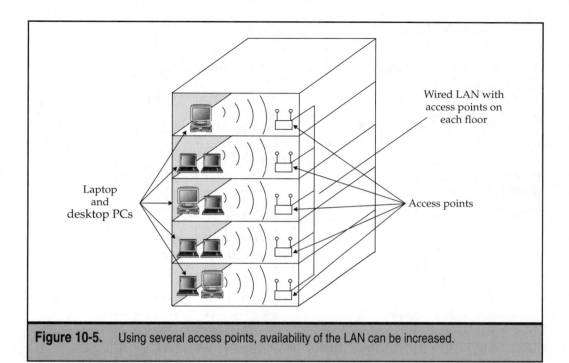

Figure 10-5.   Using several access points, availability of the LAN can be increased.

Extension points, as shown in Figure 10-6, look and act just like access points, but with one important exception—they are not tethered to the wired network. Extension points extend the range of the network by relaying signals from a client to an access point or another extension point. Extension points are necessary because signals weaken the farther they are from their receiving point. If you have clients that are far from the wired network, extension points can be strung together in order to pass along data from the clients to an access point.

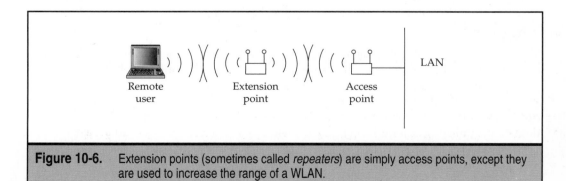

Figure 10-6.   Extension points (sometimes called *repeaters*) are simply access points, except they are used to increase the range of a WLAN.

Building-to-Building

The ultimate achievement in wireless networking comes when networks are extended between buildings in different cities. By using a wireless bridge, networks located in buildings dozens of miles away from each other can be connected into a single network.

When connecting networks between buildings with copper or fiber, there are any number of obstacles that can put the skids on a project. Roads, rivers, and politics can break a project. A wireless bridge makes physical and ideological barriers a nonissue. Transmission through the air in accordance with 802.11 requires no license and no right of way.

For deployments that do not offer a wireless alternative, organizations routinely fall back on WAN technologies. However, leasing a line from a telephone provider presents a number of headaches:

▼ Installation is expensive and takes a long time to set up.

▲ Monthly fees are expensive for high bandwidth. The additional rub is that by LAN standards, WAN speeds are very low. This is because telephone lines were designed and built for voice, not data.

One can purchase and install a wireless bridge in a single afternoon, and the cost is comparable to a T1 installation charge alone. Even better, there is no monthly charge—once a wireless connection is made, there are no recurring charges. Further, wireless bridges provide bandwidth from a technology rooted in data, not voice.

To make your building-to-building network happen, you need a directional antenna. Let's suppose you had a WLAN in Building A (the headquarters) and wanted to extend it to a satellite office in Building B, ten miles away in a neighboring city. As shown in Figure 10-7, you could install a directional antenna on the roof of both buildings with each antenna targeting the other. Building A's antenna is connected to your main LAN via an access point. The antenna on Building B is similarly connected to an access point to that facility's LAN. This configuration brings the two LANs, located miles apart, together into one, common LAN.

Because of their mobility and ease of installation, WLANs have a significant leg up on conventional LANs. They provide networking opportunities that would not be available to wired networks and are not much more expensive in the long run.

Technologies

There are a number of technologies that make wireless data transmission and receipt possible. Many of them have their roots in cellular telephony, while others have been designed solely with wireless networking in mind.

In this section, we take a closer look at three of the most popular technologies and how they impact your wireless networking needs. These technologies cover short-range data communications, long-range data transfer, and how the Internet can be accessed via cellular phones.

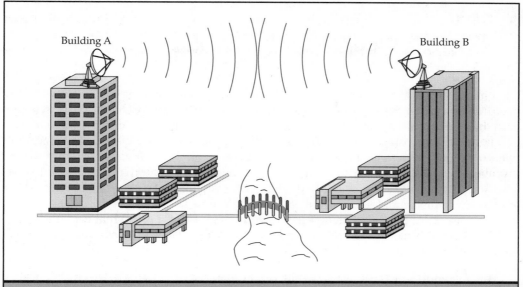

Figure 10-7.   Wireless bridges bring two networks—located miles apart—together into one network.

Bluetooth

The creators of James Bond movies must have a tough time thinking up new toys. In this day and age, there isn't much that can't already be put in a shirt pocket or integrated into a watch, but living in a world chock-full of Internet-enabled cellular telephones, wireless networking, and computers the size of a deck of playing cards has created its own connectivity problems.

Bluetooth Cuts Its Teeth   Because so many of the cool new gadgets are made by different companies with their own proprietary way of doing things, it's a challenge to get all these gadgets to interconnect. For instance, different wireless phones use their own proprietary connectors. PDAs use different technologies to sync up, and still other wireless devices use infrared communications—but they don't always match up, either. This is where Bluetooth comes into play. Bluetooth provides a low-cost, point-to-point peripheral attachment solution for computer telemetry and metering.

Bluetooth is the product of an alliance between mobile communications and mobile computing companies, as well as a standard for short-range communications. In 1998, Ericsson, Nokia, IBM, Toshiba, and Intel (among others) formed a group to develop an open specification that was given the name "Bluetooth."

NOTE: "Bluetooth" was taken from the tenth-century Danish King Harald "Bluetooth" Gormsson. During his reign, Bluetooth ruled all of modern-day Denmark and a portion of Norway. Around 986 A.D., Bluetooth was killed in battle while fighting his son, Svend Forkbeard. (Honestly, you can't even make up names like this.)

Bluetooth is a limited-distance wireless transmission technology that allows manufacturers of a variety of equipment to integrate standard and proprietary cabling schemes into their devices for a few dollars. When the cost of cabling is considered, Bluetooth represents a way to connect many devices with one, universal wireless communications method. Bluetooth's range for low-powered devices is about ten meters; in high-powered devices, about 100 meters. In 2000, the cost of integrating Bluetooth technology into a device added about $20 to the price of a device. However, this cost is expected to drop as time goes on and the technology is widely adopted.

But it isn't just the devices you carry in your briefcase and purse that have the potential for Bluetooth technology. In addition to PDAs, cellular telephones, and notebooks, Bluetooth can be implemented in:

▼ Printers

■ Desktop computers

■ Servers

■ Fax machines

■ Coffee machines

■ Keyboards

■ Joysticks

▲ Alarm systems

The scope of where Bluetooth can be implemented is only limited by one's imagination. For instance, with your Bluetooth-enabled gear, you could use your PDA to turn off your home's alarm system, brew a pot of coffee, and turn on the stereo as you pull into your driveway. In the workplace, it could be used at a meeting where all the players bring their Bluetooth-enabled PDAs and notebooks, and then can share information during the meeting.

How It Works   As you might deduce from the European and Japanese companies working with American industry, Bluetooth is intended as an international communication standard. The transceivers built into devices are designed to work in the 2.45-GHz radio band, which is unlicensed. This band provides data transmission rates up to 721 Kbps, including three voice channels.

The standard was designed to support communications even in a noisy frequency environment. To avoid interference with other devices, Bluetooth uses frequency hopping—in other words, it will jump to another frequency after transmitting or receiving a packet. It also uses Forward Error Correction (FEC), which limits retransmission due to the impact of unexpected interference. In addition to FEC, Bluetooth also supports automatic request repeat.

This allows a CRC to be computed for data packets; packets received in error (or not at all) are retransmitted to correct the error.

Bluetooth works in the background in a particular device, so its functionality is largely unnoticed by the device or the user. Each device is issued a unique, 12-byte address, and for a connection to be made, the device must know the target address. This is used to prevent data from being mistakenly transmitted to an unintended device, or an unscrupulous person from walking through the building, gathering information that is not intended for him.

Bluetooth and Networking   When it comes time for Bluetooth gadgets to interface with a computer network, the connection can be facilitated in one of four ways:

▼ **Universal Serial Bus (USB)**   A stand-alone component can be connected to a computer via the popular, high-speed USB port.

■ **RS232**   Like USB, a module can be linked into an RS232 port (albeit with much slower results than the USB port).

■ **PC Card**   A connection module can be built and included in an add-on card.

▲ **Universal Asynchronous Receiver Transmitter (UART)**   A transceiver could be built directly onto the motherboard, and then connected to the computer's UART.

Just like a conventional, wired network, Bluetooth includes its own techniques for connection setup, error detection and correction, authentication, and data transmission and reception. Let's take a closer look at some of the features Bluetooth incorporates to form its own networks.

▼ **Security**   To avoid the Pandora's box of security issues that would pop up if one Bluetooth-compatible device came within range of another (unexpected) device and had instant connectivity, designers incorporated support for authentication and encryption. Both of these security features are based on the use of a secret link key that is shared by a pair of devices. The secret key is generated the first time the devices talk together. However, a word of warning is needed—Bluetooth devices authenticate the device, not the user. Therefore, care must be taken to ensure that a Bluetooth device does not fall into any third party's evil clutches. When setting up a Bluetooth device, the owner can also restrict which devices it can interact with, limiting it to work only with the products belonging to the user.

■ **Establishing a connection**   Once a Bluetooth device is powered on, it listens to the RF spectrum every 1.28 seconds, paying attention to a set of 32-hop frequencies that are defined for the unit. How a device connects to another depends on whether the two devices have communicated before. If they have, a Page message will be transmitted. If they've never communicated before, then an Inquiry message will be sent.

■ **Piconet**   The simplest Bluetooth networking scheme occurs when two devices want to speak with each other. This is known as a *piconet*. This method involves point-to-point communications and requires that one device become the master and the other the slave. This topology can grow with up to seven active slaves (it can support up to 256 slaves that are nonactive).

▲ **Scatternet**   Depending on how much Bluetooth technology you use and how it's configured, it is highly possible that you might have piconets that would overlap in the same wireless area—for instance, an employee in one cubicle could be syncing his PDA with his PC, while an employee in the next cubicle is doing the same thing with her PDA. This doesn't mean that they will share data with each other, because each piconet will use its own frequency.

Bluetooth is an excellent, inexpensive wireless technology that is useful for small devices. However, for larger and beefier networking applications, wireless networking needs to use something that's kicked up just a few more notches.

802.11

The core technology that allows WLANs to communicate is the IEEE 802.11*x* standard. The IEEE 802.11 working group was formed in the early 1990s to develop a global standard for wireless LANs operating in the unlicensed 2.4-GHz frequency band. As we mentioned earlier, the first incarnations of 802.11*x* supported speeds of up to 2 Gbps.

The 802.11*x* standard offers different variations on the protocol for different speeds, frequency of operation, and range. The 802.11*x* LAN is based on an architecture that is very similar to the design of cellular telephone networks. Wireless LANs (WLANs) operate by connecting an *access point* (*AP*) to the server while client computers are fitted with wireless networking cards. These cards can be installed in either desktop or laptop computers, as well as other networking devices, including print servers. Some computers come with wireless capabilities built in.

There are three types of 802.11*x* networks germane to our discussion:

▼ **802.11a**   Using this specification, devices transmit at 5 GHz and send data up to 54 Mbps. Although the speed is very good, the range of 802.11a devices suffers, because their range is limited to somewhere around 75 feet in a typical environment.

■ **802.11b**   Using this specification, devices transmit at 2.4 GHz and send data at up to 11 Mbps. This was the first commercially available wireless network. The speed wasn't great, but it made it possible to connect devices without being tethered by Cat 5 cabling.

▲ **802.11g**   This is the latest incarnation of the wireless specification. It handles data communications at speeds of up to 54 Mbps and utilizes the same frequency as 802.11b devices (2.4 GHz). Because this is relatively new, look for prices on 802.11b gear to drop rather quickly as competitive products hit the shelves.

NOTE: There are other alphabet soup variations of the 802.11x standard (802.11c, 802.11d, and so forth, up through 802.11i). The rest of these variations really don't have anything to do with the current state of Cisco wireless networking.

The price gap between these technologies isn't too broad, actually. At the time of this writing, the cost of an 802.11a wireless network card was about $90, an 802.11b wireless network card was around $30, and the 802.11g card was about $45. The 802.11b access points cost approximately $60, while 802.11g access points will run about $90. Also, if you happen to have existing 802.11b gear, new 802.11g stuff will be compatible with it. Don't expect your 802.11b card to start chugging away at 54 Mbps, but at least you won't have to buy all new gear.

For easier understanding of these three protocols and how they stack up against each other, we've enumerated their similarities and differences in Table 10-1.

There are two different ways to configure an 802.11x WLAN:

▼ Ad hoc

▲ Infrastructure

Now, let's take a closer look at each of these types of WLAN infrastructure.

Ad Hoc   In the ad-hoc network, computers are brought together to form a makeshift network, like a peer-to-peer network. As Figure 10-8 shows, there is no hierarchical structure to the network. Everything is mobile and every node is able to communicate with every other node. A good example of how this would appear in the real world is to think of a meeting where everyone brought his or her own laptop.

Infrastructure   The second type of connection, shown in Figure 10-9, comes more closely in line with a conventional LAN topology. This design uses fixed network access points with which mobile nodes can communicate. The access points can be placed within range of each other to expand the range of the network.

802.11 Design

802.11 was developed with three needs in mind:

▼ The need for a media access control (MAC) and physical layer specification for wireless connectivity for portable fixes and roaming stations

■ The need for wireless connectivity to automatic machinery, equipment, or stations that require fast connectivity

▲ The need to offer a global standard

It's the third requirement that led the IEEE to embrace 2.4 GHz as the preferred frequency. It is an unlicensed frequency band that is reserved for industrial, scientific, and medical use on a global basis.

Standard	802.11a	802.11b	802.11g
Prevalence	New technology	Popular technology	New technology—expected to grow fast
Speed	54 Mbps	11 Mbps	54 Mbps
Cost	Moderately expensive.	Inexpensive.	More expensive than 802.11b, but less expensive than 802.11a.
Frequency	5 GHz—This band is uncrowded and can coexist with 802.11b and g networks.	2.4 GHz—This band is crowded and interference might occur with cordless telephones, microwave ovens, and other devices.	2.4 GHz—This band is crowded and interference might occur with cordless telephones, microwave ovens, and other devices.
Range	25 to 75 feet indoors.	100 to 150 feet indoors.	100 to 150 feet indoors.
"Hotspot" Access	As of this writing, none.	Public hotspots are popping up all over from restaurants to airports to shopping malls.	Interoperable with an 802.11b network, although it will be limited to 11 Mbps. Hotspots are likely to upgrade to the 802.11g standard.
Compatibility	Incompatible with 802.11b and g networks.	Most prevalent deployment.	Interoperates with 802.11b, but incompatible with 802.11a.

Table 10-1.   Comparing the Attributes of 802.11a, b, and g Networks

The Mechanics   The 802.11 LAN is based on the architecture that is very similar to the design of cellular telephone networks. By using a comparable network design, wireless networks can reap the same benefits as cellular, while providing high data rates.

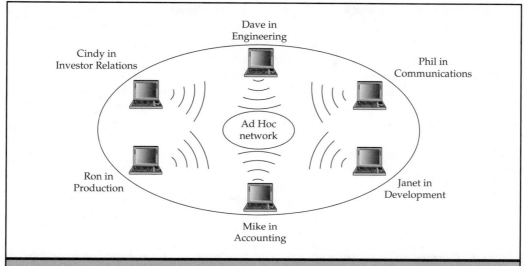

Figure 10-8. The 802.11*x* standard for wireless networking makes an ad hoc network around a conference room table possible.

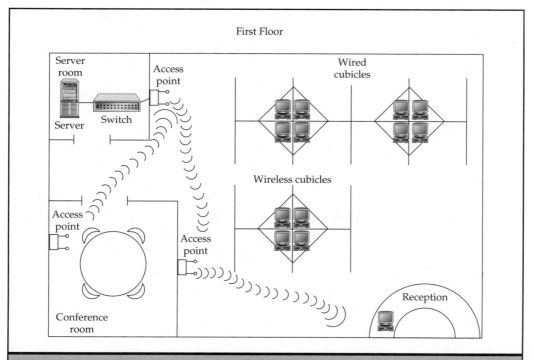

Figure 10-9. In this example, the floor plan of a company's first floor shows how access points can be deployed.

An 802.11 LAN is subdivided into cells and each cell is referred to as a basic service set (BSS). Each BSS is controlled by an access point. But because a single access point may not be capable of fulfilling the network's wireless needs, several access points can be connected to a common backbone. When a configuration of several access points is used, this is called a *distribution system.* No matter how large or small the network, no matter how many nodes are connected, the grouping of wireless equipment is viewed as a single IEEE 802.11 network to upper layers of the OSI Reference Model. In 802.11 terminology, the upper layers of the OSI Reference Model are referred to as an extended service set.

The 802.11 protocol covers the physical and media access control. But instead of a lone type of media, 802.11 supports three kinds of media: frequency-hopping spread spectrum, direct-sequence spread spectrum, and infrared. A single MAC layer supports all three physical layers. Additionally, the MAC layer provides a link to the upper-layer protocols. These functions include fragmentation, packet retransmission, and acknowledgments.

By basing wireless networking on cellular architecture, wireless devices can join, leave, or roam from cell to cell much like cellular telephones do.

Making the Connection   When it comes to actually connecting to an access point or another computer, two methods are used. The first involves a station joining an existing cell; the second entails the process of moving from one cell to another.

▼   **Joining an existing cell**   There are three different times when a wireless device will try to access an existing access point or another wireless device: when the device is powered up, after exiting sleep mode, or when it enters a new area. With each situation, the device needs to obtain synchronization information, and will locate another device to sync with via either active or passive scanning. But how does a device know that there are other wireless devices with which it can interconnect? With two different methods of scanning, as listed in the following:

■   **Active scanning**   This type of scanning requires the device to attempt to locate an access point that can receive synchronization information from that device. This is accomplished by transmitting probe request frames and waiting for a probe response packet, which is transmitted by an access point.

▲   **Passive scanning**   Devices can listen for a beacon frame that is periodically transmitted from each access point. The beacon frame contains synchronization information, so a device can use this for synchronization.

1.   After a device locates an access point and gathers synchronization information, it exchanges authentication information. The device and the access point exchange a shared key with each other, ensuring one has the right to talk to the other.

2.   Once a device has been authenticated, the two machines begin the association process. Under the association process, information about the device and the capabilities of available access points are analyzed. The current location of the device is determined, and the best access point is assigned to the device. Naturally, if there is only one access point, the association process is a done deal.

▼ **Roaming**   In the last scenario, the device connects to the access point and isn't likely to move. The connection is made and the device will most likely be associated to that access point until the user is logged off. However, if your device will be moving from one cell (access point or other wireless device) to another, this is called *roaming*. Figure 10-10 illustrates this process.

Though roaming in this situation is much like roaming with a cellular telephone, there are two important differences between the technologies. First, 802.11 supports the transmission of packets that have a specific destination address, sequence, and fragment identification. This facilitates LAN roaming because the transition between cells is at a much slower pace—walking versus driving in a car in a cellular phone environment.

Next, if there is a brief interruption in service, it is not as damaging to a voice conversation as it is in a WLAN environment. This is because with a WLAN, once packets are sent, an upper-level protocol sets a time prior to each transmission. If the timer expires without the transmitting station receiving an acknowledgment, it will resend the packets. Conversely, in a cellular telephone network, if there is an interruption in the call, voice is simply lost and there is no mechanical effort to resend it. With a WLAN, however, interruptions can mean slower times because of retransmissions.

Cells know that roaming will occur because as a device moves away from an access point, the device will observe that the signal is getting weaker. The device will use its scanning function to try and find an access point with a stronger signal. Once a new access point is found, the device will send a reassociation request. Then the new access point will send a message to the device's former access point to inform it of the new association. If the device does not receive a response to the request, it will scan for a new access point.

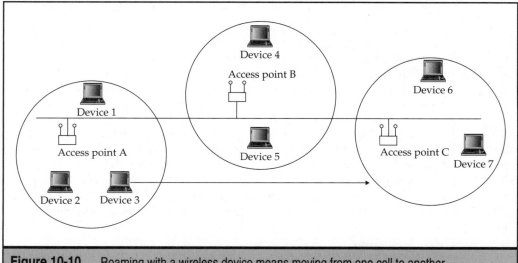

Figure 10-10.   Roaming with a wireless device means moving from one cell to another.

WAP

If you've seen Web-enabled cellular telephones that can send and receive e-mail and surf (albeit in a limited way) the Internet, then you have an idea what WAP is all about. WAP stands for Wireless Application Protocol and is a set of protocols developed to help deliver content via wireless communications to portable devices that have limited-screen displays.

Though Cisco doesn't make WAP devices for the end user, it is able to serve WAP technologies with its own equipment, which is capable of handling and processing WAP.

Roots   WAP can be traced back to 1995 when Ericsson began work on its own cellular telephone Internet protocol, called Intelligent Terminal Transfer Protocol (ITTP). A couple of years later, Nokia and Phone.com tried developing their own proprietary protocols. They soon realized that working together on a common standard would be more effective and beneficial for all. They got together with other wireless developers, and the partnership was called the WAP Forum. The goal of the WAP Forum was to develop a standard that would allow Internet communications and advanced telephone services to be supported on all digital mobile phones and other wireless terminals.

Components   As you probably know from surfing the Internet, browsing the Web uses a number of standards. For instance, the way content is displayed on your computer screen is based on the Hypertext Markup Language (HTML). The protocol that transports those Web pages across the ether and delivers them to your computer is known as the Hypertext Transfer Protocol (HTTP). WAP is very similar in its construction.

▼ **WML**   Wireless Markup Language (WML) is comparable to HTML and is used to create Web pages—in this case, on the tiny screens of cellular telephones.

▲ **WMLScript**   Like its bigger, better-known cousin, JavaScript, WMLScript is a scripting language designed to deliver content dynamically. However, WMLScript differs in important ways from JavaScript, mainly in its size and management. Because cellular telephones are not loaded with as much memory as PCs are, WMLScript employs a number of techniques to keep the script sizes small and efficient.

Architecture   The core WAP architecture was designed to use a minimal amount of bandwidth. Because of this Spartan design, WAP is able to operate over low-bandwidth wireless networks, as well as large, broadband networks. Further, it can function in any other wireless data network, making it a very popular protocol.

In Figure 10-11, you'll see how the different components of the WAP stack come together. The stack is divided into five layers. At the network layer are technologies we did not cover in this chapter—they are various kinds of wireless protocols used with cellular telephones.

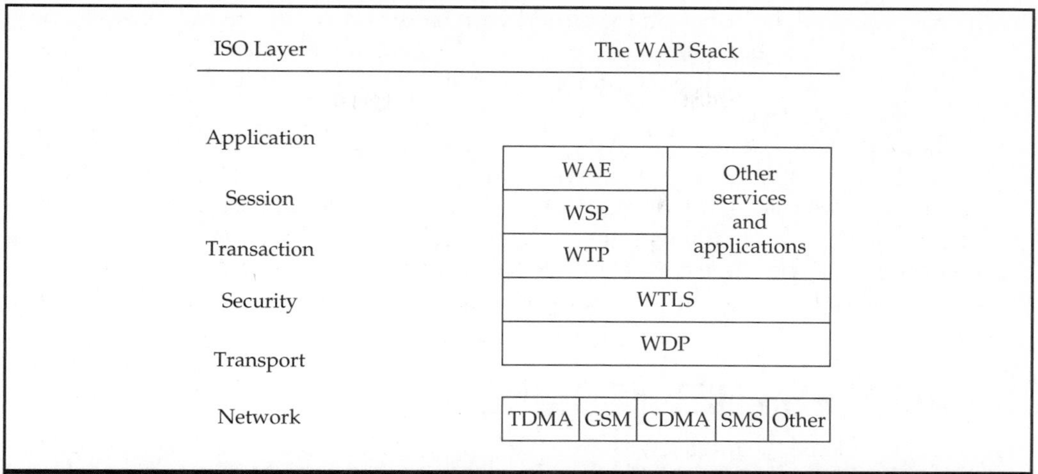

ISO Layer	The WAP Stack

Figure 10-11.   The WAP stack

The stack is quite similar—though not an exact layer-to-layer match—to the OSI Reference Model. For instance, the topmost layer—the Wireless Application Environment (WAE)—is equivalent to the application layer in the OSI Reference Model. Again, the WAP stack is not an exact match to the OSI Reference Model, but the similarities should be apparent. The column "ISO Layer" describes the function of the layer, while "The WAP Stack" names the specific protocol in use. The alphabet soup of WAP suite acronyms from Figure 10-11 is explained next:

▼   **Wireless Application Environment (WAE)**   The top of the protocol stack. The WAE consists of WML, WMLScript, and the Wireless Telephony Application Interface (WTAI), which serves as a link to telephony and network services.

■   **WAP Session Protocol (WSP)**   A session-layer protocol developed to support the exchange of data between applications. One WSP session normally consists of a series of request/response transactions that are performed by the WTP layer.

■   **WAP Transaction Protocol (WTP)**   A layer in the WAP suite that provides transaction support. Although WTP delivers information in much the same way that TCP does, it does it in a much more efficient manner.

■   **Wireless Transport Layer Security (WTLS)**   Similar to SHTTP because it offers an optional layer of security in the transport layer. WTLS can be viewed as a mechanism added to WAP that allows support for security transactions.

▲   **WAP Datagram Protocol (WDP)**   Represents the transport layer used by WAP. This layer is responsible for transmitting and receiving messages through any available bearer network.

In order for WAP information to be used with the Internet, information flowing both ways must pass through the WAP gateway. A WAP gateway is a piece of software that is normally located on a mobile operator's server and handles incoming requests from a WAP phone. Its job is compiling the WML pages into bytecode (WMLC), which can be understood by a WAP device. A WAP gateway is simply the link in the chain that makes sure everything your WAP device receives is in a format it can understand. Additionally, the gateway caches frequently used information, streamlining the process even further.

Internet-enabled cellular telephones are gaining in popularity every day, and as more consumers demand them, the need for WAP is only likely to increase. We've only scratched the surface of WAP, but it will be the protocol to watch in the next five years.

CISCO WIRELESS NETWORKING

Cisco didn't get to be the internetworking big boy by sitting around and hoping good fortune would hit the company on the head. Instead, Cisco has taken steps to stay on the cutting edge of internetworking technology. Some of the company's research and investments have paid off, while others have become costly lessons for the development team.

In this section, we'll look at how Cisco has embraced wireless technology and has groomed it as the technology for the new millennium. Then, we'll talk about the wireless networking products that Cisco has to offer.

Acquisitions

It should come as no surprise that Cisco has not only embraced wireless networking technology, but is also leading the charge. The company's recent acquisitions have come at a great time as the WLAN market heats up, and user demand for high-speed access to corporate networks is greater than ever.

Naturally, some of the market's heat is due to Cisco's own behavior. In March 2000, Cisco acquired wireless LAN vendor Aironet Wireless Communications for $799 million. In February 1999, Cisco and Motorola announced a $1 billion partnership to develop a framework for Internet-based wireless networks. To cement the standards over which wireless networks operate, in October 1999 Cisco formed a partnership with ten giant companies to drive standards for broadband wireless Internet services. In November of that year, Cisco introduced its first products based on those standards.

Then, in June 2003, Cisco bought Linksys, a company that manufactured wireless networking gear for home and small office applications. This not only got Cisco's foot in the door of the consumer market, but it also added Cisco as a major player in the multibillion-dollar home networking market.

These acquisitions afford Cisco the opportunity to rake in huge stacks of money as businesses and home network aficionados make the move to wireless connectivity, but it also helps posture Cisco to be in a good position for the development of "last mile" wireless products and services. That is, there may be a day when cable and DSL connections are supplanted by wireless connections between the consumer, the business, and their ISP. Cisco wants to be there when it happens.

Wireless Products

Cisco offers a full series of wireless products aimed at every stage of the wireless continuum. Its products start on the desktop in the form of client adapters in the back of PCs. From there, PCs can connect to a WLAN's access point. (Cisco offers two AP models, depending on what 802.11x standard you care to deploy.) Finally, if you need to connect LANs in different locations, but don't care to pay for a dedicated phone line, Cisco's line of wireless bridges can help make the connection.

Cisco Aironet Access Points

For construction of a WLAN, Cisco offers two access point models. The first is the Cisco Aironet 1100 Series Access Point. The access point uses the 802.11b or 802.11g protocols, which offer, largely, the same functionality. The difference between the two, however, comes down to the 802.11 standards used.

Cisco Aironet 1100 Access Point   The Aironet 1100 Access Point utilizes the Cisco Wireless Security Suite for beefy wireless security and Cisco IOS software for ease of use and configuration. The access point also offers a number of features, including virtual LANs (VLANs), Quality of Service (QoS), and proxy mobile Internet Protocol (IP). It also supports such basic Aironet features as hot-standby and load balancing, which allows an organization to deploy intelligent, reliable network services.

The Aironet 1100 can manage up to 16 VLANs, which allows an organization to segment its users into discrete LANs, establishing different LAN policies, services, security levels, and QoS levels.

The Aironet 1100 is managed using either the command line, or via an HTTP-based graphical user interface. The access point can be integrated with CiscoWorks solutions by using MIB I, MIB II, and SNMP for management.

The access point offers network security measures using the Cisco Wireless Security Suite. The suite is based on the 802.1x standard for port-based network access and takes advantage of the Extensible Authentication Protocol (EAP) for user-based authentication.

The Aironet 1100 Access Point sells for around $599.

The Cisco Aironet 1200 Access Point   The Cisco Aironet 1200 Access Point offers many of the same security, operation, and management functions that are afforded by the 1100 series. However, its biggest distinction is that the Aironet 1200 Access Point offers concurrent support for both 2.4-GHz and 5-GHz radios, thus allowing simultaneous operation of 802.11a/b/g networks.

The Cisco Aironet 1200 Access Point sells for around $1,259.

Cisco Aironet Wireless Bridges

Wireless bridges are used to connect two or more networks situated at different locations. For example, the bridges can be installed in different schools within a school district, and then used to connect each school's LAN into a larger network. Another application might be between floors in a building that is simply hard to wire. The benefit of a wireless bridge is that speeds greater than a T1 are achieved, but the organization need not pay for leased lines or install fiber optics.

Cisco offers two models of wireless bridges—the 350 and 1400 series.

The Cisco Aironet 350 Wireless Bridge   The Cisco Aironet 350 Wireless Bridge is used to extend your network into a hybrid of a WAN and a LAN. Though your network can be connected and configured like a LAN, bridges can be up to 25 miles apart, depending on what kind of antenna you install.

The Cisco Aironet 350 Wireless Bridge delivers 11-Mbps speeds and can be configured in point-to-point or point-to-multipoint configurations. Additionally, the bridge can be used so different locations can share a single Internet connection.

Depending on its configuration, the Cisco Aironet 350 Wireless Bridge sells from between $599 and $1,299.

The Cisco Aironet 1400 Wireless Bridge   Like its little brother, the 350 wireless bridge, the Cisco Aironet 1400 Wireless Bridge offers connectivity for campuses, metropolitan area networks, and any situation where wireless connectivity is needed between multiple buildings, or in hard-to-wire buildings.

The 1400 series differs from the 350, however, in that it supports the 802.11a standard, offering higher data rates than the 350.

Like other 802.11a devices, the trade-off for high speeds and operation in the 5-GHz band is a much shorter range than 802.11b/g deployments. The Aironet 1400 Wireless Bridge offers data rates of 54 Mbps and can be established for point-to-point links for up to 7.5 miles and point-to-multipoint connections for up to two miles. That range can be extended by using high-gain antennas and lowering the data rates.

The bridge also offers advanced features, like QoS and trunking of up to 24 Voice over IP (VoIP) circuits. The Cisco Aironet 1400 Wireless Bridge sells for around $4,999.

Client Adapters

Cisco's Aironet line offers three different types of client adapters: the Aironet 350 series (providing two different kinds of client adapters) and a 5-GHz, 802.11a adapter. All three cards use up to 128-bit encryption (in the United States) for added security.

The Aironet 350 adapters offer up to 11 Mbps of bandwidth and a range of up to 1,500 feet. The farther away you are from the access point, the slower your connection. This is illustrated in Figure 10-12.

The type of client adapter you have will depend on what kind of computer you have. Laptops and others with a PCMCIA slot will use the PC Card Client Adapter, while desktop and tower models will use the PCI/ISA Client Adapter.

PC Card Client Adapters   The Cisco Aironet 350 Series PC Card Client Adapter is a PCMCIA card radio module that plugs into any device equipped with a PCMCIA Type II or Type III slot. Because of their compactness, they can be used on a number of different machines, including the following:

▼ Desktop computers

■ Notebook computers

■ Personal digital assistants

▲ Pen-based computers

Additionally, the cards can be plugged into such peripherals as printers, adding them to your wireless network. What operating system you use will determine how complex your setup will be. If your operating system is Plug-and-Play–compliant, setup will be an easy matter. This adapter is ideal for hardware that is portable and easily moved around.

PCI/ISA Client Adapters   The PCI/ISA Client Adapter is suited for desktop and tower PCs when the actual case of the computer will have to be opened in order to install the card.

As with its streamlined, compact brother, installation is much simpler if you are installing it on a Plug-and-Play–compliant machine. Otherwise, you will be required to set DIP switches. This type of adapter is ideal for a permanent workstation that simply cannot get access to the wired network.

The Cisco Aironet 5-GHz Client Adapter   The Cisco Aironet 5-GHz Client Adapter is a PCMCIA device which is used with 802.11a networks, offering up to 54-Mbps speeds. This adapter is used in environments where the Aironet 1200 AP has been deployed.

Antennas

While wireless LANs and MANs afford the ability to connect without being leashed with Cat 5 cabling, there is still an issue of connectivity that you must consider when designing and deploying your wireless solution. In a wired network, you should spend some time

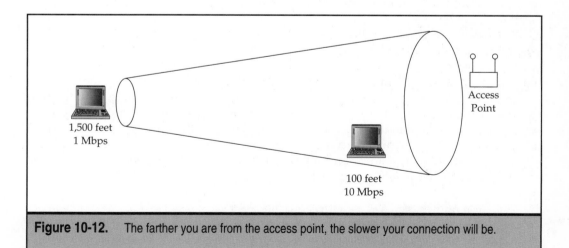

Figure 10-12.   The farther you are from the access point, the slower your connection will be.

thinking about what type of cabling is best for your system. Do you need shielded or unshielded cabling? How much cabling do you need? And so forth. However, simply because your wireless network isn't using cable doesn't mean you don't need to consider distances and interference issues.

Cisco offers a number of different antenna types for wireless deployments, either indoors or outdoors. The type of antenna you select will depend on a number of variables, including range and the device type to which it will be connected.

Table 10-2 compares antennas for Cisco access points.

Table 10-3 compares antennas for Cisco bridges.

Table 10-4 compares antennas for Cisco 5-GHz bridges.

The access points and bridges aren't the only components of a wireless network that can benefit from an antenna. Cisco also offers its AIR-ANT3351, which is a dipole antenna designed for client adapters. The antenna looks like the rabbit ear antennas on television sets (remember those?).

The Cisco Wireless IP Phone 7920

The preceding products all had wireless networking at their hearts. However, Cisco has merged wireless networking with IP telephony with its Cisco Wireless IP Phone 7920. The phone looks like a cellular telephone, but rather than access telephone service using a mobile telephone cell, it connects to an Aironet access point and serves as an IP telephone.

> **NOTE:** We'll get into more specifics on IP telephony in Chapter 11.

The wireless IP phone connects to an organization's IP network via an access point, utilizing the 802.11b protocol and Cisco CallManager. Cisco is marketing this product to organizations with mobile workforces, like hospitals, warehouses, universities, and retailers.

The wireless IP phone can utilize any 802.11b network, but voice quality is optimized when using a native Cisco network.

The problem with wireless IP phones is that—while there is a "cool" factor involved—they do not serve as multipurpose devices. That is, the wireless IP phone cannot communicate with cellular telephone networks. As such, the phone only works within the confines of the organization's wireless LAN and is not ideal for someone who wants a single phone that can be used in the office and while traveling. In the future, however, look for this to change as Cisco works with cellular phone vendors to smooth out this wrinkle.

Another potential upgrade for the next model of the wireless IP phone is the inclusion of a VPN client. That would make the IP phone usable at wireless hotspots.

Model	Physical Installation	Use	Indoor Range at 1 Mbps	Indoor Range at 11 Mbps	Beam Width
AIR-ANT5959	Omnidirectional ceiling mount	Indoor, ceiling mounted, used in high multi-path, dense cells	350 ft. (105 m)	130 ft. (45 m)	360° H, 80° V
AIR-ANT2012	Wall mount	Indoor and outdoor, applications, medium range	547 ft. (167 m)	167 ft. (51 m)	80° H, 55° V
AIR-ANT3213	Pillar mount omnidirectional	Indoor, medium range	497 ft. (151 m)	142 ft. (44 m)	360° H, 30° V
AIR-ANT2410Y-R	Yagi mast or wall mount	Indoor or outdoor directional antenna; used with access points or bridges	800 ft. (244 m)	230 ft. (70 m)	47° H, 55° V
AIR-ANT1728	Omnidirectional ceiling mount	Indoor, medium-range; normally mounted within drop ceilings	497 ft. (151 m)	142 ft. (44 m)	360° H, 38° V
AIR-ANT4941	2.2 dBi dipole antenna	Indoor, omni-directional	350 ft. (106 m)	130 ft. (40 m)	360° H, 65° V
AIR-ANT3549	Patch wall mount	Indoor, long-range and can also be used as a medium-range bridge antenna	700 ft. (213 m)	Access Point: 200 ft. (61 m) Bridge: 3,390 ft. (1,032 m)	60° H, 60° V
AIR-ANT1729	Patch wall mount	Indoor or outdoor, medium-range and can also be used as a medium-range bridge antenna	542 ft. (165 m)	Access Point: 155 ft. (47 m) Bridge: 1,900 ft. (580 m)	75° H, 65° V

Table 10-2.   Aironet Wireless Access Point Antennas

	AIR-ANT2506	AIR-ANT24120	AIR-ANT1949	AIR-ANT3338
Physical Installation	Omnidirectional, mast mount	High-gain omnidirectional, mast mount	Yagi mast mount	Dish
Use	Short-range, point-to-multipoint	Medium-range, point-to-multipoint	Medium-range, directional connections	Long-range, directional connections
Range at 2 Mbps	5,000 ft. (1,525 m)	4.6 miles (7.4 km)	6.5 miles (10.5 km)	25 miles (40 km)
Range at 11 Mbps	1,580 ft. (480 m)	1.4 miles (2.3 km)	2.0 miles (3.3 km)	11.5 miles (18.5 km)
Beam Width	360° H, 38° V	360° H, 7° V	30° H, 25° V	12.4° H, 12.4° V

Table 10-3.   Antennas for Aironet Wireless Bridges

	AIR-ANT58G9VOA-N	AIR-ANT58G10SSA-N	AIR-ANT58G28SDA-N
Physical Installation	Omnidirectional, mast mount	Sector antenna, mast mount	Dish antenna, mast mount
Use	Short-range, point-to-multipoint	Medium-range, point-to-point and point-to-multipoint	Long-range, directional
Range at 9 Mbps	8 miles (13 km)	8 miles (13 km)	23 miles (37 km)
Range at 54 Mbps	2 miles (3 km)	2 miles (3 km)	12 miles (19 km)
Beam Width	360° H, 6° V	60° H, 60° V	5.7° H, 6° V

Table 10-4.   Antennas for 5-GHz Wireless Aironet Bridges

Features of the wireless IP phone include

▼ Calling name and number display

■ Call forwarding

■ Call waiting

■ Call transfer

■ Three-way calling

■ Redial

■ Call hold

■ Call mute

■ Call park

■ Nine speed dials

■ Adaptive jitter buffer

■ Over-the-air firmware upgrades using Trivial File Transfer Protocol (TFTP)

■ SNMP Manager

■ DHCP- or static-configurable

▲ VLAN support

The wireless IP phone sells for about $595.

CONFIGURATION

Up to this point, we've talked about wireless basics, concepts, company positioning, and the handful of products Cisco has to offer. In this section, however, we'll take a more hands-on approach, and actually set up and configure a WLAN.

Given the relative complexity of setting up wired components, hooking up a wireless solution must be a nightmare, right? Happily, for installing, configuring, and using, Cisco's Aironet is as easy to use as any equipment that you'll ever have the pleasure of working with.

Access Points

When it comes to configuration, the Cisco Aironet APs are quite similar. They both follow the same basic means for setup and management. For this example, however, let's set up and configure an Aironet 1100 AP for its first use.

Before connecting and configuring your access point for the first time, it's necessary to gather a few items. The following list enumerates what's needed before configuring the Aironet 1100 AP:

▼ A system name for the AP
■ The wireless SSID for your wireless network
■ A unique IP address for the AP (unless you're connected to a DHCP server)
■ If your PC and AP are not on the same subnet, a default gateway address and subnet mask
■ If using SNMP, the SNMP community name and SNMP file attribute
▲ Your AP's MAC address (found on the bottom of the AP in a form such as 00-05-46-24-74-3c)

Once this information has been collected, you're ready to get started.

Resetting the AP to Original Settings

If, at any time during configuration, you need to reset your AP to its factory defaults, follow these steps:

1. Disconnect the AP from power.
2. Press and hold the MODE button while you reconnect power to the AP.
3. Keep the MODE button depressed until the status LED turns amber (about two seconds) then release the button.

The AP will be reset to factory defaults.

Obtaining an IP Address

The next step is to assign an IP address to the AP. There are two ways you can accomplish this. First, you can connect directly to the AP by using an Ethernet cable to connect from a PC's NIC to the AP, and then set the IP address, locally.

However, the ideal way to set the AP's IP address is to utilize a DHCP server. This will automatically assign an IP address to the AP. Once the IP address is assigned, you'll need to identify the IP address. This can be accomplished in one of two ways:

▼ Query the DHCP server using the AP's MAC address. This will identify the AP's IP address. Again, the MAC address is located on a label on the bottom of the AP.

▲ Shipped with Cisco Aironet APs is a utility called Cisco IP Setup Utility (IPSU). This tool, which is compatible with Windows operating systems, can discover the IP address of the AP.

Connecting Locally

In the event you are using the AP as a repeater, or to extend the range of your WLAN (where the AP won't be plugged into the wired LAN), you can connect directly to the AP using Cat 5 Ethernet cable.

NOTE: You do not need a crossover cable to make this connection. You can use either a regular length of Ethernet cabling, or a crossover cable.

If your Aironet 1100 has never been connected to a DHCP server and has never obtained an IP address, the factory default IP address is 10.0.0.1. When the AP is set up, it becomes a DHCP server of its own, doling out IP addresses (in the range of 10.0.0.11 to 10.0.0.30) to PCs connected to the AP's Ethernet port and wireless client devices configured to use no SSID, where no security settings are enabled.

Connecting to the AP using a PC is fairly straightforward:

1. Ensure that the PC you're using for the connection is set up to obtain an IP address automatically, or assign it an IP address somewhere in the range of 10.0.0.2 to 10.0.0.10.

2. Connect the PC to the AP using Cat 5 Ethernet cable.

3. Turn on the AP's power.

4. Configure your AP according to the steps in the next section, "Initial Settings."

Once the AP has been configured, disconnect the PC. If you are going to connect the AP to your wired LAN, do so now.

Initial Settings

Once you connect to the AP and assign its IP address, you can perform an initial configuration using the AP's Express Setup page. This page is accessed by using your Internet browser (Microsoft Internet Explorer 5.*x* and later or Netscape Navigator 4.*x* and later are recommended). Follow these steps to open the Express Setup page:

1. Enter the AP's IP address in the browser line and press ENTER. This calls up a username and password window.

2. Skip the Username field and enter **Cisco** in the password field. The password is case-sensitive, so make sure you enter Cisco and not CISCO or cisco.

3. The Summary Status page appears, as shown in Figure 10-13.

4. Click Express Setup. The Express Setup screen appears, like the one in Figure 10-14.

5. At this point, you can configure a number of settings. Table 10-5 lists the settings and a description of each.

6. Click Apply to save your settings.

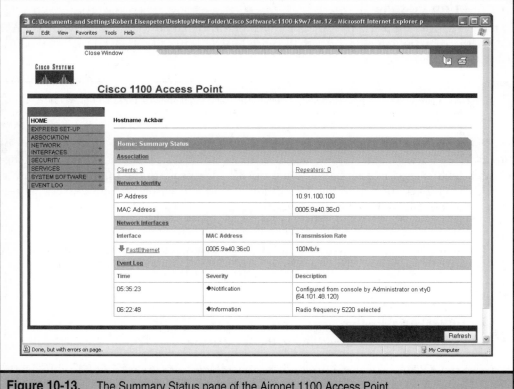

Figure 10-13. The Summary Status page of the Aironet 1100 Access Point

NOTE: If you suddenly lose your connection, don't worry. Did you change your IP address? If so, navigate to the new IP address you indicated for the AP and continue about your business.

This establishes a basic level of functionality for your Aironet 1100 AP. You can tweak it more by checking your owner's manual and making requisite adjustments.

Clients

Configuring an Aironet 350 client is refreshingly easy. In essence, all you have to do is plug in the card, load a small piece of software, and you're off. The client adapters come in two flavors:

▼ PCI/ISA Client Adapter
▲ PC Card Client Adapter

The process is a bit more complex for the PCI/ISA Client Adapter, yet it is still a straightforward setup procedure.

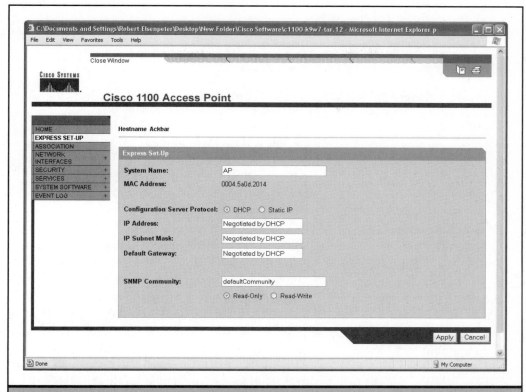

Figure 10-14. The Express Setup page of the Aironet 1100 Access Point contains a multitude of configuration options.

PC Card Client Adapters

Installation of a PC Card Client Adapter is relatively straightforward. Merely plug the PC card in an open PCMCIA port, install the driver, and you're done.

To install the driver, insert the CD-ROM that came with the card and follow the onscreen directions for installation. If you are using a non-Plug-and-Play operating system (like a musty old copy of Windows NT), you'll be asked to enter an available IRQ number. Also, you will be required to set an IP address for your computer. If you are using a DHCP server, this can be set automatically; otherwise, this information will have to be gathered before installation. Near the end of installation, you'll be asked for the card's Service Set Identifier (SSID) and your computer's client name.

NOTE: The SSID is a unique, case-sensitive identifier that is attached to selected packets sent out over the wireless network. Nodes associating to the device must use the same SSID or their association requests will be ignored.

Setting	Description
System Name	The name of the system. It helps identify the AP on your network.
Configuration Server Protocol	This is where you indicate how the AP's IP address is assigned: DHCP or static.
IP Address	If you are entering the AP's IP address statically, do so here. If the IP address is assigned dynamically, leave this field blank.
IP Subnet Mask	Enter the IP subnet mask so the IP address can be recognized on the LAN. If you are using DHCP, leave this field blank.
Default Gateway	Enter the default gateway IP address. If you are using DHCP, leave this field blank.
Radio Service Set ID (SSID)	Enter the case-sensitive SSID of your wireless network.
Broadcast SSID in Beacon	This setting allows devices that do not specify an SSID to associate with your AP. Check either "Yes" or "No."
Role in Radio Network	Select the role this AP serves in your radio network. Is it the AP connected to the wired LAN or is it a repeater, not connected to the LAN?
Optimize Radio Network For	This setting allows you to fine-tune your AP for specific functionality. There are three radio buttons: *Throughput,* which maximizes the amount of data the AP can handle (expect some range reduction, however); *Range,* which maximizes the range of the AP (expect throughput to suffer); and *Custom,* which allows you to tweak your own balance of range and throughput.
Aironet Extensions	You may want to enable this setting if yours is an all Cisco Aironet native wireless network.
SNMP Community	If your network uses SNMP, enter the community name here and indicate the attributes of the SNMP data (read-only or read-write).

Table 10-5. Configuration Options on the Express Setup Page

The PCI/ISA Client Adapter

Installing the PCI/ISA Client Adapter is a bit more involved since you will have to open the computer case to install the card. If your operating system is Plug-and-Play–compliant, the remaining part of the setup process is extremely easy—just install the card and boot up the computer. However, if you are installing the client adapter to a non-Plug- and-Play– compliant machine, you will have to make the following adjustments.

Based on the I/O Base Address and IRQ level information garnered when you in- stalled the driver for NT, set your dip switches in accordance with the values in Tables 10-6 and 10-7.

Once the DIP switches have been set and the card installed, attach the included dipole antenna and power up the computer. Since you've already installed the driver, the com- puter is set up and ready to go.

> **NOTE:**   There have been huge advances in wireless support under Windows XP. If you find yourself spending a lot of time trying to make wireless hardware and software work in older versions of Win- dows, you really should consider upgrading—if only to save a ton of time.

Client Utilities

Whereas the access point is managed via the command line, terminal, or browser inter- face, clients are managed with three utilities.

The Aironet Client Utility   The Aironet Client Utility (ACU) is the main means of configur- ing the wireless client. Its functions and features are outlined in Table 10-8.

The Client Encryption Manager   The Client Encryption Manager (CEM) is used to set up and manage security for the client. This feature is explained in more detail in the next section.

DIP Switch		Base Address (HEX)
5	4	
On	On	140
On	Off	180
Off	On	300
Off	Off	340

Table 10-6.   I/O Base Address DIP Switch Settings

DIP Switch			Interrupt (IRQ) Level
3	2	1	
On	On	On	5
On	On	Off	7
On	Off	On	9
On	Off	Off	10
Off	On	On	11
Off	On	Off	12
Off	Off	On	14
Off	Off	Off	15

Table 10-7. Interrupt (IRQ)-Level DIP Switch Settings

Feature	Function
Load New Firmware	The firmware located in the card's flash memory can be updated using this command.
Edit Properties	ACU allows you to change the configuration of your client adapter.
Statistics	This screen shows current statistics, including such details as packets received, uptime, and errors.
Status	This screen shows the current status of the client adapter. The rate at which the status is updated can be customized for more or less frequent testing.
Site Survey	This screen conducts a test that will deliver information about some of the most critical components of your wireless connection. Such statistics include transmission power, antenna location, packet size, and the interface.
Radio Off/On	The transceiver can be turned on or off using this setting.

Table 10-8. Configuration Options for a Cisco Aironet Client Adapter

The Link Status Meter The Link Status Meter (LSM) gives a graphical representation of the quality of the signal between the access point and the client. Figure 10-15 shows what this application looks like in action. Signal strength is displayed along the vertical axis of the display, while signal quality is shown along the horizontal axis. It's fun (and informative) to walk around the home or office with a wireless device and see the signal strength change.

Security

Beaming network data between the access point and client is not, inherently, secure. To enable the Aironet's encryption features, it's a simple matter of setting up a code key on both the client and the access point.

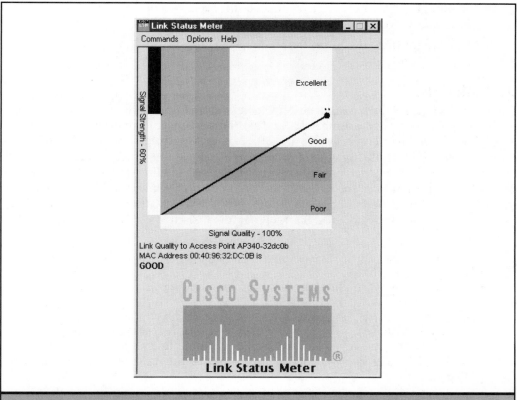

Figure 10-15. The Link Status Meter shows your signal strength and quality.

Both devices use a WEP key to encrypt and decrypt data. Some models of Aironet access points that have no WEP capabilities at all. There are others that include 40-bit encryption. Other models—sold and used only in the United States—include the beefier "128-bit" security.

NOTE: Consider that "out of the box" WEP encryption can be cracked using freely available tools like Kismet and AirSnort. While you should still employ WEP in most cases, you should also consider stronger security methods (described next and in Chapter 9) if you have valuable data to protect.

The access point and client can maintain three levels of security:

▼ **No Encryption**   Requires that the access point and client will use no data encryption

■ **Optional**   Allows clients to connect to the access point either with or without data encryption

▲ **Full Encryption**   Requires the client to use data encryption when connecting to the access point

User Interface

The screen used to set up and manage WEP looks similar for both the client and the access point. They both contain the same fields and ask for the same information; the only difference (as you can see in Figures 10-16 and 10-17) is that the access point's WEP screen is browser-based (Figure 10-16), while the client WEP screen is a window (Figure 10-17).

This screen can be opened on the access point by choosing Encryption Manager under the Security selection from the menu at the left of the browser screen. On the client, the stand-alone utility, Client Encryption Manager (CEM), is installed from the setup CD-ROM. It is accessed by choosing Start | Programs | Cisco Systems, Inc | Client Encryption Manager.

Settings

To set up and manage your client/access point data encryption, adjust the settings as follows:

▼ **Transmit with Key**   These are the buttons you click to select which WEP key you will use. Only one key can be selected at any time, and all keys can be used to receive data. The key you choose must be set before it can be selected as the Transmit key.

■ **Encryption Key**   These are the fields in which you can type in the WEP keys. To set the WEP keys on each device, you must select a hexadecimal key (including 0–9, a–f, and A–F). For 40-bit encryption, the key is ten hexadecimal digits long; 128-bit encryption requires 26 hexadecimal digits.

NOTE: It is vitally important that the keys in both the access point and the client be identical. If they are not, the association between them will be lost.

▲ **Key Size** Use this to select either a 40- or 128-bit WEP. If "Not Set" is selected, then no value will be set.

Once you've set the appropriate values, data encryption is not yet ensured. In order to finally enable the service, you must go to Properties in the Client Utility. Under the RF Network tab, select the Enable WEP check box. This is shown in the lower-left corner of Figure 10-18.

802.1*x*

Supplementing encryption as a means of wireless security is the 802.1*x* control protocol. 802.1*x* utilizes a number of authentication algorithms based on the Extensible Authentication Protocol (EAP). EAP was originally developed for dial-up PPP sessions as a way to

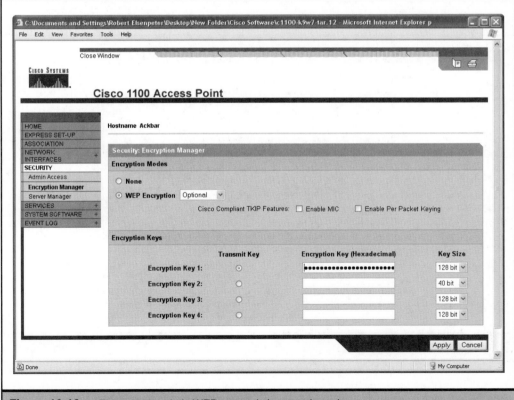

Figure 10-16. The access point's WEP screen is browser-based.

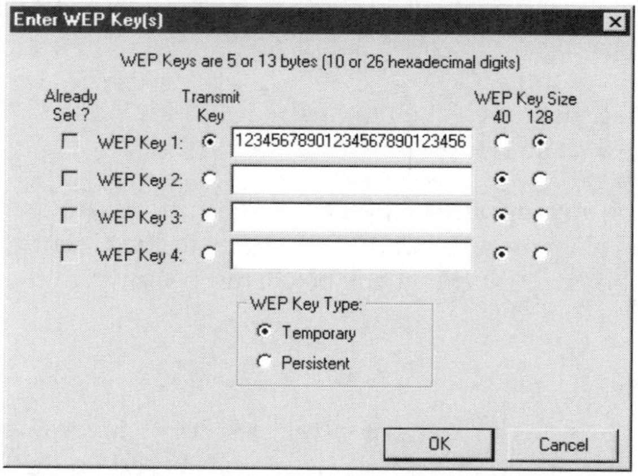

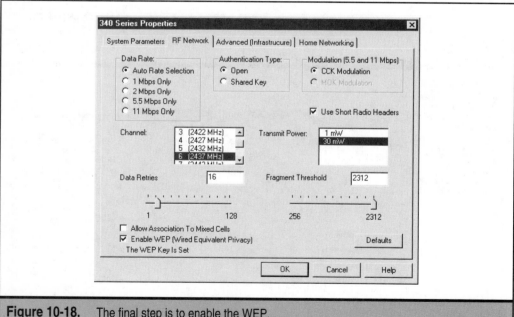

Figure 10-17. The client's WEP is managed with a security utility.

Figure 10-18. The final step is to enable the WEP.

replace PAP and CHAP authentication methods. EAP uses a flexible framework to support a number of methods of authentication, including

▼ Passwords

■ One-time passwords

■ SecurID tokens

▲ Digital certificates

In essence, EAP provides an envelope for the sender and receiver to handle authentication. What is put inside that envelope depends on the authentication method chosen.

NOTE: The wireless industry and users alike have been very concerned about the notoriously weak wireless security standards currently in use. As a result, standards that dramatically improve wireless security are being drafted and implemented as we speak. If you have wireless networks, this is one area where you should stay as current as possible.

The IEEE 802.1x standard is used to create a framework for LAN station authentication. Wireless devices and access points exchange EAP to carry out authentication, negotiate security parameters, and deliver session keys.

EAP messages are sent to a back-end authentication server (like a RADIUS server). The server then determines the appropriate authentication method and tells the client to present the requisite credentials to prove its identity. Then, based on the response, the station is either accepted or rejected onto the LAN.

Cisco's Aironet gear supports 802.1x and a number of authentication algorithms. These algorithms include

▼ Lightweight EAP (LEAP)

■ EAP-Transport Layer Security (EAP-TLS)

▲ Protected EAP (PEAP)

802.1x is a port-level access control protocol that exists between the authentication algorithms and the LAN (as shown in Figure 10-19).

802.1x translates messages from the authentication algorithm into the correct frame format of the LAN access types. Since we're talking about wireless networks, the access type is 802.11, but it can also be used to authenticate Ethernet (802.3) or Token Ring (802.5).

The choice of which authentication algorithm is used and how the key is managed is left up to the EAP authentication type. For instance, LEAP uses a per-user, per-session encryption key to supplement WEP-based encryption.

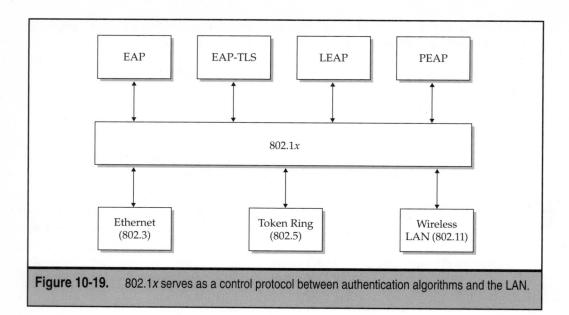

Figure 10-19. 802.1x serves as a control protocol between authentication algorithms and the LAN.

The 802.1x protocol uses a component called the Port Authentication Entity (PAE) on three components of the wireless network:

▼ The client

■ The AP

▲ The back-end authentication server

Let's follow how authentication occurs in LEAP, EAP-TLS, and PEAP authentication methods.

LEAP LEAP is beneficial because it authenticates both ways. That is, the network has to prove its mettle to the client to ensure that a rogue AP isn't trying to connect to the client. This is known as *mutual authentication*.

When a client tries to connect to the wireless network, a message is sent through the AP to the authentication server. The authentication server sends a challenge back to the client. The client runs the challenge through the LEAP algorithm, mixes the challenge and user password together and returns a value, through the AP, to the authentication server. The authentication server compares the returned value against what it believes the value to be. If the two match, the server sends a "success" message, allowing the client on the network.

The client now performs its own test, challenging the authentication server to authenticate the AP, and following the same method the authentication server used. When both devices are satisfied that they are authenticated, the authentication server generates a WEP key for that particular session, sending it to the AP. The LEAP client then uses that WEP key.

EAP-TLS   Like LEAP, EAP-TLS utilizes mutual authentication. Its basic handshaking process is similar to LEAP, but it uses digital certificates instead of usernames and passwords.

When a client requests access to the wireless network, the authentication server sends a server certificate. The client must also have a certificate, signed by an in-house or third-party certificate authority that has been authorized by the network administrator.

The client then sends its own certificate, for the sake of mutual authentication. Based on the certificate values, the EAP-TLS algorithm can generate dynamic WEP keys for the session and the authentication server can send the WEP key to the client.

Digital certificates are very secure as forgery is unheard of. However, it is more complicated and expensive than deploying a username and password authentication system.

PEAP   The new kid on the 802.1x authentication block is PEAP. Utilizing PEAP, the handshaking process between the client and authentication server is encrypted and, again, mutual authentication is required.

The client uses EAP-TLS to authenticate the server and forge a TLS-encrypted channel between the server and the client. The client uses another EAP algorithm to validate the server. The key here is that the challenge and response takes place across an encrypted channel. This ensures that the exchange will not be intercepted and exploited.

We covered quite a bit in this chapter. Even then, wireless networking is still a very young technology. Though impressive feats with wireless are possible today, it's going to be really cool to see where Cisco and the rest of the wireless community take wireless in the future.

PART III

Cisco Business Solutions

CHAPTER 11

Cisco IP Contact Center

A t the core of Cisco's offerings are its popular routers, switches, and servers. This is the meat and potatoes of Cisco's internetworking empire. Given the changing face of business in the Internet world, Cisco is staying on the cutting edge of technology and networking needs by embracing current business technologies and investing in what they think will be popular technologies of the future.

In this chapter, we take a closer look at Cisco's IP contact products and services, including Voice over IP (VoIP) and Intelligent Call Management (ICM) solution.

VoIP

If music, video, and other multimedia content can be shot across internetworks, why not conduct telephone conversations? It probably comes as no surprise that Cisco has a whole line of products to enable VoIP interaction.

One of the biggest benefits to VoIP is something that will appeal to everyone across your organization: cost savings. Consider the benefits reaped by the Minnesota Department of Labor and Industry. The department's phone system was cobbled together from five proprietary systems. After exploring their replacement options, in the fall of 2000 they decided to pursue a VoIP solution. The department installed a VoIP system with 300 phones at a cost of $435,000.

After three years, the benefits have been enormous. The department has cut their monthly phone bill by more than half—from $21,700 to less than $10,000. In 2003, seven more locations were added to the department's VoIP deployment and, currently, more branches of the Minnesota government are considering a ride on the VoIP bandwagon.

It isn't just the State of Minnesota embracing VoIP. According to an Information Week survey of 300 business-technology executives, more than 80 percent responded that their organizations are using (29 percent), testing (18 percent), or planning to deploy (34 percent) a VoIP solution. Sixty-three percent of those using VoIP say they're going to spend more on VoIP in 2004 than they did in 2003.

Further, the Gartner research firm estimates that VoIP telephony shipments will grow from 56 percent of the market, valued at $2 billion up to 97 percent of the market, valued at $4.7 billion in 2007.

As popular as it's becoming, VoIP isn't always a perfect way to get rid of your organization's desktop telephones, but it is a viable technology that is rapidly evolving. There is a good chance that you will, if you have not done so already, use VoIP to communicate with a branch office, or even an old high school friend, living on the other side of the continent. Heck, with companies like Nuvio (www.nuvio.com) selling residential VoIP in more than 24 states at the time of this writing, it's quite possible that you will have VoIP equipment in your home in the not-too-distant future.

In this section, we delve into the issues and technology surrounding VoIP, and then look at Cisco's solutions and equipment to deliver telephony across IP networks.

Introduction

One of the early promises of the Internet was the prospect of making free long-distance telephone calls. In theory, calls would be encoded by one computer, transmitted through the Internet, and then decoded by the receiver. Further, there would only be the need for one type of network—the Internet Protocol (IP) network. This would do away with the need for both dedicated voice and data networks. In practice, however, this technology had a long way to go.

The main problem was one of resources. In order for the call to go through, packets had to be received in the correct order, or Internet phone calls would come through as gibberish. Too often, packets were received in a random order, making the calls hard to understand and revealing the system to be something other than the panacea all had hoped for.

How It Works

Just what happens when you make a VoIP call? Let's take a look at the process, as shown in Figure 11-1, following the steps by the numbers:

1. The receiver is picked up and a dial tone is generated by the Private Branch Exchange (PBX).

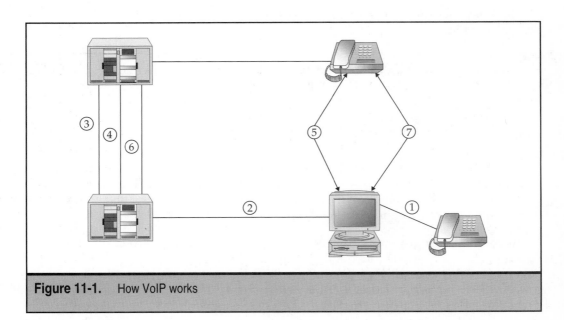

Figure 11-1.   How VoIP works

NOTE: A PBX is a device located within an organization that routes incoming telephone calls to the desired extension. It also supplies additional features like voicemail or call forwarding. We'll talk more about PBXs throughout this chapter.

2. The user dials the telephone number. (The numbers are stored by the PBX.)

3. Once enough digits are entered to match a configured destination pattern, the telephone number is mapped to the IP host. This step is accomplished via the dial plan mapper. At this point, the IP host has made a connection to either the destination telephone number or a PBX that will complete the call to its destination.

4. A transmission and reception channel are established when the session application runs the H.323 session protocol. (We talk about H.323 in more detail later in this chapter.) If a PBX is managing the call, it forwards the call to the destination telephone. If Resource Reservation Protocol (RSVP) has been configured, the RSVP reservations are made.

NOTE: RSVP clears a path across the routers between the two telephones. RSVP is one way to achieve the desired quality of service over an IP network.

5. The codecs are enabled for both ends of the connection and the conversation proceeds using RTP/UDP/IP as the protocol stack.

NOTE: Codecs are hardware or software devices that translate analog voice signals into IP packets that can be transmitted across the network.

6. Any call-progress indicators (or other types of signals that can be carried in-band) are connected through the voice path once the end-to-end audio channel has been established.

7. As soon as the phone call has ended (once either end hangs up), the RSVP reservations are torn down (if RSVP is used), the connection is broken, and the session ends. At this point, each end becomes idle, waiting for an "off hook" signal or an incoming IP phone call.

In addition to transporting the packets, the IP network must also ensure that your conversation is transported across the media in a manner that delivers the best voice quality. If packets are received in a different order than how they're sent out, then the conversation will be garbled and, ultimately, useless. Finally, the IP telephony packet stream might have to be converted by a gateway to another format. This is necessary for the sake of interoperation with either a different IP-based multimedia system or if the phone call is terminating on the conventional public telephone system.

Building VoIP Networks

There are three basic types of VoIPs. They are designed around the user's specific needs and suit a specific market.

▼ **Simple toll bypass** The most basic, straightforward use for VoIP is using it to make telephone calls without having to use the public switched telephone network (PSTN). This is ideal if you just want to use IP to transport calls between branch offices within the corporate network. The design requires minimal change to existing PBX, cabling, and handset infrastructures; is relatively easy to develop; and has no PSTN integration issues to worry about.

■ **Total IP telephony** This design relegates your existing voice systems to the dumpster. No longer will desktops have conventional telephone handsets—instead, they're traded in on IP telephones that plug into Ethernet ports. You'll use LAN servers to provide the majority of the features your PBX now provides. This is the Holy Grail of VoIP and not a journey to begin on a whim.

▲ **IP-enabled PBXs** This solution isn't as gutsy as total IP telephony, but you still get a mélange of functionality. You don't have to change the existing cabling or handsets, but you will upgrade the PBXs so that your organization's core systems can speak IP telephony protocols. PBX users will be able to communicate with other IP telephony users, but the limitation is that your PBXs will have to rely on IP telephony gateways to communicate with the conventional, public telephone system.

The easiest solution to implement is simple toll bypass, so let's take a closer look at how that works, and then we'll add some of the elements from the other two design concepts.

Simple Toll Bypass

VoIP toll bypass solutions are reasonably easy to implement. Before we start making changes, let's take a closer look at what you're likely to be starting with. Figure 11-2 shows two interconnected PBXs.

A PBX is a device located within an organization that connects phone calls coming in on trunk lines from the PSTN to their designated extensions. PBXs are also able to switch calls to extensions located on other connected PBXs. Most PBX interconnections are digital, and might even be T1 circuits, which are dedicated for the sole purpose of interconnecting PBXs. Typically, however, they are channels set up on a Time Division Multiplexing (TDM) backbone. The TDM divides bandwidth between voice and data.

The problem in having both dedicated voice and multiservice TDM lines is that bandwidth must be permanently allocated for each voice circuit, even though the voice circuits are not always in use. A better way to manage resources is to split traffic into packets so that all traffic can be commingled and use bandwidth more efficiently. This is where VoIP makes its entrance.

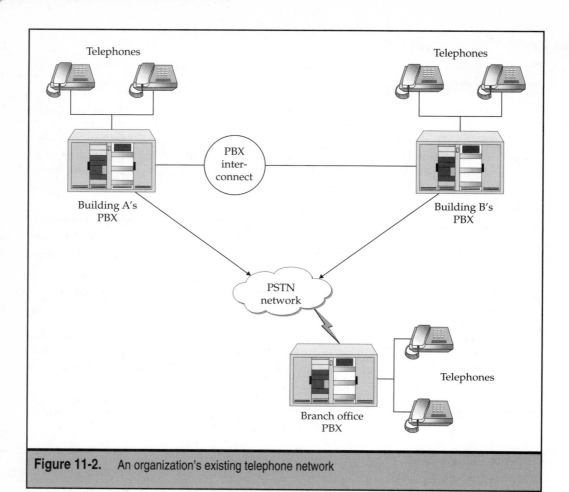

Figure 11-2.   An organization's existing telephone network

The easiest way to deploy a VoIP solution is to simply unplug the lines to the PBX and plug them into a separate unit that converts the voice signaling and transport into an IP format. These units are referred to as a *VoIP relay* and connect into a router for transport over an IP network, as illustrated in Figure 11-3.

You do not, however, have to buy a separate VoIP relay and router. Several Cisco routers (1760, 2600, and 3600, for instance) provide direct PBX interfaces. But if you want a separate VoIP relay and router, you can certainly configure your VoIP solution that way.

No matter which route you choose, there are three basic design concerns you must address.

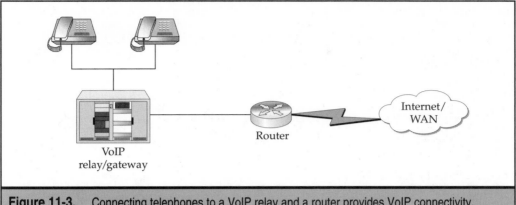

Figure 11-3.   Connecting telephones to a VoIP relay and a router provides VoIP connectivity.

▼   Make sure that VoIP gateway will relay sufficient signaling information to support the features in use on the PBXs.

■   Make sure you know which standards your solution is using. Even though some products promise H.323 compliance, there are still a number of proprietary schemes.

▲   Make sure you figure out how you're going to supply the necessary voice quality. This issue comes down to a combination of which encoding scheme you use and the QoS capabilities of your network. This is so important that we talk about it in more depth later in this chapter and QoS has its own, dedicated discussion in Chapter 7.

VoIP Solution

The toll bypass system we discussed earlier is a straightforward, cost-saving scenario that you can hook up with little or no headache. But if you want to get adventuresome, consider the design in Figure 11-4.

In a full IP telephony solution, all end-user devices (PCs and phones) are connected to the LAN. The telephone that users will come to know and love can be one of two types:

▼   Hardware IP phones that look and act just like regular telephones, except they are plugged into the network

▲   Software IP phones that rely on client software running on the PC

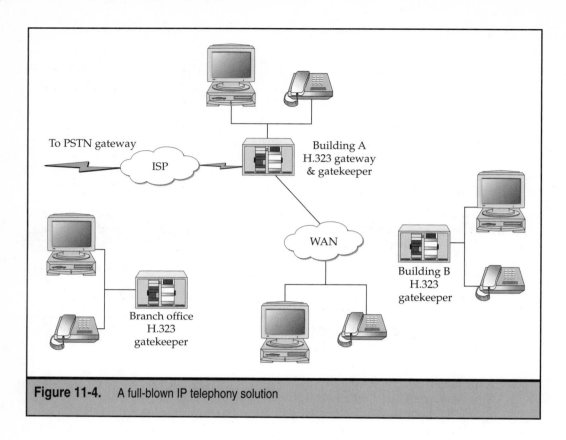

Figure 11-4.   A full-blown IP telephony solution

Consider Figure 11-5. If, for instance, Keith in Custodial Services wants to call Pat in Accounting, he picks up the IP phone and they communicate across LAN A using an IP connection. However, if Keith needs to order a drum of floor wax, his call goes through the network using IP connection B, and then is linked to a gateway. The *gateway* is a device that links VoIP calls to the public phone network.

Finally, there are servers that support IP telephony. These servers provide both basic call setup functions as well as the advanced features users have come to expect from traditional PBXs, like voicemail, hold, and call forwarding. Let's take a closer look at IP phones, gateways, and servers.

IP Telephones   At its simplest, you can set up an IP telephone by plugging in a speaker and a microphone to the PC. However, people come to expect their telephones to look and feel like telephones. As we mentioned earlier, there are hardware and software IP phones. That "telephone feel" can be accomplished with a telephone that speaks IP and can be plugged directly into a switch (a hardware phone). Alternatively, users can simply plug a specially designed handset into their PC to take advantage of the software solution.

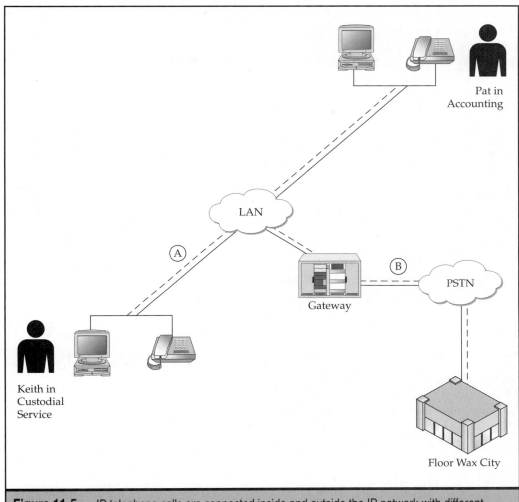

Figure 11-5.   IP telephone calls are connected inside and outside the IP network with different pieces of equipment.

Each of these phones offers the same sorts of features that a telephone connected to a PBX offers. Naturally, there are disadvantages to these solutions. Hardware IP phones will need a jack on the switch (watch out, you can run out of connections fast), and they also need their own power supply. Some switches, like the Cisco Catalyst 6500, provide power.

These pitfalls can be avoided by using a software-based IP telephone. This can be done by either plugging a telephone into a serial or USB port, or you can plug a plain old desktop analog telephone into a PC card or external adapter.

If you decide to use a software-based IP telephone (aka softphone), you must also get client software that can support IP telephony. The software can either be a stand-alone product, standards-based (make sure you buy one that matches your phone's standards), or it can be part of a package, like Microsoft's NetMeeting.

There are three issues you should keep in mind when selecting an IP telephone:

▼ When considering hardware IP telephones, make sure that the phone won't limit your ability to integrate with the desktop environment.

■ Make sure that the phones support appropriate codec and signaling standards.

▲ Make sure that the phone and your network will be able to share QoS priorities.

Gateways   Gateways serve as interfaces between PSTN telephone calls and IP telephony. PSTN consists of two separate networks—one for transporting the voice conversations and one for transporting signaling information (using the SS7 protocol).

Let's pause for a moment to consider some of the basics of the public telephone system that will be important to know for the sake of understanding gateway functionality:

▼ **Central Office**   Where local phone lines first connect into the public network

■ **Central Office Switch**   The local switch in the Central Office

▲ **Tandem Switch**   Switches that interconnect between Central Office Switches in a local area network

A Central Office Switch connects both voice and SS7 signaling trunks, which connect to Signal Transfer Points (STPs). STPs are the message switches that route SS7 signaling information. These two trunks are kept separate because it facilitates the setup and teardown of voice calls. It also streamlines the network during periods of peak usage. SS7 is also necessary for the provisioning of 800 and 888 numbers and makes such perks as call forwarding, caller-ID, and last-call return possible.

Using SS7 is not necessary for an IP telephony to PSTN Gateway connection, as long as there is in-band signaling on voice trunks, but this provides only for a telephone call from an IP telephony device to a telephone on the PSTN network. If additional functionality (like call forwarding and the like) is desired, another gateway is needed: the SS7 to IP Telephony Gateway.

Servers   A basic IP telephone call occurs when one IP telephone connects to another. However, there are a number of "behind the scenes" functions that must be managed, including such features as call routing and billing. These functions cannot be performed by either of the end users; rather they must be performed by an IP telephony server (or several servers, depending on the size of the network). Under the H.323 protocol, this set of functions is performed by a gatekeeper. (We'll explain H.323 and the gatekeeper in more detail later in this chapter in the section titled "H.323.") Gatekeepers may also include support for such extras as voice messaging and voice conferencing in the same IP telephony server.

Encoding

When you speak into a telephone, you cause air molecules to move, which bounce off a microphone and are converted into an electrical signal, which is sent across the network where it vibrates the speaker on the other telephone. Those vibrations move air molecules, which complete the transformation from sound into electricity and then back into sound.

With VoIP, another layer must be added to this process. It isn't enough for the electrical signal to be transported; it must be converted from an analog to a digital format. This conversion is exactly like the difference between records (remember them?) and compact discs.

An analog wave is pictured in Figure 11-6, in which A represents what sound looks like when it first moves through a microphone. Next, (B) the wave is sampled at regular intervals, the signal is sampled, and the numbers (C) converted into a series of zeroes and ones. This process is called *voice encoding* and the piece of software or device used to encode (then later to decode) the signal is called a *codec*. Obviously, the more frequent the sampling interval, the better the sound quality. However, the more frequent the sampling interval, the more bandwidth will be devoured.

A good rule of thumb to use when sampling is to sample at a rate at least 2.2 times the maximum frequency represented in the underlying signal. The human voice uses frequencies ranging from 300 Hz to about 4 KHz. For the sake of simple math, we can use a sampling rate of 8,000 times per second. If, for each sample, we use 8 bits to represent the signal strength, then we'll need a bandwidth of 8 bits, 8,000 times per second, or 64 Kbps. This is called Pulse Code Modulation (PCM) and is the most popular way to encode voice on public telephone networks.

Codecs provide varying qualities of speech. This quality is not a finite amount, but is rather subjective. What one person might think is perfectly clear speech might sound too muddy and electronic to someone else. The way to make the subjective world of sound

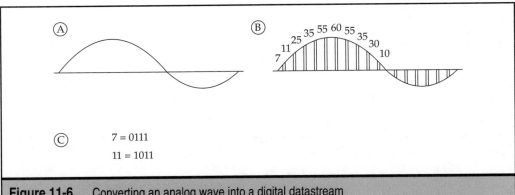

Figure 11-6.   Converting an analog wave into a digital datastream

quality more objective is through the use of the mean opinion score (MOS). Like a group taste testing a new kind of ketchup, listeners are brought together to judge the quality of a voice sample, then they rate the sound quality on a scale of 1 to 5, with 1 being "bad" and 5 being "excellent." These scores are then averaged to provide the MOS for that sample.

Table 11-1 compares the different codecs, their bit rates, compression delay, and MOS rankings.

In Table 11-1, the bit rate is used to describe the amount of data sent per second. Remember, the larger this value, the better the overall quality. You'll notice that the code with the highest bit rate—G.711—rated the highest MOS score.

Compression Method	Bit Rate (Kbps)	Compression Delay (ms)	MOS Score
G.711 Pulse Code Modulation (PCM)	64	0.75	4.1
G.726 Adaptive Differential Pulse Code Modulation (ADPCM)	32	1	3.85
G.728 Low-Delay Code Excited Linear Prediction (LD-CELP)	16	3 to 5	3.61
G.729 Conjugate-Structure Algebraic-Code-Excited Linear-Prediction (CS-ACELP)	8	10	3.92
G.729 x 2 Encodings	8	10	3.27
G.729 x 3 Encodings	8	10	2.68
G.729a CS-ACELP	8	10	3.7
G.723.1 Multi-Pulse, Multi-Level Quantization (MP-MLQ)	6.3	30	3.9
G.723.1 Algebraic Code Excited Linear Prediction (ACELP)	5.3	30	3.65

Table 11-1.   Codec Comparison

Second is the compression delay. This is the amount of time it takes, in milliseconds, for the signal to be encoded. This is an important factor to consider when selecting a codec, because lengthy encoding times will cause conversations to be difficult to understand.

There is no "best" codec to use. Depending on your need, you will have to balance these variables to get the best solution. Even though G.711 has the highest MOS score, it also consumes the most amount of bandwidth. G.723 consumes ten times less bandwidth than G.711 and is a close third in terms of MOS score. However, it takes 40 times longer to compress the signal with G.723 than G.711. These are all balls you'll have to juggle when selecting a codec for your VoIP solution.

Quality of Service

Encoding isn't the only way to ensure voice quality. By virtue of the way IP networks operate, it's important that the packets containing VoIP information arrive and are decoded in the same order in which they were sent, and without delays in excess of 120 ms. Otherwise, the conversation will be a nonsensical mélange of gibberish.

In essence, QoS (which is covered in greater detail in Chapter 7) is a means to ensure that prioritized packets (like those containing VoIP information) speed through the network ahead of packets from other, less critical applications.

Packet prioritization is usually less important to data networking, which is mostly tolerant to variable network performance. As such, networks weren't designed to ensure that packets were received expeditiously or in order—something most data applications didn't worry about too much. However, without QoS mechanisms in place, random and slow delivery is the death of VoIP.

Rather than cover QoS twice, we'd like to refer you to back to Chapter 7, but it is helpful to discuss how QoS can be implemented with VoIP in mind. From a design standpoint, there are two considerations to keep in mind when establishing how to provide your desired level of QoS. First, you must determine the capabilities of your router infrastructure and what upgrades you would have to make to support your desired QoS levels. Next, you must make sure that the IP telephony end systems will work with your QoS mechanisms.

H.323

In the world of VoIP, proprietary technologies still reign supreme, but one protocol is peeking its head up as the prevailing standard. H.323 is an umbrella recommendation from the International Telecommunications Union (ITU), which establishes standards for multimedia communications over LANs that do not have a QoS mechanism in place. Unfortunately, these kinds of networks are the norm in most organizations, which include packet-switched TCP/IP and IPX over Ethernet, Fast Ethernet, and Token Ring networks. As such, the H.323 standard is an important technology for LAN-based applications for multimedia communications.

In 1996, the H.323 specification was approved by the ITU's Study Group 16. It was followed just two years later by Version 2. The standard covers a range of technologies, including stand-alone devices and embedded personal computer technology, as well as point-to-point and multipoint conferences. In addition to hardware, H.323 addresses such management and control functions as call control, multimedia management, and bandwidth management.

Importance of H.323

The H.323 standard is all-inclusive, yet it remains flexible and can be applied to basic voice handsets or to full video conferencing workstations. There are a number of reasons that H.323 is the most popular protocol for VoIP:

▼ H.323 establishes multimedia standards for the most prominent IP-based networks. It is designed to compensate for the highly variable LAN latencies that exist in IP-based networks. By using H.323, multimedia applications can be used without having to overhaul the whole network.

■ IP LANs are getting more and more powerful. From speeds of 10 Mbps, then 100 Mbps, and now 1 Gbps, more networks are able to provide the bandwidth that H.323 applications will demand.

■ PCs continue to get more powerful because of constant improvements in processors, memory, and multimedia accelerator chips.

■ If you need to communicate between two different kinds of networks, the H.323 standard allows for internetwork functionality.

■ Increased manageability of networking can limit the amount of bandwidth that is devoured with multimedia activity. With H.323, network administrators can restrict the amount of network bandwidth available for conferencing. To be more efficient with network resources, H.323's support of multicasting reduces bandwidth consumption.

▲ In a field thick with proprietary technologies, H.323 has the benefit of many computing and communications companies supporting it. Intel, Microsoft, Cisco, and IBM are some of the biggest names backing H.323.

Key Benefits of H.323

There are a number of reasons that H.323 is standing out as the most popular way to conduct VoIP conversations:

▼ **Codec standards**   H.323 defines standards for compression/decompression of audio and video data streams. This ensures that data will be readable if it is transmitted between the products of two different vendors.

■ **Network independence**   H.323 is designed to run on top of common network architectures. As network technology evolves, and as bandwidth management techniques improve, H.323-based solutions will be able to take advantage of those enhanced capabilities.

- **Platform and application independence**   Like all standards, H.323 is not the sole purview of any single hardware or operating system vendor. Further, H.323 isn't restricted to PCs alone. H.323-compliant platforms will come in a number of forms including videophones, IP-enabled telephones, and cable TV boxes.

- **Multipoint support**   Multiconferencing is already supported by H.323, which can support conferences with three or more endpoints without requiring special equipment. However, including multipoint control units (MCU) will provide a more powerful environment for hosting multipoint conferences.

- **Bandwidth management**   Because the traffic generated by audio and video applications is bandwidth-intensive, the potential exists to clog even the most robust networks. H.323 addresses this problem with bandwidth management tools. Using the management devices, network managers can set limits on the number of concurrent H.323 connections within their network, or they can restrict the amount of bandwidth available to H.323 applications. With proper resource management, no network need ever be slowed down.

- **Multicast support**   For situations where a number of people will receive the same broadcast, H.323 supports multicast transporting. For instance, in the case of a CEO broadcasting an address to a number of branch offices, H.323 multicast sends a single packet to all the branch offices. While the data is still on the company's headquarters network, the data is not duplicated, thereby saving resources. Compare this to *unicast,* which sends multiple point-to-point transmissions, and *broadcast,* which sends to all destinations. Employing unicast or broadcast is an inefficient use of the network, because packets are replicated unnecessarily. Multicast transmission uses bandwidth more efficiently because all stations in the multicast read the same data stream.

- **Flexibility**   Not all users' computers are created equal. However, by using an H.323-compliant device, conferences can be conducted across a network that includes a variety of endpoints, each with different capabilities. For instance, a teleconference can be listened to by a user whose computer is enabled only for VoIP.

- **Internetwork conferencing**   In the last example, we talked about H.323 as a means to communicate over networks with different devices, but H.323 isn't limited to the boxes on desktops. H.323 can also be used across different kinds of network architectures, and uses common codec technology from different videoconferencing standards to minimize transcoding delays and thus deliver the best results.

H.323 defines four major components for a network-based communications system: terminals, gateways, gatekeepers, and multipoint control units.

Terminals

Terminals are the endpoint devices that clients use. The specification requires that all terminals support voice communications, but video and data are optional. H.323 specifies how different audio, video, and data terminals will work together.

Additionally, all H.323 terminals must also support H.245, which is a mechanism used to negotiate channel usage and capabilities. Terminals must also support three other components:

▼ The Q.931 protocol for call signaling and call setup

■ Registration/Admission/Status (RAS), a protocol used to communicate with a gatekeeper

▲ Support for RTP/RTCP for sequencing audio and video packets

Optional components in an H.323 terminal are video codecs, data-conferencing protocols, and MCU capabilities.

Gateways

The main function of a gateway is serving as a translator between H.323 conferencing endpoints and other terminal types. This function includes translation between transmission formats and between communications procedures. Further, the gateway also translates between different audio and video codecs and performs call setup and clearing on both the LAN side and the switched-circuit network side.

But gateways are an optional component in an H.323 conference. You don't need a gateway if you're not connecting to other networks, since endpoints can communicate directly with other endpoints on the same LAN.

As complete as the H.323 standard is, several gateway functions are left open for the manufacturer to determine. For example, the standard does not establish how many terminals can connect through the gateway.

Gatekeepers

Where gateways were an optional piece of the H.323 pie, gatekeepers are an extremely crucial component. A gatekeeper is the central point for all calls within its zone and provides call control services to registered endpoints. Therefore, an H.323 gatekeeper can be thought of as a virtual switch.

Gatekeepers perform two important control functions:

▼ Address translation from LAN aliases for terminals and gateways to IP or IPX addresses.

▲ Bandwidth management: for instance, if the network administrator has set a limit on the number of concurrent H.323 connections or a threshold on bandwidth usage, it is the gatekeeper that can refuse more connections once the threshold is breached.

Gatekeepers serve the optional function of routing H.323 calls. Routing calls through a gatekeeper allows them to be managed more effectively and efficiently. This feature is especially important at the service provider level, because they need the ability to bill for calls placed through their network. This can also help balance network resources, since a gatekeeper capable of routing H.323 calls can make decisions about managing multiple gateways.

A gatekeeper is not required for a functional H.323 system. However, if a gatekeeper is present on the network, terminals must use their address translation, admissions control, bandwidth control, and zone management services.

Gatekeepers are also used to manage multipoint connections. To support multipoint conferences, users employ gatekeepers to receive H.245 control channels in a point-to-point conference. However, when more users join and the conference switches to multipoint, the gatekeeper can redirect the H.245 control channel to become a multipoint controller.

Multipoint Control Units

For conferences between three or more users, the multipoint control unit (MCU) is employed. An MCU consists of a multipoint controller (MC), which is required, as well as multipoint processors (MP). MC and MP capabilities can be housed in a dedicated component or be part of other H.323 components.

The MC handles H.245 negotiations between all terminals and establishes the common audio and video capabilities. The MC is used to manage conference resources by determining which of the audio and video streams can be multicast.

However, the MC does not directly control any of the media streams. This task is the purview of MP, which mixes, switches, and processes audio, video, and data.

A New Protocol in Town

An alternative to H.323 that is picking up steam in the VoIP community is the Session Initiation Protocol (SIP). SIP is the IETF's standard for multimedia conferencing over IP. SIP is an ASCII-based, application-layer control protocol that establishes, maintains, and terminates calls between two or more terminals.

Table 11-2 highlights some of SIP's functionality.

SIP is a peer-to-peer protocol, which means that it doesn't need a dedicated server to manage the sessions. The peers in a session are called *user agents* (*UAs*). A UA serves in one of two roles in a conversation:

▼ **User Agent Client (UAC)**   Client applications that initiate the SIP conversation request

▲ **User Agent Server (UAS)**   Server applications that contact the user when an SIP request is received and return a response on behalf of the user

A SIP endpoint can function both as a UAC and UAS. However, they only function as one or the other on any given conversation. An endpoint will function as a UAC or UAS depending on which UA initiated the request.

Function	Description
Resolving the location of target endpoints	SIP supports address resolution, name mapping, and call redirection.
Establishing the media capabilities of the target endpoint	This is achieved by using the Session Description Protocol (SDP). SIP determines the "lowest level" of common services between the endpoints, and communications are only conducted using the media capabilities supported at both ends.
Determining the availability of the target endpoint	If a call cannot be completed because the target is not available, SIP figures out if the target is already on the phone or did not answer in the allotted number of rings. Finally, it returns a message explaining why the call was unsuccessful.
Establishing a session between the originating and target endpoint	If the call can be completed, SIP establishes a session between the endpoints. SIP also supports mid-call changes, such as the addition of another endpoint to the conference or the changing of a media characteristic or codec.
Handling the transfer and termination of calls	SIP supports the transfer of calls from one endpoint to another. During a call transfer, SIP simply establishes a session to a new endpoint and terminates the session between the transferee and the transferring party.

Table 11-2.   SIP Functionality

The physical components of a SIP network can be split into two categories: clients and servers. SIP clients include

▼ **Phones**   These devices can act as either a UAS or UAC. Softphones and Cisco SIP IP phones can initiate SIP requests and respond to requests.

▲ **Gateways**   These devices control call functions. Gateways provide a number of services, including translating functions between SIP conferencing endpoints and other terminal types. This includes translation between transmission formats and between communications procedures. The gateway also performs call setup and teardown.

SIP servers include

▼ **Proxy server**   This server provides such functionalities as authentication, authorization, network access control, routing, reliable request retransmission, and security. Proxy servers receive SIP messages and forward them to the next SIP server in the network.

■ **Redirect server**   This server tells the client about the next hop that a message should take. Next, the client contacts the next hop server or UAS directly.

▲ **Registrar server**   This server processes requests from UACs to register their current location. Often registrar servers are co-located with a redirect or proxy server.

The Future

The chief enemies of VoIP are the things that get better and better in the world of internetworking every day—speed and capacity. As organizations implement faster networking devices, the faster information can flow and the faster VoIP packets can speed downstream. Also, as the relevance and importance of QoS becomes an important issue in the minds of network administrators, the ability to deliver VoIP will only improve. Finally, manufacturers—while still embracing their own proprietary protocols—are realizing the importance of supporting other protocols, including the big dogs like H.323 and SIP.

It appears, however, that SIP is becoming the more popular protocol. It's becoming more prevalent thanks, largely, to its ability to combine voice and IP services. Another important factor is that SIP is able to coexist with existing H.323 deployments. This is important to maximize the return on current infrastructure investments, and to support new deployments that use SIP.

Implementation

There are several different ways VoIP can be implemented in your organization. Whether you are dealing with a telecommuter connecting from home or a branch office with a small complement of workers all the way to a large branch office, there are a number of ways to configure a network to enable VoIP capabilities.

Let's take a closer look at three scenarios and talk about how to design and build VoIP-enabled networks.

Telecommuter

The Internet provides exceptional opportunities to decentralize your office. Rather than pack everybody into an endless beehive of cubicles, technology has made it possible for workers to limit their commute to a walk across the living room carpet. By using VoIP technology, telecommuters can communicate with the Central Office—or anywhere else for that matter—without affecting their own home telephone bill. VoIP solves a lot of problems for telecommuters and the organization's IT staff. The most important problem it solves is the need for independent circuits for both voice and data.

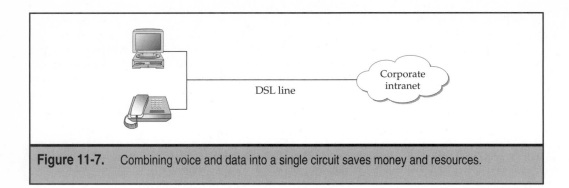

Figure 11-7. Combining voice and data into a single circuit saves money and resources.

As Figure 11-7 shows, by providing a single data circuit and H.323-compliant equipment, both voice and data can be integrated into a single circuit. They can be so well integrated, in fact, that the telecommuter can call the company operator (just by dialing 0), the voicemail system, and other telephone resources. Long-distance fees can be reduced by letting the telecommuter place H.323 calls to remote offices.

But VoIP isn't without some headaches. The tallest wall to telecommuter and SOHO VoIP involves bandwidth and network management. Users need enough bandwidth to accommodate VoIP traffic while simultaneously prioritizing, fragmenting, and queuing other data to protect the integrity of the voice transmission. If, as shown in Figure 11-8,

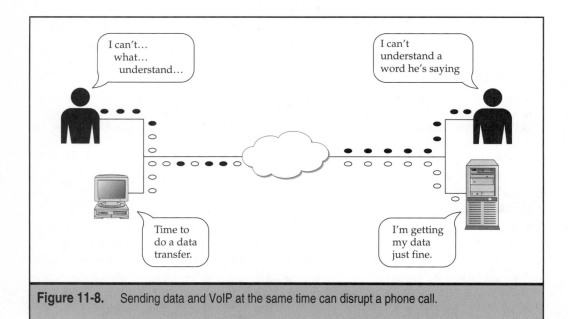

Figure 11-8. Sending data and VoIP at the same time can disrupt a phone call.

a VoIP call gets stuck in the middle of a large file transfer, the call will wind up sounding like you're talking to an alien George Lucas thought up for the next *Star Wars* movie.

Another issue to consider is that circuits to telecommuters and SOHOs must maintain full-time connectivity during business hours; otherwise, calls to the user's equipment may not be established. For instance, some VoIP devices try to gauge latency to a remote system before establishing the call. Some systems are so sensitive that ISDN's call setup times may be too long, resulting in rejected calls.

Finally, telecommuters and SOHOs will need a direct line into the internetwork, without having to be filtered through a firewall. H.323 employs negotiation techniques that aren't well suited for firewalls. This means that VoIP connections from a SOHO will need to bypass the public firewall and connect directly to the LAN.

The best solution for these issues—packet prioritization, full-time connectivity, and firewall-less connectivity—all but require using at least flat-rate ISDN or DSL (Digital Subscriber Line). However, your basic rate ISDN is only a 128-Kbps link, whereas DSL can exceed 1 Mbps.

Branch Offices

The best place to implement a VoIP solution is at the branch office level. Branch offices are ideal because they generally contain a small number of users and don't generate voluminous amounts of traffic. Further, these offices are the sites most likely to benefit from the toll-free advantages of VoIP as a replacement for long-distance services. Branch offices typically use high-speed lines like DSL or a T1 for connectivity. An example configuration is shown in Figure 11-9.

As with anything, there are few instances where everything will fall into place perfectly. For instance, your organization's branch offices may house several hundred people, and implementing VoIP can create some infrastructure challenges. Further, if your remote office is already equipped with a PBX, there isn't much need to add new equipment. Also, if your organization routes long-distance calls across a fixed-cost dedicated circuit, there may not be much cost savings back to the headquarters.

Where VoIP really makes a name for itself as a long-distance alternative is in connecting offices via the Internet. Your organization will recognize considerable cost savings by buying guaranteed services from an ISP and then routing VoIP calls across that connection, rather than paying long-distance fees or buying your own dedicated network.

By implementing a VoIP in a branch office, you can also use your corporate dialing plan, voicemail, and other features for less money than the cost of an additional PBX.

Cisco VoIP Products

Cisco offers a number of products that deliver VoIP. Some are technologies built specifically with VoIP in mind, while others are "conventional" internetworking devices that have VoIP functionality added.

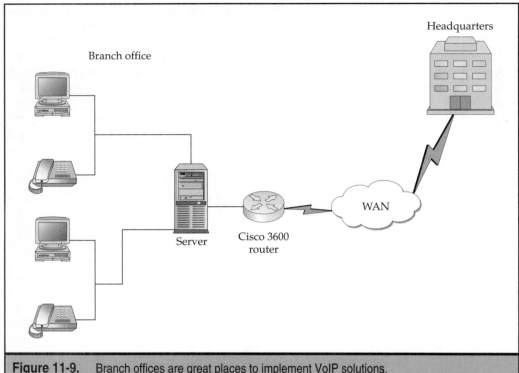

Figure 11-9.   Branch offices are great places to implement VoIP solutions.

Cisco CallManager

Cisco CallManager is the call-processing software component of Cisco AVVID (Architecture for Voice, Video, and Integrated Data). CallManager provides signaling and call control services to Cisco's integrated multimedia applications and third-party applications. CallManager can be clustered and distributed across an IP network, and as a result, it can scale to 10,000 users. In addition to serving existing applications, CallManager is also set to serve as the core of the next generation of integrated Web/voice/video applications.

The Cisco ICS 7750

The Cisco Integrated Communications System (ICS) 7750 is an integrated communications system designed for the deployment and management of data and converged voice/data applications and services. This includes VoIP, content delivery networking, and multiservice routing.

The ICS 7750 system incorporates a number of elements needed to deliver data and converged data/voice:

▼   A router/voice gateway

■   An application server with voice applications

■   Call processing software

■   Integrated single system management

▲   A data switching interface for seamless connectivity to recommended Cisco Catalyst QoS-enabled switches

The Cisco ICS 7750 is targeted at branch office and mid-market businesses.

The Cisco VSC3000

The VSC3000 is a call agent that, when coupled with a media gateway, enables the delivery of legacy and next-generation carrier voice services across multiservice packet networks. For optimal connectivity, the VSC3000 uses popular, industry-wide protocols. The VSC3000 ameliorates signaling interconnection issues through a large signaling protocol library and the Cisco Message Definition Language (MDL), which is an object-based, intuitive tool that allows for fast and easy protocol development and modifications.

Cisco Access Gateways and Controllers

Cisco Access products are a family of gateways that provide a connection between IP and circuit-switched networks. These gateways connect IP telephony systems to existing switches or analog devices using various plug-in interfaces. The use of IOS technology allows the familiar Command Line Interface (CLI) for management.

The Cisco SC2200, when combined with the AS5X00 gateways, gives service providers a solution to connect VoIP and dial access solutions to the PSTN via SS7. The Cisco SC2200 software runs on industry-standard Sun UNIX platforms.

Cisco Phones

Cisco's hardware-based IP telephones provide the feel of a "normal" telephone on a next-generation IP telephone network. Fully programmable, the family of Cisco IP telephones provides the most frequently used business features.

The newest Cisco IP phones include the following features:

▼   Streamlined user customization based on dynamic telephony needs

■   In-line power from the Catalyst switch card or the Catalyst in-line power patch panel

▲   A two-port 10/100BaseT switch interface, which delivers QoS

The telephones deliver the same audio quality that one would expect on a public network and works without being connected to a PC.

The Cisco IP Softphone

The Cisco IP Softphone is a Windows-based application for the PC. The phone can be used alone with a microphone and speaker, or in conjunction with a telephone handset. It provides the following features:

▼ **Directory integration** Integration with LDAP directories (like Microsoft's Active Directory) enables you to place calls or perform transfers with a click of the mouse. There is support for corporate and public directories, as well as a personal address book.

■ **User interface** An intuitive user interface and context-sensitive controls allow you to place calls quickly using directory entries and text fields from most Windows programs.

▲ **Virtual conference room** Participants in a conference call can be invited by dragging and dropping directory entries onto the SoftPhone's user interface, thereby creating a "virtual conference room." In addition to voice, this feature allows you to share data. You can share applications with conference call participants by selecting them from a list or dragging and dropping documents onto the virtual conference room.

Cisco Media Convergence Servers

The Cisco Media Convergence Server (MCS) 7800 series provides a server platform for Cisco AVVID. The following is a brief listing of the servers in this family.

▼ **Cisco MCS 7835H-3000** A mid-level, rack-mounted server with an Intel Prestonia Xeon 3.06-GHz processor, six hot-swap SCSI hard drives, a RAID controller, hot-swap fans, and redundant hot-swap power supplies

■ **Cisco MCS 7835I-3000** A mid-level, rack-mounted server with an Intel Prestonia Xeon 3-GHz processor, six hot-swap SCSI hard drives, a RAID controller, hot-swap fans, and redundant hot-swap power supplies

■ **Cisco MCS 7845H-3000** A high-level, rack-mounted server with an Intel Prestonia Xeon 3.06-GHz processor, six hot-swap SCSI hard drives, a RAID controller, redundant hot-swap fans, and redundant hot-swap power supplies

■ **Cisco MCS 7845I-3000** A high-level, rack-mounted server with an Intel Prestonia Xeon 3.06-GHz processor, six hot-swap SCSI hard drives, a RAID controller, redundant hot-swap fans, and redundant hot-swap power supplies

■ **Cisco MCS 7855I-1500** A high-level, rack-mounted server with two Intel Gallatin Xeon 1.5-GHz processors, up to 16 hot-swap SCSI hard drives, a RAID controller, redundant hot-swap fans, and redundant hot-swap power supplies

▲ **Cisco MCS 7865I-1500** A high-level, rack-mounted server with four Intel Gallatin Xeon 1.5-GHz processors, up to 12 hot-swappable SCSI hard drives, a RAID controller, redundant hot-swappable fans, and redundant hot-swappable power supplies

The MCS 7800 series of servers delivers a variety of IP telephony applications and functions for different-sized organizations with varying needs.

The VoIP revolution is well underway, but expect it to get bigger and better. Voice integration, interconnection, and new features will make the convergence of voice and data across a single IP network a widespread reality.

CISCO INTELLIGENT CONTACT MANAGEMENT

It would be simple enough if one's organization were able to communicate with its customers either via e-mail or by just using the telephone. However, the proliferation of computer networks and Web-based communications has made this task more feature-rich. One such way to communicate with customers is using Cisco's Intelligent Contact Management (ICM). While deploying and managing ICM isn't fodder for network neophytes, it's well worth reviewing since you'll see a lot more of this type of technology in the future. In fact, it's already commoner than you might think—it's just that most of us spend more time on the customer side.

Cisco ICM is a platform that allows customers to contact an organization's contact center, to seek help. Through multichannel contact management, computer telephony integration (CTI), and network resource monitoring, ICM can direct contact requests to the appropriate agent in a contact center.

ICM can route customer calls based on such information as the number dialed, data submitted via a Web form, or using information culled from a customer profile database. Meanwhile, the system monitors network resources—including agent skill levels and availability—and routes the contact, accordingly.

Once an agent has been selected, ICM allows customers to interact with the contact center agent via

▼ Telephone

■ VoIP

■ Text chat

■ E-mail

▲ Web collaboration

When the customer, who has already identified him or herself to the system, elects to make the contact attempt, ICM is able to compare that customer against a database, and route the call to the appropriate agent. ICM isn't a single tool. Rather, it is made up of several components.

Overview

Like any technology, ICM has been designed and built for a specific purpose (managing calls and blending online collaboration and communications methods between an enterprise and its customers). However, the ICM need not only be used by customer service—its use is limited only by an organization's need and ingenuity.

For the sake of using common terms and a simplicity of understanding, however, let's assume that ICM is being deployed by a business with a customer service contact center. Customers who need to communicate with the contact center will do so using the business's ICM-enabled Web site.

Also, before getting too deep into the function of the various widgets and gizmos that comprise ICM, it's helpful to look at each component and understand what it does in the big picture.

The Cisco Collaboration Server

The Cisco Collaboration Server (CCS) is the heart of ICM. The Web collaboration option allows your organization's agents to communicate with customers and Web site visitors with real-time voice and visual interaction.

The CCS is a Web server located outside a firewall and manages real-time Web-collaboration between a Web site visitor and a contact center agent. When the caller initiates a session, CCS sends JavaScript to the caller's browser and instructs the Cisco Media Blender (CMB) to set up a Web callback. (We'll talk about *callbacks* in more depth later in this chapter.) Once CMB establishes the callback using the selected CTI method and informs CCS of the selection, CCS gives control of the caller's browser to a call center agent.

ICM allows contact center agents to share Web pages with customers while performing voice or text chats. In addition, Web collaboration allows contact center agents and customers to complete online forms together, share Windows desktop applications, and perform one-to-one and one-to-many chats. CCS can either be deployed in a pure IP environment or can be integrated with an organization's existing telephone infrastructure.

Web collaboration features include

▼ Text chat

■ Bidirectional Web page sharing

■ Follow-Me-Browsing

■ Bidirectional FormShare

■ Real-time application sharing

■ Collaborative white boarding

▲ ScriptBuilder (for creating scripts of frequently shared Web pages or chat text)

CCS is useful for both the organization and its customers in that an easy-to-use interface is available for both the agent and the customer. Both parties use a standard Web browser, which allows for ease of use. Further, CCS can use Secure Sockets Layer (SSL) for secure chats and collaboration. Again, this is useful when filling sensitive information into a form, or for times when security is desired.

The ICM Central Controller

The ICM Central Controller is responsible for call routing decisions and configuration for the entire ICM system. This component includes the computer running the Call Management process. It also makes the routing decisions, along with a database containing information about the entire system. In addition, the ICM Central Controller stores data, providing historical and real-time data for reporting.

The Cisco Media Blender

The Cisco Media Blender (CMB) is a component which, when used with the CCS, allows you to connect customers with your organization's agents. The media blender provides the means to utilize voice or text chatting capabilities in addition to Web collaboration. CMB is located inside the firewall and is used to proxy communications between the Trailhead Web server and the ICM Web PG.

CMB works in conjunction with the CCS to provide Web callback, delayed callback, blended collaboration, and blended text chat. The Media Blender also acts as a firewall gateway service, allowing communication between the CCS (residing outside the firewall) and the ICM MR-PG, which resides within the protection of the firewall.

CMB makes these connections using three media:

▼ **Trailhead medium**   Located on the CMB, it communicates with the Trailhead server. The Trailhead medium routes requests from the Trailhead server to the ICM Web PG.

■ **ACD medium**   A Java-based software package for handling CTI messages coming from ADC, Predictive Dialer, or PBX. The same medium is used with each telephony implementation, employing a unique CTI driver for each system.

▲ **Collaboration (Web) medium**   A Java-based software package that communicates with the CCS, accepting and sharing session and agent-related events with other CMB media.

CMB provides a means for Web- and ACD-based call center systems to share CTI events. CMB acts as a backbone for blending calls and for

▼ Using HTTP tunneling and Trailhead to proxy communications between the Trailhead server and the Web PG.

■ Utilizing the CTI server, via the CallManager PG, for establishment and control of Web callbacks.

▲ Establishing blended collaborations. CMB gets its instructions from CCS to perform a Web callback. Then, CMB establishes the callback using the selected CTI method. Once the call is assigned, CMB tells CCS about the agent selection.

The Cisco Trailhead

The function of the Cisco Trailhead (CTH) is to translate incoming Web data into useful information that can be utilized by the ICM software. Once ICM has routed the call, Trailhead examines the ICM data, and then redirects the caller to the appropriate call center.

Two components make up the CTH:

▼ **Trailhead server**   Resides outside the organization's firewall

▲ **Trailhead medium**   Resides insider the firewall, on the CMB

These components communicate with each other using so-called *connections*. The Trailhead server's connections query the Trailhead media to find out if they can route calls. The Trailhead media's connection can query the Trailhead server for alerts and statistics.

There are two functions the Trailhead medium can be used to perform (either singly or both):

▼ Routing requests from the Trailhead server to the Web PG

▲ Initiating callback requests

Peripheral Gateways

A peripheral gateway (PG) is located in each contact center and is connected to each peripheral (ACD, PBX, or IVR, for example). The PG examines information from the peripheral, and then converts it into a format the ICM software can understand, afterward forwarding it to the central controller.

The Cisco ICM Web Peripheral Gateway (Web PG) allows the Trailhead medium to talk with the ICM system. The Web PG receives a route request from CMB, and then sends it to the ICM Central Controller. The ICM Web PG serves as an integration point for call requests to the ICM Central Controller for Pre-Routing.

NOTE: Pre-Routing is a function that makes routing decisions for a call while it is still in the carrier's network.

The Cisco Computer Telephony Integration (CTI) Server

The Cisco Computer Telephony Integration (CTI) Server provides third-party call control and event notification from CallManager. In essence, CTI is the use of computers to manage telephone calls. The CMB works in conjunction with the CTI server to establish and manage callbacks. When a call is assigned to a contact center agent, the CTI server uses caller information to inform the agent that a call is waiting.

Automatic Call Distributors

An Automatic Call Distributor (ACD) is a telephone facility for managing incoming calls. Once a call has been initiated, the ACD manages it based on the number called and a series of handling instructions. Often, organizations use ACDs to check callers, make outgoing calls, forward calls, allow callers to record messages, gather statistics, balance phone line use, and provide other services.

Call Flow

Now that we understand the cast of characters in Cisco's ICM solution, let's examine how a call flows through ICM—from customer to the contact center. Figure 11-10 illustrates this flow.

1. A call is initiated.

    The call flow begins when a Web site visitor clicks a link to initiate a call with a live person at the contact center. Next, Trailhead serves a callback form to the caller's Web browser. This form is used to gather necessary information to properly classify the customer. The information is used to route the call to the correct contact center agent, and provide that agent with the data needed to handle the customer's query. When the customer completes and submits the form, it is processed by the Trailhead Web server, and then formatted for delivery to the ICM Web PG.

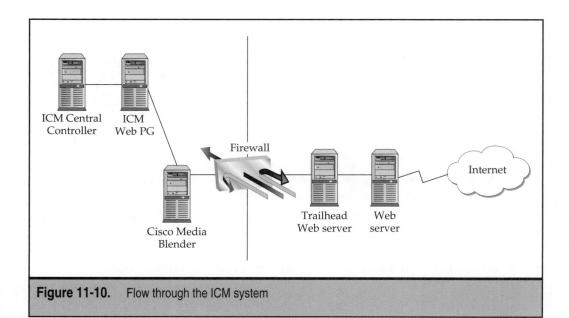

Figure 11-10.   Flow through the ICM system

2. Trailhead and the ICM Web PG translate the request for the ICM.

   The ICM Web PG is the next stop for the call flow. Web-initiated calls are sent through the ICM Web PG for Pre-Routing. CMB is used to proxy communications between the Trailhead Web server and the ICM Web PG using HTTP.

3. ICM routes the call.

   Next, the ICM Web PG forwards a route request to the ICM Central Controller. The central controller will select a routing script based on conditions and parameters established by the contact center administrator. It will route the call based on a number of dynamic, fluid factors. ICM might elect to send the call to an agent in a particular skill group based on the customer's need or on the current status of calls to the contact center. For example, let's say the customer has just purchased a new car and is having trouble getting the security system to work properly. The ICM software can route this call to an agent who has expertise with security systems, rather than someone whose expertise might be limited to car maintenance.

   Route requests are generally determined and responded with in less than a second. Route selection is then based on a number of parameters, including

   ■ CTI callback strategy
   ■ Collaboration server site
   ■ Agent skill groups
   ■ Interaction type

   The route selection is delivered to the ICM Web PG and given to the Trailhead Web server, again using CMB as a gateway through the organization's firewall. Next, the caller's browser is redirected to a URL.

4. The contact center responds to the call.

   The last step is to finally connect a contact center agent with the customer. There are three basic ways in which the two can communicate, using ICM:

   ■ **Basic callback**   The customer receives a call from the contact center agent. This is accomplished by ICM routing the Web request to the correct resource.

   ■ **Blended Web collaboration**   With this option, callers and contact center agents can share information over the Web. They are able to share Web pages, forms, and applications using a standard Web browser.

   ■ **Text chat**   The customer can perform a text chat with an agent.

Callbacks

In the event that a customer wishes to be contacted via telephone, there are two methods through which a customer can be called back from the ICM: basic callback and delayed callback. Figure 11-11 shows the components involved in a callback.

Basic Callback

The basic callback method initiates a callback, but without starting a Web collaboration session. This is a very simple contact method which is utilized when collaboration is not needed.

With basic callback, Trailhead responds to the customer's Web browser with a URL, telling the customer to expect a return call. At the same time, CMB uses the CTI server to set up the callback. As this method does not send the JavaScript component to the user's Web browser, the customer's computer is not tied up with the call.

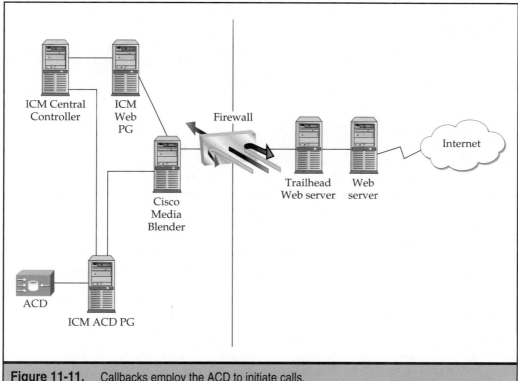

Figure 11-11.   Callbacks employ the ACD to initiate calls.

Delayed Callback

Delayed callback is similar to the basic callback method, however—as the name suggests—the callback is delayed until a time established by the customer. Generally, this delay should not be longer than 120 minutes.

Once the customer requests a callback and indicates the desired length of the delay, a form is sent to the customer, showing that the call can be expected in the number of minutes requested, plus one minute. The additional minute is added for processing time.

The CMB receives the callback request and hangs onto it for the duration of the delay. When the delay has expired, the CMB issues a Make Call request to the CTI server. CMB connects with the CTI server to establish and manage callbacks. The CMB employs several CTI policies which establish how the callback will be managed through the CTI server. These policies are managed by the contact center administrator and can be established for the whole system, or on a call-by-call basis. The caller information that was collected in the Trailhead callback form is also forwarded to the CTI server. As such, when the ACD assigns an agent, the CTI server can provide the caller information to the contact center agent.

Web Collaboration

The previous section examined methods of callbacks using ICM. When you want to provide more bang for your communications buck, ICM employs two different collaboration methods: blended collaboration and text chat with collaboration.

Blended Collaboration

The first collaboration method is blended collaboration. This method provides collaboration, along with a Web callback, establishing a telephone call and a Web collaboration session between the customer and the contact center agent. The collaboration session is initiated when the Trailhead Web server receives the route selection, then the caller's browser is pointed to the CCS. The CCS is located outside the network's firewall and manages the collaborative session between both parties.

In addition to establishing the collaborative session, the CMB and CTI server also manage the session's conference and transfer attributes. That is, if the contact center agent decides to transfer the call to another agent (or conference in someone else), the CTI server forwards the request to the CMB, and then the CMB tells the CCS to allow a second party to join the collaborative session.

Text Chat with Collaboration

In cases where a telephone call is not wanted, ICM supports Web collaboration with a text chat. This might be utilized if the customer has a dial-in connection and use of the telephone would mean losing the Internet connection.

In the event the route selection delivered to the ICM Central Controller designates a text chat, the customer is forwarded to the CCS where a phantom call is initiated. That is, the call is placed into the ACD, but when the call is assigned to a contact center agent, an outbound call is not placed. This allows the contact center agent to conduct a text chat with the customer, and use Web collaboration features.

Switching and Routing

ICM can be souped up using different routing and switching techniques. Switching can be employed if the organization's contact center is very large or spread over several locations. Routing techniques are useful for efficient call plotting.

Multiswitching

For organizations with multiple sites, ICM is quite useful. For example, if a customer is talking to a contact center agent in Memphis, but the call needs to be forwarded to an agent in Boise, multiswitching can make the transfer seamless.

In a basic phone routing configuration, there is a network interface to the public switched telephone network (PSTN), a central controller, and an ACD PG for each switch. When ICM is added to the phone system, a Trailhead Web server is also added, along with a CMB for each site. The Trailhead server collects contact requests and queries the ICM software for route requests. Figure 11-12 illustrates this.

In addition to multisite needs, multiswitching matters for large and growing organizations. CCSes can handle up to 200 contact center agents. More than that and additional CSSes are required.

Redundant Routing

Cisco Pre-Routing is a function that makes routing decisions for a call while it is still in the carrier's network. This allows the system to segment customers, balance calls, and properly route calls.

Pre-Routing can be accomplished by adding an additional Trailhead Web server. Traffic can be directed between the Trailhead servers by adding a Cisco LocalDirector to a server as a load balancer. Further, LocalDirector can query the Trailhead servers to ensure the Web link remains active. This is shown in Figure 11-13.

ICM Security Best Practices

Cisco ICM provides a couple of useful ways to keep ICM secure, locally. That is, the system employs several mechanisms to ensure that users are only able to access or modify the information for which they are authorized. ICM employs a combination of user permissions and partitioning.

User Authentication and Permissions

The first two methods of ICM security involve authenticating the user and examining the user's access privileges. Depending on how the system administrator assigns rights to different users, users can be restricted access to data based on

▼   The business entity in which the data belongs

■   The data class to which the data belongs

▲   The data object

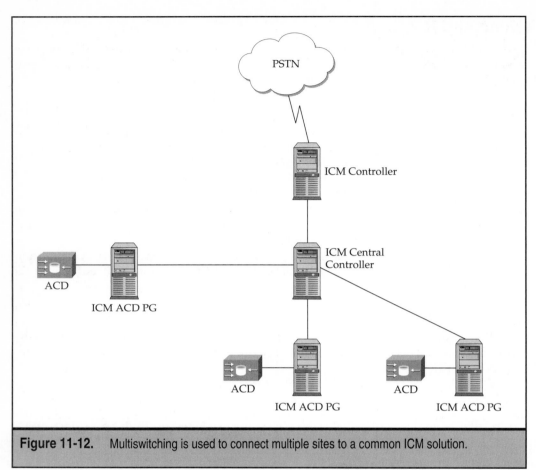

Figure 11-12. Multiswitching is used to connect multiple sites to a common ICM solution.

A user's access to data is managed based both on the user's access permissions and the permissions of the group to which the user belongs.

Access Privileges   The system administrator can manage access to each class and object in ICM by setting access privileges. Table 11-3 lists the types of access privilege levels and what the user is allowed to do at each level.

These levels of security are not one-size-fits-all affairs. It is permissible to mix different security levels. For example, users might have Read access to one layer of data, and then Reference access to subsequent layers.

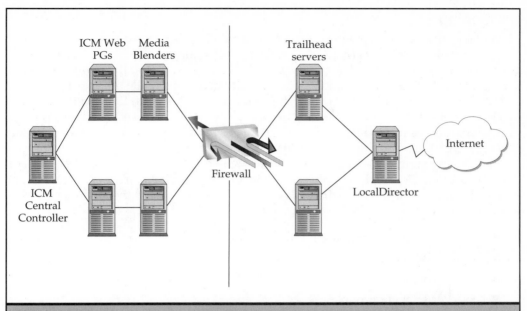

Figure 11-13.   Using LocalDirector to balance the load between multiple devices

User Groups   To make the process of managing user rights and permissions easier, it is advisable to lump like users together in a common user group. Then, each user group can be assigned the requisite set of rights. For instance, you might want to lump all shift supervisors into a category that allows them Maintenance level access, while contact center agents might only have Read level access. How you define their rights will depend, of course, on your organization and its needs.

Access Privilege Level	Description
Maintenance	The user can read, reference, create, or change data.
Reference	The user can create or modify other data that refers to the specific data, but cannot modify the specific data.
Read	The user can read data, but not make changes.
None	The user cannot see the data at all.

Table 11-3.   User Privilege Levels in ICM

Partitioning

Further, security can be managed by employing a mechanism called *partitioning*.

Even though users of ICM are able to access the data in the database, that doesn't mean that every user in the system has *carte blanche* with this data. By employing partitioning, certain users can be granted access to one set of data, while other users are permitted access to other data. Data restriction might also be used to limit who can make changes to data that affect call handling or monitoring; it might also be used to allow different departments to act independently. Whatever reason you might have for wanting data segmented, partitioning in ICM allows it.

Partitioning permits the organization to be segmented in up to five business units, or *entities*. These entities might be different divisions, departments, or special groups created for the sake of ICM management. Each business entity would then manage its own set of objects, such as:

▼ Routing and administrative scripts

■ Enterprise services

■ Enterprise skill groups

■ Enterprise agent groups

▲ Work schedules

Users can be granted or denied access to each business entity (for instance, the department manager might have the privileges to create and manage administrative scripts for that particular entity, but not for other entities), or for other ICM objects (for instance, a particular route may only be used in one entity, but not in another).

Cisco offers up a number of innovative ways for your organization to remain in contact, both internally and externally. VoIP and ICM are two ways in which your communications system and internetwork can converge for added benefit.

CHAPTER 12

Storage Tools

In the previous chapter, we talked about how the amalgamation of voice and data into a single circuit is a goal for many organizations' internetworks. As more and more data and traffic cross the network, there will be a larger demand for storage. Unfortunately, conventional means of data storage—disk arrays and tape backups connected to the server—aren't enough to keep up with the task.

Further, with the moniker "Information Age" comes the burden of storing all that data. It wouldn't be so bad if the term "information" were limited to pages of the printed word, punctuated with the occasional photograph. In recent years, however, "information" has evolved to mean rich multimedia content, mixing both graphics and sound. And organizations aren't just storing the data for archival use, either. This information is routinely accessed either internally, or served up to Web site visitors.

As wonderful as multimedia is, the storage requirements of these files take their toll. Conventional network storage gear is finding itself incapable of maintaining all this information. If that weren't enough, transferring large amounts of data creates its own problems as network bandwidth is continually challenged with other loads.

Having endured for two decades, the parallel Small Computer System Interface (SCSI) bus that has facilitated server-storage connectivity for LAN servers imposes limits on network storage. While SCSI connections are fine for desktop computers and LANs, they are not robust enough for large-scale storage needs. Adding to the limitations of SCSI is the traditional use of LAN connections for server storage backup, which takes away from usable client bandwidth.

STORAGE AREA NETWORKS

One solution to the storage dearth is implementing a storage area network (SAN). SANs are networks that are designed, built, and maintained with one purpose in mind: to store and transmit data. SANs are a burgeoning field, with impressive growth expected. According to the market research firm Gartner Group, the SAN industry is expected to grow from approximately $1.2 billion in 2002 to $4.3 billion in 2006.

In this chapter, we'll first talk about the generalities of SANs and how you can design a SAN for your own internetworking needs, then talk about Cisco's SAN solution.

Storage Needs

With the popularity of the Internet and the massive increase in e-commerce, organizations are scrambling for a means to store vast amounts of data. A popular way to maintain terabytes of information employs SANs, which interconnect storage devices with Fibre Channel hubs and switches. Even though data storage is cheap—you can add a 200GB hard drive for a couple hundred dollars—this is a reactive response to storage shortages. By creating a patchwork of hard drives, your internetwork's overhead escalates, and you slowly lose control.

SANs, on the other hand, allow you to manage all your storage needs in a proactive manner while maintaining the high availability that you need. Figure 12-1 shows an example of how a LAN and a SAN work together.

As organizations and their computing needs grow, so will their reliance on data storage. For instance, as more and more companies add server farms to manage their internal and external affairs, the more reliable the internetwork must be. To ensure high availability, servers sharing storage pools in a SAN can failover with no hiccup in service. Further, because fiber optics are the backbone of SANs, disaster recovery is pared from several hours to a few minutes or less.

By combining LAN networking models with the core building blocks of server performance and mass storage capacity, SANs eliminate the bandwidth bottlenecks and scalability limitations imposed by previous SCSI bus-based architectures. In addition to the fundamental connectivity benefits of SAN, the new capabilities, facilitated by SAN's networking approach, enhance its value as a long-term infrastructure. These capabilities, which include clustering, topological flexibility, fault tolerance, high availability, and remote management, further elevate a SAN's ability to address the growing challenges of data-intensive, mission-critical applications.

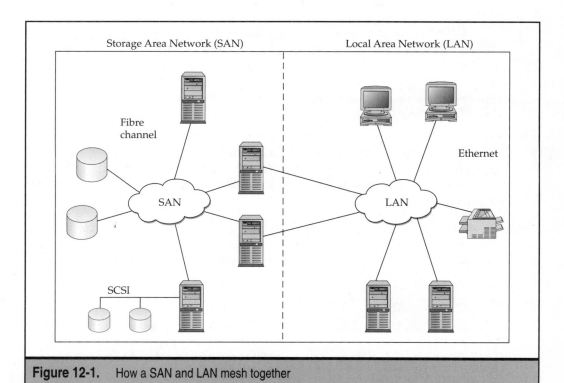

Figure 12-1. How a SAN and LAN mesh together

There are three primary components of a storage area network:

▼ **Interface**   The Interface is what allows storage to be external from the server and allow server clustering. SCSI, Fibre Channel, and Fibre Channel over IP (FCIP) are common SAN interfaces.

■ **Interconnect**   The Interconnect is the mechanism these multiple devices use to exchange data. Devices such as hubs, routers, gateways, and switches are used to link various interfaces to SAN fabrics.

▲ **Fabric**   The platform (the combination of network protocol and network topology) based on switched SCSI, switched fiber, and so forth. The use of gateways allows the SAN to be extended across WANs.

Fibre Channel

Fibre Channel is an industry-standard, high-speed serial interface for connecting PCs and storage systems. Fibre Channel provides attachment of servers and storage systems across distances up to 100 km (which is about 4,000 times farther than parallel SCSI interfaces). This allows the storage facilities to be located on another floor, another building, or in another city.

Fibre Channel carries 100 times more bandwidth than SCSI (2 Gbps vs. 20 Mbps). Further, Fibre Channel supports multiple standard protocols (like TCP/IP and SCSI) concurrently over the same physical cable. This is useful because it simplifies cabling and keeps down infrastructure costs. Because Fibre Channel allows standard SCSI packets to be transported across fiber-optic lines, existing SCSI devices can be maintained and used alongside Fibre Channel devices.

NOTE: Although Fibre Channel is most often used with fiber-optic connections, it can still be used with copper wiring. However, there are more speed and distance limitations imposed on copper deployments than on fiber. Additionally, copper can suffer performance degradation due to electromagnetic interference.

For the sake of reliability through redundancy, Fibre Channel SANs should be built around hubs and switches. This ensures that no single point of failure exists and performance bottlenecks are ameliorated. This should sound familiar, because it is a key consideration when designing a LAN.

Fibre Channel Layers

The Fibre Channel standard contains five layers. Each layer is responsible for a specific set of functions. If you think back to Chapter 2, you might notice some commonalities between Fibre Channel and the OSI model. In the Fibre Channel model, the layers are numbered FC-0 through FC4.

Table 12-1 describes the different layers of the Fibre Channel model, and Figure 12-2 illustrates this stack.

Layer	Description
FC-0: Physical Layer	Defines cabling, connectors, and the signaling controlling the data. This layer is akin to the OSI physical layer.
FC-1: Transmission Protocol Layer	Responsible for error detection, link maintenance, and data synchronization.
FC-2: Framing and Signaling Protocol Layer	Responsible for segmentation and reassembly of data packets that are sent and received by the device. Additionally, sequencing and flow control are performed at this layer.
FC-3: Common Services Layer	Provides services like multicasting and striping.
FC-4: Upper Layer Protocol Mapping Layer	Provides the communication point between upper layer protocols (like SCSI) and the lower Fibre Channel layers. This layer makes it possible for more than SCSI data to traverse a Fibre Channel link.

Table 12-1. Layers in the Fibre Channel Stack

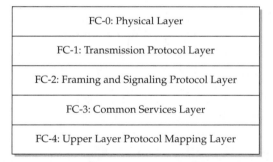

Figure 12-2. The Fibre Channel Stack

Although the stacks are different (not the least of which is that the OSI model has seven layers while Fibre Channel has five), each layer in the models relies on the layer immediately above or below.

As Fibre Channel utilizes the layer format, products and applications performing at one layer are compatible with products and applications residing at another layer, which is what the OSI model does.

Going the Distance

SCSI storage solutions had to be located next to the server because its range is limited to 25 meters. This proved to be troublesome, especially if space in a server room was at a premium. Because Fibre Channel allows for long-distance locations between servers and storage devices, the two pieces of equipment can be up to 100 km apart.

Three devices can be added to Cisco SAN devices to provide Fibre Channel connectivity. These devices employ different laser wavelengths to garner varying levels of bandwidth and distance. Those wavelengths are

▼ **Short wavelength (SWL)**   Providing connectivity up to 500 meters

■ **Long wavelength (LWL)**   Providing connectivity up to 10 km

▲ **Coarse Wavelength Division Multiplexing (CWDM)**   Providing connectivity up to 100 km

In practice, however, the ability for data to travel long distances can be useful if a storage center is constructed to maintain all the data for several departments. Further, several servers located at one campus could send their data to a central storage facility in a separate building. This allows for the creation of modular and scalable storage pools.

Increased Connectivity

Using Fibre Channel also simplifies the connectivity of multiple systems accessing a shared storage device by overcoming the limitations of parallel SCSI, including distance and number of devices per bus. Fibre Channel supports eight times more devices per loop than parallel SCSI. In practice, however, it may not be realistic to put so many devices on a single loop. However, the capability now exists for large numbers of servers to access storage devices like RAID arrays or tape libraries.

Other SAN Protocols

In addition to Fibre Channel, there are a couple other SAN protocols to be aware of. These protocols are useful in designing and deploying the optimal SAN. Let's talk about two of the currently prevalent protocols (FCIP and iSCSI) and rub our crystal ball for a look at the future of SAN protocols, iFCP.

iSCSI

The first protocol is the basket in which Cisco seemed to put all of its eggs a couple years ago—Small Computer System Interface over IP. In essence, this is simply transported data in the SCSI protocol across TCP/IP networks. SCSI is the language of disk drives, and iSCSI is a protocol that encapsulates SCSI commands and data for transport across IP networks. It is beneficial because it interoperates with existing applications and operating systems, as well as with LANs and WANs.

Products that use iSCSI allow hosts on an IP network to connect across Gigabit Ethernet networks to Fibre Channel or SCSI storage. IP storage networks are built directly on top of existing IP networks. It didn't take off like Cisco had originally hoped, but don't read this to mean that iSCSI is a dead technology. It is still a viable protocol and used in many of Cisco's (and other vendors') SAN devices.

FCIP

A new protocol is FCIP, or Fibre Channel over IP. FCIP represents two distinct technologies (storage networking and long distance networking), merged together. FCIP combines the best attributes of both Fibre Channel and the Internet Protocol to connect distributed SANs. FCIP encapsulates Fibre Channel and sends it over a TCP socket.

FCIP is considered a tunneling protocol because it makes a transparent point-to-point connection between geographically disparate SANs, utilizing IP networks. FCIP relies on TCP/IP services for connectivity between SANs over LANs, MANs, and WANs. TCP/IP is also tasked with congestion control and management, as well as data error and data loss recovery. The benefit of all this is that organizations can leverage their existing technology investments by extending the Fibre Channel fabric over an IP link.

iFCP

Just to confuse matters with FCIP, another SAN protocol is iFCP. This stands for Internet Fibre Channel Protocol. Even though the letters are the same (though in a different order), the technology is rather different. iFCP allows an organization to extend Fibre Channel across the Internet using TCP/IP. This sounds a lot like FCIP, but that is where the similarities end. While FCIP is used to extend a Fibre Channel fabric with an IP-based tunnel, iFCP is a movement away from current Fibre Channel SANs toward the future of IP SANs.

iFCP gateways can complement existing Fibre Channel fabrics, or completely supplant them. iFCP allows organizations to create an IP SAN fabric, minimizing the Fibre Channel component and maximizing the use of TCP/IP infrastructure.

While Cisco's solution, which we'll talk about in the next section, is based largely on FCIP, it is helpful to know what is on the horizon with iFCP.

Designing and Building a SAN

When it comes down to designing and building a SAN, it's necessary to consider several important factors before plugging fiber into routers and switches. You should consider such issues as what kind of applications you'll be using, the best design for the backbone, how you'll configure your topology, and what mechanisms you'll use to manage your SAN. Let's take a closer look at each of these issues.

Application Needs

When developing and designing a SAN, the first step is to figure out which applications will be served. No matter if you're designing a common data pool for a bank of Web servers, a high-performance data-streaming network, or any other needs, you must pay special attention to the SAN infrastructure. You have to take into consideration such issues as port densities, distance and bandwidth requirements, and segmentation. These are all variables that are affected by the application.

NOTE: In a mixed environment, it's important to evaluate the platforms that will compose the SAN. Hardware and software support for SANs varies depending on which platforms you use. Once you have addressed these fundamental questions, you can begin constructing the SAN.

A SAN's construction is similar to a typical Ethernet infrastructure.

A SAN comprises a few basic components: the Fibre Channel disk storage and tape libraries, fiber hubs and switches, host bus adapters (HBA), and some form of SAN management.

Backbone

As you design your SAN, a critical architectural hardware decision is whether to use arbitrated loop or switched fabric.

▼ **Arbitrated loop** Shares bandwidth and employs round-robin data forwarding. At one time, it was the only choice for SAN backbones.

▲ **Switched fabric** Dedicates full bandwidth on each port and allows simultaneous data transfers to a single node.

Your choice will be decided based largely on your scaling and performance needs. If you have modest storage needs, a simple hub should be enough to get the job done. On the other end of the spectrum, larger storage environments almost demand fiber switches.

In small groups or SOHOs, a good foundation is a Fibre Channel hub in an arbitrated-loop configuration. Hubs are well suited for this environment because they provide a high level of interoperability for a reasonably low price. Hubs support an aggregate bandwidth of 100 Mbps. Hubs can support up to 127 devices, but for optimal results, you should limit it to about 30 devices. Further, because the per-port costs of a switch are higher than those of a hub, a hub is best to fan out the core switch ports to the connecting servers.

One of the main reasons hubs are limited in their scalability is because of the way devices are added into the loop. In order to recognize other devices in the loop, each loop must perform a *loop initialization sequencer* (*LIP*) when it is first attached to the network. When this action is performed, the loop is suspended while the entire membership on the loop acquires or verifies the port addresses and is assigned an *arbitrated loop physical address.* Although the recognition process is very fast, time-sensitive traffic (like VoIP or data backups) can be negatively affected by these performance speed bumps.

On the other hand, hubs are useful because they are inexpensive, easy to configure, and interoperate well with other hubs and other vendors' products.

Fiber

If SANs are so fantastic, why are we just hearing about them now? The main factor that has brought SANs into play as a viable technology is the use of switched fiber.

Fiber switches support 2 Gbps full-duplex on all ports. Unlike hubs, which as we mentioned earlier require an LIP, a fiber switch requires nodes connected to its ports to perform a *fabric logon.* The switch is the only device that sees this logon, and this allows devices to enter and exit the fabric without providing an interruption to the remaining devices.

Devices on an arbitrated-loop hub, which is cascaded off a switch, are not fundamentally compatible with other devices on the fabric. Unlike a switched LAN environment, devices in a switched SAN environment must perform a fabric logon to communicate with other devices. However, those devices that are not built with fabric support usually cannot operate over fabric because they don't perform a fabric logon. Rather, they use an LIP.

Configuration

Just as in a LAN, there are several ways to configure switches, providing different levels of performance and redundancy. In a SAN, the basic configuration design is the tree-type model. In this scheme, switches cascade off one another and fan out throughout the SAN, shown in Figure 12-3.

The main problem with this model is its scalability constraints, due to the latency inherent with the single-port interface. This also limits bandwidth and is not ideal because it can be a single point of failure. This type of design is best as an alternative to fiber hubs for a SAN that has just a single-tier cascade.

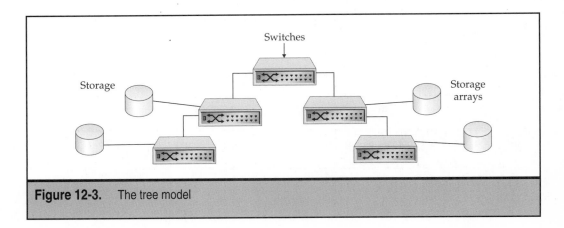

Figure 12-3. The tree model

For larger, more intricate SANs, the best choice for both high availability and performance is the mesh model. The mesh makes a large network of switches: Each switch is connected to every other switch, thereby eliminating the opportunity for a single point of failure. The mesh also reduces bottlenecks and latency. The mesh model is illustrated in Figure 12-4.

A mesh isn't perfect. The biggest problem is that it doesn't scale very efficiently. As you can tell, as more switches are added, the number of ports required to connect to all the available switches will use up most of the ports on each of the switches. Given that limitation, the mesh's strength is a good choice for midsize SANs with five or fewer switches requiring a maximum guaranteed uptime and optimal performance.

Scalability and redundancy are brought together in the next model, as shown in Figure 12-5. To ensure a redundant data path, each switch is connected to two other switches. Each switch has two different paths through the SAN, thereby eliminating a single point of failure. This configuration is an ideal solution for enterprise-class SANs.

Management

For a SAN to work at its peak, it must use centrally managed devices. SAN management is mainly a security device that ensures servers see only the intended devices and storage

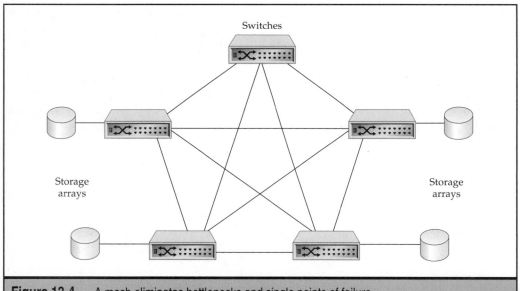

Figure 12-4. A mesh eliminates bottlenecks and single points of failure.

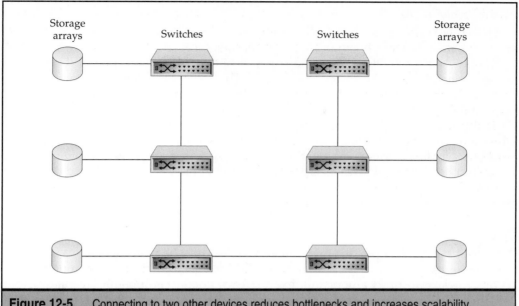

Figure 12-5. Connecting to two other devices reduces bottlenecks and increases scalability.

arrays, reducing the chance for data corruption. There are two basic ways to manage your SAN's hardware: port-level zoning and logical unit (LUN)-level zoning.

▼ *Port-level zoning* is similar to a virtual LAN (VLAN). Port zoning partitions devices based on which ports they are using on the hub or switch. Attached nodes won't be able to communicate unless individual ports are shared in a common zone.

▲ *LUN-level zoning* is similar to port-level zoning; however, it increases the granularity, thereby making it possible to partition nodes by their device ID. LUN-level zoning gives you more flexibility when it comes to communicating with devices on the edge of a SAN.

NOTE: We'll talk more about zoning with Cisco devices later in this chapter and include a discussion of virtual SANs (VSANs).

Data storage can be an ever-changing environment. Storage needs may differ drastically from one day to the next. Happily, however, managing a SAN is helpful because it gives you the ability to dynamically allocate storage to the different pools, without having to reboot the servers in your storage cluster. Additionally, you can add more storage to your SAN and reallocate it as you wish, again with no interruption.

Storage Options

When it comes down to deciding what you'll use as the storage component of your SAN, there isn't an abundance of options. An easy option, especially if you already have SCSI RAID or disk shelves, is to buy an external SCSI-to-fiber bridge. A bridge will allow you to connect almost any SCSI device to your SAN. The downside of this is that you waste all the speed that a natively attached fiber device would deliver. Bridges push between 15 Mbps and 40 Mbps.

This leads to the second option: native fiber-attached storage. Fibre Channel storage is becoming more and more popular and—as is the case with technology—the price is coming down. Fiber storage can push 2 Gbps, but even though prices are coming down, they aren't nearly as inexpensive as a SCSI RAID solution. Costwise, the hard drives are on a par with SCSI drives. It's the external Fibre Channel RAID controllers, at anywhere from $8,000 to $50,000, that jack up the price.

Backup

Fiber-optic backups are just the thing for administrators who manage networks with copious amounts of data. Not only can they offload backups from the network, but they can also share a single library among multiple servers scattered throughout several different departments. Further, resources can be allocated to the departments that have the greatest backup needs. In addition to drives, tape libraries can use SCSI-to-fiber bridges. Though tape libraries don't come close to the speed of drives and may seem a waste of fiber resources, many implement tape libraries into their SANs because backups are easier to perform.

Routers are just starting to come into their own in the world of SANs. Routers in a SAN are intelligent devices that can execute a direct disk-to-tape backup without the middleman of the server processing the information first. As you can imagine, backing up information without the server not only releases the server to perform other tasks, but it reduces backup times by removing any bottlenecks that might occur as the data filters through the server. Further, routers have the technology integrated with them to handle error recovery, as well as the capability to report problems to the backup software.

CISCO MDS SWITCHES

Cisco's SAN solution is its Multilayer DataCenter Switches (MDS). Introduced in 2003, the MDS devices are Cisco's entry into the world of SANs and SAN management. But not only has Cisco come with its own line of gadgetry, the company has also brought some new and interesting tools, technologies, and software. In this section, we take a closer look, first, at the technologies at play behind Cisco's SAN solution. Next, we'll look at the specific hardware Cisco offers for SAN switching. Finally, you can't just hook all this hardware together and expect it to work—Cisco offers a couple software packages to ease the configuration and management of its SANs.

Technologies

In addition to the core tools at play in SANs that we discussed in the last section, Cisco adds some other technologies to its SAN solution. While some philosophies are common with other vendors' SANs, Cisco dishes up some new ideas, like virtual SANs, trunking, and its own take on SAN security. Let's examine these technologies in more depth.

VSANs

Think back to Chapter 6 and our discussion of virtual LANs. The same sort of logic is at play behind virtual SANs (VSANs) and zones.

VSANs are a proprietary Cisco technology allowing independent, logical fabrics to be defined from a set of one or more physical switches. VSANs are isolated from other VSANs and function as a separate and independent fabric with its own set of fabric services, like naming, zoning, routing, and so forth.

In order to transfer data traffic between VSANs, Cisco's MDS line employs a technique called *inter-VSAN routing*. This enables the transfer of data among sources and destinations on different VSANs, as shown in Figure 12-6, but without compromising the VSANs by merging them into a single fabric. This ensures that data can be shared between VSANs, but without affecting the VSANs' scalability, reliability, and security.

Additionally, Inter-VSAN routing works across WANs using FCIP. This allows routing features to be used across long distances, which is ideal for organizations that have their assets spread across disparate locations.

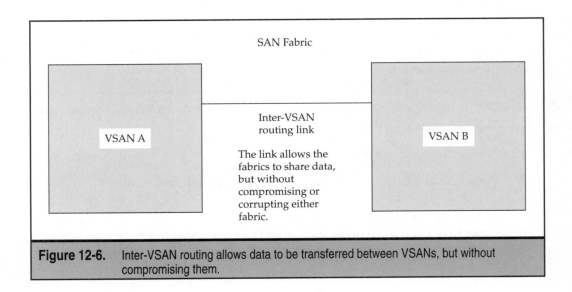

Figure 12-6.   Inter-VSAN routing allows data to be transferred between VSANs, but without compromising them.

The ability to connect VSANs across a WAN link is useful because isolated fabrics in remote data centers could be interconnected. Additionally, VSANs supplement the switch's scalability and creation of multiple SAN "islands," which eliminates the need for a separate switch for different applications.

Zoning

Zoning is another method allowing limitations on users' access to storage devices. While the users are all, technically, accessing the same devices, they are only granted permission to utilize portions of specific devices. The benefit here should be obvious: security is increased and network traffic is minimized.

Zones are a segment of SAN fabric and are used to connect groups of servers with storage devices for routine processing, but can be changed as needed. For instance, the zones can be reconfigured to allow occasional backups to storage devices residing outside the individual zones. Only members of a zone have access to the zone.

NOTE: *Zone sets* are groups of zones that interoperate on the fabric. Each zone set can accommodate up to 256 zones. All devices in a zone see only devices assigned to that zone, but any device in that zone can be a member of other zones in the zone set.

While it might sound like VSANs and zones are cut from the same fabric, so to speak, there is an important distinction between the two.

When using zoning, segmentation is not complete because it takes place within the same database on the switch enforcing zones and providing addressing and routing services. A malfunctioning node on one zone can, for example, corrupt the database and cause the whole SAN to crash.

VSANs, on the other hand, are able to segment the database. As such, each defined zone is its own unique storage network with its own dedicated database. That means if one VSAN has trouble, it doesn't affect other VSANs on the same switch.

NOTE: As a reminder, a LUN is an identifier used on a SCSI bus to distinguish among devices (logical units) with the same SCSI ID.

In a SAN, storage devices are typically zoned at the device level or LUN level.

▼ **Device level** Each user is restricted to using specific devices, like RAID arrays or specific disk drives.

▲ **LUN level** This allows the administrator to allocate resources in logical units, rather than in physical units. That is, a LUN zone could be spread out over a number of physical devices. As Figure 12-7 shows, devices could easily be the home of several zones.

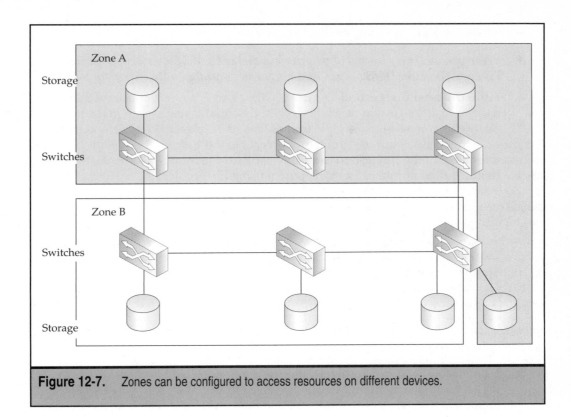

Figure 12-7. Zones can be configured to access resources on different devices.

While zoning is a great tool for managing resources, establishing zones should not be taken lightly. Like building a house, one doesn't just stumble to the hardware store, grab a few two-by-fours, a box of nails, some shingles, and then start hammering away. Zones must be carefully planned to ensure that the best use of the SAN's storage and the network's bandwidth are considered. Additionally, once zones have been put in place, it is more difficult to move storage space from one group of users (in Zone A, for instance) to another group of users (in Zone B). If this is undertaken, it is often necessary to reboot, which will cause network disruption. Even worse, there will be security holes since users in both zones might end up with access to the moved storage space.

QoS

Quality of Service is an important attribute of the MDS switch line. In earlier versions of Cisco SAN-OS (we'll talk about this operating system in more detail later in this chapter), traffic was only segmented based on whether the traffic was control data or traffic data. In the most recent release of the OS, QoS allows classification of traffic. For example, QoS can be applied so that data for latency-sensitive traffic has higher priority over throughput-sensitive applications, like data warehousing.

MDS switches provide the following QoS mechanisms:

▼ **Priority queuing**   Levels of priority are assigned to different types of traffic. Latency-sensitive traffic is granted higher priority than other types of traffic.

▲ **Fibre Channel Congestion Control (FCC)**   This is a flow control mechanism used to ease congestion on FC networks. Essentially, any switch in the network can identify congestion, sample frames from the congested queue, and then send messages about the problem upstream to the source. The switch closest to the source of the congestion can either forward the frames to other switches or limit the flow of frames from the port causing the problem.

Security

As with any internetworking device or technology, security is an essential consideration. It may be especially important in SANs, where so much of your organization's data is moving around and warehoused. The last thing you want is some thug getting into your company's archives and causing mischief.

MDS switches have a number of security features, meant to keep your data safe and secure. Let's take a closer look at the MDS switch's line of security mechanisms.

Authentication   The MDS switches provide the first layer of security through its authentication methods. Authentication comes in two forms:

▼ **User authentication**   Authentication, authorization, and accounting (AAA), which we talked about in Chapter 8, is used to validate users, grant access, and monitor activities. Once the user's ID and password have been sent, the switches perform local authentication, comparing the user's credentials against a local database, or remotely, using a RADIUS server.

▲ **Switch-to-switch and host-to-switch**   The Cisco SAN-OS utilizes Fibre Channel Security Protocol (FC-SP) for switch-to-switch and host-to-switch authentication. This is used to stifle any disruptions that would occur if an unauthorized device tried to connect to the fabric.

Port Security   Port security ensures that only an authorized device can be connected to a given switch port. Devices can be a host, target, or switch and are identified by their World Wide Number (WWN). This feature ensures that the SAN is not violated by an unauthorized device attempting connection to a switch port.

VSAN Access Control   Roles can be assigned based on the limitations of a specific VSAN. For instance, the network administrator role can be authorized for configuration setup and management duties. VSAN-administrators, on the other hand, can be granted permission only to configure and manage specific VSANs. This is a useful tool because it limits disruptions to the SAN. Rather than a misconfiguration affecting the entire SAN, it would be localized to the VSAN where the change was made.

Role-Based Access   Going hand-in-hand with user authentication is role-based access. This mechanism limits access to the switch, based on the specific permissions level granted to that user. The user can be granted full access to the device, or specific read and write levels of each command can be managed.

SPANs

A unique feature in the Cisco MDS 9000 line is the switched port analyzer (SPAN). SPAN monitors network traffic using a Fibre Channel interface. Traffic through a Fibre Channel interface can be replicated to a port known as a *SPAN destination port* (*SD port*). Any of the switch's Fibre Channel ports can be configured as SD ports. When an interface is in SD port mode it cannot be used with normal data traffic. A Fibre Channel Analyzer can be attached to the port to monitor SPAN traffic.

As the name suggests, Remote SPAN (RSPAN) allows you to monitor traffic for SPAN sources in switches throughout a Fibre Channel fabric. The SD port of a remote switch is used for monitoring. Normally, the remote switch is different than the source switch, but is attached to the same fabric. The MDS 9000 family of switches allows the remote monitoring of traffic from any switch in the fabric, as if it were the source switch.

SPAN is noninvasive, since SD ports do not receive frames; they just transmit copies of the SPAN source traffic and do not affect the redirection of network traffic. Additionally, VSANs can be specified as a SPAN source. All supported interfaces in the selected VSAN are included as SPAN sources. SPAN traffic can be monitored in two directions:

▼   **Ingress**   This refers to traffic entering the switch fabric through a source interface. This traffic is copied to the SD port.

▲   **Egress**   This refers to traffic exiting the switch fabric through a source interface. Like the ingress traffic, this is also copied to the SD port.

When a VSAN is selected as a source, then all physical ports, as well as PortChannels, are used as SPAN sources. TE ports are included when the port VSAN of the TE port is the same as the source VSAN. TE ports are ignored if the configured allowed VSAN list has the source VSAN, but the port VSAN is different.

Trunking

Harkening back to our discussion of VLANs is the term *trunking.* Trunking exists within the world of SANs much the same way that it does in the world of VLANs. Trunking refers to an inter-switch link (ISL) carrying more than one VSAN. Trunking ports send and receive extended ISL (EISL) frames, as shown in Figure 12-8. These frames contain an EISL header, which carries VSAN information. Once EISL is enabled on an E port, that port becomes a TE port.

NOTE: ISL is a Cisco proprietary protocol that maintains VSAN information as traffic flows between source and destination.

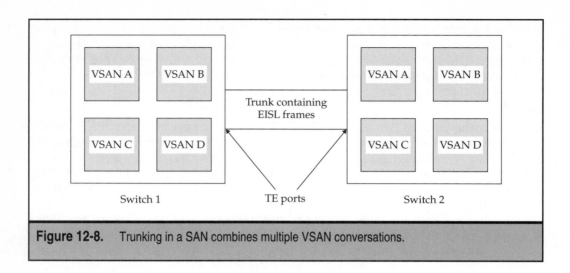

Figure 12-8.   Trunking in a SAN combines multiple VSAN conversations.

PortChannel

Multiple Fibre Channel ports can be aggregated into a single, logical port, providing high aggregated bandwidth, load balancing, and link redundancy. This is known as *PortChannel*. This allows the aggregation of up to 16 physical ports into a single logical port.

PortChannel is a useful technology because it increases the aggregate bandwidth on an ISL or EISL by distributing traffic among all links in the channel. Additionally, traffic is load balanced across multiple links. This traffic is identified by source ID (SID), destination ID (DID), or the originator exchange ID (OX ID).

PortChannel also provides redundancy for its links. If one link fails, that traffic is shifted to the remaining links. Further, if a link fails the upper protocol does not perceive the link as having failed. Rather, it simply has less bandwidth with which to work. As such, the routing tables are not affected by a link failure.

Hardware

The Cisco family of MDS products includes two Cisco MDS 9500 Series Multilayer Directors, the Cisco MDS 9216 Multilayer Fabric Switch, and the Cisco MDS 9100 Series of fixed configuration switches, in addition to several modules, providing customized functionality. These devices provide intelligent network services for SANs, including VSANs, security, traffic management, diagnostics, and a centralized management environment.

Let's take a closer look at the devices in Cisco's MDS line of multilayer storage switches.

MDS 9500 Multilayer Director Switches

The Cisco MDS 9500 Multilayer Director switches are modular devices aimed at large data-center environments. They provide a high level of scalability, security, and management.

The MDS 9500 Series includes two multilayer switches:

▼ **Cisco MDS 9506 Director** Targeted at data center environments and consisting of six slots on the chassis, two of which are reserved for supervisor modules. Four switching or services modules can be installed, providing Fibre Channel or Gigabit Ethernet services. The backplane can be directly plugged into four switching modules, two supervisor modules, two clock modules, and two power supplies.

▲ **Cisco MDS 9509 Director** Targeted at large data center environments, the chassis contains nine slots, two of which are reserved for supervisor modules. Seven switching or services modules can be installed, providing Fibre Channel or Gigabit Ethernet services. The backplane can be directly plugged in to seven switching modules, two supervisor modules, two clock modules, and two power supplies.

The supervisor modules on these directors provide high-availability and load-balancing features. A second supervisor module is available for the sake of redundancy. Additionally, the autosensing Fibre Channel ports support ISL (E ports), EISL (TE ports), loop (FL and TL ports), and fabric (F ports) connections.

The directors' small form-factor ports (SFP) are hot-swappable and can be configured for short- (500 meters) or long-wavelength (10 kilometers) connections. The ports are also individually configurable for both FCIP and iSCSI.

Table 12-2 compares the features of the Cisco MDS 9506 and the MDS 9509.

MDS 9000 Fabric Switches

The "little brothers" to the MDS 9500 series are the Cisco MDS 9000 switches. These use a similar architecture and software structure as the 9500 directors. However, where the 9500s are fully modular in design, the 9000 series is semi-modular. Within this family are two series: the Cisco MDS 9216 fabric switch and the Cisco MDS 9100 series.

The MDS 9216 Fabric Switch The chassis has two slots (one is reserved for the supervisor module). The supervisor module allows for supervisor functions and provides 16 1-/2-Gbps autosensing Fibre Channel ports. Its backplane can be directly plugged into one switching

Feature	MDS 9506	MDS 9509
Slots	6	9
Bandwidth	1.44 Tbps	1.44 Tbps
Fibre Channel ports	128	224
iSCSI and FCIP ports	24	48

Table 12-2. Comparison of Cisco's MDS 9500 Director

module. In the additional slot, another MDS 9000 family module can be installed, allowing for up to 48 ports.

Like the 9500 directors, the autosensing Fibre Channel ports support ISL, EISL, loop, and fabric connections. Further, its SFP ports are hot-swappable and can be configured for short- (500 m) or long-wavelength (10 km) connections. The ports are also individually configurable for both FCIP and iSCSI.

The MDS 9100 Series   Small- and medium-sized SANs are served with the Cisco MDS 9100 series of Fibre Channel switches. The switches (models 9120 and 9140) support 20 and 40 ports, respectively, and are fixed in terms of their expandability. Like their higher-powered brothers, the 9100 series provides high levels of scalability, availability, security, and management.

The MDS 9100 series includes built-in SAN management tools (useful for management of one or many fabric devices), including a command line and GUI tool, which we will talk about later in this chapter.

The common architecture and software structure is an important consideration when discussing the Cisco MDS devices. Because they share such a common design, it is easy to migrate from a smaller device to a larger device, or to add new switches to your fabric. Additionally, like any switches, the device can be purchased and installed, based on a specific need within the organization.

For example, a small- to medium-sized organization can use the Cisco MDS 9120 to construct their first SAN as they move from a direct-attached to a networked-storage solution. Larger organizations might use the 9120 for specific application or business functions.

Modules

Like many other Cisco products, the MDS 9000 family (save the 9100s) can be customized and configured based on your organization's particular needs. As such, there are a number of modules that can be installed in the devices. The following explains these various modules and how you can best use them in your SAN deployment.

The Cisco MDS 9500 Series Supervisor Module   The Cisco MDS 9500 Series Supervisor Module provides nondisruptive software updates and hardware redundancy for optimal availability. It can automatically restart a failed process before that process is detected at the system level. This is ideal because it reduces the number of resets to the module. However, in cases where a reset is needed, the unit's backup module will have taken over to eliminate disruption to the SAN.

With two supervisor modules installed, a 9500 series director can provide 1.44 Tbps of switching bandwidth. It also provides 1-/2-Gbps autosensing Fibre Channel ports and is compatible with future 10-Gbps modules.

Cisco MDS 9000 Family Fibre Channel Switching Modules   Cisco MDS 9000 Family Fibre Channel Switching Modules are 16- and 32-port devices. Each is a hot-swappable Fibre Channel tri-rate multiprotocol, as well as a coarse wavelength division multiplexing (CWDM) module. Individual ports can be configured with short- or long-wavelength SFPs, providing connectivity of 500 meters and 10 kilometers, respectively.

The CWDM SFP provides even great distances between devices of up to 100 kilometers. The module's interfaces operate at 1 or 2 Gbps. The ports can be configured to operate as

▼ E ports

■ F ports

■ FL ports

■ FX ports

■ Span destination (SD) ports

■ ST ports

■ TE ports

▲ TL ports

The Cisco MDS 9000 Family IP Storage Services Module   IP services can be added to the MDS 9000 family of switches through use of the Cisco MDS 9000 Family IP Storage Services Module. This module allows traffic to be routed between an IP storage port and any other port on an MDS 9000 family switch. In addition to the services available through other storage service modules (including VSANs, security, and traffic management), the Cisco MDS 9000 Family IP Storage Services Module uses IP to provide cost-effective connections to more servers and locations. This module provides FCIP and iSCSI IP storage services:

▼ **FCIP**   Provides data protection by enabling backup, remote replication, and disaster recovery across WAN connections, using FCIP tunneling. WAN resources are optimally utilized by tunneling up to three ISLs on a single Gigabit Ethernet port. Additionally, SAN complexity is ameliorated because a remote connectivity platform is not needed.

▲ **iSCSI**   One of the best attributes of the iSCSI features of the IP storage services module is its capability to use Fibre Channel SAN-based storage to IP-based servers. This is much less expensive than just using Fibre Channel. Storage and utilization is increased because IP and Fibre Channel are consolidated for storage purposes. Further, iSCSI allows the usage of legacy storage applications.

The Cisco MDS 9000 Caching Services Module   Cisco teamed up with IBM to produce the Cisco MDS 9000 Caching Services Module. This module is used to create, virtually, a storage device from disparate storage devices around the network. This provides access to more information and is managed centrally.

This module uses two nodes that are combined with IBM's TotalStorage SAN Volume Controller Storage Software for Cisco MDS 9000, allowing network-hosted virtualization and replication.

For optimal availability and reliability, each module includes 8GB of local cache, primary and backup batteries, and hard drives to protect data during power outages.

The Cisco MDS 9000 Family Advanced Services Module   Mixed storage resources can be pooled and managed using the Cisco MDS 9000 Family 32-port Fibre Channel Advanced Services Module. It allows for scalable, in-band virtualization services, utilizing integrated Veritas Storage Foundation for Networks software. The virtualized storage environment can be added to by integrating additional modules anywhere else in the fabric.

Software

There are two ways to manage MDS switches: from the command line or by using the Cisco MDS 9000 Fabric Manager, a GUI. The command-line interface (CLI) is similar to the CLI used for managing Cisco's other switches and routers. The GUI, on the other hand, provides a graphical representation of your SAN, its status, and the devices on the SAN. Before talking about the CLI and GUI, it's helpful to understand the operating system behind the MDS family: Cisco SAN-OS.

Cisco SAN-OS

The Cisco SAN-OS is the operating system for the Cisco MDS line of SAN devices. It provides storage networking features including nondisruptive upgrades, multiprotocol integration, VSANs, traffic management, diagnostics, and a unified SAN management.

The latest version of the operating system, Cisco MDS 9000 SAN-OS 1.3, includes a server-based version of the Cisco Fabric Manager, an embedded graphical management tool. This inclusion provides three important improvements: centralized management of multiple fabrics; continuous health, discovery, and monitoring; and performance monitoring.

Further, security in SAN-OS is enhanced through switch-to-switch and server-to-switch authentication, using Fibre Channel Security Protocol (FC-SP). This protects from intrusion from unauthorized devices. It also employs TACACS+ for authentication, authorization, and accounting of switches.

CLI

The first way to manage a Cisco MDS 9000 switch is using a serial RJ-45 connection on the supervisor module. This connection, like the connections made on other Cisco routers and switches, provides access to the CLI.

Whether you choose to use the CLI or Fabric Manager will depend largely on your personal taste and preference. However, there are some instances when one or the other will be preferable. For example, the CLI might be optimally employed when

▼ Initial setup routines are performed

■ Running debug and show commands for diagnostics and troubleshooting

▲ Writing and running configuration scripts

When the MDS device is connected to, locally, for the first time, the system enters a setup routine that aids in the initial configuration of the device. This step must be completed before you are able to connect to the switch or manage it with the Cisco Fabric Manager.

The CLI parser gives command help, command completion, and the ability to access previously executed commands. Entering commands is similar to the process used when entering commands into other Cisco switches. For example, the following command would be used to send a message to all users on the network that the system will be shutting down for maintenance.

```
switch# send Shutting down the system in 5 minutes. Please log off.
```

To enter the configuration mode, simply enter the following on the MDS switch:

```
switch# conf t
switch(config)#
```

Once in configuration mode, the device can be managed using a number of commands. Table 12-3 contains a very brief list of some of these commands and an explanation of what they do.

When you are done entering commands, type **end** to complete the session.

The Cisco Fabric Manager

Depending on your preference, you might prefer to manage your MDS fabric using a graphical user interface. In this case, Cisco has provided the Cisco Fabric Manager. Fabric Manager is a Java and SNMP-based network fabric and device management tool that shows real-time views of the fabric and installed devices. Cisco Fabric Manager is an alternative to the CLI for most switch management operations and is included with the switches.

Cisco Fabric Manager gathers information about the fabric topology, then sends SNMP queries to the SNMP agent running on the switch to which the Fabric Manager is connected. Once the switch has discovered all connected devices, it replies. It gathers this information using data from its FSPF database, as well as the name server database.

Command	Description
Fcc	For configuring FC Congestion Control
Fcdomain	To enter the fcdomain configuration mode
QoS	Establishes the priority of FC control frames
radius-server	For configuring RADIUS parameters
Vsan	To enter the VSAN configuration mode
Zone	To enter zone configuration commands

Table 12-3. Several Configuration Commands Used in the CLI

Fabric Manager is used to both discover and view the fabric's topology and manage zones. It is also useful for the management of:

▼ Zones and zone sets

■ VSANs

■ Port channels

▲ Users and roles

The GUI uses three views to manage your network fabric:

▼ **Device View**   Displays a current exhibit of device configuration and performance conditions for a single device.

■ **Fabric View**   Displays the current status of the network fabric, including multiple devices.

▲ **Summary View**   Displays a summary of switches, hosts, storage subsystems, and VSANs. It displays a summary of different port activity, as well as FC and IP neighbor devices.

The Cisco Fabric Manager is comprised of two network management tools, supporting Simple Network Management Protocol version 3. These tools include

▼ **Fabric Manager**   Displays a map of your entire network fabric, including not only the Cisco MDS 9000 devices, but also third-party switches, hosts, and storage devices

▲ **Device Manager**   Displays the Device and Summary Views of the fabric

SANs are a burgeoning technology and one that many organizations are expected to embrace in the coming years. While Cisco has a solid solution in its MDS line of switches, look for the company to expand its SAN offerings in the years to come. There is little doubt that there is a growing need for SANs and advanced storage, and this should be an interesting time for anyone involved in the storage arena.

CHAPTER 13

Cisco Content Networking

As the Internet continues to be a place rich with multimedia, it's apparent that an organization's single server cannot bear the entire burden on its own. For example, when hundreds of users from around the country try to access the multimedia content at a site located on a server in Kansas City, the results will be less than optimal.

However, if the content of that server were to be replicated and co-located in Seattle, New York, Chicago, Atlanta, Kansas City, and Reno, then users could get faster access to the material with fewer burdens on the network. This type of network is known as a *content delivery network* (*CDN*) and is gaining popularity with organizations that seek high availability from their internetwork.

CONTENT DELIVERY NETWORKS

Not only is the content more readily available by virtue of the fact that several servers are hosting it, but with an integrated CDN in place, a content provider can publish content from origin servers to the network edge. This frees resources on the servers, making the content easier, faster, and more efficient to locate and transfer to the user.

In this section, we talk about CDNs, how they work, and how they can be configured to help your organization. Further, we take a close look at Cisco's CDN solution, which involves several pieces of hardware and some specialized management software.

Meet the CDN

A CDN is an overlay network of content, distributed geographically to enable rapid, reliable retrieval from any end-user location. To expedite content retrieval and transmission, CDNs use technologies like caching to push content close to the network edge. Load balancing on a global scale ensures that users are transparently routed to the "best" content source. "Best" is determined by a number of factors, including a user's location and available network resources. Stored content is kept current and protected against unauthorized modification.

When an end user makes a request, content routers determine the best site, and content switches find the optimal delivery node within that site. Intelligent network services allow for built-in security, Quality of Service (QoS), and virtual private networks (VPNs).

According to International Data Corporation (IDC), the CDN market will grow from $203 million in 1999 to more than $8 billion in 2005. Fueling the growth is demand for Internet services such as Web and application hosting, e-commerce, streaming media, and multimedia applications. While user demand for such services mounts, the challenge for service providers comes in scaling their already congested networks to tap into these higher-margin opportunities.

CDN Needs

A CDN allows Web content to be cached—or stored—at various locations on the Internet. When a user requests content, a CDN routes the request to a cache that is suitable for that client. Specifically, it's looking for one that is online, nearby, and inexpensive to communicate with.

Which organizations will get the best results from a CDN? As with any technology and its usability, this is a loaded question. As we've seen time and time again, the only thing that limits how a technology is used is the imagination. However, those who would benefit most from a CDN are those who have an abundance of high-demand files or rich multimedia that would cause a strain on a single network.

However, there is a great deal of merit in using CDN principles to ensure reliability in case of a catastrophe. For instance, if you are storing content in caches in three different states, a natural disaster in your home state won't mean doom for your internetwork. Rather, users will still be able to access your information on one of the other two caches.

Using a CDN doesn't mean that all your data will be spread across the Internet. You can control where your content is located on the CDN and who will have access to it. Specified content is assigned to particular caches and only those caches are authorized to store that material. By controlling where content is cached, you increase the likelihood that requested content will be present in the cache. This is because there is enough room in the cache to store all the authorized content. Further, controlling content yields better performance results, because you can ensure that a particular cache is handling only the load associated with the content it is authorized to store.

Cisco CDN lets service providers distribute content closer to the end user and deal with network bandwidth availability, distance or latency obstacles, origin server scalability, and traffic congestion issues during peak usage periods, the company said in a statement. The system also enables businesses to expedite application deployment.

A CDN isn't a replacement for a conventional network. Rather, it's used specifically for specialized content that needs to be widely available. Dynamic or localized content, on the other hand, can be served up by the organization's own site, avoiding the CDN, while static and easily distributed content can be retrieved from the nearest CDN server. For instance, the banner ads, applets, and graphics that represent about 70 percent of a typical Web page could be easily offloaded onto a CDN.

How It Works

The need for a CDN is especially apparent when it comes to multimedia content. Because multimedia is such a bandwidth hog, a lone server cannot possibly tend to multiple, concurrent requests for rich multimedia content.

Figure 13-1 shows the basic design of a CDN.

Let's say you're surfing the Internet and want to watch a video that is online at Content Delivery Networking's Web site (a.k.a., www.cdning.com). Because that particular video is so popular, they have it deployed in their CDN. Here's what happens when you click the video's icon:

1. The user's browser requests the URL of www.cdning.com/video.mpg.

2. The DNS lookup of www.cdning.com is requested from the local DNS server.

3. The local DNS server does not have the IP address for cdning.com cached, so it sends a request to the authoritative DNS server.

4. The authoritative DNS server responds to the DNS lookup of cdning.com with IP addresses of multiple content router nodes.

5. The local DNS server transmits a request to the content router nodes for the IP address of the www.cdning.com server.

6. A content router node returns the IP address of the Content Engine (CE) to the local DNS server. There it is cached, along with a time-to-live (TTL) value.

7. The local DNS server returns the IP address of the www.cdning.com server to the browser.

8. The browser requests from the CE the file associated with the URL www.cdning.com/video.mpg.

9. The CE receives the request. If the content has been published and is stored on the CE, it is immediately served to the browser. If it is not currently stored on the CE, a pull from the origin (the www.cdning.com Web site) is initiated and the content is then served.

On the next request for content associated with www.cdning.com, the local DNS server has cached the IP address for the optimal CE, and steps 3 through 6 are skipped. When the TTL expires for the IP address in the local DNS server, then all steps are repeated.

Cisco's Solution

CDNs come in a variety of shapes and configurations, based largely on the vendor and the need. Cisco's CDN solution is based on five components—each performing its own specific function in the larger machine. Those components are

▼ Content Distribution Manager
■ Content Engine
■ Content Routing
■ Content Edge Delivery
▲ Intelligent Networking

No matter what the data being transferred—from a text file to streaming media—the content is delivered using these technologies.

Content Distribution Manager

Cisco's Content Distribution Manager is used to automatically distribute content-to-content delivery nodes, located at the network edge. This allows for global provisioning with real-time monitoring. Content Distribution Manager's products provide provisioning and policy settings for all content edge delivery nodes within the CDN. Located at the

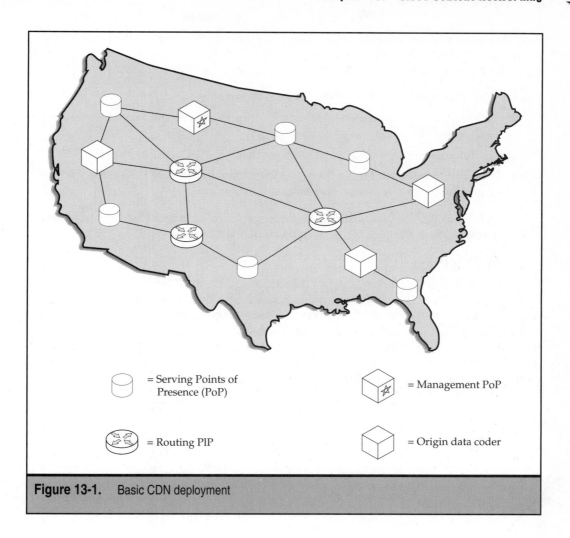

Figure 13-1.   Basic CDN deployment

logical central point of the network, Content Distribution Manager allows for the management and control of such details as:

- ▼ System policies
- ■ Network devices settings
- ■ Content control
- ■ Automatic replication of content
- ▲ Interface for live origination

The Content Distribution Manager is deployed either as a single server or as part of a redundant system. Physically, it can be located within a local cluster or distributed geographically. Other Content Distribution Manager functionality includes

▼ Central repository for real-time system monitoring

■ Management of content, including registration of Web sites and live streaming to enable delivery speed and reliability

■ Redundant configuration for fault tolerance

▲ Publishing tools that enable Web sites to easily subscribe to CDN material without extensive, hands-on setup and maintenance

The core of a Cisco content distribution system is Cisco's Content Distribution Manager, which controls the entire media distribution network.

Content Routing

Content Routing is the mechanism that directs user requests to the CDN site. This allows for high scalability and reliability. Routing is based on a set of real-time variables, including delay, topology, server load, and policies, such as the location of content and a user's authorization. Content routing enables accelerated content delivery and adaptive routing around broken connections and network congestion. Cisco's Content Router products interoperate with intelligent services in the network infrastructure, thereby ensuring content availability and providing global load balancing.

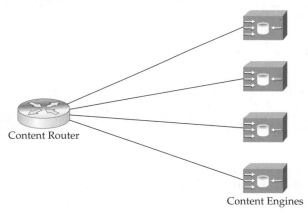

Content Router

Content Engines

The content router nodes are deployed at strategic locations within the network. Their functionality includes

▼ Real-time content request processing using standard DNS by redirecting user requests to an appropriate Content Engine, based on geographic location, network location, and network conditions

▲ Redundant configuration for multinetwork and wide-area fault tolerance and load balancing

Cisco provides a multitude of content routing protocols that enable enterprises and service providers to build content delivery networks. These protocols enable communication about content state among Cisco networking products. These protocols, which include Director Response Protocol (DRP), Dynamic Feedback Protocol (DFP), Web Cache Control Protocol (WCCP), and Boomerang Control Protocol (BCP), allow Cisco's products to work as a single, seamless system.

Content Edge Delivery

For the speediest delivery of content, Content Edge Delivery distributes content from the edge of the network to the end user. Cisco's CDN solution allows service providers to define and expand the edge of their network anywhere from a small number of data centers near the network core, out to the network edge, and just inside the firewall of a customer.

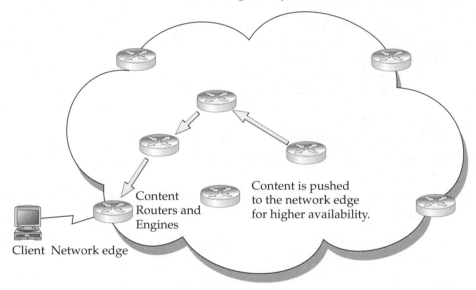

The Content Engines are located at the network edge, storing and delivering content to users. Other functionality includes

▼ Content delivery to end users and other Content Engines based on the Cisco content routing technology

■ Self-organization into a mesh routing hierarchy with other Content Engines forming the best logical topology based on current network load, proximity, and available bandwidth

■ Storage of content replicas

■ Endpoint servers for all media types

▲ Platform for streaming media and application serving

Once the right network foundation is in place, network caches are added into strategic points within the existing network, thereby completing the traffic localization solution. Network caches store frequently accessed content and then locally fulfill requests for the same content, eliminating repetitive transmission of identical content over WAN links.

Content Switching

Content switching is used to intelligently load balance traffic across delivery nodes at PoPs or distributed data centers based on the availability of the content, application availability, and server load. Intelligent content switching adds an additional layer of protection against flash crowds and ensures transaction continuity for e-commerce applications in the face of system stoppages. Intelligent content switching also allows for customization of content for select users and types of data.

Intelligent Network Services

The heartbeat of CDN is intelligent network services. This provides such functions as security, QoS, VPNs, and multicast. The Cisco CDN system integrates with existing content-aware services, which are required to build intelligent CDNs.

Key services that content intelligence provides include

▼ Content routing

■ Traffic prioritization for content

■ Services that scale economically and respond appropriately to unpredictable flash crowds

▲ The ability to track content requests and respond with content updates and replication

Because the functionality of a CDN is dependent on processing a number of variables, intelligent network services are crucial to maintaining an efficient, effective CDN.

IP Multicasting

Multicasting is a bandwidth efficient way to send the same streaming data to multiple clients. Such applications that benefit from multicasting include videoconferencing, corporate communications, and distance learning. Rather than consume large amounts of bandwidth by sending the same content to multiple destinations, multicast packets are replicated in the network at the point where paths separate. This results in an efficient way to conserve network resources.

How It Works   Multicasting is ideal when a group of destination hosts are receiving the same data stream. This group could be comprised of anyone, anywhere. It could be a training video sent to all new hires at a company's headquarters, or it could be updated benefits information sent, simultaneously, to the human resources departments at numerous branch offices. The hosts can be located anywhere on the Internet or on a private network.

We'll now examine the different types of transmission services in order to nail down, more precisely, what is going on in a multicast. Let's first consider the multicast's brothers, unicast and broadcast, shown in Figure 13-2:

▼ **Unicast**   Applications send one copy of each packet to the users requesting the information. If one user is linking to the Web server and requesting information, this isn't so bad. However, if multiple users want the same content, this gobbles up system resources as the same packets are sent to each user, simultaneously. That is, if there are 30 users requesting the same content, 30 copies of the data will be sent at the same time.

■ **Broadcast**   Applications can send one copy of each packet to a broadcast address. That is, the information is sent to everyone on the network. While this preserves bandwidth because the same content is being routed to everyone (rather than multiple copies of the content being sent at once), it suffers because there will be times when various users neither want, nor need, to see the content.

▲ **Multicast**   Applications send one copy of the packet and address it to a group of selected receivers. Multicast relies on the network to forward packets to the networks and hosts that need them. As such, this controls network traffic and reduces the quantity of processing performed by the hosts.

Multicasting has a number of advantages over unicasting and broadcasting. While it is an effective way to bring content to a single host, when the same content must be sent to multiple hosts it can cripple the network by consuming bandwidth. Broadcasting, on the other hand, is a good way to conserve network resources (a single copy of the data is sent to every user on the network). While this resolves bandwidth consumption issues, it is not useful if only a handful of users need to see the information.

IP Multicasting solves the bottleneck problems when data is being transferred from one sender to multiple destinations. By sending a lone copy of the data to the network and allowing the network to replicate the packets to their destinations, bandwidth is conserved for both sender and receiver.

Figure 13-3 shows how IP multicast delivers data from one source to multiple, appropriate, recipients. In this example, users want to watch a videocast of training for a new application. The users let the server know they are interested in watching the video by sending an IGMP (which stands for Internet Group Management Protocol) host report to the routers in the network. The routers use PIM (Protocol Independent Multicast) to create a *multicast distribution tree.* The data stream will be delivered only to the network segments that lie between the source and receivers.

Users opt in to be part of a group by sending an IGMP message. IGMP is a Layer 3 protocol allowing hosts to tell a router that it is interested in receiving multicast traffic for a particular group or groups. IGMP version 2 added the ability to leave a group. This made it easier for routers to know that a given host was no longer interested in receiving the multicast, thus freeing more network resources.

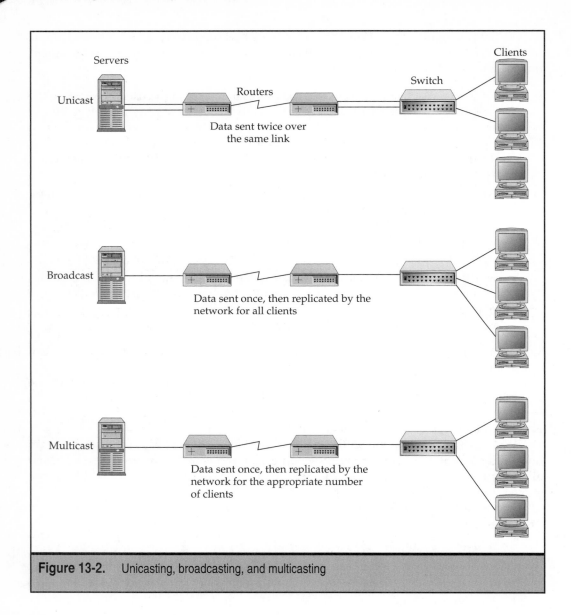

Figure 13-2. Unicasting, broadcasting, and multicasting

Addressing Addressing is an important component in the world of IP Multicasting. Once a client opts in to be part of a group, the content is delivered to a single IP address. When the data is sent to that IP address, the network, in turn, delivers it to everyone who agreed to be in the multicast group. By using a single IP address, the network can handle the task of channeling data to the appropriate clients.

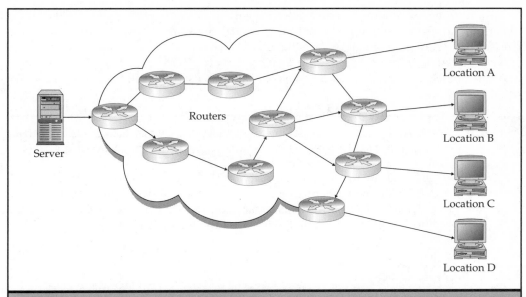

Figure 13-3. Multicast distribution trees send content to the appropriate network segments.

The Internet Assigned Numbers Authority (IANA) manages the assignment of IP multicast addresses. It has assigned the Class D address space for use in IP multicast applications. Class D address space falls between 224.0.0.0 and 239.255.255.255. There are no host addresses within Class D address space, since all hosts in the group share the group's common IP address.

However, this is not to mean that one multicast address will suit each and every need. Within the Class D address space, IP addresses have been subdivided for specialized use. The following examines how the Class D address space is further stratified:

▼ **224.0.0.0 through 224.0.0.255**   For use only by network protocols on a local network segment. Packets with these addresses should not be forwarded on by a router. Rather, they stay within the LAN segment and always are transmitted with a TTL value of 1.

■ **224.0.1.0 through 238.255.255.255**   Called *globally scoped* addresses. These addresses are used to multicast data between the source and across the Internet.

▲ **239.0.0.0 through 239.255.255.255**   Called *limited scope* or *administratively scoped* addresses. These are tied to an organization. Routers are configured with filters to prevent multicast traffic in this range from leaving the private network. Also, within the organization, this range of addresses can be subdivided within internal boundaries, thus allowing the reuse of addresses on smaller domains.

Another means of multicast addressing is called *Glop* addressing. RFC 2770 is in the experimental phase and suggests that the 233.0.0.0/8 address range be reserved for addresses by organizations that already have an Autonomous System Number (ASN) reserved. The ASN of the domain would then be converted and be made part of the second and third octets of the 233.0.0.0/8 range, to generate a static multicast address for that organization.

NOTE: An ASN is a globally unique identifier for an Autonomous System. Autonomous Systems are groups of networks that have a single routing policy, managed by the same network operators.

For instance, an organization with an ASN of 24545 would have a multicast IP address of 233.95.225.0. This conversion first takes the ASN (24545) and converts it into hexadecimal. Then, the hexadecimal value is separated into two octets, and then converted back to decimal to give us a subnet that is reserved for ASN 24545 to use.

CISCO PRODUCTS

Cisco has bolstered its CDN line the way it has with many products and devices—through company acquisitions. In 2000, Cisco delved deeper into the CDN market when, in May, it acquired ArrowPoint Communications for $5.7 billion in Cisco stock. The Acton, Massachusetts, company makes Web switches that are designed to optimize content delivery. ArrowPoint's products conduct URL- and cookie-based switching that direct traffic based on information contained in the content being requested and how often the content request occurs.

In March 2000, Cisco also bought SightPath for $800 million. SightPath, a network appliance maker in Waltham, Massachusetts, was acquired to assist Cisco customers with creating CDNs using existing Internet and intranet infrastructures. SightPath's appliances collect data on Web traffic, congestion, and server load to assist in routing traffic in the most efficient manner.

The following sections outline Cisco's CDN products, which are designed to work together to deliver an optimal CDN solution.

Content Distribution Managers

The core of a Cisco content distribution system is the Cisco Content Distribution Manager. The Content Distribution Manager controls your entire media distribution network, including all of the Cisco Content Engines, which are located at end-user sites.

The Content Distribution Manager is managed via a Web browser-based user interface, which allows you to configure and monitor Cisco Content Engines anywhere in the world. The manager allows you to preview any media and generate URLs for your intranet and extranet Web sites. Further, administrators can establish maximum bandwidth usage rates for distributing media across the WAN, as well as from content engines to end users over the LAN. This ensures that the network does not become congested with high-bandwidth traffic.

The following is Cisco's line of Content Distribution Managers:

▼ **CDM 4650** Best for a single content provider or enterprise CDN. This manager employs distribution policies for viewing and replication of video streaming and static Web content. When deployed with up to 1,000 Content Engines, the CDM 4650 provides media intranets and extranets that can be quickly deployed in branch offices, co-located or outsourced facilities, or Web-hosting services. It comes equipped with eight 18GB hard drives for system and data storage, 1GB of memory, and a single 1-GHz Xeon processor. List price: $50,000.

▲ **CDM 4630** This management device is ideal for up to 100 Content Engines at a single content provider. It offers all features available on CDM 4650 and comes equipped with two 36GB hard drives, 16MB Flash Memory, 256MB SDRAM memory, and a 600-MHz Pentium III processor. List price: $19,999.

Content Routers

A Content Router is a device that selects the best Content Engines within a CDN to serve end-user requests. Content Routers redirect requests to an appropriate Content Engine based on geographic location, network location and conditions, and content placement.

A CDN can contain up to ten Content Routers. In the event a Content Router fails, DNS proxies that would have communicated with the failed router communicate with another Content Router, and the system continues to function normally. The effect should be invisible to the end user.

The following lists Cisco's line of Content Routers:

▼ **CR 4450** This router provides Content Engine selection for large, service provider–based CDNs. It collects routing policies from the CDM 4650 and makes decisions based on the location of the user and PoPs, as well as network status and other parameters. An Oracle database is required. It comes equipped with two 18GB hard drives, 1GB of memory, and a 1-GHz Xeon processor. List price: $74,995.

▲ **CR 4430** This router provides content engine selection for small to medium CDNs (2 to 20) with multiple origin sites. This router allows for transparent insertion into edge networks and Web-hosting environments. This allows for CDN services to be expanded from the Web-hosting provider into edge ISP environments, or for creation of CDN peering services within an ISP. This model comes equipped with 1GB memory, two autosensing 10BASE-T/100BASE-TX ports, 16MB of Flash memory, and an 18GB hard drive. List price: $24,995.

Content Engines

Cisco's Content Engines are content networking products that accelerate content delivery. A Content Engine is a device that caches content in a CDN to serve end-user requests. A collection of Content Engines makes up a CDN.

The Cisco Content Engine works with your existing network infrastructure to complete your traffic localization solution. Content Engines offer a broad range of content delivery services for service providers and enterprises including streaming media, advanced transparent caching service, and employee Internet management.

The Cisco Content Engine product line covers a broad range of environments from service provider "Super Points of Presence (PoP)" down to small enterprise branch sites. Cisco's Content Engines product line includes

▼ **CE 7305**   This engine includes a default storage configuration of 144GB, and is expandable to 936GB. It runs on a 2.4-GHz Intel Pentium 4 Prestonia processor and has 2GB RAM. This engine can also be connected to the Cisco 7305 Content Engine SCSI connector, or a Fibre Channel adapter for interfacing with SANs.

■ **CE 7320**   Content delivery device for large content PoPs and co-location sites. Supports distributed Web hosting and content replication. This engine is upgradeable to support streaming media. It comes equipped with ten 18- or 36GB hard drives, 128MB Flash memory, 2GB SDRAM, and a 1-GHz Xeon processor. Its external storage is expandable to 216GB, it can handle 64,000 concurrent TCP sessions, and it delivers data transfer rates up to 155 Mbps.

■ **CE 7325**   This engine includes a default storage configuration of 432GB, and is expandable to 936GB (although no further internal storage can be added—it must be expanded externally). It runs on two 2.4-GHz Intel Pentium 4 Prestonia processors and has 4GB RAM. This engine can also be connected to the Cisco 7325 Content Engine SCSI connector, or a Fibre Channel adapter for interfacing with SANs.

■ **CE 590**   Content appliances for service provider content PoPs, co-location sites, and large enterprise sites. Upgradeable to support streaming media. It comes equipped with two 36GB hard drives. Storage is expandable up to 252GB. It has 16MB Flash memory, and 1GB SDRAM.

■ **CE 565**   The engine comes with 72GB of storage on two internal drives and can be expanded up to 396GB, using external hardware. The engine uses a 1.7-GHz Intel Pentium 4 processor, and 1GB RAM. The Cisco Content Engine 565 can be configured with Fibre Channel adapters for interfacing with SANs, or an MPEG video decoder for baseband video.

▲ **CE 510**   This engine comes with 40GB of storage and is expandable to 80GB. It does not support external storage expandability beyond its two internal drives. The engine uses a 1.7-GHz Intel Pentium 4 processor and 512MB RAM. The Cisco Content Engine 510 can be configured with Fibre Channel adapters for interfacing with SANs, or an MPEG video decoder for baseband video.

Content Switches

When Cisco first got into the CDN game, it did not develop switches that were meant just for CDNs. Rather, CDN functionality was included as a component of other types of Cisco switches. Now, however, Cisco has developed its Cisco CSS 11500 Series Content Services Switches. These switches have the functionality to work, in cooperation, with the other devices in the Cisco CDN solution.

There are three models in the Cisco CSS 11500 Series Content Service Switch line.

▼ **CSS 11501**   This model has a fixed configuration, offers 6-Gbps aggregate throughput, eight 10/100 Ethernet ports, and one Gigabit Ethernet port, through an interface converter. This model holds up to two 256MB Flash memory disks, up to two 512MB hard drives, and can conduct up to 1000 SSL transactions per second.

■ **CSS 11503**   This model has three slots, offers 20-Gbps aggregate throughput, 32 10/100 Ethernet ports, and six Gigabit Ethernet ports through interface converters. This model holds up to two 256MB Flash memory disks, and up to two 512MB hard drives.

▲ **CSS 11506**   This model has six slots, 40-Gbps aggregate throughput, 80 10/100 Ethernet ports, and eight Gigabit Ethernet ports, through interface converters. It requires one switch control module. This model holds up to two 256MB Flash memory disks, and up to two 512MB hard drives.

Cisco IP/TV

It isn't just data that can course through the veins of your IP CDN. By utilizing the Cisco IP/TV solution, networked video can be delivered. Video is integrated along with IP network services to provide live and scheduled video, video on demand, and synchronized presentations. This allows an organization to deliver content over a Web infrastructure, ensuring content management, edge delivery, content routing, content switching, and intelligent network services.

Because video is being sent across an IP network, there are a number of benefits to the delivery of content. First, IP/TV utilizes IP Multicasting to ensure bandwidth consumption is minimized when multicasting across the network. Additionally, one-to-many broadcasts are managed and controlled easier because of Source-Specific Multicasting (SSM). This makes deployment easier and alleviates address allocation problems.

To ensure content has been delivered effectively and appropriately, the IP/TV solution also includes the StreamWatch application. This allows usage monitoring from all desktops during a unicast, broadcast, or multicast. The results are generated into logs for later analysis. The reports can depict results based on quality, location, and IP address.

The Cisco IP/TV 3400 Series Video Server comes with preconfigured software, preinstalled capture cards, network interface cards, and device drivers, all of which provide a turnkey solution for video CDNs. The servers provide a range of video and audio formats, including MPEG-1, -2, and -4.

There are five models within the Cisco IP/TV 3400 Server series:

▼ **Cisco IP/TV 3412 Control Server** This model comes preconfigured with Content Manager and StreamWatch for centralized management of the IP/TV deployment. It does not contain storage for video content.

■ **Cisco IP/TV 3425 and 3425A Broadcast Servers** The model captures real-time and prerecorded content on an 18GB drive, then streams it over the network using either MPEG-1 or -2 compression. The 3425A is the same as the 3425, but offers MPEG-1 at a lower price point.

■ **Cisco IP/TV 3432 Archive Server** The 3432 is useful for environments in which prerecorded video on demand or scheduled broadcasts are used. The 75GB archive server stores 150 hours of 1-Mbps video and more than 50 Mbps of aggregate video bandwidth.

▲ **Cisco IP/TV 3417 Starter Kit** A starter device containing the capabilities of the broadcast server, control server, and archive server in a single unit. This is targeted at departmental or small group deployments and holds 18GB of video.

Global Site Selector Platform

Organizations that have their assets spread among a geographically disparate area have trouble ensuring content gets to Web visitors from the most available, closest, and appropriate site. Cisco's Global Site Selector platform makes the process of finding the appropriate data at the most available site much more effective and streamlined. This not only makes the process faster for the user, but it also eliminates any one site from being overwhelmed with requests.

The Cisco GSS 4480 adds a high-level layer of load balancing and resource accessibility to distributed data centers. This is a useful device for large organizations and service providers who have data centers distributed across a wide geographical area. The GSS 4480 selects the best site based on the load and the availability of data. This information is supplied to the GSS by the content switch, leaving the switch to select the best local sever within the data center to provide the data—again, based on data availability and current load.

The GSS 4480 also handles DNS duties (managing 4,000 DNS lookups per second). By taking on the DNS server responsibilities from traditional DNS servers, the GSS 4480 can make the process of global site selection more efficient, increase DNS responsiveness, and improve the scalability of Web sites and data centers.

CDN Software

A CDN is a constantly changing environment. Content Engines, Content Switches, and Content Routers are added and removed, and the content housed on those devices is in a constant state of flux because content providers come and go. New routed domains are defined, old ones are removed, and assignments of routed domains to Content Engines change.

To deal with the dynamics of a CDN, Cisco offers several applications to manage CDNs. Two of the more prevalent packages include Application and Content Networking System (ACNS) and CDN Enterprise Edition.

ACNS

Cisco Application and Content Networking System (ACNS) software is targeted at organizations and service providers deploying CDNs. ACNS 5.1 is the latest version of this software and combines content networking components into a common application for Content Distribution Manager, Content Engine, and Content Router. This application is useful for both small CDN deployments, as well as large ones.

ACNS can manage CDN deployments of up to 2000 Content Engines and 1,000,000 prepositioned items in Content Engines. ACNS software pulls content from a Web server or an FTP server and sends it directly to the Content Engines.

ACNS benefits from a number of features, including the ability to configure the system to run both cache and CDN applications simultaneously. Network administrators can also upgrade ACNS software, or they can downgrade to a previously installed version if they determine the new version is not as useful as a previous installation. ACNS also allows for disk provisioning, providing the management of disk space for HTTP caching and for prepositioned content.

Enterprise Edition 3.0

Cisco's CDN Software, Enterprise Edition 3.0, offers features with multimedia content and management in mind.

First, the software allows the Cisco Content Engines to be configured with an MPEG decoder for video playback to a standard monitor. This allows users to play media to analog video devices and control them from the Cisco Content Distribution Manager using VCR-like controls, including the ability to build playlists, and stop, start, and loop multimedia content.

The software's browser-based application program interface allows network administrators to establish user-level access to specific channels of content. Once this has been set up, designated users can add, modify, or delete media from their specified channels through a graphical user interface. This feature allows flexibility to the CDN and enhances security by allowing different levels of user interaction and involvement, without "giving away the keys."

CDN also employs the Self-Organizing Distributed Architecture (SODA). SODA is a Cisco proprietary technology that uses complex algorithms to route high-bandwidth media over LANs or the Internet. SODA eliminates bottlenecks that go part and parcel with multimedia streaming.

CDN's interface allows

▼ Network configuration for the Content Distribution Manager, Content Engines, and Content Routers

■ Establishment of bandwidth parameters for replication of media to the Content Engines

▲ Importing of media files to the Content Distribution Manager

CACHING

Internet traffic has been growing at a breakneck pace. Because of the sheer amount of traffic coursing across the Internet and intranets, congestion has gotten worse. ISPs and organizations are being challenged to deal with this problem, because it is difficult to ensure QoS and deliver content to clients efficiently and affordably.

While we discussed the benefits of QoS in Chapter 7, there is another solution that can help ease traffic problems on a network—caching. By localizing traffic patterns on your existing network, you get a double bonus—not only is content delivered more quickly, but the freed resources are available for additional traffic.

Content delivery is accelerated by locally filling content requests, instead of having to go across the Internet to fetch the information. This ensures the content is delivered quickly and without having to worry about bottlenecks beyond your control. Traffic localization reduces the amount of redundant traffic on your WAN connections. This allows additional network resources for more users, and for new services (like VoIP, for example).

In order to achieve this solution, it is necessary to have a network that enables transparent redirection technologies, like Web Cache Communication Protocol (WCCP). With this technology in place, network caches are added to key locations in the network to realize the traffic localization solution. Network caches store frequently accessed content, then serves them locally to deliver requests for the same content, but without having to go back across the Internet or WAN to get them. Obviously, this relieves congestion because repeated transmissions no longer need to be sent out. Figure 13-4 illustrates this process.

1. Using a Web browser, a user requests a Web page.

2. The network examines this request, and then redirects it to a local network cache. This is done transparently so the user is unaware of the redirection.

3. The cache may not have the Web page stored. In that event, the cache makes its own request of the original Web server.

4. The original Web server delivers the requested Web page to the cache, which then resends it to the user. The cache stores a copy of the page in case it is needed later.

5. When another user requests the same Web page, this time the cache has the page on hand and the request is fulfilled locally.

6. The cache delivers the Web page to the user, locally. This eliminates the need to use WAN bandwidth and delivers the content much more quickly.

Web Cache Communication Protocol

Though we mentioned several CDN protocols earlier in this chapter, Cisco's proprietary protocol for enabling transparent caching throughout a network—Web Cache Communication Protocol (WCCP)—has become the protocol on which Cisco's solution is built. This protocol uses HTTP redirects to provide functionality. The first version of WCCP allowed communicating with just one router, did not support multicasting, and was limited to HTTP traffic. The current version is WCCP v2 and resolves the shortcomings of version 1.

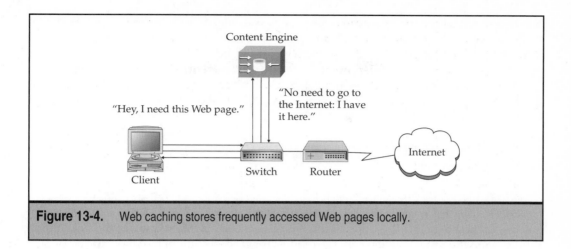

Figure 13-4. Web caching stores frequently accessed Web pages locally.

WCCP uses UDP port 2048, operating through a generic routing encapsulation (GRE) tunnel between the router and the Content Engine (or Content Engines). Once the content has been delivered, either from the Content Engine or the source Web server, the HTTP packets are delivered and are not altered.

The Content Engines maintain a list of routers with which they have WCCP communications. When the Content Engine identifies itself to the routers, it shares its list of routers. In turn, the routers reply with a list of Content Engines that they see in the *service group.* As soon as all the devices know about one another, one Content Engine becomes the lead engine and determines in what way packets will be redirected.

The Content Engines send *heartbeats* to the routers every ten seconds through a GRE tunnel. If there is a cluster of Content Engines and one of the engines fails to send a heartbeat within 30 seconds, the router informs the lead Content Engine that the engine is missing and its resources must be reallocated to the remaining engines.

NOTE: We'll talk more about the specific resources in a cluster and what clustering is later in this section.

Freshness

An obvious concern when using caching is the issue of freshness. How can you be sure that the page you're looking at contains the most current information? That is, what prevents the Content Engine from storing last Friday's visit to a newspaper Web site for perpetuity?

Each Web page is made up of a number of Web objects and each object has its own caching parameters that are established and managed by the Web page authors and HTTP standards. So, for example, our newspaper Web site will have new content, but things like the toolbars, navigation buttons, and the masthead are likely to be cacheable. As such, when the Content Engine stores the newspaper's Web site, it stores the elements that are not likely to change, then goes out to cull the new content. Content Engines deliver fresh content by obeying HTTP caching standards (which we'll talk about in a moment) and allowing the administrators to decide when content should be refreshed from the source Web servers.

Web authors can establish to what degree to allow caching. In HTTP, caching parameters for each object on a Web site can be managed. Content can be set up for caching based on three settings:

▼ The content is noncacheable.

■ The content is cacheable (the default setting).

▲ The content is cacheable, but it will expire on a given date.

HTTP 1.1 introduced a freshness mechanism called If-Modified-Since (IMS), which ensures cached data is up-to-date. Content Engines send an IMS request to the destination Web server when the engine receives a request for cached content that has expired or IMS requests from clients where the cached content is older than a percentage of its maximum age. If the content on the destination Web server determines that the content in the engine has not been updated, it sends a message to the Content Engine to go ahead and serve its stored data to the client. If the content has been updated and is no longer fresh, the Content Engine will retrieve the new content.

But freshness is not just in the hands of the Web-page creators. Network administrators can control the freshness of Web objects in their Content Engines. Content Engines have a parameter called the *freshness factor* that can be configured by the network administrator. This determines just how quickly content expires. When an object is stored in the cache, a TTL value is computed. That value is

$$TTL = (current\ date - last\ modified\ date) * freshness\ factor$$

If the content has expired, based on the aforementioned formula, the Web data is refreshed in the cache the next time an IMS request is issued.

To establish a modest freshness policy, the freshness factor can be set to a small value (like .05) so that objects will expire more quickly. This will, however, cause more bandwidth to be consumed as pages are refreshed. Setting the freshness factor higher will cause less bandwidth to be consumed.

NOTE: Freshness can also be managed by the client. The client can click the browser's Reload or Refresh button. This will cause a series of IMS requests asking for Web objects that have been refreshed. Alternatively, SHIFT-REFRESH or SHIFT-RELOAD causes Content Engines to be bypassed and have the content sent directly to the client from the Web server.

Content Engine Caching

There are three primary ways in which content can be cached in Cisco's solution: transparent, proxy-style, and reverse proxy-style. The most common means of caching utilizes the transparent style of caching. However, the other methods are also useful to understand, as they may be more relevant and useful for your organization's needs.

Transparent Network Caching

The first method of caching is known as transparent caching. We outlined the steps involved in this type of caching already—in essence, a Web browser requests a Web page. That request first runs through the WCCP-enabled router, where it is analyzed. If the router determines that a local Content Engine has the desired content cached, it sends the request to the Content Engine, which delivers the content back to the browser. If it isn't cached, the Content Engine goes to the Internet to fetch and store the page.

Because this method utilizes a WCCP-enabled router, the Content Engine functions transparently to the browser. Clients need not be configured to be pointed to a specific proxy cache. As the Content Engine is transparent to the network, the router acts in a "normal" role for traffic that does not have to be redirected.

Using a CSS switch, however, the client's request need never reach the router. In larger deployments, it makes better sense to have a CSS switch to make decisions as to whether particular content has already been cached locally. Further, large deployments might employ several Content Engines and data would be stored in each device, based on a uniform resource locator (URL).

HTTPS   The whole process of caching seems straightforward enough, especially if someone is requesting static content. However, there is a slew of content on the Internet, on your Intranet, or possibly traversing a WAN link that won't be static. For instance, there are times when a user's Web page request will have to go to the intended web server. The concept of caching is not thrown out the window in these cases. Let's consider what happens when a Secure HTTP (HTTPS) session is initiated.

1. The user initiates an HTTPS session. It is taken by the WCCP-enabled router and sent on to the Content Engine.

2. The Content Engine, configured as an HTTPS server, receives the request from the router.

3. A Secure Sockets Layer (SSL) certificate is obtained from the destination Web server by the Content Engine, and then sent back (via the Content Engine) to the client to negotiate an SSL connection.

4. The client sends HTTPS requests within the SSL connection.

5. The Content Engine analyzes the request. If the information is in its cache, HTTP request processing occurs. If the content is in the Content Engine's cache (also known as a *cache hit*), it sends the desired content back using the SSL connection.

6. If the content is not stored within the Content Engine (also known as a *cache miss*), it establishes a connection to the destination Web server and requests the content through the SSL connection.

7. If possible, the Content Engine will cache the information, and then send a copy back to the client through the SSL connection.

Content Bypassing   There are some times when the Content Engine simply has to be avoided in order to get the session that the client needs. Though there are mechanisms in place for establishing HTTPS sessions, not all secure conversations can be accepted through the Content Engine.

Some Web sites rely on IP authentication and, as such, won't allow the Content Engine to connect on the client's behalf. Content Engines can use authentication traffic bypass to avoid service disruption. Authentication traffic bypass is used automatically to create a dynamic access list for client/server pairs.

When a client/server pair go into authentication bypass, they are bypassed for a set amount of time. The default setting is 20 minutes, but that value can be changed, depending on the organization's need.

Nontransparent/Proxy-Style

The nontransparent or *proxy-style* of caching is known to the client, whereas transparent caching occurred without the client's knowledge that it was occurring. With proxy caching, the proxy cache performs the DNS lookup on the client's behalf. Proxies are used for different protocols, like HTTP, HTTPS, FTP, and so forth. Consider the network in Figure 13-5.

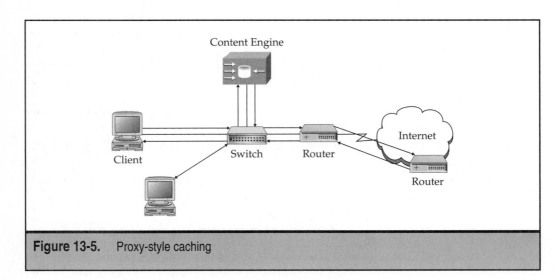

Figure 13-5.   Proxy-style caching

The client has been configured to use a proxy server for HTTP requests. Normally, port 8080 is used, but different ports can be configured for the protocol you wish to manage. The IP address of the proxy is also configured on the client. In the example, we're using address 10.1.100.100. Let's follow this method of caching step-by-step.

1. HTTP requests for content are directed to the proxy.
2. If the proxy cache does not have the content, the proxy performs the DNS lookup for the destination Web site.
3. When the DNS has been resolved, the proxy requests the content from the destination Web server, and then retrieves it.
4. The content is stored in the cache before being forwarded to the client. This ensures that the next time the content is requested, the cache will have it.

Proxy caching is useful because the cache can be anywhere in the network. Further, a measure of network security is provided in that only the client contacts the proxy, so the firewall rules can be stricter, allowing only the proxy to work through the firewall.

Reverse Proxy Caching

In the aforementioned proxy cache method, the proxy server is a proxy for the client. In the reverse proxy method, the proxy server acts as a proxy for the server. Reverse proxy caches also store selected content, whereas transparent and proxy methods story frequently requested content.

There are two cases in which reverse proxy caching is desirable:

▼ Replicating content to geographically disparate locations

▲ Replicating content for the sake of load balancing

In this scenario, the proxy server is set up with an Internet-routable IP address. That is, clients go to the proxy server based on DNS resolution of a domain name.

WCCP Servers   Consider the cache deployment in Figure 13-6. The Content Engine works with a WCCP-enabled router and is configured for reverse proxy service for a Web server. In this scenario, the router interface linked to the Internet has an IP address of 192.168.1.100. HTTP requests sent to this server are first sent to the router interface at 172.12.12.1. Once the HTTP request has been received at this interface, the router redirects the request to the Content Engine (with an IP address of 172.12.12.20). In this case, the Content Engine is in front of the Web server, helping reduce the amount of traffic on the Web server. If the information requested is not in the Content Engine, it sends a request to the Web server to locate the content.

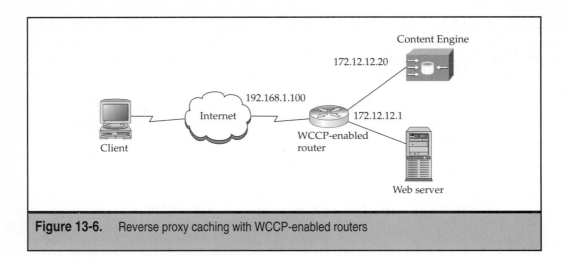

Figure 13-6.   Reverse proxy caching with WCCP-enabled routers

CSS Switches   Consider the cache deployment in Figure 13-7. Here, the Content Engines are deployed with a WCCP-enabled router and a CSS switch. Here, a user sends a request for Web page content. This is accepted at the CSS switch's virtual IP address. When the CSS switch takes the request, it forwards the request to the Content Engine. If the Content Engine does not have the requested data, the Content Engine will forward a request to the Web server.

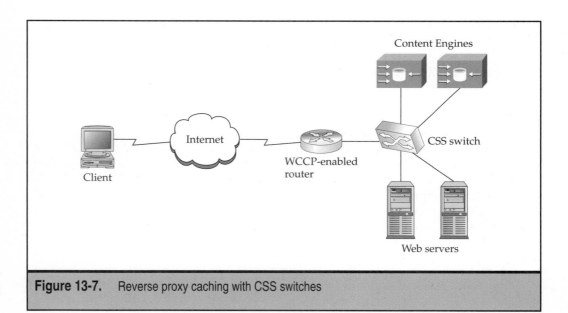

Figure 13-7.   Reverse proxy caching with CSS switches

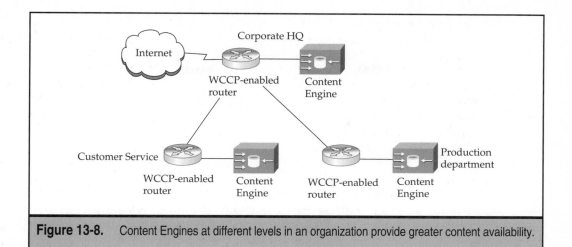

Figure 13-8.   Content Engines at different levels in an organization provide greater content availability.

Multiple Content Engine Deployment

Content Engines can be located at multiple points throughout an organization for optimal caching performance. For instance, consider the organization in Figure 13-8. In this case, the organization is served by three Content Engines. The first handles caching for the customer service department at the organization's headquarters, the second handles caching for the production department in a branch office.

If a client in the customer service department sends a Web page request that can be accommodated by the first Content Engine, it will be served by that device. If that Content Engine cannot fulfill the request, it passes the request to the end Web server. Before it gets to the destination Web server, the request is considered by the Content Engine at the main Internet point of access. This provides another chance for the content to be served before having to go out onto the Internet or across a WAN. If this Content Engine is able to fulfill the request, then it is unnecessary to go onto the Internet. In the event someone at the branch office had requested the page, it might still be located on Content Engine number three, at corporate headquarters.

This scenario is especially useful for Internet service providers. With a Content Engine serving a number of clients, if common Web sites are requested, it is unnecessary to keep getting the page from the Internet. Instead, it can be served up locally, by the Content Engine.

Clustering

Another way to manage high traffic levels is via clustering. This simply means that multiple Content Engines are set up together. For instance, one Cisco Content Engine 7325 can support in excess of 155 Mbps of traffic and up to 936 GB of data. However, if a second 7325 is added, then the cluster can handle more than 310 Mbps throughput and 1.87TB of data. Up to 32 Content Engines can be clustered together.

When a new Content Engine is added to the organization's cluster, the WCCP-enabled router detects the new device and reallocates resources for the new Content Engine.

Content Engines use so-called *buckets*. WCCP-enabled routers redirect traffic to Content Engines using a hashing procedure based on the incoming request's destination IP address, and the request is sent to one of 256 buckets. Using a hashing technique, requests are spread evenly across all 256 buckets, and therefore all Content Engines in the cluster.

When a new Content Engine is added to the cluster, the WCCP-enabled router detects the new engine, and then the number of buckets is reconfigured, based on the total number of Content Engines. For example, let's say your organization has two Content Engines. Each engine would contain 128 buckets. If a third is added, then each engine is reconfigured to contain 85 or 86 buckets.

However, since a brand new Content Engine won't have any content when it is added, it will suffer frequent cache misses until it has built up its storage. This problem is initially ameliorated because the new Content Engine sends a message to others in the cluster, seeking the requested content. If another engine in the cluster has the content, it will be sent to the new engine. Once the engine decides that it has gotten enough content from its cohorts (based on parameters established by the network administrator), it will stop bothering its peers for content requests and instead query the end server.

Reliability

Clustering is not only a good way to balance the load of caching requests, it is a good way to ensure reliability. In the event one of the Content Engines in a cluster goes down, the WCCP-enabled router steps in and redistributes that engine's load across the remaining engines. The system continues operating, but with one less Content Engine. Certainly, this is not ideal from an availability standpoint, but at least the system remains accessible until the failed Content Engine can be restored.

If the entire cluster fails, then the WCCP-enabled router will stop bothering with caching, sending Web requests to their destination Web servers. To end users, it will appear as though it is simply taking longer for Web content to arrive.

As you have probably noticed by now, there seems to be a lot of responsibility placed on the shoulders of the WCCP-enabled router. If an engine in a cluster goes down, it is easy enough to redistribute its load to the other engines. But what happens if the WCCP-enabled router fails? In such an event, and assuming the pieces are in place before a failure, a WCCP-enabled, Multigroup Hot-Standby Router Protocol (MHSRP) router pair provides routing protection. This is known as *WCCP multihoming*.

Consider the network in Figure 13-9. There are two, WCCP-enabled routers depicted. In the event one of these routers fails, the other would step in to take over for its failed brother, redirecting Web requests to the Content Engine cluster. The network in Figure 13-9 is fully redundant, because it employs both a Content Engine cluster and WCCP multihoming.

Bypassing

Multihoming and clustering are good ways to plan for problems. However, as effective as they are, they aren't perfect. There might be a time when the entire cache system must be avoided. There are two scenarios in which the cache system is bypassed.

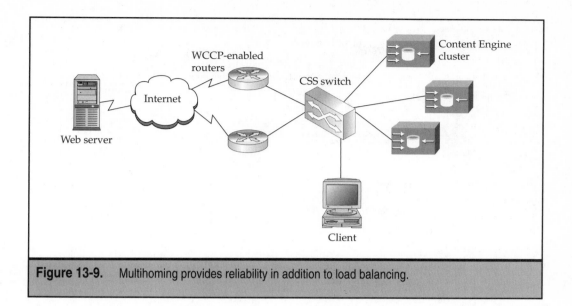

Figure 13-9.   Multihoming provides reliability in addition to load balancing.

Overload   Overload bypassing is used when there is a sudden surge of Web traffic and the Content Engine or cluster is simply overwhelmed. When this happens, the Content Engine is able to sense when it is overloaded and refuses additional requests until it can handle those already backlogged. Thus, incoming Web requests are simply forwarded to their destination Web servers, whether the content is stored in the Content Engine or not. The Content Engine continues to refuse requests until it determines that not only has the overload situation been averted, but it does not expect to become overloaded again if it takes in new requests.

If the Content Engine is so besieged with requests that it cannot communicate with the WCCP-enabled router and share status messages, then the router will logically remove that engine from the cluster, reallocating its buckets to other engines in the cluster.

Client   If a client needs to be authenticated to the Web site using the client's IP address, authentication will fail if the Content Engine's IP address is seen, and not the client's IP address. In such cases, the Content Engine will allow clients to bypass the engine and connect directly to the destination Web server.

Consider the exchange in Figure 13-10. In this figure, the client is attempting to access a Web server that insists on authentication. First, the request is funneled through the Content Engine. Seeing that the information is not stored locally, it is forwarded on to the destination Web server. If error codes are returned to the Content Engine (for instance, a 401-unauthorized request or 403-forbidden) the engine will automatically enter client bypass

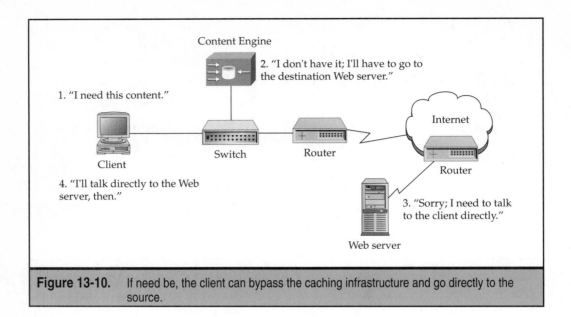

Figure 13-10. If need be, the client can bypass the caching infrastructure and go directly to the source.

mode and allow the client to interact directly with the destination Web server. Additionally, the Content Engine will store the destination IP address along with the client IP address, and the next time the client attempts to access that Web server, the Content Engine will automatically enter client bypass mode.

If you think the golden days of internetworking are behind us, you haven't seen anything yet. The future is bright as technologies and protocols are able to handle more and more. As networks become more intelligent, we can expect to see more services delivered with special attention paid to network conditions and the specific needs of the content.

PART IV

Designing Cisco Networks

CHAPTER 14

Routing Protocols

Over the preceding few chapters, we've covered the gamut of network devices. Switches sit in a data closet, taking twisted-pair cables from host devices, forming the LAN, and they also pack the power to support VLANs. Another inhabitant of the data closet is the access server, used to link remote users into internetworks via Internet VPNs or dial-in telephone lines. If a packet moves beyond its source LAN segment, it flows onto a backbone LAN where it encounters a router and (if it's a secured internetwork) a firewall. After that point is the Great Beyond. Once the packet goes past the local network, it enters a realm of seemingly infinite complexity.

Internetworks are complex because they're big and subject to endless fluctuation. An internetwork's topology is altered whenever a new switch is added, or when a router is inserted to help direct growing internetwork loads. As usage patterns evolve, traffic congestion seems to pop up in different spots every day. If network devices crash, they take their connected LAN segments down with them, and traffic must be immediately redirected—and then redirected back once the downed device is brought back online. More frequently, the network device is up but one of its network interfaces has gone down, or the interface is OK but a cable was accidentally knocked from its port. To top it all off, sometimes all the physical network equipment is running fine but things *still* go awry because a rotten config file was somehow introduced into the mix!

The point here is that large internetworks are simply too complicated to be managed by people alone. Imagine a roomful of network administrators trying to manually control each and every network event in a Fortune 500 company, and you'd see a portrait of creeping disorganization. Now imagine that same room—or even a building—filled with people attempting to corral the Internet itself, and you see unmitigated chaos. There's just too much complexity and change to handle without a constant source of reliable help—automated help.

So how does it all work? How do packets find their way across internetworks with the reliability we've come to take for granted? The answer is routing protocols.

OVERVIEW OF ROUTING PROTOCOLS

As you've learned, a *protocol* is a formalized system for exchanging a specific type of information in a certain way, and an *algorithm* is a system of rules carefully crafted to control a process that must contend with varying factors.

In our context, a *routing protocol* formalizes the ongoing exchange of route information between routers. Messages called *routing updates* pass information used by routing algorithms to calculate paths to destinations. A *routing algorithm* is a system of rules that controls an internetwork's behavior in such a way that it adapts to changing circumstances within the internetwork's topology. Ongoing changes include such things as which links are up and running, which are fastest, whether any new equipment has appeared, and so on. Each router uses its own copy of the algorithm to recalculate a map of the internetwork to account for all the latest changes from its particular perspective.

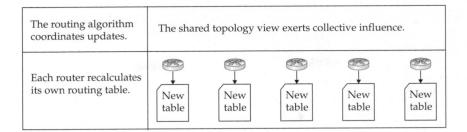

The routing algorithm coordinates updates.	The shared topology view exerts collective influence.
Each router recalculates its own routing table.	New table New table New table New table New table

Routing protocols use a peer arrangement in which each router plays an equal role. Those new to internetworking often think that routers are somehow coordinated by a centralized management server, maybe an SNMP server. They are not. There is no routing protocol server to centrally manage routing processes. Ongoing routing table maintenance is handled in real time through an arrangement in which each router makes its own route selection decisions. To configure a routing protocol for an internetwork, the routing protocol process must be configured in each router that will be involved in the arrangement. In practical terms, the IOS config file for every router must have parameters set to send and receive routing updates, run the algorithm, and so forth. Properly configured, the routing protocol is able to collectively influence all these machine-made decisions so that they work in harmony. The area within which routing information is exchanged is called a *routing domain*.

NOTE: The terms "path" and "route" are synonymous. "Path" is widely used for no other reason than it's hard to discuss routing protocols that use routing algorithms to calculate new optimal routes for distribution in routing updates sent to all routers for use in recalculating their respective routing tables. You get the point.

Routing Protocol Basics

Of the many routing protocols, some are standards-based and others are proprietary. Several are old and fading from use, a few are used only within narrowly defined market niches, and others are in such wide use that they are de facto standards. Routing protocols also differ in the type of internetworks they're designed to manage, and in the size of internetworks they can handle. Naturally, these differences are manifested in each routing protocol's algorithm. Yet all their algorithms share these two basic processes:

▼ Routers send one another update messages advising of changes in internetwork topology and conditions.

▲ Each router recalculates its own routing table based on the updated information.

Updating one another helps each individual router know what's going on. More importantly, it helps orchestrate an internetwork's routers by maintaining a common set of information with which to operate.

The Routing Table's Central Role

A *routing table* is a list of routes available to forward traffic to various destinations. Every router in an internetwork maintains its own routing table, the contents of which differ from those maintained by other routers. Each router maintains a single routing table (not one per interface). The majority of routers run just one routing protocol, although specialized border routers run two in order to pass routes between areas using different protocols (more on that later).

A routing table constitutes the router's self-centered view of the internetwork's topology—sort of its personal formula for conducting business. Every time an update is received, the routing protocol takes the information and mashes it through its algorithm to recalculate optimal paths to all destinations deemed reachable from that router. Figure 14-1 illustrates the routing table update process.

Each router must have its own routing table to account for conditions specific to its location in the internetwork. In a routing domain, the routers collectively share the same news about any change, but then each puts that information to use individually.

The Routing Protocol Is an Internetwork's Intelligence

The goal of routing protocols is to let an internetwork respond to change. They do this by providing routers a common framework for decision-making about how to respond to topology changes within the internetwork. The routing protocol coordinates the passing of updates between routers, and then each router recalculates optimal routes in its own table. If, after recalculation, all the routing tables have arrived at a common view of the topology—albeit each from its self-centered perspective—the internetwork is said to have reached *convergence* (so called because the router community has converged on a singular view of the topology). A converged topology view means all the routers agree on which links are up, down, running fastest, and so on.

Routing protocols are the quintessence of high-tech internetworking. They represent the ability of individual devices and even whole networks to help manage themselves. One could say that internetworks have become organic in the sense that routing protocols make them self-aware and self-correcting. As topologies grow from day to day or circumstances change from moment to moment, internetworks can respond because routing protocols enable the router community to converse intelligently about what to do.

A trendy marketing cliché holds that "the network is the system." If that's true, then routing protocols serve as the network's operating system. Routing protocols raise the limit on what is practical in terms of internetwork size and complexity. It's no exaggeration to state that the development of sophisticated routing protocols is what has made the Internet's explosive growth possible.

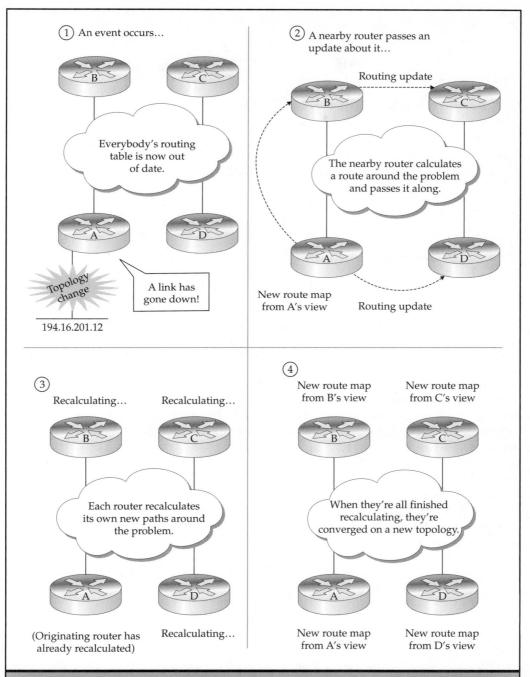

Figure 14-1. Routing update messages coordinate routing tables.

> **NOTE:**   Cisco Discovery Protocol (CDP), the Hot Standby Routing Protocol (HSRP), and other specialized protocols are sometimes also referred to as routing protocols. For our purposes, a routing protocol is a protocol that coordinates the exchange of routing updates to notify other routers of topology changes and applies an algorithm to recalculate optimal routes through an internetwork.

Comparing Routed Networks to Switched Networks

A good way to explain routing protocols is by comparison. Remember switching tables from Chapter 6? To refresh: Switches keep track of switched network topology by brute force. Every time a message arrives, the switch associates the frame's source MAC address (layer 2 physical address) with the switch port it came in on and then makes an entry into its MAC address table. In this way, the switch builds a list of destination MAC addresses for each switch port. Here's the basic layout of a switch's address table:

Destination MAC Address	Destination Switch Port
0060.2fa3.fabc	Fast Ethernet0/8
0050.0465.395c	Fast Ethernet0/4
0010.5a9b.b5e6	Fast Ethernet0/12
.	.
.	.
.	.

This isn't a particularly intelligent way to map routes because the switch's MAC address table only sees one step ahead. The table says nothing about the complete route to the destination; it merely shows you out the next door. The only way a switch can reduce the number of hops a frame must take between switches is to compile bigger and bigger MAC address tables, thereby increasing the odds that the best path will be encountered. Switch designers call this "aggregating bandwidth," but what's really being aggregated is MAC addresses. (In case you're wondering how switches choose among alternative paths, they favor those most frequently used, which appear higher in the MAC address list.)

Routers, by contrast, *can* see more than one step ahead. Routing tables give routers the ability to see farther into an internetwork without expanding their lists. Where switches substitute quantity for quality, routers apply intelligence. Here's the basic layout of a simple type of routing table:

Destination	Next Hop	Hop Count
209.98.134.126	209.126.4.38	3
	127.197.83.128	5
	202.8.79.250	9
.	.	.
.	.	.
.	.	.

This example may not look like much, but it's superior to the switch table in a fundamental way. The switch plays the odds, but the router plays it smart, because the Hop

Count column gives routers information about the entire route. Knowing how many routers a packet must hop through to reach its destination helps the sending router choose the best path to take. This kind of measurement is called a *routing metric,* or *metric* for short. Metrics such as hop count are what separate routing from the switch's abrupt "out this door, please" approach. Metrics supply the intelligence needed by routing algorithms to calculate best paths through internetworks.

Routing Updates Are Control Messages

Routed networks carry an undercurrent of specialized traffic that exchanges routing update messages. Switched networks do no such thing; they guess at what's going on by looking only at the source MAC address and incoming port of payload packets. A *payload message,* by the way, is one that carries content useful for an application instead of for the internetwork's internal operations. Figure 14-2 outlines the difference.

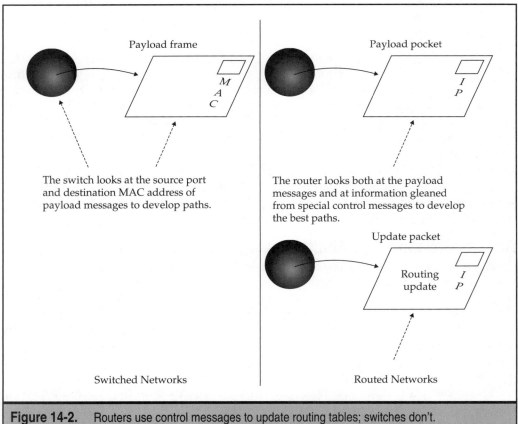

Payload frame

Payload pocket

The switch looks at the source port and destination MAC address of payload messages to develop paths.

The router looks both at the payload messages and at information gleaned from special control messages to develop the best paths.

Update packet

Routing update

Switched Networks

Routed Networks

Figure 14-2. Routers use control messages to update routing tables; switches don't.

Routing updates aren't payload messages, they're *control messages*. The content they deliver is used by the internetwork for internal operations. This second type of traffic carrying routing updates is the lifeblood of internetworking, delivering the intelligence an internetwork must have to act in a unitary fashion and survive in the face of change. Given their importance, to reach a basic understanding of routing protocols you need to know what routing updates contain, how and where they're sent, and how they're processed.

Dynamic vs. Static Routing

Before we go further, a little background is in order. There are two basic types of routing:

▼   **Static routing**   A static route is a fixed path preprogrammed by a network administrator. Static routes cannot make use of routing protocols and don't self-update after receipt of routing update messages; they must be updated by hand.

▲   **Dynamic routing**   This is the type of routing made possible by routing protocols, which automatically calculate routes based on routing update messages. The majority of all internetwork routes are dynamic.

This distinction is made here to drive home a key point. Not all routes are automatically (dynamically) calculated by routing protocols, and for good reason. In most situations, network administrators will opt to retain direct control over a minority of routes.

The best example of how static routes are used is the default gateway. A router can't possibly know routes to all destinations, so it's configured with a *default gateway* path to which packets with unknown destinations are sent. Default gateways are entered as static routes to make sure undeliverable traffic is steered to a router that has routing table entries leading outside the internetwork. Figure 14-3 shows a default gateway in action.

The ability of routing protocols to automate routing table selection is a good thing, but only in measured doses. The use of static routes as default gateways to handle unanticipated messages exemplifies this.

Routers Collaborate to Attain Convergence

Convergence is when all routers in an internetwork have agreed on a common topology. For example, if a particular network link has gone down, the internetwork will have converged when all the routers settle on new routes that no longer include that link. Yet, each router must have its own routes to account for its unique position in the network topology. Thus, the routers act collectively by sharing updates, yet take independent action by calculating their own routes. When the process is complete, they have converged in the sense that all the routes were calculated based on a common set of assumptions about the network's current topology.

This collaboration is orchestrated by the internetwork's routing protocol. Having routers work collectively gives internetworks their strength, because it may take more than one router to isolate a network problem. And, until a problem is isolated, no router has the information needed to calculate new routes around the problem.

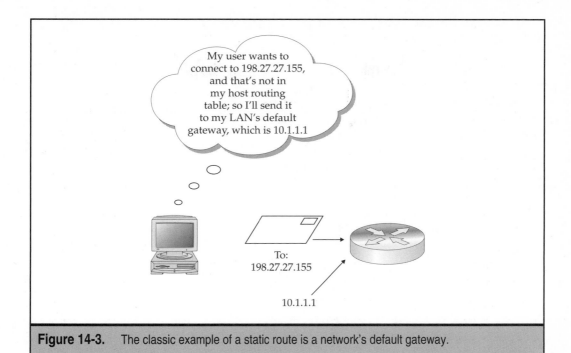

Figure 14-3.   The classic example of a static route is a network's default gateway.

How Routers Sense Topology Change

Routers use gateway discovery protocols to keep track of one another. A *gateway discovery protocol* is a system that coordinates the exchange of small "are you still there?" messages between routers in an internetwork, mainly as a way of sensing downed links.

▼   Each router broadcasts "hello" messages to its immediate neighbor routers at a fixed interval (say, once every 90 seconds).

■   If no ACK (acknowledgment message) is received back within a specified period (three minutes), the route is declared invalid.

▲   If no ACK has returned within a longer period (seven minutes), the router and its routes are removed from the sending router's table, and a routing update is issued about all routes that incorporated the nonresponding router as a link.

Gateway discovery protocols are low-overhead control protocols that in IP networks are sent via the UDP transport protocol. Figure 14-4 illustrates how they work.

In addition to sensing problems, gateway discovery protocols detect the appearance of new equipment. The four types of gateway discovery messages in Figure 14-4 are collectively referred to as *timers*.

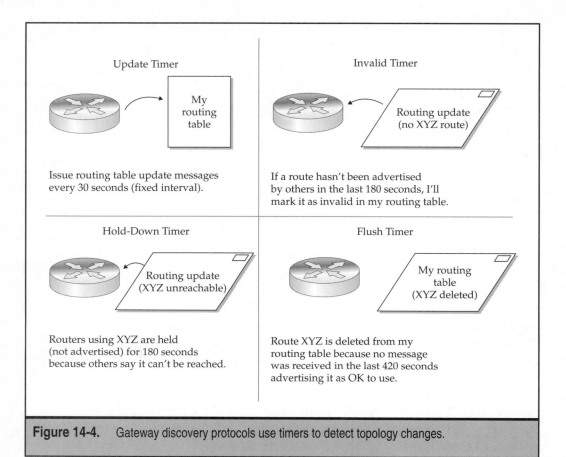

Figure 14-4. Gateway discovery protocols use timers to detect topology changes.

How Routing Updates Converge

Sensing a topology change is only the first step. From the point of discovery, routing updates must be passed until all routers can converge on a new topology by incorporating the change.

Let's take an example. Figure 14-5 shows a relatively simple four-router topology with route redundancy, in that messages have alternative paths to destinations. A message sent from Manufacturing to Accounting could travel via either the R&D or Marketing router. If packets sent from Manufacturing via the R&D router to the Expense Report server suddenly become undeliverable, the Accounting router can't be relied upon to diagnose the problem on its own. This is because there are so many potential sources for the problems, as depicted by the question marks in Figure 14-5. Here's a roundup of the most likely suspects of what caused the problem:

1. The Expense Report server has crashed.
2. The LAN connection to the Expense Report server has failed.
3. The Accounting router's interface to the Expense Report server's LAN segment has failed.
4. The Accounting router has totally failed.
5. The Accounting router's serial interface to the R&D router has failed.

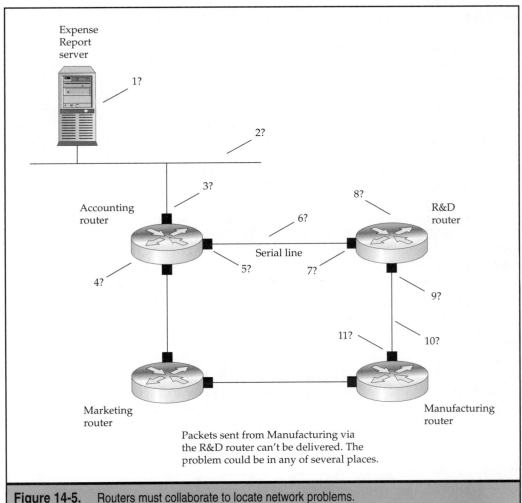

Expense
Report
server

1?

2?

3?

Accounting
router

8?

R&D
router

6?

Serial line

5?   7?

4?

9?

11?   10?

Marketing
router

Manufacturing
router

Packets sent from Manufacturing via
the R&D router can't be delivered. The
problem could be in any of several places.

Figure 14-5.   Routers must collaborate to locate network problems.

6. The serial transmission line connecting Accounting with R&D is down.

7. R&D's serial interface to the Accounting router has failed.

8. The R&D router has totally failed.

9. R&D's serial interface to the Manufacturing router has failed.

10. The serial transmission line connecting R&D with Manufacturing is down.

11. Manufacturing's serial interface to the R&D router has failed.

The Accounting router can't have definitive knowledge as to problems 1, 7, or 8 because it's not directly responsible for these network devices, and the Accounting router would be of no use at all in the event of problem 4.

Packets can't be routed to detour around the failure until the problem has been located. Also, the problem must be located in order for the routers to converge on a new (post-failure) network topology.

If, in our example topology, the serial line between Accounting and R&D has failed, both routers would sense this at about the same time and issue updates. Figure 14-6 tracks the routing update as it flows from the Accounting and R&D routers. Once the router has sensed the problem, it deletes the failed path from its routing table. This, in turn, causes the routing algorithm to calculate a new best route to all destinations that had incorporated the failed link. When these new routes are calculated, the router issues them in a routing update message sent out to other routers in the internetwork.

Updated routing tables are sent from the Accounting and R&D routers to announce they are no longer using the serial line in their routes. These are routing update messages. The Manufacturing and Marketing routers in turn replace any routes they have using the serial link. In the Figure 14-6 example, it took two routing updates for the internetwork to converge on a new topology that's minus the serial line. When the serial line is brought back online, the connected routers will also sense the topology change, and the whole route update process will repeat itself in reverse.

Short convergence time is a primary design goal when laying out an internetwork's topology. In big networks, it can take several updates to converge. The length of convergence time depends on the routing protocol used, the size of the internetwork, and where in the topology a change takes place. For example, if the problem in Figure 14-5 had occurred behind the Accounting router's gateway (say, with the Expense Report server or its LAN segment), only the Accounting router would have originated a routing update, which would have resulted in a convergence time of three updates.

Long convergence time is a symptom of a poorly functioning internetwork. Many factors can slow convergence, but the major factor in convergence times is propagation delay.

Propagation Delay

A network phenomenon called *propagation delay* is the delay between the time a packet is sent and when it arrives at its destination. Propagation delay isn't a simple matter of geographical distance or hop count; other factors can also have an influence. Figure 14-7 shows various propagation delay factors.

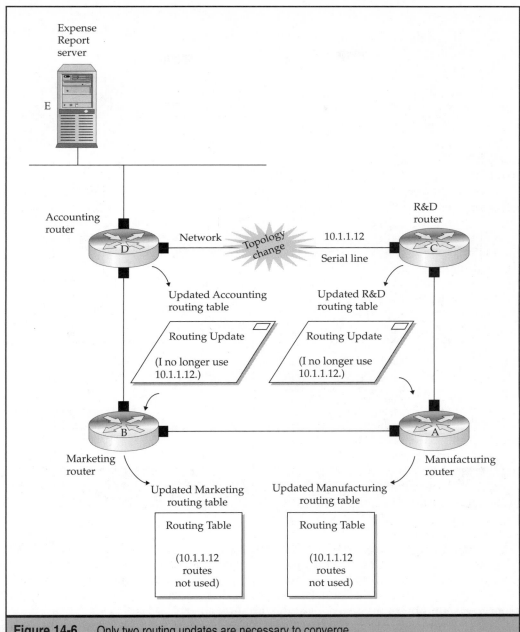

Figure 14-6. Only two routing updates are necessary to converge.

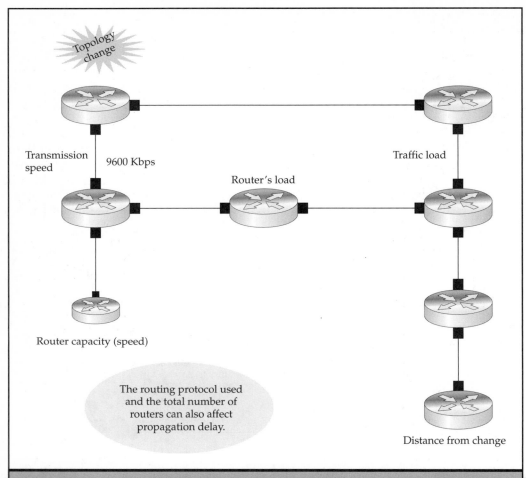

Figure 14-7. Several factors can influence the length of propagation delay.

Obviously, something as basic as the time required for data to travel over a network is important to all areas of internetworking. But propagation delay is a huge factor for routing protocols, because all routers receive a routing update at the same moment. No matter how fast the network medium, convergence takes time as a routing update is passed from router to router until it arrives at the farthest router.

The importance of propagation delay grows with an internetwork's size. Big internetworks have dozens of routers, hundreds of connected LAN segments, and thousands of hosts—each a potential source of topology change. All other things being equal, the bigger the network, the greater its propagation delay, and the more redundant paths are used, the greater the potential for confusion.

Routing Loops

Propagation delay wouldn't pose a problem to routing protocols if routers always converged before any new changes emerged. But they don't. The longer propagation delay is in an internetwork, the more susceptible it is to something called a routing loop. A *routing loop* is when payload packets can't reach their destinations because of conflicting routing table information. This happens in large or change-intensive internetworks when a second topology change emerges before the network is able to converge on the first change.

Taking the example shown in Figure 14-8, the R&D router senses that network 10.1.1.12 has gone down and issues a routing update. But before the Manufacturing router receives the update, it issues a routing update indicating that network 10.1.1.12 is still good (because the update has paths that incorporate this network). The updates from R&D and Manufacturing conflict and, depending on how the timing works out, can confuse the other routers and even each other, throwing the internetwork into a routing loop.

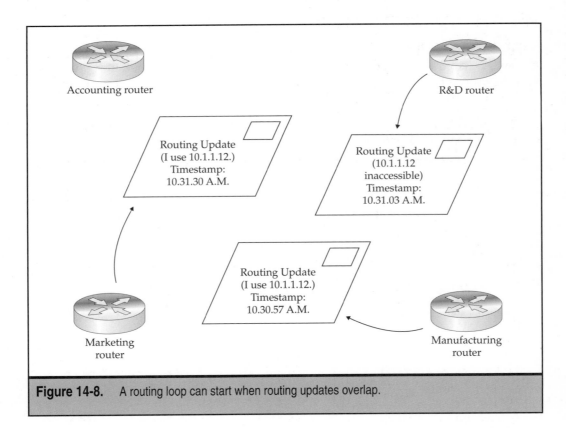

Figure 14-8.   A routing loop can start when routing updates overlap.

Routing loops can be self-perpetuating. If the conflicting routing updates are persistent enough, each repeatedly nullifies the other in route decisions made by the affected routers. If the router's primary route vacillates each time it receives an update, the internetwork has become unstable. If things go too far out of balance (for example, there are too many loops in progress and primary route selections are flapping), the protocol's collective topology can begin to disintegrate altogether. The downward spiral goes like this:

▼ Two or more conflicting routing updates cause messages to be routed via downed routes, and thus they are not delivered.

■ As the loop persists, more bandwidth is consumed by inefficiently routed payload packets and routing updates trying to fix the problem.

▲ The diminishing bandwidth triggers still more routing updates in response to the worsening throughput.

The vicious circle of a routing loop is depicted in Figure 14-9.

Mechanisms to Keep Internetworks Loop-Free

A scenario like the one just described is unacceptable to effective network operations. Routing protocols incorporate a number of sophisticated mechanisms to thwart the onset of routing loops:

▼ **Hold-downs** Suppression of advertisements about a route that's in question long enough for all the routers to find out about its true status

■ **Split horizons** The practice of not advertising a route back in the direction of the route itself

▲ **Poison reverse updates** A routing update message that explicitly states a network or subnet is unreachable (instead of a nearby router merely dropping it from its routing table for lack of use)

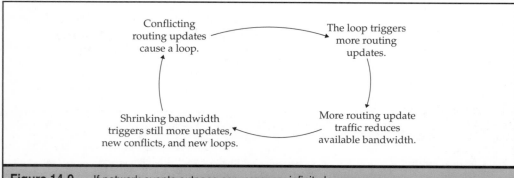

Figure 14-9.   If network events outpace convergence, infinite loops can occur.

Hold-Downs   A *hold-down* is a way to help prevent bad routes from being reinstated by mistake. When a route is placed in a hold-down state, routers will neither advertise the route nor accept advertisements about it for a specific interval called the *hold-down period*. Hold-downs have the effect of flushing information about a bad route from the internetwork. It's a forcible way to take a bad apple from the barrel to help reduce the chances of it starting a routing loop. At the extreme, a hold-down period would be an interval slightly longer than it normally takes for the entire network to learn of a routing change—its average convergence time.

But holding back the release of routing updates obviously slows convergence, so there's a harsh trade-off between the loop prevention benefit of hold-downs and the quality of network service. This is because delaying the release of an update leaves a bad route in play for a longer period. In internetworks of any size, setting hold-down intervals to match average convergence time results in frequent timeout messages to end users. In the real world, hold-down times are often set to an interval far less than the network's average convergence time to partially ameliorate loop risk, but at the same time avoid most network timeouts for users. This trade-off is depicted in Figure 14-10.

Split Horizons   A *split horizon* is a routing configuration that stops a route from being advertised back in the direction from which it came. The theory is that it's basically useless to send information back toward its source. An example of this is outlined in Figure 14-11. Router B, in the middle, received a route to network 10.1.99.0 from Router A on the left. The split-horizon rule instructs Router B not to include that route in updates it sends back toward Router A. The assumption is that Router A was probably the source of the route (given that it is in the direction of network 10.1.99.0), and, therefore, it doesn't need to be informed of the route. If Router A's interface to network 10.1.99.0 went down and it didn't have enough built-in intelligence, it might take its own routing update back from Router B and try to use it as a way around the downed interface.

Hold-downs can normally prevent routing loops on their own, but split horizons are generally configured as a backup measure because there's no particular trade-off in using them.

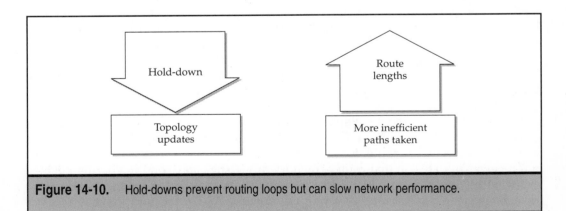

Figure 14-10.   Hold-downs prevent routing loops but can slow network performance.

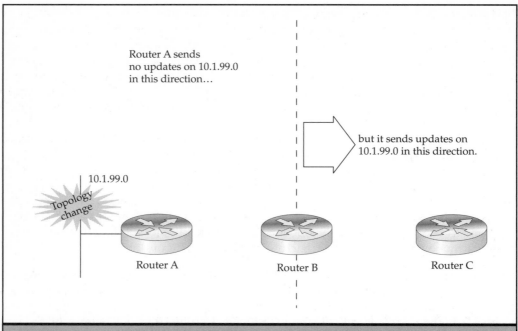

Router A sends
no updates on 10.1.99.0
in this direction...

but it sends updates on
10.1.99.0 in this direction.

10.1.99.0

Topology change

Router A

Router B

Router C

Figure 14-11. A split horizon stops a routing update from echoing back to its source.

Poison Reverse Updates By now, you've probably noticed that routing protocols work implicitly. In other words, they steer traffic around a bad link by not including routes involving that link in routing updates. *Poison reverse updates,* by contrast, explicitly state that a link is bad. Poison reverse works by having a router check for overlarge increases in metrics. Routing metrics are designed such that an increase reflects deterioration. For example, an increase in the number of hops a route must take makes it less desirable. A router compares an incoming routing update's metric for a route against what it was when the router itself had issued an earlier update including that same route. The routing protocol is configured with an acceptable increase factor that, if exceeded, causes the router to assume the route is a looping ("reversing") message. Figure 14-12 depicts the process.

In Cisco routing protocols, the default increase for a routing metric is a factor of 1.1 or greater. In other words, if a route returns in an update with a metric that is 110 percent or more of what it was on the way out, it's assumed that a loop is in progress. For example, if a router sends out an update with a route with a hop count metric of 1, and it returns in someone else's update with a hop count of 2, the assumption is that a loop is under way. When this happens, the router is placed into a hold-down state in which it neither sends nor receives updates on that route. The hold-down state stays on for a period deemed sufficiently long to flush the problem from the update system. Thus the name poison reverse: the loop is a bad metric "reversing" onto the router; the hold-down is a way of "poisoning" (or killing) updates that could contain the bad metric.

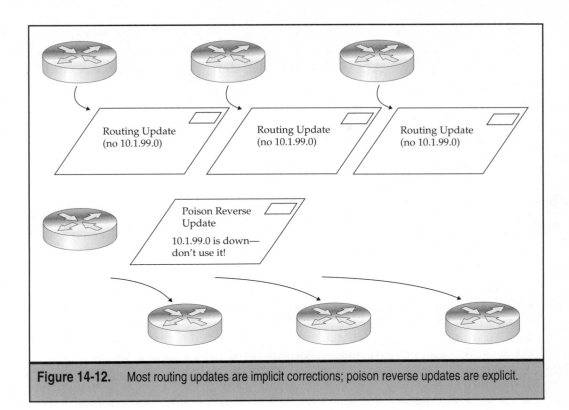

Figure 14-12. Most routing updates are implicit corrections; poison reverse updates are explicit.

Split horizons are a good way to prevent routing loops among adjacent routers. But in large internetworks in which routing updates are passed between routers far removed from one another, poison reverse updates help prevent bad routes from starting to loop before update convergence can take place. Both techniques use hold-downs.

Routing Metrics

A routing metric is a value used by a routing protocol to influence routing decisions. Metric information is stored in routing tables and is used by routing algorithms to determine optimal routes to destinations. The terminology takes some getting used to, but here are the most widely used metrics:

▼   **Cost**   Not financial cost, but a theoretical "cost" number used to represent the time, difficulty, risk, and other factors involved in a route.

■   **Distance**   Not physical distance in miles or cable feet, but a theoretical "distance" number. Most distance metrics are based on the number of hops in a route.

■ **Bandwidth**   The bandwidth rating of a network link (100 Mbps, for example).

■ **Traffic load**   A number representing the amount of traffic (such as the number and size of packets) that traveled over a link during a specified period of time.

■ **Delay**   In this context, the time between the start of a routing update cycle and when all routers in an internetwork converge on a single topology view (also called *propagation delay* or *latency*).

■ **Reliability**   A relative number used to indicate reliability of a link.

▲ **MTU**   The maximum packet size (maximum transmission units) that a particular network interface can handle, usually expressed in bytes.

NOTE: Sometimes "cost" is used as a general term for the result calculated by an equation inside the routing protocol algorithm. For example, someone might state that the overall cost of one route was more than another's, when actually the routing algorithm used metrics for distance, bandwidth, traffic load, and delay.

Some simple routing protocols use just one metric. However, usually more than one routing metric goes into determining optimal routes. For example, a two-hop route traversing a 9,600-Kbps serial line is going to be much slower than a three-hop route going over T3 circuits at 44 Mbps. You don't have to be Euclid to figure out that moving bits 4,000 times faster more than compensates for an extra hop.

Sophisticated routing protocols not only support multiple metrics, they also let you decide which to use. In addition, you can assign relative weights to metrics to more precisely influence route selection. If the network administrator sets the metrics properly, the overall behavior of the internetwork can be tuned to best fit the enterprise's objectives. Figure 14-13 shows some routing metrics in action.

All Cisco routing protocols come with default settings for metrics. These default settings are based on design calculations made in Cisco's labs and real-world experience gained in the field. If you ever get your hands on a routing protocol, think long and hard before you start changing routing metric default settings. The domino effect of a bad routing metric decision can be devastating. Out-of-balance metric settings can be manifested in the form of poor network performance and routing loops.

Routing Protocol Architectures

There are three basic types of routing protocol architectures:

▼ **Distance-vector routing protocols**   Simple algorithms that calculate a cumulative distance value between routers based on hop count

■ **Link-state routing protocols**   Sophisticated algorithms that maintain a complex database of internetwork topology

▲ **Hybrid routing protocols**   A combination of distance-vector and link-state methods that tries to incorporate the advantages of both and minimize their disadvantages

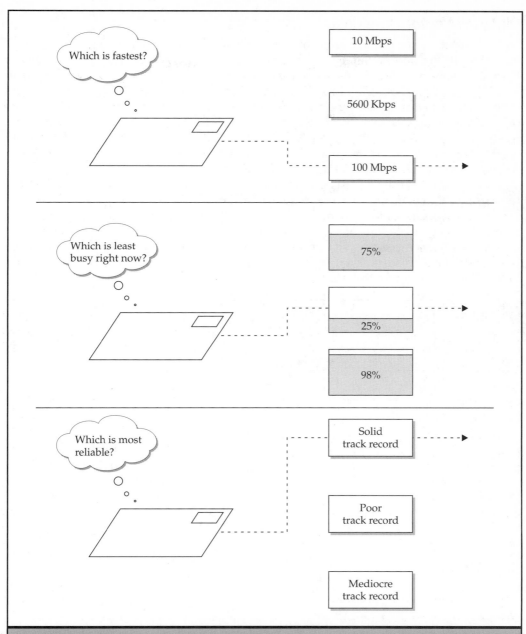

Figure 14-13.   Routing metrics are used to influence decisions that routing algorithms make.

Distance-Vector Routing

Early distance-vector routing protocols used only a so-called distance metric to calculate the best route to a destination. The distance is the number of router hops to the destination. Distance-vector algorithms (also called Bellman-Ford algorithms) operate a protocol in which routers pass routing tables to their immediate neighbors in all directions. At each exchange, the router increments the distance value received for a route, thereby applying its own distance value to that route. The updated table is then passed further outward where receiving routers repeat the process. The fundamental theory is that each router doesn't need to know all about other links, just whether they are there and what the approximate distance is to them. Figure 14-14 depicts the distance-vector routing update process.

Distance-vector routing can be slow to converge. This is because routing updates are triggered by timers to take place at predetermined intervals, not in response to a network event that causes a topology change. This makes it harder for distance-vector protocols to respond quickly to the state of a link's current operating condition. If a network link goes down, the distance-vector system must wait until the next timed update cycle sweeps past the downed link to pick it up and pass an updated routing table—minus the downed link—through the internetwork.

NOTE: The name "distance-vector" can be confusing because some advanced distance-vector protocols use routing metrics other than theoretical distance. In fact, some newer so-called distance-vector installations only partially rely on the hop count metric. The best way to think of distance-vector protocols is that they update routing topologies at fixed intervals.

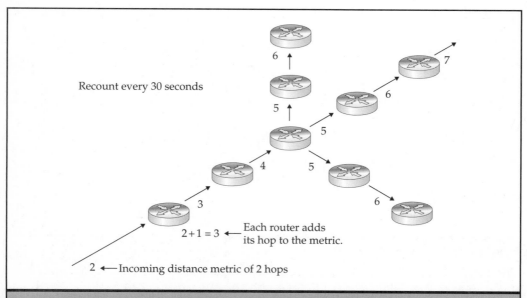

Recount every 30 seconds

$2+1 = 3$ ←— Each router adds its hop to the metric.

2 ←— Incoming distance metric of 2 hops

Figure 14-14. Distance-vector routing propagates routing updates at fixed intervals.

Relying on fixed-interval updates renders distance-vector protocols slow to converge on topology changes and, therefore, more susceptible to routing loops. Also, most distance-vector protocols are limited to 16 hops and are generally used in internetworks with fewer than 50 routers.

Despite their unsophisticated ways, distance-vector protocols are by far the most widely used. The distance-vector method is simple and easy to configure. Because it doesn't do a lot of calculating, it consumes little router CPU or memory resources. Generally, distance-vector algorithms are good enough to adapt to topology changes encountered in smaller internetworks. The most widely installed distance-vector routing protocols are RIP and IGRP.

Link-State Routing

Link-state routing is event driven. Also known as *shortest path first* (*SPF*), link-state routing protocols focus on the state of the internetwork links that form routes. Whenever a link's state changes, a routing update called a *link-state advertisement* (*LSA*) is exchanged between routers. When a router receives an LSA routing update, the link-state algorithm is used to recalculate the shortest path to affected destinations. Link-state routing attempts to always maintain full knowledge of the internetwork's topology by updating itself incrementally whenever a change occurs. Figure 14-15 depicts the link-state process.

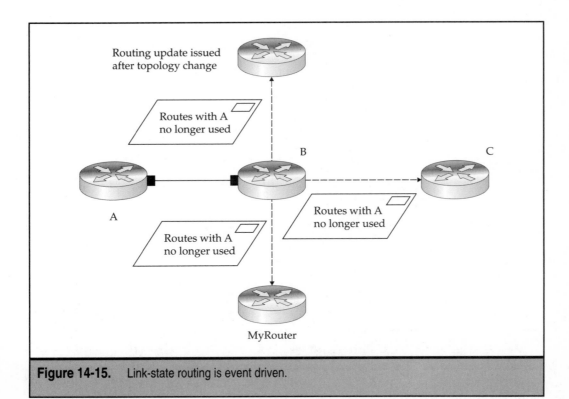

Figure 14-15.   Link-state routing is event driven.

The link-state algorithm does much more than just have a router add its local distance value to a cumulative distance. After an LSA update is received, each router uses the algorithm to calculate a *shortest path tree* to all destinations. Link-state calculations are based on the Dijkstra algorithm. This process yields entirely new routes instead of merely applying new distance values to preexisting routes. Think of it this way: distance-vector routing places a new value on the same old route; link-state routing's SPF algorithm builds whole new routes piece by piece, from the link up. SPF is able to do this because the link-state database contains complete information on the internetwork's components and its topology.

New routes calculated by SPF are entered into the updated routing table. These entries include recalculated values for all metrics configured for use in the link-state implementation. Possible metrics include cost, delay, bandwidth, reliability, and others, with their values updated to reflect the new route. This is done by rolling up metric information for each link incorporated into the newly calculated route. Figure 14-16 shows how the SPF algorithm picks the best route.

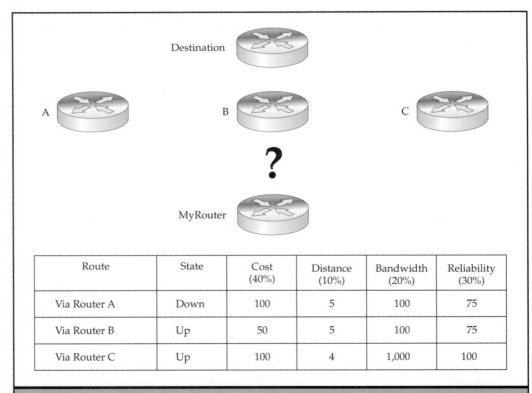

Route	State	Cost (40%)	Distance (10%)	Bandwidth (20%)	Reliability (30%)
Via Router A	Down	100	5	100	75
Via Router B	Up	50	5	100	75
Via Router C	Up	100	4	1,000	100

Figure 14-16. Link-state routing's SPF algorithm builds the shortest paths from the link up.

There are two other advantages to link-state routing; both have to do with bandwidth conservation. First, because LSA updates contain only information about affected paths, routing updates travel faster and consume less bandwidth. Second, in distance-vector routing, most update cycles are wasted because they take place even though there was no topology change. Unnecessary update cycles not only increase bandwidth overhead but also boost the odds that conflicting routing updates will be converging simultaneously. By issuing LSA updates only when required, link-state protocols diminish the opportunity for the self-perpetuating conflicts of routing loops.

Because link-state protocols are event driven, adaptation to topology change need not wait for a series of preset timers to go off before the convergence process can begin. This not only makes link-state protocols less prone to loops but also makes them more powerful in that there is no limit on the number of hops in the routes they calculate.

The drawbacks to link-state routing protocols mainly have to do with logistics and expense. During the initial stages of implementation, LSA traffic tends to flood an internetwork with database-building control messages, making implementation expensive. Because it does so much more calculating, link-state routing also can consume considerable router CPU and memory resources when recalculation is necessary. This means that those considering an upgrade to a link-state routing protocol must face the prospect of spending big money on equipment upgrades. Yet perhaps the biggest hurdle to link-state protocols is that they're complicated. These are sophisticated routing protocols that can be intimidating to network administrators, especially those set in their ways. Most known are OSPF and IS-IS.

Hybrid Routing

Hybrid routing protocols use more accurate distance-vector metrics in a protocol designed to converge more rapidly. Although open standards have been developed for so-called hybridized routing, the only Cisco product based on the concept is the Enhanced Interior Gateway Routing Protocol (EIGRP).

How Routing Protocols Are Implemented

Much like firewalls, routing protocols take their own particular view of the internetwork landscape. To a firewall, networks are either *inside* or *outside,* and connections are controlled accordingly. Routing protocols have as their overriding concern the gathering and dissemination of updated topologies, not connections. Thus, routing protocols define the networking landscape in terms of *interior* and *exterior,* where one routing domain ends and another begins. This is because a router needs to know which other routers are part of its own routing domain (are in the interior) and, therefore, should share routing updates.

Autonomous Systems

Administrative control is defined as who controls the configuration of equipment in a network. Because the Internet interconnects so many organizational entities, it has developed the concept of an autonomous system. An *autonomous system* is defined as a collection of networks that are under the administrative control of a single organization and that share a common routing strategy. Most autonomous systems are internetworks operated by corporations, Internet service providers (ISPs), government agencies, and universities.

Looking at the three autonomous systems in Figure 14-17, each regards the other two as exterior (or external) autonomous systems. This is because the other two are under the administrative control of someone else, and they are running a separate routing strategy. A *routing strategy* is a term used to describe the fact that routing updates are being exchanged under a common routing protocol configuration. Thus, a routing strategy implies running a single routing process to exchange updates and sharing other configuration parameters, such as the relative settings of each path's metrics.

The three autonomous systems in Figure 14-17 could be running the same routing protocol software—even the same *version* of the same routing protocol—but because the autonomous systems aren't within the same routing process of update messages and relative metrics settings, they don't share a common routing strategy. In other words, they're in the same autonomous system, but in different routing domains.

The Difference Between Interior and Exterior Gateway Protocols

So what we have, then, is a nice neat little package where routing domains and administrative domains overlay one another, right? Well, as always seems to be the case in internetworking, things aren't quite so tidy. If routing strategy were as simple as configuring one routing protocol for every administrative domain, there could be no Internet. After all, if everything were internal, who or what would coordinate routing updates between the millions of autonomous systems making up the Internet?

The answer is exterior gateway protocols. An *exterior gateway protocol* runs on routers sitting at the edge of an autonomous system and exchanges routes with other autonomous systems. These edge routers are also called *border routers, boundary routers,* or *gateway routers.* A routing protocol that operates within an autonomous system is an *interior gateway protocol.* Figure 14-18 shows the two side by side.

In practical terms, the most obvious difference between the two is where the routers running the protocol sit in the topology. Exterior routers sit at the edge of autonomous systems; interior gateway routers sit toward the middle. A closer inspection of how the exterior protocols are implemented brings out more fundamental differences:

▼ An exterior protocol lets an autonomous system designate certain other routers as peers. The border router exchanges updates with its peer routers and ignores other routers (in interior protocols, all routers participate in router updates).

■ Routing tables maintained by exterior protocols are lists of autonomous systems (interior protocols keep lists of LAN segments).

▲ Exterior protocols simply insert a new route received for a destination into the routing table; no recalculation of new best paths is computed after an update is received (interior protocols recalculate new routes based on weighted metrics).

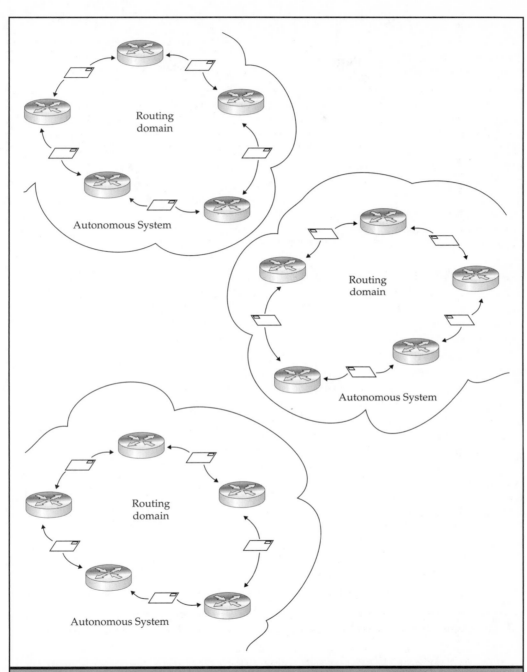

Figure 14-17.   Routing protocols draw maps largely based on administrative control.

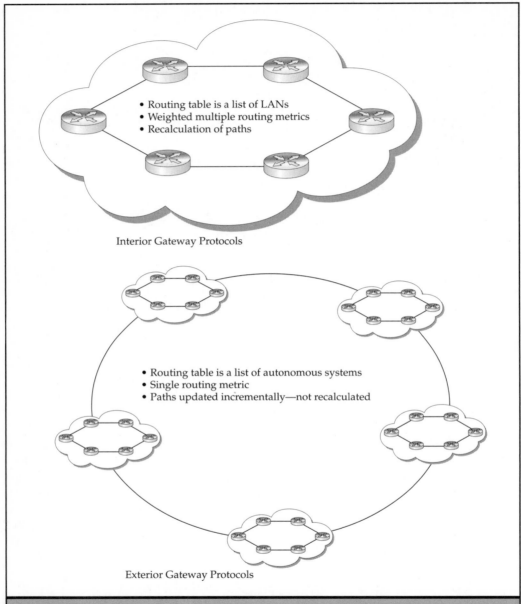

Figure 14-18. Differences between interior gateway protocols and exterior gateway protocols.

Methods that Let Autonomous Systems Interconnect

Reaching beyond an autonomous system invites potential trouble. For a firewall, the potential trouble is a security breach. For an exterior gateway protocol, the trouble can be either bad information about routes to other autonomous systems or just too much information to handle. The problems inherent in connecting to the outside also hold for exterior and interior protocols alike:

▼ Without some way to filter route exchanges, exterior protocols would be overwhelmed by a torrent of traffic flowing in from the Internet.

▲ Interior protocols could be confused about the best connections to take to the outside without being able to identify and select from various sources providing new routes.

Interior and exterior gateway routing protocols use a set of techniques to handle these problems. As a group, these techniques are intended to cut down on the volume of routing information and to boost the reliability of new route information that is received:

▼ **Route summarization**   A technique that divides an internetwork into logical areas, with the area's border router advertising only a single summary route to other areas, thereby cutting down on the size of routing tables.

■ **Route filtering**   Also called *administrative distance,* an add-on metric that rates the relative trustworthiness of individual networks as a source from which to learn optimal routes.

■ **Route tagging**   A technique that tags a route in a number of ways to identify the source from which it was learned. Tags can include router ID, autonomous system number, exterior protocol ID, and exterior protocol metric.

▲ **Router authentication**   In effect, this requires a communicating router to present a password before the receiving router will accept routing updates from it.

It's notable that some of the techniques are implemented in both internal and external systems, not just one or the other. This is done to enable interior and exterior routing domains to act in concert as messages flow between the autonomous system and outside world. Another notable fact is that some of these techniques are applied between interior routing domains where differing routing protocols are being run within the same autonomous system (for example, route summarization between OSPF and RIP routing processes).

Routing Domains, Routing Areas, and Administrative Domains

A *routing domain* is a group of end systems within an autonomous system. An autonomous system, in turn, is defined as an administrative domain, where there exists singular administrative control over network policy and equipment.

Most routing protocol architectures coordinate the exchange of *complete* route information between all routers in the routing domain. However, this practice can become inefficient as internetworks grow, because that means more update traffic traveling longer distances.

State-of-the-art routing protocols use the concept of routing domain areas. A *routing area* is a subdivision of a routing domain into logically related groups, with each area uniquely identified by an area name or number. The primary benefit of areas is that route information can be summarized when exchanged between areas, cutting down on network overhead and enhancing control over traffic flow. Routing domain areas are also used to unify several smaller routing domains into a single, larger routing process.

Routing area	Routing area	Routing area
Routing domain		

The typical global enterprise implements a single routing domain worldwide. This is done so that employees on one continent can connect to company colleagues and resources anywhere in the world. So it would follow, then, that there is always a one-to-one relation between a routing domain and an administrative domain. And, until recently, this was the case.

A new phenomenon called external corporate networks extends routing domains across administrative domains. An *external corporate network* is a configuration in which two or more enterprises build a unified routing domain to share routes between their respective organizations. The shared routing domain is the subset of each enterprise's overall autonomous system, and contains the resources and users that are to participate in the shared business process. Figure 14-19 illustrates how such a configuration is set up.

The thing to focus on with external corporate networks is that routes are being freely exchanged between enterprises—at least within the shared routing domain area in the middle. The external corporate network configuration enables routers within two or more enterprises to keep up an ongoing dialog on how to route cross-border connections. This is a relatively new internetworking practice. Not that long ago, the idea of directly trading route information between autonomous systems was unthinkable, not only out of concern for system security, but also for competitive reasons.

This is the most advanced form of extranet, in that one *system* is allowed behind another's firewall. Think of it this way: most extranets involve a person logging through a firewall by entering a username and password. In the Figure 14-19 example, the system of one enterprise is able to freely conduct business behind the firewall of another, system to system (not person to system). Harking back to Chapter 9's coverage of firewalls, in an external corporate network the extranet is *route-based*, not *connection-based*. Put another way, routes are shared between enterprises for long-term use. In the traditional extranet relationship, a user is allowed to connect to a resource on a per-session basis.

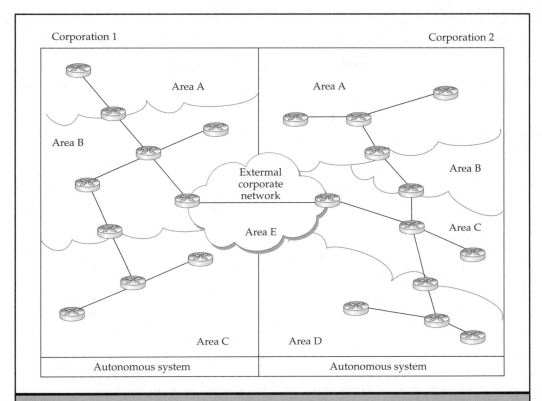

Figure 14-19. An external corporate network is a routing domain across autonomous systems.

OVERVIEW OF CISCO ROUTING PROTOCOLS

When internetworking started to take off during the mid-1980s, internetworks were smaller and simpler. The interior gateway protocol of choice back then was Routing Information Protocol (RIP). At that time, the two predominant proprietary networks were IBM SNA and Digital Equipment's DECnet implementation of Ethernet, each with its own routing scheme. But at the time, the "open" networking market was booming, with UNIX servers connecting to Novell's NetWare IPX LANs. RIP shipped with most UNIX server systems and emerged as the de facto standard. Thus, RIP is an open standard, not a Cisco proprietary technology.

RIP is simple to understand, easy to configure, and works well enough for small, homogenous networks. To this day, RIP is still the most widely installed routing protocol in the world.

But the early versions of RIP were limited to just the hop count metric. This didn't provide the routing flexibility needed to manage complex environments. Also, RIP was slow to converge, and thus limited to a maximum hop count limit of 16. Configure a longer route and the user will encounter a "destination unreachable" message. As a distance-vector protocol, RIP issues routing updates at a fixed interval. (The default update interval for most RIP products is every 90 seconds.)

Cisco's Interior Gateway Routing Protocol

It gradually became apparent that RIP was a roadblock to continued internetwork expansion. The 16-hop limit, single-metric scheme constrained network size and capacity. Cisco seized the opportunity by devising a replacement routing technology that did away with most of RIP's disadvantages: a more robust distance-vector protocol named IGRP (Interior Gateway Routing Protocol).

IGRP, a company-proprietary extension of the open RIP standard, was first released by Cisco in 1986 for IP only. In the succeeding years, IGRP implemented support for other network layer protocols (IPX, AppleTalk, and so on), and it became the standard in customer shops using only Cisco equipment. By around 1990, RIP's limitations had become apparent, and IGRP was positioned as its general replacement for client-server networks.

Many observers regard IGRP as the single most important factor behind Cisco's explosive growth. The competition had devised OSPF as their primary replacement to RIP—but it was (and still is) limited to IP-only networks. IP-only compatibility is acceptable in some enterprises, but the reality is that most internetworks still run multiple protocols (IPX, AppleTalk, DECnet, and so on). Cisco was able to couple IGRP's superior functionality with the 1990s' UNIX/Internet juggernaut to attain the market dominance it enjoys today.

IGRP was a major departure in that it used multiple metrics: distance, delay, bandwidth, reliability, and load. This advance was a big deal because it enabled network administrators to get a handle on increasing network complexity and provide better service. Figure 14-20 compares IGRP's features with RIP's.

A big virtue of IGRP is the granularity of its metrics. For example, being able to set parameters for reliability or load to any value between 1 and 255 gives administrators the granularity needed to finely tune IGRP route selection. IGRP's ability to specify alternate routes boosts reliability and performance. This provides redundancy, so that if a link goes down, the IGRP routing algorithm dynamically begins to steer traffic to the secondary route. Multipath routing also introduced *load balancing*—the ability to dynamically shift traffic between alternate routes depending on how busy each is. These were important benefits during a period when most internetworks were in their infancy and prone to slowing to a crawl or going out altogether.

In 1994, Cisco augmented IGRP with a product called Enhanced Interior Gateway Domain Protocol. EIGRP is a substantial advance over its predecessor—so much so that Cisco touts it as a hybrid routing protocol instead of a mere distance-vector protocol. Although competitors might disagree, most observers now regard EIGRP as the new de facto standard for interior gateway protocols.

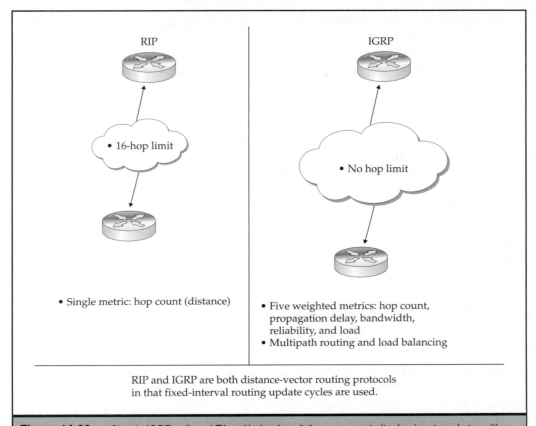

RIP   IGRP

• 16-hop limit

• No hop limit

• Single metric: hop count (distance)   • Five weighted metrics: hop count,
                                               propagation delay, bandwidth,
                                               reliability, and load
                                             • Multipath routing and load balancing

RIP and IGRP are both distance-vector routing protocols
in that fixed-interval routing update cycles are used.

Figure 14-20.   Cisco's IGRP eclipsed RI and helped vault the company to its dominant market position.

EIGRP combines the advantages of link-state protocols with those of distance-vector protocols. It provides superior convergence properties and operating efficiency. Here are the key EIGRP features:

▼ **DUAL finite state machine**   The software engine used by the EIGRP algorithm. DUAL (Diffusing Update Algorithm) is used to provide loop-free operation at every instant throughout a route computation. DUAL allows routers to synchronize route changes and does not involve routers unaffected by the change. The key architectural feature is that routers running DUAL store all of their neighbors' routing tables (called *neighbor tables*) so that they can more intelligently recalculate alternate paths in order to speed convergence.

■ **Variable-length subnet masks (VLSMs)**   The ability to automatically summarize subnet routes at the edge of a subnet. Before VLSM, routing protocols such as RIP could not build routes with subnet addresses included. All subnets had to be the same.

- ■ **Partial updates** Also called *event-triggered updates,* this means routing updates are issued only when the topology has changed. This saves control message overhead.

- ■ **Bounded updates** The method whereby routing update messages are sent only to those routers affected by the topology change. This saves overhead and helps speed convergence.

- ▲ **Reliable Transport Protocol (RTP)** A protocol guaranteeing the orderly delivery of priority update packets to neighbor routers. RTP works by classifying control message traffic into four priority groups: Hello/ACKs, updates, queries and replies, and requests. Only updates and queries/replies are sent *reliably.* By not sending Hellos and ACKs or requests reliably, resources are freed to guarantee the delivery of message types more critical to EIGRP's internal operations.

It is commonplace for enterprises using Cisco hardware to migrate their internetworks from IGRP to EIGRP over time. EIGRP routers can be operated as compatible with IGRP routers. The metrics between the two are directly translatable. EIGRP does this by treating IGRP routes as external networks, which allows the network administrator to customize routes to them. EIGRP advertises three types of routes:

- ▼ **Internal routes** Routes between subnets in a network attached to a router's interface. If the network is not subnetted, no interior routes are advertised for that network.

- ■ **System routes** Routes to networks within the autonomous system. System routes are compiled from routing updates passed within the internetwork. Subnets are not included in system routing updates.

- ▲ **External routes** Routes learned from another routing domain or those entered into the routing table as static routes. These routes are tagged individually to track their origin.

Figure 14-21 shows the interplay between these three types of EIGRP routes. Breaking down routes into these three categories facilitates advanced functions within the EIGRP algorithm. The internal routes designation enables EIGRP to support variable-length subnet masks; external routes make it possible for EIGRP to exchange routes that are discovered outside the autonomous system.

General Cisco Routing Protocol Configuration Steps

Configuring any Cisco routing protocol is largely a matter of setting its options. The number of steps is a function of how many options the routing protocol has for you to set. The more options a routing protocol has to set, the more commands there are for you to use. Because all Cisco routing protocols are implemented within IOS software, the initial steps

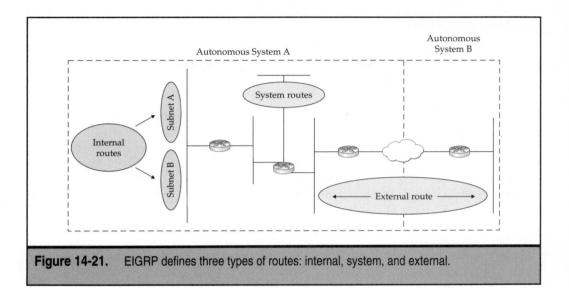

Figure 14-21.   EIGRP defines three types of routes: internal, system, and external.

of configuring Cisco routing protocols are the same. Table 14-1 explains the standard IOS routing protocol configuration steps.

Routing domains are built router by router. In other words, because routing protocols are peer arrangements, the routing process must be configured in each router that will be included in the routing domain. This is done by working with each router's configuration file individually. Once all the routing processes are configured on all the routers in the internetwork, the routing domain is complete.

Configuration Step	Description
Initialize and number the routing process.	The routing protocol must be turned on in a router so it can begin exchanging routing updates with other routers. This is done using the **router** command and giving the new routing domain an autonomous system number.
Configure LANs into the routing domain.	The **network** command is used to configure networks into the routing domain.
Set other routing protocol parameters.	Once the routing domain is constructed, its behavior is specified by using the routing protocol's various commands from the (config-router)# prompt.

Table 14-1.   Initial Steps to Configure Cisco's Various Routing Protocols

Configuring EIGRP

The **router** command initializes the routing process on a router. In this example, an EIGRP for autonomous system 999 is turned on in a router called MyRouter:

```
MyRouter(config)#router eigrp 999
MyRouter(config-router)#
```

An autonomous system number must be given in order to start a routing process. IOS uses the autonomous system number to distinguish one routing process from others. Notice that the IOS prompt changed to MyRouter(config-router)# when the **eigrp 999** routing process was invoked. All routing protocol parameters are set from this prompt.

The **network** command is used to start the routing protocol running over specific networks. Sticking with our example, the following command would make network 10.1.13.0 part of the routing process:

```
MyRouter(config-router)#network 10.1.13.0
```

The preceding command initializes EIGRP across network 10.1.13.0. If MyRouter is a four-port router and the other three LAN segments are also to run EIGRP, the **network** command must be used to make them part of the **eigrp 999** routing process also:

```
MyRouter(config-if)# network 10.1.14.0
```

```
MyRouter(config-if)# network 10.1.15.0
```

```
MyRouter(config-if)# network 209.168.98.32
```

Now the EIGRP routing process is running across all four of MyRouter's LAN segments, subnets 10.1.13.0–10.1.15.0, and network 209.168.98.32.

Each routing protocol has its own command set. These commands reflect the protocol's particular capabilities. Once a routing protocol is initialized, its commands are used to set various parameters in the configuration file to tune the behavior of the routing process as it operates in that router. EIGRP's command set is listed in Table 14-2.

Given that this is an introductory guide, we won't go into the commands for EIGRP or the other Cisco protocols—each one has its own complete command reference manual. But looking at the commands in Table 14-2 gives you a notion of how the concepts introduced in this chapter are implemented. Let's take one example of an advanced command to give you an idea of how things work:

```
MyRouter(config-router)#metric maximum-hops 25
```

What the preceding command does is set a maximum network diameter for the routing domain. *Network diameter* is a limit on how many hops a route may have before the routing protocol stops advertising it. The setting in this use of the **maximum-hops** command will enforce a limit of 25 hops. Should the router receive a routing update with 26 or more hops

EIGRP Command	Description
auto-summary	Enables automatic network number summarization
default	Sets a command to its defaults
default-information	Controls distribution of default information
default-metric	Sets the metric of redistributed routes
distance	Defines an administrative distance
distribute-listeigrp	Filters networks in routing updates (used with commands that are specific to EIGRP)
maximum-paths	Forwards packets over multiple paths.
metric	Modifies IGRP routing metrics and parameters
neighbor	Specifies a neighbor router
network	Enables routing on an IP network
offset-list	Adds or subtracts offset from IGRP or RIP metrics
passive-interface	Suppresses routing updates on an interface
redistribute	Redistributes information from another routing protocol
timers	Adjusts routing timers
traffic-share	Computes traffic share for alternate routes
variance	Controls the load-balancing variance

Table 14-2.   EIGRP's Command Set (Each Routing Protocol Has Its Own)

indicated in its distance metric, the router will decline to enter it into its routing table. The **maximum-hops** command is an easy way to limit the kind of traffic a router will carry.

Configuring RIP 2

Although the severe limitations of early RIP versions opened the door for EIGRP, the competition fought back. The Internet Engineering Task Force (IETF) oversaw the release of the RIP 2 open standard in 1997. RIP 2 has most of the advanced functionality of other state-of-the-art interior gateway protocols such as EIGRP and OSPF. None of the improvements are unique to RIP 2, but they go a long way toward catching up RIP's functionality with other routing protocols. The IETF felt this was a good thing because RIP has such a huge installed base and is still quite useful for small internetworks.

But even with its advances, the use of RIP 2 is still limited to smaller internetworks by its 16-hop limit. Also, RIP 2 still issues routing updates on a fixed-interval cycle, causing it to converge more slowly than EIGRP or OSPF.

Configuring RIP 2 involves the same generic commands as other Cisco routing protocols, where the commands must be used to initialize the routing process on the router and its networks:

```
MyRouter(config)#router rip
```

```
MyRouter(config-router)#network 209.11.244.9
```

You'll notice that no autonomous system number was entered (as in **router rip 999**) since neither RIP nor RIP 2 supports autonomous system numbers. Also, the command to initialize RIP 2 is **router rip** (not **router rip2**), because the version of RIP you can run is a function of the version of IOS the router has loaded.

Once the RIP 2 process is launched, configuring it is a matter of setting its other parameters. In RIP 2, these include router authentication using the **rip authentication** command, route summarization using the **auto-summary** command, and validation of the IP addresses of routers sending routing updates using the **validate-update-source** command.

Let's take a look at an example RIP 2 command that's more generic in nature. The **timers basic** command is used to set the routing update intervals within an RIP routing domain. The default is 30-second intervals. If you wanted to change routing update frequency to every 25 seconds, you'd enter the following command:

```
MyRouter(config-router)#timers basic 25
```

Changing basic metrics such as this is discouraged. Making updates five seconds more frequent will help speed convergence, but will increase network overhead by causing more routing messages.

Configuring Open Shortest Path First

In 1991, the industry moved to establish an open standard replacement for RIP. The result was OSPF (Open Shortest Path First), which, as the name implies, is an open standard used to seek out shortest path routes just like RIP. But that's where the similarities end. OSPF is a link-state, not distance-vector, routing protocol. OSPF converges faster than RIP and operates under the link-state concept, in which each router keeps a database of all links in a network and information on any delays it might be experiencing. In addition, OSPF saves control message overhead by issuing routing updates only on an event-driven basis.

OSPF Routing Areas

Most OSPF features are designed to help cope with internetwork size. The central concept behind OSPF is internetwork areas. As stated earlier in the chapter, an *area* is a zone within an autonomous system that is composed of a logical set of network segments and their attached devices. The areas are used by the routing system as a strategy to control traffic flow and sift out unwanted routing table details. Every OSPF domain must have a backbone area with number 0. Areas are created by using the keyword **area** as an argument with the **network** command, as shown next:

```
MyRouter(config-router)#network 10.0.0.0  0.255.255.255 area 0
```

This command puts the subnet 10.0.0.0 into OSPF area 0. It's possible to run a one-area OSPF network, having only an area 0. Figure 14-22 shows a three-area OSPF network.

A key functionality of OSPF is that it can redirect routing updates between areas. *Redirect* is a routing update that passes through one or more areas of a routing domain, usually through a number of filters designed to cut down routing update traffic.

Variable-Length Subnet Masks

OSPF networks are frequently used to tie together preexisting routing domains such as RIP internetworks. This is done by creating an OSPF area for each RIP domain and passing routing updates between them through the OSPF backbone (area 0). The routers at the edges of the areas are called *autonomous system boundary routers* (or *ASBRs,* for short). The ASBRs sit between the OSPF autonomous system and the RIP networks, and run both OSPF and RIP protocols.

Variable-length subnet mask (VLSM) support is a critical feature for OSPF. Respective areas often have their own subnet schemes that fit their particular needs. In Figure 14-23, all the serial line–based networks in Area 0 use the .252 subnet mask, typical for long-distance connections. This is because the .252 mask allows up to 64 subnets, but only two hosts per subnet. This is ideal for networks composed of a serial-line connection because only two hosts are needed: one at each end of the line.

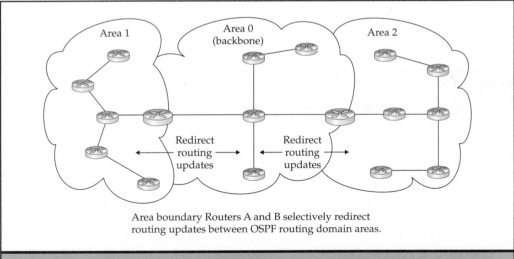

Area boundary Routers A and B selectively redirect
routing updates between OSPF routing domain areas.

Figure 14-22.   OSPF implements routing areas and redirects routes between them.

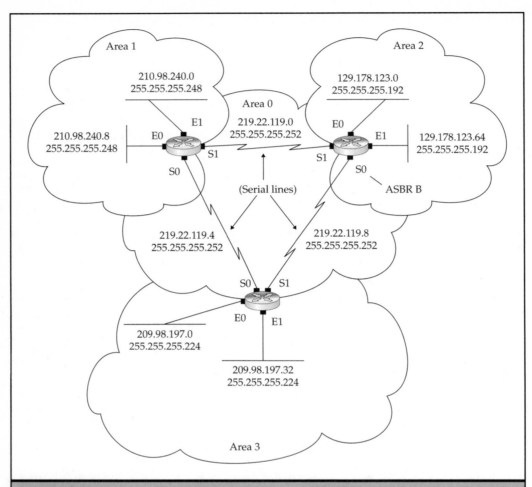

Figure 14-23. The variable-length subnet mask feature helps make areas possible.

Each of the other end-system areas uses its own scheme. Area 1 uses the .248 mask (yielding a maximum of 32 subnets and six hosts each), Area 2 uses the .192 mask (up to four subnets with 62 hosts each), and Area 3 uses the .224 mask (up to eight subnets with 30 hosts each).

VLSM support means that the routes exchanged in updates passed between the OSPF areas can include the subnet addresses (instead of just the network address). This is an important feature because it allows complete routes to be shared across areas using differing subnet schemes, which means each area can use only the amount of address space required for its needs. For example, in Figure 14-23's Area 0, there are only a few hosts connected to the serial lines, and being able to use the .248 masks lets Area 0 use up only a few addresses (a .248 mask has only six hosts per subnet).

Even with all of OSPF's power, it would be hard to scale internetwork size very much without VLSM. This is because most LANs use subnetted addressing schemes in order to conserve precious IP address space. OSPF areas make possible large-scale expansion of routing domains and, therefore, internetwork size. VLSM enables routers to have full address visibility between areas, and thus route traffic within internetworks with much greater efficiency.

Border Gateway Protocol

The Border Gateway Protocol (BGP) is the high-level routing protocol that makes the Internet possible. Optimized to coordinate internetworking between autonomous systems, BGP is, at this point, virtually the only exterior gateway protocol in use today.

There are several versions of BGP, and Cisco IOS supports all of them. BGP Version 2 is defined in RFC 1163, version 3 in RFC 1267, and version 4 in RFC 1771. It's a worthwhile read for those interested in digging deeper into BGP. But for now, let's keep it above ground.

EIGRP and OSPF let network operators scale their internetworks to large capacities, but it is BGP that ties them all together along so-called Internet trunks, or peer networks. Most networking types will never work with BGP; its use is mainly left to ISP administrators concerned with discovering routes across high-speed backbones. However, it's helpful to briefly review how BGP fits in.

The predominance of a single exterior routing protocol is unsurprising in light of the fact that the world's network operators need a single standard to integrate the millions of autonomous systems operating in the world. If the industry hadn't settled on BGP as the common platform, some other exterior gateway protocol would be the de facto standard instead.

BGP Routing

Like interior gateway protocols, BGP uses routing update messages and metrics to maintain routing tables. BGP is a modified link-state architecture routing protocol, but obviously is radically different in architecture to be able to scale to Internet growth. BGP's architecture is characterized by the use of route aggregation and the ability to work with interior gateway protocols. BGP supports three types of routing:

▼ **Inter-autonomous system**   Inter-autonomous system routing is the basic function of BGP in the Internet routing operations.

■ **Intra-autonomous system**   Intra-autonomous system routing is performed by BGP when two or more BGP routers operate inside the same autonomous system. This is generally seen in cases in which it's necessary to cross a large internetwork from one edge to the other.

▲ **Pass-through autonomous system**   Pass-through autonomous system routing occurs when it is necessary for BGP traffic to traverse a non-BGP autonomous system in order to connect to another BGP autonomous system.

As an exterior gateway routing protocol optimized to scale to Internet size, BGP differs sharply from interior protocols in some fundamental ways:

▼ **Peer routers**   The network administrator specifies a list of BGP routers representing other autonomous systems (usually other ISPs or large internetwork portals). This is done because it isn't feasible to pass routing updates through a worldwide routing domain.

■ **Routing table contents**   A table entry in BGP is an autonomous system (not a LAN, as it is in an interior gateway protocol). Each route consists of a network number and a list of autonomous systems that must be passed through, called an *AS path.*

■ **Single routing metric**   BGP uses a single metric to determine the best path to a given network. This metric consists of an arbitrary number to weight the degree of preference to a particular link. It's not dynamic; it must be input and updated by a network administrator.

▲ **Incremental route updates**   When a routing update is received, BGP simply replaces the old route with the new one. No best path recalculation is done, because to maintain a link-state database on the Internet's topology is not feasible.

Cisco's implementation of BGP supports each router establishing a set of neighbors, or peers, with which to exchange reachability information. A variety of techniques are used to aggregate routes to help simplify route processing and to reduce the size of routing tables. One is the use of *route maps*—a practice that restricts the dissemination of routing updates to certain routers. Another is the use of a simplified form of administrative distance where, instead of having the choice among 255 relative weightings, a route can take on any of three trustworthiness ratings depending on the topology position of the router.

BGP's key facet is its ability to filter, reduce, and simplify the routing information it gathers from the Internet.

Mulitprotocol Label Switching

Another way to route packets through an internetwork is with a protocol that streamlines the whole process. Multiprotocol Label Switching (MPLS) is a way to forward packets through an internetwork. Routers, situated on the edge of a network, apply simple labels to packets. Then, routers, switches, or other network devices within the network can switch packets based on the labels. This process is ideal, because it requires minimal lookup overhead.

How It Works

Conventional layer-3 IP routing is based on the exchange of network availability information. As a packet winds its way through a network, each router makes decisions about where the packet will be sent next. This information is based on information in layer 3 of the header and is used as an index for a routing table lookup to determine the packet's next hop. This process is repeated at each router in the network. At each hop, the router has to resolve the next destination for the packet.

The downside of this process is that the information within the IP packets—like information about precedence or VPN data, for example—is not considered when forwarding packets. For best performance, only the destination address is considered, but, because other fields within the packet could be relevant, an in-depth header analysis must take place at each router along the packet's path.

MPLS streamlines this process by placing a *label* on each packet. Think of conventional IP routing like addressing a letter. It tells the post office where to send the letter. MPLS takes addressing to another level by adding extra instructions—like writing "Perishable" or "Do Not Bend" on the envelope.

The label includes important information about the packet:

▼ Destination

■ Precedence

■ A specific route for the packet, if one is needed

■ Virtual private network membership

▲ Quality of Service (QoS) information

MPLS causes the layer-3 header analysis to be performed only twice—at the edge label switch router (LSR) as it enters and exits an internetwork. At the LSR, the layer-3 header is mapped into a fixed-length label and applied to the packet. Figure 14-24 shows how a label is applied to a packet.

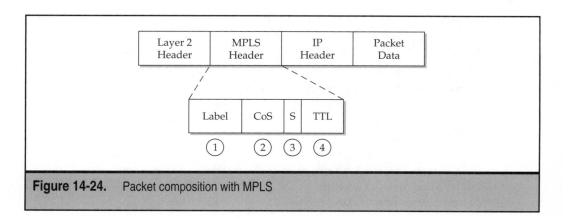

Figure 14-24.   Packet composition with MPLS

The 32-bit MPLS header contains the following fields, as numbered in Figure 14-24:

1. The label field (20 bits) carries the actual value of the MPLS label.
2. The Class of Service (CoS) field (3 bits) can affect the queuing and discard algorithms applied to the packet as it is transmitted through the network.
3. The Stack (S) field (1 bit) supports a hierarchical label stack.
4. The TTL (time-to-live) field (8 bits) provides conventional IP TTL functionality.

Next, as the packet crosses the routers in an internetwork, only the label needs to be read. Once it reaches the other end of the network, another edge LSR removes the label, replacing it with the appropriate header data linked to that label.

A key result of this arrangement is that forwarding decisions based on some or all of these different sources of information can be achieved by means of a single table lookup from a fixed-length label. Label switching is the merger of switching and routing functions—it combines the availability information of routers with the traffic engineering benefits of switches.

Benefits

MPLS offers many advantages over traditional IP and ATM routing protocols. Label switching and hardware switching work together to deliver high degrees of performance. For multiservice networks, MPLS allows a switch to provide ATM, Frame Relay, and IP service on a single platform. This is ideal, because supporting all these services on a single platform is not only cost-effective, but it also simplifies provisioning for multiservice providers.

The following benefits highlight some of the usefulness of MPLS:

▼ **Integration**   MPLS combines IP and ATM functionality, making the ATM infrastructure visible to IP routing and eliminating the need for mappings between IP and ATM features.

■ **VPN performance**   With an MPLS backbone, VPN information need only be processed where packets enter and exit the network. Additionally, BGP is used to deal with VPN information. The use of both MPLS and BGP makes MPLS-based VPN services easier to manage and much more scalable.

■ **Reduction of burden on core services**   Because MPLS examines packets when they enter and exit a network, internal transit routers and switches need only process the connectivity with the provider's edge routers. This prevents the core devices from becoming overwhelmed with the routing volume exchanged over the Internet.

▲ **Traffic engineering capabilities**   MPLS's traffic engineering capabilities enable network administrators to shift the traffic load from overburdened sections to underused sections of the network, based on traffic destination, type, load, and time of day.

The MPLS Network Structure

An MPLS network has three basic components. They are

▼ **Edge label switch routers**   Edge LSRs are situated at the physical and logical boundary of a network. These devices are usually routers (like the Cisco 8500) but can also be multilayer LAN switches (like the Cisco Catalyst 6500) or a proxy device.

■ **Label switches**   These devices switch packets based on the labels. In addition, label switches may also support layer-3 routing or layer-2 switching. Some label switches include the Cisco 6500, the Cisco 8540 Multiservice Switch Router, and Cisco 8500.

▲ **Label Distribution Protocol**   The Label Distribution Protocol (LDP) is used alongside network layer routing protocols and distributes label information between MPLS network devices.

MPLS provides internetworks with an unprecedented level of control over traffic, resulting in a network that is more efficient, supports more predictable service, and can offer the flexibility required to meet constantly changing networking situations.

Cisco's Routing Protocol Strategy

The move around 1990 to replace RIP with a more robust interior gateway protocol was a key moment in the history of the internetworking industry. (Keep in mind that 1990 is ancient history in Internet time.) The ability to scale beyond 16 hops or a network diameter of 50 routers was sorely needed. Faster convergence was also on the critical list because loops were becoming a pressing problem.

Cisco exploited the moment by promoting IGRP as a RIP replacement. This was a risk because IGRP was (and is) a proprietary standard. But the strategy was wildly successful because it solved customers' needs to continue internetwork expansion and, at the same time, persuaded network managers to standardize on Cisco equipment. Most of those that did have since migrated to EIGRP.

OSPF is an IP-only routing protocol. The technology planners on the OSPF Working Group were right to promote a RIP replacement. And they were probably right that one day all networks will be based on the Internet Protocol, but that won't happen for another ten years. It was only ten short years ago that many were pointing a finger at Novell and complaining that Novell held a monopoly on client-server LAN operating systems. There are millions of IPX LANs to this day. The reality is that most enterprises still have a mix of network-level protocols and need to support them using an interior gateway technology like EIGRP. This was the marketing window Cisco exploited.

Cisco supports an OSPF product as a complement to its EIGRP strategy. OSPF is a powerhouse in its own right. Most ISPs (and an increasing number of enterprises) are running large IP-only routing domains, and given the standards-setting clout of the Internet, many think that one day everybody will be IP only. OSPF has built the mission-critical infrastructure surrounding and sustaining the BGP peer networks. Without OSPF, BGP peer networks probably wouldn't be possible. Both are enabling technologies that made the explosive growth of internetworks and the Internet possible.

Further, Cisco support of MPLS streamlines routing through internetworking. As we've seen, by affixing a header on a packet when it enters your network, then stripping it as it leaves, MPLS improves network functionality and eases the burden on core network devices. The use of MPLS is certainly beneficial when issues of network performance and capacity are involved.

Comparing the functionality of current routing protocols can be confusing. Although RIP is the lowliest of the interior gateway protocols, it has been so heavily enhanced that it now shares much of the advanced functionality available with EIGRP and OSPF. Further confusing the routing protocol landscape is that RIP and other protocols are being subsumed into OSPF domains as routing domain areas. Things get more clouded because OSPF is so scalable that it has a lot of the size-scaling functionality associated with BGP.

Suffice it to say that today's routing protocols overlap so much that they're hard to keep straight. Just keep in mind that the essential distinctions are distance-vector versus link-state architectures and interior gateway protocols versus exterior gateway protocols.

CHAPTER 15

Network Management

We've now covered the major pieces of technology that compose internetworks. Routers, switches, firewalls, and access servers are cabled together to form network topologies. Most configurations run over twisted-pair copper feeding into fiber-optic backbones that move data at speeds from 100 Mbps up to a mind-boggling 10 Gbps. While network devices vary in type and size, most look like PCs or servers in that they have memory, CPUs, and interface cards. They are, however, diskless, seldom have monitors, and use their interfaces to connect networks instead of peripherals.

Cisco's software infrastructure to make it all go is the Internetwork Operating System (IOS). IOS is a lean package of commands, protocol software, and the all-important config file. IOS software images differ greatly depending on the type of device. The switch has a modest version of IOS, while the behemoth Cisco 12000 Series Gigabit Router is loaded with protocols and specialized management software packages. Yet, regardless of device type or IOS functionality, network behavior is controlled by setting parameters in the config file.

As we saw in the previous chapter, perhaps the most sophisticated internetworking technology of all is the routing protocol. Routing protocols give internetworks a level of self-awareness and self-adaptation without which large-scale configurations wouldn't be practical. They do this by constructing a hierarchy of LANs and autonomous systems to find optimal paths to get across the office campus—or to the other side of the world.

It takes more than optimal routes to run an internetwork, though. The ability to self-operate is only part of the network management equation. Routing protocols may be able to handle most minute-to-minute issues, but internetworks still require constant management effort from people. Without persistent review and intervention from administrators, an internetwork's ability to self-operate will be overwhelmed by a progressive deterioration in operating conditions. Internetworks must be constantly updated and even upgraded to accommodate problems, growth, and change. Network teams need tools for managing change and anticipating problems (and, hopefully, avoiding them).

If left alone, even a perfectly configured internetwork will degrade under the strain of added users, increased loads, shifting traffic, new hardware and software versions, and new technology. Network administrators must monitor, reconfigure, and troubleshoot without end. The recent boom in users—and the increase in the amount of traffic generated per user—has left network teams scrambling to keep up. Routing protocols and other automated features only make effective internetwork management feasible, they don't make it easy. Network management tools are needed also. The industry's response has been a stream of standards, technologies, and products focused on the configuration and operation of internetworks.

OVERVIEW OF NETWORK MANAGEMENT

Network management can be confusing to newcomers. By its nature, the field involves a daunting list of tasks. Figure 15-1 outlines the range of chores performed by the typical network management team.

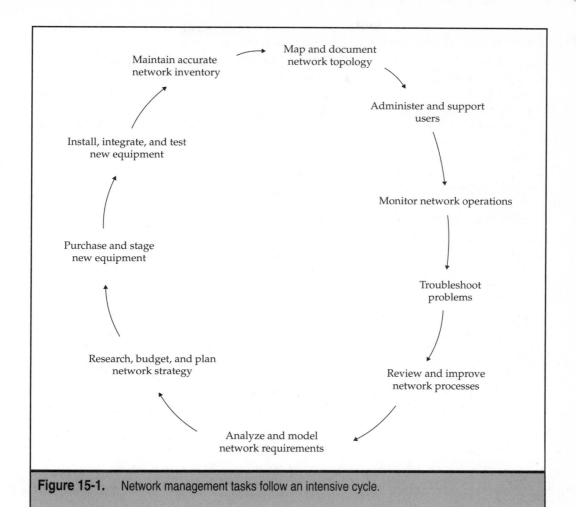

Figure 15-1.   Network management tasks follow an intensive cycle.

Internetworks must be planned, modeled, budgeted, designed, configured, purchased, installed, tested, mapped, documented, operated, monitored, analyzed, optimized, adjusted, expanded, updated, and fixed. That's a lot. No single tool can do all these things, at least not yet. Suffice it to say that network management products and services is an industry unto itself, composed of a complex array of technologies, products, and vendors providing everything from simple protocol analyzers that measure a single link to worldwide network command centers.

NOTE: You may have noticed that the term "network management" is used in connection with internetworks. (Almost nobody manages just one LAN anymore.) The term has held on since the rise of internetworking and is still in universal use. There is no real difference between network management and internetwork management.

The Evolution of Management Tools

Historically, the problem with computer management tools has been delivering true multivendor support. In other words, it's hard to find a single tool that can handle equipment from different manufacturers equally well. Multivendor configurations—the norm in virtually all enterprise IT (information technology) infrastructures today—are tough to manage using a single tool because of subtle differences in each manufacturer's equipment.

Computer management tools have evolved from opposite poles of the computing industry: systems and networks. The goal is to bring all computing assets under the management control of a single tool, and the prevalence of placing host systems on networks is driving existing system and network management tools into one another's arms.

Traditional System Management Consoles

Sophisticated computing management systems called *system consoles* have been around for decades. These consoles were generally hooked up to mainframes sitting in a data center and used to schedule jobs, perform backups, and fix problems. Over time, they developed more and more capabilities, such as managing remote computers.

The best-known product from the data center mold is Unicenter from Computer Associates (CA). Unicenter is actually an amalgamation of products that CA has woven into a single management solution. Unicenter evolved from a sophisticated console for managing IBM mainframes and disk farms to an integrated management system with support for all the important hardware and software platforms. Most Unicenter product growth has been achieved by acquisition, understandable given the product scope.

The key to Unicenter and other system consoles is the ability to handle the various computer architectures that enterprises are likely to put into a configuration.

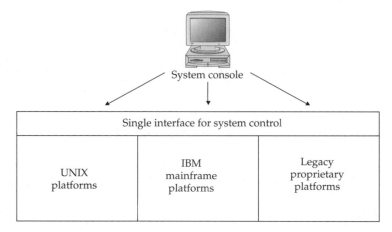

Network Management Systems

Over the past decade, a second breed of management tool emerged in the form of network management systems. These tools focus on network infrastructure instead of the data center. They use the networks they manage as the platform for monitoring events and are controlled from a console referred to as the network management station (NMS).

The leading NMS is OpenView from Hewlett-Packard (HP). There's a bit of history as to how HP ended up in this enviable position. HP had committed to UNIX as its strategic operating system in the mid-1980s—years earlier than other enterprise platform vendors. (Don't give HP too much credit; they did so out of desperation because their proprietary 16-bit operating system had run out of gas.) By that time, UNIX and IP had become closely linked in the market, mostly because IBM and other big system vendors were still pushing their proprietary networking schemes. Around 1990, HP seized the moment, and OpenView rode the UNIX bandwagon to become the predominant network management tool. There are now over 100,000 OpenView installations.

As with Unicenter, the key to OpenView's success is its ability to work with devices from various manufacturers, but HP had a built-in design advantage in the form of a then-new IP network management standard called SNMP (Simple Network Management Protocol). Instead of having to design to dozens of proprietary interfaces, HP was able to let the network equipment vendors design products to the SNMP standard. OpenView was the first major management product to implement SNMP.

Network management station (e.g., HP Open View or IBM NetView)					
Device inventory	Configuration	Topology mapping	Device monitoring	Troubleshooting	Analysis
SNMP/RMON					
Routers	Switches	Hubs	Access servers	Servers	
CiscoWorks		Nortel Optivity	Others (e.g., Castle Rock, NetScout, etc.)		
Resource mgr. essentials	CWSI				

The defining difference between system and network consoles is the level at which they operate. System management tools focus on operating systems, transactions, data files, and databases as they exist across servers, storage controllers, and disks. Network management tools focus on packets and connections as they exist over network devices, interfaces, and transmission links.

System and network consoles are now converging into a single technology class some call enterprise system management (ESM) tools. Convergence into ESM is inevitable as the line between network and computer blurs and enterprises complete the shift to client-server architectures that move resources from the data center out into their internetwork topologies.

The focus of this book is internetworking, so we'll cover only the networking components of ESM.

Network Management Tools Today

It has proven to be very difficult to manage an internetwork using a single tool. The problem has been the inability to collect consistent data from the variety of devices that exist in most enterprise IT infrastructures. The problem isn't so much old versus new equipment, although that's part of it. The major hang-up is that most network management systems are shallow in their implementations; in other words, they can manage only a few aspects of device operation, and leave some devices unmanaged altogether.

This is so despite the fact that all major network equipment makers bundle SNMP into their device operating systems. The base SNMP infrastructure is there, but device manufacturers seldom implement it fully in their products. There are a variety of reasons for this:

▼ **Consumption of resources by network management**   Every CPU cycle spent gathering a measurement or sending an SNMP message is a cycle not used for payload traffic. Network management extracts a cost either in slower performance or extra hardware.

■ **Spotty standards support by manufacturers**   It would be expensive for device makers to build complete compliance into their products. Device hardware would need to be beefed up to handle the additional SNMP work, pushing up prices in the process. In addition, some manufacturers prefer a dash of SNMP incompatibility to steer customers toward standardizing on their product line because implementing SNMP from one manufacturer is easier than bringing devices of different manufacturers under the same management regime.

■ **Labor**   A lot of time and attention is required for enterprises to implement and operate a network management system. Management teams are hard-pressed just to keep up with network growth. Few have the manpower to make greater use of SNMP-based systems.

▲ **Price-conscious customers**   Customers are fixated on low price points. The network half of IT shops is regarded as infrastructure, and managers demand commodity pricing. The relentless focus on driving down the cost per port looks good on paper, but incurs hidden costs in the form of poorly utilized assets.

For these reasons, most SNMP implementations gather only high-level information. Fewer processes—called *objects*—are monitored, samples are smaller, polling cycles are less frequent, and so on.

Often, even when an enterprise *does* want more network management controls, blind spots are still created by noncompliant devices. Blind spots occur when a policy cannot be enforced in part of a network because a device doesn't support it. Blind spots often occur at backbone entryways, especially to switched backbones. Take the scenario depicted in Figure 15-2. The part of the topology on the bottom has implemented a policy to manage traffic usage between a pair of communicating hosts. But the switch in the middle is not configured to monitor that, leaving that SNMP policy unenforced beyond the switch.

The IETF (Internet Engineering Task Force) is responsible for the SNMP standard, and it has a tough job. The implementation of any standard requires coordinated acceptance from both manufacturers and users. This is difficult to pull off because manufacturers are wary of market acceptance and the potential loss of competitive advantage. Understandably, then, standards-setting is always a tricky process. Yet the goal of an integrated NMS console has proved to be particularly elusive for these reasons:

▼ **Hardware dependencies**   Any computer standard must contend with various architectures used for CPUs, buses, device interfaces, drivers, and the like. This both complicates the standards-setting process and makes it more expensive for manufacturers to comply with. The problem is exacerbated by the internetworking industry's habit of using so many different parts in their product lines. Remember all the different CPU architectures that go into Cisco's router line?

■ **Converging technology**   Until recently, telecommunications, data networking, and computing were viewed as separate and distinct industries. Each had its own industry bodies, standards, and so on. But nowadays, all of this equipment has fallen under the purview of network managers. This has increased the scope of the standards and brought together different engineering fields, which creates increasingly more complex work environments for network managers.

▲ **Technology onslaught**   Relentless technology advances in all quarters of computing (telecommunications, operating systems, CPUs, cabling, and so on) have presented the IETF with a constantly moving target, and a manufacturer that has won a hard-earned advantage is often reluctant to fall into line with standards and make life easier for competitors.

Progress has been slow. Yet the lack of integrated management hasn't impeded the explosive growth in the size and use of networks. To accommodate this conflict, management teams use several products to track different parts of their internetworks. Most big enterprises have an ESM, but they augment it with dedicated tools to manage critical parts of internetworks. Figure 15-3 illustrates a typical scenario, with OpenView used to watch the overall network and manufacturer-specific tools to manage critical assets.

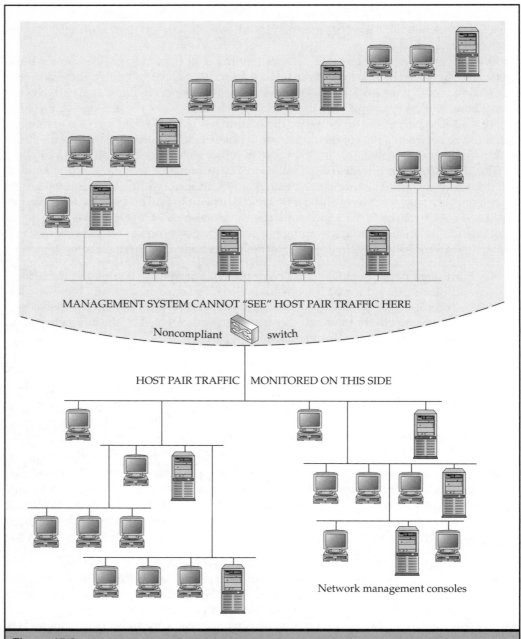

MANAGEMENT SYSTEM CANNOT "SEE" HOST PAIR TRAFFIC HERE

Noncompliant switch

HOST PAIR TRAFFIC | MONITORED ON THIS SIDE

Network management consoles

Figure 15-2. Partial SNMP management causes network management blind spots.

HP Open View		
Generic applications	CiscoWorks	Optivity
Shallow SNMP	Deeper SNMP and RMON instrumentation of device manufacturer's own products	
Device inventory high-level MIBS	Device inventory, high-level MIBs, "deep," device-specific, private MIBs (e.g., monitor device cooling, fan, etc.)	

Figure 15-3.   Most network teams use several tools to manage their internetworks.

The most significant manufacturer-specific tool is CiscoWorks, with broad enough functionality to be considered an ESM unto itself—but only as long as you're strictly running Cisco gear. For that reason, CiscoWorks is usually snapped into an ESM suite like OpenView or NetView.

NOTE: Management standards aren't just a problem in internetworking. An industry group called the Distributed Management Task Force (DMTF) has been trying for years to get a standard called the Desktop Management Interface (DMI) implemented. The purpose of DMI, aimed at distributed PCs and small servers, is to let consoles monitor inventory—disks, drivers, BIOS versions, memory configurations, and so on—and to perform remote upgrades. DMI 2.0 products include Compaq's Insight Manager, IBM's Universal Management Agent, Intel's LANDesk Manager, HP's TopTools, and others. Trouble is, these products pretty much work only with platforms of their own manufacture. Microsoft has weighed in with an open standard called WBEM (Web-Based Enterprise Management), now under the auspices of the DMTF. Intel is working on a complementary standard at the hardware level called WfM (Wired for Management). For now, you either restrict the number of vendor product lines you use, or use individual tools to manage each of them. Sound familiar?

Trends in Enterprise System Management

ESM tools have been criticized as difficult to implement, labor intensive, expensive, slow, and ineffective. They're priced at up to $250,000 and cost at least that much again to implement. As far as specialized management hardware, RMON probes can cost over $10,000 each. The expense has left most small- to medium-sized internetworks relying on multiple tools, each usually specific to the major equipment manufacturers used in the configuration. A second result is that fewer things are monitored, diminishing proactive network management.

The market for tools is robust anyway because the potential for savings from NMS tools is enormous. Some estimate that during a typical IT infrastructure's lifecycle, 75 percent or more of all costs are spent on operations. There is a double benefit of enabling network administration personnel to be more productive and getting better results in available bandwidth. NMS tools help enterprises reduce costs and boost service at the same time.

There are now many major NMS tools. In addition to OpenView and Unicenter, other notables are IBM's Tivoli NetView (IBM acquired Tivoli Systems several years ago), Aprisma's Spectrum (Aprisma is the Cabletron spin-off that took Spectrum with it to distance the product from Cabletron's hardware business), Nortel Networks' Optivity, Bull's OpenMaster, and Sun's SunNet Manager.

Microsoft entered the fray with the introduction of Microsoft Management Console (MMC) in its Windows 2000 release. Ever expanding, MMC is a key management interface in Win Server 2003. It's not only used for Microsoft management tools, either. Third-party vendors have been creating their own snap-ins for the MMC as well. See Figure 15-4 to chart how different management tools interrelate.

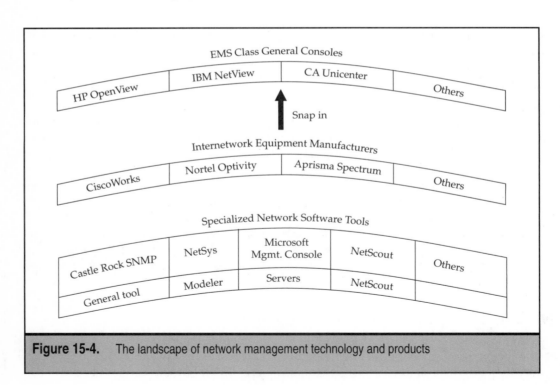

Figure 15-4.   The landscape of network management technology and products

The cast of contenders comes from three sources: computer platform makers such as HP and IBM; network device manufacturers like Cisco and Nortel Networks; and software companies in the form of Microsoft, Castle Rock, and others. Who prevails will tell which is most important: the wire, the desktop, or the mainframe. Regardless of vendor, NMS technology is headed toward these goals:

▼ **More coverage**   As greater management control is placed on devices and network processes, faster device hardware will be required and more data will be available.

■ **Simplicity**   As internetworking has exploded in popularity among small- and medium-sized enterprises, more networks are being operated by nonexperts.

■ **Automation**   As underlying network management technologies improve, more management tasks are being automated to improve Quality of Service (QoS).

▲ **Proactive management**   A new breed of tools helps isolate emerging problems and avert major network problems by taking early corrective action.

Nearly all progress in computing results directly or indirectly from industry standards. Internetworking ushered in the era of open computing with the help of several standards: the seven-layer OSI reference model, IP, Ethernet, UNIX, HTTP, SQL, and others. Now it's time to bring it all under control with integrated management technology driven by SNMP.

SNMP IS IP'S COMMON MANAGEMENT PLATFORM

Almost all modern internetwork management suites are built atop the Simple Network Management Protocol. Thus, before discussing the Cisco management applications, a look at their underlying network management technology is in order.

What Is SNMP?

SNMP is a TCP/IP protocol purpose-built to serve as a communications channel for internetwork management operating at the application layer of the IP stack. Although SNMP can be directly operated through the command line, it's almost always used through a management application that employs the SNMP communications channel to monitor and control networks. As Figure 15-5 shows, SNMP has two basic components: a network management station and agents.

Agents are small software modules, residing on managed devices, that can be configured to collect specific pieces of information on device operations. Most of the information

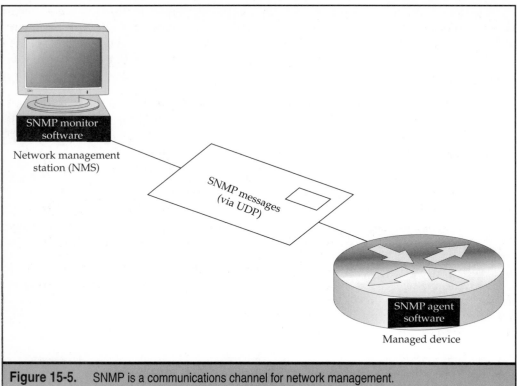

Figure 15-5.   SNMP is a communications channel for network management.

consists of totals, such as total bytes, total packets, total errors, and the like. Agents can be deployed on the panoply of devices, such as:

▼ Routers

■ Switches

■ Access servers

■ Servers (Windows, UNIX, Linux, MVS, VMS, and so on)

■ Workstations (Windows PCs, Macs, UNIX, and Linux desktops)

■ Printers

▲ UPS power backup systems

The idea is to place agents on all network devices and manage things according to the status information sent back. A piece of equipment with an SNMP agent loaded onto it is referred to as a *managed device* (also called a *network element*).

The NMS is the internetwork's control center. Usually, there's just one NMS for an autonomous system, although many large internetworks use more than one NMS—usually arranged in a hierarchy. Most NMSs today run on dedicated UNIX or Microsoft servers.

SNMP Polling and Managed Objects

SNMP is a fairly simple request/response protocol. It works by having the NMS periodically poll managed devices for fresh information. The polling frequency is a matter of configuration choice, but it usually takes place once every few minutes or so. There are three types of polling:

▼ **Monitor polling**   To check that devices are available and to trigger an alarm when one is not

■ **Threshold polling**   To detect when conditions deviate from a baseline number by a percentage greater than allowed (usually plus or minus 10 percent to 20 percent) and to notify the NMS for review

▲ **Performance polling**   To measure ongoing network performance over longer periods and to analyze the data for long-term trends and patterns

The agent responds to the poll by returning a message to the NMS. It's able to do this by capturing and storing information on subjects that it has been configured to monitor. These subjects are usually processes associated with the flow of packets. A process about which the agent collects data is called a managed object. A *managed object* is a variable characteristic of the device being managed. The total number of UDP connections open on a managed device, for example, could be a managed object. One open UDP session on a specific interface is an *object instance,* but the total number of simultaneously open UDP sessions on the device (say, a router) is a managed object. Figure 15-6 shows our example UDP connections as managed object and instances.

Managed objects are usually operating characteristics of managed devices. The managed devices can be anywhere in the topology—backbone devices, servers, or end systems. Most objects are physical pieces, such as a network interface, but a managed object isn't necessarily a physical entity. An object could also be a software application, a database, or some other logical entity.

The MIB

The agent stores the information about objects in specialized data records called *MIBs* (*management information bases*). An MIB is the storage part of the SNMP agent software. Information stored in MIBs is referred to as *variables* (also called *attributes*). MIBs usually collect information in the form of totals for a variable during a time interval, such as total packets over five minutes. Figure 15-7's example shows variables being extracted from instances and processed through managed MIBs and the managed object—in this example, a count of total Ethernet packets going through a router's interface. Again, the packet

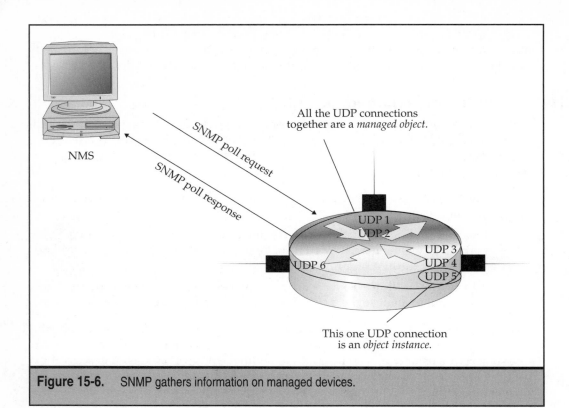

All the UDP connections together are a *managed object*.

SNMP poll request

SNMP poll response

NMS

UDP 1
UDP 2
UDP 3
UDP 6
UDP 4
UDP 5

This one UDP connection is an *object instance*.

Figure 15-6.   SNMP gathers information on managed devices.

count from each interface is a managed object instance; the count for all three interfaces is the managed object.

By collating data from multiple objects, the MIB lets the agent send the NMS information concerning everything on the device that is being monitored.

Types of MIBs

MIBs are prefabricated to perform specific jobs. They're often called MIB objects. Basic MIBs usually come packaged inside the network device operating system. For example, IOS comes packaged with MIB objects for most network management jobs.

Generally, MIBs are named using a convention that indicates the MIB category.

For example, a Cisco MIB object that deals with a specific network interface will have *if* in its name (from the letters *i* and *f* in interface). The ifInErrors MIB object monitors incoming packet errors on an interface; ifOutErrors monitors the outgoing errors. sysLocation reports a device's network location, and so on. In and Out specify whether the MIB object is to measure incoming or outgoing traffic. Table 15-1 shows five basic MIB categories used in most SNMP systems.

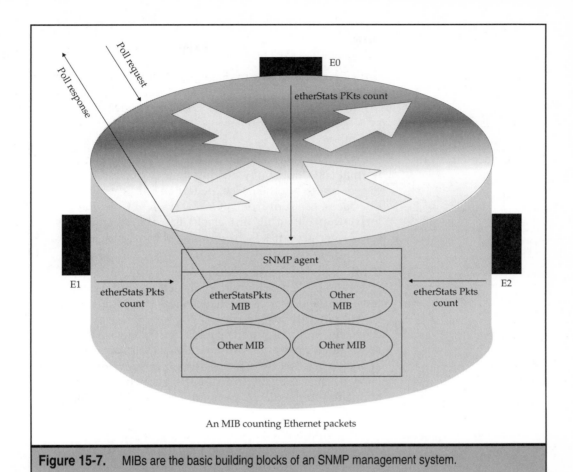

Figure 15-7.   MIBs are the basic building blocks of an SNMP management system.

It is possible to set an MIB to gather information on a single object instance only, called a *scalar* object. Most managed objects, however, are composed of several related instances. This practice, called *tabular* objects, is the rule in most MIBs because it's more efficient to manage as much as possible from a single data collection point. As the name implies, a tabular MIB keeps the information straight by storing it in rows and tables.

NOTE: MIB lingo can be confusing. You'll hear references to the MIB as if it were a single MIB object. But that's not the case. For example, the Cisco MIB is not an MIB as such; it's actually the root of about 400 private Cisco MIB objects.

Category	Description and Examples
Configuration	MIBs that report basic management information such as device name, contact person, device location, and uptime. MIB configuration objects are sysName, sysDescr, sysContact, sysLocation, sysUpTime, ifNumber, romID, and others.
Interface error rates	MIBs that monitor specific interfaces. Packet errors are a normal condition, but watching their trends indicates device health and helps isolate faults. For Ethernet interfaces, use ifInErrors, ifOutErrors, locifCollisions, locIfInRunts, locIfInGiants, locIfCRC, and others. For serial interfaces, use locIfInFrame, locIfInAbort, locIfInIgnored, locIfResets, locIfRestarts, and others.
Bandwidth	ICMP is a layer-3 protocol that reports on IP packet processing. It's best known for its **echo** command used to verify the presence of other devices by pinging them. Timed pings are used to determine how far away a device is (much like in the submarine movies). SNMP sends ping input and output messages to measure available bandwidth. Cisco's MIB objects for this are icmpInEchos and icmpInEchoReps, and icmpOutEchos and icmpOutEchoReps. Generally speaking, these are the only SNMP messages not sent as UDP messages.
Traffic flow	Performance management is largely a matter of measuring traffic flow. There are Cisco MIBs to measure traffic rates both as bits per second and packets per second: locIfInBitsSec, locIfOutBitsSec, locIfInPktsSec, and locIfOutPktsSec.
Unreachable address	The object to measure how often a router is asked to send messages to an unreachable address is icmpOutDesUnreachs.
SNMP data	There are even objects to measure how much time the router spends handling SNMP messages. The objects include snmpInGetRequests and snmpOutGetRequests, snmpInGetResponses and snmpOutGetResponses, and others.

Table 15-1.   Basic Cisco MIB Objects Commonly Used in SNMP Implementations

What Makes SNMP Machine-Independent

We don't want to get too technical in this book, but you should understand how the SNMP standard makes itself machine-independent. In other words, how is it able to run on different brands of equipment, each with its own proprietary operating system?

The SNMP standard requires that every MIB object have an object ID and a syntax. An object ID identifies the object to the system and tells what kind of MIB to use and what kind of data the object collects. Syntax means a precise specification a machine can understand in binary form.

To understand a field's contents, IOS must know whether the field contains a number, text, a counter, or other type of data. These are called data types. *Data types* specify the syntax to be used for a data field. A *field* is any logical piece of data, such as a model number or temperature reading. In the same way that a field has its own box on an input screen, it has its own position in a computer file. A file represents data in binary (zeroes and ones), and a set of binary positions are reserved for each field within the file. All fields must be declared as some data type or another, or else the machine cannot process the data held there.

Computer hardware architectures, operating systems, programming languages, and other environmentals specify the data types they're willing to use. A data type represents the layer where software meets hardware. It tells the machine what syntax to use to interpret a field's contents. A different syntax is used for floating-point numbers, integer numbers, dates, text strings, and other data types.

SNMP makes itself independent by declaring its own data types. It does so in the form of the Structure of Management Information (SMI) standard. SMI is a standard dedicated to specifying a machine-independent syntax for every data type. These data types are independent of the data structures and representation techniques unique to particular computer architectures. SMI specifies the syntax for data types such as object IDs, counters, rows, tables, octet strings, network addresses, and other SNMP elements.

MIBs are programmed by vendors using an arcane programming language called ASN.1, created just for programming SMI data types. ASN.1 (Abstract Systems Notation One) is an OSI standard, from the same people that brought us the seven-layer reference model. Figure 15-8 shows how SMI data types universalize MIB information.

SMI tries to let vendors code "write-once, run anywhere" MIB objects. In other words, someone should be able to write a single piece of MIB software—a packet counter, for example—and the counter MIB should be able to run on any device that supports the SMI syntax definition for a counter.

SMI data types are SNMP's building blocks at the lowest level. They are used to construct MIB object formats in a syntax any machine can understand. From there, object instances are measured and rolled up into managed objects, which in turn are reported by the SNMP agent to the NMS. This is how NMSs can operate across disparate device architectures.

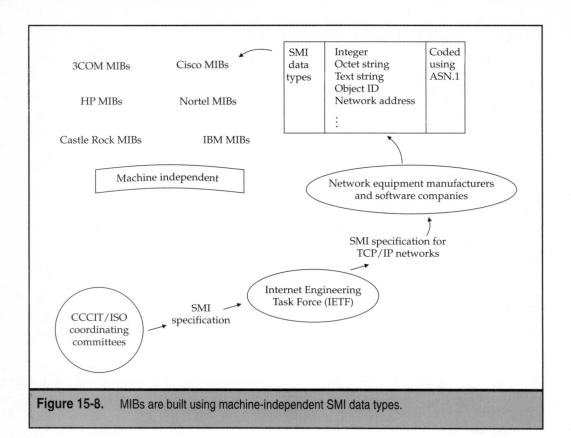

Figure 15-8. MIBs are built using machine-independent SMI data types.

Standard MIBs and Private MIBs

The current MIB standard is MIB-II, which has nearly 200 standard MIB objects. The standard is implemented as a hierarchy that starts from a root and continues to branch down from the source MIB to the root Internet MIB. Looking at Figure 15-9, you see that each branch is marked both by a name and a number (the numbers are used to build object IDs).

Figure 15-9 also shows the players in the history of the Internet. ISO is the International Standards Organization, and DoD is the U.S. Department of Defense (which started it all with ARPANET). CCITT is the Consultative Committee for International Telegraph and Telephone. The CCITT is only a distant cousin of the Internet, handling telephony and other communications standards. The CCITT is now known as the ITU-T (for Telecommunication Standardization Sector of the International Telecommunications Union), but you'll still see the CCITT acronym attached to dozens of standards.

Because they're more user-friendly, text strings are usually used to describe MIB objects in directories. Object IDs are mainly used by software to create compact, encoded representations of the names.

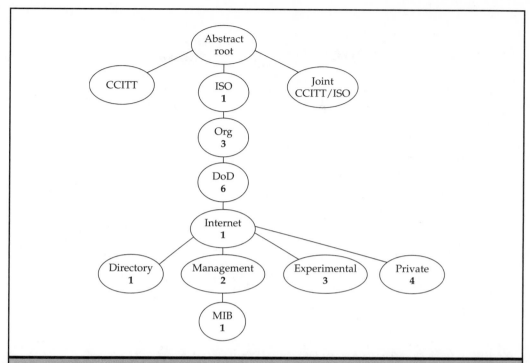

Figure 15-9. The Internet's family lineage yields the standard Internet MIB hierarchy.

Working from the tree structure in Figure 15-9, the Internet root's object ID is 1.3.6.1, named iso.org.dod.internet. The two main branches beyond the Internet root are the management and private MIBs. Industry-standard MIBs go through the management branch to become iso.org.dod.internet.mgmt.mib with the object ID 1.3.6.1.2.1. Private MIBs become iso.org.dod.internet.private and 1.3.6.1.4. Cisco's private MIB is represented as iso.org.dod.internet.private.enterprise.cisco, or object ID 1.3.6.1.4.1.9.

Vendors can build private MIBs by extending standard MIB branches. In this way, they can customize MIBs to better fit their particular needs. Figure 15-10—Cisco's private MIB hierarchy—shows how private MIBs extend from the standard Internet MIB.

Many of the object groups within the Cisco Management, Temporary Variables, and Local Variables subgroups measure Cisco proprietary technology. For example, the Cisco Environmental Monitor group in the Cisco Management subgroup—object ID 1.3.6.1.4.1.9.9—looks after such things as the operating temperature inside the device. This type of information is the "deep" stuff we were talking about that management applications from other manufacturers have trouble getting at.

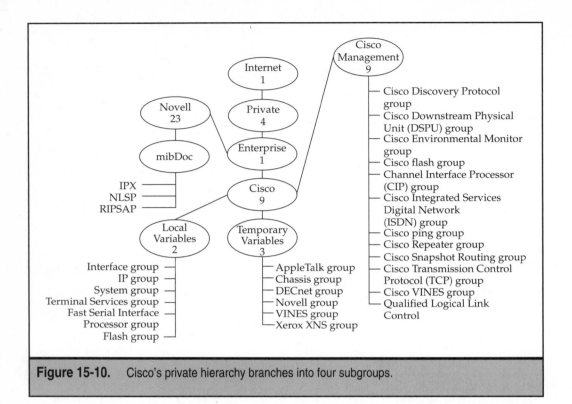

Figure 15-10.   Cisco's private hierarchy branches into four subgroups.

Another important thing to see in Figure 15-10 is support for legacy desktop protocols. Novell NetWare IPX, VINES, AppleTalk, DECnet, and even Xerox XNS networks can be managed using Cisco MIBs. These are legacy in that the IP LAN specification seems to be steamrolling the market, but the others are still in use and therefore important to their customers.

Polling Groups and Data Aggregation

MIBs are frequently placed into polling groups to facilitate SNMP data collection. A *polling group* is a set of logically related managed objects that are reported and analyzed as a cohesive entity. For example, Figure 15-11 shows polling groups for three different classes of equipment in an internetwork: the backbone switches, routers, and application servers. Different MIB variables are likely to be collected for each type, so each gets its own polling group. In this way, logically related management information is compiled and stored into the SNMP database under group names.

Grouping simplifies the network administrator's job. In the Figure 15-11 example, thresholds can be set to fit tolerances appropriate for each group. For example, a network

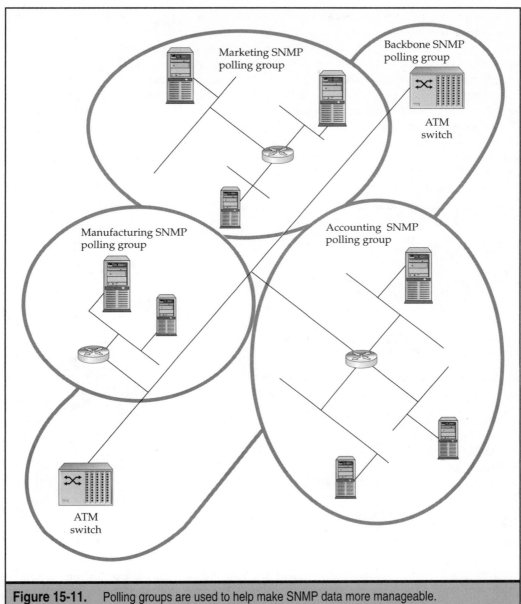

Figure 15-11.   Polling groups are used to help make SNMP data more manageable.

team is likely to set alarm variables to be more sensitive for the backbone switches because trouble with them could bring the entire internetwork down. Polling similar MIBs en masse simplifies SNMP operations and helps assure data that's consistent, trustworthy, and easier to assimilate.

Groups also make it easier to limit the amount of information stored in the NMS database. SNMP could build mountains of data on every device in a network, but doing so would be neither practical nor worthwhile. Storing information on related MIB groups facilitates the movement of raw data through a cycle of aggregation and purging. Figure 15-12 shows a typical scenario, in which MIB variables in a group are polled and stored in the NMS database every five minutes. Each midnight, the data is aggregated into minimums, maximums, and averages for each hour, and stored in another database. The data points are purged from the database weekly, leaving behind only the aggregated data.

The collect-aggregate-purge cycle has several benefits. It keeps disk space open on the NMS server for storing new MIBs and maintains statistical integrity of the data record. At the same time, it also keeps a consistently fresh picture of network operations.

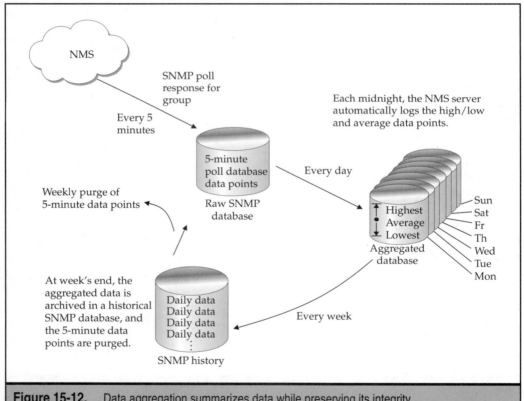

Figure 15-12. Data aggregation summarizes data while preserving its integrity.

SNMP Commands

The *simple* in Simple Network Management Protocol comes from the fact that the protocol has just six root commands. They're used to set SNMP parameters within the device's config file. Here are the root SNMP commands:

▼ **Get**   Used by the NMS to retrieve object instances from an agent.

■ **GetNext**   Used to retrieve subsequent object instances after the first instance.

■ **GetBulk**   New for SNMP version 2, the **GetBulk** operation retrieves all instances in a managed object (replacing the need for iterative **GetNext** operations).

■ **Set**   Used to set values for object instances within an agent (such as a threshold).

■ **Trap**   Used to instruct an agent to unilaterally notify the NMS of an event (without being polled).

▲ **Inform**   New for SNMP version 2, this command instructs one NMS to forward trap information to one or more other NMSs.

NOTE: Most of the time, SNMP commands are used by computer programs rather than by people directly. For example, if an administrator enters the location of a router in an inventory screen in the Essentials console, a process is launched from Essentials that invokes the **set snmp location** command in IOS inside that router.

SNMP's two basic commands are **get** and **set.** The **set** command is used to set managed parameters in managed objects. The following code snippet shows a command that configures the managed device to supply its geographical location if polled for it.

```
MyRouter>>set snmp location ""St. Paul""
```

The **get** command is used to fetch stored variables from agents and bring them back to the NMS. This example requests a specific MIB object be reported by calling out a specific object ID of a private Cisco MIB:

```
MyRouter>>getsnmp 1.3.6.1.4.1.9.9.13
```

SNMP needs to be simple in order to make itself supportable by disparate architectures. Doing so is a practical requirement for SNMP interoperability.

Thresholds

A *threshold* defines an acceptable value or value range for a particular SNMP variable. When a variable exceeds a policy, an *event* is said to have taken place. An event isn't necessarily an either/or situation, such as a switch going down. Events are usually operational irregularities that the network team would want to know about before service is affected.

For example, a network administrator may set a policy for the number of packet errors occurring on router interfaces in order to steer traffic around emerging traffic bottlenecks. Thresholds can be set either as a ceiling or as a range with upper and lower bounds. The two types of thresholds are depicted in Figure 15-13.

The shaded portions of the graph in Figure 15-13 are called *threshold events*. In other words, an event is when something has taken place in violation of the set policy. A *sampling interval* is the period of time during which a statistic is compiled. For example, an MIB object can store the total number of packet errors taking place during each five-minute period. Intervals must be long enough to gather a representative sample, yet short enough to capture events before they can substantially affect network performance.

Events and Traps

When an event occurs, the network administrator can specify how the SNMP agent should respond. The event can either be logged or an alarm message can be sent to the NMS. An SNMP alarm message is called a *trap*, so named because it catches (or traps) the event at the device. A trap contains information about the event. Figure 15-14 shows the course of events leading up to an alarm.

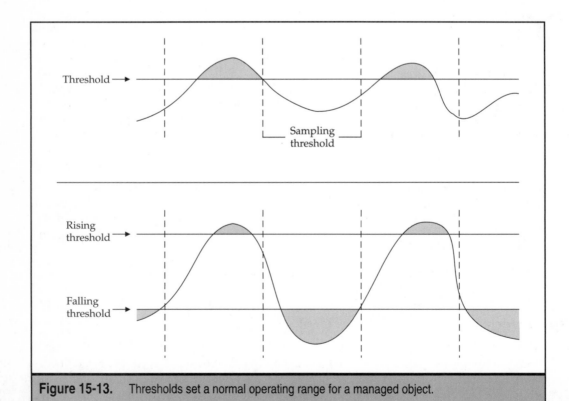

Figure 15-13.   Thresholds set a normal operating range for a managed object.

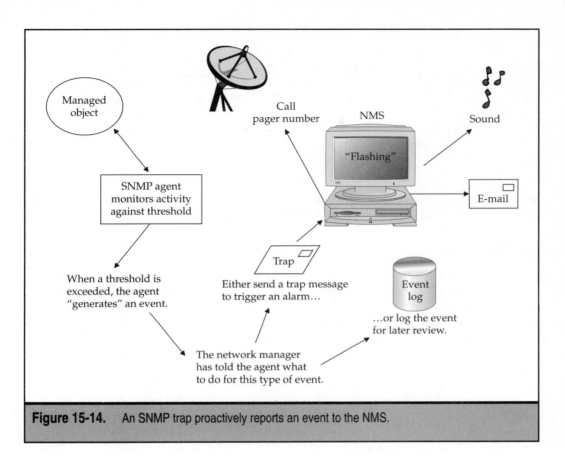

Figure 15-14. An SNMP trap proactively reports an event to the NMS.

Alarms can take many forms. They're often configured to show themselves as a blinking icon on the NMS console, but you could have a noise generated. Networks that don't have administrators present at the NMS all the time have the trap dial a pager or send a priority e-mail to alert the person on response duty at the time.

Traps aren't used just to send alarms. As an internetwork grows in size, SNMP overhead traffic will increase along with it. Network managers can reduce SNMP overhead by stretching the polling frequency, but doing that makes the NMS less responsive to emerging network problems. A better way to limit SNMP overhead is to use traps. Given that they're unsolicited messages instead of SNMP poll responses, traps consume a negligible amount of bandwidth.

The following code snippet is from a Cisco router's config file. It shows the SNMP settings made for the device. RO and RW are the read-only and read-write community strings that make the device a member of a particular management group.

```
MyRouter(config)#snmp-server community yellow RO
MyRouter(config)#snmp-server community blue RW
MyRouter(config)#snmp-server enable traps snmp
MyRouter(config)#snmp-server enable traps isdn call-information
MyRouter(config)#snmp-server enable traps config
MyRouter(config)#snmp-server enable traps bgp
MyRouter(config)#snmp-server enable traps frame-relay
MyRouter(config)#snmp-server enable traps rtr
MyRouter(config)#snmp-server host 10.1.1.13 traps vpi
```

A number of SNMP traps are enabled in this config file. This tells the SNMP agent on the device to send trap messages if anything changes. The last line gives the IP address of the NMS, so the agent knows where to send the trap messages.

RMON: Hardware Probes for Switched Networks

RMON (short for *remote monitoring*) is a separate but related management standard that complements SNMP. RMON is similar to SNMP in several ways: it is an open standard administered by the IETF, it uses SMI data types and the root MIB format, and it collects device data and reports it to an NMS. But RMON differs from normal SNMP in these fundamental ways:

▼ RMON is instrument-based, in that it uses specialized hardware to operate.

■ RMON proactively sends data instead of waiting to be polled, making it bandwidth-efficient and more responsive to network events.

▲ RMON allows much more detailed data to be collected.

RMON instrumentation is more powerful, but more expensive. Consequently, RMON probes tend to be placed on critical links such as network backbones and important servers.

RMON and Switched Networking

The movement toward RMON-based network management is closely linked to the rise of switched networking. While LAN switching is on the rise as the way to improve network performance, it poses special problems for conventional SNMP management methods. In a network formed using hubs, a LAN analyzer has full visibility because the medium is shared by all nodes. But a switched LAN isn't a shared medium, so to maintain the same level of visibility, the analyzer would have to be placed on each switched port. The solution is to incorporate the analyzer (or at least the sensor part of it) directly into the switch's hardware. That's what an RMON probe is. Figure 15-15 shows a switched network managed with and without RMON.

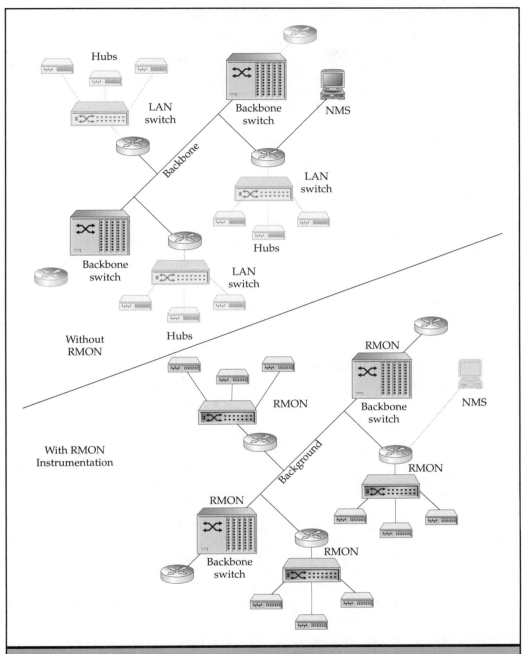

Figure 15-15.   RMON probes provide management visibility across switched networks.

RMON became a standard in 1992 with the release of RMON-1 for Ethernet. The RMON-2 standard, the current version, was completed in early 1997. While RMON-1 operated only at the physical and data-link layers (layers 1 and 2) of the seven-layer OSI reference model, RMON-2 adds the capability to collect data at higher layers, giving it more reporting capability. The ability to monitor upper-layer events has been a boon to the popularity of RMON. For example, RMON-2 can report what's happening with IPX traffic as opposed to IP on a multiprotocol LAN segment.

RMONs replace expensive network analyzer devices that must be physically attached to the approximate area of a network problem. RMON probes come in different forms, depending on the size and type of device to be monitored:

▼   An RMON MIB that uses the monitored device's hardware (called an *embedded agent*)

■   A specialized card module inserted into a slot within the monitored device

■   A purpose-built probe externally attached to one or more monitored devices

▲   A dedicated PC attached to one or more monitored devices

Having specialized hardware remotely located with a monitored device brings advantages. RMON probes can yield a much richer set of measurement data than that of an SNMP agent. The dedicated hardware is used as a real-time sensor that can gather and analyze data for possible upload to the NMS.

The Nine RMON MIB Groups

Another advantage RMON enjoys is its freedom as a separate standard. The root RMON MIB defines nine specialized MIB groups (and a Token Ring group). The nine groups let RMON collect more detailed and granular management information than can be collected using SNMP. Figure 15-16 charts the RMON MIBs.

RMONs, at a minimum, come with the Events and Alarm groups. Most come with four groups needed for basic management: Events, Alarms, Statistics, and History. Because of hardware expense and response time concerns, resource-intensive groups such as the Traffic Matrix group are infrequently deployed.

The Alarm RMON MIB is a more powerful mechanism for event management than SNMP. For example, because there's a separate MIB just to keep track of events, RMON can adjust itself to avoid sending too many alarms. In addition, the Matrix MIB can monitor traffic on a "conversation" basis. In other words, it can be set up to monitor connections between pairs of MAC addresses and report on what's happening with each connection. For example, if a Matrix MIB was set up to watch an expensive link, say, between New York and London, and someone was using it to play a transatlantic game of Doom, the MIB could see that and alert the NMS that valuable bandwidth was being wasted.

The problem with RMON is that it's expensive. It takes extra hardware to store and analyze packets in real time, and that costs money. Consequently, RMON is being put to use to manage links that are mission critical or expensive.

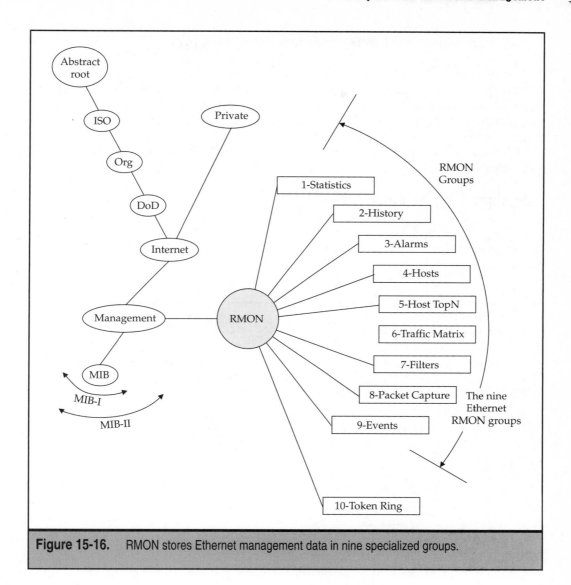

Figure 15-16.   RMON stores Ethernet management data in nine specialized groups.

Trends in Network Management Technology

SNMP compliance issues have left new versions of the standard mired in political infighting. In addition, the fast development of powerful RMON-based tools is pushing the approach to network management in a new direction. The technology underpinnings of network management applications exhibit these trends:

▼ More powerful data collection (more information reported faster)

■ More proactive management

■ Improved built-in hardware support for management

▲ Better security for protecting management tools themselves

The trend toward more intensive management of internetworks is coming up against the same old problem: every management message is overhead that consumes precious bandwidth. This dilemma is what's pushing the industry toward RMON, because that technology captures better information and works locally (instead of via NMS polling).

The other trends have to do with making management systems more efficient and providing SNMP itself with better security.

Advanced SNMP Commands

The evolution of SNMP can be seen in the **GetBulk** and **Inform** commands. **GetBulk** makes it easier for the agent to fetch MIB information from multiple object instances. **Inform** makes it easier to use a hierarchy of NMSs to manage complex internetworks, as shown in Figure 15-17.

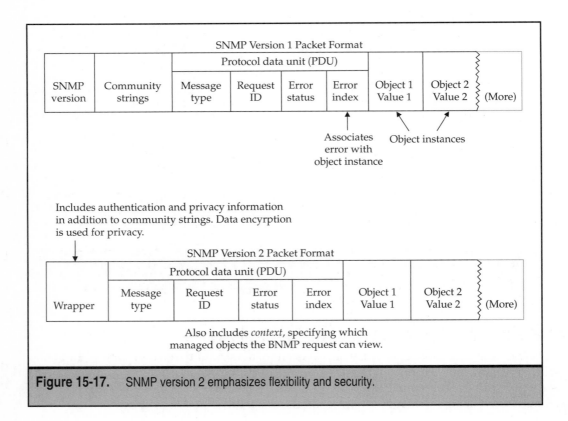

Figure 15-17.   SNMP version 2 emphasizes flexibility and security.

SNMP's support for protocols beyond IP is a substantial change. Doing this will extend the reach of SNMP into non-IP topologies. This is a very important advance for network managers overseeing multiprotocol internetworks. Don't forget that big parts of many sophisticated internetworks run legacy network architectures, such as Novell NetWare IPX, AppleTalk, and DECnet, and will continue to do so for the foreseeable future. Extended SNMP protocol support will help bring these topologies under the control of centralized NMSs.

SNMP Version 1 vs. SNMP Version 2

Keeping track of standards can be confusing because they overlap. For example, right now the majority of all SNMP implementations are of version 1 (SNMPv1). Improvements have been incorporated in SNMPv2, which is just now being implemented by the major vendors. Yet the security pieces of version 2 were found wanting, so a third version of SNMP is under active consideration even before most have implemented SNMPv2. Whatever the version, here are the components of the basic SNMP message format:

- ▼ **Version**   The SNMP version being used.

- ■ **Community String**   The equivalent of a group password used by all devices in the same administrative domain. The SNMP message is ignored without the proper community string.

- ■ **Protocol Data Unit (PDU) Type**   The instructions about what to do. The PDU specifies the operation to be performed (**GetBulk**, **Trap**, and so on) and the object instances on which to perform the operation.

- ■ **Error Status**   This field defines an error and error type.

- ■ **Error Index**   This field associates the error with a particular object instance.

- ▲ **Variable Bindings**   Don't be intimidated by the fancy name; a variable binding is the data collected on the object instance—it's the SNMP packet's payload.

SNMPv2 enhances the message format with these changes:

- ▼ **Wrapper**   This includes destination and source party identifiers for SNMP message authentication and privacy and also identifies context in the form of the managed objects on which the PDU is to perform its operation.

- ■ **Enhanced PDU**   The **GetBulk** and **Inform** operations.

- ▲ **Multiple transport protocols**   Originally, all SNMP packets were transmitted via UDP (User Datagram Protocol). SNMPv2 supports Novell NetWare IPX, AppleTalk DDP, and OSI CLNS.

The enhancements in SNMPv2 reflect the demand for more powerful controls and better security.

Better Security for SNMP Messages

Support for SNMP has been hindered by security concerns. A smart hacker armed with a protocol analyzer would like nothing more than to intercept SNMP messages. Instead of just getting some user's file download, hacking an SNMP system could yield a virtual blueprint of the internetwork topology.

Today, most networks rely on a combination of access lists and SNMPv1 community strings to secure their management systems. If a hacker somehow obtains the community string for an SNMP system, he might navigate around the access list controls and retrieve data on all network devices. Worse, knowing the Read-Write community strings would allow a hacker to alter config file settings on the community's network devices. This would be a devastating security breach, especially if community strings on **set** operations were stolen, because that would hand over control of all devices configured for remote management.

Both customers and manufacturers called for more stringent SNMP security. Keep in mind that a *user* here doesn't necessarily have to be a person; it could just as easily be an automated process (such as a **get** request) as part of an SNMP poll. In SNMPv2 format, the wrapper contains authentication information that identifies approved destination and source parties to the SNMP transaction. The authentication protocol is designed to identify the originating party reliably. Beyond authentication, SNMPv2 makes it possible to specify which managed objects can be included in a message. Figure 15-18 outlines measures taken to secure SNMPv2 messages.

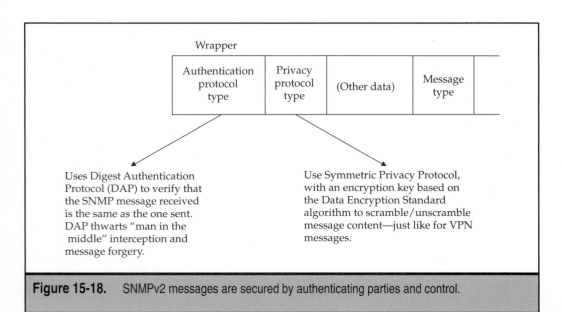

Figure 15-18.   SNMPv2 messages are secured by authenticating parties and control.

SNMPv3

SNMPv1 and SNMPv2 are the big dogs on the management block. However, they are not perfect. As noted earlier, neither version offers tight enough security features. To be more precise, neither version is able to authenticate the source of a management message, nor provide encryption. Without authentication, it is possible for outsiders to use SNMP functions. Without encryption, it is possible for your network's management commands to be monitored.

Because of this shortcoming, many SNMPv1 and v2 implementations allow just read-only capability. This reduces their usability to serve only as a network monitor. SNMPv3 looks to correct this deficiency.

The SNMPv3 functionality has been described in its IETF drafts as "SNMPv2 plus administration and security." SNMPv3 adds three services:

▼ **Authentication**   This ensures that SNMP commands are being issued by the appropriate person or application.

■ **Privacy**   Encryption enables network administrators to ensure that their SNMP commands are not being eavesdropped upon.

▲ **Access control**   Different levels of access to the agent's MIB can be established for different managers. Agents can restrict access to its MIBs by either allowing read-only access, or by limiting the actions that can be taken upon the MIB.

These services are delivered through a concept called a *principal.* This is the entity on whose behalf services are provided or processing takes place. A principal can be an individual acting in a certain role; a group of individuals, each acting in a certain role; an application or group of applications; or any combination of these.

A principal operates from a management station and issues SNMP commands to the agents. The identity of the principal and the target agent, together, determine which security features will be used. Because a principal is used, security policies can be tailored to the specific principal, agent, and information exchange, allowing flexibility to the network administrator.

Cisco ships full SNMPv3 support starting in IOS version 12.0(3)T. It is implemented for all IOS platforms that have 12.0(3)T-based images.

Cisco's SNMP and RMON Implementations

Cisco claims unparalleled SNMP and RMON capability. Virtually all the company's devices ship with SNMP agents and most switches with RMON. As the internetworking industry's powerhouse, Cisco sits on the major standards-setting committees and is among the first to release products supporting new standards.

Cisco and SNMP

Cisco includes SNMP support in the form of agent software on every router and communications server it makes. According to the company, its SNMP agents can communicate successfully with OpenView and NetView. Cisco supports over 400 MIB objects. Cisco's private MIB objects feature support for all the major LAN protocols, including IP, Novell NetWare IPX, Banyan VINES, AppleTalk, and DECnet.

Cisco uses its private MIB to enhance system monitoring and management of Cisco devices. For example, Cisco routers can be queried both by interface and by protocol. You can query for the number of runt packets on a network interface or query for the number of IPX packets sent or received from that interface. This kind of information is invaluable to baselining the traffic profile of a network. Average CPU usage statistics are sampled by five-second, one-minute, and five-minute intervals to ascertain whether a router is being properly utilized. Physical variables are also measured. Air temperature entering and leaving a device or voltage fluctuations can be monitored to assure continued device operation. Cisco's private MIB includes chassis objects to report the number of installed modules, module types, serial numbers, and so on. Figure 15-19 depicts some of Cisco's advanced SNMP features.

To help secure SNMP messages, IOS provides the ability to prohibit SNMP messages from traversing certain interfaces. SNMP is further secured by the option to designate certain community strings as read-only or read/write, thus restricting the ability to configure certain devices remotely. Also, a device can be assigned more than one community string, enabling key routers or switches to fall under multiple SNMP regimes (sometimes used in large internetworks).

Cisco has committed to making their routers "bilingual" in their simultaneous support of both SNMPv1 and SNMPv2. The coexistence strategy uses two techniques—a proxy agent that translates messages between versions, and the support of both versions in a single NMS platform.

Cisco and RMON

Cisco integrates RMON into all its platforms. The greatest RMON capabilities are packaged into the high-end Catalyst 6500, but RMON capability is built into the LightStream ATM switch line cards also.

RMONs for Catalyst Switches   The Catalyst simultaneously acts as a LAN switch and a network probe because of its multiprocessor design. One CPU does the switching, and the other handles management data collection and forwarding duties. The Catalyst can be configured to collect traffic data in either of two modes:

▼ **Standard RMON mode**   The RMON agent collects data for up to all nine RMON groups across all attached switch ports.

▲ **Roving RMON mode**   A focused mode that collects more detailed data for just one or two RMON groups across all eight ports, and then focuses on a single LAN when an event takes place there.

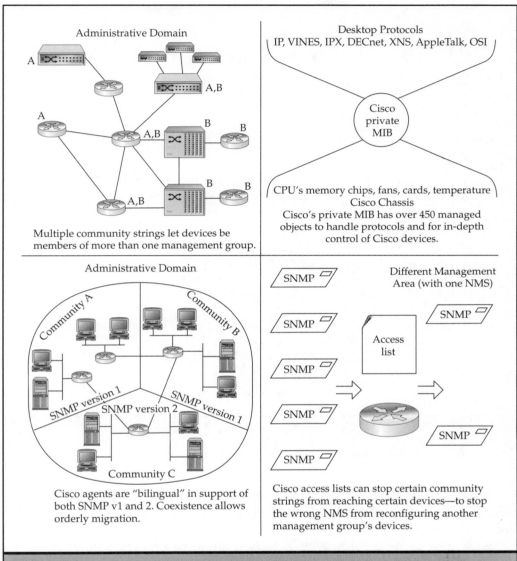

Figure 15-19. Cisco's SNMP implementation supports several advanced functions.

In either mode, the RMON follows a structured course of action to enforce thresholds, generate events, and send alarms. Figure 15-20 depicts the structure.

The concurrent RMON configuration is the normal mode. Its ability to see across all connected LANs is particularly valuable for troubleshooting, especially client-server applications in which the communicating hosts are on different LANs.

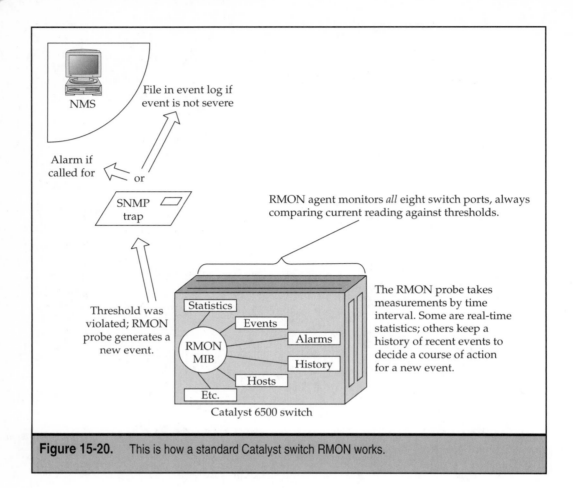

Figure 15-20.   This is how a standard Catalyst switch RMON works.

Catalyst's roving RMON is as advanced as it gets. Normally, it works at collecting detailed historical information on a per-port and even per-host level. But when a trap is sent, the stripped-down, two-group RMON spawns a fully configured nine-group RMON probe that automatically begins collecting troubleshooting data just from the offending connected LAN. Figure 15-21 depicts how a roving RMON changes to handle an event.

By the time the administrator responds to the alert, the roving RMON has already reconfigured itself and started intensive monitoring of the LAN segment in which the problem emerged.

Cisco offers a complete line of RMON probes for various situations. Fast EtherChannel configurations are instrumented using so-called Mini-RMONs, which are built-in agents that monitor channel utilization and launch SNMP traps when necessary. Mini-RMON agents are also packaged into Catalyst Token Ring ports.

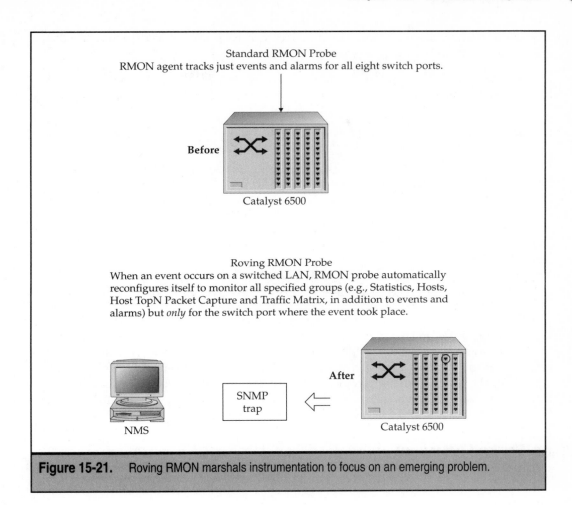

Standard RMON Probe
RMON agent tracks just events and alarms for all eight switch ports.

Before

Catalyst 6500

Roving RMON Probe
When an event occurs on a switched LAN, RMON probe automatically reconfigures itself to monitor all specified groups (e.g., Statistics, Hosts, Host TopN Packet Capture and Traffic Matrix, in addition to events and alarms) but *only* for the switch port where the event took place.

After

SNMP
trap

NMS

Catalyst 6500

Figure 15-21.   Roving RMON marshals instrumentation to focus on an emerging problem.

Cisco offers a family of stand-alone RMONs called SwitchProbes. These are physical devices with hardware tuned to serve as instrumentation. Usually customers attach them to critical links or diagnostic ports. The SwitchProbe product line comes in either a small or a large chassis, ranging from 1 to 12 ports and 4MB to 32MB. There are SwitchProbe models for Fast Ethernet, FDDI, WAN or HSSI (High-Speed Serial Interconnect), Ethernet, and Token Ring.

CISCOWORKS

CiscoWorks is Cisco's NMS suite. It contains over a dozen network management applications based on SNMP and RMON infrastructure. CiscoWorks to some degree is more packaging than a cohesive product because it comes in several pieces (like those described next), each with its own user interface:

▼ **Resource Manager Essentials** A Web browser-based suite of seven applications designed for managing switched networks, operated through a topology map

■ **CWSI Campus** A Windows-based suite of four applications operated through a network topology map

▲ **CiscoView** A Windows-based application in which you interact with a lifelike color image of the actual device

The applications share common device inventory database and other background processes. Baseliner was acquired by Cisco and is just now being integrated into the larger product suite. CiscoWorks packs a lot of powerful tools that are invaluable once you learn how to use them.

Although it boasts full SNMP and RMON compliance, CiscoWorks is used only for Cisco products. And don't let the name fool you, CiscoWorks runs on UNIX platforms in addition to Microsoft Windows.

Given Cisco's dominance of the world router market, CiscoWorks should be regarded as the most important manufacturer-specific tool in the industry. This isn't surprising, given that routers are the most critical element in internetworks. Network teams use a variety of tools to manage big internetworks, and Cisco's tools are front and center more often than not. The commonest management scenario these days is to use HP OpenView as the base enterprise system management (ESM) platform, employ CiscoWorks to manage Cisco routers and switches, and use several smaller tools for narrower duties.

CiscoWorks Overview

CiscoWorks is a product family, not a point product. In other words, it's a common software platform that serves as a framework from which optional applications can be operated. Some call the applications that plug into suites *snap-ins*. The goal of product suites is to integrate snap-in applications by letting them share data. The suite's infrastructure shares a database and various background processes such as SNMP polling, configuration checking, and so on. CiscoWorks can import data from HP OpenView, IBM NetView, Sun Microsystem's SunNet, and other ESM suites.

Browser	Windows	
Essentials	CiscoView	CWSI Campus
Device inventory database		

CiscoWorks has been around for a few years. The original incarnation—called CiscoWorks for Windows—featured only two snap-in applications:

▼ **CiscoView**   An interactive graphical tool in which a screen image of the actual device is used to monitor and configure the device.

▲ **Configuration Builder**   A GUI-based tool that prompts the user through the process of configuring network devices.

Configuration Builder is an older, cruder version of Cisco ConfigMaker, covered in Chapter 5. The only plus to Configuration Builder is that it handles Token Ring devices. We anticipate that Configuration Builder will be phased out as ConfigMaker matures.

A product called CiscoWorks2000, released in 1999 (its latest incarnation is known simply as CiscoWorks), is more than a mere replacement for CiscoWorks for Windows—it's a full-fledged management environment. It is so big that it would take a veteran network administrator weeks to learn all its applications. With CiscoWorks, Cisco's management tools are finally catching up with its burgeoning product line. CiscoView is a stand-alone application that will eventually be integrated into the following management suites:

▼ **Resource Manager Essentials**   Called Essentials for short, these are the foundation applications for monitoring, controlling, and managing Cisco devices. Essentials has tools for remote device installation, SNMP monitoring, configuration management, software deployment, path analysis, device inventory, and so on.

▲ **CiscoWorks for Switched Internetworks (CWSI)**   Pronounced "swizee" and usually called CWSI Campus, this is a suite of integrated applications for management of Cisco switched networks. CWSI handles VLAN configuration, real-time device management, RMON-based traffic analysis, and ATM connection and performance management.

CiscoWorks installs and operates on a normal computer platform—not a specialized network device. The platform must have a minimum of 1GB memory and at least 40GB of disk storage. In addition to the Microsoft Windows 2000 Server platform, CiscoWorks can be installed on the IBM AIX, HP PA-RISC, and Sun Solaris operating systems. The software ships with a run-time version of the Sybase database management system.

CiscoWorks Resource Manager Essentials

Resource Manager Essentials (we'll call it Essentials hereafter) provides the CiscoWorks environment and several tools for everyday network management chores. The centerpiece is the device inventory database that keeps a record on individual Cisco devices.

The inventory database is kept up-to-date via SNMP polling and serves as the basis for network management. Essentials is composed of several applications:

▼ **Inventory Manager**   Maintains an up-to-date database of Cisco devices. Can import device records from HP OpenView, IBM NetView, CWSI, or a flat file. From there, polls for additional SNMP data such as chassis type, installed memory, interfaces, IOS version, and so on.

■ **Configuration Manager**   Archives router and switch configurations. Configuration Manager is *active* in that it senses device changes and keeps a running file of who did what. Configuration Manager passes change information to the Change Audit Service application and others. Configuration Manager is frequently used to compare config files in different devices automatically.

■ **Change Audit Service**   Provides a central view of all configuration changes. It records who changed what, how, and when, and whether the change was made from the device console, Telnet, or CiscoWorks.

■ **Software Manager**   Simplifies version management and deployment of IOS software images. Provides a wizard-assisted planning tool that validates proposed changes. Software Manager can reduce time to do software upgrades from hours to minutes.

■ **Syslog Analyzer**   Filters syslog messages logged by routers, switches, access servers, and Cisco IOS firewalls. Syslog Analyzer displays probable causes and recommends corrective actions.

▲ **Cisco Management Connection**   This application delivers a toolkit and program to integrate new network management applications, using Internet-based technologies. The toolkit allows the connection of Web-based management applications to Essentials, allowing application developers to make their Web-based applications linkable through a system certified through Cisco.

These applications share the Essentials management console (user interface) and work from the same device inventory.

NOTE: There are dozens of screens and hundreds of options in CiscoWorks—far too many to cover here. We'll cover key items and concepts in this chapter.

The User Interface for Resource Manager Essentials

Essentials provides one user environment through which several management applications can be operated. The management console is Web-based, which is to say that it's used through a browser. Shown in Figure 15-22, the key to the console is the login window in the left pane, where you select which applications to run. At any given moment, the login window only displays the navigation tree for one of three option groups: Tasks, Tools, and Admin.

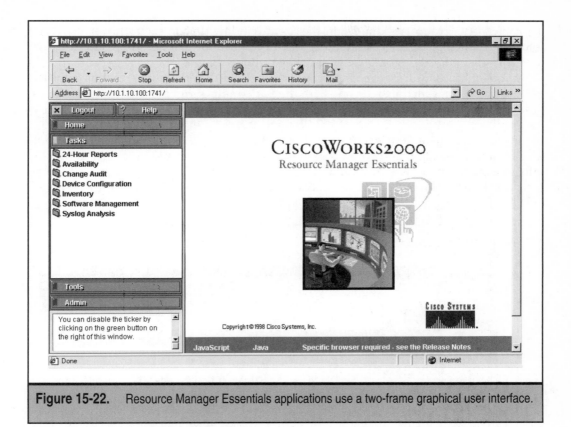

Figure 15-22.   Resource Manager Essentials applications use a two-frame graphical user interface.

In Figure 15-22, the login window is pointed to the Tasks group. The console uses a Microsoft Windows Explorer-style navigation tree interface with drawers and folders. Essentials' three menus are organized as follows:

▼ **Tasks**   Applications used to perform various management tasks: Daily Reports, Availability Manager, Change Audit, Device Configuration, Inventory, Software Management, and Syslog Analysis.

■ **Tools**   Support mechanisms to research problems. Tools that connect to www.cisco.com are Case Management, CCO Tools, Contract Connection, and Management Connection Certification. Local tools are Connectivity Tools and Device Navigator.

▲ **Admin**   Basic tools for the applications in the Tasks menu. This is where you select application options. For example, Syslog Analysis is in both the Tasks and Admin drawers. Tasks is where you see data logged about network events; Admin is where you go to tell Essentials what you want Syslog to collect.

Each menu group is a drawer in the login window. Inside each drawer there is a folder for each application. Click a folder and the application's options pop out (as shown in Figure 15-23) for the Availability reporting option.

If you look closely at Figure 15-23, you'll notice three different types of icons to the left of the application functions: the one with the folded upper-right corner indicates a program, the icon with horizontal lines is for reports, and the icon with three vertical bars is for graphs.

Double-click an option to start it. As a Web application, Essentials responds by downloading the information into your browser or starting a background process to gather the information. Essentials is a slow-running application because it is implemented as Java applets that must download from the NMS server to your PC. It's made even slower by the

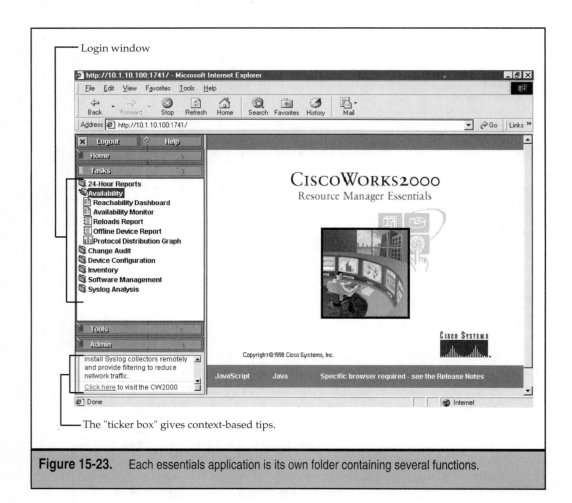

Figure 15-23.   Each essentials application is its own folder containing several functions.

fact that it needs to gather the necessary data. When using Essentials, you'll find yourself looking at the hourglass cursor a lot, so be patient. Response time depends on the size of the network you're managing, your LAN connection speed, and the configuration of your PC.

Adding Devices to Essentials

Even with everything installed properly, Essentials is of no use until network devices are loaded into its database. This is usually done by importing them from other applications, such as HP OpenView, Castle Rock Computing's SNMPc, a CiscoView database, or even an earlier version of CiscoWorks. Importing is the preferred method because inputting dozens or hundreds of network devices by hand is laborious and error prone. For illustration purposes, Figure 15-24 shows the Essentials screen for entering a device record by hand. The User Fields can be used for whatever items the network team wishes to store on a device—in this example, the contact person, the asset number, and the serial number.

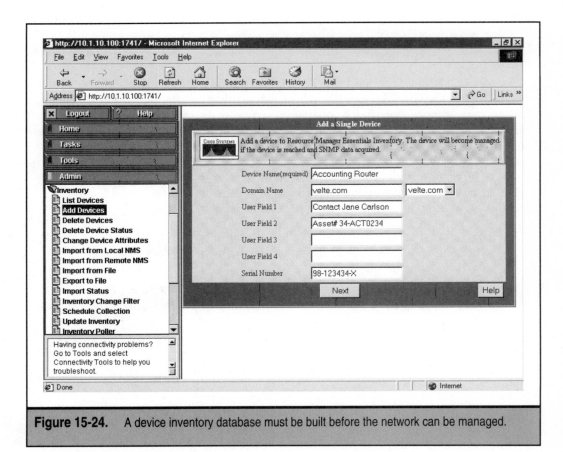

Figure 15-24.   A device inventory database must be built before the network can be managed.

Figure 15-24's screen is followed by others for inputting SNMP community strings and TACACS+ passwords (TACACS+ is a security application we covered in Chapter 9). Notice that Essentials uses the Start | Next | Finish paradigm you know from the Install Programs Wizard in the Microsoft Windows Control Panel. Essentials uses a three-step routine to do things: select the application option, choose the devices to report on, and then display the reported information. Sometimes the output is displayed in the right pane; for other reports, a separate browser instance is started.

CiscoView: The Tool for Managing Individual Devices

Cisco's most basic management tool is CiscoView. It is the tool used to work with individual Cisco devices. It's a sophisticated RMON-based monitoring application that communicates to the NMS through the SNMP communications channel. A real-time image of the device is presented, displaying two kinds of information:

▼ **Configuration**   The CiscoView interface can be used to configure the device.

▲ **Performance**   Real-time monitoring information is displayed to help with device management.

CiscoView, also incorporated into CWSI Campus, is the place to go to check on the status of a Cisco device. For example, if you suspect that a particular router is causing a network performance bottleneck, open a CiscoView image of that device and click around with your mouse to check its operating status. The other major role of CiscoView is to set RMON thresholds.

When CiscoView is started, a small window called the CiscoView Desktop appears. This is the jumping-off point from which you can move among managed devices.

The CiscoView desktop opens with an image of the device chassis, along with several selections allowing you to invoke various tools. Those tools include

▼ **Tools bar**   Located at the upper-right corner of the screen, this allows you to log out of a CiscoView session, get online help, or see which version of CiscoView you are running.

■ **Options bar**   Located about a third of the way down the screen, this allows you to change your CiscoView preferences, start a Telnet session to the device, or send a message to the Cisco Technical Assistance Center.

■ **Activity bar**   Located beneath the options bar, the activity bar indicates the progress and end result of device polling, refreshes, and other information. In the event an error occurs, it will be displayed in the activity bar.

■ **Chassis view**   Located in the center of the window, this is a graphical representation of your device. This shows either the device's front or back panel. Components follow a color-coded scheme to indicate their status. We'll explain the color coding later in this section.

▲ **Object selector handle**   Located on the leftmost side of the window, this item opens and closes the Object Selector, which is used to choose which device you wish to manage.

Viewing a Device

To select a device, simply click the Object Selector handle. The Object Selector lists all the devices that Essentials can manage. Before a device can be viewed with CiscoView, it must be imported into the Essentials database.

Selecting the device you wish to view uses a simple Windows drop-down list. When you click the Object Selector handle, a list of all viewable devices will be displayed. Simply select your device from the list and your choice will be displayed in the CiscoView desktop.

Once a device is opened, CiscoView presents a color image of it. The image isn't just a pretty picture, it's interactive. In other words, the administrator can point at and click the image and enter commands into the individual device's config file.

NOTE: If you have a lot of devices from which to choose, you can enter a partial IP address, then click **Go.** This filters your device list so only those matching the partial IP address will be displayed.

It's hard not to like CiscoView, not only because it's neat to look at, but also because the interface is so intuitive. The interface is a natural way to work with devices because it's like being physically present with them—even though you might be hundreds of miles away. Actually, in some ways CiscoView is better than the real thing because of the intelligence added to the display. For example, the status of each port in the device is reported by presenting the ports in one of six coded colors:

▼ **Cyan**   The port cannot pass packets, but is in a "waiting" state for an external event to bring the port back online.

■ **Orange**   The port is administratively down.

■ **Green**   The link is up.

■ **Purple**   The link is being tested.

■ **Yellow**   There is a problem—an SNMP policy is violated and an alarm was sent.

▲ **Red**   There is no status reported.

CiscoView supports most Cisco routers, switches, and access servers. As you might suspect, all actions taken from the CiscoView image are executed by operating equivalent commands in the device's IOS command line. In other words, selecting something on a CiscoView menu executes an IOS command in the background.

Navigating a Device via CiscoView   The image display is the equivalent of using the **show** command in the IOS command-line interface, but it's a lot more powerful because it shows many parameters instead of just one at a time. This makes for better monitoring and troubleshooting because at a glance you can check the status of most components in the device.

Double-click a component to see details about it. A dialog box will appear displaying information about the component's status and configuration. All this information is gathered from the router via SNMP polling.

The dialog box reports the interface's operating status, speed, MAC address, and so on. Clicking the Interface button will bring up a different dialog box that details what's happening on the LAN connected to the interface. In either of these dialog modes, CiscoView lets you manually turn things on and off—for example, you can bring an interface administratively down, restart the network, and so on.

Threshold Manager

The place in CiscoWorks to make config file settings is the Threshold Manager application. Network administrators use events to monitor what's going on inside the device. Setting thresholds tells the SNMP agent software what you consider noteworthy. The agent keeps statistics on the managed object for each time interval, and it reports when polled. However, once the statistic crosses the threshold, an event is said to have taken place, and the agent can take proactive measures, such as triggering an alarm. Essentials uses the RMON alarm and event groups to operate.

Using Threshold Manager

Once you've started CiscoWorks, click the Threshold Manager link and the Threshold Manager Device Details window appears.

This window contains a number of links across the top of the screen. Clicking Event Logs displays a list of all policies in effect for the device. You can create new policies and modify existing ones from the Device Thresholds tab. Earlier in this chapter, Figure 15-13 depicted how rising and falling thresholds define an acceptable operating range to monitor events. Event monitoring is the basis for deciding what gets monitored and reported via SNMP. A threshold setting is a value for the "sampled statistic" of a managed object's variable, such as input interface utilization, runt packets, fragmented packets, and so on.

When the current sampled value of the statistic is greater than or equal to the threshold value, a single event is generated. A *falling threshold* is a technique to make sure only one event is generated. After a rising threshold is crossed, a new event for that object cannot be generated until its sampled value falls below the falling threshold. In other words, things must return to normal for the managed object before a new abnormal report—event—can take place. Otherwise, an unlimited number of events would be generated during the time the sampled statistic is above the threshold value. An event causes a trap message to be sent. You have an option to either log a type of event to a file or trigger an alarm on the NMS console.

How Cisco Implements SNMP

Cisco implements SNMP and RMON in a three-tier arrangement. At the top is the template, in the middle are threshold template files, and at the bottom are the actual templates.

A *template* is a group of threshold policy files covering the community of managed devices. Threshold Manager supports two types of standard templates:

▼ **System**   Threshold policy files to track system-level information, such as CPU capacity events, available memory, buffer failures caused by lack of memory, and so on.

▲ **Interface**   Threshold policy files specific to an interface, such as the number of connections, internal resets, and so on.

A template file is a collection of one or more policies that define threshold values for specific MIB variables. Cisco ships 11 standard policy files that cover the most commonly monitored variables. They come with default threshold values, but can be customized if desired. Table 15-2 lists the standard template files and shows the kinds of issues network administrators deal with on a daily basis. (Going back to Chapters 4 and 5, you'll recognize the *if* mnemonic as standing for interface.)

Resource Manager Essentials Applications

Seven applications are packaged with Essentials:

▼ **Availability**   A device's recent track record for availability and response time

■ **Change Audit**   What was changed in a config file, who made the change, when it was made, and from which management application

■ **Device Configuration**   Tools to centrally search and manage config files

■ **Inventory**   Central repository of all data stored on every device in the network, updated automatically

■ **Software Management**   Tools for managing and upgrading IOS images and other Cisco software products

■ **Syslog Analysis**   Tools used to keep a running history of network events, and to sort and analyze them in order to diagnose problems

▲ **Cisco Management Connection**   Used to integrate new third-party network management applications, using Internet-based technologies

Threshold Policy File	Description	Default Threshold
avgBusy5	Average CPU utilization during last five minutes	90 percent
avgBusy1	Average CPU utilization during last minute	70 percent
FreeMem	Free DRAM memory	Falling 500K
IfInOctets	Utilization of input bandwidth on an interface	50 packets
ifOutOctets	Utilization of output bandwidth on an interface	50 packets
locIfCarTrans	Number of carrier transitions on an interface	10/minute
locIfReliab	Reliability of an interface expressed as a score within a defined worst-to-best range of values	Falling 240
locIfResets	Number of resets on an interface	10/minute
locIfRestarts	Number of restarts on an interface	10/minute
bufferFail	Buffer allocation failures	5/half-minute
bufferNoMem	Buffer creation failures	5/half-minute

Table 15-2.   Default Event Threshold Template Files Shipped with Cisco Devices

The inventory database is the key to everything. This is where a central record is kept on everything having to do with an individual device: its serial number, what cards it has installed, who's responsible for it, where it is, its IOS version, and so on. Hundreds of data items are stored on every piece of equipment. All CiscoWorks applications revolve around the inventory database.

NOTE: Essentials has a feature called Report Filters. A filter is a reusable format that tells the application what fields to report, and in what order. Filters are used to customize the data that is collected for reports. Instead of specifying the information you want every time you generate a report, a filter can be reused.

Availability Manager

Availability Manager keeps statistics on device reachability and response time. Availability Manager can monitor current status or give an availability history for one or more selected devices. The Reachability Dashboard shows current device availability status down to the interface level. The Protocol Distribution Graph depicts the device as a bar chart or pie chart showing level-3 protocol packet types going through a device—a useful feature because most large internetworks are multiprotocol. The Availability Monitor, shown in Figure 15-25, gives reachability and response time track records for a device.

This report is handy for troubleshooting. When there is a problem in part of an internetwork, the administrator looks at devices in that area for likely suspects. Knowing a device's recent availability track record is usually a pretty good clue.

Configuration Manager

Managing a good-sized internetwork means keeping track of hundreds of config files, and keeping track of parameter settings in that many devices can be a nightmare. Configuration Manager keeps an active archive of config files in all managed devices. *Active* means the database can be updated automatically. Administrators use this application as a search tool and reporting tool. The most popular report is comparing configurations. For example, if a router is having problems, it makes sense to compare its running config file against one that you know is good, to highlight parameter settings that might be causing the trouble.

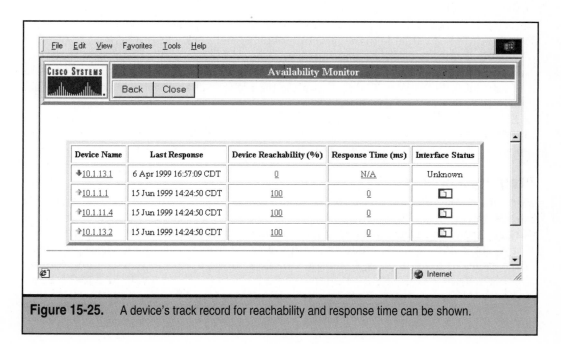

Figure 15-25. A device's track record for reachability and response time can be shown.

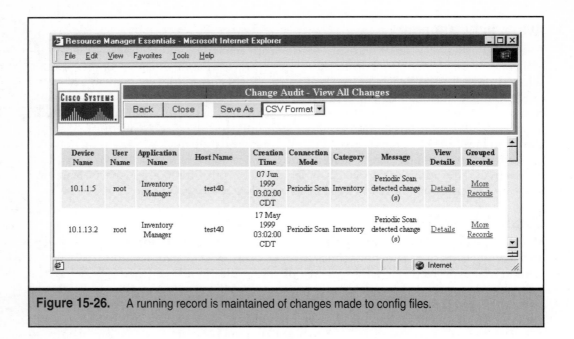

Figure 15-26.   A running record is maintained of changes made to config files.

Change Audit

Essentials automatically maintains a running record of who changed what in a config file. Change Audit is a valuable management tool in big network teams where it can be hard to keep track of things. When something comes up with a config file, before you change it, you want to make sure you're not breaking something that was put in there for a reason of which you're not aware. Change Audit is the place to check before making a change. Figure 15-26 shows the audit history screen.

Even in smaller network teams, it's useful to have a record of something that was done in the past. A busy administrator works on so many devices that it's not possible to remember the reason every setting was made.

Inventory Manager

Inventory Manager is the foundation of CiscoWorks. It acts as the central repository for information about devices. Closely related to the Software Manager and Configuration Manager applications, Inventory Manager produces reports and graphs that give the big picture about the devices making up a topology. For example, the Chassis Summary Graph tallies utilization by type of router—a good thing to look at when setting routing protocol metrics to steer traffic through various parts of the topology. Figure 15-27 shows the kinds of basic inventory facts maintained on Inventory Manager.

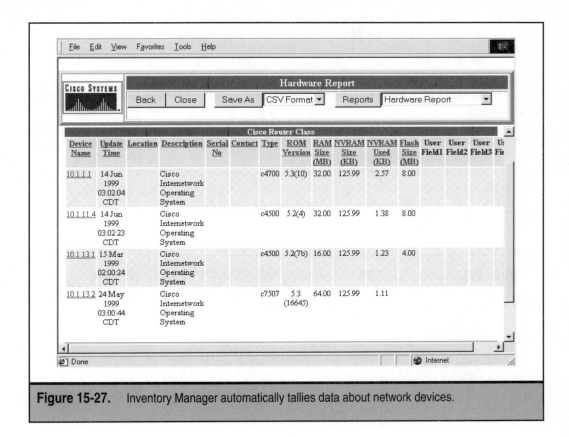

| File | Edit | View | F_avorites | Tools | Help | | |

Hardware Report

| Back | Close | | Save As | CSV Format ▾ | | Reports | Hardware Report ▾ |

Cisco Router Class

Device Name	Update Time	Location	Description	Serial No	Contact	Type	ROM Version	RAM Size (MB)	NVRAM Size (KB)	NVRAM Used (KB)	Flash Size (MB)	User Field1	User Field2	User Field3	U: Fic
10.1.1.1	14 Jun 1999 03:02:04 CDT		Cisco Internetwork Operating System			c4700	5.3(10)	32.00	125.99	2.57	8.00				
10.1.11.4	14 Jun 1999 03:02:23 CDT		Cisco Internetwork Operating System			c4500	5.2(4)	32.00	125.99	1.38	8.00				
10.1.13.1	15 Mar 1999 02:00:24 CDT		Cisco Internetwork Operating System			c4500	5.2(7b)	16.00	125.99	1.23	4.00				
10.1.13.2	24 May 1999 03:00:44 CDT		Cisco Internetwork Operating System			c7507	5.3 (16645)	64.00	125.99	1.11					

Done   Internet

Figure 15-27. Inventory Manager automatically tallies data about network devices.

Inventory Manager can generate reports and graphs by device type, IOS version, domain name, and so on. Cisco leverages its private MIB to report device configurations right down to the chassis slot level.

Inventory data is collected by periodically scanning the network for new devices and changes in existing devices. The scans are usually scheduled to avoid disrupting traffic during business hours. Scanning a big internetwork can take hours and consumes a lot of bandwidth.

Software Manager

Software Manager handles IOS upgrades and troubleshooting. It's not unusual for several version levels of IOS to be in use in an internetwork at the same time. Things are made more complicated by the fact that individual devices are configured with different IOS feature sets. Software Manager performs two main functions:

▼ Analyzing IOS images for conflicts both within and between devices.

▲ Maintaining a library of IOS software images for downloading and installing onto devices.

Figure 15-28 shows the screen for setting up distribution jobs. Software Manager can deploy an image on more than one device in a single job.

Because of interdependencies, administrators work to keep IOS versions synchronized throughout the network. Because IOS has so many features and options, keeping everything straight can be an enormous job. Software Manager performs dependency checks to make sure the software will work with the hardware on which it's being installed.

Cisco offers an online upgrade analysis from its Web site. (Again, CCO stands for Cisco Connection Online, the name of the cisco.com site.) Registered customers of CCO can have a device's IOS image analyzed for necessary patches or upgrades. Like any computer company, Cisco releases minor fixes to its operating system on an almost daily basis, and CCO helps customers keep up with changes. For example, if a major bug is found in a certain type of IOS image, CCO Tools can be used to tell where to install the code patch that Cisco released as a fix.

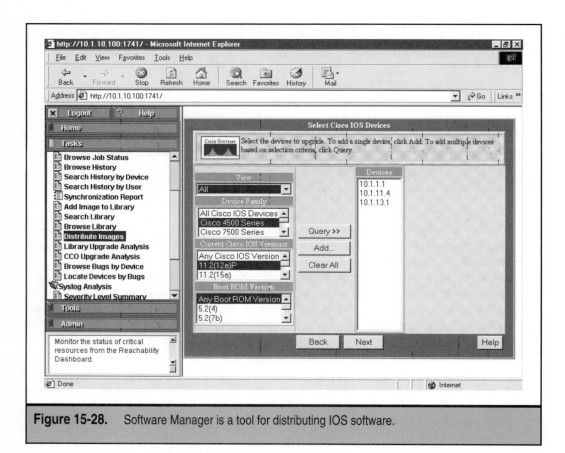

Figure 15-28. Software Manager is a tool for distributing IOS software.

Syslog Analyzer

Almost every Cisco device logs unusual events to a system file. Syslog Analyzer automatically collects error messages from devices and uploads them to the Essentials database on the NMS. Syslog Analyzer lets you selectively filter events—such as a link-down or a device reboot—by type and severity level. There are six severity levels, ranging from informational to emergency.

Syslog Analyzer is configurable. For example, you can define how long a device stores error messages, how frequently a remote collector uploads syslog files to the NMS, and so on.

Cisco Management Connection

When third-party developers create new network management applications and they want to integrate these with Essentials, Cisco Management Connection provides a toolkit with which to create the application. This toolkit allows the connection of Web-based management applications to Essentials, permitting developers to make their applications linkable through a system certified by Cisco. So far, more than 30 vendors—including Computer Associates, Hewlett-Packard, and Sun Microsystems—have created certified Cisco Management Connection applications for their systems.

CiscoWorks for Switched Internetworks

CiscoWorks for Switched Internetworks (CWSI) is the part of CiscoWorks used to manage switched networks. It's a sister management suite to Essentials. In fact, before you can install CWSI, Essentials must already be installed on the same computer.

Why a separate management suite just for switched networks? Because—as discussed in Chapter 6—a switched network's behavior is fundamentally different from network behavior in normal LANs, which run on truly shared LAN media. This is not so on a switched network where, at any given instant, the medium is shared only between a pair of MAC addresses. If you monitor a routed network, the traffic making up all the logical connections (sessions) are visible to the SNMP agent. On a switched network, sessions are visible only for a series of tiny instants, making them harder to detect. These RMONs provide the sensor instrumentation necessary to monitor switched bandwidth.

CWSI Campus is actually a product from a company called NetScout Systems, and Cisco resells it. Cisco packages it to work closely with Cisco devices by implementing private Cisco MIB and RMON objects into the data discovery process. When CWSI Campus discovers a device configuration or status, it's able to look deeper into the device and measure such things as whether the cooling fan is running, what the air temperature is within the device, and so on. Like Essentials, CWSI Campus uses proprietary protocols to track things: Cisco Discovery Protocol to find hardware, Virtual Trunk Protocol to identify VLANs, and others.

CWSI Campus is an end-to-end solution for switched internetworks that lets network teams monitor switch traffic and view VLANs as they exist atop physical topologies. Also, because it monitors at layer 2—where it sees frames instead of packets—CWSI Campus can monitor ATM (Asynchronous Transfer Mode) transmission media—the network specification of choice for most high-speed backbones.

CWSI Management Applications

CWSI Campus comes in the form of three Director applications:

▼ **VLAN Director**   An interactive tool to display, modify, and manage VLANs.

■ **Traffic Director**   An application that provides usage monitoring for troubleshooting performance problems.

▲ **ATM Director**   Used to work with ATM switches, this application discovers switches, physical links, and virtual circuits, and both monitors performance and analyzes traffic within RMON-enabled Cisco ATM switches.

CWSI Campus comes packaged with CiscoView for inspecting individual devices, but the CWSI Campus Map shows the big picture and serves as the interface through which the Director applications are operated.

NOTE: As a reminder, LANE (LAN Emulation) is a technology that allows an ATM network to function as a LAN backbone. Remember, ATM is a networking specification equivalent to Ethernet or Token Ring, but fundamentally different in its use of fixed-size packets (called *cells*), instead of dynamically sized packets. For ATM to work with another technology, such as Ethernet, it must perform address mapping (MAC-to-ATM) and adapt to the other protocol's most essential conventions (such as Ethernet's rules for managing virtual or permanent circuits).

The CWSI Campus Map   The CWSI Campus Map diagrams switched networks in an interactive color graphical display. Figure 15-29 shows the map as it appears after CWSI Campus has been started and it has completed the network device discovery process. A key function of CWSI Campus is to discover and document all Cisco devices in the network topology. Remember, discovery goes beyond the whole device level to detail individual cards, interfaces, RMONs, and even software. These things constantly change, so network teams rely on tools like CWSI Campus and Essentials to keep things up-to-date.

The CWSI Campus Map can pan, zoom, refresh its contents, drill down into individual devices, and use other navigation techniques. The key to the CWSI interface, however, is filtering. You can see the device and link filters in the Map Highlighting pane to the right of the map. Click the check box next to a type, and that kind of device or link is incorporated into the map. This is good for finding resources. For example, if you're trying to decide where to locate a server that will consume a lot of bandwidth, you might want to filter out all devices except Catalyst 6500 switches to find the throughput power necessary to avoid a bottleneck. In the Map Highlighting window to the right, "C" stands for Catalyst and "LS" for LightStream.

Notice that the list of device types in the upper-right corner includes Cisco router model numbers. This is because switched internetwork topologies generally include routers to augment switching intelligence. As covered in Chapter 6, multilayer switching (MLS) is an advanced technique in which routing tables are used to dynamically identify and verify a new optimal path and then "bump" nearby switches to place that path at the top of its MAC address table for use. To configure and monitor a switched network, then, you must be able to view and configure routers in addition to the switches.

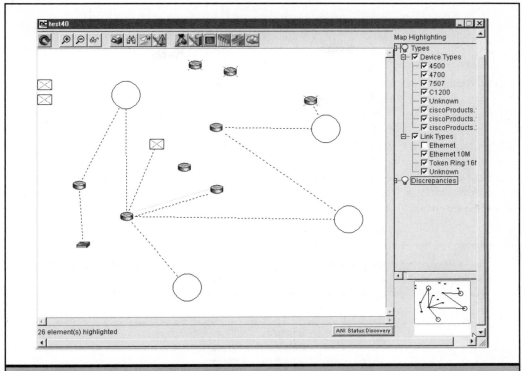

Figure 15-29. The CWSI Campus Map documents devices and links in switched networks.

The CWSI Campus Map uses filters to control its contents. Five filters are available to select what will be included in the topology:

▼ **Device and link filters**   Displays a specific set of devices or network links, such as all Token Ring networks.

■ **VLAN management filter**   Displays a specific VLAN by highlighting it in color on the map.

■ **LANE management filter**   Same as the VLAN filter, but displays a specific ATM VLAN by highlighting it in color on the map.

■ **Multilayer switching filter**   Displays multilayer switching devices—layer-3 routing devices that act in conjunction with switched networks.

▲ **Discrepancy filter**   Displays configuration discrepancies in the network.

When the VLAN Director application is started, the LANE management and VLAN filters are automatically turned on in the map display. In essence, each Director application takes ownership of the map and populates the diagrammed topology from its perspective.

Traffic Director   Traffic Director is a console providing 14 functions. The console, shown in Figure 15-30, is divided into three parts. Hardware can be analyzed by device and even down to the port level. Indeed, many Traffic Director functions—such as App Monitor—*must* have ports selected. Data also can be gathered from a specific RMON agent or a group of agents. In Figure 15-30's example, HTTP traffic is being analyzed for port 04 on switch2900x1. Functional analysis can be performed for a number of things, such as application traffic now or over a historical period, conversations (sessions), and what's called TopN talkers. *TopN* is for the host pair that talked the most during the most recent sampling interval.

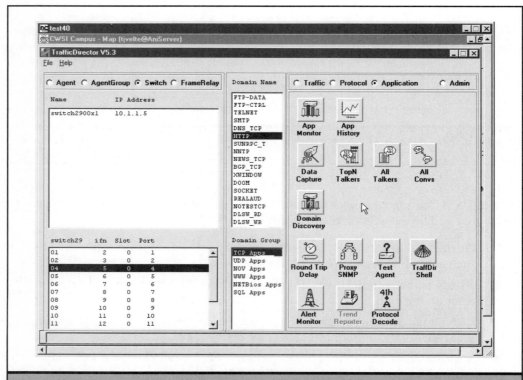

Figure 15-30.   Traffic Director can monitor traffic up to the application level.

Traffic Director can look at traffic by application, by network protocol, or view it as raw traffic. The buttons in the top half of the Traffic Director console change, depending on which mode is selected. In traffic mode, the App Monitor button shown in Figure 15-30 changes to the Traffic Monitor button—sorting traffic by TCP, UDP, or other low-level traffic types instead of by network application type. In protocol mode, Traffic Director's console changes to let you sort traffic statistics by network protocols such as IP, IPX, AppleTalk, and others.

VLAN Director   VLAN Director is used to configure and manage VLANs. Remember, a virtual LAN is not defined by a shared medium such as a switch. It is instead defined by a network administrator, who assigns users VLAN memberships according to enterprise policy. A VLAN cannot be seen by looking at a physical topology map, so a key benefit of CWSI Campus is VLAN Director's ability to discover and display VLAN topologies on the map.

VLAN Director performs the gamut of tasks that must be done to manage virtual LANs: assign membership, look up VLAN switch device statistics, and track movement of end users.

When VLAN Director is on, the map displays Spanning-Tree Protocol (STP) configurations. STP is the control protocol that uses an algorithm to stop loops from appearing as MAC address tables are exchanged between neighbor switches (the equivalent of routing loops, but in a switched internetwork). When performance slows in a switched internetwork, frequently the cause is a looping MAC address that is causing connections to be made over bad paths. When this happens, the network administrator can view the STP information and tweak the settings to steer traffic back in the right direction.

ATM Director   ATM Director is used to configure, display, and monitor ATM topologies by displaying virtual channels in the same way VLAN Director displays virtual LANs. Because switched networks are less intelligent than routed ones, network administrators often intercede and manually *merge* or *separate* ATM groupings in order to steer traffic. Figure 15-31 shows the ATM Director's dialog box for building a group or fabric of ATM switches.

ATM Director also can be used to assign circuits within fabrics. Remember that in a switched network, a connection (session) is normally made dynamically in the form of a switched virtual circuit, or SVC. But sometimes a permanent virtual circuit (PVC) should be configured. For example, if a pair of communicating hosts exchange heavy traffic over an ATM backbone, a PVC should be configured because it's always busy.

VLANs can be configured and managed using ATM Director. It lets you specify hosts and interfaces to run the LAN Emulation (LANE) translation process. Once configured, LANE clients then talk to a LANE server that provides joining, address resolution, and address registration for the clients in the ATM-VLAN.

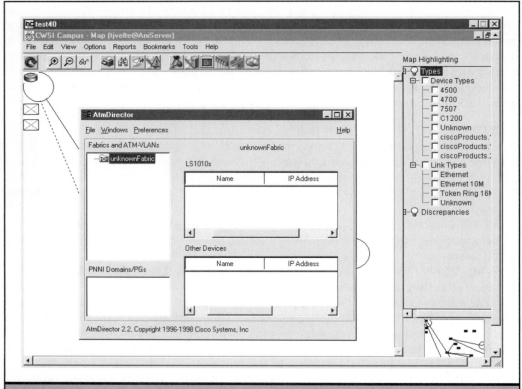

Figure 15-31. ATM Director can configure and monitor ATM switch fabrics.

Network management is an incredibly important task to keep up on. The work on a network doesn't stop once it's been built and configured. Networks are dynamic environments and it is necessary to constantly monitor your network's performance and make the requisite tweaks. Happily, Cisco offers a number of applications to keep on top of your network's behavior.

CHAPTER 16

Network Design Process

We've now covered the components that make up an internetwork. In this chapter, we'll put this knowledge to work by examining the network design process and configuring networks to fit various design scenarios.

As you've seen, there is no shortage of technologies and products to choose from—even in Cisco's product line alone. You've also seen how there is no free lunch in networking: every design move brings a trade-off of one kind or another. Trade-offs can come in the form of reduced bandwidth to carry payload traffic, increased complexity, additional expense, or other disadvantages. When designing a network, you need to know not only what the options are, but also how to juggle them to strike the best possible balance.

Each year brings so many new products and advances in technology that just keeping the acronyms straight is difficult. In this chapter, we'll sort things out a bit by applying Cisco's array of products to real-world problems. Looking at internetwork configuration problems will help put things into perspective and bring those critical trade-offs into sharper focus.

INTERNETWORK DESIGN BASICS

Internetworking is geographical by nature, so most design practices have to do with matching topology to needs. (Recall from Chapter 6, a topology is a map of an internetwork's physical layout.) The layout of an internetwork largely dictates how it will perform and how well it can scale. In networking, *scale,* or *scalability,* means how much an internetwork can grow without having to change the basic shape of its topology (that is, without having to replace or excessively reconfigure an existing infrastructure).

Internetworking Basics Reviewed

One last run-through of what we've learned thus far is in order. Doing so is especially important here, because in this chapter we'll be looking at a variety of design factors and options. Therefore, we need to be clear on the various components that make up an internetwork.

LAN Segments

Switches form LAN segments, the basic building block of every internetwork. A LAN segment could be a departmental LAN or a high-speed LAN backbone servicing dozens of other LAN segments within an enterprise.

> **NOTE:** To review, a LAN segment is a physical medium shared among a group of devices. Most LAN segments are formed by hubs or switches. Strictly speaking, a LAN segment is a LAN. Usually, though, the term LAN is used to refer to a local network consisting of many LAN segments.

Collision and Broadcast Domains

A collision domain is a shared network medium in which Ethernet packets are allowed to collide; a broadcast domain is the area within which messages may be sent to all stations using a so-called broadcast address. Collision domains should be kept small because collisions limit the use of bandwidth. The more hosts that are connected to a LAN segment, the slower the traffic moves.

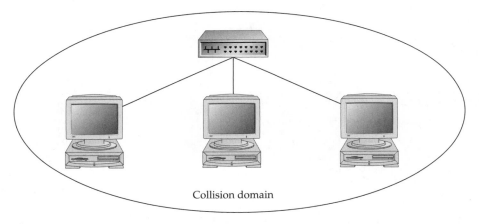

Collision domain

Most collision domains are formed by hubs that connect host devices to the internetwork. Hubs are the functional equivalent of the Ethernet cable segments used in the early days of local area networking.

A broadcast domain is the network area in which broadcast messages are forwarded. To review, broadcasts use the reserved dotted decimal IP number 255; therefore, a message to be forwarded to every device within network 298.92.182.0 would be addressed 298.92.182.255. Some broadcasts are useful, but too many can bog down a network in useless overhead traffic—an unwelcome phenomenon called a *broadcast storm*. Broadcast domains are, by default, the same as a network's collision domain for shared media (in other words, hubs), but the scope of broadcast addresses can be made smaller than a collision domain using switches. Routers normally limit broadcasts, but a broadcast domain can be extended by configuring a router to let broadcast messages pass.

Shared Bandwidth vs. Switched Bandwidth

Switches also connect hosts to networks, but in a fundamentally different way. A switch "time slices" network access among its attached hosts in such a way that each switch port forms a channel with a collision domain of one. This is called *switched bandwidth,* as opposed to the *shared bandwidth* of hubs. Switched networks are estimated to be ten times faster than shared networks over the same medium.

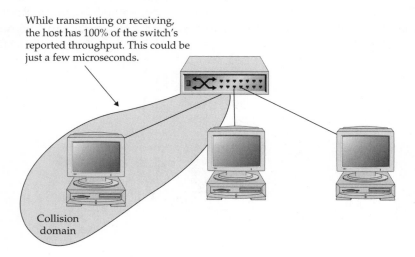

While transmitting or receiving, the host has 100% of the switch's reported throughput. This could be just a few microseconds.

Collision domain

Moreover, switched networks support virtual LANs (VLANs), enabling administrators to group users rationally instead of being forced to group them according to which host devices they are attached.

In addition to forming them by connecting hosts, larger switches connect LAN segments to form internetworks. To avoid confusion, the two types of switches are sometimes called access switches and LAN (or backbone) switches.

Routers Control Internetworks

The third basic device in internetworking is the router. Routers connect LAN segments instead of hosts, as do hubs and access switches. Routers are used to isolate intramural traffic and to provide internal security. In addition, they can extend broadcast and multicast domains to specified LAN segments, to help bind those networks into a functional unit.

Routers are deployed both inside internetworks and at the edge of autonomous systems. Inside routers are sometimes called internal routers or access routers. Routers that concentrate on communicating with the outside are called edge, or gateway, routers. For example, an Internet service provider (ISP) will use gateway routers to connect to the Internet. By contrast, a big company will place at least one internal router at each of its major sites to help manage in-house traffic.

Routers are more intelligent than hubs and switches because they are able to interpret network addresses. They read network addresses in order to filter traffic, control access to networks or services, and choose the best path to reach a destination. Routers bring internetworks to life. It's no coincidence that the three most basic devices in internetworking operate at different levels of the seven-layer OSI reference model, as illustrated here:

Level 3 Network layer		209.98.123.74 IP address

Level 2 Data-link layer		4254.1d83.ec07 MAC address

Switch

Routers operate at the network layer (layer 3). Today, most internetworks use IP network addresses—all Internet routers do. But many internal routers must still use legacy desktop protocols such as IPX, AppleTalk, or DECnet. For that reason, Cisco and its competitors have invested heavily in engineering multiprotocol products to allow legacy LANs to interoperate with IP. Cisco's IOS feature sets exist mostly to give network designers options in purchasing system software that fits their network protocol needs.

Routers Use Layer-3 Network Addresses

Whether IP or a legacy layer-3 protocol, network addresses are inherently hierarchical. As a router works its way rightward through an IP address, it zeros in on the LAN segment to which the destination host is attached. Over long-haul routes, moves through the address are manifested in hops between routers. A one-hop route would require only finding the LAN segment on which the destination resides.

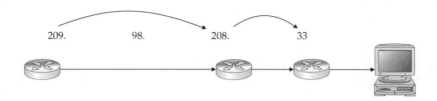

Routes are often summarized before being shared with other routers. This improves performance by greatly reducing the number of address entries carried inside a router's route table. Route summarization, called *route aggregation,* works by relying on a gateway router to know the target LAN segment's full address, allowing interim routers to carry fewer entries in their respective routing tables, thereby improving performance. Address translation is also frequently used, where internal addresses are either altered or grouped into a global address in packets sent outside an internetwork. Mechanisms such as Port Address Translation (PAT) and Network Address Translation (NAT) are used at edge routers or firewalls to make these translations in the packet address fields in both directions.

Switches Use Layer-2 MAC Addresses

Switches operate at the data-link layer (layer 2), dealing in MAC addresses instead of network addresses. A MAC address is a long number that uniquely identifies physical hardware devices. MACs combine a manufacturer code with a serial number. Even routers use MAC addresses for a message's last step—resolving an IP address to the physical MAC address to locate the destination host within the LAN segment.

MAC addresses are topologically flat. The logical profile of a MAC address appears as if all hosts are connected to the same cable; it offers no clue as to where hosts are located because it's basically a serial number. Switched networks, therefore, must operate by brute force, flooding broadcasts of MAC addresses to all ports when a destination MAC is unknown.

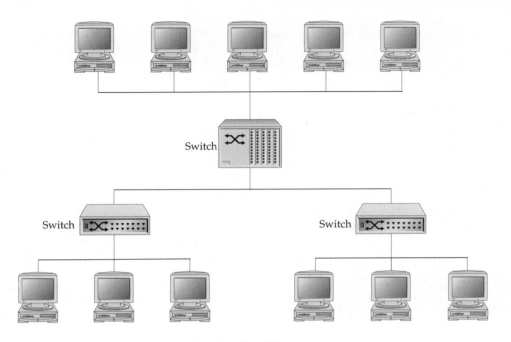

Broadcast Flood Zone

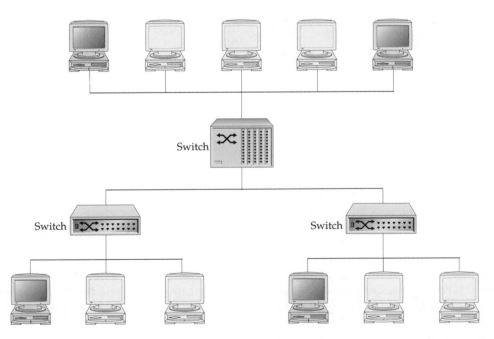

VLAN Broadcast Flood Zone

VLANs give switched networks hierarchy by limiting broadcasts to discrete groups of users. This combines the speed of switched bandwidth with the hierarchical topology heretofore available only in shared bandwidth networks. In addition, VLANs flexibly assign users to logical workgroups instead of having to group users by device.

Path Optimization

Internetworks use control protocols to route messages. There is so much dynamic change in internetworks—through growth, changing traffic patterns, a device going down, and the like—that they must self-operate to some degree by constantly updating device routing tables. Routed networks rely on routing protocols to keep track of paths through internetworks. For example, many small internetworks use RIP 2; most large ones use EIGRP or OSPF (EIGRP is Cisco proprietary, OSPF is an open standard). These trade in lists of routes, mostly within an autonomous system, and are used to connect LAN segments. BGP trades in lists of autonomous systems and is used to connect the Internet.

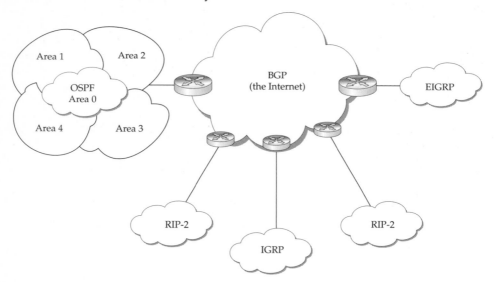

As you've learned, internetworks maintain a degree of self-awareness by way of discovery protocols, which find new devices and keep checking the status of known ones. These protocols—Cisco Discovery Protocol (CDP) is an example—are the supporting cast to routing protocols. When an event takes place, it's discovered and the news is passed around until the device population converges on a new list of routes. Sometimes loops appear where a suggested route turns back toward its source device, creating nonsensical routes that can slow or even crash an internetwork. Routing protocols use metrics to tune internetworks. RIP uses only hop count, but the more sophisticated protocols use several metrics that can be combined into a weighted matrix to steer traffic along desired links.

Switched networks aren't so sophisticated. Switches exchange only lists of MAC addresses, with the most recently used MACs appearing toward the top, the highest one being the first choice. Switched networks use the Spanning Tree Protocol (STP) to prevent loops.

Internetwork Architectures and Applications

In just the past few years, the design requirements of the typical enterprise have changed radically. These changes have occurred at opposite ends of the topology. At the bottom, segmentation using hubs and access switches has greatly increased the number of LAN segments and, therefore, the amount of traffic to go over the backbone between segments. At the top, whole new computing architectures are becoming standard, with Web-based intranets replacing traditional client-server management systems, extranets transforming traditional electronic data interchange (EDI) systems, and virtual private networks (VPNs) replacing leased-line wide area networks (WANs).

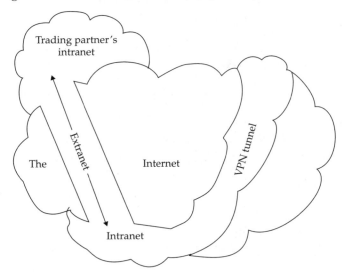

Driving even more change is the fact that new network applications have changed traffic characteristics. For example, videoconferencing is becoming popular, increasing the need for configurations optimized to handle multicasts—where a single copy of a message is forwarded to a subset of destination hosts.

The Three-Layer Hierarchical Design Model

Hierarchical topologies are inherently better than flat ones for a number of reasons, the main one being that hierarchy contains traffic to its local area. The rule of thumb designers use is that broadcast traffic should not exceed 20 percent of the packets going over each link—the implication being that segmentation will naturally boost throughput by isolating traffic to its most likely users. This rule of thumb applies only to the amount of broadcast packets in the traffic mix, and is not to be confused with the 80/20 rule. The 80/20 rule states that 80 percent of all traffic stays home and only 20 percent goes beyond the local area.

A flat topology—one in which each device does more or less the same job—increases the number of neighbors with which an individual device must communicate. This increases somewhat the amount of payload traffic the device is likely to carry and greatly increases overhead traffic. For example, each time a router receives a broadcast message, its CPU is interrupted. For many small internetworks, a flat topology is sufficient, and the added expense and complexity that hierarchy requires isn't warranted. But it doesn't take many LAN segments to hurt an internetwork's performance and reliability, with devices and hosts bogged down in unnecessary traffic.

This is why the industry adheres to a classical hierarchical design model. The model has three layers: the access, distribution, and core layers. This separates local traffic from high-volume traffic passing between LAN segments and areas and lets network devices at each layer concentrate on doing their specific job. The hierarchical model is depicted in Figure 16-1.

Hierarchy is made possible by segmentation—the practice of dividing hosts into smaller LAN segments. Fifteen years ago, most LAN segments were actual cable spans running through walls and ceiling plenums. Today, most are formed by "cable-in-a-box" hubs and access switches. Segmentation and hierarchical topology yield several benefits:

▼ **Performance** Traffic is isolated to source areas, thereby narrowing Ethernet packet collision domains and speeding throughput.

■ **Reliability** Most faults are isolated to the segment from which the problem originated.

■ **Simplicity** By separating dissimilar areas, network elements can be replicated as needed throughout the internetwork.

■ **Scalability** Modular design elements can be added as the internetwork grows over time, with minimal disruption of existing networks.

▲ **Security** Access can be controlled at well-defined junctures between the layers.

Internetworks naturally tend toward a two-level hierarchy. Hubs and switches connect host devices into LAN segments, and the backbone connects the segments into a local network, whether within a floor, building, office campus, or even a metropolitan area. This is a relatively flat topology in the sense that, even though collision domains are limited, excessive broadcast traffic still chews into available bandwidth. This makes the distribution layer the key. By isolating traffic, the distribution layer also isolates problems and complexity.

Hierarchy also helps reduce costs. By dividing hosts and traffic, variations are limited to fewer LAN segments, or even a single segment. Variations include such things as desktop protocols (IP, IPX, AppleTalk), traffic volumes (workgroup versus backbone), and

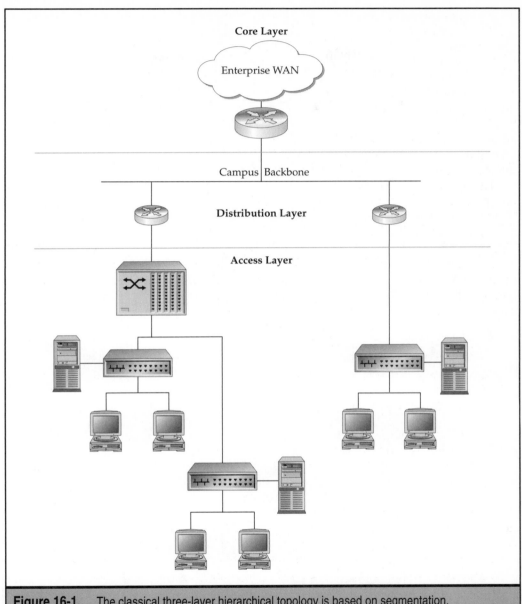

Figure 16-1. The classical three-layer hierarchical topology is based on segmentation.

traffic type (big graphical files, e-mail, HTTP). Hierarchy allows the network designer to tune the configuration for the particular job at hand. Adjustments are made in the model of network device purchased and in how it is configured in terms of memory, modules, software, and config file parameter settings.

The Access Layer

The access layer is made up mostly of hubs and switches, which serve to segment host devices such as PCs and servers into many LAN segments made up of either shared or switched bandwidth. This is where MAC-layer filtering can take place.

If an internetwork has remote sites, such as branch offices or home offices, the access layer would also include access servers. WANs must use some type of long-distance transmission medium. There is a wide selection of media now, such as leased digital T1 or T3 lines and Frame Relay public digital networks. Dial-in remote users employ analog modem lines and, in certain areas, higher-bandwidth technologies such as Digital Subscriber Line (DSL) and Integrated Services Digital Network (ISDN). Figure 16-2 shows access-layer functionality.

In large internetworks, the access layer can include routers. These internal routers serve mostly to isolate overhead, control traffic, and enhance internal security. The access layer encompasses a mix of technologies in most internetworks. Dial-on-demand routing (DDR) has become popular for remote connections because it keeps a link inactive except when traffic needs to be sent, thereby reducing telecommunication costs.

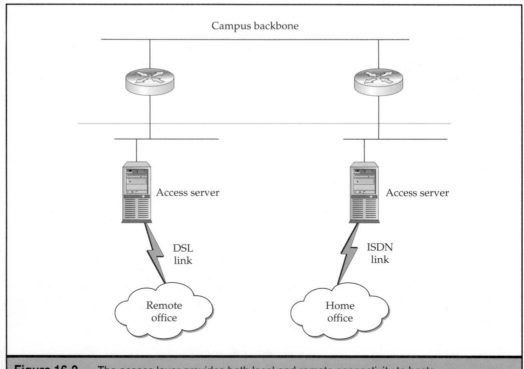

Figure 16-2.   The access layer provides both local and remote connectivity to hosts.

Most enterprises have legacy technologies that are being gradually phased out as new ones are implemented. For example, many big companies still use their leased-line T1 WANs alongside growing VPNs, substituting shared network usage for dedicated leased lines. From a practical standpoint, this is necessary because the routers must be upgraded along each VPN link.

The Distribution Layer

The distribution layer is made up mostly of routers. They're used to separate slow-speed local traffic from the high-speed backbone. Traffic at the access layer tends to be band-width-intensive because that's where most LAN and host addresses reside. Network overhead protocol traffic for discovery protocols, SNMP, routing protocols, and other network control systems is heavier at the access layer.

Because routers are intelligent enough to read network addresses and examine packets, they also improve performance by sending traffic as directly as possible to its destination. For example, distribution-layer routers define broadcast and multicast domains across LAN segments. Domains are, by default, limited to LAN segments; routers can extend domains across segments as the hierarchy design dictates. Figure 16-3 depicts distribution-layer functionality.

In configurations using multilayer switches, distribution-layer devices route messages between VLANs. *Multilayer switching* is a relatively new technology in which packets are filtered and forwarded based on both MAC and network addresses. The Catalyst 5000 is perhaps the best example of a multilayer switch, incorporating route switch modules (RSMs) in addition to those with typical switch electronics.

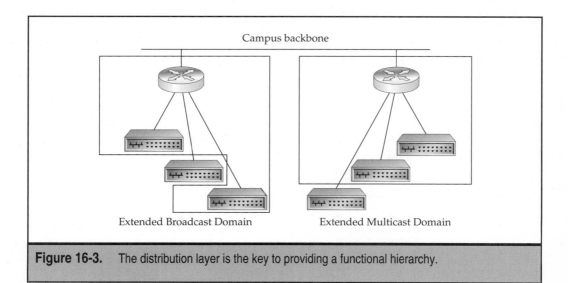

Figure 16-3.   The distribution layer is the key to providing a functional hierarchy.

Most value-added services are provided by devices at the distribution layer. Address translation takes place at this layer, usually on a gateway router or a firewall (itself a type of router). Address aggregation also takes place here, as well as area aggregation if the internetwork is running OSPF routing domains. Other services are also performed on distribution-layer routers: translation between protocols such as IPX and IP; encryption for VPN tunneling; traffic-based security using access lists and context-based firewall algorithms; and user-based security using security protocols such as RADIUS, TACACS+, and Kerberos.

The Core Layer

The core layer is the backbone layer. In large internetworks, the core incorporates multiple backbones, from campus backbone LANs up through regional ones. Sometimes special backbone LANs are configured to handle a specific protocol or particularly sensitive traffic. Most backbones exist to connect LAN segments, usually those within a particular building or office campus. Figure 16-4 depicts how the core layer might look in a typical large enterprise internetwork.

To run fast, a backbone LAN should be configured to experience a minimum of interruptions. The goal is to have as many backbone device CPU cycles as possible spent transferring packets among segments. The distribution layer makes this possible, by connecting workgroup LAN segments and providing value-added routing services. A minimum of packet manipulation should occur at this level. This is why most new backbones are switched LANs. The need for address interpretation at the core is minimized by the processing already performed by distribution-layer routers, so why not use switching technology to move data over the backbone much faster?

ATM (Asynchronous Transfer Mode) and Gigabit Ethernet are doing battle to become the switched backbone technology of choice. ATM has an edge for multimedia applications because it uses fixed-sized cells instead of Ethernet's variable-length packets. The obvious advantage of Gigabit Ethernet switched backbones is easier compatibility with the millions of Ethernet LANs already installed throughout the world.

ATM is an international cell relay standard for service types such as video, voice, and data. The fixed-length 53-byte cells speed data transfer by allowing processing to occur in hardware. Although ATM products exist to take data all the way to the desktop, the technology is optimized to work with high-speed transmission media such as OC-48 (2.5 Gbps), T3 (45 Mbps), and T3's European counterpart, E3 (34 Mbps).

Design Methods

Over the years, the networking industry has developed a set of concepts and best practices for use in internetwork design. Most internetworks are works in progress; very few are designed from a clean sheet of paper. As internetwork topologies evolve through time and circumstance, it becomes difficult to maintain a rigorous hierarchical network design—especially in large enterprises with distributed management structures, or in shops that have high personnel turnover in their network teams.

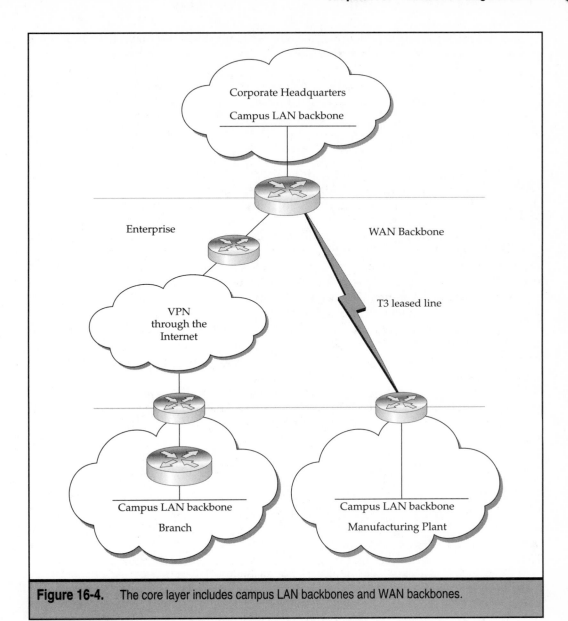

Figure 16-4. The core layer includes campus LAN backbones and WAN backbones.

Redundancy and Load Balancing

Redundancy is the practice of configuring backup equipment. This is done to provide fault tolerance, where traffic will shift to the backup device if the primary unit fails, a process called *failover*. For example, most high-speed backbones have dual-configured switches at each end in case the primary switch goes down. Another common safeguard is to have redundant power supplies within a device, so that if one fails, the device keeps running.

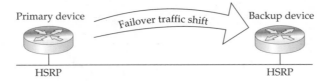

Cisco's technology to support redundancy is the Hot Standby Router Protocol (HSRP), a suite of commands in IOS. *Hot standby* is a computer industry term meaning that the backup unit is always up and running, thereby allowing automatic failover in the event of a failure. HSRP works by creating a group of routers where one is elected as the active router, and another is elected as the standby, or "phantom" router. They all share a virtual IP and MAC address that the active router will serve. The active router is monitored by others in the group, and should it fail, the standby router will take over the traffic processing duties, and another backup router (if more than two) will be elected as the new standby router. Failovers are achieved with no human intervention and are generally accomplished in a few seconds.

Because redundant configurations are expensive, fault-tolerant configurations are usually limited to critical devices. Redundancy is most commonly configured into backbone devices and firewalls, where device failure would have the broadest effect on the overall network.

Load balancing is a configuration technique that shifts traffic to an alternative link if a certain threshold is exceeded on the primary link. Load balancing can be achieved through various means, such as tuning routing metrics in router config files within routing protocol domains.

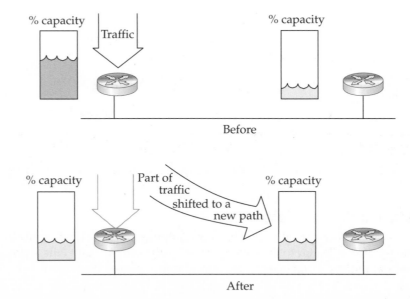

Load balancing is similar to redundancy in that an event causes traffic to shift directions, and alternative equipment must be present in the configuration. But in load balancing, the alternative equipment isn't necessarily *redundant* equipment that only operates in the event of failure.

Topology Meshing

A good design will incorporate a meshed topology to achieve redundancy and load balancing. A *mesh* is where two network devices—usually routers or switches—are directly connected. In a fully meshed topology, all network nodes have either physical or virtual circuits connecting them to every other node in the internetwork. You can also have a partially meshed topology, in which some parts of the topology are fully meshed, but some nodes are connected only to one or two other nodes. Figure 16-5 depicts the two.

At first blush, all meshing seems to be an inherently good thing. Looking at the example in Figure 16-5, you can readily see the benefits in the full-mesh topology:

▼ **Performance**   It's only a single hop to any network attached to one of the other routers, and the fewer the hops, the faster the speed.

■ **Availability**   Having redundant paths means that if any one router goes down, one or more alternate routes are always available.

▲ **Load balancing**   Alternative paths can also be used for normal operations, where routing parameters can be configured to use alternate paths if a preset traffic load is exceeded on the primary router.

The partially meshed internetwork on the bottom of Figure 16-5 doesn't have these advantages. For example, to go from router A to C takes two router hops, not one. If routers on both sides of router F go down, it will be unable to communicate with the rest of the internetwork. Also, fewer mesh connections reduce opportunities for load balancing. However, although meshing can bring benefits, it must be used carefully, because it comes at the following costs:

▼ **Expense**   Every router (or switch) interface dedicated to meshing is one that can't be used to connect a LAN segment. Meshing consumes hardware capacity.

■ **Overhead traffic**   Devices constantly advertise their services to one another. The more mesh links a device has, the more advertisement packets it broadcasts, thereby eating into payload bandwidth.

■ **Vulnerability**   Meshing makes it more difficult to contain problems within their local area. If a misconfigured device begins propagating indiscriminate broadcast messages, for example, each element in a mesh will cause the broadcast storm to radiate farther from the source.

▲ **Complexity**   Additional connections make it more difficult to isolate problems. For example, it would be harder to track down the device causing the broadcast storm in a fully or heavily meshed internetwork, because there would be so many trails to follow.

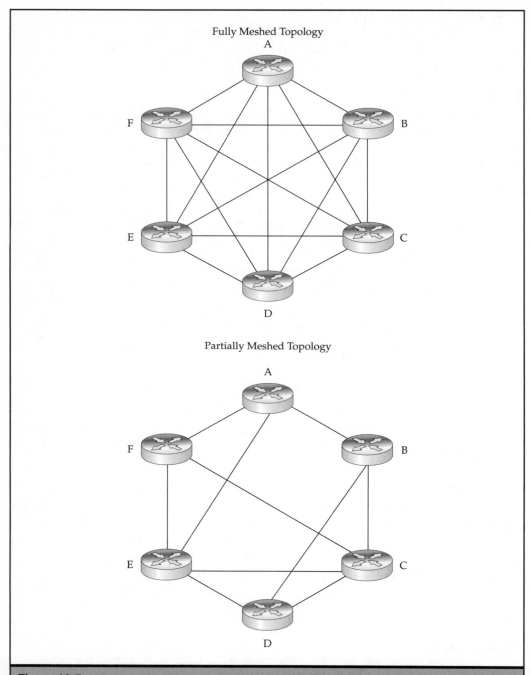

Figure 16-5. Fully meshed vs. partially meshed topologies

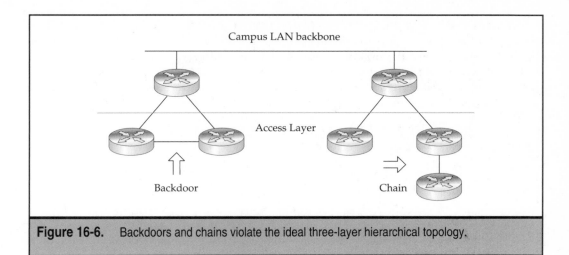

Figure 16-6.   Backdoors and chains violate the ideal three-layer hierarchical topology.

For these reasons, few internetworks are fully meshed. The general practice is to fully mesh the backbone portion of topologies to provide fault tolerance and load balancing along these critical links, but only partially mesh the access and distribution layer topologies.

Backdoor and Chain Configurations

Circumstance sometimes dictates deviating from the strict hierarchical model. The two commonest topology deviations are so-called backdoors and chains. A *backdoor* is any direct connection between devices at the same layer, usually the access layer. A *chain* is the addition of one or more layers below the access layer. Figure 16-6 depicts the two.

Sometimes it makes sense to configure a backdoor. For example, you might want to directly link two remote sites if the links to the distribution-layer routers are costly or slow. Backdoors also provide a degree of redundancy: if the backdoor link goes down, the two remote sites can failover to the distribution-layer router and keep communicating. More often than not, however, backdoors and chains emerge because of poor network planning or a renegade manager who installs networking equipment without involving the network team.

DESIGNING TO FIT NEEDS

You'd be surprised how many internetworks—even big sophisticated ones—have grown haphazardly. Unmanaged network growth occurs for any number of reasons. The most common one is that things simply happened too fast. Keep in mind that realities we now take for granted—client-server computing, intranets, the Web, extranets—were mere concepts until the last decade. This left many IT managers unprepared to formulate well-researched, reasoned strategic network plans for their enterprises.

In many cases, a plan wouldn't have done much good. Management fads come and go, but one fad that stuck is the credo "If I pay, then I have the say." The management trend has been toward flat organizational structures, with minimum layers between the CEO and worker. Most IT departments are now "budgeted" by individual divisions, groups, or even departments. In other words, IT decisions are increasingly being made from the bottom up by the entity that owns the budget, not the central IT department.

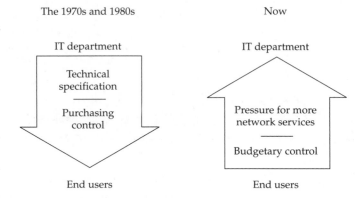

This kind of distributed decision making has been magnified by the slowness of many IT departments to respond to emerging customer demands driven by such things as business process reengineering, mergers, acquisitions, and trading partner cooperatives. So it got to the point where many end-user managers simply threw out the corporate technical architecture, picked up the phone, and ordered new networks on their own.

The trend over the last several years has been for IT departments to break off networking into a separate group called *infrastructure*. Separate the chip heads from the wire heads, so to speak. This is being done because internetworking has simply become too big and too complicated to be left to a manager who, say, has a background in COBOL and mainframe software project management. Networking is its own game now. It is fast becoming its own discipline with its own set of best practices—some of which we'll review in the remainder of this chapter.

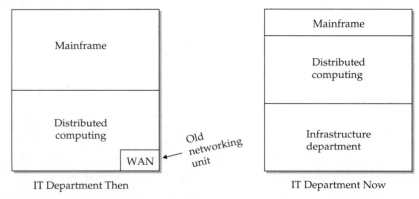

Methodologies have been developed to help bring network planning under control. Not surprisingly, these bear a strong resemblance to data processing methodologies. First and foremost, of course, is to fit the solution to the business needs through some form of needs assessment—both present and future.

Understanding Existing Internetworks

As mentioned earlier, few network designs start from scratch. Although it would be nice to work from a blank sheet of paper, most designs must accommodate a preexisting network. Most are incremental redesigns to serve more users or to upgrade bandwidth capacity, or both. A common upgrade, for example, is to insert a layer of routers between the LAN backbone and the layer at which hosts access the network. This is being done in many enterprises to improve performance and accommodate projected growth. Whatever the change, the pre-existing infrastructure must be thoroughly analyzed before even considering a purchase.

The next section describes methods for network planning and design. They focus on establishing a baseline of how the network will look upon implementation. To refresh on the subject, a baseline is a network's starting point, as expressed in traffic volumes, flows, and characteristics. Allowances are made for margins of error and projected growth over and above the baseline.

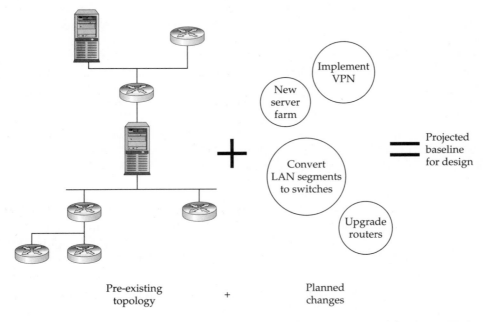

When designing an entirely new network area, you must arrive at a design baseline based on well-researched assumptions, often derived from paperwork or other nonnetworked data traffic already in place. If an existing network topology is being upgraded, the baseline is taken by measuring its characteristics. If the design scenario encompasses nonnetworked and networked elements, then the two must be compiled together. Whatever the case, the principles and methods of good network design remain the same.

Characterizing Networks

There are several methods for understanding an internetwork well enough to formulate a proper design. These methods apply whether it's an existing internetwork or a topology to be built from scratch. As you might expect, the methods focus on geography and traffic—in other words, where network nodes are and what travels between them. A network node is any device in the topology, including network devices such as routers and payload hosts such as servers. For our purposes, when designing a network from scratch, a node could be a noncomputer entity such as a desk or a file cabinet. The point is to identify where the users are and what they're using.

Quality of Service

Characterizing networks is good for managing as well as designing. The industry is pushing the concept of Quality of Service (QoS)—an approach largely based on characterizing traffic. As discussed in Chapter 7, QoS is the technique of assuring throughput for traffic through an internetwork. QoS is more sophisticated than just guaranteeing that a certain link will run at a certain throughput level. Most QoS guarantees are associated with a particular type of traffic, say, prioritizing video multicasting for distance learning over e-mail and other less critical traffic.

As you might imagine, QoS policy implementation relies heavily on information gathered via SNMP and RMON and presented through NMS consoles such as Resource Manager Essentials and CWSI Campus. Like those console applications, QoS uses the client-server model by storing a QoS database, and it implements policies through purpose-built applets such as QoS Policy Manager, QoS Distribution Manager, and Cisco Assure.

Cisco's QoS Policy Manager creates abstract commands that group individual IOS commands to perform a task from the Cisco Policy Manager GUI. As with other NMS console applets, when you push a button, one or more commands are put to use on the client network device being configured. Some QoS subcommands are generic IOS commands (the **interface** command, for example); others are QoS-specific. The major QoS abstract commands are as follows:

▼ **WFQ**   Stands for *Weighted Fair Queuing*. Combines the **interface** and **fair-queue** commands to let network managers prioritize how a mix of traffic types will flow through certain areas of the topology. For example, e-mail might be given a higher priority on Lotus Notes servers, but not elsewhere.

■ **WRED**   Stands for *Weighted Random Early Detection*. Combines the **interface** and **random-detect** commands. (The **random-detect** command accepts a weight value to represent the relative importance of a traffic type.) WRED tries to control traffic congestion as it begins to emerge.

▲ **CAR**   Stands for *Committed Access Rate*. CAR is the fundamental QoS bandwidth control technology. It uses a sophisticated RMON MIB to recognize traffic types, set priorities, and limit packet rates as needed.

QoS techniques are mostly applied at the network interface level, and make heavy use of access control lists to filter packets. The idea is to differentiate traffic types within topology areas and influence network behavior—a technique dubbed *traffic shaping*. The goal of traffic shaping is to guarantee minimum levels of end-to-end service for various types of traffic. There are several other QoS abstract commands dealing with special areas such as Frame Relay links and Fast EtherChannel bandwidth aggregation. But, for now, many operational areas don't yet have meaningful QoS infrastructure in the form of commands and RMONs. Many hope that QoS will come to fruition with IP's next major release, IP version 6.

Understanding Traffic Flow

Understanding and documenting traffic flow is the first step in network design. Drawing an analogy to highway design might seem too obvious, but the two are remarkably similar. A road designer must know where the roads should be, how wide, covered with what type of surface, and what traffic control rules are to be applied. All these things are largely a function of traffic flow.

Traffic characteristics are largely a matter of directionality, symmetry, packet sizes, and volumes. A unidirectional flow does most communicating in one direction; a bidirectional flow communicates with roughly the same frequency in both directions of a connection. An asymmetrical flow sends more data in one direction than the other; a symmetrical flow sends roughly equal amounts of data back and forth. For example, an HTTP session's flow is bidirectional and asymmetric because a lot of messages are sent both ways, but data is mostly downloaded from the Web server to the browser client.

Identifying Traffic Sources To understand traffic flow, you must know its sources. This is done by identifying groups of users, not individual persons. In the parlance of computer methodology, a group of users is often called a *community* (probably because the obvious term, *user group,* is already used by customer associations; for example, the Cisco User Group).

An inventory of high-level characteristics, such as location and applications used, should be gathered. This isn't to say that one would go around with a clipboard gathering the information. Most network designers would pull this information off a database from such tools as Resource Manager Essentials or NetSys Baseliner. The following example shows a form that might be used to gather user information:

Community	# Persons	Locations	Applications	Host Type
Accounting	27	St. Louis	AR, AP, GL	AS/400
Customer Service	200	Minneapolis	Call Center	Windows NT 4.0

You can gather whatever information you want. For example, you might not want to document the type of host the group uses if everybody has a Pentium PC. On the other hand, if there's a mix of dumb terminals, thin clients, PCs, and souped-up UNIX/LINUX workstations, you might want to know who has what. This information can help you more accurately calculate traffic loads.

If you're analyzing an existing network, this information can be gathered by turning on the record-route option in IOS. This information can also be gathered using Resource Manager Essentials or CWSI Campus.

Identifying Data Sources and Data Sinks   Every enterprise has major users of information. The experts identify these heavy data users as *data sinks* because it's useful to trace back to the data sources they use to help identify traffic patterns. The most common sources are database servers, disk farms, tape or CD libraries, inventory systems, online catalogs, and so on. Data sinks are usually end users, but sometimes servers can be data sinks. The following illustration shows information to gather on data sinks:

Data Sink	Locations	Applications	User Communities
Server farm 3	St. Louis	AR, AP, GL	Accounting
CCSRV	Denver	Call Center	Customer Service

Documenting which communities use each data sink enables you to correlate traffic. You can now begin connecting user desktop hosts to data sink servers. Combining the information in the preceding two illustrations lets you begin drawing lines between client and server. Correlate every user community to every data sink, and an accurate profile of the network's ideal topology begins to emerge.

Identifying Application Loads and Traffic Types   Most network applications generate traffic with specific characteristics. For example, FTP generates unidirectional and asymmetric traffic involving large files. Table 16-1 is a sampling of typical message types and their approximate sizes. Obviously, sizes can vary widely, but these are industry rules of thumb useful for estimating traffic loads.

Beyond traffic loads, it's also useful to know the traffic type. Traffic types characterize the kinds of devices connected and how traffic flows between them:

▼ **Client-server**   Usually a PC talking to a UNIX/LINUX or Windows server, this is the standard configuration today. In client-server types, traffic is usually bidirectional and asymmetrical.

■ **Server-to-server**   Examples include data mirroring to a redundant server backing up another server, name directory services, and so on. This type of traffic is bidirectional, but the symmetry depends on the application.

■ **Terminal-host**   Many terminal-based applications run over IP, even IBM terminal connections to mainframes. Another example is Telnet. Terminal traffic is bidirectional, but symmetry depends on the application.

▲ **Peer-to-peer**   Examples include videoconferencing and PCs set up to access resources on other PCs, such as printers and data. This type of traffic is bidirectional and symmetric.

Understanding what types of traffic pass through various links gives a picture of how to configure it. The following illustration shows information used to identify and characterize traffic types.

Application	Traffic Type	User Community	Data Sinks	Bandwidth Required	QoS Policy
Web browser	Client-server	Sales	Sales server	350 Kbps	CAR
TN3270	Terminal	Purchasing	AS/400	200 Kbps	WRED

Frequently, a link is dominated by one or two traffic types. The Bandwidth Required column in the preceding illustration is usually expressed as a bit-per-second estimate and could be Mbps or even Gbps. Once all the applications in an internetwork are identified and characterized, the designer has a baseline from which to make volume-dependent configuration decisions. Traffic typing is especially useful for knowing where and how to set QoS policies. In other words, you must identify which applications go through a router before you can properly set QoS parameters in its config file.

Message Type	Approximate Size
Web page	50KB
Graphical computer screen (such as a Microsoft Windows screen)	500KB
E-mail	10KB
Word processing document	100KB
Spreadsheet	200KB
Terminal screen	5KB
Multimedia object (such as videoconferencing)	100KB
Database backup	1MB and up

Table 16-1.   Typical Message Types and Sizes

Understanding Traffic Load

After the user communities, data sinks and sources, and traffic flows have been documented and characterized, individual links can be more accurately sized. The traffic flow information in the following illustration ties down the paths taken between sources and destinations.

	Destination 1	
	Link	**Mbps**
Source 1: Accounting	Frame Relay	0.056
Source 2: Call Center	Point-to-Point	1.54

	Destination 2	
	Link	**Mbps**
Source 1: Accounting	Frame Relay	0.256
Source 2: Call Center	Frame Relay	1.54

	Destination 3	
	Link	**Mbps**
Source 1: Accounting	Frame Relay	0.256
Source 2: Call Center	Frame Relay	0.512

Designing internetworks to fit needs is more art than science, though. For example, even after having totaled the estimated bandwidth for a link, you must go back and pad it for soft factors such as QoS priorities, anticipated near-term growth, and so on.

CISCO NETWORK DESIGNS

Designing networks is largely a matter of making choices. Most of the choices have to do with selecting the right technologies and products for the job. Even design elements over which you have no control may still leave choices to make. For example, if the company's art department uses AppleTalk and has no intention of changing, you must decide whether to run it over multiprotocol links or break it off into one or more AppleTalk-only LAN segments.

Once the present and future needs of the enterprise have been researched and documented, the next step is to choose technologies for various functional areas:

▼   **Backbone technology selection**   A variety of backbone LAN technologies exist, chosen mostly based on the size of the internetwork and its traffic characteristics.

■   **Protocol selection**   It's assumed here that IP is the network protocol, but choices remain as to which routing and other network control protocols to use.

▲   **Access technology selection**   A mix of hubs and switches is usually configured to best fit the needs of a workgroup or even a particular host.

After the underlying technologies are chosen, specific products must be configured to run them. After that step, more design work must be done to implement the configuration. For example, an IP addressing model must be configured, a name services subsystem must be set up, routing metrics must be tuned, security parameters must be set, and so on.

Internetwork design takes place at two levels: the campus and the enterprise. Campus designs cover the enterprise's main local network, from the desktop up to the high-speed backbone to the outside. The enterprise level encompasses multiple campus networks and focuses on WAN configurations—whether a private leased-line WAN or an Internet-based system tunneled through the Internet.

Logical Network Design

An internetwork design is defined by both a physical and a logical configuration. The physical part deals with topology layout, hardware devices, networking software, transmission media, and other pieces. Logical configuration must closely match the physical design in three areas:

▼   **IP addressing**   A plan to allocate addresses in a rational way that can conserve address space and accommodate growth

■   **Name services**   A plan to allow hosts and domains to be addressed by symbolic names instead of dotted-decimal IP addresses

▲   **Protocol selection**   Choosing which protocols to use, especially routing protocols

Internetwork design should always start with the access layer, because higher-level needs cannot be addressed until the device and user population are known. For example, estimating capacity is virtually impossible until all hosts, applications, and LAN segments have been identified and quantified, and most of these elements reside in the access layer.

From a practical standpoint, the three logical design elements of addressing, naming, and routing are good first steps in nailing down how the physical hardware should be laid out. Each of the three requires forethought and planning.

IP Addressing Strategies

The number of available addresses is called *address space.* Enterprises use various addressing schemes to maximize address space within the block of IP addresses they had assigned to them by their ISPs. Various addressing strategies have been devised, not only to maximize address space, but also to enhance security and manageability.

Private IP Address Blocks   An enterprise receives its public IP address from the Internet Assigned Numbers Authority (IANA). The IANA usually only assigns public addresses to ISPs and large enterprises, and then as a range of numbers, not as a single IP address. In actual practice, the majority of enterprises receive their public IP addresses from their ISP. When designing IP, the IETF reserved three IP address ranges for use as private addresses:

▼   10.0.0.0 through 10.255.255.255

■   172.16.0.0 through 172.31.255.255

▲   192.168.0.0 through 192.168.255.255

These three IP address blocks were reserved to avoid confusion. You may use addresses within any of these reserved blocks without fear of one of your routers being confused when it encounters the same address from the outside, because these are private addresses that never appear on the Internet.

Private IP addresses are assigned by the network team to internal devices. Because they'll never be used outside the autonomous system, private addresses can be assigned at will as long as they stay within the assigned range. No clearance from the IETF or any other coordinating body is required to use private addresses, which are used for these reasons:

▼   **Address space conservation**   Few enterprises are assigned a sufficient number of public IP addresses to accommodate all nodes (hosts and devices) within their internetwork.

■   **Security**   Private addresses are translated via PAT or NAT to the outside. Not knowing the private address makes it tougher for hackers to crack into an autonomous system by pretending to be an internal node.

- **Flexibility**   An enterprise can change ISPs without having to change any of the private addresses. Usually, only the addresses of the routers or firewalls performing address translation need to be changed.

▲ **Smaller routing tables**   Having most enterprises advertise just one or perhaps a few IP addresses helps minimize the size of routing tables in Internet routers, thereby enhancing performance.

This last item perhaps explains why the IETF settled on a 32-bit IP address instead of a 64-bit design. Doling out infinitely greater address space would discourage the use of private addresses. The use of global IP addresses would be rampant, engorging routing tables in the process. This would create the need for routers to have faster CPUs and lots more memory. Back when IP was designed, during the 1970s, network devices were in their infancy and were very slow and underconfigured by today's standards.

Obtaining Public IP Addresses   Registered IP addresses must be purchased from the nonprofit IANA, which is responsible for ensuring that no two enterprises are assigned duplicate IP addresses. But few enterprises obtain their IP addresses directly from the IANA; most get them indirectly through their ISP.

```
           ╭─────────────╮
          (  Available IP  )
          (  address pool  )
           ╰─────────────╯

              InterNIC

                 ⇓

       Tier-1    ISPs

         ⤡          ⇲
     Large        Tier-2   ISPs
   enterprises
                     ⇓

            Smaller enterprises
```

For example, Tier 1 ISPs such as UUNET or Sprint secure large blocks of IP addresses from the IANA. They in turn dole them out to Tier 2 ISPs (there are probably dozens in your town alone), who in turn assign them to end-user enterprises. Most large companies deal directly with Tier 1 ISPs. IP addresses are doled out in blocks. The bigger your enterprise, the larger the range of IP addresses you should obtain.

Dynamic Addressing   Dynamic addressing is a technique whereby end-system hosts are assigned IP addresses at login. Novell NetWare and AppleTalk have had built-in dynamic addressing capabilities from the beginning. That's not the case with IP, though.

Remember, desktop protocols such as NetWare IPX were designed with client-server in mind, while IP was originally designed to connect a worldwide system, the Internet. IP dynamic addressing came to the fore only in the mid-1980s to accommodate diskless workstations that had nowhere to store permanent IP addresses.

A couple of earlier dynamic IP address assignment protocols led to the development of the Dynamic Host Configuration Protocol (DHCP). DHCP, now the de facto standard, uses a client-server model in which a server keeps a running list of available addresses and assigns them as requested. DHCP can also be used as a configuration tool. It supports automatic permanent allocation of IP addresses to a new host and is even used for manual address assignments as a way to communicate the new address to the client host. Figure 16-7 depicts DHCP's processes.

Dynamic allocation is popular because it's easy to configure and conserves address space. DHCP works by allocating addresses for a period of time called a *lease,* guaranteeing not to allocate the IP address to another host as long as it's out on lease. When the host logs off the network, the DHCP server is notified and restores the address to its available pool.

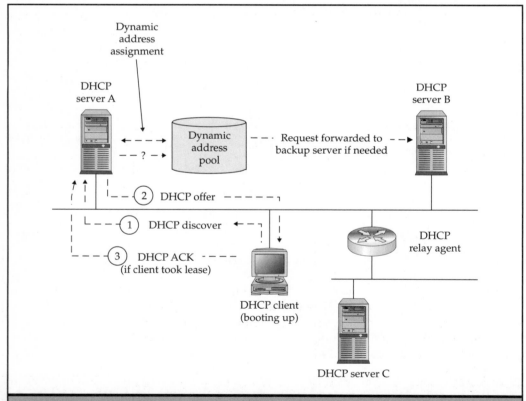

Figure 16-7.   DHCP can dynamically assign IP addresses to end-system hosts.

To assure service, multiple DHCP servers are often configured. When the host logs in, it sends a DHCP discover message across the network to the server specified by the DHCP identifier field of the message. The DHCP server responds with a DHCP offer message or passes the discover request to a backup server. The client accepts the offer by sending the server a DHCP ACK message as acknowledgment.

If the offer is accepted, the server locks the lease in the available address pool by holding the assignment in persistent memory until the lease is terminated. Lease termination occurs when the client logs off the network (accomplished usually by the user turning off his or her PC at day's end). If the identified DHCP server is down or refuses the request, after a preset timeout period the client can be configured to send a discover request to a backup DHCP server. If the server isn't on the same subnet, a router can be configured as a DHCP relay agent to steer the request message to the LAN segment on which the server resides.

Domain Name System

As discussed in our review of internetworking fundamentals in Chapter 2, people almost always reach network nodes by name, not by address. Think about it—how many times have you typed a dotted-decimal IP address into the address field in your browser? In most cases, you type in a URL instead, or simply click one sitting beneath a hypertext link on a Web page.

The service used to map names on the Internet is called the Domain Name System (DNS). A DNS name has two parts: host name and domain name. Taking toby.velte.com as an example, *toby* is the host (in this case, a person's PC), and *velte.com* is the domain. Up until 2000, domain names had to be registered with InterNIC (which stands for Internet Network Information Center), a U.S. government agency. However, that responsibility was transferred to several private companies, taking the government out of the URL business.

The IETF has specified that domain name suffixes be assigned based on the type of organization the autonomous system is, as listed in Table 16-2.

Domain	Autonomous System Type
.com	Commercial company
.edu	Educational institution
.gov	Governmental agency
.org	Nonprofit organization
.net	Network provider

Table 16-2. IETF Domain Name Suffixes

There are also geographical top-level domains defined by country. For example, .fr for France, .ca for Canada, .de for Germany (as in Deutschland), and so on.

For domain names to work, they must at some point be mapped to IP addresses so routers can recognize them. This mapping is called *name resolution*—a task performed by name servers. Domain Name Systems distribute databases across many servers in order to satisfy resolution requests. A large enterprise would distribute its DNS database throughout its internetwork topology. People can click their way around the Internet because their DNS databases are distributed worldwide. Figure 16-8 depicts the name services process.

When a client needs to send a packet, it must map the destination's symbolic name to its IP address. The client must have what's called *resolver software* configured in order to do this. The client's resolver software sends a query to a local DNS server, receives the resolution back, writes the IP address into the packet's header, and transmits. The name-to-IP mapping is then cached in the client for a preset period of time. As long as the client has the mapping for a name in cache, it bypasses the query process altogether.

Name Server Configuration   Many internetworks have multiple DNS servers for speed and redundancy, especially larger autonomous systems on which hosts frequently come and go. Usually, name services are handled from the central server within the internetwork. For example, NT networks have so-called primary domain controller (PDC) servers, which are responsible for various housekeeping duties, including logon requests.

Besides DNS, the other two major naming services are the Windows Internet Name Service (WINS) and Sun Microsystems' Network Information Service (NIS). While DNS is optimized for Internet mappings, WINS and NIS manage name services at the internetwork level. WINS servers use DHCP to field requests, because DNS doesn't lend itself to handling dynamic names. (It wants them stored permanently.) NIS performs similar duty among UNIX hosts.

DNS is an important standard. You're able to click between hosts throughout the world because there are hundreds of thousands of DNS servers across the globe, exchanging and caching name mappings across routing domains so that it takes you a minimum of time to connect to a new Web site.

Campus Network Designs

The term *campus network* is a bit of a misnomer. What's meant is any local internetwork with a high-speed backbone. For example, the local network of a company's headquarters located entirely in a skyscraper is an example of a campus network. The term has had such heavy use in computer marketing that it's stuck as the term for medium-to-large local networks. Whatever it's called, a number of models have been developed for how to configure campus networks. We'll review them here.

The Switch-Router Configuration

The so-called switch-router configuration covers the access and distribution layers of the three-layer hierarchical network design model. The two layers are considered together because the distribution routers are generally located in the same building as host devices being given network access.

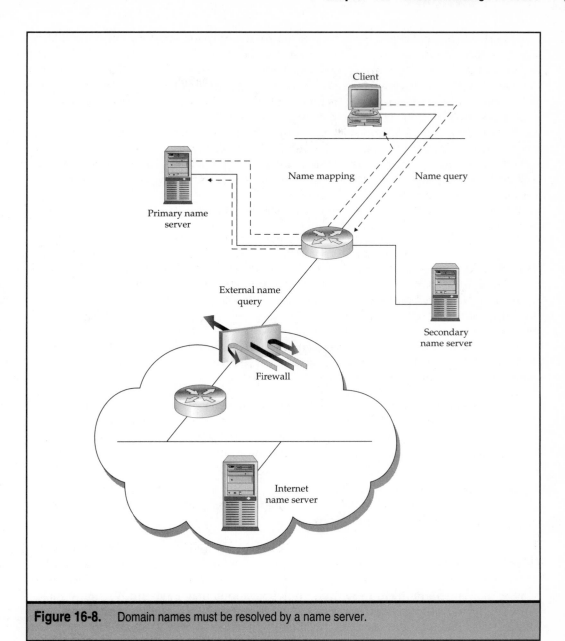

Figure 16-8. Domain names must be resolved by a name server.

Access-Layer Configuration   The access layer of the three-layer hierarchical model is largely a function of the so-called switch-router configuration. The major exception to this is remote access, covered later in this chapter (see the section titled "Connecting Remote Sites"). Configuring the access layer is largely a matter of wiring together hosts in a department or floor of a building. As far as physical media, we'll assume that Category 5 unshielded twisted pair (UTP) cable is used to wire hosts into access devices.

An important consideration, when configuring the access and distribution layers, is what type of network you'll be deploying. Most access-layer LAN segments being designed today run over Fast Ethernet specification, the 100-Mbps variant of the Ethernet standard. Token Ring has by all appearances lost the standards war to Ethernet, its use limited to IBM-dominated customer enterprises.

These decisions dictate what Cisco products to configure and to some extent how to lay out your topology.

Selecting Access-Layer Technology   Nowadays, if you have a choice, it's pretty much a given that you'll use Fast Ethernet for the access layer. It's fast, cheap, and the talent pool of network administrators knows this LAN specification best. If you have 4- or 16-Mbps Token Ring or 10-Mbps Ethernet, your choices are somewhat more limited. You also must be careful that any existing cable plant meets the physical requirements specified by the LAN technology.

Exactly how you lay out the access layer is a little more complicated. If you've gathered the needs analysis information discussed earlier, that data will go a long way toward telling you two important things:

▼   **Workgroup hierarchy**   Large homogenous workgroups lend themselves to flat switched networks. For example, large customer service departments or help desks tend to connect to a fairly consistent set of hosts to run a limited set of applications. These shops are great candidates for flat (non-VLAN) switched networks.

▲   **Traffic loads**   If traffic volumes will be heavy and QoS policies stringent, you might want to look at a VLAN switched network, or at least high-bandwidth routed network configurations.

As you answer these two questions for various areas across the topology, the configuration begins to take shape. Quite often, this process is iterated floor by floor and building by building. This shouldn't surprise you. After all, networking isn't the only field of endeavor that is geographical in nature. So is operations management; it usually makes sense for managers to group certain types of workers and/or certain types of work tasks into one physical location.

Physical Layout   The classical access-layer topology is the data closet-MDF layout. A *data closet* (also called a *wiring closet* or *phone closet*) is a small room housing patch panels connecting hosts to hubs or access switch ports. The patch panel is where networks start. A *patch panel* is a passive device with rows of RJ-45 jacks similar to the RJ-11 jacks for telephones. The host device's unshielded twisted pair (UTP) cable plugs into one jack, and a cable from another jack plugs into the switch port. This modular arrangement gives flexibility in moving devices between ports.

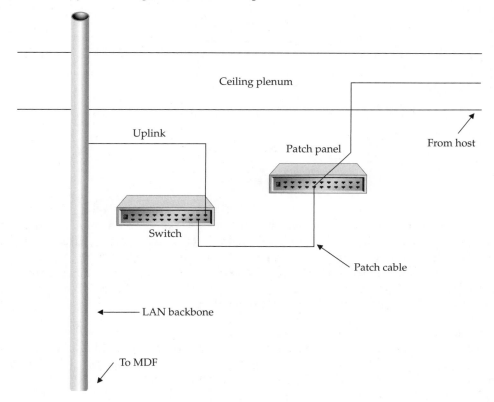

Signals go through the switch by going out its uplink port to connect to the building's riser. *Riser* refers to the bundle of individual cables running from each floor down to a termination point. An *uplink* connects the switch "up" in the logical sense, in that the riser is headed toward a larger piece of equipment—usually a router or a LAN switch.

MDF stands for *main distribution facility*—usually a room in a secure location on the building's first floor. The MDF serves as the termination point for the wiring emanating from the data closets, often equipment for both voice and data. The trend has been to locate the MDF in the enterprise's computer room if there's one in the building. Depending on the building's setup, the backbone travels either through holes punched through the floors or through the elevator shaft.

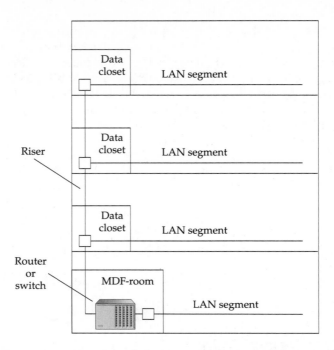

A riser's medium is almost always fiber-optic cable in larger buildings. The main reason for using fiber is that it can carry data more than 100 meters and is unaffected by electrical noise in buildings. But there's also a physical reason: because a riser hangs, over time the inexorable force of gravity will pull the twists out of a twisted pair cable by causing the copper wire strands to unwind, deteriorating its electrical properties. Fiber-optic glass won't suffer that fate because it isn't twisted.

The Switch Configuration   Various rules of thumb are applied when configuring the access layer. UTP cable can span up to 100 meters from the data closet. This is almost always more than enough on the horizontal plane. (Few work areas are wider than a football field is long.) If the data closet is located at the center of a floor, the effective span would be 200 meters. As shown in Figure 16-9, not all buildings are vertical. Many are large horizontal structures of one or two floors, such as manufacturing plants and warehouses. For very large floors, the practice is to place data closets on either side.

From a logical standpoint, it doesn't make sense to place a router or LAN switch on every floor. Doing so would be prohibitively expensive and, just as important, would waste precious IP address space, because each LAN segment must have a unique IP address. The strategy, then, is to minimize the number of router interfaces servicing a given number of hosts. Switches fulfill this.

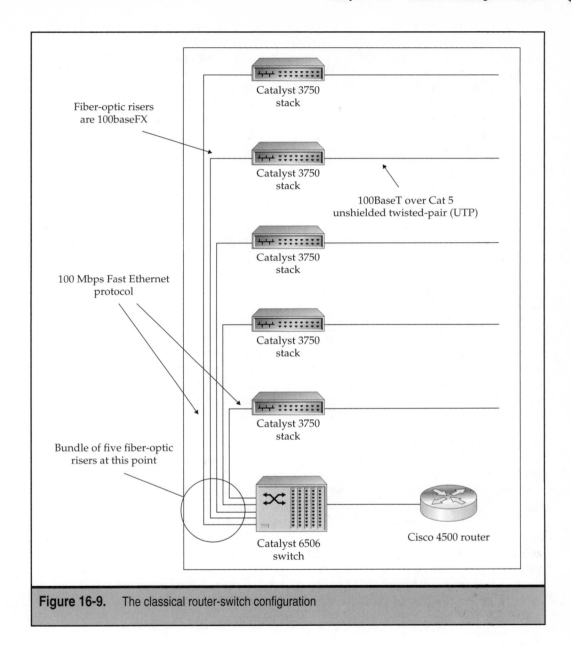

Fiber-optic risers
are 100baseFX

Catalyst 3750
stack

Catalyst 3750
stack

100BaseT over Cat 5
unshielded twisted-pair (UTP)

Catalyst 3750
stack

100 Mbps Fast Ethernet
protocol

Catalyst 3750
stack

Catalyst 3750
stack

Bundle of five fiber-optic
risers at this point

Cisco 4500 router

Catalyst 6506
switch

Figure 16-9.   The classical router-switch configuration

Figure 16-9 shows a configuration for a medium-sized company holding a few hundred employees in a building. To connect users on each floor, at least one Cisco Catalyst 3750 is placed in each data closet. Catalyst 3750 models connect 12, 24, or 48 hosts per unit and are stackable up to nine units per stack. The size of the stack depends on the number of employees on the floor. Which particular Catalyst 3750 model you use depends on the population density: some models support 12 ports for a stack density of 108 ports, and others support 48 ports for a density of 432 ports. If the population goes beyond 432, simply put another stack in the data closet to increase the number of ports.

The bottom left of Figure 16-9 shows how a riser is not a backbone in the proper sense of the term. The uplink running out of the Catalyst 3750 on the ground floor expands the riser bundle to a total of five fiber cables, which are essentially long wires used to avoid having to put a terminating device on each floor. Think of riser cables as "feeder wires" instead of as a backbone.

The LAN technology throughout the example building is Fast Ethernet, which runs at 100 Mbps. That speed is plenty for connecting most individual host devices. In practical terms, this means our riser is heading into MDF with 500 Mbps raw bandwidth, so a fast device is needed to handle the connections. We've configured a Cisco Catalyst 6506 switch for the job. With a 32-Gbps backplane, the Catalyst 6506 has plenty of horsepower to maintain satisfactory throughput for traffic from the five LAN segments. This box has six module slots, but a single 12-port 100FX card will handle all five LAN segments, leaving plenty of room for growth. A second slot is used to connect to the outside, leaving three open slots.

Figure 16-9 draws out the inherent advantages of LAN switching. You'll remember from Chapter 6 that a switch is roughly ten times quicker when it has a MAC address in its switching table. Our example company has 300 employees, and the Catalyst 6506 has more than adequate memory and backplane speed to handle a switching table of that size. (It can handle thousands.) Because the switch is talking to all 300 hosts, it has their MAC addresses readily available, so why go through the relatively slow process of processing their IP addresses in a router?

The Access Switch Configuration   We've mentioned that most people think eventually hubs will give way to switches. What they're talking about here is *access switching*, as opposed to the LAN switching example in Figure 16-9. An access switch connects hosts to a LAN segment. This extends switched bandwidth all the way out to the desktop or server. Figure 16-10 shows a typical access switch configuration.

It wouldn't be practical to run a fiber-optic cable all the way down to the MDF for every switched host. As Figure 16-10 shows, an interim step can be configured using an access switch such as the Cisco Catalyst 2820, able to connect up to 24 devices. A lower-end switch isn't used here because it doesn't have an FX port for connecting to a fiber-optic riser.

It should be pointed out that in high-density environments, users are faced with either configuring high-end Catalyst switches in the data closet or running riser cables to the MDF.

The Switch-Router Configuration   To be able to internetwork, users need to be routed at some point. The standard practice is to configure a local router in the MDF room. That way, users inside the enterprise are connected to the enterprise internetwork for intramural communications, and to the firewall to access the Internet.

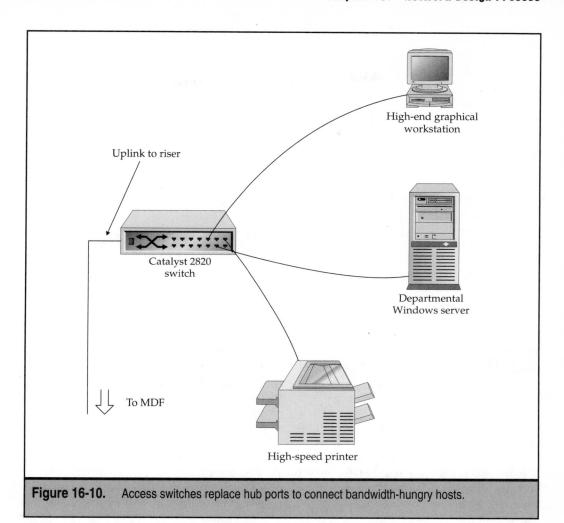

Figure 16-10.   Access switches replace hub ports to connect bandwidth-hungry hosts.

Figure 16-11 zooms in on our example company's MDF room. A Cisco 3700 router is configured in this situation because it has eight module slots that can accommodate LAN or WAN modules. One slot is filled with a one-port 100BaseTX LAN module to connect the Catalyst 6500 switch; the other houses a one-port T1 WAN module, connecting the building to the outside world.

If you're thinking that with all the bandwidth floating around the building, a mere 1.544-Mbps pipe to the outside might not provide sufficient capacity, you're catching on.

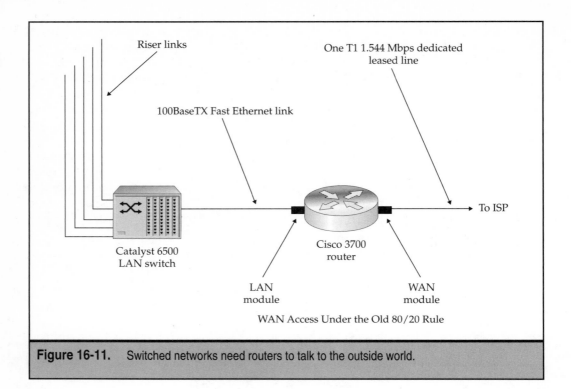

Figure 16-11.   Switched networks need routers to talk to the outside world.

A T1 link indeed might not be enough, depending on how much of the local traffic load flows to the outside.

The New 80/20 Rule   Remember the 80/20 rule discussed earlier in the chapter (see the section "The Three-Layer Hierarchical Design Model")? The traditional dictum has been that only 20 percent of the traffic goes to the outside. But things have changed. Now the gurus are talking about the "new 80/20 rule," also known as the 20/80 rule, where as much as 80 percent of traffic can go to the outside as users reach into the Internet to download files, talk to other parts of the enterprise intranet, or even deal with trading partners via an extranet.

The single biggest driver turning the 80/20 rule on its head is e-commerce, where networked computers are taking over traditionally human-based sales transactions. Web sites such as Amazon.com and E*TRADE are famous for cutting out the middleman, but electronic business-to-business trading—called electronic data interchange (EDI)—is generating more IP traffic with each passing day.

Assuming the new 80/20 rule holds for our example enterprise, the MDF room might be configured along the lines of Figure 16-12, where a much fatter pipe is extended to the outside in the form of a T3 line—a 43-Mbps leased-line digital WAN link medium.

Now the router is bigger and the switch is smaller. If the users are talking to the outside 80 percent of the time, there's less need to switch traffic within the building. We've configured a Cisco Catalyst 2900 switch instead of the Catalyst 6500 because there's less LAN switching work to do. The high-end Cisco 7206 router is configured for greater throughput capacity, with a faster processor and a six-slot chassis.

At 45 Mbps, T3 runs nearly 30 times faster than a T1 line. More and more enterprises are turning to T3 to make the point-to-point connection to their ISPs. Few, however, need all that capacity, so most ISPs resell a portion of the bandwidth to individual customers according to their needs, a practice called *fractionalizing,* in which the customer signs up for only a fraction of the link's capacity.

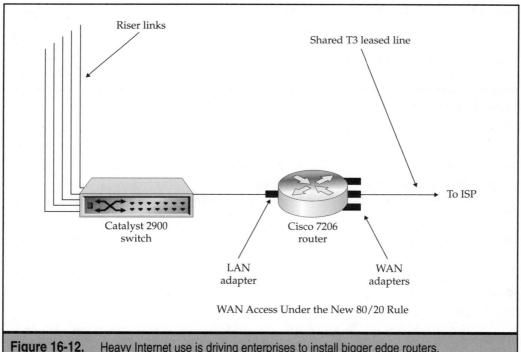

Figure 16-12. Heavy Internet use is driving enterprises to install bigger edge routers.

Choosing a High-Speed Backbone

Backbones are used to connect major peer network nodes. A backbone link connects two particular nodes, but the term *backbone* often is used to refer to a series of backbone links. For example, a campus backbone might extend over several links.

Backbone

Backbone links move data between backbone devices only. They don't handle traffic between LAN segments within a site. That's done at the distribution layer of the three-layer hierarchical model by LAN switches and routers. Backbones concentrate on moving traffic at very high speeds over land.

Campus backbones obviously cover a short distance, usually via underground fiber-optic cabling. WAN backbones—used by big enterprises and ISPs—move traffic between cities. Most WAN backbone links are operated by so-called Internet backbone providers, although many large enterprises operate their own high-speed long-distance links. WAN links run over high-speed fiber-optic cable links strung underground, on electrical py-lons, and even under oceans. Satellite links are also becoming common. Regardless of transport medium, and whether it's a campus or WAN backbone, they share the following characteristics:

▼ **Minimal packet manipulation**   Such processing as access control list enforcement and firewall filtering are kept out of the backbone to speed throughput. For this reason, most backbone links are switched, not routed.

■ **High-speed devices**   A relatively slow device like a Cisco 4500 would not be configured onto a high-speed backbone. The two ends of a backbone link generally operate over a Catalyst 6500 link or faster.

▲ **Fast transport**   Most high-speed backbones are built atop transport technology of 1 Gbps or higher.

The two main backbone technologies now are ATM and Gigabit Ethernet. FDDI is more widely installed than either, but with a total capacity of only 100 Mbps, few new FDDI installations are going into high-speed backbones.

ATM Backbones   Asynchronous Transfer Mode (ATM) uses a fixed-length format instead of the variable-length packets Ethernet uses. The fixed-length format lends itself to high-speed throughput because the hardware always knows exactly where each cell begins. For this reason, ATM has a very positive ratio between payload and network control overhead traffic. This architecture also lends itself to QoS—a big plus for operating critical backbone links.

Figure 16-13 shows a campus backbone built over ATM. The configuration uses Catalyst 6500 LAN switches for the outlying building and a high-end Catalyst 8500 Multiservice switch router to handle traffic hitting the enterprise's central server farm.

A *blade* is an industry term for a large printed circuit board that is basically an entire networking device on a single module. Blades plug into chassis slots. For a Catalyst switch to talk ATM, the appropriate adapter blade must be configured into the chassis. The LightStream 1010 blade is used here because it's designed for short-haul traffic—there are other "edge" ATM blades for WAN traffic. One reason for this is to allow Cisco to support different technologies in a single product.

Cisco ATM devices use the LAN emulation (LANE) adapter technology to integrate with campus Ethernet networks.

Switched WAN backbones run over very high-speed fiber-optic trunks running the SONET specification. Most new trunks being pulled are OC-48, which run at about 2.5 Gbps. OC stands for Optical Carrier, and SONET stands for Synchronous Optical Network. This is a standard developed by Bell Communications Research for very high-speed networks over fiber-optic cable. The slowest SONET specification, OC-1, runs at

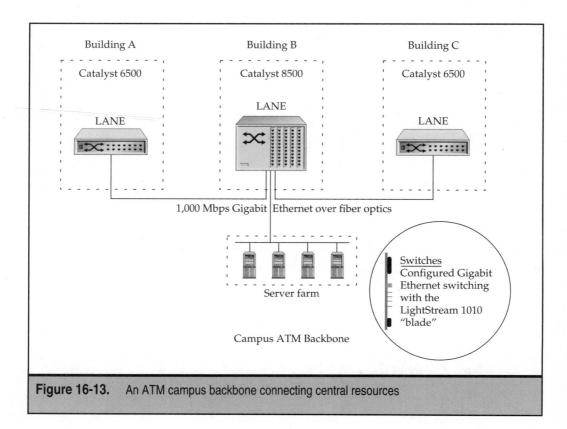

Figure 16-13.   An ATM campus backbone connecting central resources

52 Mbps—about the same speed as T3. OC SONET is an important technology because it represents the higher-speed infrastructure "pipe" the Internet needs to continue expanding. We mention this here because ATM and Gigabit Ethernet R&D efforts are carried out with the SONET specification in mind, and it's the presumed WAN link transport.

Gigabit Ethernet Backbone   Although Gigabit Ethernet is a much newer technology than ATM, many network managers are turning to it for their backbone needs instead of ATM. Figure 16-14 shows that a Gigabit Ethernet backbone can be configured using the same Catalyst platforms as for ATM. This is done by configuring Gigabit Ethernet blades instead of ATM blades. Note, also, that the same fiber-optic cabling can be used for Gigabit Ethernet, but the adapters must be changed to those designed to support Gigabit Ethernet instead of ATM.

As you might imagine, the technology-specific blades and adapters represent the different electronics needed to process either variable-length Ethernet packets or fixed-length ATM cells.

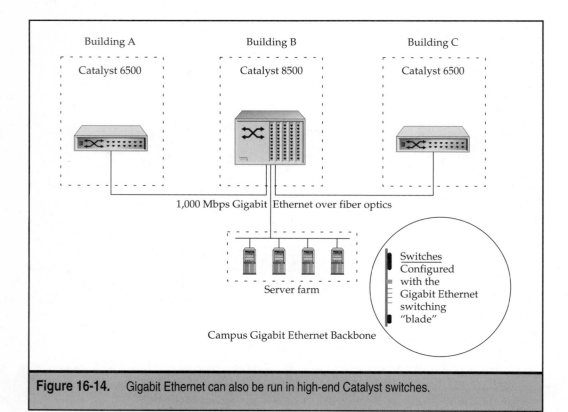

Figure 16-14.   Gigabit Ethernet can also be run in high-end Catalyst switches.

Connecting Remote Sites

There are two kinds of remote locations: the branch and the small office/home office (SOHO). The defining difference between the two is the type of connection. Because they have only one or two users online at any given moment, SOHO sites use dial-in connections, while branch sites use some form of a dedicated circuit. Three major remote connection technologies are configured here. You might want to flip back to Chapter 2 to review how these respective technologies work.

Frame Relay   Frame Relay is ideal for "bursty" WAN traffic. In other words, dedicated leased lines such as T1 or T3 only make economic sense if they're continually used. Frame Relay solves that problem by letting users share WAN infrastructure with other enterprises. Frame Relay can do this because it's a packet-switched data network (PSDN), in which end-to-end connections are virtual. You only need to buy a local phone circuit between your remote site and a nearby Frame Relay drop point. After that point, your packets intermix with those from hundreds of other enterprises.

Normally, a device called a FRAD is needed to talk to a Frame Relay network. FRAD stands for Frame Relay Assembler/Disassembler, which parses data streams into the proper Frame Relay packet format. But using a mere FRAD only gets you connected and offers little in the way of remote management, security, and QoS. Cisco has built Frame Relay capability into many of its routers to provide more intelligence over Frame Relay connections. Figure 16-15 shows a typical Frame Relay configuration using Cisco gear.

Because Frame Relay uses normal serial line connections, no special interfaces need be installed in a router to make it Frame Relay–compatible. The Cisco 2600 router is a cost-effective solution for the stores in Figure 16-15's example, because they have sufficient throughput capacity to handle traffic loads these remote locations are likely to generate.

Integrated Services Digital Network   Integrated Services Digital Network (ISDN) can be used for either dial-in or dedicated remote connections. It provides much more bandwidth than normal analog modem telephone connections, but must be available from a local carrier to be used on your premises. ISDN has channel options called BRI and PRI. BRI has two so-called B-channels to deliver 128-Kbps bandwidth and is usually used for dial-in connections from home or small offices, or for backup in case the main connection fails. PRI packages 23 B-channels, for about 1.48-Mbps bandwidth, and is generally used for full-time multiuser connections. This is commonly referred to as a T1.

Figure 16-16 shows a typical Cisco ISDN configuration. The Cisco 800 series router is targeted to connect ISDN users. The 804 has four ports, and the 801 has one port. If, however, VPN connection is required, the Cisco 1721 Access Router must be configured. It's more costly, but it has the electronics and software to handle encryption/decryption that VPN networking requires.

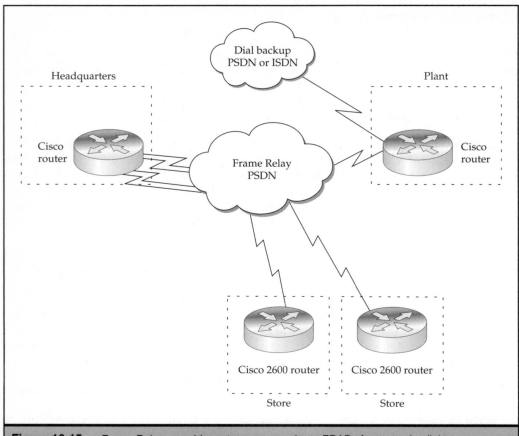

Figure 16-15. Frame Relay–capable routers are superior to FRADs for managing links.

Digital Subscriber Line   Digital Subscriber Line (DSL) is competing with ISDN for the small office/home office market. To use DSL, you must be serviced by a local telephone switch office that supports DSL and be within a certain distance of it—usually a few miles.

▼   **ADSL**   Characterized by asymmetrical data rates, where more data comes down from the phone company than the user can send back up. This means that ADSL should be selectively used where traffic characteristics match this constraint—in other words, where the user does a lot of downloading but not a lot of uploading. This is the case with most Internet users, though, and ADSL has become very popular where the phone companies offer it.

■ **SDSL** Characterized by symmetrical data rates, where the same amount of data goes either way. This is usually a more expensive solution than ADSL.

▲ **IDSL** A slower symmetrical solution to locations that are not close enough to the local telephone switch office, it offers a maximum throughput of 144 Kbps in both directions.

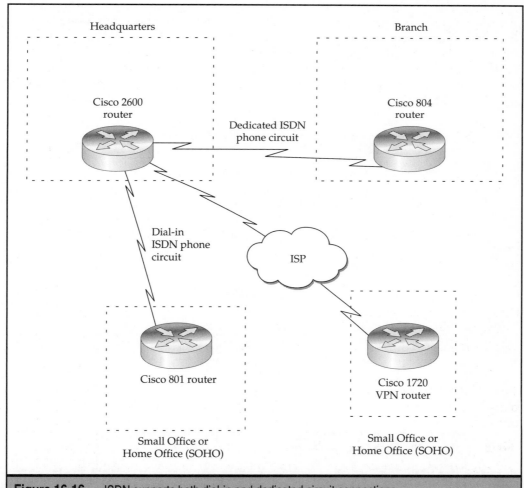

Figure 16-16. ISDN supports both dial-in and dedicated circuit connections.

The configuration in Figure 16-17 shows a Cisco 827 ADSL (Asymmetric Digital Subscriber Line) router. The Cisco 827 looks like a fat radar detector, but has an Ethernet interface on the back to connect local users.

Cable Modem   Cable modems are good alternatives if traffic needs to flow downstream. Users can expect rates from 500 Kbps to 1.5 Mbps to be sent to their computers; however, this speed is not achieved going back upstream. This is because cable modems send traffic—as the name implies—across the cable television infrastructure. Since your television set never sends information back to the cable company, the system was never designed to accommodate two-way traffic. In order to send information back to the ISP, traffic must be sent across a dial-up telephone line.

One such modem is the Cisco uBR905 Cable Access Router. It features downstream speeds of up to 41.4 Mbps, but this rate is variable, depending on how many other subscribers are sharing bandwidth on the cable line.

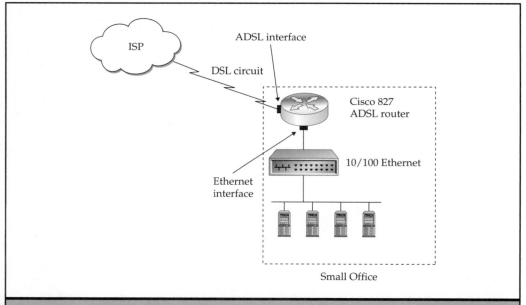

Figure 16-17.   The Cisco Speedrunner 675 is ideal for DSL connections.

CHAPTER 17

Troubleshooting Cisco Networks

Keeping an internetwork going is a full-time job. As you saw earlier, problems emerge with such frequency that the industry invented routing protocols to deal with them automatically, not even waiting for a network administrator to intervene. They do a pretty good job, at least with problems that can be ameliorated by detouring to a new route. But changing routes is only a temporary solution. In order for a network to run effectively, all its components must be running properly and constantly. After all, delivering available bandwidth to users under normal circumstances is hard enough without having a LAN segment out of commission or a router at partial capacity.

For this reason, a big part of a network team's time is spent troubleshooting. Problems range from a single user unable to access a service, to an entire LAN segment crashing. Troubleshooting isn't just a matter of finding and fixing broken parts; much of it is dedicated to fixing performance bottlenecks. When a problem emerges, the network administrator often has no idea which device is causing the trouble. And once the problem device is identified, the cause of the problem must be diagnosed. Then decisions must be made on how to fix the situation.

A methodical approach should be taken to troubleshooting; otherwise, a lot of time can be wasted trying to figure out what's causing the problem. Like a doctor, the troubleshooter must recognize the symptoms, associate them with a set of probable causes, and then progressively narrow down the list until the culprit is finally identified. From there, a proper action plan must be devised and implemented. That's troubleshooting.

In this chapter, we'll review how to troubleshoot problems in a variety of Cisco configurations by running through some troubleshooting scenarios. For simplicity's sake, we'll assume IP as the network protocol and the Microsoft Windows platform as the host. Although the terminology can vary, networking problems are largely the same, regardless of the protocol or host environment. We'll also restrict the examples to troubleshooting routers, which is where most of the action is.

THE MECHANICS OF NETWORK TROUBLESHOOTING

In internetworks, trouble is often caused either by failing device hardware or a configuration problem. The location of most problems can be identified remotely, and to some extent the problems can also be diagnosed and even fixed remotely (but the hardware must still be running for that). By "fixing remotely," we mean without walking over and actually inspecting and touching the device; we don't necessarily mean being geographically removed. If, say, an enterprise's campus internetwork is experiencing a problem, network administrators usually do most troubleshooting tasks without even leaving their desks.

In Cisco environments, remote work can be done through a network management console or by logging directly into a device's IOS command-line environment via Telnet. As you learned, the Cisco NMS consoles—Resource Manager Essentials and CWSI Campus—use their graphical interfaces to indirectly manipulate IOS commands inside the remote device. Thus, most of the real troubleshooting work takes place inside the device's IOS environment. Here are the major IOS commands used to perform most troubleshooting tasks:

▼ **ping**   Indicates whether "echo" packets are reaching a destination and returning. For example, if you enter **ping 10.1.1.1,** IOS will return the percentage of packets that echoed back from the 10.1.1.1 interface.

■ **trace**   Reports the actual path taken to a destination. For example, if you enter **trace ip 10.1.1.1**, IOS will list every hop the message takes to reach the destination 10.1.1.1 interface.

▲ **show**   Reports configuration and status information on devices and networks. For example, the **show memory** command displays how much memory is assigned to each network address and how much is free.

The source of problems must be in either device or network media (cabling, connectors, and so on), even if the trouble is in a cable, the way to it is through IOS. The **ping** and **trace** commands are used to locate problems. If the device is still running, the **show** and **debug** commands are employed to diagnose them. Actual fixes are done by changing either the hardware or its configuration. The **debug** command is similar to **show,** except it generates far more detailed information on device operations—so much so that running **debug** may greatly slow device performance.

Network Troubleshooting Methods

Problems are usually brought to a network administrator's attention by users. They want to know why they can't access a service within the enterprise's internetwork, or they complain that performance is slow. The location and nature of the complaint are themselves strong clues as to what's causing the problem. Many times, the administrator immediately knows what's wrong and how to fix it, but oftentimes an investigation must be launched to figure out which device is the source of the trouble, what's causing it, and what the best way to fix it is. The network administrator must find answers by methodical troubleshooting. As you might imagine, troubleshooting largely works by a process of elimination, as in the following:

▼ **What are the symptoms?**   Usually this boils down to users not being able to reach a destination. Knowing both endpoints of a network problem—the source and destination addresses—is the base information in most troubleshooting situations.

■ **Where do I start looking?**   Does the scenario fit a known pattern that suggests probable causes? For example, if a server isn't responding to service requests from a client, there could be a problem with the server or the client itself. If the server is working okay for other clients, then it might be the client device. If not that, then the problem must reside somewhere between the two.

■ **Where do I start?** There are rules of thumb that short-list what's most likely causing a certain type of symptom. The administrator should diagnose "best-candidate" causes first. For example, if a server accessed via a WAN link seems slow to remote dial-in users, the link could be going bad, usage could be up, there could be a shortage of buffer memory in the router interface servicing the link, or the hosts could be misconfigured. One of these probable causes will explain the problem 95 percent of the time.

▲ **What's the action plan?** Finding the exact cause of a problem in a malfunctioning device means dealing with one variable at a time. For example, it wouldn't make sense to replace all network interface modules in a router before rebooting. Doing so might fix the problem, but it wouldn't define the exact source or even what fixed it. In science, this is called changing one variable at a time. The best practice is to zero in on the source by cutting variables down one by one. That way, the problem can be replicated, the fix validated as a good one, and the exact cause recorded for future reference.

Most internetwork problems manifest themselves as either seriously degraded performance or as "destination unreachable" timeout messages. Sometimes, the problem is widespread; other times, it's limited to a LAN segment or even to a specific host. Let's take a look at some typical problems mapped to their probable causes. Table 17-1 outlines problems with host connectivity. (Hosts are usually single-user PCs, but not always.)

Unfortunately, most internetwork problems aren't limited to a single host. If a problem exists in a router or is spread throughout an area, many users and servers are affected. Table 17-2 outlines a couple of typical network problems that are more widespread.

Many times, networks and services are reachable, but performance is unacceptably slow. Table 17-3 outlines factors that can affect performance within a local network. It doesn't address WAN links, however. They're covered separately later in this chapter because serial lines involve a slightly different set of technologies and problems.

Symptoms	Probable Causes
Host can't access networks beyond local LAN segment.	Misconfigured settings in host device, such as bad default gateway IP address or bad subnet mask. The gateway router is malfunctioning.
Host can't access certain services beyond local LAN segment.	Misconfigured extended access list on a router between the host and the server. Misconfigured firewall, if the server is beyond the autonomous system.

Table 17-1. Typical Host Access Problems and Causes

Symptoms	Probable Causes
Most users can't access a server.	Misconfigured default gateway specification in the remote server. Misconfigured access list in the remote server.
Connections to an area can't be made when one path is down.	Routing protocol not converging within the routing domain. All interfaces on router handling alternative path not configured with secondary IP addresses (discontinuous addressing).

Table 17-2. Typical Router Problems and Causes

Troubleshooting Host IP Configuration

If a user is having trouble accessing services and the overall network seems to be okay, a good place to start looking for the cause of the problem is inside that person's computer. There are a couple of things that could be misconfigured in the user's host computer:

▼ **Incorrect IP Information** The IP address or subnet mask information could be missing or incorrect.

▲ **Incorrect Default Gateway** The default gateway router could be misconfigured.

To refresh on the subject, every host has a default gateway specified in the host's network settings. A *default gateway* is an interface on a local router that is used for passing messages sent by the host to addresses beyond the LAN. A default gateway (also called a *gateway of last resort*) is configured because it makes sense for one router to handle most of

Symptoms	Probable Causes
Poor server response; hard to make and keep connections.	Bad network link, usually caused by a malfunctioning network interface module or LAN segment medium. Mismatched access lists (in meshed internetwork with multiple paths). Congested link, overwhelmed by too much traffic. Poorly configured load balancing (routing protocol metrics).

Table 17-3. Campus LAN Performance Problems and Their Causes

a host's outbound traffic in order to keep an updated cache on destination IP addresses and routes to them. A host must have at least one gateway, and a second one is often configured for redundancy in case the primary gateway goes down.

Checking the Host IP Address Information

Misconfigured network parameters in desktop hosts are usually attributable to a mistake by the end user. Keep in mind that—on Windows computers, at least—any user can easily access and modify network settings. To check the hosts in Windows XP, for example, click the Start button on the menu bar, then choose Connect To | Show All Connections. From the resulting list of network connections, right-click the appropriate network icon, and then select Properties. Select the General tab and in the This Connection Uses the Following Items box, click both Internet Protocol (TCP/IP) and Properties. In Windows NT/2000, click the Start button on the menu bar, and then choose Control Panel | Network | Configuration, and, finally, TCP/IP Properties. This will allow you to set the IP address and default gateway.

The protocol will usually point to a network interface card (NIC) connecting the host to the LAN, as is the case with the TCP/IP Ethernet PC card highlighted in Figure 17-1.

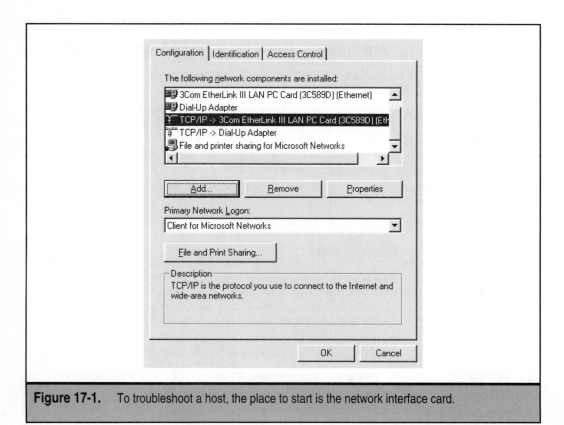

Figure 17-1.   To troubleshoot a host, the place to start is the network interface card.

(If the host dials into the internetwork, the protocol that points to the dial-up adapter should be selected instead.)

Once you're pointed at the right NIC, start by making sure that the host is identifying itself correctly to the network. To do that, choose Network | IP Address to review the settings in the IP Address tab. The example in Figure 17-2 shows a statically defined IP address and subnet. These must match what's on file for the host in the config file of the router serving as the default gateway. If the Obtain An IP Address Automatically selection is checked, the host's IP address is dynamically assigned by a server—a Dynamic Host Control Protocol (DHCP) server. If DHCP or an equivalent is in use, misconfigured host IP information is less likely, but the troubleshooter could check the situation at the address server.

Next, make sure the host's declared IP address is the right one by logging into its gateway router and entering the **show arp** command. You'll remember that ARP stands for Address Resolution Protocol, a utility that maps the physical device's media access control (layer 2) address to its assigned IP (layer 3) address in order to handle the final stage of delivery between the gateway router and the host. Figure 17-3 shows the ARP table in

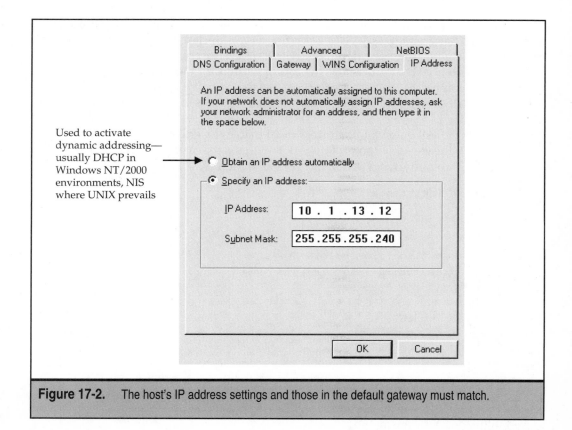

Figure 17-2. The host's IP address settings and those in the default gateway must match.

```
                                   MAC address
                                        ↓
vsigate#show arp
Protocol   address      Age (min)   Hardware Addr   Type   Interface

Internet   10.1.13.11       0       0050.0465.395c  ARPA   Ethernet1
Internet   10.1.11.1       12       0060.3eba.a6a0  SNAP   TokenRing0
Internet   10.1.13.12       9       00a0.c92a.4823  ARPA   Ethernet1
Internet   10.1.11.2        –       0006.f4c5.5f1d  SNAP   TokenRing0
Internet   10.1.11.3      190       0006.c1de.4ab9  SNAP   TokenRing0
Internet   10.1.12.3        –       0006.f4c5.5fdd  SNAP   TokenRing1
Internet   10.1.13.12      15       0050.04d7.1fa4  ARPA   Ethernet1
```

Figure 17-3.   The host's IP address must match the one for the gateway router in the ARP file.

the config file of our example gateway router. The shaded line shows that the Ethernet interface indeed has an address 10.1.13.12 on file, as was declared in the host's IP Address tab. The host itself is uniquely identified by the MAC address of its NIC.

Another potential host problem is the config settings for the default gateway itself. In other words, you have to make sure the host has the correct IP address configured as its default gateway router. To do that, click the Gateway tab in the Network dialog box, shown in Figure 17-4.

The host's default gateway IP address must match the one set for the network interface module on the gateway router. To check that this is the case, go to the gateway router and enter the **show interfaces** command, as shown here:

```
MyRouter#show interfaces
.
.
.
Ethernet1 is up, line protocol is down
 internet address is 10.1.13.1/28
 ip accounting output-packets
 ip nat inside
 ip ospf priority 255
 media-type 10BaseT
.
.
.
```

As you can see, our example interface, Ethernet1, is indeed addressed 10.1.13.1, as declared in the host's Gateway tab.

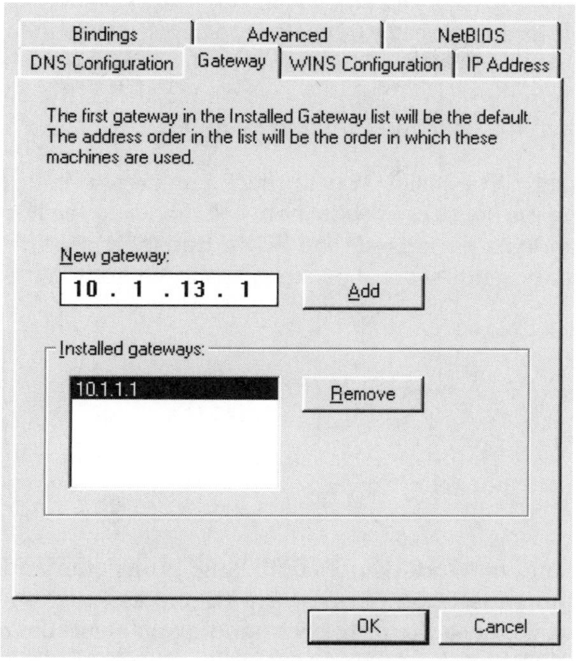

Figure 17-4.   Check to make sure the correct default gateway IP address is configured.

This is also where you can check to make sure the host's declared subnet mask matches the one on file in the gateway router. Mask/28 is also correct, because it matches the one (255.255.255.240) declared in the host's IP Address tab.

Obviously, if any of the host's network settings are incorrect, the administrator should adjust them to match the gateway router's settings, reboot the PC, and try to make a network connection. On the other hand, if the PC's settings are OK, the troubleshooter must work outward from the operable host to identify the source area of the problem.

Isolating Connectivity Problems

Most network problems have to do with the inability to connect to a desired host or service. Connectivity problems—also called "reachability problems"—come in many forms, such as attempted HTTP connections timing out, attempted terminal connections getting no response from the host, and so on. As just outlined, the troubleshooter should first make sure the host reporting the problem is itself properly configured, and then work outward. To draw an analogy, the troubleshooter must work the neighborhood door to door, much like a cop searching for clues.

Checking Between the Host and Its Gateway Router

If the host's network settings are configured properly, the next step is to work outward from the host to the gateway router. This should be done even if the host's problem is failing to connect to a remote server. Before working far afield, the best practice is to first check the link between the host and its gateway router.

Using the ping Command   The easiest way to check a link is to use the **ping** command. This command sends ping packets to a specific network device to see if it's reachable. In technical terms, **ping** sends its packets via the ICMP transport protocol instead of through UDP or TCP. It actually sends several packets, as shown here:

```
MyRouter#ping 10.1.1.100

Type escape sequence to abort.
Sending 5, 100-byte ICMP Echos to 10.1.1.100, timeout is 2 seconds:
!!!!!
Success rate is 100 percent (5/5), round-trip min/avg/max = 1/1/1 ms
MyRouter#
```

Host computers and network devices both have **ping** commands. The preceding example was taken from a Cisco router, and the ping successfully reached the destination. But one could just as well use the **ping** command available in the command line of the host. We're using a Windows host for our examples, but other platforms—such as Macs, the various UNIX platforms, IBM's OS/400, and other proprietary server architectures—all have **ping** and other basic network commands built into their operating systems.

Usually, the first ping test from a host is the link to its gateway router. On a Windows XP machine, check this by clicking the Start button in the menu bar and choosing All Programs | Accessories | Command Prompt to open a DOS command line window. Then check to see if the gateway router is responding by entering the **ping** command, as shown in the following code snippet:

```
Microsoft Windows XP [Version 5.1.2600]
(C) Copyright 1985-2001 Microsoft Corp.

C:\Documents and Settings\Tony>ping 10.1.13.1

Pinging 10.1.13.1 with 32 bytes of data:

Request timed out.
Request timed out.
Request timed out.
Request timed out.
```

```
Ping statistics for 10.1.13.1:
    Packets: Sent = 4, Received = 0, Lost = 4 (100% loss),

C:\Documents and Settings\Tony>
```

The preceding example shows that four ping packets were sent to the gateway router, which failed to respond. This tells the troubleshooter a few things:

▼ The host PC's NIC is good; otherwise, MS-DOS would have generated an error message when the card failed to respond to the **ping** command.

■ The Ethernet LAN segment might be down—a condition often referred to as a "media problem." (The shared medium is apparently not working.)

▲ The network interface module on the gateway router might be faulty.

If the host checks out okay, the troubleshooter must move outward. As mentioned, the investigation should start with the link to the gateway router.

Extended Ping   As useful and utilitarian as the **ping** command is for troubleshooting, it does have its limits. When using **ping**, the source address of the **ping** is the IP address of the interface that the packet uses as it exits the router. If you need more precision out of your **ping**, you can upgrade to the *extended ping* command.

Extended ping performs a more advanced check of your system's ability to reach a particular host. This command works only at the privileged EXEC command line, whereas a regular **ping** command works in both user EXEC and privileged EXEC modes.

Usage of extended ping on Cisco routers is fairly straightforward. Simply enter **ping** at the command prompt, and then press ENTER. You will be prompted with a number of conditions and variables. The default setting is enclosed in brackets. If you like the default, simply press ENTER; otherwise, enter your preferred setting.

The following shows an example of an extended ping at work:

```
Router>ping
Protocol [ip]:
Target IP address: 64.66.150.248
Repeat count [5]: 100
Datagram size [100]:
Timeout in seconds [2]:
Extended commands [n]:
Sending 100, 100-byte ICMP Echos to 64.66.150.248, timeout is 2
seconds:
!!!!!!!!!!!!!!!!!!!!!!!!!!!!!!!!!!!!!!!!!!!!!!!!!!!!!!!!!!!!!!!!!!!!!!!!!!
!!!!!!!!!!!!!!!!!!!!!!!!!!!!!!!!
Success rate is 100 percent (100/100), round-trip min/avg/max =
12/19/280 ms
```

NOTE: The command also exists in its own form in Windows and UNIX/LINUX environments. Simply add the switches –s (UNIX/LINUX) or –t (Windows) after the **ping** command.

Using the show interfaces Command   To check whether the problem is the gateway router's interface or the LAN segment's medium, log into the gateway router, and enter the **show interfaces** command to obtain the following report:

```
MyRouter#show interfaces
Ethernet1 is up, line protocol is down
  Hardware is MyRouter, address is 0060.2fa3.fabd (bia 0060.2fa3.fabd)
  Internet address is 10.1.13.1/28
  .
  .
  .
```

In the preceding example, the router reports both that the Ethernet1 network interface module is up and the line protocol is down. The term *line protocol* denotes both the cable into the router and the LAN protocol running over it. A line protocol reported as down probably indicates that the LAN segment's shared medium—a hub, an access switch, or a cable—is faulty. From there you would physically check the medium to identify the hardware problem. (How to do that is covered later in this chapter in the section "Troubleshooting Cisco Hardware.")

Another potential condition could be that a network administrator has turned off either the interface or the line, or both. This is routinely done while a piece of equipment is being repaired, upgraded, or replaced. Notifying IOS that a piece of equipment is down for maintenance avoids having needless error messages generated by the router. The following example shows the report when a network interface module is administratively down:

```
MyRouter#show interfaces
Ethernet1 is administratively down, line protocol is down
  Hardware is MyRouter, address is 0060.2fa3.fabd (bia 0060.2fa3.fabd)
  Internet address is 10.1.13.1/28
  .
  .
  .
```

Whether a piece of equipment is down by design or because of a malfunction, it still stops traffic. So it's important to know when a piece of equipment is being worked on in order to make sure an alternative path is available to handle traffic.

If both the gateway router interface and line protocol are up and running fine, the cause of the connectivity problem probably resides in a link to another network.

Troubleshooting Problems Connecting to Other Networks

Things get a little more complicated beyond the home LAN segment. If the host can't connect beyond the gateway router, there are at once both more potential sources and more types of trouble to check out. What's meant by potential problem *sources* here is that many more hardware devices must be considered as potential causes of the reachability problem. What's meant by potential problem *types* is that such things as access lists, routing protocols, and other factors beyond hardware must now also be considered.

Using the trace Command to Pinpoint Trouble Spots   Instead of pinging outward from the host one link at a time, the route between the host and the unreachable server can be analyzed all at once using the **trace route** command. In our example Windows host, do this by choosing Start | Programs | MS-DOS Prompt to get into the host's DOS prompt. Once there, enter the **tracert** command, Microsoft's version of the **trace route** command. The example in Figure 17-5 shows the route being traced from the host PC to www.PayrollServer. AcmeEnterprises.com, which is an internal server several hops away. It's optional to use either the domain name or the IP address. Each line in the **tracert** command represents a hop along the path to the destination.

```
Microsoft(R) Windows NT(TM)
(C) Copyright 1985-1996 Microsoft Corp.

C:\>tracert www.PayrollServer.AcmeEnterprises.com

Tracing route to www.PayrollServer.AcmeEnterprises.com [10.1.22.19]
over a maximum of 30 hops:

  1    <10 ms    <10 ms    <10 ms   10.1.13.12   ◄──────── Host's gateway router
  2    <10 ms     12 ms    <10 ms   10.1.5.3
  3     17 ms     20 ms     19 ms   10.1.17.22
  4     22 ms     19 ms     23 ms   10.1.31.2                 Slow response indicates
  5    768 ms    831 ms    790 ms   10.1.49.12   ◄────────── that this router is probably
  6     31 ms     40 ms     42 ms   10.1.22.19                the culprit.

Trace complete.

C:\>
```

Figure 17-5.   The **trace route** command is a great way to pinpoint the source of a problem.

In TCP/IP internetworks, **trace route** commands work by sending three trace packets to each router three times and recording the echo response times. As with the **ping** command, trace packets use the ICMP transport protocol. However, trace packets differ from ping packets in that they have a time-to-live (TTL) field used to increment outward from the host one step at a time. The TTL field causes the packet to die when the counter hits zero. The **trace route** command uses the TTL field by sending the first trace packet sent to the nearest router with a TTL of 1, to the next router with a TTL of 2, and so on. This process is repeated until the destination host is reached—if it's reachable. The network administrator can put a limit on how many hops the trace may take to automatically stop the process if the destination proves unreachable.

The *ms* readings are milliseconds, and you can see that nearby routers naturally tend to echo back faster. Under 10 ms is fast; anything over 100 ms or so is getting slow—but one must always adjust the timings according to how many hops removed the router is. As you can see, the router in the shaded line in Figure 17-5 is the likely suspect for the slow service because of its slow response times. The probable explanation is that the router's interface or the LAN segment attached to it is either congested or experiencing hardware faults. The next step would be to Telnet into router 10.1.49.12 (if possible) and diagnose the system, the involved network interface, and so on. If making a Telnet connection isn't possible, the troubleshooter must go in through the Console or AUX port, which of course requires that somebody be physically present at the device, unless a dial-in maintenance solution has been configured beforehand.

Sometimes a trace route will locate a node that's stopping traffic altogether. An example of this is shown in Figure 17-6, where 10.1.49.12 now is dropping trace packets instead of merely returning them slowly. The asterisks indicate a null timing result because nothing came back, and the message "request timed out" is inserted. Take note that this does not necessarily mean the entire router is down. It could be that only the network interface or LAN segment that connects the suspect router may be down, or configured not to respond to pings.

If possible, first try to Telnet into the router through one of its other interfaces. If this doesn't work, the next move depends on the router's proximity. If it's nearby, go to it and log in through the Console or AUX port. If it's remote, you should contact the person responsible for dealing with it and walk that person through the diagnosis steps.

NOTE: Troubleshooting almost always takes place within the enterprise's internetwork. This is because the network team can control events only within its autonomous system. The **trace route** command is a good example of this. If you traced a route through the Internet—say, to troubleshoot a VPN connection—most lines between your gateway router and the destination node will return asterisks instead of timings, and "request timed out" messages instead of IP addresses. This is because almost all edge routers are configured by their network teams not to respond to trace routes. This is done as a security precaution. The point here is to highlight the trade-off a VPN must incur: Loss of control is exchanged for very low-cost WAN links; you generally can't troubleshoot somebody else's network.

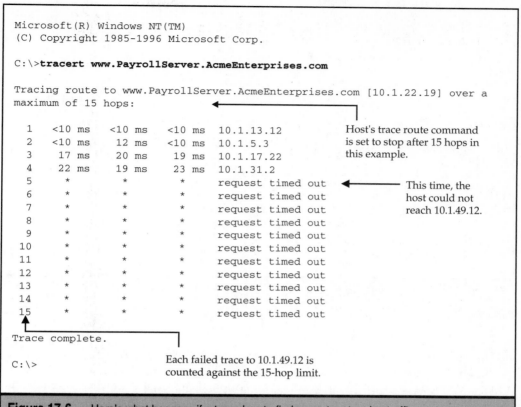

```
Microsoft(R) Windows NT(TM)
(C) Copyright 1985-1996 Microsoft Corp.

C:\>tracert www.PayrollServer.AcmeEnterprises.com

Tracing route to www.PayrollServer.AcmeEnterprises.com [10.1.22.19] over a
maximum of 15 hops:

   1    <10 ms    <10 ms    <10 ms   10.1.13.12          Host's trace route command
   2    <10 ms     12 ms    <10 ms   10.1.5.3            is set to stop after 15 hops in
   3     17 ms     20 ms     19 ms   10.1.17.22          this example.
   4     22 ms     19 ms     23 ms   10.1.31.2
   5       *         *         *     request timed out       This time, the
   6       *         *         *     request timed out       host could not
   7       *         *         *     request timed out       reach 10.1.49.12.
   8       *         *         *     request timed out
   9       *         *         *     request timed out
  10       *         *         *     request timed out
  11       *         *         *     request timed out
  12       *         *         *     request timed out
  13       *         *         *     request timed out
  14       *         *         *     request timed out
  15       *         *         *     request timed out

Trace complete.

C:\>                          Each failed trace to 10.1.49.12 is
                              counted against the 15-hop limit.
```

Figure 17-6.   Here's what happens if a traced route finds a router stopping traffic.

Using the show interfaces Command   Once the suspect network interface module has been identified, the troubleshooter must diagnose what's causing the problem. The best way to do that is to run the **show interfaces** command and review the latest statistics on the interface's operations. Remember, this information not only reflects on the interface module itself, but also gives a rich set of clues as to what's happening out on the network.

An example **show interfaces** report is given in Figure 17-7. Don't let its size and cryptic terminology intimidate you. There is indeed a lot of information in it, but nothing that takes a rocket scientist to understand.

This report is a snapshot of the interface at a particular instant in time. To check for trends, the troubleshooter must run the **show interfaces** command intermittently to look for changes. The interface is identified by private IP address 10.1.49.12/28. Remember, usually only routers on the edge of an autonomous system—firewalls, Web servers, FTP servers, and the like—use public Internet addresses. The /28 notation lets other routers know that

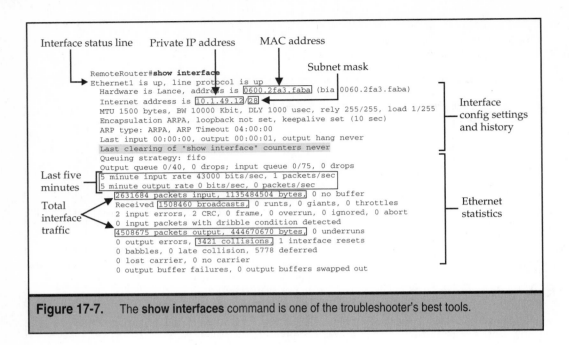

Figure 17-7. The **show interfaces** command is one of the troubleshooter's best tools.

LAN segments attached to RemoteRouter are subnetted using the 255.255.255.240 subnet mask. The notation uses 28 because the 255.255.255.240 mask has 28 bits available for network addressing (as opposed to hosts). As mentioned earlier, mismatched subnets often cause problems.

The first thing to look at is the seventh line of the **show interfaces** report that reads "Last clearing of show interfaces counters never" (highlighted in Figure 17-7). The example states that nobody has reset the report's counters to zero since the last time the router was rebooted. The length of time since the statistics were last cleared is very important because most of the statistics are absolute numbers, not relative values such as percentages. In other words, the longer IOS has been compiling the totals, the less weight the statistics should be given. For example, ten lost carriers in a day is a lot, but the same total over six months is not. To see when the last reboot was, use the **show version** command, as shown here:

```
RemoteRouter#show version
Cisco Internetwork Operating System Software
IOS (tm) 4500 Software (C4500-IS-M), Version 11.2(17),
RELEASE SOFTWARE (fc1)
Copyright (c) 1986-1999 by Cisco Systems, Inc.
Compiled Mon 04-Jan-99 18:18 by etlevynot
Image text-base: 0x600088A0, data-base: 0x60604000
```

```
ROM: System Bootstrap, Version 5.3(10) [tamb 10],
RELEASE SOFTWARE (fc1)
BOOTFLASH: 4500 Bootstrap Software (C4500-BOOT-M), Version 10.3(10),
RELEASE SOFTWARE (fc1)

RemoteRouter uptime is 2 weeks, 3 days, 13 hours, 32 minutes
System restarted by power-on
.
.
.
```

The second-to-last line in the preceding example shows that the router has been up for about two and a half weeks. Knowing this lets the troubleshooter more accurately judge whether certain error types are normal or excessive.

NOTE: Historically, there have been a wide range of interoperability issues identified between different versions of IOS. When troubleshooting, one should make note of the IOS versions running in the environment and assess the impact of running different versions.

The exception to this sampling window is the two lines sitting in the middle of Figure 17-7. These report input and output to the interface over the five minutes prior to the report having been run. A troubleshooter trying to discern a trend in traffic patterns would periodically generate the **show interfaces** report and look at these numbers.

Statistics differ on what constitutes excessive. For example, Ethernet arbitrates media access control by collisions, so it's normal for them to occur to some degree. The count of 3,421 collisions in Figure 17-7's example is OK for a period of two weeks or so, but a figure of 50,000 would indicate congested bandwidth. Broadcast packets are also normal, because they perform positive functions such as alerting routers of topology changes and providing other useful updates—again, within limits. There are over one and a half million in Figure 17-7's report, which might be excessive. What's excessive is subject to so many variables that it must be left to the judgment of the troubleshooter. That's where experience comes into play.

Many statistics should ideally be very low or even at zero (depending on the time period reported). For example, *runts* and *giants* are malformed packets sometimes caused by a poorly functioning network interface card. In a WAN link, lost carrier events probably indicate a dirty line or a failing telecommunications component.

Table 17-4 defines many of the items reported using the **show interfaces** command. Knowing the items will help you understand how they can be used to diagnose problems.

Now that we're introduced to the various statistics compiled in the **show interfaces** report, let's review how to read it. Figure 17-8 shows the Ethernet statistics portion of the report, this time with some of the more important variables highlighted. These are the variables an experienced network administrator would scan first for clues.

Statistic	Explanation
Five-minute rates (input or output)	The average number of bits and packets passing through the interface each second, as sampled over the last five-minute interval.
Aborts	Sudden termination of a message transmission's packets.
Buffer failures	Packets discarded for lack of available router buffer memory.
BW	Bandwidth of the interface in kilobits per second (Kbps). This can be used as a routing protocol metric.
Bytes	Total number of bytes transmitted through the interface.
Carrier transitions	A carrier is the electromagnetic signal modulated by data transmissions over serial lines (like the sound your modem makes). Carrier transitions are events where the signal is interrupted, often caused when the remote NIC resets.
Collisions	The number of messages retransmitted due to an Ethernet collision.
CRC	Cyclic redundancy check, a common technique for detecting transmission errors. CRC works by dividing the size of a frame's contents by a prime number and comparing the remainder with that stored in the frame by the sending node.
DLY	Delay of the interface's response time, measured in microseconds (µs), *not* milliseconds (ms).
Dribble conditions	Frames that are slightly too long, but are still processed by the interface.
Drops	The number of packets discarded for lack of space in the queue.
Encapsulation	The encapsulation method assigned to an interface (if any). Works by wrapping data in the header of a protocol to "tunnel" otherwise incompatible data through a foreign network. For example, Cisco's Inter-Switch Link (ISL) encapsulates frames from many protocols.

Table 17-4.   Definitions of Some Ethernet Statistics

Statistic	Explanation
Errors (input or output)	A condition in which it is discovered that a transmission does not match what's expected, usually having to do with the size of a frame or packet. Errors are detected using various techniques such as CRC.
Frame	The number of packets having a CRC error and a partial frame size. Usually indicates a malfunctioning Ethernet device.
Giants	Packets larger than the LAN technology's maximum packet size—1,518 bytes or more in Ethernet networks. All giant packets are discarded.
Ignored	Number of packets discarded by the interface for lack of available interface buffer memory (as opposed to router buffer memory).
Interface resets	When the interface clears itself of all packets and starts anew. Resets usually occur when it takes too long for expected packets to be transmitted by the sending node.
Keepalives	Messages sent by one network device to another to notify it that the virtual circuit between them is still active.
Last input or output	Hours, minutes, and seconds since the last packet was successfully transmitted or received by the interface. A good tool for determining when the trouble started.
Load	The load on the interface as a fraction of the number 255. For example, 64/255 is a 25 percent load. This counter can be used as a routing protocol metric.
Loopback	Whether loopback is set to on. *Loopback* is where signals are sent from the interface and then directed back toward it from some point along the communications path; used to test the link's usability.
MTU	The maximum transmission unit for packets passing through the interface, expressed in bytes.
Output hang	How long since the interface was last reset. Takes its name from the fact that the interface "hangs" because a transmission takes too long.

Table 17-4.   Definitions of Some Ethernet Statistics *(continued)*

Statistic	Explanation
Overruns	The number of times the router interface overwhelmed the receiving node by sending more packets than the node's buffers could handle. Takes its name from the fact that the router interface "overran" the sender.
Queues (input and output)	Number of packets in the queue. The number behind the slash is the queue's maximum size.
Queuing strategy	FIFO stands for "first in, first out," which means the router handles packets in that order. LIFO stands for "last in, first out." FIFO is the default.
Rely	The reliability of the interface as a fraction of the number 255. For example, 255/255 is 100-percent reliability. This counter can be used as a routing protocol metric.
Runts	Packets smaller than the LAN technology's minimum packet size—64 bytes or less in Ethernet networks. All runt packets are discarded.
Throttles	The number of times the interface advised a sending NIC that it was being overwhelmed by packets being sent, and to slow the pace of delivery. Takes its name from the fact that the interface asks the NIC to "throttle" back.
Underruns	The number of times the sending node overwhelmed the interface by sending more packets than the buffers could handle. Takes its name from the fact that the router interface "underran" the sender.

Table 17-4. Definitions of Some Ethernet Statistics *(continued)*

More often than not, connectivity problems are caused by some type of configuration problem, not by a piece of failing equipment. Depending on the Ethernet statistic that's high, the interface may be overwhelmed by incoming traffic, have insufficient queue size configured, have insufficient buffer memory, or be mismatched with the speed of a network sending input.

Checking Access Lists for Proper Configuration   The classic example of a device malfunctioning even though its hardware is running fine is the misconfigured access list. You'll recall that access lists are used to restrict what traffic may pass through a router's interface, thereby cutting off access to the LAN segment attached to it. The basic access list does this by inspecting for source and destination IP addresses—a way of controlling who may go

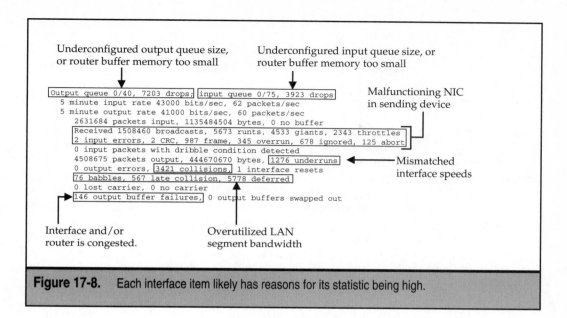

Figure 17-8.   Each interface item likely has reasons for its statistic being high.

where. The extended access list also uses application layer port numbers, to further restrict which applications may be run once you're admitted. Indeed, access lists are the most rudimentary form of internetwork security, used as a kind of internal firewall. Not all use of access lists has to do with security; sometimes they're used to steer traffic along certain routes in order to "shape" traffic to best fit the internetwork's resources.

The first step in checking for access list problems is to determine whether a suspect router—or a suspect interface on a router—is even configured with an access list. To find this out, log into the router and enter the **show access-lists** command to see if all the access lists are configured:

```
RemoteRouter#show access-lists
Extended IP access list 100
    deny    ip any host 206.107.120.17
    permit ip any any (5308829 matches)
Extended IP access list 101
    permit tcp any host 209.98.208.33 established
    permit udp host 209.98.98.98 host 209.98.208.59
    permit icmp any host 209.98.208.59 echo-reply
    permit tcp any host 209.98.208.59 eq smtp
    permit tcp any host 209.98.208.59 eq pop3
    permit tcp any host 209.98.208.59 eq 65
    permit tcp any host 209.98.208.59 eq telnet
```

```
permit tcp host 209.98.208.34 host 209.98.208.59
permit tcp any 209.98.208.32 0.0.0.15 established
permit icmp any 209.98.208.32 0.0.0.15 echo-reply
.
.
.
```

Looking at the preceding example, access list 100 explicitly denies traffic to a certain IP address. This is frequently done to stop outbound traffic to a known undesirable IP address, or some other type of router that could allow hackers a crack at the enterprise's edge router. Access list 101 is more sophisticated, with a series of permit rules to control which applications may be used between hosts. The application's IP port is defined behind each **eq** modifier, such as **eq smtp** for e-mail or **eq 65** for TACACS+ database service. (Certain ports can be identified by an acronym; others must be identified by a number.) Also note that access list 101 has only permit rules. This is possible because if a packet's request for service isn't explicitly permitted, it will be denied by the "implicit deny" rule when it reaches the bottom of the access list.

It could be that the inadvertent deny rule or lack of a permit rule is causing the problem. The troubleshooter would scan the access lists for any rules that might be causing the problem at hand. For example, if a person can't connect to the mail server, the troubleshooter would look for statements containing **eq smtp** or the mail server's IP address. The next step would be to go to the interface connecting the network experiencing the problem to see if the **access-group** command was used to apply the questionable access list to it. To do this, you must enter privileged EXEC mode and go into configure interface mode pointed to the interface in question, as shown here:

```
MyRouter#enable
Password:
MyRouter#show running-config
.
.
.
interface Ethernet1
 ip address 10.1.13.1 255.255.255.240
 ip access-group 100 in
 ip access-group 101 out
 .
 .
 .
```

If the questionable access list is in force, temporarily disable it to see if traffic can pass the router without it. There are two access lists in our example, so we would disable them both to see if the problem is being caused by access lists. Disable access lists on the interface as follows:

```
MyRouter#config terminal
MyRouter(config)#interface ethernet1
MyRouter(config-if)#no ip access-group 100 in
MyRouter(config-if)#no ip access-group 101 out
```

In case you forgot, the **in** modifier at the end of each access-group statement configures the access lists to be applied to inbound packets only. An **out** modifier would do the opposite; the absence of a modifier applies the list to both inbound and outbound traffic.

Once the access lists are disabled, attempt to make the connection between the host and the server reported as nonresponding. If the traffic goes through with the access lists disabled, then a statement somewhere in one of the access lists is probably the cause. The next step is to see which list contains the problem by reenabling one of the two. Access list 101, with all its rules, is the most likely culprit. To find out if this is the case, put it back into force with the following command:

```
MyRouter(config-if)#ip access-group 101 out
```

Now try to connect to the server again. If the problem has returned, you've established that the problem resides somewhere inside access list 101.

To debug the access list, carefully review it to find the offending rule. It could be a misplaced deny rule, but a missing TCP or UDP port in a permit rule could also be the problem. Remember, each access list rule must declare to which IP transport protocol it applies: TCP, UDP, or ICMP. Most often, however, offending application ports are the source of the problem, simply because there are so many of them and network applications being used change so much. For example, if users are having a problem making a connection to a Web server, look to make sure that HTTP port number 80 is permitted between the host and server addresses.

It's also possible that the traffic is being denied before getting to the permit rule designed to let it through. Remember that Access Control Lists read from the top down until a match is found. If this is the case, the sequence in which rules are listed should be adjusted accordingly by putting the priority rules nearer the top.

Redirecting Traffic from Congested Areas   Sometimes traffic becomes congested in a particular router. This could be the result of new hosts having been added in the area, new network applications coming online, or other causes. When this happens, log into the congested router and enter the **show ip traffic** command to generate the following report:

```
MyRouter#show ip traffic
IP statistics:
  Rcvd:  7596385 total, 477543 local destination
         0 format errors, 0 checksum errors, 96 bad hop count
         0 unknown protocol, 1 not a gateway
         0 security failures, 0 bad options, 0 with options
```

```
Opts:    0 end, 0 nop, 0 basic security, 0 loose source route
         0 timestamp, 0 extended security, 0 record route
         0 stream ID, 0 strict source route, 0 alert, 0 cipso
         0 other
Frags:   0 reassembled, 0 timeouts, 0 couldn't reassemble
         0 fragmented, 0 couldn't fragment
Bcast:   53238 received, 280 sent
Mcast:   205899 received, 521886 sent
Sent:    738759 generated, 6113405 forwarded
         13355 encapsulation failed, 374852 no route
  .
  .
  .
```

In addition to reporting IP traffic, the **show ip traffic** command reports traffic generated by transport protocols, routing protocols, ARP translation requests, and even packet errors. The report also breaks out broadcast and multicast messages. It's a quick way to understand the loads being put on a router and what options you might have to lighten the load.

For example, if broadcast traffic seems excessive, you might look into tightening restrictions in the access lists governing the surrounding routers. But, if it appears that all or most of the heavy traffic is legitimate, traffic affecting neighbor routers should also be analyzed. If there is an inequity in loads between routers of similar power, perhaps load balancing is in order. In most cases, this makes more sense than buying more powerful hardware.

One way to balance traffic loads between routers is to log into the congested router and enter config-router mode by calling up the routing protocols; then set individual distance metrics for each router to steer traffic away from the congested router to its less congested neighbor. Let's take an IGRP example:

```
MyRouter(config)#router igrp 3
MyRouter(config-router)#distance 255
MyRouter(config-router)#distance 120 10.1.13.1 0.0.0.255
MyRouter(config-router)#distance 80 10.1.14.1 0.0.0.3
MyRouter(config-router)#
```

As covered in Chapter 14, routing protocols choose best routes based on theoretical cost. The **distance** commands in the preceding code snippet make routes through 10.1.13.1 more costly than those using 10.1.14.1 by boosting its administrative distance relative to its neighbor.

To explain, the **router igrp 3** statement places the router into config-router mode in order to set parameters for the router's behavior within IGRP routing protocol domain number 3. The **distance 255** statement, by having no IP address, instructs the router to ignore all routing updates from routers for which no explicit (nondefault) administrative distances have been set. Then, the statement **distance 120 10.1.13.1 0.0.0.255** sets the congested router's distance metric to 120. (Cisco routing protocols use inverse masks, thus the **0.0.0.255** modifier.) Finally, the **distance 80 10.1.14.1 0.0.0.3** statement sets the neighboring router's distance metric to 80, making it one-third "cheaper" to use than the congested router. This routing metric tweak will automatically steer traffic away from 10.1.13.1 toward 10.1.14.1.

Troubleshooting WAN Links

Troubleshooting WAN problems entails using a slightly different set of tools. This is because most connections into WAN links must go through a serial line. To refresh on the subject, a serial line connects a CSU/DSU unit to a router. Telephone networks don't transmit signals using a data-link layer (layer 2) network technology such as Ethernet. Routers aren't telephone switches, so the transitions between the two technologies must somehow be made. The CSU/DSU-to-serial-line interface gives the router signals it can understand.

NOTE: A CSU/DSU is like a modem, but it works with digital lines instead of analog ones. CSU stands for channel service unit, an interface connecting to a local digital telephone line such as a T1 (instead of a modem connecting to an analog phone line). DSU stands for data service unit, a device that adapts to the customer end of the connection, usually into a router or LAN switch.

Serial links have an obvious importance because they extend internetworks beyond the office campus to remote locations. A remote link of any size requires using a digital telephone circuit of some kind, ranging from a fractional T1 up to a full T3 (DS3) line.

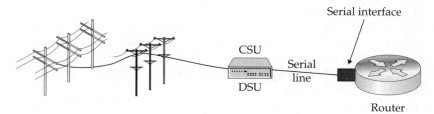

Even though a serial line is only a short run of cable, it provides a window through which its entire WAN link can be diagnosed. In other words, not only can you analyze the serial line and its interfaces, but by looking at the traffic it carries, you can also diagnose the digital phone loop and, to some extent, what's happening at the remote end of the link.

Differences in the show interfaces serial Report

Cisco provides a special tool for troubleshooting serial links in the **show interfaces serial** command. It's largely the same as the normal **show interfaces** command, but with some important differences, as highlighted in Figure 17-9.

```
RemoteRouter>show interface serial0
Serial0 is up, line protocol is up
  Hardware is HD64570
  Internet address is 10.1.14.1/30
  MTU 1500 bytes, BW 1544 Kbit, DLY 20000 usec, rely 255/255, load 217/255
  Encapsulation HDLC, loopback not set, keepalive set (10 sec)
  Last input 00:00:00, output 00:00:00, output hang never
  Last clearing of "show interface" counters never
  Input queue: 0/75/390 (size/max/drops); Total output drops: 54920
  Queueing strategy: weighted fair
  Output queue: 0/1000/64/12921 (size/max total/threshold/drops)
     Conversations  0/1/256 (active/max active/max total)
     Reserved Conversations 0/0 (allocated/max allocated)
  5 minute input rate 39000 bits/sec, 52 packets/sec
  5 minute output rate 36000 bits/sec, 48 packets/sec
     26405 packets input, 1977458 bytes, 0 no buffer
     Received 12385 broadcasts, 0 runts, 0 giants, 0 throttles
     1294 input errors, 0 CRC, 0 frame, 0 overrun, 0 ignored, 397 abort
     4783008 packets output, 2510565558 bytes, 0 underruns
     0 output errors, 0 collisions, 9172 interface resets
     0 output buffer failures, 0 output buffers swapped out
     12 carrier transitions
  DCD=up  DSR=up  DTR=up  RTS=up  CTS=up
```

Figure 17-9.   Most WAN links still use serial lines to connect routers to phone loops.

One way serial links differ is that encapsulation must be used over digital telephone loops. The High-Level Data-Link Control (HDLC) encapsulation protocol is indicated in the top shaded box in Figure 17-9. Encapsulation is necessary to maintain Ethernet packets over the digital telephone link. Sometimes encapsulation may have been inadvertently turned off, so the Encapsulation field should be checked.

Another difference is that conversations (sessions) are reported in the **show interfaces serial** report. WAN links have less bandwidth than local shared media. To wit, a T1 (DS1) circuit has a data rate of 1.544 Mbps, and a T3 (DS3) has a rate of 45 Mbps. Most enterprises use fractional T1 or T3 by purchasing channels within them (T1 has 24 channels, T3 has 672). WAN bandwidth therefore is limited compared to, say, a 100-Mbps LAN segment, and sometimes a particular user session takes more than its share. Therefore, when troubleshooting a WAN link, it helps to know how many conversations are going on. In case you're wondering, the Reserved Conversation field has to do with the Resource Reservation Protocol (dubbed RSVP). RSVP is an industry standard designed for use in QoS tools to help guarantee service levels.

NOTE: For more information about QoS, flip back to Chapter 7.

The box at the bottom of the figure shows a third difference in the **show interfaces serial** report. These five fields are the same as the blinking lights you may have noticed on external modems. For example, DTR stands for Data Terminal Ready, an EIA/TIA-232 (née RS-232) circuit that is activated to notify the data communications equipment at the other end that the host is ready to send and receive data. DCD stands for Data Carrier Detect, which is important because it senses the actual carrier signal (the modem noise you hear when making a modem connection). The five modem circuits are included in the **show interfaces serial** report for troubleshooting serial links that run over analog/modem lines instead of digital lines.

Key Diagnostic Fields in the show interfaces serial Report

Serial links differ by nature from LAN segments, so diagnosing them takes a different focus. Certain things that are to some extent taken for granted in LAN segment links are often the cause of performance problems or even failures in serial links. Figure 17-10 highlights the items that troubleshooters look at first in a serial interface.

As you can see, troubleshooting serial links emphasizes looking at errors and line activity. This is natural, given that the middle part of a WAN link—the telephone circuit—is basically invisible to networking equipment.

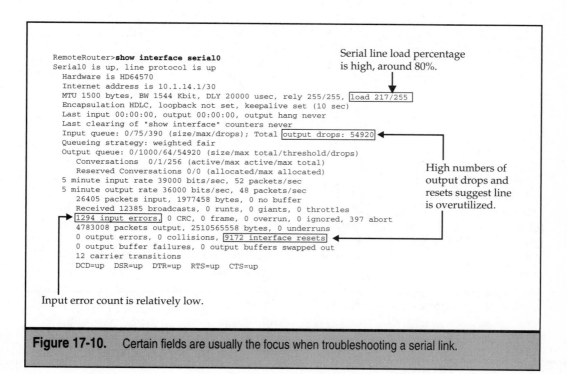

Figure 17-10.   Certain fields are usually the focus when troubleshooting a serial link.

Looking at Figure 17-10, we see a case in which input traffic seems to be going okay, but a lot of output packets are being dropped. Given that the serial line is being pushed hard, running at about 80 percent of available bandwidth, we can conclude that the drops are being caused by overuse, not by faulty hardware in the link.

Troubleshooting Serial-Line Input Errors   One of the most common causes of serial-line problems is input errors—in other words, data inbound from the remote site. Probable causes of serial-line input errors, with suggested actions, are outlined in Table 17-5.

Troubleshooting Serial-Line Output Errors   Another clue to serial-line problems is an increase in dropped packets at the interface. A *drop* occurs when too many packets are being processed in the system and insufficient buffer memory is available to handle the packet. This applies to both input and output drops, as outlined in Table 17-6.

Input Error Symptoms	Probable Causes and Suggested Actions
Input errors along with CRC or frame errors	A dirty line, where electrical noise interferes with the data signal. Serial cable exceeds maximum length specified for the type of phone circuit. Serial cable is unshielded. The phone circuit itself may be malfunctioning. **Actions:** Reduce cable length. Install shielded cable. Check phone loop with a line analyzer. Clocking jitter in line where data signal varies from reference timing positions, or clocking skew where device clocks are set differently. **Actions:** Make sure all devices are configured to use a common-line clock.
Input errors along with aborts	The transfer of a packet terminated in midtransmission. Usually caused by an interface reset on the router being analyzed. Can also be caused by a reset on the remote router, a bad phone circuit, or a bad CSU/DSU. **Action:** Check local hardware, then remote hardware. Replace faulty equipment.

Table 17-5.   Input Errors Causes and Actions

Packet Drop Symptoms	Probable Causes and Suggested Actions
Increase in dropped input packets	Input drops usually occur when traffic is being routed from a local interface (Ethernet, Token Ring, FDDI) that's faster than the serial interface. The problem usually emerges during periods of high traffic. **Actions:** Increase the interface's input hold queue size in the router's config file.
Increase in dropped output packets	Output drops happen when no system buffer is available at the time the router is attempting to hand the packet off to the transmit buffer during high traffic. **Actions:** Increase the interface's output hold queue size. Turn off fast switching. Implement priority queuing.

Table 17-6. Dropped Packet Causes and Actions

Drops taking place in one direction but not the other (input versus output) can point the troubleshooter toward the problem's source. If they're happening both ways, the router or its serial interface is probably the culprit.

Troubleshooting Serial Links   Most of us have used modems long enough to know that sometimes an established connection can falter, or even be broken. This goes for serial lines, too, usually because of interface resets or carrier transitions, as outlined in Table 17-7.

Although they're not LAN segments per se, serial links are integral to geographically distributed internetworks. Don't forget to consider them, even when a serial-line problem is not initially apparent. For example, when evaluating performance problems, it could be that a faulty serial link is shifting traffic loads elsewhere within the internetwork.

Client-Server VPNs

As we've discussed already, VPNs are a cost-effective way to use the Internet as your own private WAN. If you're having trouble getting a VPN to work, there are four areas in which VPN problems generally fall:

▼ Blocked VPN traffic

■ Bad Internet connections

■ Configuration errors

▲ Network Address Translation (NAT) tunneling problems

Line Error Symptoms	Probable Causes and Suggested Actions
Increasing carrier transitions	Interruption in the carrier signal. Usually due to interface resets at the remote end of the link. Resets can be caused by external sources such as electrical storms, T1 or T3 overuse alerts, or faulty hardware. **Actions:** Use breakout box or serial analyzer to check hardware at both ends. Then check router hardware. Replace faulty hardware as necessary. No action required if problem was due to external cause.
Increasing interface resets	Interface resets result from missed keepalive messages. They usually result from carrier transitions, lack of buffer, or a problem with CSU/DSU hardware. Coincidence with increased carrier transitions or input errors indicates a bad link or bad CSU/DSU hardware. **Actions:** Use breakout box or serial analyzer to check hardware at both ends. Contact leased-line vendor if hardware is okay.

Table 17-7.   Serial Line Error Causes and Actions

At the risk of insulting anyone's intelligence, when problems arise (not only VPN issues), the first thing to do is to check for loose cables. Wiggle the cables on the client's modem, the router, and firewall to ensure they are seated properly. It's also a good idea to make sure you're using straight-through Cat 5 cabling, and didn't pick up a length of crossover cable.

Blocked Traffic

The next step is to ensure your Internet service provider (ISP) allows IPSec VPN traffic. Most ISPs do allow IPSec VPN traffic, but if yours does not, it will not matter if your VPN is properly configured, because the packets won't be going anywhere. If your ISP does not allow IPSec VPN traffic, you might have to consider changing ISPs.

Check your firewall to ensure that it isn't blocking IPSec or PPTP traffic. To make a VPN connection, it is necessary to configure outbound IPSec traffic on the firewall. To do this, you must configure your firewall to enable IPSec, then create a rule allowing the passage of traffic between the LAN and WAN. If that's not possible, it might be necessary to locate the client in the DMZ, or consider investing in a different router or firewall.

Not only can hardware firewalls block traffic, but so can software firewalls. This is another easy place to check, especially for clients that are traveling or trying to connect from locations that aren't equipped with hardware firewalls, but that are set up with software firewalls. Just disable the software firewall and see if that works. Some software firewalls will ask you if they should allow VPN traffic to be passed and you can add the desired destination IP address to the trusted-zone setting.

NAT

Make sure your NAT is tunneling correctly. A good place to start is by making certain you have the most current firmware updates and software. Out-of-date firmware may not support IPSec when NAT is used. What happens is that when IPSec tries to verify the packets' integrity, NAT changes the source IP address to the firewall's WAN address to properly navigate the Internet. Unfortunately, this causes problems with IPSec because the packets fail an integrity check.

You can get a listing of your NAT translations and an overview of your NAT statistics by using two simple EXEC commands:

▼ **show ip nat translations verbose** This displays the active NAT translations with additional information for each translation table, including how long the entry has been used.

▲ **show ip nat statistics** This displays a variety of NAT statistics, including the number of active translations, interfaces, and total translations.

Configuration

Configuration can also be the culprit when trying to track down VPN problems. Ensure that the correct IP addresses are being used. For client VPN's, checking and reconfiguring the IP address in Windows is accomplished by opening a command prompt, and then entering **ipconfig.**

If the IP address issued by the network administrator to connect to the VPN does not fall within the range shown, then the IP address is not valid. To correct this, renew the lease. This is accomplished by typing **ipconfig/renew.** In Windows, this generates a dialog box. Select the network interface card from the drop-down menu, and click the Renew button.

NOTE: If the client is using PPPoE to connect to the ISP—they'll be using PPPoE if a static IP address has not been assigned—make sure the client is connecting to the Internet using whatever connection application is needed.

Send a **ping** command to your VPN server's IP address. If you get a response, then you know the client is connected to the Internet and able to see the VPN server. Next, you should rule out any DNS configuration problems. This time, conduct a ping test, but use the domain name (for example, www.velte.com). If you get a response, the Internet connection is working fine. If not, it means your DNS is misconfigured.

The client and the VPN server must be able to speak the same language to get the job done. As such, it's important to make sure that the encryption settings on both the client and VPN server are the same. Authentication algorithms must be configured properly on both the client and VPN server. Both devices will need the shared secret, or, if using certificates, the correct public key is necessary.

Bad Connections

Next, check whether the client is trying to connect over a slow connection. Latency can cause your VPN connection to fail, because they like consistent traffic; otherwise, they tend to drop off. You're most likely to see this as an issue with satellite connections where latency can run from half a second to several seconds.

Connection speed can be checked with the ping tool. Using the "-t" switch, you can get a continuous test of connection speeds between the client and the VPN server. For instance:

```
ping 68.93.44.123 -t
```

This produces a list of the test's efforts to send packets to the address. The test is ended by using CTRL-C. Take a look at the results. If you see the stray "Request timed out" error messages, try increasing the timeout value so you can accurately gauge how much latency your connection suffers. This value can be changed by using the "-w" switch. For instance:

```
ping 68.93.44.123 -t-w 7000
```

This increases the timeout value to 7,000 ms. This should be enough to indicate how much latency is present on your link. Connection times at 1,500 ms and above will cause the VPN link to fail.

NOTE: It might not sound important at first blush, but if the VPN server and client are not in the correct time zones and have the correct time settings, they might not be able to hook up. This is because correct time settings are necessary for key expiration.

TROUBLESHOOTING CISCO HARDWARE

When the probable location of the problem has been identified, the first step is to physically examine and test the suspect device. This will identify the problem's cause in a surprising number of troubleshooting situations. Sometimes the problem is caused by something as simple as a loose component; other times, something is damaged.

Inspecting Devices

Once a suspect device is identified, it should be physically inspected. This is routine procedure. (Even when a suspect or troubled device is in a remote location, a contact person is sent to make an inspection.) Earlier, we stated that most troubleshooting tasks are done from the administrator's desk, and that's true. Most tasks are done from the administrator's PC or an NMS console. However, there's no substitute for actually looking at a device to see what's going on. The two parts of inspecting a device are reading its LEDs and inspecting the device's components.

Reading Device LEDs

If the device is still online, the first thing to do is to read the LEDs (light-emitting diodes). You probably recognize LEDs as those blinking lights on the front of many electronic devices. Virtually all network devices have LEDs to assist in troubleshooting. The LED bank arrangement follows the device layout:

▼   *Access devices with a bank of ports on the front, with a twisted-pair cable plugged into each port using an RJ-45 phone-style jack.* Products from the Cisco Catalyst 2800 to the Catalyst 4500 Switch fit this description. There is usually one LED per port.

■   *Motherboard-based routers with LAN segments plugged into the back, usually via twisted-pair cable, but also fiber-optic cables for uplinks.* The Cisco 6400 Router fits this description. LEDs on these devices appear behind smoked-plastic panels on the front of these boxes.

▲   *High-end routers and switches of the bus-and-blade configuration, again with networks plugged into the back, both fiber-optic and twisted-pair cable.* The Cisco 7500 Router and Catalyst 6500 Switch fit this description. LEDs on these devices appear both behind smoked-plastic panels on the front and on the blades (card modules) themselves on the back (remember, a *blade* is basically an entire router or switch on a board).

LEDs are also called *activity lights.* Each LED on an access device represents a host. Router and LAN switch LEDs represent entire LAN segments.

LEDs blink and change colors according to the port's status. Green means okay, and orange means the port is coming up. If the port is down, its LED goes dark. The port's LED blinks when packets are passing through it. A common practice is to press RESET to see what happens. LEDs temporarily go orange or even red if they encounter trouble during the power cycle. They will eventually go green, but the temporary error condition may indicate a nonfatal configuration error.

The rule is that if an activity light is green, the line is good and the problem must stem from some type of configuration problem. If the light is orange, the line is operating but malfunctioning. If the activity light is off, the line is down.

Physically Inspecting Devices

The next step is to physically inspect the device itself. Start by making sure the device is offline, and then remove the cover from the top of the device chassis and inspect the interior, looking for the following:

▼ **Loose connections**   Look for any loosely attached card (module) or cable. Reseat any that are found.

■ **New cards**   If you know any card to be new, reseat it into its connection several times. New cards are more prone to oxidation or carbon film buildup on their backplane connections.

■ **Burned or damaged parts**   Look for any burned wires, ribbon cables, or cards. Also look at the backplane to see if it's okay. Closely inspect the wires leading to the device's power supply. Also look for any crimped wires.

▲ **Dirty device interior**   If the device has dust and lint in the interior, turn off the device and clean it. Devices can accumulate a lot of foreign substances from the air in dusty or dirty environments, which sometimes can affect performance.

After completing the inspection, try rebooting the device to see if power-cycling it will fix the problem. One important caution: Don't change anything in the configuration. Doing so before rebooting can make it very difficult to determine the problem's source afterward; it only adds more variables to the mix.

The Reboot Test

If no severe problem was found inspecting the device, the next step is to try a power-cycle test to see how it responds. *Power-cycle* means to turn a device off and then turn it on again, which you probably know as the cure-all for Microsoft Windows. As we saw in Chapter 4, rebooting devices can tell a lot about the status of a device, and in some cases, it even makes the problem go away.

When you reboot, if the configuration in memory is mismatched with the hardware, a variety of problems can ensue. Ports might hang, bus timeout errors may occur, and so on. If the device reboots and prompts for a password, the circuitry and memory are working properly. Some major symptoms and probable causes are outlined in Table 17-8.

When hardware problems this extreme are encountered, it's time to call in support from Cisco or a third-party maintenance organization with which your enterprise has contracted. Typically, devices are shipped into the maintenance center for bench repair. Only end-user enterprises with spare parts, Cisco-trained personnel, and proper instruments attempt to repair networking hardware devices in-house.

Reboot Symptom	Probable Causes
No response	Bad power supply; blown fuse; bad breaker; bad power switch; bad backplane
Won't reboot	Bad or miswired power supply; bad (or poorly seated) processor card; bad memory board; bad IOS image in NVRAM; shorted wires
Partial or constant reboot	Bad processor, controller, or interface card; bad backplane; bad power supply; bad microcode
No cards show up in boot display	Bad processor, controller, or interface card; bad backplane; cards not seated in backplane; bad power supply

Table 17-8.   Typical Reboot Problems and Their Probable Causes

TROUBLESHOOTING NETWORK CONFIGURATIONS

As your network grows and evolves, you'll likely encounter some LAN segments that have wireless capabilities—and their own set of problems. Additionally, you'll more than likely want to track down issues related to your network's overall performance. In this section, let's take a closer look at how to track down and resolve problems with a wireless network, and some good methods for locating and fixing problems stemming from performance issues.

Wireless Networks

Wireless networks provide a whole new level of convenience to the world of networking. The ability to connect computers without having to worry about wiring—not to mention the ability to take your laptop anywhere in the office—and still maintain network connectivity is a huge plus.

Many wireless deployments fire up as soon as you connect your access point and wireless card. For example, if you're using a Plug-and-Play capable version of Windows (like Windows XP, for example) most times the wireless card will be instantly recognized and, security issues aside, you'll have access to the network with no problems. Regrettably, it doesn't always work that smoothly.

Encryption

An easily overlooked component of wireless networking is enabling encryption on your access points and clients. As we mentioned in Chapter 10, this is extremely important for the sake of protecting your data.

If encryption is not enabled, it is relatively easy for someone to sniff the wireless network traffic and glean all sorts of information from user ID and password information, to the contents of e-mails being sent and received.

Wireless Equivalent Privacy (WEP) is the most common encryption protocol available today. It uses a key that you establish on the access point and then enter into your wireless- enabled devices. This key is used to encrypt the data being transmitted and decrypt incoming data. Without the key, no one else can "see" the data as it's transmitted.

The next level of wireless security is WiFi Protected Access (WPA). It's like WEP but provides a much higher level of encryption and authentication security. It's not available on older access points, and it may take an upgrade on the client side to enable it there. If you can't use WPA, at least run WEP—some encryption is way better than none at all.

NOTE: It is wise to become familiar with the encryption and overall security features available on your hardware and software—the standards and technology are advancing quickly in the wireless arena and sometimes a more secure environment is only a firmware or software update away.

With encryption, however, comes its share of problems. If your encryption scheme is incorrectly set on either the access point or clients, then expect problems.

If you're having problems getting your wireless clients to connect, the first place to stop is by checking encryption settings. Follow these steps to ensure your encryption settings are correct:

1. **Turn off encryption.** I know, we just said it was important to have encryption enabled. However, if you shut down encryption and are still having problems, then you know encryption isn't to blame. If it turns out that everything is running fine, move on to step 2.

2. **Count characters.** Check your access point and WiFi card's instructions to make sure you're entering the correct number of characters for the encryption key. For instance, when using a 40-bit WEP key, our Cisco Aironet 350 requires five ASCII or ten hexadecimal characters for its encryption key (this is shown in Figure 17-11). Also, check to see if you must specify whether you are using an ASCII string or hexadecimal string for the key. Table 17-9 shows how many characters are needed for various bit-lengths of keys.

3. **Configure authentication methods.** When using WiFi, there are two types of authentication employed: *open system* and *shared key*. Reconfigure the access point and client to allow open system, thus disabling WEP. When you enable WEP, change over to the shared key authentication. This provides optimal security.

4. **Match your WEP levels.** Although it's possible to mix environments in which 40/64-bit and 128-bit devices are operating (we'll talk about that more in a moment) it's best to make sure everyone is using the same level. That said, if it turns out you need to work in a mixed environment, 128-bit devices can talk to 40/64-bit WEP devices only if they are set to use 40-bit keys.

5. **Check your passphrases.** Some WiFi vendors (including Cisco) allow you to enter *passphrases* for key generation. That is, you don't have to come up with a string of hexadecimal characters. If you like, you can come up with a simple phrase. (For instance, Figure 17-12 shows the passphrase "chunkymonkey" turned into a hexadecimal WEP key.) This is a convenient tool, because when setting up the key, you don't need to remember a series of meaningless letters and numbers. "chunkymonkey" is easier to remember than "63B27312BB". When you use passphrases, there are a couple things you should keep in mind. First, keep the passphrase string short. You don't need to come up with phrases like "supercalifragilisticexpialidocious"—it won't result in a key that is any more secure than one generated with a shorter passphrase. Second, use letters and numbers only—don't throw spaces, punctuation, or other symbols into the mix.

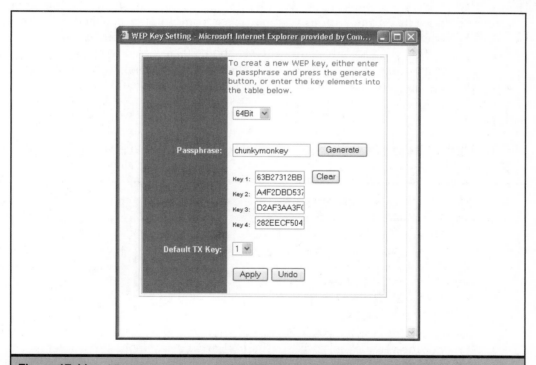

Figure 17-11. Mistyping a character in the WEP can cause WiFi networks to fail.

WEP Bit Levels	ASCII	Hexadecimal
40/64	5 characters	10 characters
128	13 characters	26 characters

Table 17-9.   The Number of Characters Needed in Various Key Lengths

Antenna Placement and Interference

With a wired network, you don't need to worry too much about interference from other devices. For instance, running the photocopier probably won't cause any trouble with your wired workstations, but curiously, it may cause your wireless connection to drop out. And even though your wireless-enabled laptop affords you the freedom to go anywhere in your office, you can only be from 100 to about 300 feet from your access point. After that, interference from walls, floors, and other obstructions will cause connections to slow appreciably or drop out altogether. Of course, this still beats the pants off a wired connection, which only lets you roam as far as the Cat 5 tether allows, which might be no further than one corner of your desk. Wireless networking can be worth doing, just remember to keep in mind where your wireless devices will be in relation to an access point. In most cases, try and locate your access point as centrally as possible to the clients.

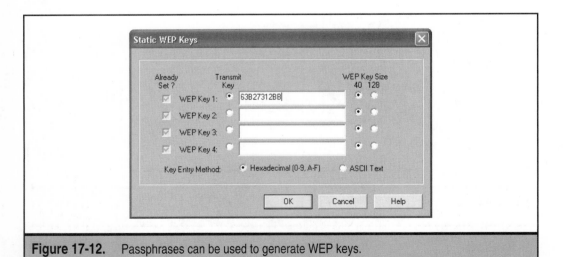

Figure 17-12.   Passphrases can be used to generate WEP keys.

No matter where you place your access points, always be aware of sources of interference. We've mentioned earlier that photocopiers have been known to reduce connectivity in WiFi networks, but be mindful of other devices that can wreak havoc on your system. A main culprit comes in the guise of the 2.4 GHz cordless telephone. Since this operates on the same frequency as 802.11b/g, it can cause some headaches. If you suspect a cordless phone or other 2.4 GHz device, try using other WiFi channels to see if things improve.

Extending Your Wireless Network's Range   What if you just can't get a good signal in some areas of your space and you really want wireless there? After ruling out interference from another device, repositioning your antenna(s), and perhaps relocating your access point, you may just want to buy an additional access point. This extra access point can be used to extend the range of your wireless network, as Figure 17-13 shows.

When using an access point to extend range, you can do so without needing a wired connection by configuring the access point as a bridge from an existing access point. Just make sure you are monitoring performance and capacity as your user count grows because the wired access point could become saturated with network traffic and become a network bottleneck.

Checking Your Levels   A simple way to check your connectivity levels is to start the client in the same room or location as the access point. When you've got the two devices communicating, it's easy enough to start moving the client away from the access point. This will give you a quick and dirty idea of the range between the two.

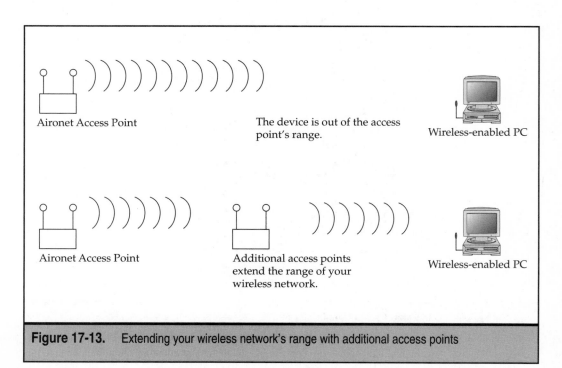

Figure 17-13.   Extending your wireless network's range with additional access points

However, you can plot your devices' connectivity with a little more finesse by using the Cisco Aironet Client Utility. Once started on your client, this application, shown in Figure 17-14, shows the quality and strength of your wireless signal.

Point-to-Point Troubleshooting   If your wireless bridge link stops working, it is possible that there is a problem with your system's antennas, cabling, or connectors. Check your antennas and ensure they have not come out of alignment.

Also, antennas and connections can be damaged by moisture. If the antennas are not sealed properly when they're installed, moisture can condense inside the antenna feedhorns, ultimately filling them with water. Moisture that makes its way into coaxial cabling can be even more problematic. Coax cables have a foam internal dielectric. This can act like a sponge, sending moisture along the length of the cable.

NOTE: If you determine that coax cabling has been compromised and is sucking up moisture, replace the entire length, rather than snipping off a few feet and replacing the connector.

When problems manifest themselves in outdoor systems, the effect will appear on both ends of the link, to the same degree. This is relevant to know because if you see a degraded signal on one end of your link, don't automatically think you've found the location of the problem. It might very well be on the other side of the link. Check both ends.

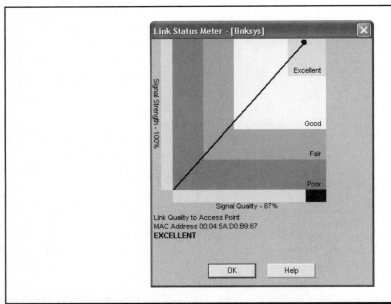

Figure 17-14.   The Cisco Aironet Client Utility shows your signal strength and quality.

On the other hand, if the receive-signal is low on one end, but not the other, generally this is a problem caused by misconfiguration of the radio units, or by interference. As such, don't make a bad situation worse by realigning antennas. If you determine that the setup is correct and the equipment is working properly, check for anything that might cause interference before adjusting the antennas.

If you suspect interference as the culprit, examine your system and its behavior. Is the problem there continuously, or is it intermittent? Most often, interference occurs intermittently, when the source of interference becomes active.

For point-to-point wireless networks, determining the source of interference can be a horrendous chore. First, look around the antennas at each end of your link. Are there any other antennas present? If so, do a little sleuthing to determine who owns it, who operates it, at which frequency it operates, how much power it is transmitting, and what type of antenna polarization is being used.

Once you've tracked down this data (it could be just as simple as asking around in the building on which the antenna is mounted), the next step is to ask the owner if he or she would be willing to help you determine if their system is the source of your system's interference.

When you have all the pertinent information about the interfering source, you can much more easily resolve the problem. First, consider your own antennas. Are any of them pointed at the other system's antennas? Is it possible to reposition your antennas so they are out of the other system's broadcast path?

Often, changing the polarization of your antennas to the opposite polarization of the interfering system will fix the problem. This is an easy and inexpensive solution to try first, as it doesn't require the repositioning of any equipment.

If that doesn't work, try changing the frequency of your system. Systems on different frequencies tend not to interfere with each other. One simple way to change your frequencies is to simply swap the transmit and receive frequencies on your system.

Troubleshooting Network Performance

If you're trying to pinpoint and troubleshoot problems in network performance, the first, best advice is to laboriously test and document your system, its configuration, maintenance, and anything else that you do to it. That way, should the network start operating in a sub-par fashion, you have a history with which to compare it.

Change Management and Your Network

There are two ways you can approach troubleshooting a network with performance problems. The first is to go in, oblivious to any changes and modifications that have been made to the system. That is, you go in to fix the problem, but have no clue what has already been done. When this happens, the best you can do is start making changes here and there, based on your guesses, not on fact. The second, and obviously better, solution is to gather basic performance trend information and refer to your network's change management log.

A change management log is a document where you record each and every change and bit of maintenance that is performed on your system, no matter how big, no matter how small. If you installed a new router, that should be in the document, but so should someone going into the server room to reset a device.

> **NOTE:**   There's a story about a network technician performing the simple task of blowing dust out of a router's fan. Ultimately, the dust was worked deeper into the fan, causing it to intermittently stop and cause the router to overheat. Since the technician didn't record this "simple" task in a change management document, it was never thought to be checked, until it was too late and the router burned up.

It is also helpful, when making changes to your network's configuration, to make as few changes at once as possible. That way, if your network either takes a performance hit, or goes down altogether, it's easier to undo than if you've performed a dozen different things.

If you have a change management document, and know when the system started having problems, you can start analyzing changes that were made to the network and its devices. You might discover that a new routing protocol was introduced, or a new quality of service policy was implemented. If you were to shoot blindly in the dark, it could take you weeks to find these issues. If you have a change management document, however, it's much easier to pin down the problem.

An effective, well-implemented change management plan has a number of useful attributes that will help your overall network management and also aid in troubleshooting. Benefits include the following:

▼ A checkpoint that allows you to measure performance both before and after changes are made to the network

■ A journal of network updates, maintenance, and reconfigurations, allowing you to compare your network and its changes to previous configurations in your network's history

▲ A rollback tool, which makes it easier to restore your system to an optimal configuration if the performance of a new configuration does not live up to your expectations

For best results, you'll have the proper software and hardware devices that will help you gather and analyze your performance metrics. For some suggestions, flip back to Chapter 15.

Router Performance Problems

If you suspect there are performance problems with your router, consult your change management document. Have you changed anything recently? Once a networking device has been set up and is working, problems generally stem from a person trying to improve the device's performance. Assuming there isn't some hardware problem (an unplugged cable or network card improperly seated) then the next place to look is if there were any changes made to the device's configuration.

NOTE: Don't dismiss hardware problems too quickly. It is always possible that someone went to perform a seemingly unrelated task and accidentally pulled a power cord a bit too hard, or pinched a network cable with a floor tile or the rack door. Always inspect your hardware before you commit hours of your time to sorting through configuration files. One of the biggest sources of network snafus is cabling plugged into the wrong ports. Don't be sheepish about preparing a map showing which cables go where between your devices. It beats the tedious alternative: pulling on cables to see where they go.

Hopefully, you backed up your router's configuration file. Taking the few seconds to back up the file when it is working optimally will save you untold hours trying to restore the system. The time to back up the configuration file is when everything is working well.

NOTE: If you do not have a backup of your router's configuration file, put this book down right now and go make one. Don't worry, we'll wait for you.

If you don't have a backup of the configuration file, the next step is to study your change management documentation. This documentation should describe all the changes that have been made to the router. Examine the document and see which changes might be responsible for your router's problems. You might have to go back to the router's configuration file and undo those changes, one-by-one, until the problem has been resolved.

The culprit might also be changes in the device's OS. If you've recently upgraded your OS or applied a patch, that's a good place to check. Before adding new operating systems or applying patches, you should understand just how you can rollback the OS to the previous, operational OS if something goes wrong. Remember, however you attack a troubleshooting problem, the goal is to "follow the wire" and track the source of the problem down to the end.

Keep in mind that the most important thing to do when troubleshooting is to proceed carefully and logically. Don't change several variables at the same time. Make a change, observe, document if necessary, and then proceed to the next step. Fixing problems in complex systems is more about process than luck. That said, we wish you the best of luck in troubleshooting and in life.

INDEX

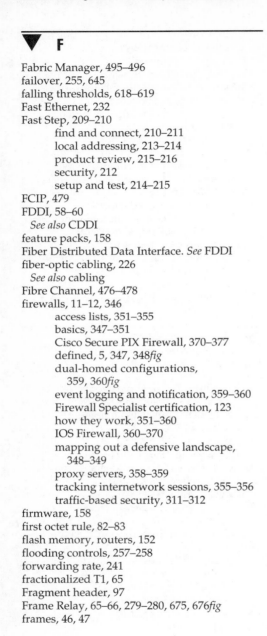

INTERNATIONAL CONTACT INFORMATION

AUSTRALIA
McGraw-Hill Book Company
Australia Pty. Ltd.
TEL +61-2-9900-1800
FAX +61-2-9878-8881
http://www.mcgraw-hill.com.au
books-it_sydney@mcgraw-hill.com

CANADA
McGraw-Hill Ryerson Ltd.
TEL +905-430-5000
FAX +905-430-5020
http://www.mcgraw-hill.ca

**GREECE, MIDDLE EAST, & AFRICA
(Excluding South Africa)**
McGraw-Hill Hellas
TEL +30-210-6560-990
TEL +30-210-6560-993
TEL +30-210-6560-994
FAX +30-210-6545-525

MEXICO (Also serving Latin America)
McGraw-Hill Interamericana Editores
S.A. de C.V.
TEL +525-1500-5108
FAX +525-117-1589
http://www.mcgraw-hill.com.mx
carlos_ruiz@mcgraw-hill.com

SINGAPORE (Serving Asia)
McGraw-Hill Book Company
TEL +65-6863-1580
FAX +65-6862-3354
http://www.mcgraw-hill.com.sg
mghasia@mcgraw-hill.com

SOUTH AFRICA
McGraw-Hill South Africa
TEL +27-11-622-7512
FAX +27-11-622-9045
robyn_swanepoel@mcgraw-hill.com

SPAIN
McGraw-Hill/
Interamericana de España, S.A.U.
TEL +34-91-180-3000
FAX +34-91-372-8513
http://www.mcgraw-hill.es
professional@mcgraw-hill.es

**UNITED KINGDOM, NORTHERN,
EASTERN, & CENTRAL EUROPE**
McGraw-Hill Education Europe
TEL +44-1-628-502500
FAX +44-1-628-770224
http://www.mcgraw-hill.co.uk
emea_queries@mcgraw-hill.com

ALL OTHER INQUIRIES Contact:
McGraw-Hill/Osborne
TEL +1-510-420-7700
FAX +1-510-420-7703
http://www.osborne.com
omg_international@mcgraw-hill.com

Sound Off!

Visit us at **www.osborne.com/bookregistration** and let us know what you thought of this book. While you're online you'll have the opportunity to register for newsletters and special offers from McGraw-Hill/Osborne.

We want to hear from you!

Sneak Peek

Visit us today at **www.betabooks.com** and see what's coming from McGraw-Hill/Osborne tomorrow!

Based on the successful software paradigm, Bet@Books™ allows computing professionals to view partial and sometimes complete text versions of selected titles online. Bet@Books™ viewing is free, invites comments and feedback, and allows you to "test drive" books in progress on the subjects that interest you the most.

OSBORNE DELIVERS RESULTS!

McGraw Hill

OSBORNE
www.osborne.com

Designed for people. Not clocks.

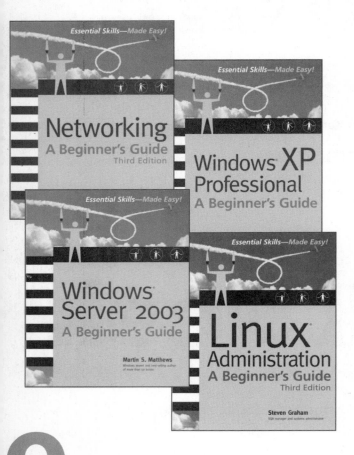

People learn at their own pace. That's why our Beginner's Guides provide a systematic pedagogy. Real-world examples from seasoned trainers teach the critical skills needed to master a tool or technology.

Osborne Beginner's Guides: Essential Skills—Made Easy

Solaris 9 Administration:
A Beginner's Guide
Paul A. Watters, Ph.D.
ISBN: 0-07-222317-0

UNIX System Administration:
A Beginner's Guide
Steve Maxwell
ISBN: 0-07-219486-3

Dreamweaver MX:
A Beginner's Guide
Ray West & Tom Muck
ISBN: 0-07-222366-9

HTML: A Beginner's Guide,
Second Edition
Wendy Willard
ISBN: 0-07-222644-7

Java 2: A Beginner's Guide,
Second Edition
Herbert Schildt
ISBN: 0-07-222588-2

UML: A Beginner's Guide
Jason Roff
ISBN: 0-07-222460-6

Windows XP Professional:
A Beginner's Guide
Martin S. Matthews
ISBN: 0-07-222608-0

Networking: A Beginner's Guide,
Third Edition
Bruce Hallberg
ISBN: 0-07-222563-7

Linux Administration:
A Beginner's Guide,
Third Edition
Steve Graham
ISBN: 0-07-222562-9

Red Hat Linux Administration:
A Beginner's Guide
Narender Muthyala
ISBN: 0-07-222631-5

Windows Server 2003:
A Beginner's Guide
Martin S. Matthews
ISBN: 0-07-219309-3

9 proven learning features:

1 Modules
2 Critical Skills
3 Step-by-Step Tutorials
4 Ask the Experts
5 Progress Checks
6 Annotated Syntax
7 Mastery Checks
8 Projects
9 Network Blueprints

OSBORNE DELIVERS RESULTS!

McGraw Hill **Osborne**
www.osborne.com